DATE DUE

JA 17 '94	MY 2 8 98		
AP 1 '94	NO 19 '98		
AP 29 '94			
	AP 24 00		
JE 17 '94	JE 1 8 00		
	AG 7 '00		
	DE 00		
OC 14 '94	JE 00		
DE 23 '94			
MR 31 '95	MY 7 '01		
	MY 20 08		
MY 12 '95	JE 19 08		
MY 26 '95			
NO 9 '95	JE 12 09		
AP 15 '96	MY 7 1		
MY 24 '96			
NO 18 '96			
MY 21 '97			
98			

DEMCO 38-296

INFORMATION FREEDOM and CENSORSHIP

WORLD REPORT 1991

Preface by William Shawcross

ARTICLE 19

INTERNATIONAL
CENTRE ON
CENSORSHIP

AMERICAN LIBRARY ASSOCIATION
CHICAGO

ica by

Kingdom by

Library Association Publishing Ltd
7 Ridgmount Street
London WC1E 7AE

First published 1991

Library of Congress Cataloging-in-Publication Data

Information freedom and censorship : world report 1991 / Article 19 :
   preface by William Shawcross : introduction by Frances D'Souza.
        p.   cm.
   Includes bibliographical references (p.   ) and index.
   ISBN 0-8389-2156-6
   1. Censorship 2. Freedom of information 3. Article 19
(Organization) I. Article 19 (Organization) II. American Library
Association.
Z657.I52   1991   90-29177
323.44'5--dc20   CIP

Typeset by ARTICLE 19
Printed and made in Great Britain by Billing & Sons, Worcester

ARTICLE 19
The International Centre on Censorship

ARTICLE 19 is an independent and impartial human rights organization established in 1986 to promote freedom of expression and to combat censorship worldwide. Taking its name and mandate from the nineteenth article of the Universal Declaration of Human Rights, the organization promotes freedom of opinion and expression as universal human rights guaranteed by international law and fosters and defends these rights across national, cultural, religious, racial, ideological and language boundaries.

❝Everyone has the right to freedom of opinion and expression; this includes freedom to hold opinions without interference and to seek, receive and impart information and ideas through any media and regardless of frontiers.❞

Article 19 of the Universal Declaration of Human Rights

ARTICLE 19 is developing networks which will help to raise national and international awareness of attacks on freedom of expression and their consequences and ensure effective monitoring and action on behalf of the many victims of censorship: individuals who are physically attacked, threatened by violence, unjustly imprisoned, banned or restricted in their movements or dismissed from their jobs; publications which are censored or banned, media outlets closed, suspended from operation or threatened with closure; organizations which are denied a democratic voice.

ARTICLE 19 can only succeed if it generates worldwide support and International action. If you wish to join, give financial support or would like further information please write to:

ARTICLE 19
90, Borough High Street, London SE1 1LL, UK.
Tel: 071 403 4822 **Fax**: 071 403 1943

Director: Frances D'Souza

Acknowledgements

This book was edited and prepared by the following ARTICLE 19 staff who also undertook additional research:

Editorial Team: Frances D'Souza (Director), Carmel Bedford (Editor), Annelise Jespersen (Assistant Editor).

Special thanks are due to Kevin Boyle (Consultant Editor).

Staff: Elizabeth Cleary-Rodríguez (Latin America Research Co-ordinator), Said Essoulami (Middle East and North Africa Research Co-ordinator), Dominic Ruston and Gary Sangha (Design and Typesetting), Sandra Coliver (Legal Officer), Helen Darbishire (Campaigns and Publicity Officer), Susan Hay (Membership Co-ordinator), Ann Naughton (Programme Co-ordinator), Liz Schofield (Administrative Officer).

Index created by Carmel Bedford, Annelise Jespersen and Dominic Ruston.

ARTICLE 19 World Report maps by Tony Hall.

Temporary and Volunteer Staff: David Agnew, Farimah Daftary, Silvester Edwine, Nina Feldman, Karen Mayo, Angela Stocker, Janice Welch.

ARTICLE 19 thanks Ciarán Ó Maoláin for sub-editing assistance and Alison Roberts and Andrew Taylor for compiling the statistics.

ARTICLE 19 wishes to thank the many individuals and the other human rights organizations that have contributed to the production of this Report, including:

Mike Adjei, Hassan Bahey el-Din, Jamal Ben Omar, Zuzana Bluh, Thorsten Cars, Alberto Arons de Carvalho, Richard Carver, Ellen Dahrendorf, Ghaleb Darwish, Donna A Demac, Shirley Eber, Roberto Espindola, David Flint, Michael Freeman, Nils Petter Gleditsch, David Goldberg, Duncan Green, Philip Gunson, Zuheir al-Hashimi, Karen Hatherley, Charles Hebbert, Werner Kastor, Udo Janz, Lene Johannessen, Erik Lykke, Allan McChesney, Gilbert Marcus, François Misser, Ahmed Motala, Mariana Musat, Makau Mutua, Geoffrey Mulgan, Hugh Pope, Elizabeth Philipson, Matthew Piette, Shamlal Puri, Murray Rankin, Jiri Rohan, Eduardo San Martin, Lawrence Shimba, Ricky Singh, Martin Smith, Gerardo Sotelo, K S Venkateswaran, Tim Westcott, Elizabeth Winter, Steingrim Wolland and Kenta Yamada;

Amnesty International, Anti-censorship Action Group, Caribbean Rights (CAMWORK), Committee to Protect Journalists, Human Rights Watch (Africa Watch, Americas Watch, Asia Watch, Helsinki Watch, Middle East Watch), Index on Censorship, Interights, International PEN Writers in Prison Committee, Lawyers Committee for Human Rights, Latin American Bureau and Minority Rights Group.

ARTICLE 19 wishes to acknowledge the support of the J Roderick MacArthur Foundation and UNESCO.

Contents

Africa, South of the Sahara

The Americas

Asia

Europe

Middle East and North Africa

Oceania

Themes and Issues

Rights of Others, National Security, State Security, Sedition, Public Interest, Public Health and Welfare, Public Morals, Public Order, Violence, Racism, Sexism, Religious Intolerance, Linguistic and Cultural Hegemony, Propaganda, Media Bias, Copyright and Intellectual Property, Contractual Obligations to Maintain Secrecy, Protection of Sources, Corruption, Special Situations.

Press Laws, Licensing, Attacks and Restrictions on Journalists, Censorship of Materials, Media Concentration, Closure of Media Outlets, Economic Pressures, Restrictions on Equipment, Restrictions on Access to Information, Self-regulation, Restrictions on Freedom of Assembly and Association, Banning of Individuals, Illiteracy.

Media Workers, Writers and Academics, Human Rights Defenders, Political Opponents, Prisoners, Speech, Correspondence, Telephone Communications, Newspapers and Journals, Electronic Media and Technologies, Artistic Expression, Education and Research, Advertising, Environmental Information, Historical Information.

Non-governmental Organizations, Inter-governmental Organizations, International Measures to Protect Journalists, National Law and Practice, Literacy Programmes, Development Issues, Pluralism.

Preface

by William Shawcross
Chairman, ARTICLE 19

In November 1989 I was fortunate to be amongst ecstatic crowds in Wenceslas Square, Prague, cheering the end of the communist dictatorship in Czechoslovakia. The dragon was dying there, as elsewhere in the Soviet bloc. "No More One-party Rule" was the first slogan of the revolution and the party's official censors were the first people to pack their bags.

Suddenly people dared to speak on the telephone again. All at once the papers and television began to tell the truth - to be on the side of the people. It was a fabulous and exhilarating moment.

Many things contributed to the liberation of Eastern Europe in 1989. Amongst the most important was the ceaseless and immensely courageous war which people like Vaclav Havel fought against censorship. All over the world there are individuals like Havel who understand that the truth sets people free and that lies and censorship incarcerate them. ARTICLE 19 exists to defend and help the Havels wherever they are.

Censorship not only imprisons, it also kills. It does that both directly and indirectly. In 1990 a new and awful famine hit the Sudan and Ethiopia. These are both countries without a free press and that is one reason why their poorest and most vulnerable people are dying of starvation. In India there is malnutrition and poverty, but politicians are held accountable by a free press operating in a pluralist society, and famines no longer occur.

In China the threat is different. Since the massacre around Tiananmen Square, the government has fought to deny and destroy the truth of what happened there and has killed many of those who bore witness to the movement for democracy.

But today, that truth can no longer be easily suppressed. Even as Tiananmen happened, the events were instantly relayed all over the world by satellite, and they have since been constantly replayed on thousands and thousands of video cassette recorders. That knowledge is free and no amount of government lies can capture it again. This is one of the great gains of the communications revolution in which we are immersed.

Similarly, in Wenceslas Square, along with the throngs of people there was a large truck bearing a huge white dish which was beaming information to and from a satellite six miles up. New technology is undoubtedly helping to destroy the monopoly that authoritarian governments try to impose on news. Computers, faxes, satellite communications - all seem so far to be working on the side of the people against oppression and censorship. ARTICLE 19 will do everything it can to assist and increase that momentum.

But in countries of sub-Saharan Africa and elsewhere in the less developed world such technologiocal progress has not yet had great impact. There our task is harder.

It is to try to keep the tragedies and distortions that censorship creates at the forefront of minds in the relatively uncensored world, and to try and convince the governments which censor that their practices are both destructive and doomed. More and more people are coming to understand that censorship is totally incompatible with an economically developed society, let alone a humane one. As we continue to defend the victims and expose the abuses of censorship, we will proselytize in a brazen manner. Censorship is a monster which kills. But it is a dragon which we can all help slay.

London 1991.

Introduction

Freedom of Expression 1988-1991

This ARTICLE 19 World Report on Information Freedom and Censorship in 77 countries covers a remarkable period of extremes; the crumbling of authoritarian rule in Eastern Europe; the flowering of *glasnost* in the Soviet Union; the end of emergency rule in South Africa; the return to civilian rule in four Latin American countries: and, in other countries, an inexorable tightening of all forms of censorship. In Myanmar, a government defeated in the May 1990 elections tenaciously clings to power by means of stringent censorship; in China, the aftermath of the 1989 Democracy Movement includes charging key demonstrators with treason, a capital offence; in Sri Lanka, killing has become the chief form of censorship; and, in April 1990, Turkey introduced Special Decree 424 which has outlawed debate on the Kurdish issue. In Kenya and other African countries, calls for an end to one-party rule are brutally suppressed and in Guatemala the level of violence directed towards the media guarantees a high degree of self-censorship.

Many major world events during the past two years have had at their heart the issue of freedom of expression: the democracy movement in China began as a concerted demand for freedom of expression; the chain-reaction collapse of authoritarian governments in Eastern Europe was initiated and sustained by popular insistence on the freedom to demonstrate against repression, injustice and corruption; in South Africa, it was the insistent demand that the black majority have a democratic voice. A review of the statistics, however, provides a less sanguine picture.

Censorship Statistics

In 62 of the 77 countries surveyed in this book, people remain in detention for having peacefully expressed their opinions and, in these same countries, people or their works, or both, continue to be banned because of the beliefs they express. Ethnic and/or religious conflicts and consequent suppression of freedom of expression exist in 51 of the countries reported and, of these, 27 currently operate under State of Emergency or Prevention of Terrorism legislation which allows those governments to arbitrarily suspend the right to freedom of expression.

In 27 countries in the report, people, including journalists, continue to be tortured, killed, or otherwise maltreated on account of their opinions. The government retains ownership or direct control of the press in 22 countries. Extra-legal censorship operates in 72 countries including the United States, the United Kingdom and most of Western Europe. Mechanisms range from tacit agreements between government ministers and newspaper editors, and appointment of trusted friends or relations to positions of power, particularly in the press, to the assassination by death squads of those who express beliefs or opinions contrary to the government.

Censorship Mechanisms

The mechanisms of censorship are many and diverse but the underlying and connecting theme is that any form of censorship not only suppresses information but also serves as a reminder to toe the government line. In Turkey, political trials can last for more than a decade, severely disrupting the defendant's daily life and livelihood and serving to keep the threat of censorship very much alive in the public's mind. Since the 1980 coup in Turkey, more than 85,000 people have been tried for "freedom of expression crimes" and more than 3,000 remain in detention, awaiting trial for having expressed their beliefs. In Pakistan, during the late General Zhia's military rule, fully half the prime-time evening television news was devoted to the activities of the government, leaving little time for coverage of foreign or other news. In Iran, all plays are required to pass through seven stages of censorship, each judged by a different official, a practice which has effectively extinguishd independent theatre in that country. In 1987, the BBC World Service reported a massive bomb explosion half a mile from the Sri Lanka Broadcasting offices, which killed hundreds of people. Sri Lankan news editors delayed reporting the outrage for several hours until it had been confirmed by the official news agency.

In some areas of China, permission of the local party organization is required before a lawyer can present a not-guilty plea on behalf of a client. In India and many other countries, the government controls the allocation of newsprint and often discriminates against its critics by supplying inadequate amounts or charging exorbitant prices. In Cuba, only the government newspaper is distributed nationally, due to a growing shortage of newsprint. In many countries, the widespread use of the telephone to censor the media (a practice so routine in Malaysia that it has acquired the title of "budaya telpon") enables the government to exert direct control.

What is Censored?

Governments often react swiftly and drastically to threats to their authority or to perceived threats to national security or religious orthodoxy. In Sudan, organizing or even calling for a strike is punishable by death. In Taiwan, security legislation makes it an offence to reveal the number of pigs on the island, due to the fear of invasion and possible threat to the island's food supply; a television editor was imprisoned for seven and a half years for having shown a video-tape of a communist military parade. In Vietnam, a 58-year-old poet, who has spent half his life in prison, was re-arrested in 1979 for handing a poem to a foreign diplomat. He remains in detention. In Malawi, a government minister fearing the consequences of an accurate press report of a speech she had given, ordered the arrest of seven journalists; three remained in detention without charge for one year. In the Israeli Occupied Territories, newspaper and magazine editors may have to submit up to 30 pages of text (including sports reports and crossword puzzles) to the military censor in order to achieve a 12-page edition after censorship. In Indonesia, a newspaper was summarily closed down by the government after having published the results of a survey on the most admired person, which placed the prophet Mohammed in only eleventh place; this was interpreted as an insult to Islam. In Saudi Arabia, a woman was tortured to death for being in possession of a Shi'a prayerbook and a photograph of the late Ayatollah Khomeini.

As this book goes to press a Ugandan radio journalist faces charges of defamation (despite the fact that the law only punishes libel) for having asked visiting Zambian President Kenneth Kaunda about his sons' involvement in murder and corruption. In Morocco, a comic duo was banned from TV after a sketch in which they lampooned the criteria used in selecting artists for television appearances. In Spain, satirizing the Pope is strictly prohibited and, in 1987, a journalist received a six-year prison sentence for insulting the King. In Japan, criticism of the Emperor provokes death threats from paramilitary groups. In the UK a journalist was convicted of contempt of court for refusing to reveal his sources for an unpublished article.

Censorship can also be proactive. In North Korea, all citizens are required to wear a badge of Kim Il Sung and to hang portraits of him and his son in their homes on a wall bare of other decoration. Imported radios have their dials fixed to prevent reception of foreign programmes. In Malaysia, the onus is on journalists to prove that their information is not restricted by security laws *before* publication. This practice undoubtedly discourages journalists from investigating alleged malpractice in the public sector. School textbooks are comprehensively censored by the Ministry of Information in Japan to conceal the activities of the armed forces furing World War II. In Guatemala, a wave of killings of members of the University Students' Association began in late 1989; in April 1990, 19 students disappeared and 11 corpses have since been found. In Peru, an eight-year-old boy, arrested in June 1988, remains in detention without charge and his parents are denied access even to information on his whereabouts let alone on their visiting rights.

Obsolete laws, long on the statute books, can be resurrected and used to restrict freedom of expression. In Hong Kong in July 1990, peaceful pro-democracy activists were fined for using loudhailers, under an ancient and rarely used ordinance which also prohibits the shoeing of horses in public. In Pakistan, a law originally formulated in 1876 by the colonial government continues to be used to control freedom of expression in the theatre. In the UK, blasphemy laws dating from the Middle Ages are still used to ban books and films.

The Culture of Secrecy

Freedom of expression rests upon the principle that it is an inalienable right and the foundation of democracy. Without freedom of expression, governments can and do act with impunity. The culture of secrecy breeds more secrecy. Because of censorship, the international media can fail to report on the true extent of repression and violation of human rights.

It is only recently, for example, that the international media have begun to report on conditions in Myanmar and Kenya. The Sudan government's persistent refusal to acknowledge the extent of the famine sweeping across that country and its strict censorship of both the national and foreign media will undoubtedly lead to thousands of needless deaths. In Iraq, arguably one of the most censored nations in the world, the lack of reliable information about what has been happening there over the past decade and more has allowed a distorted and dangerous assessment of that country and its intentions.

Despite liberal laws, governments can and do exert tight control. The lack of formal laws in East Germany, for example, was striking and yet censorship was both severe and ubiquitous. Nor do reports on freedom of expression in the newly-liberated Eastern European countries and in the Soviet Union give a picture of unmitigated progress. Democracy and freedom of expression are by no means guaranteed and although there may no longer be formal censorship laws, this does not, nor can it ever, guarantee that freedom of expression will flourish. Censorship persists in informal mechanisms which, by means of their opaque and often subtle nature, are more difficult to resist and certainly to protest.

The world over, there are serious challenges to the right of freedom of expression amongst which the threats of racism and new technology will contribute. The reverberations of *The Satanic Verses* case in the UK, in India and in many Islamic countries, highlights those areas of censorship requiring sustained debate. The novel was first published in the autumn of 1988 and had an immediate global resonance, largely due to the new technology which facilitated its publication simultaneously in different parts of the world.

The growth of satellite communications, including TV, which inevitably cross borders in ever-increasing networks, will represent further challenges to closed societies which do not wish to admit beliefs other than those they espouse. It is no coincidence that the Romanian revolution and the downfall of Ceausescu began in Timisoara, a region able to receive Yugoslav television and, thus, witness nightly the astonishing events occurring in other Eastern European countries, in particular the destruction of the Berlin Wall. These cross-border pictures, virtually impossible to censor, contributed to people's confidence in pursuing their demands to the bitter end. Nowhere was this brave confidence more graphically reflected than in the patent disbelief expressed on the late President Ceausescu's face as he at first dismissed and then was forced to acknowledge the barracking from the crowd as he spoke from his balcony. This event marked the beginning of the end of 40 years of brutal repression.

Conclusions

At the beginning of 1990, it seemed as if the Doom Watch clock had been turned back at least a few minutes and that the world was a safer place. The role of communications in effecting the changes which had occurred and in helping to shape new political systems in which basic human rights would prevail is not to be underestimated. The obliteration of censorship in the Soviet Union, for example, has allowed a reunification of language. Words and concepts, such as democracy, justice and law, now have a shared meaning between East and West and there is the hope of universal human values which transcend the interests of social class.

As the millenium approaches, there are also new and complex areas of potential conflict. ARTICLE 19, as the international centre on censorship, will both provoke and participate in the debate on these areas of censorship. These are likely to include religious and racial incitement. Perhaps one of the most urgent areas for concern will be the right of access to information and the need for international *glasnost*. If it is truly the goal of all nations to achieve international security, then states will have to explicitly acknowledge the right to know in order to protect against terrorism and other life-threatening conditions such as AIDS, famine, the destruction of the environment and the proliferation of chemical weapons.

Much work is being done in these and other areas to formulate laws to protect individuals against censorship, but this report bears testimony to the fact that while laws are clearly vital, they alone cannot protect against the frequent and widespread infringements catalogued in this book. Laws are too often used by the powerful and by the majority to prosecute the weak and the minorities and are sometimes used for purposes other than those for which they were intended. Freedom of expression is a fragile right and maintaining it is difficult enough. The task of developing an open culture where it follows on from many years of stringent restriction is even more difficult. The ingredients include a constitutionally enshrined right to freedom of expression, legal redress in the event of any infringement, technical resources to transfer information freely and, above all, the building of confidence which comes from successful challenges to existing or potential restrictions.

What is needed is a positive formulation of the right to freedom of expression and a positive commitment to openness on a global level. Censorship often has small beginnings and, by necessity, proliferates. It is only when the culture of secrecy (so evident in the vast majority of the countries surveyed in this book) begins to fade that people will develop the necessary confidence to challenge any infringement, however peripheral, and have some real expectation that their challenges will be successful. Decades of repression have, in so many countries including Eastern Europe, bred an apathy which is the death knell for true democracy.

ARTICLE 19 will continue to support and amplify the call for freedom of expression throughout the world and to campaign relentlessly against its restriction.

Frances D'Souza
Director, ARTICLE 19
London, January 1991.

Country Reports

This section of the Report contains studies on the state of freedom of expression in 77 countries representative of all regions and of various political and ideological systems. The countries were chosen to reflect the diverse issues and challenges raised by the violation of freedom of expression and information in all parts of the world. Countries are not rated or classified. Reports were updated to November 1 1990.

Where ARTICLE 19 has taken action in a particular case or on behalf of a person, this has been summarized at the end of each country report.

Statistics were taken from *The Europa World Year Book 1990, UNESCO Statistical Year Book 1990*, the United Nations Human Development Index and from ARTICLE 19's International Centre on Censorship. Countries that have not ratified the International Covenant on Civil and Political Rights are marked "No". For other countries the year of ratification is given.

Africa, South of the Sahara

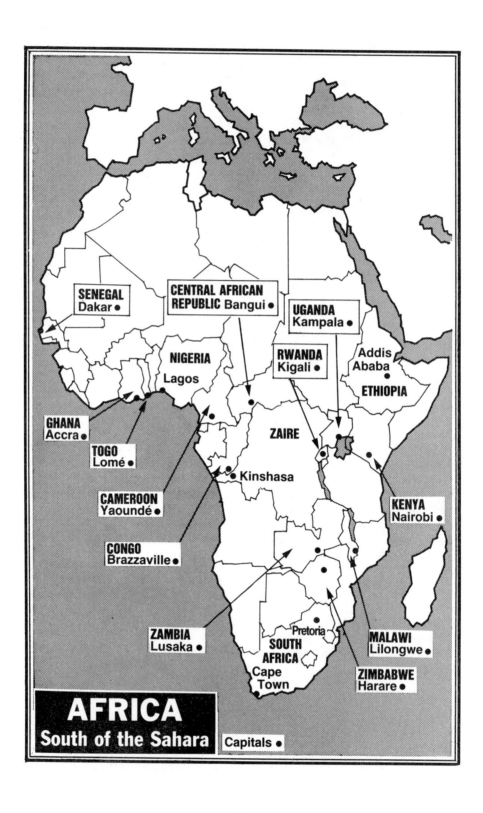

SENEGAL
Dakar •

CENTRAL AFRICAN
REPUBLIC Bangui •

UGANDA
Kampala •

NIGERIA

Lagos

RWANDA
Kigali •

Addis
Ababa

ETHIOPIA

GHANA
Accra •

ZAIRE

TOGO
Lomé •

• Kinshasa

CAMEROON
Yaoundé •

KENYA
Nairobi •

CONGO
Brazzaville •

ZAMBIA
Lusaka •

Pretoria

SOUTH
AFRICA

MALAWI
Lilongwe •

Cape
Town

ZIMBABWE
Harare •

AFRICA
South of the Sahara

Capitals •

Cameroon

Freedom of expression is enshrined in the Constitution along with the freedom to form political parties, but President Paul Biya, who has ruled Cameroon by decree since 1982, has enforced a one-party system. The ruling Rassemblement Democratiqué du Peuple Camerounais (RDPC) has dominated the country since its independence in 1960, and the rival Union des Populations du Camerounaises (UPC) has been banned. Since a coup attempt in 1984, which was brutally crushed, the country has been governed under emergency powers.

In May 1990, a new party, the Social Democratic Front (SDF), was launched. Its inaugural rally, planned for May 21 in the provincial capital of Bamenda, was prevented from taking place by government troops. A State of Emergency was declared and the local radio station warned that people who left their homes risked being shot. When the rally eventually took place, five days later, police opened fire on the crowd, killing six people. At the end of the month a French minister, Jacques Pelletier, cancelled an official visit, apparently to register France's protest at the police action.

In July, President Biya announced that Cameroon would attempt to introduce political pluralism "quite quickly", and that all political prisoners would soon be released. In the same month Albert Mukong, a writer and one of the SDF leaders, lodged a plea with the United Nations to send a delegation to monitor constitutional changes.

	Data	Year
Population	10,821,746	1987
Life expectancy (M/F)	49.2/52.6	1985
GNP (US$ per capita)	1,010	1988
Main religion(s)	Christianity	
	Animism	
	Islam	
Official language(s)	French	
	English	
Illiteracy %	45.9	1990
(M/F)	33.7/57.4	1990
Daily newspapers	1	1986
Non daily newspapers	3	1984
Radio sets	1,300,000	1987
TV sets	120,000	1987
Press agencies:		
	Camnews	
ICCPR:	YES	1984

Freedom of Political Expression

In June 1986, the Supreme Court refused an application to compel the government to recognize the UPC. The petitioner, Dr Sende, was detained for four months in 1985 when he presented the petition and was re-arrested in July 1988 and held for nine days.

The Subversion Ordinance In May 1989, a senior police officer warned against abuse of freedom of expression, referring to a 1962 Ordinance on Subversion, thought to be defunct, which punishes "lack of respect for the authorities" by up to five years' imprisonment. Albert Mukong was detained for 11 months under this ordinance after giving an interview to the BBC World Service in which he criticized the April 1988 parliamentary elections and government corruption. In February

1990, he was re-arrested, together with 11 others, including Yondo Black, a lawyer, two months after they had met to discuss forming a political party. In April, six were acquitted, including Albert Mukong; Yondo Black was sentenced to three years' imprisonment for subversion. The defendants were charged under the 1962 Ordinance and under Article 153 of the Penal Code, which provides for up to five years' imprisonment for contempt of the President of the Republic.

The Media

The *Cameroon Tribune*, published daily in French and weekly in English, is government-controlled. Ten other publications appear weekly and seven fortnightly. CAMNEWS, the official news agency, is owned by the government company SOPECAM. Private publications face major hurdles: newsprint is expensive, there are no government subsidies and SOPECAM has a printing monopoly.

Attempts by the independent press to report on demands for multi-party democracy resulted in bannings and arrests in 1990. The April 24 and May 22 issues of *Le Messager* were banned, apparently in connection with articles about a multi-party system, the release of political prisoners and the short-term detention of television journalists in May. The paper's editor-in-chief, Pius Njawe, was briefly detained by police while covering the SDF's inaugural rally in Bamenda on May 26.

Paddy Mbawe, editor-in-chief of the *Cameroon Post*, and Jerome Gwellem, editor-in-chief of *Cameroon Outlook*, were detained on May 25 and 27 respectively, allegedly for possessing an SDF press release criticizing government attempts to disrupt its rally.

The *Cameroon Post* was banned in mid-May, without explanation, after it published an interview with SDF leader Ni John Ndi Fru, a letter by Albert Mukong and a report on the detention of TV journalists.

Press Law The Press Law requires all publications to obtain prior authorization from the censors. Publisher Charles Ndi Chea has been detained several times since 1983 for publishing a newspaper without prior authorization. Article 11 of the Press Law requires publications to submit proofs to the Interior Ministry before printing. SOPECAM will only print publications bearing the censor's stamp and newspaper vendors are forbidden to distribute publications without a second stamp from the censor, after printing. Only the private press is subject to this censorship machinery; official newspapers are expected to exercise self-censorship. If a publication is passed by the censor, there is no guarantee that it will not be seized. Newspapers containing articles which may "disturb public order or peace" can be seized, temporarily or permanently. In April 1989, *Le Messager* published an article which displeased the President and copies were seized. Its director and editorial advisor were interrogated by the police for two weeks.

Use of Criminal Law In April 1988, the security service arrested four journalists and an academic and questioned them for five days on the grounds that they had committed contempt against the head of state and public officials. Joseph Neyimbe, director of *Le Combatant*, and Samuel Zang des Joies, a journalist at the magazine, were detained for four months for criticizing former French President Valery Giscard d'Estaing during his visit to Cameroon in January 1988. Former Radio Cameroon journalist Sam Nuvala was charged with defamation for calling parliamentarians "a bunch of monkeys, idiots and hand clappers" while reading the news. He was given a suspended sentence.

Radio and Television   Radio and TV are run by the state-owned Office de Radiodiffusion Télévision Camerounaise (CRTV), and strict government control is maintained over the content of broadcasts. The Director General of CRTV was dismissed in 1988 after broadcasting a story on poor housing conditions for university students.

In May 1990, TV journalist George Tanyi was arrested and sacked after a programme in which he co-ordinated a studio discussion on multi-party democracy. Eleven other journalists were also arrested and some had their pay suspended for eight days, the maximum allowed under the Constitution.

Foreign Media   Most Cameroonians rely on foreign media for news about events in their country, although the government does censor the foreign media. At least two issues of the French magazine *Jeune Afrique* were banned in 1988, and the May 1989 issue was delayed for a week. In November 1989, an issue of *West Africa* was confiscated, as was an issue of *Nouvel Afrique-Asie* three weeks later. They contained articles critical of President Biya's record. An issue of *Les Marchés Tropicaux*, containing the same information, was also banned.

Actions

In January 1989 ARTICLE 19 asked its members to write to the government protesting the detention of Albert Mukong, and on February 20 1989 ARTICLE 19 wrote to the government calling for his release. He was freed on May 5 and charges were dropped. (See text)

In its 1989 Commentary to the Human Rights Committee ARTICLE 19 said that the constitutional provisions on press freedom and freedom of expression are rendered ineffective by a system of law and procedure which imposes censorship on all media, information and ideas. ARTICLE 19 called for an entire review of such laws and procedures.

On March 20 1990 ARTICLE 19 wrote to the government protesting the arrest of 12 people after they had met to discuss forming a political party. (See text)

Central African Republic

The Central African Republic (CAR) is a one-party state, with the Rassemblement Démocratique Centrafricain (RDC) the sole legal party. General André Kolingba, who came to power in a bloodless coup in 1981, was elected in 1986 to a six-year term as head of state. Multi-party systems have been condemned by President Kolingba as "the root cause of division and destabilization", but varying trends are allowed inside the RDC, at least in theory. France wields considerable influence through high-level advisers and troops stationed in the country.

The 1986 Constitution grants the President exceptional powers "to adopt measures warranted by circumstances to restore public order", if territorial integrity, national independence and the normal functioning of the institutions are seriously threatened (Art.14). At such times, however, the National Assembly cannot be dissolved, nor the Constitution altered.

	Data	Year
Population	2,740,000	1986
Life expectancy (M/F)	41.4/44.6	1985
GNP (US$ per capita)	330	1988
Main religion(s)	Animism	
	Christianity	
Official language(s)	French	
Illiteracy %	62.3	1990
(M/F)	48.2/75.1	1990
Radio sets	163,000	1987
TV sets	6,000	1987
Press agencies:		
Agence Centra-africaine de Presse		
ICCPR:	YES	1981

The Constitution proclaims a set of 10 human rights principles, but makes no specific mention of freedom of opinion, nor freedom of the media. The "right of expression" is included but, according to the authorities, is restricted to exclude "insults against the representatives of the public authorities".

Freedom of Expression

In recent years a number of former dissidents have returned to the government's ranks, some obtaining high-level positions.

In September 1989, 12 opposition activists living in exile in Benin were forcibly transferred to prisons in Bangui, the CAR capital. They had been arrested by the Benin authorities in July 1989 and were flown to Bangui in a Zaïrean military plane. Among those seized was General Francois Bozize who heads the opposition Rassemblement Populaire pour la Reconstruction de la Centrafrique (RPR). A high-ranking official under former Emperor Jean-Bedel Bokassa, he was later Information Minister under President Kolingba. Six others were members of another opposition group, the Front Patriotique Oubanguien-Parti du Travail (FPO-PT), led by Abel Goumba.

Another noted dissident in jail in Bangui is Jeanne-Marie Ruth Rolland, who was sentenced by a special court to a three-year-term in 1987 for incitement. She was released in September 1989, two months before the end of her sentence, but re-arrested in December.

Journalist Thomas Koazo, jailed in October 1986 for insulting the head of state, was released in September 1989. Employed by the CAR news agency, the Agence Centrafricaine de Presse (ACAP), he had sent a dispatch to the Pan African News Agency (PANA) in Senegal, in which he recounted a secret meeting between President Kolingba and former Emperor Bokassa.

Former Emperor Bokassa was brought to trial in Bangui in 1986 and was sentenced to death but, in March 1988, President Kolingba commuted the sentence to life imprisonment.

In September 1990, Nicolas Tiangaye, who was Francois Bozize's defence lawyer, went on trial accused of making "seditious statements" against the armed forces. The judge, Faustin Gabriel Gbodov, began the trial behind closed doors.

The Media

The media are mostly state-owned. Offical surveillance and control is legal and operates along lines laid down by decrees and directives issued over the years by successive governments. Control over the state-run media is exercised by the Ministry of Communication, Arts and Culture which is located in the same building complex in Bangui as the radio and television stations.

Newspapers The printed media are the least developed. The sole daily paper, *E Le Songo*, published in French in Bangui since 1986, prints about 2,000 copies. *Balao*, a quarterly French-language paper carrying cartoons, prints some 10,000 copies. Other papers, with a readership of less than 1,000, are the weeklies, *Renouveau Centrafricain* and *Terre Africaine*, and the monthlies, *Bangui Match* and *Ta Tene*.

Two privately-owned papers are also published in Bangui: the monthly *Demain Le Monde* and the economic weekly *Le Pari du Développement*, both in French.

Radio and Television Radio is the main form of communication in a country with high illiteracy and a large and sparsely populated countryside. Radio broadcasts run to 130 hours a week, with one third of the programmes in French and the remainder in Sango: a specifically rural orientated radio station is being planned. The sole radio station was ordered to give maximum coverage to the speeches of President Kolingba and other senior officials during the period leading up to the 1986 constitutional referendum and presidential election. The station did not report a 1986 trial of student protestors, but the trial of former Emperor Bokassa was broadcast without any censorship.

Television broadcasting began in December 1983 and there are now programmes for up to 36 hours a week; half are in French and half in Sango.

News Agencies The Agence Centrafricaine de Presse was re-established in May 1974 under the authority of the Ministry of Communication, Arts and Culture.

Foreign Media All foreign news reports, including those obtained from foreign news agencies, require the approval of the authorities before publication. Foreign newspapers can be distributed only after official clearance. There are no regular foreign correspondents apart from the Soviet news agency TASS. However, the 1986 trial of former Emperor Bokassa was widely covered by foreign correspondents.

Books and Films There is no censorship of books, paintings or musical compositions, but there is no book production in the CAR. Legislation governs the showing of foreign films, and a 1972 presidential ordinance forbids "westerns" and films featuring banditry and war. A permanent censorship committee for films was created in 1972, but it appears to exist in name only.

President Kolingba took French author Roger Delpey to court in Paris for his book, *Affaires Centrafricains*, because he was offended by two of the chapters, "Kolingba and the Forty Thieves" and "The Last Honour of General Kolingba". In November 1987, the court ordered Roger Delpey to pay FF5,000 (US$900) in damages to President Kolingba.

Actions

In its 1988 Commentary to the Human Rights Committee ARTICLE 19 expressed grave concern that the single-party system does not allow a free exchange of opinions when all meetings outside the ruling party are unlawful. It called upon the government to implement its own proposals for freedom of the press, to review the operation of the High Court in treason and state security trials, and to abolish the crime of insult of public officials.

Congo

There were great changes in Congo's political and economic structures in 1989, echoing change elsewhere in the world, particularly Eastern Europe. In July, more than 20 members of the ruling Parti Congolais du Travail (PCT) Central Committee were removed. They were reported to be Marxist-Leninist hardliners opposed to President Denis Sassou-Nguesso's moves to end the state monopoly of the economy by privatizing the main sectors, as advised by the International Monetary Fund and the World Bank.

In September, for the first time since 1973, people other than PCT members were allowed to stand in the National Assembly elections, and more than half of those elected were non-PCT members. In November, President Sassou-Nguesso presented the PCT Central Committee with a Bill to revise the 1979 Constitution to incorporate the economic and political changes, but continued to say that multi-party democracy was not an option for Congo. However, in July 1990, the PCT Central Committee announced that it had decided to end one-party rule and said it would draw up legislation on multi-party politics in 1991.

Freedom of expression and of the press are guaranteed by the Constitution, but in practice the PCT exercises direct control over all communications, including theatres and artists, through the Censorship Commission.

	Data	Year
Population	1,843,421	1984
Life expectancy (M/F)	44.9/48.1	1985
GNP (US$ per capita)	930	1988
Main religion(s)	Animism	
	Christianity	
	Islam	
Official language(s)	French	
Illiteracy %	43.4	1990
(M/F)	30.0/56.1	1990
Daily newspapers	2	1990
Non daily newspapers	2	1986
Periodicals	10	1986
Radio sets	220,000	1987
TV sets	6,000	1987
Press agencies:		
Agence Congolaise d'Information		
ICCPR:	YES	1983

The Media

The Press Of the five government-owned daily newspapers listed in the 1988 ARTICLE 19 World Report (*Courrier d'Afrique*, *L'Eveil de Pointe-Noire*, *Le Journal de Brazzaville*, *Journal Officiel* and *Mweti*), only *Mweti* is known to be still published, and that only about three times a week. In addition to the PCT's weekly *Etumba*, there is a weekly sports paper, *Le Stade*, and *Congo Magazine*, previously a monthly but now published about four times a year.

The poor literacy levels and declining economy make it virtually impossible for newspapers to survive without subsidy. The only independent newspaper is the Roman Catholic weekly, *La Semaine Africaine*. Even with a government subsidy, economic constraints caused the daily bulletin of the Agence Congolaise d'Information to cease circulation for 19 months until May 1989.

Three issues of the French magazine *Jeune Afrique* were seized during 1989. Issue 1496 was seized because it published an article by Jean-Baptiste Placca about the deteriorating economic situation in Congo; issue 1499 was seized because it included a report of the arrest of Jean-Baptiste Placca and issue 1502 because of an editorial about the seizure of issue 1499.

Front commun, produced by the opposition group, Mouvement Patriotique du Congo, remained banned in Congo and in France, but continued to be published clandestinely. Most of its recent issues concerned the detention without trial of civilians and military officers arrested in 1987 and 1988 in connection with an alleged coup plot, which the government claimed to have foiled in July 1987.

Radio and Television Radio and TV are owned by the state and do not broadcast material that is critical of government or party policies and practices. Radio is the most important source of information for the majority of the population. There is one station, la Voix de la Revolution Congolaise, which broadcasts in French, English, Portuguese, Lingala, Kikongo and Subia. TV began transmission in 1963 and now operates for 46 hours per week with most programmes in French and some in Lingala and Kikongo.

Treatment of Journalists In August 1989, two journalists, Jacques Lumbwele Boy Buta, an Agence France Presse correspondent, and Jean-Baptiste Placca of *Jeune Afrique*, were arrested in Brazzaville. Placca, who had gone to Congo to cover the PCT National Congress, was allegedly carrying a letter smuggled out of prison by a political prisoner, journalist Lecas Atondi Monmondjo. He was interrogated for a day and subsequently expelled. Jacques Lumbwele Boy Buta, a Zaïrean refugee, was detained for two weeks and then ordered out of the country. He was reported to have been granted asylum by the USA. He had previously been detained from October to December 1987 together with about a dozen other Zaïrean refugees.

Foreign Journalists Foreign journalists are allowed to visit Congo but they need special permits to travel beyond the major towns. Most interviews by journalists are restricted to senior government and party officials.

Freedom of Expression and Opinion

The Constitution guarantees freedom of thought and religion "within the framework established by law". The Jehovah's Witness movement is banned and the Baha'i faith may hold services but is prohibited from organizing and preaching publicly. Only the PCT and affiliated social and political organizations are allowed to hold political meetings. Special permission is required to set up any clubs or organizations. Only one trade union, the *Confederation Syndicale Congolaise*, which is affiliated to the PCT, is allowed by law. In September 1990, workers held a general strike in support of the principle of independent trade unions.

Current Prisoners

Lecas Atondi Monmondjo, a journalist who had once been on the PCT Central Committee, and about 25 other political prisoners arrested in 1987 and 1988 were still detained in 1990 in Brazzaville without charge or trial. More than 70 people of the Kouyou ethnic group had originally been arrested but most of them have since been released. A group of more than 40 political detainees was released in November 1989. Those still held in mid-1990 included former president Joachim Yhomby-Opango and a Catholic priest, Father Joseph Ndinga. Since being arrested, the detainees have had neither access to legal counsel nor any opportunity to challenge the legality of their detention. The President announced in November 1989 that those who remained in prison would soon be brought to trial but this has not yet materialized.

Actions

In its 1987 Commentary to the Human Rights Committee ARTICLE 19 expressed concern over the denial of the right to hold political opinions other than those acceptable to the PCT, and over the censorship enforced by the PCT on all forms of expression. ARTICLE 19 called on the government to abolish the Censorship Commission and to allow full freedom and distribution to all media.

Ethiopia

The People's Democratic Republic of Ethiopia was officially proclaimed with a new Constitution in 1987. Under the Constitution, freedom of the press is stipulated and Ethiopian citizens are guaranteed freedom of conscience and religion (though not in a manner contrary to the interests of the state), of speech, assembly, peaceful demonstration and association, as well as freedom of movement and secrecy of correspondence. These have little meaning in practice, however, and are offset by other clauses of the Constitution, including the obligation to do national military service, the observance of socialist law and the acceptance of the Workers' Party as the guiding force of society.

	Data	Year
Population	47,882,000	1988
Life expectancy (M/F)	39.3/42.5	1985
GNP (US$ per capita)	120	1988
Main religion(s)	Christianity	
	Islam	
	Animism	
Official language(s)	Amharic	
Illiteracy %	37.6	1983
Daily newspapers	3	1986
Non daily newspapers	7	1986
Periodicals	4	1986
Radio sets	8,700,000	1989
TV sets	70,000	1987
Press agencies:		
	Ethiopia News Agency	
ICCPR:	NO	

Background   Ethiopia is ruled by a Military Administrative Council (*Derg*) which assumed power in September 1974 after overthrowing Emperor Haile Selassie. In 1976, the *Derg* elaborated a reform programme which included land reform, nationalization, elected local urban and rural associations (*kebeles*), and the reorganization of trade unions. Mengistu Haile Mariam seized power in 1977 and presided over a major struggle for control of Ethiopia, which became known as the "Red Terror", during which thousands died and tens of thousands were detained, tortured and brutally rehabilitated.

The Workers' Party of Ethiopia, a Marxist-Leninist party, was established in 1984 but its members were recruited on the basis of personal loyalty rather than on ideological grounds. A personality cult emerged, with huge portraits of the leader in all public places and idealized displays of official art showing the masses moving foward under the "leadership of Comrade Mengistu".

The country's economic problems were exacerbated by a series of droughts between 1982 and 1988, and by draconian government policies including enforced villagization resettlement programmes. Adding to these problems, the government is waging war against two secessionist movements, the Eritrea People's Liberation Front (EPLF) and the Tigrayan People's Liberation Front (TPLF).

After an unsuccessful coup attempt in May 1989, involving many senior armed forces officers, the government was forced into negotiations with the EPLF and the TPLF. In March 1990, President Mengistu made a series of concessions. He suggested renaming the party the Ethiopian Democratic Unity Party and appeared to open the way to a multi-party system. In May, 12 generals involved in the failed coup were executed, leading to unprecedented demonstrations in Addis Ababa against the President. University students went on strike and the university was sealed off and armed police took away 300 alleged ring-leaders. According to one source, a student was killed and several injured.

The Media

All forms of the media are controlled by the Workers' Party, acting through the Ministry of Information and National Guidance (MING). The Ministry registers, administers and controls all government newspapers and supervises all private newspapers and magazines. It also controls the radio, television, audio-visual service and the Ethiopian News Agency which reports all domestic news. Content is regulated by an Information Policy Committee, at ministerial level. Other constraints include the government's control of newsprint imports and of distribution.

During the 1980s the media was severely restricted in what it could print or broadcast about the famine that was afflicting the country, especially in the north. While the *Ethiopian Herald* reported appeals by the government's Relief and Rehabilitation Commission (RRC) in January and March 1984, there was no coverage between July and September, which was a crucial period for the development of the famine. Even the RRC Food Aid Appeal in August was not reported. In effect, the government concealed the existence of the famine from its own people.

Foreign journalists were also restricted. During most of 1983 and 1984, journalists could not travel to the heart of the famine zone in Tigray and northern Wollo because the TPLF was active in those areas but also because the government considered a famine to be an embarrassment and humiliation to the revolution. During the 10th anniversary celebrations of the revolution, in September 1984, restrictions were particularly severe. No foreigners at all were allowed to travel north, as it was feared that coverage of the famine would detract from the celebrations of the supposed advances of the revolution.

Newspapers There are two national daily papers, *Addis Zemen* (in Amharic), and the *Ethiopian Herald* (in English). *Addis Zemen* normally prints 30,000 copies, although this can double on special occasions; the *Ethiopian Herald*'s normal run is 6,500. There is also *Hibret* (in Tigrinya), a daily paper published in Asmara, the Eritrean capital, with a circulation of about 4,000. Four weeklies are published by MING, *al-Alem* (in Arabic); *Berisa* (in Oromo); *Ethiopia* and *Yezareitu Ethiopia* (both in Amharic). Another weekly, *Serto Addo*, is published by the Workers' Party and claims a circulation of 100,000. The party also publishes *Maskaram*, a theoretical quarterly. The police and the army put out fortnightly papers, and the Orthodox Church also publishes two papers, *Maedot* and *Tinsae*.

Distribution is inadequate because of lack of transport. Of the 101 provinces in the country, 45 do not get any daily paper, nor do 234 of the 324 urban areas, even in times of peace. The capital, Addis Ababa, takes nearly 50 per cent of the output of the two main papers, and nearly 80 per cent of the English language daily.

Ethiopian journalists are expected to belong to the Ethiopian Journalists' Association which is headed by Workers' Party members. Its code of conduct, although undeclared, is powerful and infringements can mean losing one's job or liberty. Self-censorship is extensive. At least one journalist, Martha Kumsa, was held without trial for over eight years until September 1989, on apparent suspicion of having links with another ethnic opposition group, the Oromo Liberation Front.

Foreign newspapers and magazines are available, although subject to censorship. However, because of the presence of the Economic Commission for Africa and the Organization of African Unity headquarters in Addis Ababa, it is relatively easy for uncensored foreign publications to enter the country.

Foreign Press Several foreign news agencies report from Addis Ababa. AFP and Reuters have stringers (correspondents for both agencies were expelled in the 1970s), as have TASS and APN (USSR), ADN (Germany), ANSA (Italy), Tanjug (Yugoslavia), Prensa Latina (Cuba), and Xinhua News Agency (China). MING issues visas for foreign journalists whose movements are carefully monitored; Western journalists are infrequent visitors.

In May 1989, two BBC reporters and a Reuters photographer, who entered the country to cover an attempted coup, were expelled with no reason given. Two other Reuters reporters, who arrived to cover events immediately after the coup attempt, were denied entry.

Travel inside the country, for both visitor and resident, remains limited and has to be carried out under government auspices and with government officials present on every visit. Similar restrictions apply to trips with the opposition movements, particularly with the EPLF and TPLF. However, there have been no investigative reports on the widespread human rights abuses that dissident members of these groups claim have been carried out by the EPLF and TPLF.

Books One major success of the government has been its literacy campaign, launched in 1979. In 10 years the literacy rate has risen from around 6 per cent to nearly 80 per cent (though all figures should be treated with some caution because of the difficulty in collecting accurate information due to civil wars). Much of the teaching is in Amharic, but the campaign has also been accompanied by publications in a number of other languages.

Western books are imported, though not in large quantities. Works on Ethiopia are normally banned, whether considered favourable or not. Larger numbers of books are imported, mainly from Moscow, through the government-owned Kuraz Publishing Agency. A considerable number of "ideologically sound" works have been translated into Amharic and are widely available. The few private presses are careful of what they print, as is the University of Addis Ababa Press which publishes academic works.

A number of novels about the revolution have been published in Amharic. It has been rare for anything critical, or even mildly unfavourable, to get past the controls. One of the very few was *Oromai* by Baalu Girma, the deputy Minister of Information. *Oromai* was an account of the disastrous Red Star campaign (hailed by President Mengistu as the final victory over the Eritrean Rebels) in Eritrea in 1982. Baalu Girma had been the head of propaganda for the campaign and his novel was a cynical report on the leadership and organization of the campaign. Cleared for publication by the head of the ideology department of the Workers' Party (who had been opposed to the Red Star campaign), the book reportedly sold 500 copies in 24 hours before being withdrawn and subsequently banned. Two months later Baalu Girma was abducted from his car. He has not been heard of since and it is widely believed that he has been killed.

Radio and Television Radio and TV, like the rest of the media, are used for political mobilization and propaganda. In 1986, it was estimated that 59 per cent of radio time was spent on such activity, as a means to educate the masses and form a new kind of social consciousness. Radio Ethiopia broadcasts in nine languages. The national service goes out in Amharic, Orominya, Somali, Tigre and Tigrinya. The international service broadcasts in English , French, Arabic, Somali, Afar and Amharic (in 1986 these broadcasts amounted to a total of 161 hours a week).

The capital, Addis Ababa, has by far the largest concentration of radios, TVs and telephones. The 1984 census estimated that 62 per cent of its 260,000 housing units had radios, though only 15 per cent possessed TVs.

Censorship of Communications It is widely believed that considerable phone tapping goes on and although there is little specific evidence for this, the rumours have induced caution in most users.

Similarly, while there is no great difficulty in sending and receiving mail from abroad, or within Ethiopia, enough examples of interference have been reported to suggest that the authorities wish to deter correspondence. Mail is interfered with, and magazines with foreign post-marks are delayed or never arrive.

Travel Travel restrictions are considerable. Movements between areas run by different *kebeles* are controlled both in towns and in the countryside and permission has to be obtained for overnight stays outside a home area. Road blocks are frequent on all major roads. Internal travel has been seriously affected by the wars, particularly in the northern regions of the country. It is difficult to obtain permission for overseas travel; substantial financial guarantees have to be pledged and are forfeit if the traveller does not return. Pilgrims are allowed to go to Mecca on the *Hajj*, but the application has to be approved by local *kebele* officials.

Freedom of Expression

Religious Groups The government has given little encouragement to religion in its policies, though persecution has fallen short of systematic anti-religious campaigns. Some recognition was given to Islam by the granting of Muslim holidays and both the Patriarch of the Orthodox Church and the Imam of the Grand Mosque in Addis Ababa are on the Central Committee of the Workers' Party. The Orthodox Church was seriously affected by the land reform measures in 1975 and the then Patriarch Theophilus was arrested and accused of embezzlement in the mid-1970s. He subsequently "disappeared" and is assumed to have been killed. During the villagization campaign of the late 1980s, the creation of new villages often meant the disappearance of the local church or mosque.

The Evangelical churches have been more commonly targetted. These include the Ethiopian Mekane Yesus Evangelical Church (affiliated to the Lutheran World Federation), Meseret Christos Church (a member of the Mennonite World Conference), the Kale Hiwot (World of Life) Church, Jehovah's Witnesses, and Mullu Wongel (Full Gospel) Church. Worst affected has been Mekane Yesus, many of whose members have been detained and which has had numerous churches closed, less for religious reasons than for the Church's alleged involvement in Oromo dissidence; the Church is strong in Oromo regions.

Eritrea and Tigray By early 1990, the EPLF and the TPLF controlled much of Eritrea and all of Tigray. Both opposition movements today publish a variety of papers and pamphlets, and broadcast via the EPLF radio station. All output is strictly controlled and no private publications of any kind are permitted by either organization. Any indications of dissent appear to be suppressed. In March 1989, Mehari Missegina, a journalist for Radio Ethiopia known for his opposition to Eritrean secession, was shot dead by the EPLF. The EPLF also denies the existence of several other Eritrean organizations, while the TPLF calls for the elimination of "bourgeois opposition movements".

Actions

In April 1990 ARTICLE 19 published *Starving in Silence*, a report on the effects of censorship on famine in Ethiopia, Sudan and China. It demonstrated that censorship and disinformation can delay or prevent famine relief and prolong the effects of famine. It also pointed out that it is highly unlikely that famine would occur in a country with a free press, as even the suggestion of food shortages would become a topic for public debate and thus for preventive action.

Ghana

On December 31 1981, Flight-Lieutenant Jerry Rawlings staged his second *coup d'etat*, toppling the government to which he had handed power in 1979, suspending the Constitution he had signed, dissolving parliament and banning all political parties in the country. Executive and legislative powers were subsequently vested in the Provisional National Defence Council (PNDC) which has ruled the country since.

In July 1987, the PNDC announced plans for district council elections to be held by the end of 1988. When the elections were finally held voting was staggered over a three-month period in three zones in December 1988, and

	Data	Year
Population	13,391,000	1987
Life expectancy (M/F)	50.3/53.8	1985
GNP (US$ per capita)	400	1988
Main religion(s)	Christianity	
	Animism	
Official language(s)	English	
Illiteracy %	39.7	1990
(M/F)	30.0/49.0	1990
Daily newspapers	5	1986
Radio sets	4,000,000	1987
TV sets	171,000	1987
Press agencies:		
	Ghana News Agency	
ICCPR:	NO	

January and February 1989. It has been alleged that this interval was to ensure rigging in an election in which the government nominated a third of the candidates. Even though the election was billed as a non-party event, government agents had powers to determine who should stand for election. Candidates were not allowed to canvass for votes independently except under the supervision of, and at the times, venues and format decreed by government agents.

The Preventive Custody Law 1982, which empowers the government to hold indefinitely anyone suspected of threatening state security, has been used extensively by the PNDC to suppress its critics, political opponents and personal enemies. While most politicians detained after the 1981 coup were released within a year, a handful of ministers, some believed to be personal enemies of people in government, were held for five years without trial. In 1990, at least 50 people, mostly members of the armed forces arrested in previous years following alleged coup attempts or conspiracies against the government, remained in detention without charge or trial.

The Media

There are no laws telling Ghanaian journalists what they can or cannot write: most members of the press resort to self-censorship. As one person put it: "The only freedom in Ghana is the freedom to praise." Those who cannot praise are summarily dismissed.

Government-Owned Media The government owns the two major dailies, the *People's Daily Graphic* and the *Ghanaian Times*, and the two main weeklies, the *Mirror* and the *Weekly Spectator*. Radio and television are both wholly state-owned. Opponents and critics of the government are rarely allowed access to these media. Editors and some media personnel are appointed either directly by the head of state or through the Ministry of Information. On assuming power in early January 1982, the PNDC fired all but one of the top editors and some administrative personnel in the various media. Their replacements were journalists who shared similar political credos to those in government.

The Ministry of Information supervises the media and from time to time meets editors to discuss issues affecting the media. With the coming to power of the PNDC, the Press Commission, whose existence had been guaranteed by the 1979 Constitution, was replaced by the Castle Information Bureau, officially the press unit of the Office of the Head of State. This organization competes with the Ministry of Information to control the media. It writes editorials, news commentaries, commissions feature articles and issues instructions to journalists. The latter are not permitted to publicly acknowledge its existence.

Since January 1982, there has been a ban on the reporting of opposition political activity. Although there are repeated calls for national discussion of political issues, the columns of the media, with the exception of *The Mirror*, do not reflect any serious debates. One-sided views are published, with the state-owned media in many cases refusing to publish the views of opposition groups. It is common to read editorials condemning workers in industrial conflicts and failing to offer the public information on the specific grievances voiced by the workers involved.

Independent Press The brunt of government displeasure with the media has been borne by the independent press and their employees. In March 1990, there was only one privately-owned newspaper, *Pioneer*. However, this paper is often not published for lack of newsprint, sometimes for as long as six months at a time. *The Monitor* was launched in September 1989 and folded in March 1990.

The *Palaver* closed down in early 1982 when its editor-in-chief fled the country in the wake of the 1981 coup. In July 1982, the offices and press of the weekly *Echo* were attacked and the editor-in-chief, John Dumoga, fled into exile in Nigeria. In February 1985 the editor of the Kumasi-based *Pioneer*, Baffour Ankomah, and his news editor, Osei Tutu, were taken to Accra. At the military headquarters of the PNDC they were subjected to beatings and humiliation by soldiers for allegedly getting a name wrong in a story. The editor was hospitalised for three months and later fled into exile. In July 1985, the publisher of the *Free Press* was detained with about 20 others, probably for reviving the paper which was closed down when he was detained in June 1983. He was released in November 1985.

On December 13 1985, the government revoked the licence of the *Catholic Standard*, a weekly paper critical of its actions. An attempt to murder its editor, the Reverend Dr Palmer Buckle, failed in a case of mistaken identity: the body of the priest who was abducted instead was found on the Accra beach the following day. This spate of attacks intensified self-censorship by journalists. In April 1987, the head of state decried what he called the "culture of silence" in the country and roundly denounced both the populace and journalists for not debating conditions in the country. No mention was made of attacks against the press.

Newspaper Licensing Decree On March 27 1989, the government introduced two new laws, the Newspaper Licensing Regulations Law (PNDCL 211) and Legislative Instrument L11417, requiring all newspapers and magazines in the country to re-apply for licences. "Bad taste and cultural pollution" were cited as the reason for the laws. Once issued, a licence is valid for 12 months, unless it is revoked.

There had been an upsurge in the number of sports papers published, apparently profitably. By the end of 1989 there were about 13 such papers, most of them weeklies. In addition to sporting news many commented on political issues and printed cartoons considered by the government to be licentious. Many consider that the PNDC's motive for the new laws was to further control avenues for disseminating information critical of its performance. Its first victim was a new publication, the *Independent*. This paper and its sister publication, *Sports Guide*, have been refused licences. Government-owned papers were all available the day after the law came into force.

Foreign Newspapers Legislative Instrument L11417 requires vendors of foreign newspapers and magazines to obtain licences before selling them. After the licence is approved, the vendor must apply to the Ministry of Information for permission to remove the papers from the airport. If approval is given, the vendor must provide the Ministry with four copies of the publication within 24 hours of clearance. Imported magazines and newspapers carrying articles critical of the government are banned.

Religion In June 1989, the government took the unprecedented step of attempting to control the Churches. It banned the Latter Day Saints (Mormons), the Jehovah's Witnesses, and two local sects, the Jesus Christ of Dzowulu and the Nyame Sompa. All Churches and sects in the country were ordered to register, but the main Christian Churches, Catholic, Anglican, Methodist and Presbyterian, refused. In a pastoral letter entitled "A Message from the Christian Council of Ghana and the Ghana Catholic Bishops' Conference", a copy of which was sent to the government on November 10 1989, Church leaders said that PNDCL 221 (Religious Bodies Registration Law) "in its present form constitutes an infringement of the fundamental human right of the freedom of worship. For this reason we are of the view that our Churches would be surrendering both our present membership and for future generations a fundamental and inalienable human right, if we registered in accordance with this law".

Actions

On May 10 1989 ARTICLE 19 wrote to the Ghana government urging it to withdraw the decree which requires all publications to obtain authorization in order to publish, and all foreign publication to obtain authorization for distribution. (See text)

Kenya

Kenya is a single-party state. Since a constitutional amendment to this effect was passed in the National Assembly in 1982, the sole party, the Kenya African National Union (KANU), has increasingly imposed its influence. The party is supreme and the National Assembly and the government are described as agents of party decisions. President Daniel arap Moi wields great personal influence, and appoints High Court judges, and both provincial and district commissioners.

Although section 79 of the Constitution guarantees freedom of opinion and expression, as well as the flow of information and ideas, and privacy of correspondence, the President can suspend such rights and institute extensive censorship under the Preservation of Public Security Act.

	Data	Year
Population	21,163,000	1986
Life expectancy (M/F)	51.2/54.7	1985
GNP (US$ per capita)	360	1988
Main religion(s)	Animism	
	Christianity	
	Islam	
Official language(s)	Kishwahili	
Illiteracy %	31.0	1990
(M/F)	20.2/41.5	1990
Daily newspapers	5	1989
Non daily newspapers	5	1989
Periodicals	37	1989
Radio sets	1,900,000	1989
TV sets	200,000	1989
Press agencies:		
	Kenya News Agency	
ICCPR:	YES	1972

Since early 1990, President Moi has faced growing opposition from an alliance of politicians, lawyers, journalists and grassroots communities, and church leaders wrote an open letter to him denouncing political murders. Members of opposition groups have faced imprisonment and violence, including an armed attack on the home of Kenneth Matiba when his wife and daughter were seriously injured. Mr Matiba resigned from the government in 1988, and in May 1990 launched a campaign with Charles Rubia for multi-party elections. In June, a press conference held by the lawyer for the two men, at which he called for greater freedom of speech, was broken up by police who reportedly confiscated film and a BBC reporter's notebook. The same day, George Mbugguss, managing editor of the *Daily Nation*, was briefly detained, apparently because of his paper's reporting of debates for a multi-party system. The Commissioner of Police later announced that the police would vet future press conferences "to determine whether they were genuine or illegal meetings".

At the beginning of July Kenneth Matiba and Charles Rubia were arrested along with Gitobu Imanyara, editor-in-chief and publisher of *Nairobi Law Monthly* and international board member of ARTICLE 19, John Khaminwa and Mohammed K Ibrahim, both lawyers, Raila Odinga, son of former vice-president Oginga Odinga, and five of Kenneth Matiba's employees. They were detained without charge under the Public Security Regulations until July 25 when all except Matiba, Rubia and Odinga were released. Gitobu Imanyara was re-arrested on July 26 and charged with sedition in connection with articles in his magazine on multi-party democracy. He was released on bail six days later but Matiba, Rubia and Odinga remained in detention without charge. Kenneth Matiba's lawyer and family have not been allowed to see him since August 25.

On August 14, one of Kenya's most outspoken church leaders, Bishop Alexander Muge, was killed in a road accident, three days after Peter Okondo, the Minister for Labour, had warned him not to visit Busia District or "he might not leave alive". The Bishop went ahead with the visit and was killed in a head-on collision with a lorry on his return. A week later, after pressure from government ministers, church leaders and lawyers, Peter Okondo resigned.

President Moi is also facing a possible threat to his credibility from an investigation by UK detectives, requested by the President himself, into the murder of Robert Ouko, a former foreign minister. The British police submitted their report in September and, a month later, the Kenyan government began its own inquiry into the murder. Following anti-government protests after the minister's death in February 1990, all demonstrations were banned. In March, the Reverend Lawford Ndege Imunde was sentenced to six years' imprisonment for possession of seditious publications; the prosecution maintained that personal notes in his desk diary contained "offensive words" against the President. The contents of the diary were not disclosed on grounds of state security, but they are believed to relate to rumours about Mr Ouko's death. In June, dozens of people were arrested in Nairobi for playing cassettes of anti-government songs including one called *Who Killed Robert Ouko?*

Government actions against dissidents continued in October with the arrest of Kogi wa Wamwere, who had been in political exile in Norway since 1986, and two lawyers, Rumba Kinuthia and Mirugi Kariuki. Mr Wamwere was in jail for 11 days without access to a lawyer before being charged with treason, an offence punishable by death. In the same month, Norway, one of Kenya's major aid donors, announced that it was reducing its aid because of concern at President Moi's human rights record. In response, Kenya broke diplomatic relations with Norway, accusing it of conspiring with dissidents to overthrow the government.

The Media

Newspapers The best selling newspaper is the *Daily Nation* with a circulation of 200,000. It is published by the Nation Group of Newspapers, owned by the Aga Khan, spiritual leader of the prosperous Shia Ismaili community. In recent years, Kenyans have been offered shares in the company but major editorial decisions still come from the Paris headquarters. The oldest English-language newspaper, established in 1917, is *The Standard*, published by the London-based Lonrho. Its circulation is about 49,000. Africa's only full-colour newspaper, the *Kenya Times*, was first published in 1983, and is jointly owned by the ruling KANU Party and the London-based Maxwell Communications Corporation. Its circulation is around 40,000.

The Nation Group publishes the best-selling Kiswahili daily, *Taifa Leo*, while the Kenya Times Media Trust publishes East Africa's first full colour Kiswahili newspaper, *Kenya Leo*. There are also a number of weekly and monthly publications, such as the *Nairobi Law Monthly*, which are lively platforms for debate.

On June 28 1989, Members of Parliament unanimously banned the Nation Group of Newspapers from covering parliamentary proceedings. The ban, lifted four months later, was the outcome of President Moi's consistent criticism of the newspaper. On June 1, the President warned Kenyans to avoid reading some newspapers, particularly the *Daily Nation*. He said any Kenyan who still read the newspaper was "playing with fire".

During the period of the ban, the state-owned Voice of Kenya radio station was instructed to drop the *Daily Nation* from its programme, *The Press Today*, which highlights the contents of the daily press.

In June 1990, three journalists from The Standard Group of Newspapers were charged with publishing material "likely to cause fear, alarm and despondency to the public" after reporting deaths in a battle between police and residents during a slum clearance in Nairobi. The government claims there were no deaths.

Censorship There are no written rules on how much a journalist can criticize those in power. Most rulings are on the whim of the authorities, and the President does not hesitate in taking *ad hoc* measures against offending journalists.

Day-to-day control of newspapers' content and perspective is exerted by the Office of the President, either through telephone calls from the President's Press Secretary or written instructions conveyed through the ruling KANU party. If these instructions are disobeyed, journalists are threatened, arrested and imprisoned. Privately-owned newspapers face the added fear of the withdrawal of government advertising revenue, vital for the survival of many publications.

Journalists being trained at the University of Nairobi are made aware that certain subjects must not be covered. Any criticism of the President or his policies is taboo. KANU leaders often seek to prove their loyalty and enhance their standing by reacting harshly to newspaper reports which dare to attempt even veiled criticism of the President's policies. It is difficult to know what, in the eyes of the authorities, will be construed as "unsuitable" on any given day.

In March 1988, the monthly publication of the National Christian Council, *Beyond*, was banned after alleging that "political thuggery" was used in the selection of candidates for the general election. Its editor, Bedan Mbugua, was sentenced to nine months' imprisonment, but his sentence was quashed by the High Court after he had served two weeks in jail. The official reason given for his original sentence was that he had failed to submit proper returns of sales for his magazine. In April, Gitobu Imanyara, was charged with offences similar to Mbugua's; his case is still pending in the courts.

In April 1989, the *Financial Review* was banned after criticizing government and economic policy, and a new economic magazine, *Development Agenda*, was banned after only two issues.

On September 28 1990, the *Nairobi Law Monthly* was banned, and possessing even back issues became a criminal offence, after the magazine had printed a number of articles on multi-party democracy. The courts overturned the ban on October 8 but the government has appealed this decision.

Generally, journalists are apprehensive when it comes to writing political stories. Their practice is to tune to the Voice of Kenya radio news bulletins for clues on what topics to cover. News editors also rely on the output of the Kenya News Agency.

Several journalists have lost their jobs after the authorities accused them of "bold reporting". Investigative reporter William Onyango was eased out of his post on the *Kenya Times* after he exposed scandals linking several influential figures to a textile imports scandal. He was named Journalist of the Year by a Kenya press club but the honour was withdrawn after pressure on the organizers of the event. Today, Onyango freelances for business magazines.

The unpredictability of the authorities' attitude is such that civil servants up to the level of permanent secretary will not comment on even the most mundane matters nor provide basic information for news stories for fear of reprisals. This leaves the Office of the President as the sole source of information for anything from political events to Kenyan agricultural statistics. Generally, editors heap lavish praise on President Moi on the front pages of their newspapers.

Even journalists on the KANU-owned *Kenya Times* have not been spared the wrath of the authorities. In 1986-1987, the ruling party dismissed Mitch Odero, Acting Managing Editor of *Kenya Times* and Chairman of *Kenya Times* Management Committee, after he gave an interview on the situation in Kenya to the BBC World Service while visiting London. The authorities said the interview was "outspoken and outrageous". In 1989, two district reporters were warned that severe action would be taken against them by local government officers if they did not stop writing "rubbish" about the districts they were based in.

Foreign Correspondents The Kenyan capital, Nairobi, is the base for nearly 150 foreign correspondents. Between them they represent predominantly, but not exclusively, the Western European press, broadcasting stations and news agencies. From here, they cover large parts of Africa, including news flashpoints such as Ethiopia, Somalia, Uganda, Zaïre and even southern Africa. Kenya has been the traditional base for foreign correspondents because it has good international communications and travel facilities.

Traditionally, Kenya-based foreign correspondents avoid writing any news or analysis critical of Kenya so as not to jeopardize their position. For example, foreign correspondents do not touch stories of corruption which circulate freely within the country. President Moi has often warned foreign correspondents about negative coverage of his country's affairs. These warnings have come privately and through the Kenyan media. When BBC correspondent Colin Blane filed a story about the arrest, in breach of government policy, by a local chief of a Kenyan, who failed to attend a national celebration in Murang'a, the authorities responded through the columns of the *Kenya Times*, criticizing Blane and the BBC for wasting precious airtime on parochial matters.

Few foreign correspondents have been expelled, but they have been threatened with expulsion. Recently, Mary Anne Fitzgerald, the Nairobi-based stringer of several British and American publications, was expelled from the country.

The Foreign Press British and American publications are sold in cities such as Nairobi and Mombasa within three days of publication. Expatriates in up-country towns obtain their newspapers through private subscription. A government censor vets the content of all publications for mass circulation when they arrive at the airport. The Office of the President also issues orders to the Post Office to vet pages of magazines and newspapers containing articles or news items critical of Kenya, particularly those addressing issues of human rights violations or those critical of government practice. Foreign current affairs magazines have sometimes appeared on the newsstands minus the pages the censor finds offensive. It is not uncommon for private subscription publications to be intercepted. The Kenya Times Media Trust vets copy from all international wire news agencies before relaying it to the Kenyan media; previously, this work was done by the Kenya News Agency.

Radio and Television Kenya's sole broadcasting authority, the Kenya Broadcasting Corporation (KBC), is state-owned. No private radio or TV transmitters have ever been approved but on November 16 1989, the Kenya Times Media Trust announced that it was setting up Kenya's second TV channel, KTN Channel 62, a 24-hour global commercial channel open to subscribers only. Radio and TV programming is strictly controlled in terms of political content and perspective and a censorship board vets both foreign and locally produced material before it goes on the air. A majority of the output is produced in Kenya but some 45 per cent is purchased from Britain and the USA. The bulk of radio output is allocated to government news broadcasts and the President's speeches, and creative programming is non-existent. The radio service is divided into national, general and vernacular. Both local and foreign music is played but songs deemed provocative or containing political lyrics are censored, thwarting a rich oral narrative tradition.

Prohibited Publications Among banned publications are Salman Rushdie's *The Satanic Verses*, Amnesty International's report on torture and imprisonment in Kenya, and any literature produced by the underground Mwakenya movement or the opposition organization UMOJA. Other banned periodicals include those published by the Kenya Socialist Group.

Actions

On August 25 1988 ARTICLE 19 wrote to the government protesting the imprisonment of Bedan Mbugua, editor of *Beyond*, and on May 10 1989 ARTICLE 19 urged the government to lift a ban on the *Financial Review* and the declaration which makes possession of it an offence.

On July 6 1990 ARTICLE 19 wrote to the government expressing concern at its actions denying individuals the right to freedom of expression, and calling for the release of 11 people, including its international board member, Gitobu Imanyara, Kenneth Matiba and Charles Rubia, who were arrested and detained without charge (see text). In the same month, an appeal letter was sent to ARTICLE 19 members urging them to write to the government protesting the arrests.

On July 12 1990 ARTICLE 19 wrote to the UK government requesting it to make representations to the Kenyan government in order to secure the immediate release of Gitobu Imanyara and other political detainees. ARTICLE 19 received a series of letters from the UK Foreign and Commonwealth Office in response to the release and re-arrest of Gitobu Imanyara.

On October 28 1990 ARTICLE 19 wrote to the government requesting that it lifts the banning order issued against the *Nairobi Law Monthly* and stops harassing editor-in-chief Gitobu Imanyara.

On November 11 1990 ARTICLE 19's international board wrote to the High Court in Nairobi in support of Gitobu Imanyara's application for his passport in order to travel to ARTICLE 19's board meeting in London. The passport was not returned.

Malawi

Since shortly after Malawi's independence in 1964, the free exchange of information has been severely circumscribed both in law and in practice. Malawi has a single-party political system headed by Dr Hastings Banda, President-for-Life (since 1970) of both the country and the ruling Malawi Congress Party (MCP). Any expression of political dissent is severely repressed: leaders and active members of opposition parties are either imprisoned or in exile; journalists and academics, including the country's leading poet, are also imprisoned. People imprisoned for attempting to exercise their freedom of expression are known to have been tortured, and some have been denied medical treatment. In March 1990, police shot dead 20 people in the capital, Lilongwe, after protests against the hushing up of a murder case which allegedly involved the bribing of a senior policeman.

	Data	Year
Population	7,983,000	1987
Life expectancy (M/F)	38.1/41.1	1977
GNP (US$ per capita)	160	1988
Main religion(s)	Animism	
	Christianity	
Official language(s)	English	
Illiteracy %	58	1985
Daily newspapers	1	1986
Non daily newspapers	5	1986
Periodicals	43	1986
Radio sets	1,500,000	1987
TV sets	4,000	1986
Press agencies:		
	Malawi News Agency	
ICCPR:	NO	

The 1965 Public Security Regulations make it an offence, punishable by up to five years' imprisonment, to publish anything likely "to undermine the authority of, or public confidence in, the government". Since 1973 life imprisonment has been the penalty for sending "false information" out of the country which may be "harmful to the interests or to the good name of Malawi". President Banda has extensive personal powers of indefinite detention without charge under the Public Security Regulations.

In February 1989, Fred Sikwese, a senior economist in the Ministry of Foreign Affairs, was arrested and taken to Lilongwe Central Prison. He is alleged to have photocopied documents relating to the sensitive issue of Malawi's relations with South Africa. On March 10, he died, apparently from starvation. His family did not see the body and there was apparently no post mortem examination. At about the same time Frackson Zgambo, a businesman, was arrested for allegedly trying to pass documents copied by Sikwese to a magazine in Britain. A few days after Sikwese's death he was transferred to Mikuyu Prison, where he remains in detention without charge.

The Suppression of Intellectual Life

The ruling MCP maintains a tight control on all aspects of life, and intellectual freedom is closely circumscribed. Intimidation is so complete that nowhere in Malawi (university, parliament, newspapers, church) can there be found any discussion whatsoever of Malawi's recent past or possible future when President Banda, who is elderly and frail, dies. Many of the country's most talented writers have chosen exile, often after spending time in jail, as in the cases of Felix Mnthali (now in Botswana), Innocent Banda (now in Zimbabwe) and Frank Chipasula (now in the USA).

The Censorship and Control of Entertainment Act 1968 established a censorship board which sets the conditions under which newspapers operate and all publication takes place. The Act makes it an offence to publish or distribute any publication "likely to give offence to the religious convictions or feelings of any section of the public, bring anyone into contempt, harm relations between sections of the public or be contrary to the interests of public safety or public order". The Act makes provision for any member of the public to complain, anonymously if they wish, about material which has "caused offence". All scripts for plays also have to be approved by the censor.

Banned Books All books, foreign or local, are subject to clearance from the official censorship board. Publications can also be suppressed without actually being banned. Hundreds are banned however, including works by George Orwell, James Baldwin, Bernard Malamud, Wole Soyinka, Okot p'Bitek, Ernest Hemingway, Tennessee Williams, Simone de Beauvoir and Graham Greene. Possession of these books is punishable by imprisonment. In a trial in 1976, one of the allegations against a former secretary general of the MCP, Albert Muwalo, was that he had been found in possession of a copy of Orwell's *Animal Farm*. He was also found to possess books on the politics and economics of the USSR and other communist countries. Unlike *Animal Farm*, these were not banned, but the judges were in no doubt that had they been imported "in the regular manner", they would have been banned.

Jack Mapanje Jack Mapanje, Malawi's foremost poet, was arrested in Zomba in September 1987 and has been detained without charge in Mikuyu Prison ever since. The authorities have given no reason for his imprisonment, although it is known that at the time of his arrest he was preparing a volume of his poetry for publication and had just accepted a position as Writer in Residence at the University of Zimbabwe. Jack Mapanje is not affiliated to any of the exiled opposition groups, nor does his work display any specific political viewpoint. However, in recent years his poems had become more openly critical of President Banda and his entourage.

An earlier volume of his poetry, *Of Chameleons and Gods*, was published in London in 1981. It was not prohibited by the censorship board, but neither was it cleared for sale. This meant that it could not be found in Malawian bookshops, but it was not an offence to possess a copy. At about the time of Mapanje's arrest, however, the book was forbidden for use in schools and colleges.

As well as being a poet, Mapanje is head of the Department of English Language and Literature at the University of Malawi. After his arrest, one of his colleagues in the English department, Blaise Machila, suffered a nervous breakdown and was admitted to a psychiatric hospital. There he was interrogated by Special Branch police officers. Machila denounced John Tmebo, uncle of the President's Official Hostess, and her brother Dr D Zimani Kadzamira, Principal of Chancellor College in the University, as responsible for Jack Mapanje's imprisonment. He was promptly discharged from hospital, arrested and detained in Mikuyu prison himself. He remains there, reportedly in solitary confinement and in great mental distress.

The Crisis in Education

Under British colonial rule, the Tumbuka-speaking people of northern Malawi received a better standard of education than groups from the south and centre of the country. As a result, they have tended to dominate Malawi's civil service and educational system. Since 1964 the country's leadership has been dominated by Chichewa-speakers from the central region, notably President Banda himself. Chichewa is an official language of the country, along with English, whereas Tumbuka is not. Only the official languages are permitted on the radio or as a medium of instruction in schools. The political elite from the central region resent the widespread employment of Tumbuka speakers in government service and make periodic efforts to purge them. 1988 and 1989 have been marked by just such an anti-northern purge, signalled in a series of public speeches by the President. One of the effects has been to cause chaos in the country's educational system.

In a speech on February 13 1989, President Banda accused teachers from the north employed in schools in central and southern regions of deliberately teaching badly in order that their students would do less well academically than northern students. He ordered all teachers to be transferred to schools in their region of origin. At least one man, Thoza Konje, an area manager with the Sugar Company of Malawi, is reported to have been detained for having commented that the redeployment of teachers was unworkable. The remark was made while he was having a drink with friends and was presumably overheard by government informers, a common hazard which inhibits the open discussion of political issues.

Restrictions on Religious Freedom

President Banda is an elder of the Church of Scotland and presents his rule as moral and God-fearing. (Another elder of the Church of Scotland, Orton Chirwa, a former Attorney-General, is serving a life sentence for treason after a grossly unfair trial.) However, religious freedom is not extended to those of whom the government disapproves. Notably, the Jehovah's Witnesses have been banned since 1967 as an "unlawful society". Jehovah's Witnesses refuse to salute the national flag or to join the MCP. In 1972 possibly as many as 100 Jehovah's Witnesses were killed by party militants and more than 20,000 fled to Zambia. In the 1980s repression against the sect appears to have eased although reports are still received of Jehovah's Witnesses being imprisoned. There is a large Muslim minority, some 20 per cent of the population, centred among the Yao people of south-eastern Malawi, who have been largely neglected by the Church-dominated education system.

The Media

There is no free press in Malawi. With the exception of one or two Church papers, the mass media are owned and controlled by the government. In the Malawi Broadcasting Corporation (MBC), the Malawi News Agency (MANA), the *Daily Times* and the weekly *Malawi News*, not the faintest suspicion of critical comment is allowed. Journalism in Malawi is a hazardous business, even for those resolved not to step out of line. In 1985, a number of journalists from MANA, the MBC and the

Daily Times (including its editor) were detained because they had accurately reported a speech by a member of the government. Unfortunately, the speaker subsequently had second thoughts about a speech that she feared would be deemed critical of the President and ordered the journalists' arrest for "misquoting" her. Three of the journalists remained in detention without charge for a year.

In October 1989, Mkwapatira Mhango, an exiled Malawian journalist living in Lusaka, Zambia, died as a result of a firebomb attack which also killed nine other people, including his two wives and five of his children. Despite Malawian government allegations that the killings were the result of feuding among opposition groups, there are many circumstantial factors which point to the government itself being responsible.

Foreign Press Reporting Foreign journalists attempting to report on Malawi face less extreme but nonetheless effective sanctions. In 1972, a British journalist was expelled for gathering information on Malawi's relationship with South Africa and a Rhodesian journalist was expelled for writing about the persecution of the Jehovah's Witnesses. A year later a senior expatriate editor at the MBC was deported.

In recent years there have been visits to Malawi by representatives of a number of western papers. In 1988, two foreign correspondents, Mike Hall and Melinda Ham, established offices in Lilongwe, the first time this had happened for many years. They survived for about a year on a diet of purely economic stories until there was a delay in renewing their work permits in October 1989 when they were forced to leave the country for two weeks. The apparent reason was that Hall had reported that pregnant women were sometimes obliged to buy party cards for their unborn children. In January 1990, they were expelled from the country without explanation.

Human Rights Monitoring

No indigenous human rights groups operate in Malawi, and no international human rights mission has visited the country since 1983 when an Amnesty International delegate tried, unsuccessfully, to observe the trial of Orton Chirwa and his wife Vera. In November 1989, the government publicly denounced an Amnesty International report on political imprisonment in Malawi. In September 1989, an official denounced Africa Watch's reporting on the country and in December turned down a request from the organization to visit Malawi.

Nigeria

Freedom of expression lacks a secure foundation in Nigeria. Having survived long stretches of military rule, the press remains under the watchful eye of the present military government which is set to hand over to civilian rule in 1992.

The overall picture of the Nigerian press is nevertheless still one of high quality. The fastest growing press in Africa, there are now more than 100 newspapers and magazines. The proliferation of publications has also spurred the emergence of a new generation of journalists, better paid, better educated and more respected. But the profession has been brought into disrepute by some reporters who succumb to the "brown envelope" phenomenon, the buying of positive publicity through cash "gifts" to journalists.

	Data	Year
Population	104,957,000	1988
Life expectancy (M/F)	46.9/50.2	1985
GNP (US$ per capita)	290	1988
Main religion(s)	Islam	
	Christianity	
	Animism	
Official language(s)	English	
Illiteracy %	49.3	1990
(M/F)	37.7/60.5	1990
Daily newspapers	19	1986
Radio sets	16,600,000	1987
TV sets	5,600,000	1989
Press agencies:		
News Agency of Nigeria		
ICCPR:	NO	

Although most dailies are government-owned, an increasingly significant proportion is owned by private individuals and organizations. Radio and television are, however, still wholly owned and controlled by the government.

The Media and the Military

In the mid-1970s the military government compulsorily acquired a majority shareholding in the then independent Daily Times Publishing. Its approach was to try to co-opt the press through monthly confidential press briefings for senior editors. In the ensuing months, the government banned *Newbreed* magazine and laid the foundations of a Press Council to "regulate operations of the press". Its brief was to register all journalists and impose fines on erring reporters and editors. The Nigerian Press Organization (NPO) refused to participate and the council exists today in name only.

By far the most draconian measures against the media were taken by the military regime of Major General Muhammadu Buhari. Under Decree 4 of 1984 any journalist who published a story considered injurious to a public office holder was liable to a minimum of two years in jail, however true the story. Trial was by military tribunal specially constituted to handle such cases.

The Decree's first victim was *The Guardian* newspaper and its two journalists, Tunde Thompson and Nduka Irabor, accused of publishing a story predicting the posting of Nigerian diplomats abroad. They were each sentenced to one year in prison and their newspaper was fined Naira 50,000 (US$6,850).

When Major General Ibrahim Babangida came to power, following the bloodless coup that ousted Buhari in August 1985, he stated that Nigeria's press could look forward to a new relationship with the government. He abrogated Decree 4 and pardoned the journalists from *The Guardian* who had by then served their sentences. The euphoria in Nigerian newsrooms was short-lived for, within months, cracks began to appear in the relationship between the media and the new government.

On October 19 1986, the editor-in-chief of *Newswatch* magazine, Dele Giwa, was killed by a parcel bomb at his home. The government was immediately accused of using violent means to eliminate an editor who it believed was critical of its policies. The government denied that it was behind the murder. Before Dele Giwa's murder, his magazine was proscribed for six months by the government for publishing what was termed "classified information" (a report on the government's plan for guidelines for the return to civilian rule). The Nigerian media saw the report as a major scoop. Critics of the government alleged that Dele Giwa had angered the authorities by threatening to publish more classified information. The Nigeria Union of Journalists (NUJ) called for a commission of inquiry into the Giwa murder, which was quickly rejected by the government.

Gregory Onwuneme, editor of the state-run daily, *The Nigerian Observer*, fled the country after being sacked. The paper was closed down in October 1988 after an editorial criticizing a Commissioner in charge of sport but re-opened in February 1989. The newspaper is now censored and its staff has been cut from 547 to 400.

Journalists on *The Republic* were arrested and detained after publishing a story on June 15 1989, alleging that the Chief of General Staff, Vice Admiral Augustus Aikhomu, had been involved in a US$3.5 million scandal. The newspaper's offices were closed.

Security agents also detained and questioned Ikpe Etokudo, managing editor of the independent *New Horizon* magazine and Tunde Ogungbile, an assistant editor, in connection with an interview with human rights lawyer Chief Gani Fawehinmi.

Tony Ukpong, a business journalist on the *Weekly Metropolitan*, was detained for eight months without charge and without his offence being disclosed to him under Decree 2 of 1984. He was released from detention in mid-1989.

Femi Aborisade, editor of *Labour Militant*, was also detained without charge under this decree from February 6 1989 to September 30 1989 in connection with an October 1988 article calling for the release of all imprisoned trade unionists.

An attempted coup on April 22 1990 resulted in severe measures being taken against the press. Although the coup was suppressed within hours, a week later several journalists were arrested and *The Punch* was closed down. *The Punch* had condemned the coup attempt as "ill-conceived, thoughtless and unpatriotic" but apparently angered the government by urging it to examine the issues which might have given rise to the rebellion. It was eventually re-opened on May 20.

Chris Mamah, deputy editor of *The Punch*, was detained, along with Chris Okojie, deputy editor of the *Vanguard*, Willy Bozimo, deputy general manager of the News Agency of Nigeria, Onoise Osunbor, a senior journalist on the *African Concord* weekly magazine, Bassey Ekpo Bassey, a former political editor on *The Chronicle*, and Tolu Olanrewaju, a Radio Nigeria journalist who was believed to have been on duty when the rebels temporarily took over the radio station. Chris Okojie was released without charge on May 11; Bassey Ekpo Bassey, Willy Bozimo and Chris Mamah were all released around June 21.

Several other publications have also been closed down. The *Lagos News, Lagos Evening News* and *Sunday News* were closed on May 1, apparently because of an editorial comment in the *Sunday News* of April 27 on the coup attempt, which the government considered to be "negative and critical". *Newbreed*, a bi-weekly news magazine, was closed for two weeks in June, apparently because of publication of a letter written by Chief Great Ogboru who the government accuses of financing the coup attempt. Chief Chris Okolie, the publisher and editor-in-chief, was also arrested and detained for 16 days. The *Vanguard* and *Champion* were both closed down for three days in June for reporting apparent ethnic discrimination in Lagos State, and several journalists were arrested and detained for several days.

Laws Restricting Freedom of Expression

Various laws restrict the freedom of the Nigerian press. The Official Secrets Act of 1962, though rarely invoked, greatly limits the extent of investigative journalism concerning government activities. Many Nigerian editorials have called for a freedom of information law.

The State Security (Detention of Persons) Decree More popularly known as Decree 2 of 1984, this has been used by the government as an instrument for muzzling the press. Under the law, the government can detain anyone indefinitely and without trial for "reasons of state security"; journalists have been detained for up to eight months. The government refuses to say how many people are held under this decree but the President of the Nigerian Bar Association, Alao Aka-Bashorun, claims there are 30 detainees, including prominent politicians.

Media Council Decree The Media Council Decree of 1988 provides for an 18-member Media Council (a successor to the Press Council) whose chairman, secretary and 10 council members will be appointed by the President. The NUJ will have four representatives, and the Newspaper Proprietors' Association and the Guild of Editors will each have two. The Council has the power to register journalists and to discipline them for misconduct. The decree defines journalists as graduates of approved institutions with five years' experience in recognized media. They alone will be allowed to practise journalism, while those who are not qualified will face stiff fines. There is no provision for freelance journalists, stringers or photographers. One prediction is that some 70 per cent of the country's several hundred journalists will lose their work.

The NUJ does not support the Media Council and claims that the government had reneged on an agreement allowing the union to register bona-fide journalists and expose anyone who fraudulently claimed to be a reporter. The NPO has rejected the Decree, calling it an "infringement of the fundamental rights of Nigerians to inform and be informed".

Libel Human rights lawyer Chief Gani Fawehinmi has campaigned to bring to justice two top government security officials he thought were behind the 1986 murder of Dele Giwa, editor-in-chief of *Newswatch*.

Fawehinmi sought to prosecute them for their alleged role in the murder. The Supreme Court rejected his application, reiterating an earlier court decision that a citizen cannot bring a private prosecution against another for murder. Instead, a High

Court in Ikeja decided that by accusing the security officials, Fawehinmi had libelled them and awarded them damages of Naira 3 million (US$410,950) each.

In January 1990, Fawehinmi was sentenced to 12 months in prison for contempt of court after he claimed that the judge who found him guilty of libelling the security chiefs was a "government judge".

Two newspapers, *The Punch* and its editor Ademola Osinubi, and the *African Concord* and its editor Lewis Obi, were also sued for publishing stories relating to the original case, but the charges were later dropped.

Chief Fawehinmi had been detained in June 1989 after an interview of his was published in the March issue of *New Horizon*, criticizing the government and its economic programme. Both Chief Fawehinmi and the publishers of *New Horizon* were tried under Decree 19 which forbids statements that could "jeopardize" the military government's transition to civilian rule. On October 14 1989, Fawehinmi was released after four months in detention. On January 30 1990, the charges against him were dropped, but he remained in prison serving his contempt of court charge. On February 15 1990, he was released pending the outcome of his appeal.

The Media

The Nigerian mass media is made up of 26 daily newspapers, 36 weekly newspapers and magazines, 40 English-language periodicals, the News Agency of Nigeria, Federal Radio Corporation of Nigeria and the Nigerian Television Authority. The industry is still growing.

Newspapers A majority of Nigerian publications are still owned by federal and state governments. Of the 26 dailies, the governments own and run 13 and an equal number of weeklies. The country's oldest newspaper, the *Daily Times*, and its weekend publication, the *Sunday Times*, are owned by Daily Times Publications, a company 60 per cent government-owned. The 61-year-old group remains the biggest and richest publishing company in Nigeria, with more than 10 publications, ranging from daily newspapers to monthly magazines.

There has been a steady growth of private newspapers since the early 1980s, launched to compete against poorly-funded and inefficiently managed government newspapers and the well-established privately-owned dailies, the *Nigerian Tribune* and *The Punch*.

However, the press has been adversely affected by the country's economic programme. Devaluation of the country's currency, the Naira, has made it difficult for the Nigerian Newsprint Manufacturing Company to import raw materials, leading to severe shortages. High newsprint prices have raised prices of newspapers, and numerous publications have been forced out of business.

The *Nigerian Tribune* was launched by the late politician Obafemi Awolowo in 1947, mainly to promote his political ideals. This paper, with a circulation of 109,000, has been the most outspoken critic of recent government policies. *The Punch*, launched in 1976 by Chief Olu Aboderin, has a circulation of 150,000, has remained an alternative voice in the crowded media scene and has been labelled a "popular tabloid" due to its inclusion, until recently, of pictures of semi-nude women.

The first serious contender to challenge the circulation of the *Daily Times, The Nigerian Tribune* and *The Punch* emerged in 1980 when millionaire Moshood Abiola launched the *National Concord* and the *Sunday Concord*. They have a combined circulation of more than 200,000. Another millionaire businessman, Alex Ibru, entered the scene in 1983 with the publication of *The Guardian*, which has a circulation of 80,000. Both the Concord and Guardian groups have, in addition to dailies and weeklies, set up financial papers and news magazines vying for sales in Nigeria and overseas.

Radio and Television The federal and state governments own all radio and TV stations. There were an estimated 20 million radio receivers in use in 1987 and an estimated two million TV sets. The Federal Radio Corporation of Nigeria has 29 radio stations in the country. Established in 1978 to replace the Nigerian Broadcasting Corporation, it is controlled by the federal government and divided into five zones, Lagos, Enugu, Ibadan, Kaduna regions and external services for transmissions in six languages. The domestic service broadcasts in 13 local and regional languages.

The Nigerian TV Authority, established in 1976, is controlled by the federal government. It has 32 regional TV stations and broadcasting facilities are generally well-developed, but coverage is principally government-biased.

Self-Censorship

Journalists publishing offensive articles are regularly invited for "chats" (a euphemism for brief detentions) with security agents. Editors of private newspapers must also avoid publishing articles contradicting the views of their proprietors, if they are to retain their jobs. Thus, many editors tread softly, imposing substantial self-censorship. Nigerian newspapers fear that they are gradually losing press freedom.

Actions

On October 3 1988 ARTICLE 19 raised with the Nigerian authorities the case of Patrick Wilmot, a lecturer at Ahhmadu Bello University, who was abducted in March and put on a plane to the United Kingdom. A reply from the High Commissioner in London said that he had engaged in activities "incompatible with his status as a lecturer".

On April 10 1989 ARTICLE 19 wrote to the government protesting the detention without charge or trial of Femi Aborisade, editor of *Labour Militant*. (See text)

On April 28 1989 ARTICLE 19 wrote to the government about the cancellation of a rock concert because of police action.

On June 7 1989 ARTICLE 19 wrote to the government about recent measures curtailing political activity. A reply from the High Commissioner in London included an offer to meet ARTICLE 19 representatives.

Rwanda

In October 1990, a rebel force, predominantly ethnic Tutsis exiled in Uganda, invaded Rwanda. The rebels, led by Fred Rwigyemra, a major general in the Ugandan army, claimed they were fighting for democracy and an end to corruption. Within days, at least 500 civilians from the Tutsi minority in Rwanda had disappeared and are believed to be held in detention. These include priests and intellectuals suspected of sympathy with the rebels. As this report goes to press, the fighting continues.

Rwanda is a single-party state, whose Constitution guarantees freedom of expression, thought, conscience and religion. It does not guarantee the separate freedom to hold opinions without interference, a right declared in the International Covenant on Civil and Political Rights which the country has ratified.

	Data	Year
Population	6,274,000	1985
Life expectancy (M/F)	45.1/47.7	1978
GNP (US$ per capita)	310	1988
Main religion(s)	Animism Christianity	
Official language(s)	French Kinyarwanda	
Illiteracy %	49.8	1990
(M/F)	36.1/62.9	1990
Daily newspapers	0	1986
Non daily newspapers	4	1984
Periodicals	8	1984
Radio sets	411,735	1988
Press agencies: Agence Rwandaise de Presse		
ICCPR:	YES	1975

The Mouvement Révolutionnaire National pour le Développement (MRND) is the sole political organization, outside of which no political views can be expressed or political activity exercised and to which all Rwandese citizens automatically belong. The government justifies the one-party system by reference to the country's serious conflicts between its minority Tutsi and majority Hutu population.

The Tutsi minority suffers discrimination which includes a quota policy restricting access to schools, universities, and public sector posts to 10 per cent, even in regions like the province of Butare where they represent more than 30 per cent of the population. Criticism of the quota system within Rwanda goes unreported by the media.

Brochures, pamphlets and publications published in exile by members of the estimated 1.5-2.5 million Tutsi refugees are banned.

Dissent No one can avoid the influence of the MNRD which extends even to those in exile. In 1988, the German press reported that Rwandese security agents had attempted to kidnap a refugee, Jean Barahinyura, who was working in Germany on a book about the President, Major General Juvénal Habyarimana. Barahinyura has been protected by the German police ever since.

Former judge Dr Donat Murego, accused of "distributing documents which advocated the overthrow of the government", was imprisoned in November 1981 and remains in jail. The documents were in fact "open" letters which circulated in Kigali in 1980.

Innocent Ndayambye, a student at Rwanda National University, was arrested in 1986 apparently because he criticized the government. He has been detained in Kigali central prison without charge or trial.

In October 1986, 296 defendants were charged with offences relating to their activities as members of religious sects. All were sentenced to prison terms of two to 10 years because their religious beliefs did not allow them to participate in MRND activities. By the end of 1989, however, they were believed to have been released.

Aloys Sebiziga, a medical doctor, was detained from May 1989 to April 1990 when he was tried on charges of having links with former minister Alexis Kanyarengwe, now a political refugee in Tanzania, who opposes the government. He was acquitted along with Callixte Sinaruhamagaye and Claude Bahintasi, who had been detained since December 1987, and Kanyarengwe's daughter and son-in-law.

The Media

The Rwandese authorities pay particular attention to the Burundese media; both countries have approximately the same ethnic mix. Since ethnic conflicts in Burundi in August 1988, the Tutsi minority have held power but have adopted a more balanced share with the Hutu majority and have allowed more open debate on ethnic issues.

Radio and Television Radio is a particularly important means of communication in Rwanda where the illiteracy rate is around 50 per cent. The national radio broadcasts daily in Kinyarwanda, Rwanda's national language, and in Swahili and French. Following the example of neighbouring Burundi, the government plans a second station to broadcast exclusively in the national language.

The Rwandese authorities have, until recently, resisted a national TV station, officially for financial reasons, but also fearing outside influence on the Rwandese population. President Habyarimana's decision to introduce TV may have been due to the growing availability of Burundese and Zaïrean television in the south of Rwanda. The programmes of the Rwandese TV station, which was due to start broadcasting in 1990, will focus on education and culture.

Newspapers No press code exists. In November 1987, the government informed the UN Human Rights Committee in Geneva that a new law governing the press was in preparation. However, no legislation has yet been presented to parliament. In the absence of legal rules, the Service Central de Renseignements (the country's secret service) has imposed its own system of censorship.

The printed press is limited: Rwanda has no daily newspaper. The two principal newspapers are the weekly *Imvaho*, which is state-owned and has an estimated circulation of 51,000, and the fortnightly *Kinyamateka* (linked to the Roman Catholic Church authorities) with a circulation of some 11,000. Both are published in Kinyarwanda. There is also a weekly independent paper, *IWAC*, and the monthly *Kanguka*. The government publishes a French-language weekly, *La Relève*. The national press agency, Agence Rwandaise de Presse, issues a daily bulletin in French which is distributed only within the public administration. Government control of the media is maintained through an office of the MRND, the Organisme d'Information Rwandaise.

Periodicals A number of periodicals appear in French (a language which the majority of the population does not speak) in which some criticism and debate is tolerated.

However, the media abstain entirely from criticizing the constitutional system, the role of the MRND and the status of the President. Self-censorship is pervasive. Nine out of 10 professionals are employed by the state. Professionals and intellectuals have a clear understanding of how far the discussion of critical issues can be taken and what can be printed.

Le Dialogue, a bi-monthly university periodical, has a circulation of 1,900 and receives its main support from the Roman Catholic Church. The magazine is subject to pressure from the Roman Catholic hierarchy as well as the government but remains one of the main forums of intellectual discussion and debate. The monthly *Cahiers du Bureau Social*, published by Caritas-Rwanda, provides analysis and debate of social issues such as AIDS and urbanization in Kigali.

Foreign Media There are few restrictions on access to foreign media by Rwandese citizens, provided they do not contain critical reports on Rwanda. The Belgian daily, *La Libre Belgique*, which carried a story on Rwanda in October 1989 entitled "Atmosphere de fin de regne", was banned.

Restrictions on the Press

In an interview with ARTICLE 19, shortly before his death in November 1989, Father Sylvio Sindambiwe, chief editor of *Kinyamateka* until 1987, claimed that the lack of a daily newspaper exacerbated censorship. He suggested that if a daily paper existed, the security agents who control publications would be overworked and less effective.

In the 1960s *Kinyamateka* was suspended several times. Recently, new methods of intimidation have been used. Fr Sindambiwe explained that since his interview with President Habyarimana in 1985, over the detention of two prisoners of conscience, he had been subject to close surveillance. In 1987, after several articles criticizing corruption in the administration, Fr Sindambiwe was called in by government officials. Later, a security agent poured a bucket of excrement over him. After months of such harassment, Fr Sindambiwe resigned from the paper.

However, *Kinyamateka* has pursued its attempts to report fairly and independently. In late 1989, it reported public criticism of an increase in the salaries of top officials and MPs.

In December 1989, the Minister for Justice, acting on the orders of the President, summoned journalists from *Kinyamateka* and *Kanguka* who had "defamed public officials" and warned them that they could face court action if their articles were not toned down.

In 1990, the authorities appear to have increased pressure on the press. Among journalists prosecuted were Fr Andre Sibomane, director of *Kinyamateka*, Awastase Sweuvamba of the weekly *IWAC*, and Francois Hangimana, who published an article in *Kanguka* about the trial of former Finance Minister Vincent Ruhamanya. Hangimana was tried in March and sentenced to two months' imprisonment but released because he had already been detained for longer than that.

In July, Vincent Rwabukwisi, editor of *Kanguka*, was arrested after meeting Rwanda's former king, Kigeri Ndahindurwa, in Kenya, and charged with "threatening state security" which carries a sentence of 10-20 years' imprisonment. In the same month Hassan Ngeze, editor of *Kangura*, was arrested after publishing an editorial about the balance of economic power between the two main ethnic groups and reportedly printing letters written by the former king. He was charged with subversion and faces up to 10 years in prison. The trials of both men have been postponed because of insufficient evidence.

Actions

In its 1987 Commentary to the Human Rights Committee ARTICLE 19 called on the government to respect the religious and political beliefs of all individuals and groups and, in particular, to release people detained solely for having expressed their beliefs and opinions.

Senegal

Senegal attained independence from France on August 20 1960 and a revised Constitution, strengthening the position of the President, was approved by referendum in 1963. The Constitution was again amended in 1976 allowing for political pluralism and the creation of three parties, but the widely-based Rassemblement National Démocratique (RND) was refused recognition. In December 1978 the Mouvement Républicain Sénégalais (MRS) was granted recognition.

In December 1980, President Léopold Sédar Senghor resigned and handed over power to Abdou Diouf who immediately set about reorganizing the political institutions in the country. Restrictions on political activities were lifted in April 1981 and the

	Data	Year
Population	6,882,000	1988
Life expectancy (M/F)	41.7/44.9	1985
GNP (US$ per capita)	630	1988
Main religion(s)	Islam	
	Christianity	
Official language(s)	French	
Illiteracy %	61.7	1990
(M/F)	48.1/74.9	1990
Daily newspapers	1	1986
Non daily newspapers	9	1986
Radio sets	850,000	1990
TV sets	60,000	1986
Press agencies:		
Agence de Presse Sénégalaise,		
Pan-African News Agency		
ICCPR:	YES	1978

Constitution was amended to allow more than four political parties, with the result that there are now 18 parties in the country. Coalition parties are prohibited. In the 1983 election the President won 83 per cent of the vote.

A general election was held in February 1988, following renewed appeals for electoral reforms, and preliminary results indicated massive victories for the President and his Parti Socialiste Senegalais (PS). The opposition Parti Démocratique Sénégalais (PDS) alleged electoral fraud and rioting broke out in the Dakar area. As a result, a State of Emergency was declared, public gatherings were banned, educational institutions closed and an overnight curfew was imposed in the capital. Abdoulaye Wade, leader of the PDS, Amath Dansoko, leader of the Marxist-Leninist Parti de l'Independance et du Travail (PIT), and 12 other oppostion leaders were arrested and detained. Official results of the election gave the President 73 per cent of the votes, and Wade 26 per cent.

In March 1988, the National Assembly voted to extend the State of Emergency for an indefinite period but schools and colleges were allowed to re-open. The curfew was lifted in April and the State of Emergency ended in May when an amnesty was granted to those detained after the election.

In April 1989, the President announced changes to the electoral code, including a fairer system of voter registration and the shortening of electoral campaigning from three to two weeks. Access to the state-owned media was also granted to all opposition parties.

Laws Affecting Freedom of Expression

Article 8 of the Constitution guarantees everyone the right to freedom of expression and opinion, "subject to the limitation imposed by laws and regulations".

A substantial amount of legislation concerns the media. Article 49 of Act 79-44 of 1979 requires a journalist to handle information objectively and impartially. Article 50 prohibits "defamation, accusations made without established proof, falsification of documents, distortion of facts, deliberate inaccuracies, and the use of any kind of deception in order to extort information or undermine anyone's good faith".

Article 51 prohibits "signing articles for the purpose of disguised advertising, practising plagiarism, reproducing or quoting texts without indicating the author ... " as being incompatible with "professional dignity". Journalists are also required to refrain from breach of confidence, "within the limits set by law".

Criminal Code Article 248 of the Criminal Code defines the mass media as: "Radio, television, the cinema, the press, bill-posting displays, distribution of written matter or pictures of any kind, speeches, chants, shouts or threats uttered in public or meetings and in general any technical process intended to be seen or heard by the general public".

The Criminal Code allows for heavy penalties for infringement of the press laws. Article 255 states that the publication, dissemination, or reproduction or any such attempt by any means of "inaccurate reports, fabricated or forged documents, or documents wrongfully attributed to third parties ... when the said publication, whether or not it is in bad faith, leads to the violation of the laws of the country or casts discredit on the public institutions" will be punishable by imprisonment for one to three years and a fine of between 100,000 and 1.5 million francs (US$300-4,500). Preventive detention can also be imposed on people suspected of disseminating false news.

Prison sentences of up to two years and fines of up to 300,000 francs (US$900) can be imposed on those involved with the publication, possession or distribution of material "of an indecent nature". These penalties apply to the publication and dissemination of any material intended to cause racial hatred, or incite racial, ethnic or religious discrimination.

Regionalist Propaganda The Constitutional Act No 63-22 of March 7 1963 makes any regionalist propaganda a punishable offence. These provisions have been invoked to restrict news of the independence movement in Casamance Province. Since 1982 Casamance, a small region of Senegal, has demanded independence. Led by the Mouvement des Forces Démocratiques de la Casamance (MFDC), the separatists demonstrated in Ziguinchor in December 1983 and at least 25 people were killed. Several hundred people were arrested for political reasons between 1982 and 1989, some just for calling for independence. Many of those arrested are alleged to have been tortured by members of the security service; several have died in police custody.

Defamation Under Article 259 of the Criminal Code the penalty imposed on those who defame politicians or public officials is greater than for defamation of the private individual. The official explanation for this disparity is that private individuals can commence legal proceedings quickly to defend their reputations, while public officials have less privacy and need permission to take legal action.

The Media

The Press There is only one national daily newspaper, *Le Soleil*, the paper of the ruling PS. There are six weekly papers: *Le Temoin, Sud Hebdo*, both privately owned, *Le Cafard Libere, Le Politicien*, both independent satirical papers, *Wal Fadjiri*, an Islamic publication, and *Daan Doole*, belonging to the PIT. *Le Temoin* was founded in the spring of 1990 by journalists who had resigned or been dismissed from *Sopi*, the PDS newspaper which publishes bi-weekly.

In 1990, the price of newsprint increased by 34 per cent, leading the Union of Communications and Information Professionals to declare that rising costs of production constituted a danger for democracy and the dissemination of diverse information.

Article 13 of the Press Code affirms freedom from prior restraint. However, there is a provision (Art.43) that before publication a declaration must be submitted and five copies of any publication have to be deposited with the respective authorities, including the Ministries of the Interior, Information and Justice. The ministers have a constitutional right to restrict the publication of certain articles, but since 1979 no press organ has been refused authorization.

Radio and Television There are two radio networks which broadcast in French, Portuguese, Arabic, English and in six vernacular languages. There is one TV station, established in 1973. Both radio and TV are owned by the state company Office de Radiodiffusion-Télévision du Sénégal.

Opposition parties have uninhibited and equal access to radio and TV only during elections. Broadcasting is controlled by the government, except during the weekly parliamentary debate programme when all views expressed in the National Assembly are broadcast. Despite this, opposition PDS members of the Assembly boycotted sessions in mid-1989, accusing the state-owned media of partial coverage of parliamentary debates.

The Foreign Press The foreign press is subject to prior restraint. Before distribution every foreign publication must be deposited at the Ministry of the Interior and the Ministry of Information (Art.31). Any two ministers can jointly decide to prohibit any foreign publication. Failure to observe the compulsory deposit requirement is an offence punishable by imprisonment.

Sopi On November 17 1989, Cheikh Koureyssi Bâ, publisher of *Sopi*, was sentenced to six months in prison and fined one million francs ($3,000) for allegedly publishing false news. He was released pending appeal. On March 10 1989, the paper had claimed that, contrary to the declared result, PDS leader Abdoulaye Wade had won the 1988 presidential election. The defence's attempts to subpoena regional governors to testify in the case were disallowed on the grounds that it was against the penal code procedure.

On August 11 1989, *Sopi* printed an article about army officers' dissatisfaction with their military equipment. The editor, Mamadou Omar N'Diaye, refused to name his sources of information and both he and Mbagnick Diop, a *Sopi* journalist who worked on the article, were charged with "provoking the military". Diop was sentenced to six months in prison and N'Diaye to three months but were released pending appeal. Restrictions were imposed on the paper's production (Art.255) and its usual print run of 70,000 copies was reduced to 6,000.

The next issue of *Sopi* carried a story by Ousmane Ngom of the PDS about Minister of State Jean Collin. Khadre Fall, a freelance journalist, who had contributed to the article, was convicted of "offending a head of state" and sentenced to six months in prison. Cheikh Koureyssi Bâ was sentenced to one year for spreading false news, offending a head of state, provoking the military and defamation. Both were released pending appeal.

In October, *Sopi* journalist Madior Sokhna N'Diaye published a letter purported to have been written by the secretary-general of GOPEC, Malick Djibril N'Diaye. The letter, critical of Jean Collin, turned out to be false. Madior Sokhna N'Diaye was arrested and held for two months on charges of complicity in the dissemination of false news.

All journalists involved in these cases received further sentences in early 1990. In January, Mamadou Oumar N'Diaye, Khadre Fall and Mbagnik Diop were jailed for one year but, along with Cheikh Koureyssi Bâ, were released pending further appeal. In February, Ousmane Ngom and Cheikh Koureyssi Bâ stood trial for the article on Jean Collin but both were released. In the same month Madior Sokhna N'Diaye was released. In May, Bâ lost an appeal against conviction in connection with publication of the false letter and in July began a six-month prison sentence.

Actions

In its 1987 Commentary to the Human Rights Committee ARTICLE 19 noted the positive freedom from prior authorization for the publication of newspapers as "a distinctive and important feature of the Constitution". However, it called on the government to remove the offence of dissemination of false information, and to abolish the special penalties for defamation of public officials.

On May 4 1989 ARTICLE 19 wrote to the government urging it to withdraw charges made against Cheikh Koureyssi Bâ, director of *Sopi*, after the publication of an article alleging electoral fraud.

On May 10 1989 ARTICLE 19 wrote to the government protesting the banning of a demonstration organized by Abdoulaye Wade, leader of the opposition PDS.

South Africa

What has been termed the "New Enlightenment" in South Africa dates from February 2 1990 when President FW de Klerk announced a range of initiatives designed to remove obstacles to negotiation with the country's majority population. The African National Congress (ANC), the Pan African Congress (PAC) and the South African Communist Party (SACP) were unbanned, restrictions on organizations such as the United Democratic Front (UDF) were lifted and the release of Nelson Mandela along with other political prisoners was promised.

	Data	Year
Population	33,747,000	1988
Life expectancy (M/F)	51.8/55.2	1985
GNP (US$ per capita)	2,290	1988
Main religion(s)	Christianity	
Official language(s)	Afrikaans	
	English	
Illiteracy %	30	1985
Daily newspapers	24	1986
Radio sets	10,550,000	1987
TV sets	3,200,000	1987
Press agencies:		
	South African Press Agency	
ICCPR:	NO	

These momentous developments were accompanied by the withdrawal of the media emergency regulations almost in their entirety. For the first time since the National Party came into power in 1948, the government stepped back from its efforts to determine ideas and information in circulation and organizations such as the ANC were able to be seen, heard and read by the white population. The transformation was most dramatic in the case of the South African Broadcasting Corporation (SABC), which had long acquiesced in the role of government mouthpiece (the dismissal of SABC chief Riaan Exsteen in April 1988 was widely seen as a measure of the network's subordination to the government). News and current affairs programmes now feature interviews in which organizations and individuals who have fought apartheid debate with representatives of the administration which had harassed and silenced them.

In June 1990, the leading "alternative" newspaper, *The Weekly Mail*, which had battled against censorship since its inception in 1987, became a daily "mainstream" paper, *The Daily Mail*. However, owing to a lower than expected circulation and higher than anticipated overheads, the liberal daily folded three months later, but the *Weekly Mail* continues.

Despite the new freedoms, journalists continue to suffer in their attempts to cover the news. Between February and July, one journalist was shot dead, four were seriously wounded, several were arrested and detained under the Internal Security Act, films and notebooks have been confiscated, and access to the townships was prevented by the police. Bombs have exploded at opposition newspaper offices and visitors have received death threats. Five foreign journalists were denied entry visas, sometimes several times. Peaceful demonstrations have been brutally dispersed by the police using tear-gas on at least five occasions and baton charges twice. These attacks have resulted in 19 deaths, several hundred wounded and over 300 arrests.

The Media

Radio and Television Although state-controlled TV and radio in South Africa are no longer so openly propagandist, broadcasting is still seen to be promoting the government's policies. In terms of existing legislation (notably the Radio Act of 1952 and the Broadcasting Act of 1976), broadcasting is totally under the control of the government in South Africa. The state-run SABC holds a virtual monopoly of TV and radio, running 23 of the 30 internal radio stations (six of the remainder are owned by the governments in the Bantu homelands) and four of the six TV channels. One of the other two TV stations is owned by the Bophuthatswana homeland government and has an extremely limited transmission area, while the other, M-Net, is owned by the Big Four newspaper groups.

The government also exercises control, through legislation, over those few broadcast media it does not own as the state has exclusive licensing rights on all broadcast media. Under the terms of its licence, for example, M-Net is not allowed to broadcast news and current affairs.

In 1990, the government announced the establishment of a Task Force to investigate the restructuring of broadcasting. It is widely believed that the Task Force has been briefed to investigate deregulation. The move however, is not being welcomed as it is seen as an attempt to deny access by a post-apartheid government to the currently highly centralized SABC, and to avoid the monopoly becoming the subject of constitutional negotiations.

One of the major criticisms of the Task Force is its composition. It is made up mainly of government-linked white Afrikaaner males and has a high concentration of security personnel represented. Opposition groups calling for a moratorium on the work of the Task Force say decisions on the deregulation of broadcasting in the country cannot be taken without consultation with organizations representing the majority of South Africans.

Withdrawal of Emergency Regulations Comprehensive restrictions on the media had been introduced under the State of Emergency re-imposed in 1987. The effect of the regulations and their enforcement was that entire areas of news were removed from public knowledge, many journalists were detained and foreign journalists expelled. The restrictions were intended to prevent the transmission of information, particularly TV coverage, on the conflict in the townships between the security forces and people.

Following the withdrawal of the restrictions the media were free to report and comment without fear of suspension or seizure. However, the ban on publication of photographs or film that depict the consequences of unrest or security action, including damage or destruction of property and pictures of dead or injured persons, continues. Although journalists are no longer legally barred from scenes of confrontations, police officers have continued to take action against them and have prevented them from entering townships. Some have had their film confiscated while others have been arrested and detained for several hours.

In September, police announced that journalists would be barred from areas of unrest under a mini state of emergency implemented under the Public Order Act. Twenty-seven townships were designated areas of "unrest". Despite assurances by Law and Order Minister Adriaan Vlok that the new "unrest" regulations would not be used against journalists, several have been arrested and briefly detained and one film crew member has been charged under the Public Order Act.

At the height of the media restrictions in 1988-1989, five newspapers were temporarily closed, *The Weekly Mail*, *New Nation*, *South*, *Grassroots* and *New Era*, and others charged or threatened with prosecution (including *The Star*, *Natal Witness*, *Sowetan* and *Weekly Mail*). In November 1989, the editors of *The Star*, *Sowetan* and *Sapa* were threatened with subpoenas requiring them to disclose sources. Newspapers and publications were seized, sometimes in large numbers: some 10,000 copies of *Cosatu News* were confiscated in April 1989; *Crisis News*, published by the Western Provincial Council of Churches, had 1,500 copies seized in June and *Saamstan* had more than 300 copies of the paper seized.

Detention of Journalists   Zwelakhe Sisulu, editor of *New Nation*, and Brian Sokuto, freelance journalist, remained in detention during 1988. They were released in late 1988 but served with restriction orders, which were lifted from Mr Sokuto in November 1989, and Mr Sisulu in December 1989.

There were no convictions of journalists in 1988. However, in August and September 1989, an unprecedented number of journalists were arrested throughout the country, mostly at scenes of unrest or protest. This included the holding of 82 journalists during a protest in Cape Town. Many foreign journalists were expelled from the country during the State of Emergency and more than 200 were refused visas to enter. In early 1990, two foreign journalists were ordered to leave.

Permanent Laws

Despite the government's moves towards more freedom of political expression and for the mass media to relay, and comment on, current political developments, the formidable code of permanent censorship laws remains untouched and threatens the gains that have resulted from the scrapping of the emergency restrictions.

Internal Security Act (ISA)   Despite the unbanning of the ANC and the SACP, existing laws nevertheless curtail the ability of both organizations to propagate their message openly and lawfully. It remains an offence under the ISA (Internal Security (Amendment) Act, 66 of 1986), punishable by up to 10 years' imprisonment, to advocate, advise, defend, or encourage the achievement of any of the objectives of communism. "Communism" is extensively defined and includes "any doctrine, ideology or scheme which is based on, has developed from or is related to the tenets of Karl Marx, Friedrich Engels, Vladimir Lenin or Mao Tse Tung, or of any other recognized theorist in connection with, or exponent of, those tenets, and which aims at the establishment of any form of socialism or collective ownership". The ANC and the SACP (which re-launched itself openly in South Africa in June 1990) cannot, therefore, lawfully advocate nationalization and other policies for which they have long campaigned.

This Act also makes it a serious offence to incite or commit an act of civil disobedience; and despite the removal of the prohibition on subversive statements which included calls for civil disobedience, it remains a crime. It also contains the powers to ban organizations and to "list" and thereby silence individuals, through house arrests and banning the publication of their names, statements or writings.

The Publications Act Under the Publications Act (most recently amended in 1986) thousands of publications and books have been banned on the basis that they constitute a "threat to the security of the state, the general welfare and the peace and good order". The Act continues to regulate all publications (except newspapers which are members of the Newspaper Press Union), including those of previously unlawful organizations.

The official publication of the SACP, *The African Communist*, as well as the official publication of the ANC, *Sechaba*, were banned in perpetuity, but have recently been unbanned. Although the London based anti-apartheid International Defence and Aid Fund for Southern Africa is now a lawful organization, a decision was taken in 1980 under this Act whereby none of its publications could be imported into South Africa, except on the authority of a permit. Not all of its publications were banned but many of those that were have now been unbanned.

The "alternative" press has the most to fear from this statute since these publications are not affiliated to the Newspaper Press Union. In the past, community newspapers such as *Grassroots*, *South* and *New Nation* have been victims of banning under the Publications Act.

Nevertheless, the Publications Board established under the Act has developed an independent and increasingly liberal approach towards censorship in recent years. One reason advanced for the emergency censorship restrictions in 1987 was alleged concern over the Board's policies which had led to the unbanning of a number of newspapers, journals, books and films. In 1988, security police confiscated copies of the film *Namibia: No Easy Road to Freedom* and all copies of the film *Cry Freedom* under the 1987 Media Emergency Regulations. Both films had been passed by the Publications Board.

In November 1988, Salman Rushdie's novel, *The Satanic Verses*, was banned by the South African government after protests from Muslim organizations. An invitation to Salman Rushdie to address a book fair, organized by the *Weekly Mail*, on the subject of apartheid and censorship was hastily cancelled following threats of a "holy war" against the newspaper and several bomb threats at the paper's editorial offices in Johannesburg.

Newspaper and Imprint Registration Act 1971 This Act requires all newspapers to register and for registration to lapse if a newspaper fails to come out once a month. Under the Internal Security Act, a newspaper must deposit up to R40,000 (US$15,600) with the government if the Minister of Justice believes it may be banned at any stage. This is clearly designed to discourage the registration of small opposition newspapers. In 1988, an Eastern Cape news agency was forced to abandon plans to start a newspaper when the minister demanded a R40,000 deposit, and the device was recently used against two other publications, *The New African* and *Vrye Weekblad*.

Police Act 1958 Section 27B of this Act prohibits the publication of any untrue statement concerning the action of the police and makes such publications a criminal offence. The onus is on the publisher to prove the truth of any statement and the offence carries a maximum fine of R10,000 (US$3,900), five years' imprisonment or both.

Prisons Act 1959 It is an offence to publish "any false information concerning the behaviour or experience in prison of any prisoner or ex-prisoner or concerning the administration of any prison, knowing the same to be false or without taking reasonable steps to verify such information". Again, the onus of proving that reasonable steps were taken to verify the truth of the information in question lies with the publisher.

Defence Act 1957 Section 118 of this Act prohibits the disclosure of any information, by any means of publication, of the composition, movements or disposition of the South African Defence Force or Navy or any of its equipment. The Act prohibits the taking of photographs and making sketches of military premises or installations. It is also an offence to use any language or to act with intent to encourage any other person to refuse to do military service.

It is equally an offence to publish any statement, comment or rumour relating to any member of the defence forces calculated to prejudice or embarrass the government in its foreign relations, or to alarm or depress members of the public unless the Minister of Defence authorizes such publication.

Protection of Information Act 1982 This Act prohibits the obtaining, possession and disclosure of certain information. The Act defines "security matters" very broadly as any matter dealt with by the National Intelligence Service. It also prohibits the possession of certain official documents which may be prejudicial to the security of the Republic. On October 3 1990, Max du Preez, editor-in-chief of *Vrye Weekblad*, was convicted of contravening the Act for an article on February 2 alleging that Stellenbosch University's Institute for Soviet Studies is a front for the National Intelligence Services (NIS). (The NIS have since confirmed that this is true.) During the trial, which was held in camera, the defence was denied access to classified testimony by prosecution witnesses. Max du Preez was fined R2,000 (US$800) and the newspaper's owner, Wending Publikasies, was fined R5,000 (US$1,950).

The Armaments Development and Production Act 1968 This Act prohibits the disclosure of any information relating to the acquisition, manufacture or marketing of armaments and associated technology, except with the consent of the Minister.

Disclosure of Foreign Funding Act Under this Act, which came into effect in August 1989, any organization or person thought to be receiving funds from abroad can be declared a "reporting" organization or person. This requires the disclosure of the amount and source of external funding and for what purpose it is to be used. There are penalties of R40,000 (US$15,600) and/or up to 10 years' imprisonment for failure to comply with the provisions or for using foreign funding for a purpose other than the one declared to the registrar. The Wilgespruit Fellowship Centre was declared a reporting organization in January 1990 and several others are under consideration.

Academic Research

An important by-product of the lifting of restrictions on those listed under the ISA is that previously inaccessible academic research material may now be quoted and disseminated. Amongst those listed were academics of distinction, such as Albie Sachs, Jack Simons and Harold Wolpe, as well as eminent authors like Alex La Guma and

Bloke Modisane. These works are now at least theoretically accessible, both for purposes of research and as sources of information for journalists.

Not all the names have been removed from the list: some individuals convicted of certain security offences since 1989 remain on the list and may not be quoted without ministerial permission. A number of publications remain banned under the Publications Act. Access to such literature is only possible subject to stringent conditions.

Actions

ARTICLE 19 has taken many actions in support of its international board member Zwelakhe Sisulu, editor of *New Nation*, including the publication of a pamphlet highlighting his case entitled "An Editor in Prison", updated in 1989 to "Released But Not Free".

On September 29 1988 ARTICLE 19 wrote to the South African government expressing concern over the detention and health of Mr Sisulu. On December 3 1988 a letter was sent to the government welcoming the release of Mr Sisulu but protesting against the restrictions placed on him including one preventing him working as a journalist. In the same month an appeal letter was sent to ARTICLE 19 members urging them to write to the government protesting the restriction order.

On October 13 1988 ARTICLE 19 wrote to the South African government protesting the detention of journalist Veliswa Mhlawuli who had appeared in a BBC documentary about the alleged torture of children in detention.

On October 25 ARTICLE 19 wrote to the government protesting the *Weekly Mail* being charged with publishing "subversive articles".

On November 1 1988 ARTICLE 19 wrote to the government protesting the banning of the *Weekly Mail*.

On February 21 1989 ARTICLE 19 wrote to the government protesting the closure for three months of *New Era* and *Grassroots*; the threatened closure of *Work in Progress* and *Al-Qalam*; and general attacks on and prosecutions of the press.

In July 1989 an appeal letter was sent to ARTICLE 19 members urging them to write to the government protesting the confiscation of books from David Phillip Publishers, Learn and Teach Publications, and from the University of Witwatersrand.

On November 15 1989 ARTICLE 19 wrote to the government protesting the threatened closure or prior censorship of *New Nation*.

On January 25 1990 the director of ARTICLE 19 met, by invitation, the South African ambassador to the UK to discuss the threatened closure of *New Nation* and censorship in general.

On January 30 1990 ARTICLE 19 wrote to the ambassador about the case of Gabu Tugwana, acting editor of the *New Nation*, who was being prosecuted for having published the name of a banned person while the editors of the *Sunday Times* and the *Weekly Mail*, who did likewise, had their cases quashed.

Togo

During the 1970s and early 1980s, hundreds of political prisoners were detained for having criticized the one-party state, censorship and the general lack of democratic freedoms. While there has been an improvement in the human rights situation since 1987 and there are now fewer arrests, state censorship still prevails.

President General Gnassingbe Eyadema, who is also President of the Rassemblement du Peuple Togolais (RPT), the sole party allowed in Togo, has wide powers, including the right to dissolve the National Assembly. The Constitution states that all political activity, including the right to vote, has to be exercised exclusively within the RPT. This has led in practice to the prosecution of anyone engaged in independent political activities.

	Data	Year
Population	3,247,000	1988
Life expectancy (M/F)	48.8/52.2	1985
GNP (US$ per capita)	370	1988
Main religion(s)	Animism	
	Christianity	
	Islam	
Official language(s)	French	
	Kabiye	
	Ewe	
Illiteracy %	56.7	1990
(M/F)	43.6/69.3	1990
Daily newspapers	1	1986
Radio sets	560,000	1987
TV sets	17,000	1987
Press agencies:		
Agence Togolaise de Press		
ICCPR:	YES	1984

Despite government statements during 1989 that freedom of expression is guaranteed in Togo, no practical steps have been taken to end its absolute control over the media; journalists and writers exercise self-censorship before submitting their material in order to obtain the authorities' approval for publication.

On October 5 1990, Logo Doddouvi and Doglo Agbelenko were sentenced to five years' imprisonment for distributing anti-government pamphlets but, a week later, the two men were pardoned by the President. After their trial their supporters were forcibly removed from the court by soldiers; in the demonstration that followed, army violence left four people dead and 34 injured. In response, the country's lawyers staged a three-day strike in protest at the army action and also called on the government to implement a multi-party system.

Freedom of Expression

The Constitution guarantees "the rights and freedoms of the human person, the family and local communities, as well as political, philosophic and religious freedoms", but makes no reference to freedom of expression and opinion or freedom of the media and of publication. The Penal Code makes it an offence to violate the confidentiality of correspondence or of telephone conversations, but recent information indicates that the mail and telephone conversations of suspected government opponents and also of some high-ranking government officials are routinely monitored by the Togolese security service.

Insulting Public Authorities Article 140 of the Penal Code provides for up to two years' imprisonment for anyone who, by any means, abuses or insults a magistrate, civil servant or any other citizen in charge of public services. Under Article 141, the punishment can be five years' imprisonment if the insult is made publicly. This law has been used over many years against people who have tried to expose corruption or publicize government maladministration. Many people, including writers, who have been arbitrarily detained and ill-treated have had their imprisonment justified by reference to this offence.

"Attacks Against the President" Article 26 of the Act of July 29 1881 (which is actually the French press code and was adopted as part of Togolese law and amended over the years) has been consistently applied in a way which makes all criticism of the President a penal offence. The Article, "Offence against the Republic", provides for up to one year's imprisonment and a fine for "an attack against the President" through "speech, screaming, threats, writing, printing, drawing, engraving, painting, emblems, images or any other medium".

Defamation Under Article 29, the offence of defamation is defined as "allegations or imputations of fact which attack the honour or dignity of a person or a corporate body". It is also an offence if a person or corporate body, though not explicitly named, can be identified from incriminating remarks. Article 30 extends protection from defamation to "courts, tribunals, the armed forces, the constituted body and public administrations". Anyone who makes criticisms or unfavourable comments about government-created public institutions risks imprisonment of up to one year and a fine. Although this Article appears under offences against individuals, it seems to be designed to prohibit criticism of state bodies. The punishment provided for in Article 30 also applies, in Article 31, to defamation of "one or many members of any ministry or the assembly or any civil servant or against any agent of public authority or any minister of religion employed by the state". Insult of those mentioned in Articles 30 and 31 is punishable by imprisonment of up to two months and a fine.

The Media

The media, which comprises a daily newspaper, *La Nouvelle Marche*, a monthly magazine, *Togo Dialogue*, one TV station and two radio stations, are government-owned and access to information of all kinds is regulated by the government. All journalists are civil servants and those who hold managerial positions in the media are appointed by the RPT. Allegiance to the party and loyalty to the President are the main criteria for appointment. The media reports only views which support the government and is used to promote a positive image of the President with regard to both his domestic and foreign policies. The government does not permit publication or circulation of any critical news and reports concerning corruption in the government are published only with prior authorization from the President. Foreign news on Togolese radio and TV reflects government foreign policy. In October 1989, Togolese media reported the publication of Amnesty International's annual report but focused mainly on the fact that 20 prisoners were executed in Ghana, a neighbouring country with whom relations are tense.

Foreign Press Foreign news is carefully selected from international news agency reports and the foreign news which is published usually reflects the diplomatic efforts of the President in furthering international relations. All foreign publications are scrutinized before distribution and those which carry articles on Togo's political and economic situation are confiscated. Where an issue of a publication is found to be unacceptable, the government usually buys all the copies sent for distribution in Togo so as to avoid criticism from abroad of its censorship practices. Opposition newspapers published in Paris are banned and possession of these papers is a criminal offence punishable by imprisonment for up to 11 months. Foreign news on subjects other than Togo is mostly unrestricted.

Recent Developments

In October 1989, the National Commission for Human Rights (CNDH), a government institution created by decree in 1987, organized its annual seminar on the theme "freedom of expression and press within the respect due to the rights of others".

The choice of freedom of expression as its theme reflected important political developments in the country. The government has unofficially encouraged individuals to set up independent publications for the first time since President Eyadema came to power in 1967. However, it appears that no-one has come forward. Most Togolese intellectuals who have been approached by government officials have expressed cynicism about government intentions given that, in the past, hundreds of people suffered imprisonment for the expression of views critical of government policies.

Civil servants are reported to have been dismissed or disciplined for expressing views critical of the President and the one-party system. Dr Adani Ise, professor at the University of Benin in Lome, was dismissed from his post in 1989 for submitting a paper on the debt question in Africa at an academic conference. He had apparently criticized the economic policies of the government.

In September 1989, Nyaledome Kodjo was arrested by security police for seeking information. During a seminar, he had asked government officials to explain their decision not to celebrate April 27 as a national day and why they avoided talking abut Togo's history between 1960 and 1967 when President Eyadema took power following a military coup. He was reported to have been released later following pressure from the CNDH.

Religious Freedom Fourteen religious associations in Togo complained to the CNDH about a government ban on their activities. The government outlawed these associations in May 1978 and Jehovah's Witnesses were particularly targetted. The CNDH organised a public seminar entitled "Religious freedom and public order" and a number of recommendations were then submitted to the government. To date, however, the 14 religious associations who approached the Commission are still not allowed to organize religious activities.

Actions

In its 1989 Commentary to the Human Rights Committee ARTICLE 19, referring to the inadequate safeguarding of freedom of opinion and expression at constitutional level, called for a review of legislation affecting these rights. It also called for clarification of the machinery and practices of censorship and on the role of the CNDH in investigating censorship.

Serious concern was expressed at the plight of writers, the denial of academic freedom, the control on all media and the general atmosphere of intimidation which denies freedom of opinion and expression to the population as a whole.

In June 1989 Yawo Agboyibor, President of the CNDH, visited ARTICLE 19 to respond to the points made in the Commentary. A response was also received from Yaovi Adodo, head of the Department of Legal and Political Affairs at the Togo Foreign Office.

Uganda

Uganda has been plagued by a series of undemocratic governments, military coups, and rigged elections for more than two decades and has suffered gross abuse of human rights.

Since January 1986, following a four-year guerrilla war, Uganda has been governed by the National Resistance Movement (NRM) under the Presidency of Lieutenant-General Yoweri Museveni. In March 1986, political parties were ordered to suspend all active operations although they were not proscribed.

In February 1989, the first national elections since 1980 were held. The National Resistance Council (NRC), the ruling body of the NRM, was expanded from 98 to 278 members, to include 210 elected members. Among these were many Democratic Party (DP) members, one of whom, Paul Ssemogerere, is President of the NRC and also the Foreign Minister. In the same month, President Museveni appointed a committee to review the Constitution and to present, within 24 months, a new draft constitution.

	Data	Year
Population	13,225,000	1988
Life expectancy (M/F)	47.4/50.7	1985
GNP (US$ per capita)	280	1988
Main religion(s)	Christianity	
	Islam	
Official language(s)	English	
Illiteracy %	51.7	1990
(M/F)	37.8/65.1	1990
Daily newspapers	7	1989
Radio sets	375,000	1986
TV sets	90,000	1990
Press agencies:		
	Uganda News Agency	
ICCPR:	NO	

In October 1989, the NRC approved draft legislation, to prolong the government's term of office by five years from January 1990, when its mandate was due to expire. One member of the NRC resigned in protest, two others abstained. In March 1990, the NRM extended the national ban on party political activity for a further five years. President Museveni has been quoted as saying: "There is no reason why a single political party cannot be democratic."

The new administration has brought a measure of political stability to Uganda and at the outset demonstrated a commitment to human rights by setting up two organizations, the office of the Inspector General of Government (IGG) (to investigate abuses by the present government) and the Human Rights Commission (HRC) (whose role is to investigate abuses by the former government). These initiatives have been supported by non-governmental efforts and have helped to raise levels of awareness of these issues among Ugandans. However, their work has suffered from drastic underfunding and a failure to make clear recommendations. The IGG operates with a degree of independence, although its effectiveness is limited. For example, if a case is already being challenged in the courts, the IGG cannot take any action. Furthermore, the IGG has never been successful in taking a minister to court for corruption, although some have subsequently been sacked.

In February 1990, *The New Vision* newspaper reported that dissatisfaction had been expressed by HRC members at what they see as laxity on the part of the Criminal Investigation Department in investigating cases to be brought before the courts.

The Media

In 1983, the NRM published the *Ten Point Programme*, a manifesto for the rehabilitation of the country, promising to restore democracy. President Museveni's government has guaranteed greater freedom of speech than was the case under previous administrations, although there has been tension on occasions between the government and the press. At a press conference in Entebbe in February 1987, the President warned the media: "I am putting journalists on notice that if they malign the good name of the National Resistance Army (NRA), they will be locked up under the detention laws."

In April 1988, Kahinda Otafiire, Minister of State for Internal Affairs, singled out five newspapers which he said were "misleading the nation by writing lies" and threatened to "close such irresponsible newspapers". Otafiire was dismissed from office in 1988 after an article in *The New Vision* which claimed he had threatened someone whilst drunk.

In May 1989, the President stated: "Two types of criminals interest me; journalists and common criminals. They think they are above the law." In September he said: "There are some people who deal with form rather than substance, who talk about mere appearances and not substance. These are our friends the newspapers. And I think that there will be a conflict between us and the papers."

In February 1990, *The Guide* reported that the Ministry of Information had proposed the introduction of a press council with powers to suspend publications and prohibit journalists from practising for a given period or indefinitely. As of October 1990, the council has not been established.

The Press About 30 publications are distributed in Uganda but less than a dozen are published regularly. These include *The New Vision*, *Weekly Topic*, the *Citizen*, *Financial Times*, the *Star*, and *Shariat*. Several of them, including *Shariat* and *The Citizen*, are overtly hostile to the government. Those papers which continue a tradition of investigative journalism include *The New Vision*, the only daily in the country, and the *Weekly Topic*. Self-censorship is endemic and coverage of government corruption and abuses by the military in the war zone are taboo. Although articles about these subjects regularly appear in the press, they are usually "watered down". There appears to be little solidarity among journalists and it is therefore unlikely that they will jeopardize their jobs by taking risks.

Financial Constraints Newsprint is imported and is prohibitively expensive, especially in view of foreign exchange problems which have existed since 1986. Most newspapers buy paper locally from agents who import it from Kenya. These include daily and weekly newspapers like the *Star* and *Weekly Topic*. Independent newspapers such as *The Light*, *Finance and Trade* and *Focus* (which publish once a month at the most) find difficulty in obtaining the necessary government approval for their importation applications.

The official government newspaper, *The New Vision*, claims to be a neutral corporation and is established by Charter. It has many rural correspondents, some of whom are government employees and teachers, and is known to investigate failures of government, and to expose corruption and human rights abuses. Communication with rural areas is too costly for most newspapers who may not have a telephone, a telex, or even a permanent address and who depend on traders and the commuting public for information.

In addition, few people can afford newspapers (one month's supply of daily newspapers costs about twice the average monthly wage), and they rarely reach rural areas with low levels of literacy. The resulting lack of revenue prevents newspapers publishing at regular intervals.

Due to general lack of resources, journalists tend to be underpaid, undertrained, and inexperienced, resulting in reporting which may be inaccurate or out of date. Such inaccuracies often provide the government with justification for taking punitive measures against offending newspapers.

Books Apart from the government publishing house, there are several independent publishers including Marianum Press, Makerere-Printery, New Vision Printing and Publishing Corporation, Uganda Publishing House Ltd and the Anglican Church-owned Centenary Publishing House; their output is small and authors are expected to pay the cost of their own publications.

Legal Constraints The Penal Code, instituted in 1900, defines the crime of "sedition and false news" which carries a term of five to seven years' imprisonment (Cap.106, para 41). Newspapers can be banned under paragraph 47 of the Penal Code. Other charges brought against journalists who have fallen foul of the government include theft, criminal libel and treason. In August 1988, the NRM introduced an amendment to the Penal Code allowing the prosecution of anyone publishing information regarded as endangering the armed forces. In most cases, these charges are either dropped or never come to trial. Journalists have, so far, been charged under the criminal law rather than being detained under the extensive powers to imprison people without charge or trial which the government can exercise under the Public Order and Security Act.

Arrest of Journalists In March 1986, Sully Ndiwalana Kiwanuka, the editor of *Focus*, a Muslim-owned newspaper, was arrested following his paper's report that the army was experiencing problems in rebel areas. He was charged with sedition but was released three days later.

In June, the *Weekend Digest* reported that the DP was plotting with the governments of West Germany and Italy to overthrow the government. The paper was banned and its editors, Jesse Mashate and Wilson Wandera, were charged with publishing false rumours. As of October 1990, the Attorney General was still unsure whether charges against Kiwanuka, Mashate and Wandera were still pending.

In October 1986, Anthony Ssekweyama, editor of *The Citizen*, was arrested on a charge of treason against the newly-formed government; he had allegedly attended a meeting where a coup was being planned. He was acquitted and released in March 1988. John Kakooza, *The Citizen*'s acting editor-in-chief in Ssekweyama's absence, was arrested on December 29 1987 and charged with sedition. The charge related to three separate items that had appeared in *The Citizen* (a news report which stated that opposition guerrillas controlled tracts of territory in the Teso region; a commentary on the political lessons of the "Holy Spirit" rebellion led by Alice Lakwena; and a line-drawing of President Museveni which was deemed disrespectful). Kakooza was released on police bail but re-arrested on April 7 1988 and charged with sedition, this time for criticizing the delay in bringing to trial the murderer of former energy minister Andrew Lutakome Kayiira. He was released six days later on bail.

His deputy, Joseph Kiggundu, was also arrested and charged in connection with the same article but was later released on bail. The charge of "publishing false news" was withdrawn on December 15 1989. John Kakooza has left journalism and now works for a government organization.

Joseph Kiggundu was also editor of *Munnansi* (the Luganda-language version of *The Citizen*) and, as of May 1990, has been released on bail of 50,000 Ugandan shillings (25 times the average monthly wage). He faced a criminal libel charge instigated by Prime Minister Samson Kisseka for a 1988 article he wrote alleging that the Prime Minister might not be serving another term in office after the elections. The Uganda Editors' Guild has described Kiggundu's article as "fair political comment and analysis".

Kiggundu has appeared in court at least 30 times in connection with this case. Since his release on bail, he has been required to report to the police once a month but had stopped doing so in September 1990. Kiggundo also faces at least 11 civil libel cases, one dating back to 1986.

In August 1990, Kiggundu resigned as editor of *The Citizen*, stating that he was tired of being forced to print false stories by the proprietors of the paper. The chief sub-editor and the sports editor resigned with him. Kiggundu is now the editor-in-chief of the *Activist* magazine, published by the Uganda Human Rights Activists.

In November 1987, the *Sunday Review* (a newspaper which published information and views from rebel areas) carried a hypothetical interview with Alice Lakwena. Francis Odida, its editor and a supporter of the party of former President Milton Obote, the Uganda People's Congress (UPC), was arrested in December and charged with sedition and later with treason (punishable by a mandatory death sentence). After eight months' detention he was released on bail of 200,000 Ugandan shillings, the highest ever paid by a journalist. The bail was raised by fellow journalists and newspapers. The charges of sedition and publishing false information were dropped in January 1990. *Sunday Review* has since ceased publication.

Two *Sunday Review* reporters, George Ongaya and Ben Kitara, detained at about the same time as Francis Odida, have not been heard of since. Disappearances are uncommon in Uganda and there is speculation that the two reporters may have fled the country, but this is unconfirmed.

On December 10 1987, Professor Charles Kagenda-Atwooki, the UPC Secretary for Information, Research and Publication, gave an interview to the BBC, criticizing the NRA's human rights record. He was arrested by police and handed over to military intelligence who held him incommunicado for some weeks. In March 1988, he was charged with terrorism and unlawfully possessing seditious publications. He was released on bail and the terrorism charge was dropped but, as of March 1990, he was still awaiting trial on two sedition charges.

Three journalists have been tried on criminal libel charges of defaming a foreign dignitary. On January 29 1990, at a press conference in Kampala for visiting President Kenneth Kaunda of Zambia, Hussein Abdi Hassan, the Uganda correspondent for the Swahili-Somali service of the BBC, asked President Kaunda about allegations that his son had murdered a woman and about another son's involvement with a cargo and airline company. Hassan was arrested on February 10 in Kampala and charged with defaming President Kaunda. He was finally granted bail on March 30. On September 26, Justice A R Soluade of the High Court dropped the charge after accepting the defence lawyer's argument that Section 51 of the penal code was not applicable because the journalist's questions had not been published, only spoken. According to Section 51, an individual is guilty of the misdemeanor after "publish[ing] anything intended to be read ... with intent to disturb peace and friendship between Uganda and the country to which such ... dignitary belongs". However, in October 1990, the Director of Public Prosecution announced his intention to appeal the decision.

Similar cases are pending against Alfred Okware, a journalist with Third World Media Services and associate editor of the newly launched magazine *Newsdesk*, and Festo Ebongu of *The New Vision*, both of whom also asked President Kaunda questions at the news conference. Both were charged with defamation under Section 51 of the Penal Code. Alfred Okware was also charged with possessing seditious materials. In February, the defamation charges were dismissed and both journalists were released, but Okware was immediately redetained. He was released several days later. The state's appeal to reinstate defamation charges against the two was denied in March and the charge against Okware of possessing seditious materials was withdrawn. Two months later, however, the initial ruling was reversed and the defamation charges against the journalists were reinstated. Alfred Okware was scheduled to appear in court on October 11. A hearing date had not yet been set for Festo Ebongu.

Latigo Lapoti, a senior information officer in the Ministry of Information and Radio Uganda, was arrested on February 2 1990. He reportedly had a weekly Acholi-language radio programme. Some believe he may be held because of his ethnic origin (he is a Northerner), and his suspected rebel activities. He was originally held in Lubiri barracks and reportedly transferred to Katabi barracks in May or June; his current whereabouts are unknown. He is still being held without charge.

Radio and Television The government-owned Radio Uganda, established in 1953, broadcasts in 22 languages, has an estimated audience of more than 12 million and is the only radio station. Radio Uganda rarely risks incurring government disapproval and is the channel through which the government broadcasts its official statements. The station is seriously under-equipped. Attempts to establish an alternative radio station have, thus far, not been permitted.

Uganda Television Service is also government-owned and was first broadcast in 1962. Its equipment, however, is now obsolete. The Presidential Press Unit provides the station with coverage of President Museveni's activities. Occasionally, the station carries some financial programmes, sponsored by businesses for promotional purposes.

Journalists' Organizations The Uganda Journalists' Association (UJA), established in 1967, but only registered in 1987, exists to unite journalists but is riven by internal disputes. The Association has intervened to help arrested journalists; it persuaded the Inspector General of Government to drop a libel charge against the newspaper *Finance and Trade*, following publication of an article alleging that the government had dealings with an insurance company. In March 1990, the UJA adopted a constitution and a code of professional conduct described as "tough" by the *Weekly Topic*. Promotion of patriotism and national unity, public responsibility and accuracy are included in the adopted rules.

In May 1989, the East African Journalists' Association (EAJA) was formed in Kampala, with representatives from more than 10 countries of the East African region. However, the fact that it has requested a "donation" from the Ugandan government for the organization's office and a grant of US$500,000 does not bode well for its future independence. Most Ugandan journalists believe the head of the EAJA, UJA president James Namakajo, is linked to the government.

In February 1990, the Uganda Newspaper Editors and Proprietors Association (UNEPA) was established.

The Minister of Information and Broadcasting, Kintu Musoke, one of three government ministers who own the *Weekly Topic*'s publishing house, is a member of all three of the above press organizations. In November 1989, he proposed the establishment of a cross-media Editors' Commission.

Other, smaller, media organizations include an Editors' Guild, Uganda Media Women and the Catholic Broadcasters' Association.

Public Health

Uganda was the first country in the world to have a National AIDS Control Programme organized by the World Health Organization and established in 1987.

A national survey of HIV infection was completed in early 1988, the first such in Africa and the only one to be published. The results were not disclosed until the end of 1989; the report was initially withheld because the information was so shocking that it was thought it might create a sense of helplessness among Ugandans. The survey claimed that 790,522 people were HIV positive, including 29 per cent of urban adults in the western region and 12 per cent of rural adults in the central region. At the time the report was issued, the country's Health Minister, Zak Kaheru, said that by 1989 one million Ugandans, or six per cent of the population, might have been infected.

Zaïre

The Constitution guarantees the right to freedom of expression, free opinion and association. These rights, however, are nullified by the authority of the sole legal political party, the Mouvement Populaire de la Révolution (MRP). Each Zaïrean becomes a party member at birth.

Political discussions and sometimes even innocent references to state structures are punishable. Any expression of independent political thought or action may be punished severely. However, in April 1990 President Mobutu Sese Seko announced the re-introduction of a multi-party system under a transitional government, led by a new prime minister, with presidential elections planned for 1991. In July, a law was passed allowing for only three legally-recognized political parties, but in October the President announced that a full multi-party system would be allowed.

	Data	Year
Population	33,458,000	1988
Life expectancy (M/F)	48.3/51.7	1985
GNP (US$ per capita)	170	1988
Main religion(s)	Christianity	
	Animism	
Official language(s)	French	
Illiteracy %	28.2	1990
(M/F)	16.4/39.3	1990
Daily newspapers	4	1986
Non daily newspapers	9	1984
Periodicals	106	1984
Radio sets	3,400,000	1988
TV sets	20,000	1988
Press agencies:		
Agence Zairoise de Presse,		
Documentation et		
Informations Africains		
ICCPR:	YES	1976

Freedom of Opinion

The most concerted recent effort to create an opposition organization was the founding of the Union pour la Démocratie et le Progrès Social (UDPS). Hundreds of UDPS members have been arrested, detained without charge and tortured since its formation in 1982. In September 1989, Baudoin Mangala, editor of the UDPS's clandestine magazine *Le Combat*, was detained after meeting in Kinshasa with a delegation from the US-based Lawyers' Committee for Human Rights. In January 1990, he was moved to house arrest.

Demonstrations In January 1988, the UDPS held a rally several thousand strong in Kinshasa. According to eye-witness accounts, security forces attacked the crowd using clubs, batons and live ammunition. The attack left several people dead. More than 500 people were reportedly detained for up to several months.

Zaïrean security forces also violently suppressed a small peaceful demonstration of women in downtown Kinshasa in April 1988. The women were subsequently banished to remote areas and some of their property was destroyed by government agents. In a television speech after the incident President Mobutu called on Zaïrean youth to intervene personally and forcibly suppress such demonstrations in the future.

In February 1989, students in institutions of higher education in Kinshasa and other major cities began to protest over deteriorating economic conditions. These protests culminated in major demonstrations on February 14 and 15. Security forces moved in and dozens of students were arrested, and many injured. Organizers said 14 students had been killed in Kinshasa alone but the government acknowledged only that one student was killed in Lubumbashi. The universities were closed until mid-March. In February, Elvis Asana, a journalist for the national newspaper *Elima*, was arrested. On July 27 1990, the International Federation of Journalists reported that he had not been seen or heard of since his arrest and that his wife believed he had been arrested for his articles on student unrest.

On May 9 1990, anti-government demonstrations broke out in several universities and became particularly violent in Lubumbashi when students attacked police informers and reportedly killed two. Members of the security forces attacked the university and witnesses said that more than 50 students were killed between May 10 and May 12. Later reports said that there may have been up to 150 deaths and several hundred wounded.

Article 209 Article 209 of the Criminal Code provides for up to three years' imprisonment for circulating material which may "harm the national interest". Over the past several years, the government has arrested and detained many citizens under Article 209.

Kalengayi Kadima was arrested in April 1988 and held for seven months. He was in possession of a letter to the Zaïrean government, signed by 47 US Congressmen, expressing concern about the suppression of the UDPS demonstration in January. He was released provisionally in November 1988, but was detained again in November 1989 for a month.

In July 1989, two UDPS activists, Joseph Bula and Luc Alingabala, were arrested for possession of the UDPS newsletter *Le Combat*. By the end of 1989, they were still detained in Makala prison.

In early August 1989, Nzembela Kankongolo, an employee of the Central Bank of Zaïre, was arrested for possessing copies of an article which implicated the government in the death of the Roman Catholic prelate, Cardinal Malula. His arms were reportedly broken during interrogation. Several other employees of the bank were held for up to five days in connection with the article.

Following a visit by the US-based Lawyers' Committee for Human Rights in August 1989, at least six people who had contact with the delegation were arrested. The government had assured the Committee that citizens were free to speak with them. Four of the six men were apparently held for possession of UN documents discussing human rights treaties which Zaïre has ratified. The six were detained for periods ranging from several weeks to several months without charge or trial. Several of them were physically abused.

The Media

Dissemination of information through the mass media is tightly controlled. In theory, the press is regulated by the Press Law of 1981, Article 1 of which proclaims that the printing, publication and distribution of written materials shall be unrestricted. This provision of the Press Law is largely irrelevant in practice, however.

Article 19 provides that "no written material published in a newspaper or periodical may jeopardize public order, morality, *bonnes moeurs* or the honour or dignity of the individual". Whether private or public, the media is dependent on the state. Moreover, security forces have, in the past, acted swiftly and without regard to the law when journalists have attempted to exercise their rights under Zaïrean law. As a result, journalism is dominated by the national news agency, Agence Zaïroise de Presse (AZAP), and journalists practise self-censorship. Most news consists of reports of official positions without commentary.

Books The main independent publishers of books in Zaïre have traditionally been the Christian publishing houses. They have periodically published books which support an independent political vision, but only within the context of religious interpretation. Their presses have also been subject to government pressure and periodic censorship.

Newspapers All major newspapers are privately-owned, although the hand of the MPR is evident in most of them. There are four dailies and 10 periodicals. The owners of the papers are closely linked to the government and party hierarchy and believed to depend on the MPR for financial support. *Salongo* and *Elima*, the two principal daily papers, are particularly pro-government and are virtually indistinguishable from AZAP's official daily news bulletin. Another daily, *Analyste*, which is only available by subscription, is regarded as the most independent paper.

All journalists must belong to the National Union of Journalists, which issues a press card without which a journalist cannot work. The fear of denial of a press card causes extensive self-censorship. It is through this mechanism that the MPR exercises unseen control over the press.

Press articles rarely criticize officials, and never the President or the security forces. Most information regarding the opposition goes unreported. For example, newspapers did not report any of the demonstrations discussed above, nor the subsequent closure of universities.

On August 4 1989, Jacques Lumbwele, an Agence France Presse reporter, was detained after he gave a letter from Lecas Atandi, a political prisoner detained since August 1987, to the foreign press and human rights organizations. Lumbwele was released on September 12 1989.

Radio and Television Radio is the most important communication medium in Zaïre. The government runs and controls most radio stations, although at least one small church-affiliated educational station broadcasts from the Kivu Region. The state also controls and runs TV.

Radio and TV are dominated by government news and programmes, and the government is extremely sensitive about what news is reported. In late 1989, for example, radio and TV blacked out all coverage of the overthrow of President Nicolae Ceausescu in Romania. In May 1990, a total black-out was imposed for at least three weeks following the massacre of students in Lubumbashi and clashes between students and security forces in other cities.

In March 1989, two journalists from the Zaïrean Office of Radio and TV, Makoko Mucheni and Kafuka Rujamizi, were arrested and detained for four days. Makoko had broadcast on TV information about a crisis in Zaïre's relations with Belgium. He was fired for "irresponsible reporting". Kufuka, a radio journalist, was detained after he announced a government-approved rise in fuel and transport costs.

Foreign Media The government controls the circulation of foreign publications, and security agents often seize copies of those deemed critical of the government as soon as they enter the country. Foreign journalists require permission to operate in Zaïre and are often detained, expelled or denied entry for reporting views contrary to the government. On April 22 1990, Colette Braeckman of the Belgian paper *Le Soir* was denied an entry visa because her writings on Zaïre were considered to be "too partisan". At least one Belgian journalist was also refused a visa during 1989.

Music

Zaïrean music is arguably the most popular in Africa and the Zaïrean authorities regard it as an important means of communication. A special set of laws for the censorship of music was passed in 1967 and a Censorship Commission of Music, whose members include the President, judges, parents, musicians and representatives of the recording industry, monitors songs. Only authorized songs can be performed or recorded. This has ensured that songs critical of the state are not heard by the general public.

Actions

In its 1990 Commentary to the Human Rights Committee, ARTICLE 19 recommended, among other things, that the Penal Code should be amended to delete articles which deny freedom of speech or criticism of the government, and that the Censorship Commission of Music be abolished. ARTICLE 19 also called for an end to the penalizing of journalists and publishers for reporting views and accounts of events contrary to those of the government.

Zambia

Zambia became an independent republic in 1964. In 1972, the National Assembly voted unanimously (after a walk-out by members of the opposition) to ban opposition parties and establish President Kenneth Kaunda's United National Independence Party (UNIP) as the sole legal party.

In May 1990, President Kaunda announced that there would be a referendum on the introduction of multi-party democracy but warned that an end to one-party rule could threaten stability and undermine the country's economic reform programme.

In June, widespread protests and riots against the doubling of food prices left 23 people dead. Armed troops raided the University of Zambia campus in Lusaka to put down protests and all the students were ordered to leave; the university was shut down, its third closure in six months. At one stage during the protests several soldiers seized the national radio and declared, falsely, that President Kaunda had been overthrown. The President blamed the disturbances on supporters of a multi-party system but confirmed that the referendum on the introduction of such a system would be in October.

	Data	Year
Population	7,531,000	1988
Life expectancy (M/F)	49.6/53.1	1985
GNP (US$ per capita)	290	1988
Main religion(s)	Christianity Animism	
Official language(s)	English	
Illiteracy %	27.2	1990
(M/F)	19.2/34.7	1990
Daily newspapers	2	1986
Non daily newspapers	12	1986
Radio sets	550,000	1987
TV sets	110,000	1987
Press agencies:		
	Zambia News Agency	
ICCPR:	YES	1984

In September 1990, UNIP endorsed proposals by President Kaunda to hold multi-party elections in 1991, with Mr Kaunda as the sole presidential candidate. However, in October police prevented the Movement for Multi-Party Democracy from holding a meeting in Lusaka to establish the first legal opposition party for 17 years. Police refused to grant a permit to hold the meeting, despite assurances by the government that opposition parties could hold meetings.

The Constitution guarantees freedom of expression and the freedom of the individual to hold opinions without interference, but these rights are undermined by the doctrine of party supremacy and by the prohibition of any manifestation of political views except within the fold of the UNIP. The government has created for itself a constitutional mandate for unchallengeable censorship, a mandate which it has not hesitated to use.

The UNIP Constitution, now appended to the Constitution of Zambia, forbids criticism of the party and party functionaries. Local journalists are instructed that it is their "duty" to write "constructively" in order to assist in the process of national development. The ever-present threat of repercussions has led the media to exercise self-censorship.

Prohibited Publications Under the Penal Code, the President may prohibit any publication published within or outside Zambia "as contrary to the public interest".

In February 1989, President Kaunda used this power to ban Salman Rushdie's book *The Satanic Verses* while on a visit to Iran.

Information, possession, sale or distribution of a prohibited work is punishable by fine or imprisonment. There are powers to censor foreign songs and films and a Censorship Board, responsible to the Minister of Information and Broadcasting, vets such material.

Defamation It is an offence to defame the President by writing, print, word of mouth, or in any other way, and is punishable by three years' imprisonment.

False News It is an offence to publish "false news with intent to cause fear and alarm to the public". The penalty is three years' imprisonment. In July 1989, Augustine Phiri, a reporter, was arrested and prosecuted for reporting that a baby had been trampled to death in a state shop as women scrambled to buy maize meal, which had been in short supply for some time. Phiri was accused of causing fear and alarm and of embarrassing the government. The Commonwealth Press Union and the Press Association of Zambia hired a lawyer to defend him. Although he was acquitted, the trial served notice on other reporters to tread even more cautiously.

The Media

Zambia's two daily newspapers, *The Times of Zambia* and the *Zambia Daily Mail*, both initially owned by foreign enterprises, are now owned by the state, which appoints the editors. In 1988, the state tightened its grip on the media by creating a conglomerate called the National Media Corporation (NAMECO) and placing both dailies and the Zambia Publishing Company under its control. NAMECO is headed by Milimo Punabantu who, until 1989, was Minister of Information and Broadcasting and, before that, had served as President Kaunda's special assistant for press affairs.

The Zambia News Agency (ZANA), owned by the government, is the sole distributor of foreign news in Zambia. It has the role of "gate keeper" and passes on to its subscribers only news that it regards as fit for publication.

Radio and Television Zambia Broadcasting Services, which runs both radio and TV, is state-owned and funded. There are an estimated one million radio receivers and 234,000 TV receivers in use. Radio programmes are provided in English and seven of the 73 Zambian languages. There are two TV channels, one of which is dedicated totally to educational and in-school services. The news bulletins for both radio and TV are prepared by ZANA.

Restrictions on Journalists Working as a journalist in Zambia is difficult because of the economic crisis besetting the country and the political sensibilities this crisis has engendered, particularly in the last two years. Growing disenchantment among the population is a source of worry for the political leadership which has become increasingly sensitive to news which might "cause fear and alarm" and influence the people against the government.

In February 1988, police were sent to the premises of the Zambia Forestry and Forest Industry Corporation (ZAFFICO) in Ndola where workers had gone on strike. Howard Musonda, a photographer for *The Times of Zambia*, who was taking pictures of the striking workers, was roughed up by police and had his film confiscated.

In the first week of July 1989, the government increased the prices of maize meal and fuel, barely a week after devaluing the Kwacha by 60 per cent. This sparked off food riots and looting in several towns on the Copperbelt. The press was told not to report anything about the situation and Zambians outside the Copperbelt heard about the riots and looting from BBC reports. The only time the government acknowledged there had been such incidents was when Alex Shapi, Defence and Security Minister, accused the BBC of "misleading reports" and blowing events out of proportion.

Investigative reporting in Zambia is rendered additionally difficult by the fact that workers in public service institutions are not allowed to give information to reporters. This has become the exclusive responsibility of official spokesmen who give only "doctored" information calculated to show their organization's activities in the best possible light.

Actions

In its 1987 Commentary to the Human Rights Committee ARTICLE 19 called on the government to abolish laws which unfairly restrict freedom of expression, including the offences of the publication of false news and defamation of the office of President.

Zimbabwe

When Zimbabwe attained independence in 1980, the country's Declaration of Rights guaranteed freedom of expression, specifically "freedom to hold opinions and to receive and impart ideas and information without interference". Such an assurance was especially important since the pre-independence Rhodesian state had systematically violated these rights.

Independence meant unprecedented political freedom for the majority of the population. However, internal political conflict led the government to circumscribe a number of important freedoms in the mid-1980s. There was little critical reporting by the government-controlled daily and weekly press, and two editors were removed from their posts because they were regarded as too inde-

	Data	Year
Population	8,880,000	1988
Life expectancy (M/F)	54.0/57.6	1985
GNP (US$ per capita)	660	1988
Main religion(s)	Animism	
	Christianity	
Official language(s)	English	
Illiteracy %	33.1	1990
(M/F)	26.3/39.7	1990
Daily newspapers	3	1986
Non daily newspapers	4	1986
Radio sets	750,000	1987
TV sets	193,000	1987
Press agencies:		
	Zimbabwe Inter-Africa	
	News Agency	
ICCPR:	NO	

pendent in their views. Foreign journalists were expelled or excluded from the country for reporting human rights violations by the security forces in the conflict-ridden area of Matabeleland in the west of the country. Hundreds of members of a minority political party were detained without charge, including members of parliament. Symbolically perhaps, in early 1989 a planned meeting on "The need for *glasnost* and *perestroika* in Zimbabwe" was cancelled on the orders of the ruling party.

In December 1987, the two main political parties, the ruling Zimbabwe African National Union-Patriotic Front (ZANU-PF) and the minority Zimbabwe African People's Union (ZAPU), agreed to begin a process of unification: ZANU-PF's stated objective has long been the formation of a one-party state. The initial effect of the December 1987 unity agreement was to create new space for popular criticism. In parliament, elected members from both major parties were openly critical of aspects of government policy and especially of high-level corruption. Sections of the press pursued investigative stories for the first time, while at the university, students and academics also criticized official corruption. From late 1988, however, the government began to suppress this brief flowering of popular expression.

President Robert Mugabe had been keen to establish a one-party state but, on August 2 1990, 22 members of the 26-strong ZANU-PF Cabinet opposed moves to legislate one-party rule.

State of Emergency In July 1990, the government lifted the 25-year-old State of Emergency, renouncing powers which included the right to detain an individual indefinitely without trial "in the interests of public safety and public order". During 1989, the emergency powers were used to detain political, student and trade union critics. The government justified the continued State of Emergency on grounds of national security but the majority of those so detained appear to have been peaceful critics.

The University A year-long confrontation between the government and its critics at the University of Zimbabwe culminated in the three-week closure of the university in October 1989.

In September 1988, students at the university and Harare Polytechnic attempted to organize a demonstration against official corruption. They were prevented from doing so by riot police, who went onto the campuses firing teargas and beating students. A number of students and lecturers were arrested and charged with public order offences, although all charges were finally dropped. A law lecturer, Shadreck Gutto, a Kenyan political exile, was summarily deported.

A year later, the Student Representative Council (SRC) tried to organize a seminar to mark the anniversary of the demonstration. Again police came onto the campus and broke up the meeting. On October 2 1989, the SRC issued a statement condemning the police action as a violation of academic freedom. Two days later police arrested Arthur Mutambara and Enoch Chikweche, SRC president and secretary-general. As news of the arrests spread, angry students gathered, there were violent clashes with police and the Vice-Chancellor announced the closure of the university which lasted until October 23. The two students successfully challenged their detention orders in the High Court but they were then charged with issuing a subversive document. They were released on bail before the end of the month and were due to stand trial with nine other students.

On October 6 1989, Morgan Tsvangirai, Secretary-General of the Zimbabwe Congress of Trade Unions (ZCTU), was arrested after issuing a statement condemning the university closure and arrest of student leaders. He was held for nearly six weeks under emergency powers, despite two High Court orders for his release.

Freedom of Political Activity In October 1988, shortly after the first student protest against corruption, a former ZANU-PF secretary-general, Edgar Tekere, added his voice to those criticizing government corruption. He was promptly expelled from ZANU-PF. In April 1989, he announced the formation of a new political party, the Zimbabwe Unity Movement (ZUM). From the outset the new party faced official harassment. Fifteen ZUM officials were detained in June 1989 as the party prepared to contest its first by-election at Dzivarasekwa in Harare. In October, another 11 were detained in the course of a by-election campaign at Kariba in the north of the country and there were further detentions in the wake of a general election in March 1990.

In the general election, ZANU-PF won 116 out of the 120 contested parliamentary seats and Robert Mugabe won 78 per cent of the presidential votes cast. ZUM candidate Patrick Kombayi was widely believed to have an assured victory in the Gweru central constituency against ZANU's Vice-President, Simon Muzenda. A week before voting, the constituency boundaries were re-drawn to remove half of Mkoba township, the centre of Kombayi's support. Kombayi was later shot and gravely wounded, along with five other ZUM members, allegedly by Muzenda's bodyguards.

The government-owned press scarcely reports ZUM activities or statements, unless it is to denounce the new party's supposed links with South Africa. There has been little coverage of the opposition's activities or policies, even in the context of the general election campaign. ZUM representatives have frequently alleged that they have been denied paid advertising space in the government-owned press and on television and radio.

Human Rights Monitoring Because of its long and reputable history of monitoring human rights abuses by the former Rhodesian administration, the Catholic Commission for Justice and Peace has been able to operate freely in post-independence Zimbabwe. A major exception occurred in 1986 when the Commission's director, Nicholas Ndebele, was detained without charge for two weeks on suspicion that he was passing information to Amnesty International.

The Media

Newspapers and Magazines Zimbabwe has a variety of newspapers and magazines of varying degrees of outspokenness. The daily and Sunday press are entirely under government control. Soon after independence, the government bought a controlling interest in these papers for the Mass Media Trust. The papers, the *Herald* and *Sunday Mail* (Harare), *Chronicle* and *Sunday News* (Bulawayo) and *Manica Post* (Mutare), were previously owned by the South African Argus Group. The Mass Media Trust is nominally independent, although experience has shown that the opinion of the Minister of Information is decisive.

There are a number of independent journals. These range from magazines such as *Parade* and *Prize Africa* (which deal in fashion and football but also sometimes tackle sensitive political stories) to the *Financial Gazette*. The latter is a small circulation weekly aimed at the business community, whose coverage of political issues is much sharper than the official press. *Moto*, a monthly Catholic-funded magazine, is prepared to be highly critical of the government and has Zimbabwe's liveliest letters column.

The government's tolerance of criticism in independent journals does not compensate for its tight control of the official press. It is from the daily press and radio that most Zimbabweans get their news. When editors step out of line they are dealt with swiftly. In 1985, Willie Musarurwa, editor of the *Sunday Mail*, was sacked because, according to a letter from the head of Zimbabwe Newspapers: "The government, through the Minister of Information, Posts and Telecommunications, has taken the view that the *Sunday Mail*, under your editing, has acted like an opposition newspaper." Thus, the pretence that the Mass Media Trust was an entity separate from the government was abandoned. In 1987, Musarurwa's successor, Henry Muradzika, was also sacked over a contentious story. Again, the Mass Media Trust was not consulted.

The Chronicle In February 1989, Geoffrey Nyarota, editor of the Bulawayo *Chronicle* was removed. Under his editorship, the *Chronicle* ran a number of investigative stories about corruption. In October 1988, it broke the "Willowgate" story: government ministers were using their positions to buy scarce new cars assembled at the Willowvale plant in Harare, re-selling them at several times the legal price. The resulting scandal obliged President Mugabe to set up a judicial commission of inquiry, which confirmed the *Chronicle*'s allegations, as a consequence of which a number of ministers and officials resigned.

President Mugabe, however, publicly criticized Nyarota for "overzealousness" and the Minister of Information stated that Zimbabwe was not yet ready for investigative journalism. Under pressure from the government, Zimbabwe Newspapers Ltd removed both Nyarota and his deputy from their posts.

Three months after their removal, the government prevented the *Chronicle* from publishing an interview with ZUM leader Edgar Tekere.

In November 1988, when the *Chronicle* was running its "Willowgate" stories, one of its reporters, Gibbs Dube, was investigating the gold mining interests of the Governor of Matabeleland South, Mark Dube. (The two are not related.) After an interview at the Governor's house the reporter and his driver, Philip Maseko, were pursued by the Governor, detained and assaulted. Gibbs Dube was then released, but Maseko was held overnight. Press outrage at this incident was unanimous, but President Mugabe publicly defended Governor Dube, who was convicted of assault and fined Z$150 (US$45) in September 1989.

Foreign Press Harare enjoys good communications with the outside world and a high standard of living for its white population. These twin attractions have made it the main centre for the international press in the region outside South Africa. Foreign correspondents have in the past been expelled, notably when they have reported on human rights abuses, but there were no expulsions in 1988 or 1989.

Radio and Television Radio in Zimbabwe, as elsewhere in Africa, is the most important news medium: Zimbabwe Broadcasting Corporation is under close government control. On May 18 1989, two radio journalists, Robin Shava and Nyika Bara, interviewed lecturer Kempton Makamure about the government's new investment code. Makamure was critical of the code, probably the first critical voice to be heard on this issue in the government-controlled media. The two journalists were called before the Information Minister the following day and suspended from duty. They were later reinstated in non-journalistic posts. Zimbabwe TV (ZTV) is watched primarily by the urban population in Harare and Bulawayo and is confined largely to a diet of imported programmes. As with radio, ZTV news coverage is entirely devoted to presenting the government position.

Censorship of Books Harare has a number of active novelists, poets and local publishing houses, although these are constrained by shortages of foreign exchange. The import of books suffers from foreign exchange shortages, but is also restricted by the activities of a censorship board, inherited from the Rhodesian government, which approves all imported titles. In November 1989 the government announced plans to reform the censorship board and ease restrictions on the import of books.

Actions

On April 20 1989 ARTICLE 19 wrote to the Zimbabwean government protesting the removal of Geoffrey Nyarota from his post as editor of the Bulawayo *Chronicle* following the publication of an article on high-level corruption. A reply from the High Commission in London acknowledged ARTICLE 19's letter.

The Americas

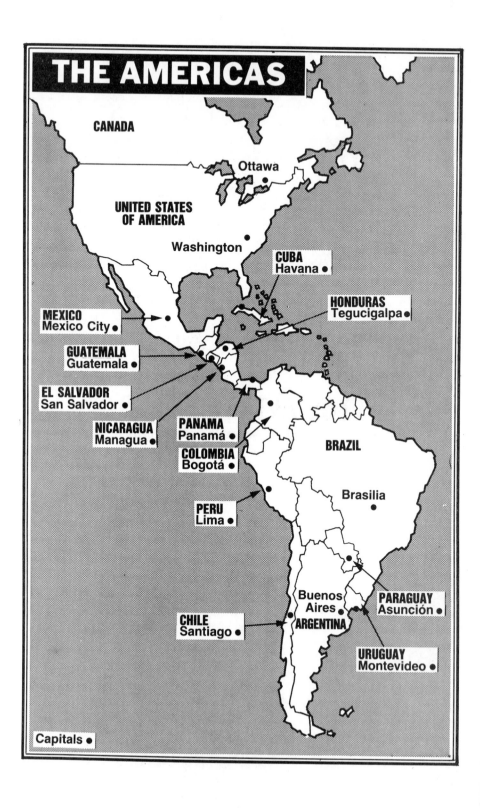

THE AMERICAS

CANADA

Ottawa

UNITED STATES
OF AMERICA

Washington

CUBA
Havana •

HONDURAS
Tegucigalpa •

MEXICO
Mexico City •

GUATEMALA
Guatemala •

EL SALVADOR
San Salvador •

NICARAGUA
Managua •

PANAMA
Panamá •

COLOMBIA
Bogotá •

BRAZIL

Brasilia

PERU
Lima •

PARAGUAY
Asunción •

Buenos
Aires

CHILE
Santiago •

ARGENTINA

URUGUAY
Montevideo •

Capitals •

Argentina

Since 1988, there have been instances of interference with and opposition to the exercise of freedom of expression, potentially threatening the continuation of the relatively open and free debate within the country.

The Constitution, promulgated in 1853, affirms freedom of the press and the right to publish without prior censorship (Arts.31 and 14). Courts have interpreted this to cover other forms of expression, including artistic expression. Since 1930, however, these rights and guarantees have frequently been suspended, both by military governments installed by *coups d'etat* and by elected governments resorting to the state of siege provisions of the Constitution in times of internal turmoil.

	Data	Year
Population	31,963,000	1988
Life expectancy	69.7	1985
GNP (US$ per capita)	2,640	1988
Main religion(s)	Christianity	
Official language(s)	Spanish	
Illiteracy %	4.7	1990
(M/F)	4.5/4.9	1990
Daily newspapers	218	1986
Radio sets	20,500,000	1987
TV sets	6,750,000	1987
Press agencies:		
	Agencia TELAM SA,	
	Diarios Y Noticias,	
	Noticias Argentinas SA	
ICCPR:	YES	1986

Declaration of a state of siege does not automatically impose prior censorship, but its effect on free expression has generally been very negative.

In the period covered by this report, President Raúl Alfonsín of the Radical Civic Union (UCR) governed until July 7 1989, when an economic crisis led to the transfer of power (five months ahead of schedule) to Peronist President-elect Carlos Saúl Menem. Debate immediately prior to the May 1989 elections had been free and open, but incidents affecting freedom of expression began in the last few months of Alfonsín's tenure, and have continued under President Menem.

On August 15 1990, the Senate approved a proposed amendment to the Penal Code which would make it an offence to publish information of an economic, political, financial, industrial or military nature without appropriate authorization. Although this refers primarily to state officials, there is concern that the proposed law might limit journalists' access to information other than through official channels. The amendment has yet to be approved by the Chamber of Deputies.

In September, an investigation was being conducted into "leaks" to the press by civil servants after an article by Horacio Verbitsky appeared in *Pagina 12* (an independent Buenos Aires daily newspaper) on September 4. This included excerpts of a statement made to a parliamentary commission by the Minister of Works and Public Services, Roberto Dromi, which criticized Economy Minister Erman Gonzalez. At Sr Dromi's request, the Attorney General ordered an investigation into a "possible crime against national security" against whoever passed on the recorded conversation to *Pagina 12* even though Sr Dromi confirmed that the meeting was not secret.

In light of the proposed amendment to the Penal Code, the investigation could intimidate the press and promote self-censorship in cases of official information received other than through approved channels.

The Media

Media Suspensions In February 1989 the sale in Argentina of a Uruguayan daily newspaper was suspended for several days. The paper, *La República*, had published two press statements attributed to a left-wing guerrilla group claiming responsibility for an attack on a Buenos Aires army base on January 29. The group claimed that some of its members had been killed after surrendering. Argentine journalists' efforts to investigate the official version of events at the base were reportedly impeded. The origin of the suspension order has not been established, but it occurred as President Alfonsín, under pressure from the armed forces, was creating an advisory National Security Council.

In April 1989, shortly before the elections, the UCR-linked Fundación Plural prepared a two-part television documentary on the last 20 years of Argentine history. The programme, *El Galpón de la Memoria* (Storehouse of Memories), featured well-known TV personalities. After the first part was broadcast, and following complaints from the army high command alleging anti-army bias, a government minister met the board of the foundation which decided to withdraw the second programme "temporarily", just hours before it was due to be screened. The second part was never shown, but the minister involved, Carlos Bastianes, denied responsibility for the decision.

Government Interference in the Media Official interference with the broadcast media continued into the first weeks of Menem's presidency. The new administration placed right-wing activists in key positions in some radio and TV stations owned or operated by the federal government, and several programmes were subsequently cancelled on political grounds. In one major station, Radio Belgrano, all news and talk shows were overhauled, with the cancellation of some programmes and dismissals of presenters, announcers, producers and researchers. Among those abruptly dismissed was Enrique Vázquez, a journalist well-known for his spirited opposition to the military authorities in the early 1980s.

At the official federal radio network, Radio Nacional, which has 38 stations throughout the country, the new director dropped several shows and reportedly instructed presenters of media comment and analysis programmes not to quote from or mention *Página 12*.

The paper was also pressurized by the new administration when it mentioned the criminal indictment by a Venezuelan court of the economy minister, Néstor Rapanelli, arising from his previous executive role with an Argentine multinational company. According to the paper's editor, the head of the State Intelligence Service, Juan Yofre, made direct threats to *Página 12* and tried to persuade some of its advertisers to withdraw their business.

There have also been attacks and threats against individual journalists and media. In the case of telephone threats it is difficult to establish responsibility, but those affected have attributed them to members of the intelligence services.

Responsibility for some unsolved bomb attacks on the media has been claimed by little-known right-wing organizations. In February 1989, a small bomb exploded in the city of La Rioja, in a house adjoining that of its presumed target Leandro López Alcaraz, publisher of the local newspaper *El Independiente*. The attack may have occurred because of the paper's condemnation of a resurgence in terrorist activity in La Rioja province, then governed by Menem.

On October 9 1989, factionalism in the labour movement was the apparent cause of the petrol-bombing of the offices of *El Pregón* newspaper in Lanus, a southern suburb of Buenos Aires. Leaflets left at the site attributed the attack to the Comando Libertadores de América and accused the paper of "poisoning the public with the disease that infects all communications media: the promotion of Ubaldinism". (Saúl Ubaldini was general secretary of the main labour federation and head of a faction rivalling that of President Menem.) The bombing followed a series of telephone threats.

The Comando Libertadores de América made similar threats to the mass-circulation daily *Clarín*, to Radio Mitre of Buenos Aires, and to Magdalena Ruiz Guiñazú, political commentator and host of a popular radio talk show. Ruiz Guiñazú served on the National Commission on Disappearance of Persons, chaired by writer Ernesto Sabato, and testified at the trial of General Jorge Rafael Videla and other members of the military juntas. In the 1970s, the Comando, then operating mainly in Córdoba province, was one of two notorious death squads; the involvement of military officers in its kidnappings and murders was disclosed in the 1980s during trials arising from the so-called "dirty war".

Protection of Journalists' Sources A legal saga arising from the alleged mistreatment of an army recruit has created an unfortunate precedent in the field of protection of sources. In December 1986, the daily *La Arena* of Santa Rosa, La Pampa province, carried a story based on a reader's letter complaining that a young conscript had been obliged to undertake a very long journey in a sealed railway wagon along with two horses belonging to an officer.

Military authorities maintained that the soldier had chosen to travel in that fashion, and his complaint of criminal "reduction to servitude" was thrown out of court four months later, leading to impeachment proceedings against the judge involved. The federal judge of Santa Rosa then subpoenaed Raúl D'Atri, the 82-year-old founder and publisher of the paper, ordering him to identify the two journalists who confirmed the story. D'Atri twice refused to comply, citing constitutional guarantees of freedom of expression. In early 1989, he was prosecuted for disobeying the court order, but refused for two weeks to report for fingerprinting until the police executed an arrest warrant. His case was taken up by newspaper trade organizations, and the prosecutor requested his acquittal, but in June 1989 he was convicted and given a suspended prison sentence of two months.

Libel Jorge Lanata, editor of *Página 12*, is currently being sued for criminal libel by former army intelligence agent "Paqui" Forese, allegedly a torturer in the "Automotores Orletti" camp in Buenos Aires during the "dirty war" (although charges against him were dropped under the 1987 Due Obedience amnesty law). After Forese was photographed during 1988 riots, apparently involving *agents provocateurs*, *Página 12* published details of a 1975 murder case in which he was acquitted.

Government Advertising The manipulation of official advertising under the present government, as under its predecessors, allows scope for interference with freedom of expression. All publicity for federal agencies and for many provincial and municipal governments has, since the military era, been commissioned by Telam, the official news agency. The relevant law states that Telam must distribute advertising evenly among all media, but in practice there are wide discrepancies. Given the paucity of commercial advertising, dependence on state patronage could unduly influence editorial content.

Control of Newsprint In 1976, under the Videla military government, three major Buenos Aires dailies (*Clarín*, *La Nación* and *La Razón*) created the Papel Prensa corporation to manufacture newsprint. The federal government subsidises the company and owns half its stock. The company is free to sell to any newspaper, but favours its own and allied papers and refuses to sell to some newspapers. As a result, some papers have to buy newsprint at US$650 a ton, while Papel Prensa sells to its clients at US$400.

Media Concentration In late 1989, the Menem administration repealed Article 45 of the Broadcasting Law, which had prohibited cross-ownership of radio and television channels by enterprises owning print media. Article 45 was already widely circumvented; front companies for at least two major newspaper companies have bought one radio and one TV station in the past few years. The repeal of Article 45, however, paved the way for new media conglomerates. Simultaneously, the government privatized TV Channels 11 and 13 in Buenos Aires, taken over in the mid-1970s. Channel 13 was sold to the company that owns both *Clarín*, the country's biggest-selling daily, and Radio Mitre, one of the main radio stations in Buenos Aires. Channel 11 was sold to a holding company that includes Editorial Atlántida (Argentina's largest magazine publisher) and the pro-military Bahía Blanca newspaper *La Nueva Provincia*. Channel 2 of La Plata (screened throughout the metropolitian area) has long been controlled by Hector García, owner of the major tabloid *Crónica*.

Newspaper managements have hailed the repeal of Article 45 as a "triumph for freedom", but the new administration provides no control over the process of concentration of media ownership. Small independent media outlets are disappearing because of economic pressures and there are no mechanisms to ensure editorial independence in the major enterprises.

Actions

On September 8 1990 ARTICLE 19 wrote to the government expressing concern at a proposed amendment to the Penal Code which would make it an offence to publish economic, political, financial, industrial or military information without appropriate authorization. (See text)

On September 12 1990 ARTICLE 19 wrote to the government expressing concern over an investigation into leaks to the press by civil servants. (See text)

Brazil

Since early 1985, when a civilian became President after 25 years of military rule, Brazil has enjoyed greater freedom of expression than at any other time in its recent history. In October 1988, a new Constitution guaranteed the rights to free expression, information and assembly. Political groupings operate and publish freely and are allowed broadcasting time during electoral campaigns.

The last time a major radio station was taken off the air was in 1982, during coverage of a strike in the car industry. Thereafter, the rights to political expression gradually increased. Since 1985, there has been no major act of political censorship; the 1988 Constitution formalized the freedom of expression that already existed in practice. The section covering "social communication" guarantees non-interference in the free expression of thought and information in all media. However, the federal government has the duty to regulate broadcasting, public performances and screenings.

	Data	Year
Population	144,428,000	1988
Life expectancy	63.4	1985
GNP (US$ per capita)	2,280	1988
Main religion(s)	Christianity	
Official language(s)	Portuguese	
Illiteracy %	18.9	1990
(M/F)	17.5/20.2	1990
Daily newspapers	322	1986
Non daily newspapers	1,307	1985
Periodicals	3,782	1985
Radio sets	52,000,000	1987
TV sets	27,000,000	1987
Press agencies:		
Editora Abril SA, Agencia ANDA,		
Agencia o Estado de Sao Paulo,		
Agencia Folha de Sao Paulo,		
Agencia Globo,		
Agencia Journal do Brasil		
ICCPR:		NO

Ideological, political or artistic censorship is explicitly prohibited and the right of reply is guaranteed. The Constitution also commits broadcasters to encouraging regional culture and prohibits monopolistic or oligopolistic ownership of the media (although in practice Rede Globo, owned by Roberto Maninho, is allowed what is clearly an oligopolistic position in print and broadcast media). All media companies must be wholly Brazilian-owned and may not accept any foreign investment. The advertising of alcoholic drinks, tobacco, fertilisers and medicines is restricted by law.

While print media companies can be freely established, radio and television stations need a government licence, renewable every 10 years for radio stations and 15 years for TV stations. The withdrawal of a licence requires the approval of two-fifths of the National Congress.

Censorship The end of official political censorship after 1985 has not meant the end of censorship as a whole, but rather a significant mitigation of the process operating in the years of authoritarianism. The five years since transition were marked by infrequent but consistent censorship in popular music, theatre, radio and television.

Some pornographic publications have been banned and minimum age limits for films are enforced. Although Brazil's attitude in such matters is still regarded as liberal, films and plays have continued to be cut and banned on the grounds of pornography or blasphemy. In March 1990, the new government of Fernando Collor de Mello, elected in December 1989, prohibited total nudity in the carnival parade, broadcast live nationally. The justice minister, Bernardo Cabral, has expressed concern about pornography and has announced plans to impose tighter controls over sexually explicit material on television.

Freedom of expression concerning sexual issues was generally allowed by successive military governments from 1964-1985, which financed the development of a popular soft-porn comedy genre of Brazilian film, the *pornochancada*. The 1970s saw a parallel growth in the production of printed pornography. However, thousands of films were cut and around 1,000 books and plays, some by classical authors, were banned for "pornographic content".

Traditionally, censorship and age classification has been the responsibility of a branch of the Federal Police. In the 1964-1985 period, as in the Vargas era (1930-1945), there was close liaison with the political police. From 1975, the government tried unsuccessfully to involve members of the intelligentsia in a consultative council on censorship. Until 1982, election propaganda was limited to live speeches, printed matter and audio broadcasting; on TV, only stills of the candidates were allowed with pre-recorded voice-overs.

The Media

The present legally guaranteed freedom of expression and information is a major advance on conditions during the military era. Nowadays, all shades of opinion are represented and print and broadcast media are free to comment on any subject. The press has exposed corruption, sometimes instigating congressional investigations; its main complaint concerning its right to inform is the ban on news of ransom kidnappings until the cases are solved.

The press is mainly regional, and the best selling newspaper prints 400,000 issues at most, a small circulation in a population of 140 million. The free circulation of information is further restricted by high illiteracy: although education is considered "a right of everybody and a duty of the state", only primary schooling is guaranteed.

Self-Censorship A 1989 Gallup poll found that most respondents felt that they were frequently misled or not told the whole truth and that major media, printed or electronic, were too linked to "economic interest groups". Even in the quality press, there are often complaints of omissions and incomplete reporting, sometimes not the fault of owners or editors but of a traditional method used by the state to co-opt journalists: their employment in second or "ghost" jobs is tolerated by owners as a way to keep salaries relatively low.

The broadcast media, which are the main information sources for most of the population, tend not to make full use of their present freedom, possibly because they operate under temporary licences from the federal government. There is a recognized problem of self-censorship in broadcasting as a whole. Controversial political programmes are broadcast mainly late at night; the major news programmes rarely discuss government wrongdoings, and usually only in regional or provincial administrations, not at federal level.

Newspapers and Magazines In recent years, the only overt act of official censorship concerned the weekly humour magazine *O Pasquím*, which had one issue withdrawn from sale for offensive language against government officials in September 1989. Quality newspapers and magazines have made use of the wider freedom of expression available after 1985. Daily papers, like *A Folha de São Paulo* and *Jornal do Brasil*, and weekly current affairs magazines like *Isto é-Senhor*, took the lead in scrutinizing the performance of the transitional government and denouncing corruption and nepotism. They did not suffer official censorship, but experienced restricted access to government information and some political and financial pressures. During 1987-1988 *Jornal do Brasil* had difficulties in obtaining permits to import new technology. There have been no major cases of bribery of journalists other than by the need for second jobs.

Books Enjoying tax incentives and total freedom from censorship, book publishing experienced a revival during 1985-1987, with more than 10,000 titles launched yearly. These included many of the 500 books banned in the military era, but it was only in 1989 that the last of these, *Feliz Ano Novo* by Rubem Fonseca, was able to be re-issued, 11 years after it was banned for alleged violent content. A new trend is the publication of memoirs of well-known radical figures, including former guerrillas.

Radio and Television Organizacoes Globo is thought to be the fourth-largest private TV group in the world, with assets of US$1,000 million and an annual turnover in excess of US$700 million. Its TV network has been operating since 1965 and now has 63 stations covering the entire country. The radio network has 16 stations, plus 34 affiliated stations. Its publishing branch includes books and 36 newspaper and magazine titles (including the major daily *O Globo*) and a national news agency. TV Globo has produced many award-winning science programmes and exports soap operas to over 40 countries.

Radio and TV have been more restrained in criticizing the government or social problems than the print media. TV Globo's news programme, *Jornal Nacional* with 60 million viewers, has rarely criticized the government in its 20 years of broadcasting. Small state-owned stations like TV Cultura (São Paulo) have been more incisive in their reporting than their private-sector rivals. However, major channels now produce mass-audience soap operas on themes unthinkable a few years ago, such as the struggles of landless peasants and the underground years of a veteran communist leader.

Television is the main forum for political propaganda. Since the 1930s, the government has broadcast a daily one-hour official news and information programme on radio. The current President is himself a regional media owner, and was supported for the whole of his campaign by the main national network. Popular TV presenter Silvio Santos, who launched himself as a presidential candidate in the last 15 days of the campaign, managed to secure around 20 per cent support in several opinion polls before being disqualified by the Electoral Court.

Public Entertainment In 1986, the film *Je Vous Salut Marie*, by Jean-Luc Godard, was banned as blasphemous. Popular music, after two decades of tight control of lyrics, is now unrestricted, but no longer has as strong a political content as in the 1960s and 1970s.

Canada

Prior to the proclamation of the Canadian Charter of Rights and Freedoms as part of the Canadian Constitution of 1982, freedom of speech and of the media in Canada was preserved more by tradition than by constitutional or judicial protection. Section 2(b) of the Canadian Charter now guarantees "freedom of thought, belief, opinion and expression", including freedom of the media. This provision applies to the federal Parliament and government, and to the legislatures and governments of the 10 provinces and two territories.

The press is independent of the government and there is no censorship of political discussion at public meetings or in radio and television broadcasts. While strenuous political dissent exists, it should be noted that ownership of the private popular media is concentrated in a few hands. The sharpest criticism of government tends to be found in publications with modest means and limited circulation. However, this is balanced somewhat by the state-funded but predominantly independent Canadian Broadcasting Corporation (CBC) which operates national radio and TV networks, both in English and in French. Pluralist political commentary and even scathing satire are regularly featured in programming. Concern has been expressed at the federal government's reduction of financial support for the CBC in recent years.

	Data	Year
Population	26,218,500	1989
Life expectancy (M/F)	71.8/78.9	1982
GNP (US$ per capita)	16,760	1988
Main religion(s)	Christianity	
Official language(s)	English	
	French	
Illiteracy %	1	1985
Daily newspapers	116	1986
Non daily newspapers	1,295	1986
Periodicals	1,322	1986
Radio sets	24,624,000	1987
TV sets	14,895,000	1987
Press agencies:		
	The Canadian Press	
ICCPR:	YES	1976

Language Rights

The right of everyone to express him or her self in either of Canada's two official languages is protected by the Canadian Charter. Sections 16-22 guarantee equal status for English and French in all institutions of Parliament and federal government and those of New Brunswick, the only officially bilingual province. Similar language rights are also constitutionally protected for certain judicial proceedings and educational purposes, and protected by ordinary legislation in Quebec, Ontario, and some other jurisdictions. There is an active programme to promote language equality in the federal sphere, overseen by the Commissioner of Official Languages, who is an independent officer of Parliament with security of tenure.

Apart from Ontario, Quebec, and New Brunswick, there are limited circumstances in which francophones can communicate with provincial government services and participate in public life in their first language. In Quebec, on the other hand, the francophone majority has reinforced French language rights in law and practice in the last 15 years. This has led to a diminution of the opportunity for non-francophones to work, carry on business, advertise in English, or to have children educated in that language. During the 1970s, there was a resulting exodus of anglo-phones from Quebec. In 1988, the Supreme Court of Canada (in *Ford v Quebec*) considered a law restricting the use of English in Quebec, and upheld a right to post signs and notices in English under freedom of expression safeguards in the Canadian Charter and in Quebec human rights legislation, observing that choice of language is closely related to true freedom of expression. The Supreme Court stated that the Quebec government might be justified in seeking to protect the French language, for example, by allowing French to predominate in commercial signs, but a requirement of "French only" was considered to be excessive.

The Quebec government responded to the *Ford* judgement by disallowing the display of information in English outside business premises. Information could be in any language but French would predominate inside a commercial establishment. To protect itself from further constitutional litigation, Quebec declared that its "sign law" would be immune from challenge "notwithstanding" that it might violate free-dom of expression under the Canadian Charter. This declaration of exemption is al-lowed under section 33 of the Canadian Constitution. One individual (Gordon McIntyre), supported by others, has complained to the Human Rights Committee, asserting that Quebec's action violates minority language rights under Article 27 of the International Covenant on Civil and Political Rights, to which Canada is a signa-tory.

Meech Lake Accord   Though Québécois leaders consider the "sign law" (Bill 178) necessary to protect French expression rights in primarily English-speaking North America, it was viewed as draconian by many anglophones in Canada. Their angry reaction was reflected in the national debate in 1990 over a proposed package of amendments to the Constitution, known as the Meech Lake Accord. If ratified, this would have recognized Quebec as a "distinct society" within Canada, and this was perceived as strengthening francophone language rights. Some municipalities in other provinces declared themselves to be "English only". The Accord was not, in fact, ratified but the strong sentiments generated by the national debate are likely to have continued impact on rights of expression.

Indigenous Peoples   Sections 25 and 35 of the Constitution can be interpreted as af-firming language rights for Canada's indigenous peoples. Until 1984, the govern-ment of the Northwest Territories had two official languages, English and Inuktitut ("Eskimo"), and has been endeavouring to make greater official use of other aborig-inal languages. The imposition (by the federal government) of French as an official language in 1984 was not welcomed by territorial peoples. The Northwest Terri-tories plan to phase in the use of French and eight aboriginal languages in the governmental and educational systems over the next few years.

In the federal domain, the 1990-1991 budget eliminates the Natives Communica-tions Programme, which had sustained 15 aboriginal language newspapers, and re-duces spending by 16 per cent on the Northern Native Broadcast Access Pro-gramme, which supports television and radio broadcasting in remote parts of the country. Section 27 of the Canadian Charter requires that the Charter be interpreted "in a manner consistent with the preservation and enhancement of the multicultural heritage of Canadians". Section 14 guarantees the right to an interpreter "in any proceedings", for those who cannot understand or speak the language used.

The Media

The Press The daily press in Canada is primarily local in distribution and influence. Through the use of satellite transmission, a national edition of the *Toronto Globe and Mail*, established in 1981, is available throughout the country. In 1988, the *Financial Post* also began publication of a national edition. In March 1989, there were 110 daily papers in Canada with a combined circulation of over 5.8 million, representing 63 per cent of the country's households. More than 1,000 weekly and twice-weekly community newspapers reached an estimated 5.2 million people, mainly in the more remote areas of the country. Over 80 daily and weekly publications in over 20 languages catered to the indigenous and immigrant population.

Private press councils have been established to consider complaints concerning abuses such as stereotyping and unfair representation. The press councils are voluntary bodies and have no statutory powers of enforcement.

Ownership Concern over the lack of competition among the press has led to two extensive federal reviews, a Senate Study on the Mass Media (1970), and the (Kent) Royal Commission on Newspapers (1981). The Kent Report found that eight organizations controlled about 75 per cent of Canada's newspapers, with two corporations controlling about 60 per cent of English-language circulation. One family controlled all the English-language dailies in New Brunswick (as well as owning many broadcast outlets there). The press opposed the Kent Commission recommendations, which were designed to ensure greater competition, and the report had little eventual impact. Newspaper ownership has subsequently become even more concentrated.

Harassment of Journalists During a tense stand-off (caused by a land rights dispute) between members of the Mohawk community and the police and army at Oka, Quebec, in the summer of 1990, many journalists entered the Mohawks' encampment to cover the siege and began filing radio and press reports by cellular phone. The police obtained a court order allowing them to cut off and jam cellular transmissions by journalists, and the army also prohibited reporters inside the encampment from receiving food, blankets, and work supplies. All journalists leaving were searched and coercive attempts were made to interrogate them about the situation there and the Mohawks' plans. CBC reporters had video and audio cassettes seized and many journalists had their vehicles searched.

Newspapers filed suit but, on the day the siege ended (September 26), a Federal Court judge ruled that the journalists' constitutional rights had not been violated and so it would be inappropriate to interfere with the military operation regarding journalists' supplies. The judge also ruled that freedom of the press had not been violated because news stories had continued to emerge from behind the lines.

Media Regulation Under the 1968 Broadcasting Act, radio and TV frequencies are considered to be public property in Canada, and owners of stations and networks (including CBC) must obtain and periodically renew licences. A broadcast licence, issued by the Canadian Radio-TV and Telecommunications Commission (CRTC), is accompanied by conditions. Licence approval hearings are public, and enable public interest organizations to attempt to attach conditions which benefit their constituencies. Legislation proposed in 1990 would have removed the obligation for the CBC to promote "national unity", which critics had argued allowed the government to exert improper influence on the Corporation. Under the new Broadcast Act, the CBC would only have been required to "contribute to shared national consciousness and identity". The CRTC imposes rules requiring policies designed to ensure that both programming and advertising reflect the increasingly diverse nature of Canadian society, and do not exhibit stereotypes of women or minorities. Private TV broadcasters have generally shown a desire to maximize profit by purchasing cheap and popular US shows in order to sell more advertising time. Newspapers, books and magazines are not subject to similar supervision. Complaints concerning stereotyping or unfair representations may be made to "press councils", but these are voluntary bodies with no powers of enforcement.

Government efforts to ensure a diverse cultural sector are considered a necessity, because of the scale of the ubiquitous US entertainment industry. Only 20-30 per cent of films distributed to cinemas are Canadian. There have been recent cutbacks in tax concessions, postal subsidies, and government grants to assist Canadian publishing and film production, but a new federal grants scheme, announced in July 1990, gives new hope to the Canadian publishing, recording and film/video sectors. "Canadian content" quotas require that a high percentage of Canadian-produced programmes be broadcast on TV. The "Canadian content regulations" also apply to the playing of music on radio. These rules have checked the domination of US and UK artists in this field and have enabled Canadian performers and composers to gain wider recognition in the last two decades.

Cultural nationalists voiced strong opposition to the new Free Trade pact between Canada and the US which allows US publications to compete directly with Canadian ones. It appears that preferential postal rates available for Canadian magazines are being extended to US magazines merely printed in Canada and a tariff protecting Canadian sound recording industries (records, tapes and CDs) is being phased out.

Disabled People As people with disabilities have asserted their rights to equity in recent years, public bodies at all levels have moved to increase their opportunities to communicate and receive information through "alternative format material" or through enhanced delivery systems. Innovations have been made in print media, telecommunications, and TV broadcasting. In 1988, the House of Commons Committee on the Status of Disabled Persons recommended measures for ameliorating stereotyping in print and electronic media and for improving access to these media for disabled persons. One innovation can be traced to the Committee Report; *No News is Bad News* is a weekly programme presented by and about people with disabilities, on CBC TV's all-news channel.

Broadcasting Legislative Sessions For some years, TV broadcasts of legislative proceedings, including the federal Parliament, have been routine. Nova Scotia, however, forbids TV cameras in its legislature. A trial judge in that province recently held that this denial of access violated the freedom of expression guarantee (section 2(b)) of the Canadian Charter. His decision was based partly on earlier Canadian judgements that relied on international human rights conventions which defined free expression to include access to information.

Defamation In Canada, honour and reputation are protected by non-criminal statutes which seriously restrict free speech. In all jurisdictions except Quebec (the only "civil law" province), "common law" defamation doctrines also apply.

Of significant concern is an ongoing civil action for defamation brought by the wealthy and powerful Reichman family against a journalist and *Toronto Life* over an article in the magazine. The courts have refused to permit a jury trial and have obliged the writer to produce the first draft of her book on the same subject. The case has reportedly deterred other publications contemplating critical articles about powerful people. It is said that the interests of companies which insure publishers against libel suits act as a further restraint.

Freedom of Expression

Hate Expression In the (federal) Canadian Human Rights Act (CHRA), there is a section proscribing "hate" messages. The CHRA prohibits telephone communication likely to expose people to hatred or contempt as a result of cases dealing with anti-semitic taped messages played through the telephone by one organization. After repeated refusals to comply with an order by a tribunal to cease, the main perpetrator, John Ross Taylor, was sentenced to a prison term. In appeal proceedings, the defence argued that the CHRA "hate message" section violated the "freedom of expression" protection in the Constitution. Section 1 of the Constitution allows a government to impose reasonable limits, however, and the judges ruled that the section in question and the manner of its enforcement were reasonable and justifiable.

Under the Criminal Code, offences that relate to hate propaganda include: advocating genocide; publicly inciting hatred against an identifiable group where such incitement is likely to cause a breach of the peace (harm to a person or property); wilful promotion of hatred against an identifiable group; and wilful publishing of false news or statements which the publisher knows to be false and which could or does cause injury to "a public interest" (Section 177, now 181).

The sensational trial of Ernst Zundel in 1985 involved Section 177. Zundel had distributed pamphlets worldwide denying that six million Jews had died in the Nazi holocaust. The seven-week trial provided Zundel with extensive exposure of his theories. His conviction was overturned on appeal because of procedural errors, and a new trial was ordered (in which Zundel was later reconvicted). The Ontario Court of Appeal found, however, that the section did not violate the Canadian Charter, holding that "the maintenance of racial and religious harmony is certainly a matter of public interest" and that "spreading false news is the antithesis of seeking truth through the free exchange of ideas". The Supreme Court of Canada refused leave to appeal this judgement further.

The Zundel case bolstered the long-standing arguments by commentators, including newspaper editors and the Law Reform Commission of Canada, for removal of the "false news" section, seen as an unnecessary restriction on free speech and, where prosecution occurs, as giving bigots a public platform. Other commentators have said that an important public service had been performed by the prosecution of Zundel arguing that Canadians have had a chance (through expert testimony) to see just how baseless Zundel's "holocaust fraud" theories are.

In *R v Keeqstra*, a teacher was convicted of telling anti-Semitic lies to his students, thereby wilfully promoting hatred "against an identifiable group" (Jews) contrary to the Criminal Code. The Alberta Court of Appeal overturned the conviction, ruling that the Criminal Code section was an unconstitutional infringement of freedom of expression. The Court concluded that at least some error or untrue speech must be protected by the freedom to ensure free exchange of political discussion and that the Code made a crime of "imprudent speech". The Alberta Prosecutor has appealed to the Supreme Court of Canada.

Obscenity Provincial administrative bodies classify films as being suitable for certain age groups, and may require advertisements to include warnings as to their content (for example, "violence and coarse language" or "some nudity"), or may ban a film from distribution. The standards vary considerably from province to province.

Such censorship is opposed by civil liberties groups, cinema owners, and members of the artistic community. In a leading case, the Ontario courts decided that the province was justified in having a board of censors, but that its terms of reference were too vague and, therefore, violated the Constitution. The legislation was amended accordingly.

Federal legislation permits Customs officers to suspend importation of books and magazines temporarily, pending determination of their compliance with the Criminal Code. Publishers can obtain an advance opinion permitting them to excise material that would prevent importation. Some books with homosexual themes have been prohibited. There is little monitoring of printed matter published in Canada. Video rental businesses and the tapes which they offer are also virtually unregulated. Nevertheless, an important case in 1985, which tested Criminal Code provisions on obscenity, concerned a rental business called Red Hot Video Ltd. The Code outlaws distribution of obscene material, "a dominant characteristic of which" is the "undue exploitation" of sex, or of sex linked with violence or cruelty. The judges ruled that the degrading treatment of women portrayed in the offending video tapes was "unacceptable by any reasonable Canadian community standard". The court found that the restriction on freedom of expression was acceptable under Canada's Constitution, given growing community concern over exploitation of women and children in some publications and films.

Official Secrets The principles surrounding governmental secrets are based largely on the United Kingdom Official Secrets Act (not including its recent revisions). In addition to federal law on state secrets, there are federal and provincial laws which restrict the release of information held on individuals (for personal privacy) and on business corporations (to keep information from competitors and employees). There has been a gradual movement towards greater openness and improved public access to official information.

In a judgement that attracted much attention, the Supreme Court of Canada upheld the dismissal of a federal employee for criticizing aspects of government policy. It was decided that he had displayed a lack of loyalty incompatible with his public service duties.

Early in 1990, the national government enacted rules which prohibited demonstrations or distribution of literature within 50 metres of Parliament. Two men were arrested for protesting within the prohibited zone. One was conducting an anti-abortion vigil and the other protested alleged federal government corruption. The rules and the arrests were condemned by an all-party parliamentary committee.

Access to Information The federal government, the Yukon government, and the majority of provinces have procedures for members of the public to obtain unpublished government information. The key federal statutes are the Access to Information Act and the Privacy Act. The former allows (with a number of exceptions) citizens or permanent residents and some others to seek access to any documentary or computer record under the control of a government institution. The latter allows individuals access to information or opinions recorded about themselves and to request that errors be corrected. Each Act is overseen by a Commissioner whose tenure permits some independence in acting as a type of adjudicator. Where access to information cannot be obtained even with the help of the Information Commissioner, an applicant can seek an order from the Federal Court.

Under these Acts, there are a number of categories of data not available for public scrutiny including: most commercial data; information originally obtained by a foreign government or by a previous domestic one; information that could harm defence, diplomatic, or trade interests or that pertains to law enforcement; and records connected with the operation of the federal Cabinet. Some critics say that, in effect, these exemptions weaken Canadian access law. Others, including the Information Commissioner, have suggested that the legislation is fine, but that government bureaucracy sometimes endeavours to hamper its application. Several leading newspapers employ journalists who have become specialists in seeking information through the access law.

In her 1989 and 1990 annual reports, Information Commissioner Inger Hansen criticized the government for failing to implement the recommendations to improve the Act that were unanimously adopted by an all-party parliamentary committee in 1987. One of her recommendations was that Canada follow the Swedish example and enshrine Canadians' "right to know" in the Constitution. Commissioner Hansen's tenure was not renewed by the government when her seven-year term expired in 1990. There are suggestions that the government now intends to impose higher fees on those who apply for information under the Act.

Open Justice Two cases involving refugee claimants are of particular interest. *Southam v Minister of Employment and Immigration* concerned immigration detention review hearings involving migrants from a ship docked in Nova Scotia, all of whose passengers claimed to be refugees from India. The Federal Court confirmed that freedom of the press encompasses a right of access to judicial proceedings and overruled an order denying access to the media. Certain newspapers are currently challenging an Immigration Act provision under which they have been refused access to deportation hearings involving Mahmoud Mohammad, a Palestinian convicted of terrorism who had entered Canada without disclosing his criminal record.

Commercial Speech Commercial expression is a protected right under section 2(b) of the Charter. This was decided by the Supreme Court of Canada in the *Ford* case noted above. The court found that commercial expression includes "listeners" as well as "speakers", and plays a significant role in enabling individuals to make informed economic choices. Nevertheless, the Court upheld a restrictive Quebec law designed to protect children, finding it to be a reasonable limit in a free and democratic society. The Quebec government had enacted a Consumer Protection Act severely curtailing advertisements directed at children under 13 years of age. A toy manufacturing company unsuccessfully challenged the legislation.

Contempt of Court In 1987, the Ontario Court of Appeal reversed a contempt of court conviction against a lawyer. Harry Kopyto had been assisting a client who was suing police officers for alleged misconduct against him. The case was dismissed. Kopyto made a statement, reported by a journalist, alleging that the courts in Canada were "warped in favour of protecting the police", and that "courts and the police stick so close together you would think they are stuck together with 'krazy glue'". He was convicted of contempt of court. The Ontario Court of Appeal ruled that the contempt order violated his freedom of expression, and the common law contempt offence of scandalizing the Court was declared to be unconstitutional. The Canadian judicial system, the Court said, was strong enough to withstand such criticisms.

Actions

In its 1990 Commentary to the Human Rights Committee ARTICLE 19 recommended, among other actions, that the government should amend Article 33 of the Canadian Charter to add section 2's protection of freedom of expression to the list of fundamental rights that may not be infringed by provincial legislation.

Chile

On December 14 1989, Patricio Aylwin, the Christian Democratic leader of an opposition coalition, was elected President. He took office on March 11 1990, ending 16 years of military rule under General Augusto Pinochet. In August 1988, the Pinochet government had lifted all emergency legislation, although discretionary powers limiting freedom of expression, provided for in the 1980 Constitution and its 29 transitory articles, remained. Article 41 permits suspension and restriction of freedom of information and opinion in a declared state of emergency, during which the President may suspend publications or broadcasts deemed harmful to national security for a specified period.

	Data	Year
Population	12,748,000	1988
Life expectancy	72	1987
GNP (US$ per capita)	1,510	1988
Main religion(s)	Christianity	
Official language(s)	Spanish	
Illiteracy %	6.6	1990
(M/F)	6.5/6.8	1990
Daily newspapers	74	1986
Non daily newspapers	25	1983
Periodicals	118	1983
Radio sets	4,200,000	1987
TV sets	2,050,000	1987
Press agencies:		
Orbe Servicios Informativos		
ICCPR:	YES	1972

In July 1989, the Constitution was amended and a number of oppressive elements removed, including the transitory articles and Article 8 which banned the expression of certain ideologies. Its replacement, Article 19 Clause 15, has similar intent but refers to actions rather than ideas. Clause 12 of Article 19 provides for freedom of expression and private operation of the media and provides a right of correction for persons "offended or unjustly alluded to" in any medium. The state is prohibited from establishing a monopoly in media, and prior censorship is only allowed to uphold "general norms" concerning "artistic activities".

Laws Affecting Freedom of Expression Law 12.927, the Law for Internal Security, is probably the one most frequently used to repress free expression. It criminalizes any calls for disruption of public order or for illegal strikes. Article 6(b) punishes defamation, libel, or slander of the President, members of the armed forces and public officials; 6(f) refers to proponents of propaganda for doctrines, systems or methods which promote violence as a means for political, economic or social change.

Law 18.313 of May 1984 makes it an offence to publish damaging or potentially damaging material concerning the private life of an individual. The law, which provides for a jail sentence and does not allow truth as a defence, was modified in 1985 by Law 16.643 on Abusive Publication, which stipulates some 14 laws, decrees and resolutions affecting freedom of expression.

The government has stated that it intends to repeal some 15-20 regulations passed under Gen Pinochet and to introduce a modern press law based on consensus. The delay arises partly from the fact that Gen Pinochet appointed five of the seven Supreme Court judges and the members of the National Security Council which has powers to overrule all three branches of government.

Political Expression The electoral law introduced for the October 1988 plebiscite, which approved the return to civilian rule, limited campaigning (by press, radio, television and leafletting) to a 28-day period ending two days before polling. Other forms of campaigning were illegal at any time, including posters and wall-painting, traditionally an important form of communication (and allowed in practice for government slogans). Similar rules were enforced for the 1989 elections. On July 8 1989, Raúl Valdés, a member of a Socialist Party faction (PS-Almeyda), was killed by a security guard while painting slogans.

Although the Communist Party of Chile (PCCh) and the PS-Almeyda were outlawed by the Constitutional Court under Article 8, the establishment of the Broad Left Socialist Party (PAIS) coalition permitted members of proscribed organizations to contest congressional seats. Following the repeal of Article 8, the PCCh was legalized on October 22 1990, and the unified Socialist Party is also seeking legal status.

Human Rights and the Courts A painful issue in the transition to civilian rule has been that of accountability for human rights violations during military rule. A National Commission of Truth and Reconciliation, established in May 1990, is empowered to investigate the extent of, but not individual liability for, such offences by opposition as well as government forces. On June 21, President Aylwin indicated that military personnel, including Gen Pinochet, could be prosecuted for proven abuses.

The legal system is to be reformed by the new government. Under the Pinochet administration Judge René García, an outspoken supporter of human rights, was dismissed by the Supreme Court for "inappropriate behaviour". During the 1988 plebiscite campaign, film of García denouncing torture was censored from opposition TV advertisements.

An important obstacle to freedom of expression is the power of military courts to try journalists and others for defamation of the armed forces, under Art. 417 of the Code of Military Justice. In December 1988, the interior ministry dropped all such charges against journalists in the civil courts, but some 29 military prosecutions are continuing. In the first week of May 1990, an army judge ordered *La Epoca* journalist Manuel Salazar to be arrested and held incommunicado after he had tracked down a secret agent involved in the assassination of a former minister. Salazar was released after one night, and President Aylwin joined protests at his detention. Osvaldo Muray, political editor of the magazine *Fortín Mapocho*, is on bail on charges of insulting the police in his report on the death of journalist Juan Bertolo.

In September, there were further arrests and detentions of journalists by the military. Juan Pablo Cárdenas, director of *Analisis*, was charged with "offences and injuries" against Gen Pinochet for an interview that was printed on March 19; Alfonso Stephens of the same magazine was also detained.

Juan Andrés Lagos, editor-in-chief of *El Siglo* (newspaper of the Communist Party), was arrested for refusing to appear before a military court to answer questions concerning articles in his paper. *El Siglo's* editor, Guillermo Torres, who is national secretary of the College of Journalists, was also facing charges.

In addition, Fernando Paulsen, of *Analisis*, had a prison sentence ratified for alleged "offences against the armed forces", and Jorge Donoso, chief editor of *Fortín Mapocho*, received a 60-day suspended sentence and had restrictions imposed on his movements for an article published in May 1984.

In January 1990, Amnesty International reported that the military courts had used a 1978 amnesty law to close three investigations involving over 100 "disappearance" cases. Human rights lawyers have appealed the decision.

Official Secrecy The secret police of the National Information Centre (CNI) have now been absorbed into the Ministry of Defence, losing their autonomy and powers of arrest but retaining political files on 12 million citizens. The identification of 900 CNI agents in *El Siglo* on April 15 1990 was a considerable embarrassment to the army high command and led to legal action and threats against the paper. Two other lists, one naming CNI professionals (lawyers, doctors, etc) and the other military personnel, are said to be awaiting publication.

The Media

In addition to the diverse local media, foreign newspapers and periodicals are freely available. Under President Pinochet, there was a vigorous opposition press, although attacks on the media were frequent. There are approximately 80 daily or weekly newspapers and 22 major periodicals. Several formerly proscribed publications, such as *El Siglo*, have now reappeared on newstands. In May 1990, a non-governmental Committee for Freedom of Expression and of the Press was formed, including public figures such as actors, journalists, members of the Senate and representatives of the Catholic Church.

Radio In early 1990, there were some 42 radio stations representing several shades of opinion. They were formerly monitored and "advised" by the *Dinacos*, National Directorate of Social Communication, and self-censorship was reportedly practised to avoid state harassment. Unofficial interference also occurred in that radio stations were vulnerable to attack or takeover by guerrilla groups wishing to broadcast political messages. From late 1989, the role of *Dinacos* was limited to television. There were a number of "pirate" radio stations but, in October 1990, the government ordered the suspension and dismantling of equipment of all stations without the appropriate licence.

Television TV was strictly controlled by the Pinochet administration, although less so after the 1988 plebiscite. The state channel, Televisión Nacional (TVN), is the only one with near-national coverage. Other stations are run by universities whose rectors were appointed by the previous government. The Pinochet government announced plans to privatize TVN, now suffering a serious financial crisis partly because of programmes paid for and not broadcast, over-staffing and substantial spending on government propaganda during the 1989 election. Many workers have recently been dismissed, officially for budgetary reasons although most were supporters of the former government. Observers report that TVN now covers human rights stories and has innovative cultural programmes.

Books Under the new administration, a number of books have been published which document injustice during the Pinochet era. There has been a reported upsurge in book publishing since June 1990.

Attacks on the Press The Committee to Protect Journalists recorded some 70 cases of arson, bombings and other attacks or threats against media organs, media workers or their property in 1988, and 31 for 1989. In 1990, a number of journalists were attacked and threatened, among them Héctor Mérida who was assaulted by Gen Pinochet's bodyguards in northern Chile on May 15; he was punched and had his camera broken. On February 10 1990, Juan Bertolo, journalist for the San Antonio daily *Proa Regional* and correspondent for the Santiago-based Radio Cooperative and *Las Ultimas Noticias*, died in police custody. One month prior to his detention, Bertolo had released information about the alleged involvement of Carabineros (military police) in a robbery which had led to the arrest of two police officers. On March 31, British journalist Jonathan Moyle, editor of *Defence Helicopter World*, was found hanged in a wardrobe in a Santiago hotel. He was investigating alleged links between a Chilean arms manufacturer and Iraq.

Actions

On August 12 1989 ARTICLE 19 wrote to the government about the welfare of Alvaro Rojas, news editor of *Análisis*, who was arrested and charged with "offending the armed forces" in an article published in February. A reply dated August 22 said that he was released on August 17.

On October 12 1988 ARTICLE 19 wrote to the government protesting police attacks on journalists following the defeat of President Pinochet in a plebiscite.

In its October 1989 Commentary to the Human Rights Committee ARTICLE 19 expressed deep concern at the continued illegality of sections of political opinion, and the continued repression of media and journalists. It concluded that the rights to freedom of opinion, expression and information continue to be denied in Chile.

On August 20 1990 ARTICLE 19 wrote to the government expressing concern at death threats received by four journalists, Manuel Cabieses of *Punto Final*, Libio Perez of *Pagina Abierta* and Juan Andres Lagos and Guillermo Torres of *El Siglo*.

On October 10 1990 ARTICLE 19 wrote to the government expressing concern at the arrest and detention of journalists in connection with "offences against the military", and urging the release of those in detention (see text). On November 12 1990 ARTICLE 19 received a reply from the Chilean government stating their inability to legally intervene in the cases of journalists currently appearing before military tribunals. The letter also stated that President Alywin's government fully supports freedom of expression and is seeking diverse legislative reforms through parliament.

Colombia

Both the ICCPR and the American Convention on Human Rights have been ratified by Colombia and incorporated into domestic law. The Constitution cites war, social instability and public disorder as conditions which may permit the suspension of freedom of expression. These conditions have plagued Colombia for generations.

Violence and Freedom of Expression Freedom of political expression and opinion is at particular risk. According to the UN Commission on Human Rights, explicitly political killings over the 21 months from January 1988 totalled 4,256; these are direct attacks on the rights upheld by Article 19 of the Universal Declaration. Whilst much of the violence is perpetrated by drug traffickers, there is evidence of the involvement of members of the armed forces in torture, disappearances and murders of trade union leaders, human rights workers, teachers, priests, peasants and members of the judiciary. From 1986-1989, 99 members of the teachers' union and some 350 other trade union activists were murdered; another 1,000 teachers had to abandon their homes and jobs because of death threats. Since the founding of the Patriotic Union Party (UP) in 1985 by former guerrillas, over 1,000 of its members have been murdered. During 1988-1989, 76 members of the Social Conservative Party (PSC) were killed, as were 163 members of the Liberal Party (PL) and 255 members of the UP.

	Data	Year
Population	30,241,000	1988
Life expectancy	65	1987
GNP (US$ per capita)	1,240	1985
Main religion(s)	Christianity	
Official language(s)	Spanish	
Illiteracy %	13.3	1990
(M/F)	12.5/14.1	1990
Daily newspapers	46	1986
Radio sets	5,000,000	1987
TV sets	3,250,000	1987
Press agencies:		
	Ciep-El Pais, Colprensa	
ICCPR:	YES	1969

Presidential Elections On May 27 1990, César Gaviria Trujillo (PL) was elected President, to take office in August. During the campaign, violence was directed particularly at the left although all parties suffered harassment and murders. Three presidential candidates were murdered: Luis Carlos Galán (PL) on August 18 1989, Bernardo Jaramillo (UP) on March 22 1990 and Carlos Pizarro Leongómez (the M-19 movement) on April 26. The murder of the UP leader, the second in just over two years, led the party to withdraw from the elections.

The Drugs Trade Colombia supplies 80 per cent of the world's cocaine, and the violence associated with the trade has severely curbed free expression. Cocaine provides more export earnings than coffee and has created a new, unrestrainedly brutal class of billionaires. Corruption and fear have penetrated nearly every institution, including the judiciary, military, police, and the legislature. The press practises self-censorship on the issue and those who speak out against the traffic may suffer the consequences: journalists have been murdered and newspaper premises bombed. An anti-drugs offensive, launched by outgoing President Virgilio Barco, met with limited success: some middle-level traffickers were extradited to the United States, a major producer was killed by police and over 1,000 men were dismissed from the armed forces.

Although most newspapers are, understandably, circumspect in their coverage of the drugs mafia, an exception is the daily *El Espectador*. Its editor, Guillermo Cano, was murdered in 1985; many other staff members have been killed, kidnapped or forced to flee the country. In September 1989, its editorial and distribution offices in Bogotá were bombed. In October 1989, its head of distribution and its administrative director in Medellín were killed by gunmen. Despite the onslaught, the newspaper has, without fail, published daily but in March 1990 it stopped editorial comment on the drug barons.

The Media

The Press Law Under a 1975 law, journalists must hold a relevant degree from an institution approved by the Ministry of Education and must carry press cards which can be suspended or cancelled if they break laws regarding journalism or are convicted of harming third parties by their work.

Article 11 of the Press Law provides for the protection of sources but, on February 26 1988, a judge in Bucaramanga ordered the weekly magazine *Voz* to provide information on an interview with a hired killer, including the name of the journalist responsible and details of the distribution of *Voz*. Protesting that the order was contrary to Article 11, staff stated that the content of the magazine was a collective responsibility and that since the interview was conducted by telephone they could give no useful information.

Other Legislation For almost 40 years, emergency legislation has restricted press freedom. New laws introduced to combat drug trafficking have limited the flow of information on narcotics; a law on political parties restricts the publication of political advertising, and an eight per cent import tax on newsprint has had a particularly serious effect on smaller newspapers.

The Anti-Terrorist Statute, Decree 20/180 of January 27 1988, covers the reporting of guerrilla activity. Article 49 forbids transmission of any recording or information identifying witnesses to terrorist acts. Article 50 forbids live broadcasts from the location of terrorist action; Article 51 permits the suspension of radio frequencies in the case of infringements. The Decree has also operated in such a way as to inhibit and restrict non-violent political expression. On March 19 1988, soldiers from the Bombona Batallion in Medellín invoked the Anti-Terrorist Statute to detain María Luisa Parra, charging her with distribution of the Communist Party weekly newspaper *Voz*.

Press There is considerable diversity in the national press. The main dailies are *El Tiempo* and *El Espectador*, with circulations in excess of 200,000 each. Newspaper ownership is concentrated in a number of influential families including those of former presidents and leading members of the PL and the PSC.

Radio Radio, which is the most influential news medium, is state-regulated with frequencies licensed to private companies. The three largest radio networks are Cadena Radial Colombiana Caracol, Radio Cadena Nacional and Todelar.

Television TV is also regulated by the state, with most channels licensed for one to four years to private companies, the largest of which include Caracol, RTI and Punch. Guidelines ensure equal time for candidates during electoral periods; because of violence against them during the 1989-90 presidential election, candidates were given additional TV air-time to conduct their campaigns. Curiously, all the major news programmes are directed by the children of ex-presidents: *Noticiero de la 7* by Felipe López Caballero, son of López Michelsen; *Noticiero 24* by Mauricio Gómez, son of Gómez Hurtado; *Noticiero Crypton* by Diana Turbay Quintero, daughter of Turbay Ayala; *Noticiero TV Hoy* by Andrés Pastrana, son of Pastrana Borrero; and *Tele Noticiero de Mediodía* by María de Rosario de Ortíz Santos, of the family of ex-President Eduardo Santos which also owns *El Tiempo*.

Attacks on Journalists Nineteen journalists were killed during 1989, more than is known to have been killed in any other country; in 1988, four were murdered. On February 26 1990, journalist Silvia Duzan was murdered in Santander along with three peasant activists whom she was interviewing. Attacks on the press since 1988 have been relentless with many kidnappings, threats, arrests and forced departures for exile. Premises have also been attacked by unofficial and state forces, most recently when police ransacked the Student Press Office in the National University on May 16 1990. One effect of the violence is to create no-go areas for journalists, thus limiting public access to information.

Actions

In its 1988 Commentary to the Human Rights Committee ARTICLE 19 called for an end to attacks on journalists, for investigation into the murders of journalists, and the withdrawal of Decree No. 180 of January 27 1988 which regulates media reporting on guerrilla activity.

On April 28 1989 ARTICLE 19 wrote to the government calling for an investigation into the April 22 murder of Luis Daniel Vera López of Radio Metropolitana de Bucaramanga.

On June 5 1989 ARTICLE 19 wrote to the government calling for an investigation into the murders of two journalists, Carlos Enrique Morales Hernández of *Grupo Radial Colombiano* and *Radar Colombiano*, and Adolfo Pérez Arosemena, who was employed by the Red Cross.

On November 30 1989 ARTICLE 19 wrote to the government protesting the increasing number of attacks on civilians by members of the armed forces, in particular the detention of Guillermo Ramírez of the Santander Teachers' Union, an attack on Popular Front candidate Nurdín Díaz and a raid on the San Isidro Foundation.

In April 1990 ARTICLE 19 wrote to the government condemning the deaths of three presidential candidates prior to the May elections. (See text)

In June 1990 ARTICLE 19 wrote to the government expressing concern about a violent raid on a university student press office by members of the security forces on May 16 which caused extensive damage.

Cuba

Freedom of speech and of the press are guaranteed, provided they are exercised "in accordance with the goals of the Socialist State". The Constitution also proclaims that "artistic creation is free", unless its content is "contrary to the Revolution". In practice, the application of these restrictions together with the hostile relationship with the United States has resulted in several forms of censorship: state censorship, social control applied by peer groups, and self-censorship.

Prior to Fidel Castro's victory in 1959, the dictatorship of Fulgencio Batista operated a mixture of formal respect for the rule of law and unofficial terror carried out by security forces and government supporters. Those publishing or expressing opinions contrary to

	Data	Year
Population	10,402,000	1988
Life expectancy (M/F)	72.6/76.1	1984
GNP (US$ per capita)	1,509	1988
Main religion(s)	Christianity	
Official language(s)	Spanish	
Illiteracy %	6.0	1990
(M/F)	5.0/7.0	1990
Daily newspapers	17	1986
Non daily newspapers	1	1986
Periodicals	85	1986
Radio sets	3,378,000	1986
TV sets	1,957,000	1987
Press agencies:		
Agencia de Informacion Nacional,		
	Prensa Latina	
ICCPR:	NO	

the government could be fined or imprisoned, but were just as likely to be beaten, tortured and killed. President Castro's new government guaranteed freedom of expression, allowing *Diario de la Marina*, *Prensa Libre* and other newspapers to voice opposition. However, in January 1960, the government instructed newspapers to publish statements "clarifying" stories that were critical of the new administration. The unions of printers, journalists, television and radio personnel became *de facto* censors within their own media. Such censorship soon began to affect even the media which officially supported the government, as divisions appeared within the revolutionary ranks.

In March 1960, the destruction of the French freighter Coubre (which had brought arms for the new government) marked the beginning of US operations aimed at overthrowing the revolutionary state. Subsequently, criticisms of the government were regarded as tantamount to attacks on the nation and its security. In May, *Diario de la Marina* was closed down and other papers were taken over by the state. As the diverse groups in the government began to unite and become the Organizaciones Revolucionarias Integradas in 1962 and then the Partido Comunista de Cuba (PCC) in 1965, the media fell under the control of a system in which the state was identified with the PCC.

As opposition was eliminated and Cuba became a one-party state, constraints extended to other channels through which freedom of expression could manifest itself, such as the Roman Catholic Church and universities. The former was denounced as counter-revolutionary and the state took tight control of the latter.

Artistic expression, which had blossomed during the first year of the revolution, became constrained by the requirement that art be an instrument in the construction of socialism and a weapon in the conflict with the US. In several Latin American countries, Cuban posters, literature and music were censored as potentially "subversive", but in Cuba they represented an orthodoxy which admitted no deviations.

During its first decade, the revolutionary administration underwent severe crises, some exogenous (Bay of Pigs invasion, missile crisis, US clandestine operations, exclusion from the Organization of American States) and others of a more domestic origin (shifts in economic policy and political infighting). By the early 1970s, political and economic systems had become consolidated, as had censorship which was characterized by a lack of formal structures but a high level of effectiveness.

The Media

The Press The Cuban press has had a well-deserved reputation for dullness. There are several national newspapers: *Granma*, the official voice of the government, published daily by the PCC's central committee; *Trabajadores*, a daily published by trade unions; and *Juventud Rebelde*, published by the PCC youth organization. Among magazines, the most important are *Verde Olivo*, published by the armed forces, and the traditional general interest magazine *Bohemia*, published by the PCC.

Political control of publications is exercised through a variety of agencies, including the organizations publishing them, the office of President Castro and the Departmento de Orientación Revolucionaria (DOR). The DOR is constituted by media editors and decides media policy rather than engaging in specific censorship. The most influential source of day-to-day censorship is the editorial staff, through their local branch of the Unión de Periodistas de Cuba (UPEC), which analyses coverage and has a major voice in editorial policies. These forms of control have allowed for significant differences in editorial policy to develop between publications. In late 1979, *Trabajadores* pursued a line critical of a new middle class of state bureaucrats which other papers neither followed up nor challenged; eventually, the criticism was adopted by the PCC and the government undertook a major purge of middle-rank officials.

Opina, founded in 1979 by the Institute for the Study of Internal Demand, is a consumer advice magazine which investigates consumers' complaints and criticizes government officials and the service industries. It provided a blueprint for the type of investigative journalism which appeared as part of the process of liberalization in 1984 and was based on the rule that anyone could be criticized apart from President Castro and the PCC leadership.

The process of liberalization was short-lived and, in 1986, President Castro, on the ground that economic liberalization was creating a new "petty bourgeoisie", replaced it with a policy of "rectification of past errors and negative tendencies". This tightened state control, emphasized "revolutionary morality" and "popular participation", and encouraged criticism of corruption and inefficiency. Although President Castro's "rectification" encourages investigative journalism, *Opina* has been penalized in recent years for incidents as trivial as including an advertisement from a senior PCC official in its "lonely hearts" column. *Somos Jovenes*, which appeared in the wake of the liberalization process, had an issue withdrawn when it reported on the dangers to young people posed by prostitution and drugs.

In October 1990, Julio García Luis, president of Cuba's Journalists' Union, called for more freedom and openness in Cuban journalism. He claimed that official interference, excessive bureaucracy, and a false uniformity had broken communication between the Cuban people and its press.

Independent Publications In recent years, some independent publications have appeared. The first, and so far the most important, was *Noticias Religiosas de Cuba*, published and edited since 1987 by the Roman Catholic intellectual Enrique López, taking advantage of the rapprochement between Church and state. Financed through subscriptions by foreign diplomats and foreign correspondents, and distributed free in Catholic and university circles, its small circulation and unofficial connection with the Catholic Church explain why it is tolerated by the authorities. However, López has suffered harassment, being openly watched by his neighbours and having his telephone cut off when important foreign visitors are in Havana, as happened during the 1988 visit of the UN Commission on Human Rights.

During 1989, several other independent publications appeared, more clearly linked to political dissidents, and were promptly declared illegal: *Franqueza*, published by the underground Human Rights Party, *Paz, Amor y Libertad*, published by the dissident group of that name, and *Disidente*, published by the Union of Dissident Writers and Artists of Cuba. Those involved in producing *Franqueza* were arrested and charged with "clandestine printing" and, in January 1989, Lidia and Manuel González and their son Manuel were given jail sentences of up to one year and Isis Pérez Montes de Oca was fined.

Since the 1989 scandal of the involvement of several police and armed forces officers in drug trafficking and their subsequent trial and execution, the authorities have taken a tougher line with such journals. *Noticias Religiosas* has had to suspend publication, unable to obtain newsprint and spare parts for its duplicator. Three prominent activists involved in producing underground dissident magazines have been arrested and charged with the criminal offence of "spreading false news", punishable by up to four years' imprisonment under Article 115 of the Penal Code.

News Agencies The main source of foreign news is the state-owned Prensa Latina (PL) agency, which has an extensive network of correspondents throughout the world. It is closely linked to the foreign ministry and PL personnel are often given diplomatic appointments abroad; they are also in charge of the foreign ministry's press department, which provides escorts for foreign correspondents. Local news is supplied by the Agencia Interna de Noticias. Although the Cuban media receive the services of international agencies such as Reuters, EFE and IPS, most of their overseas coverage originates from PL. Until 1987 PL provided little "real" news but in recent years the broadcasts of the US-financed and Florida-based Radio Martí have forced it to improve its coverage. This has meant, for instance, that the collapse of governments in Eastern Europe and the changes taking place in the Soviet Union have been well covered in the Cuban media.

Foreign Journalists Thirty years of conflict with the US have created a fairly impenetrable state bureaucracy, suspicious of foreign reporters, and a comprehensive police system to monitor foreigners. Established foreign correspondents are able to obtain information through leaks and gossip, but find it impossible to verify stories for accuracy. Correspondents can be expelled as verified by the expulsion of Reuters correspondent Giles Trequesser in July 1989 and Radio Prague correspondent Michael Cermak in January 1990. These risks lead some established correspondents to exercise a form of self-censorship, filing only stories which have appeared in the local press or which have already been published abroad. Foreign journalists frequently complain of the obstructions imposed by the authorities when they apply for visas, in sharp contrast with the facilities provided when the government wants them to attend a stage-managed event. There is an obvious policy to limit the numbers of visiting journalists in order to exercise some control over coverage of Cuba in the foreign media.

Television and Radio All forms of broadcasting are state-controlled through the Instituto Cubano de Radio y Televisión (ICRT). Control over editorial content is exercised by ICRT, in association with DOR and the local branches of UPEC, although the influence of the latter is less than in the case of the press.

Until 1985, radio and TV were as dull as the Cuban press, relying on a diet of locally-made, Soviet and East European drama series, films, and music programmes which excluded musical forms associated with the US and considered to be decadent. News bulletins were heavily censored. In 1985, the launching of Radio Martí from Florida forced Cuban broadcasters to compete for their audience. Initially, the areas mainly affected were news bulletins and popular music, where Radio Martí enjoyed clear advantages, but by 1986 these areas of Cuban broadcasting had been thoroughly overhauled.

This process coincided with criticisms voiced by UPEC and has resulted in a new approach to TV programmes. Since January 1990 there has been a weekly news programme produced by the US Cable News Network which, so far, has not been censored; 40 per cent of foreign films shown are US films and popular music programmes include a range of salsa and rock music produced in the US.

Transmissions of TV Martí from Florida have been jammed and Cuban officials have announced that they intend to continue jamming them, arguing that they constitute a breach of international agreements on broadcasting and violate their territorial integrity and political independence. There has been no conclusive evidence of jamming of Radio Martí and its broadcasts can be received throughout the island. In 1990, the Cuban authorities threatened to broadcast to the US to create problems there for smaller radio stations.

Book Publishing Several books by Cuban and foreign writers have been banned for containing criticisms of President Castro or the revolution. Banned foreign writers include those, such as Jean Paul Sartre, who denounced the government over the Padilla affair; the poet Heberto Padilla was censured by the Writers' Union of Cuba (UEC) in 1968 and later engaged in what appeared as a painful exercise in self-criticism. Distinguished writers such as Guillermo Cabrera Infante and Padilla himself have gone into exile.

The state controls all local publishing houses and the importation of books, although censorship can take place long before the publishing stage. Writers are encouraged either to read their manuscripts at UEC-organized workshops, where their work is criticized, or to submit work to annual competitions; these forms of peer-group censorship are essential to ensure publication.

Although the government has done much to ensure literacy and to improve educational standards, as well as making books accessible through subsidies, it keeps a tight control over what is published, and some topics are clearly out-of-bounds. This is most evident in the area of history. Periods in the 1930s and early 1940s, when the "old" (pre-1959) Communist Party (Partido Socialista Popular) co-operated with the emergent military leader Fulgencio Batista, are avoided by historians. Two senior historians decided not to publish accounts of the 1960s after being advised that their views did not coincide with those of President Castro.

Artistic and Cultural Life Artists work under constraints similar to other intellectuals, with the state controlling the means of artistic production. In music and the plastic arts, resources are directed exclusively to those artistic forms which have official approval. This has driven underground those artistic expressions frowned upon by the government; some painters are unable to exhibit and have to rely on informal networks for the sale of their work, and "heavy metal" bands are unable to obtain recording facilities. The production of posters and prints, an area where Cuban artists enjoyed a high reputation, is also subject to strict government control and some 11 artists were imprisoned between 1980 and 1987 for producing posters considered to be anti-government.

The state's total control of the educational system means that dissent is swiftly suppressed. An exception has resulted from improved state-Church relations, the appointment of Enrique López as a part-time history professor at the University of Havana. Expressions of dissent among students, on the other hand, have recently led to the imprisonment of a number of students and put at risk their careers in a society where practically all professional jobs are in the hands of the state.

Actions

On April 18 1990 ARTICLE 19 wrote to the government expressing its concern about the jamming of TV Marti. (See text)

El Salvador

Under Article 6 of the 1983 Constitution, all persons may freely express their beliefs and opinions so long as they do not subvert public order or damage the morals, honour or privacy of others, and the right of reply is guaranteed. Such expression shall not be subject to prior censorship. The Constitution also states that privately-owned media cannot be expropriated or nationalized.

Journalists were nonetheless severely restricted until January 1987, when a state of siege was lifted. By the time the Christian Democratic (PDC)

	Data	Year
Population	5,107,000	1988
Life expectancy (M/F)	62.6/67.1	1985
GNP (US$ per capita)	950	1988
Main religion(s)	Christianity	
Official language(s)	Spanish	
Illiteracy %	27.0	1990
(M/F)	23.8/30.0	1990
Daily newspapers	7	1986
Radio sets	2,000,000	1987
TV sets	410,000	1987
ICCPR:	YES	1979

President, José Napoleón Duarte, left office in June 1989, the media had achieved freedom to report on previously restricted topics although occasional arrests, threats and killings still occurred. The real damage to the practice of journalism had occurred in the early 1980s when 26 journalists were killed in the course of their work. Consequently, as the news director of a television station stated two months before the inauguration of the new President, Alfredo Cristiani of the Arena party, "We cover everything but we don't investigate".

Although there are now few legal restrictions on the media, military personnel have attempted to impose *de facto* limits. During and after the State of Emergency declared in the course of a November 1989 offensive by the left-wing Farabundo Martí Liberation Front (FMLN) guerrillas, the armed forces intimidated and harassed media workers.

An Anti-Terrorist Decree passed by the National Assembly on November 24 1989 included articles which would severely curtail freedom of expression, but President Cristiani vetoed the measures as contrary to "the spirit of the 1983 Constitution". Even more repressive measures proposed on June 23 in a Bill to amend the penal code, including a 10-year maximum prison sentence for "communications which subvert public order", were effectively abandoned after attracting widespread domestic and international criticism.

The Media

Although no formal system of prior restraint exists, self-censorship occurs widely as a result of government pressure and violence against the media. The last major papers critical of military repression were forced to close after sustained intimidation and violence (*La Crónica del Pueblo* in 1980 and *El Independiente* in 1981). More recently, however, *El Mundo* and *Diario Latino* have been able to report on previously taboo subjects.

Television In recent years TV stations, particularly Channels 6 and 12, have actively sought to extend coverage of the range of political opinion. However, reporters who take an overly critical line of the government may be dismissed, as happened on August 11 1989 to journalists' union activists Joel Burgos and Sandra Idalia Reyes of Channel 6 news.

On November 14, the Treasury Police searched the offices of the Centro de Comunicadores, a freelance TV news agency, and seized papers, videotapes and a photograph of a guerrilla press conference. The police circled the faces of some journalists in the photograph.

Radio Given widespread illiteracy, radio is one of the most important mass media. There are several privately-owned commercial stations, but the government retains the right to revoke a station's operating licence at any time. Radio Sonora and Radio YSU carry frequent news broadcasts. The armed forces run Radio Cuscatlán, and a clandestine station, Radio Venceremos, is operated by the FMLN.

Newspapers Most newspapers have tended to have a pro-government bias but two of the main dailies, the conservative *El Mundo*, and *Diario Latino*, now strive for greater balance and occasionally criticize the government. However, one *El Mundo* reporter, Guillermo Mejía (a union activist), was fired after a junior minister complained about his coverage of economic policies. *Diario Latino*, formerly pro-government, is now run by its staff and seeks to provide access to views excluded from the other print media.

The mass-market pro-government *La Prensa Gráfica* reproduces, without comment, the statements of the Press Committee of the Armed Forces (COPREFA). Another daily, *El Diario de Hoy*, is strongly pro-Arena. Both papers are owned by traditionally influential Salvadorean families. The newest daily, *Noticiero*, specializes in sensational news stories.

The FMLN Offensive

On November 12 1989, the day after the launch of the FMLN offensive, the imposition of a State of Emergency suspended constitutional guarantees of freedom of expression and correspondence, not reinstated until February 8 1990. Emergency regulations prohibited the publishing of rebel communiques and obliged the media to use statements of the official press service, the National Information Centre (CIN), in all military or political reporting.

The FMLN offensive, and the government's reaction to it, led to a series of attacks on the media including the murders of at least seven full-time journalists. Many journalists received threatening telephone calls and one foreign journalist consequently left the country. Several journalists were wounded during the offensive, others were arrested and many had their offices and homes searched. Moreover, the emergency regulations were themselves excessive; the Committee to Protect Journalists has stated that although international law permits certain press restrictions during periods of national emergency, "the measures adopted in El Salvador were extreme and arbitrary and constituted a clear pattern of abuse".

Broadcast Media For the first three weeks of the guerrilla offensive, all radio stations were required to join the government network led by the military Radio

Cuscatlán, which was in effect a propaganda channel which transmitted telephoned death threats against popular organizations and leftist politicians. Threats were also made against Jesuit priests associated with the University of Central America, six of whom (including three involved in journalism) were murdered days later. Radio stations that did not immediately link up with the military network received threatening calls until they complied.

Channel 12 TV news was criticized more than 20 times in two days on Radio Cuscatlán, with some callers accusing Channel 12 of FMLN sympathies. Channels 12 and 6 both received calls from government officials who stated that certain news programmes could not be broadcast. TV news directors were later told officially that all political or military news would have to be approved by the government. On November 15, a government censor was assigned to Channel 12's news programme, *Al Día*, which went off the air in protest for a week from November 22.

Print Media During the emergency period many newspapers refused, or were forbidden, to accept paid advertising from opposition or human rights groups. The December 2 issue of *Diario Latino* carried the message "CENSURADO" across a space booked by the National Revolutionary Movement.

Attacks on Journalists On November 17 1989, David Blundy of the UK *Sunday Correspondent* was shot dead by a sniper in San Salvador. It is widely believed that government troops were responsible but it is not known if he was the intended target.

On November 21, a Reuters bureau chief was wounded by gunfire, possibly from guerrillas, as he drove through San Salvador's wealthy Escalón neighbourhood (where there was no fighting in progress) in a vehicle clearly marked as belonging to the press. On November 25, a Salvadorean cameraman working for the US Cable News Network and a Mexican journalist were wounded by guerrilla fire while travelling in a military helicopter on a reporting mission.

On November 29, five TV journalists with the state information agency CIN (Aníbal Dubón, José Ceballos, Oscar Herrera, Elibardo Quijada and Alfredo Melgar) disappeared from a building seized by the FMLN. Their bodies were never found, but a guerrilla commander reportedly claimed responsibility for killing five "security agents" in the building. On the same day, a Salvadorean soundman with Univision was wounded by an unidentified gunman while driving through Escalón in a clearly marked press vehicle.

On December 1, a Salvadorean photographer for Agence France-Presse, Eloy Guevara, was killed by apparently indiscriminate machine-gun fire after entering an area of Soyapango where there was no combat in progress.

There were also numerous reports of the detention and harassment of journalists by security forces during the offensive. On November 14, a US photographer was held for two hours and assaulted by police in Zacamil. On November 16, one US and one Australian journalist were arrested, blindfolded and brought to Treasury Police headquarters, where they were searched and released.

On November 19, a journalist with the Canadian magazine *Maclean's* was arrested by the air force in Colonia Guadalupe, Soyapango. He was transferred twice and held for 14 hours, and his hotel room was searched on November 20. On December 3, a Spanish journalist was detained while reporting on events in a San Salvador church in which dozens of guerrillas were blockaded. He was released after an hour at the request of the Spanish ambassador. On December 8, one US and one Italian reporter were detained for seven hours by police in San Salvador.

Previous Attacks on Journalists Although the November offensive markedly increased attacks and harassment against media personnel, there have been several other incidents since 1988.

On March 28 1988, a group of 15 foreign correspondents were arrested in Morazán province after attending an FMLN press conference. They were searched and verbally abused at army headquarters in San Francisco Gotera, and materials were confiscated or copied before they were released. On May 11, the correspondent of a Soviet daily, *Komsomolskaya Pravda*, was expelled after being refused a press card by the military press office, COPREFA. On September 13, some 20 foreign reporters were threatened by armed police while covering a demonstration in the capital, and some film was confiscated.

On March 18-19 1989, the day before and day of the presidential elections, the armed forces shot dead Reuters photographer Roberto Navas Alvaraz and TV soundman Mauricio Pineda Deleón of Channel 12, and wounded another Reuters photographer. In addition, when Dutch cameraman Cornel Lagrouw was injured in crossfire, military aircraft strafed the press vehicle taking him to hospital, where he was pronounced dead on arrival. Investigations into these incidents have not resulted in any charges.

In May, soldiers detained three *New York Times* personnel for several hours near San Salvador. On July 14, a San Salvador photographer was abducted by plainclothes Treasury Police while on his way to cover a rally. He was released the next day without charge.

On August 19 1989, Sara Cristina Chan Chein, journalist and member of the National Federation of Salvadorean Workers, was detained by the air force which later claimed to have handed her over to the Treasury Police. The police denied holding her in custody and she remains "disappeared".

Foreign Press The Salvadorean Press Corps Association (SPCA), established by journalists, seeks to negotiate better access to authorities and freer travel for foreign correpondents. Local military commanders frequently deny access to journalists who have obtained the safe-conduct passes formerly needed to visit war zones but required from early 1990 by anyone wishing to travel anywhere in the interior of the country. Journalists must obtain their passes from the COPREFA offices, where they are interviewed twice before their visit and once on returning. They must also obtain permission from the local (departmental) authorities, and the procedure may take so long that the ability to provide up-to-date news reports is greatly diminished. Often, therefore, the only available version of events is that of COPREFA.

The SPCA also tries to assist foreign journalists in obtaining visas into El Salvador; visa denial is not a common problem, but has prevented at least one visit by a US photographer in March 1990.

Actions

On April 7 1989 ARTICLE 19 wrote to the government expressing concern at the deaths of three journalists covering the presidential elections, Roberto Navas Alvaraz, Mauricio Pineda Deleón and Cornel Lagrouw. (See text)

On July 6 1989 ARTICLE 19 wrote to the government protesting proposed amendments to the criminal code which would curtail the right to freedom of expression.

On November 17 1989 ARTICLE 19 wrote to the government calling for an investigation into the deaths of six Jesuits (see text); and expressing concern at recent attacks on the media, including a death threat to a US journalist, the arrest of another journalist, and a security force raid on a press office.

On June 15 1990 ARTICLE 19 wrote to the government expressing its concern about the harassment of staff members of *Diario Latino* by armed forces personnel. ARTICLE 19 also raised its concern about a press release issued by the Armed Forces Press Office in which two El Salvador-based US correspondents were named as sources for a US Congressional report linking human rights abuse to military commanders in El Salvador.

Guatemala

Guatemala, like so many countries in Latin America, continues to be marked by high levels of violence involving the military, conservative economic forces and opposition movements. The return to a civilian government led by Vinicio Cerezo Arévalo on January 14 1986, the first in 16 years, brought with it renewed hope that the new government could break with the tradition of widespread repression exercised during two decades of military rule. It was in Guatemala that the phenomenon known as "disappearances" originated, a method of terror which was rapidly adopted by military governments throughout the region. It has

	Data	Year
Population	8,681,078	1988
Life expectancy	63	1987
GNP (US$ per capita)	880	1988
Main religion(s)	Christianity	
Official language(s)	Spanish	
Illiteracy %	44.9	1990
(M/F)	36.9/52.9	1990
Daily newspapers	9	1986
Radio sets	550,000	1987
TV sets	315,000	1987
Press agencies:		
Inforpress Centroamericana		
ICCPR:	NO	

been estimated that from 1970-1979 there were between 50,000 and 60,000 victims of political violence in Guatemala. Censorship of the press was imposed following a declared state of siege in July 1982 and was not lifted until August 1983 when General Oscar Mejía Victores, the Defence Minister, led a successful coup deposing Gen Efrain Rios Montt. Under Gen Mejía Victores, it was estimated that more than 100 political assassinations and 40 abductions were carried out each month. The civilian government of Vinicio Cerezo Arévalo has adopted a more tolerant approach with political opponents free to express their opinions. However, the violence has escalated, exacerbated by guerrilla activity by groups from across the political spectrum. There have been two attempted coups against the government of Vinicio Cerezo Arévalo, in May 1988 and May 1989.

The new Constitution, promulgated in May 1985, took effect in January 1986. Article 35 of the 1985 Constitution provides ample guarantees for freedom of expression, prohibits censorship or licensing requirements and establishes that criticism of public officials in the course of duty does not constitute libel. The Law on Emission of Thought, based on Article 35, covers defamation and insult and requires that all media dealing with national politics be Guatemalan-owned and managed. The Law also establishes a right of correction or reply for anyone injured by a false report in the media. The government of President Vinicio Cerezo Arévalo has made much use of its right of reply in a running battle with the right-wing daily *Prensa Libre*.

Only once in the past two years has the government taken official action against the media. In May 1988, the government suspended Canal 3 television for broadcasting "material dangerous to the state" when a news editorial urged viewers to support a coup attempt. The station was eventually allowed to resume broadcasting, but without that news programme.

Despite the absence of official censorship, freedom of expression is limited by the fear born of years of military violence against the press and critics of the government. According to the New York-based Committee to Protect Journalists, 48 Guatemalan journalists were abducted or killed between 1976 and 1985. Violence remains at a sufficient level to guarantee self-censorship, particularly relating to military abuses. In the first seven months of 1989, some 1,598 Guatemalans were murdered, 2,517 were tortured and 806 forcibly "disappeared".

The Media

The Press With an illiteracy level of 45 per cent in Guatemala, newspaper readership is relatively low. The scope of news reporting widened with the inauguration of a civilian president in January 1986, but remains narrow even by Central American standards. Investigative reporting is a lost art and, while the press reports violence in lurid detail, it generally avoids mention of security force crimes. This discretion is exercised even when abuses are publicly denounced or reported in the international press. In January 1988, when the Mutual Support Group of relatives of the disappeared held a press conference on military violations of human rights, the main daily *Prensa Libre* published nothing, while a second, *El Gráfico*, reported only those accounts which implicated civilian officials. In July, the Guatemalan press ignored articles in the *Miami Herald* on the illegal detention for five days of a woman in the Huehuetenango military base following her return from the United States. An exception to the rule was the outspoken tabloid weekly *La Epoca*, founded in February 1988 and forced out of business later that year.

The Guatemalan press generally lies to the right of the Christian Democratic Party (PDCG) government of which it is harshly critical. It has, however, been more willing to cover human rights matters than when under direct military rule. Reporting on violence is generally sensationalistic and unhelpful in establishing the facts of individual cases of murder, torture or kidnapping.

Radio and Television There are five government and six educational radio stations. In 1989, radio licences, which previously were valid from five to 25 years, were replaced by provisional 30-day permits. Stations which do not conform to government policy have their licences rescinded. There are four commercial and one government television channels.

Books In August 1989, the Congressional Human Rights Attorney declared that the impounding by Customs of a box of books sent to a human rights activist constituted censorship and violated the constitutional guarantee of "free emission of thought". Copies of the book, *Guatamala: Eternal Spring, Eternal Tyranny* by Jean-Marie Simon, were released. A similar intervention by the Attorney, two years earlier, led to the release of 100 imported books which had been seized by the army.

Attacks and Threats In May 1988, correspondents for the Soviet and Cuban agencies, Tass and Prensa Latina, were forced to leave the country by threats from Mano Blanca, a military-linked death squad. On May 18, the home and office of the Tass correspondent were bombed by another death squad, the Secret Anticommunist Army, which in June threatened to kill "communist" journalists, particularly those who had returned from exile.

On May 27, a reporter for both *La Epoca* and the Italian agency Inter Press Service was abducted by three armed men in Guatemala City after disclosing details of a coup plot. He was drugged and interrogated, but released alive. On June 10, the offices of *La Epoca* were burnt to the ground, reportedly on the orders of a named high-ranking military officer. Although the staff voted to continue publishing, threats forced the paper's editor and a staff writer to leave the country temporarily and *La Epoca*, after only 14 issues, closed down. On October 26 1990, Byron Barrera, former editor-in-chief of *La Epoca*, and his wife were shot by unknown gunmen. Barrera survived; his wife was killed.

On July 19 1989, an explosion in the broadcast tower of Channel 7 killed a night watchman. The station had been due to broadcast an interview that night with Nicaragua's President, Daniel Ortega. That same month, a grenade exploded at the home of the editor of *Patrullaje Informativo*, a leading radio news programme.

Danilo Barillas, a senior PDCG leader and a writer and shareholder in *Por Que?*, a new weekly magazine, was shot dead by five armed men in Guatemala City on August 1 1989. Several motives have been suggested, including his investigation of alleged drug-trafficking by other PDCG members. *Por Qué?* closed later that month after its owner and editorial staff received death threats. The owner left the country temporarily.

Reporters at the weekly *7 Días*, including some recently returned from exile, also received threats in August. Former exiles are viewed with suspicion by the military and the right and several have been harassed, detained or killed. Late in August, a student journalist at the daily *La Hora* sought refuge at the Red Cross after being threatened. Several other members of the University Students' Association (AEU) were murdered or disappeared in August and September. A further attack on AEU members in April 1990 led to the disappearance of 19 students; 11 corpses were later found.

In early October 1989, a *Prensa Libre* writer was beaten and threatened, apparently in retaliation for his coverage of a bus crash. In mid-December, distribution vehicles for *Prensa Libre* and *El Gráfico* were attacked. Thousands of newspapers and a truck were set on fire.

A journalist who had received a series of threatening telephone calls and other messages from September 1989 was again threatened after a January 18 1990 meeting with the US human rights group Americas Watch.

On September 18 1990, Mirna Mack, a journalist for Inforpress and researcher with the Association for the Advance of the Social Sciences in Guatemala, was stabbed to death and robbed. At the time of her death, she had been researching the killing of street children and government policy on this issue, but it is not known whether her murder was connected with her work.

Another two journalists were murdered in separate incidents on October 15. Miguel Angel Cospín, a founder member of the Guatemalan Journalists' Association, was stabbed and it is understood that his killing may have been politically motivated. Humberto González Gamarra, owner of several radio stations and general secretary of a newly-recognized left-wing political party, the Democratic Revolutionary Union, was shot by several men with machine guns.

Freedom of Expression

Military and paramilitary groups have also targeted trade unionists, peasant leaders, university students and human rights activists. Since 1988, four rights workers have been murdered and six have disappeared following abduction by soldiers. Since a wave of killings and disappearances of students and teachers began in August 1989, 18 persons from the University of San Carlos have been abducted; nine were found dead and six remain disappeared.

The theatre group Dos Que Tres (2Q3) was formed by trade unionists during a 376-day occupation of the Coca-Cola plant in Guatemala City in 1984-1985. Its plays ridiculed the army, landlords and corrupt politicians and called on workers and peasants to unite in defence of their rights. In 1989, members of 2Q3 began to receive threats and on February 25 an actor was shot in the leg, in circumstances suggesting security force involvement, as he left a performance by the musical group which accompanies 2Q3. Other members of the group were subsequently assaulted and threatened and on July 2 the injured actor's brother, 2Q3 member José Rolando Pantaleón, was kidnapped by three armed men, tortured and shot dead. His wife remains in Guatemala, a victim of death threats. The other members of 2Q3 and their families have fled the country.

The Guatemalan Human Rights Commission reported that in the first eight months of 1990, 585 persons were killed by security and paramilitary death squads.

Actions

On September 18 1990 ARTICLE 19 wrote to the government expressing concern at the murder of journalist Mirna Mack and requesting a full investigation into her death. (See text)

On October 23 1990 ARTICLE 19 wrote to the government condemning the murders of two journalists, Miguel Angel Cospin and Humberto González Gamarra, and requesting an inquiry into their deaths. (See text)

Honduras

The Constitution, under Article 72, provides for free expression of thought through any medium and without prior censorship. Communications media may not be confiscated, closed or interrupted for any offence relating to such expression (Art.73), nor censored indirectly through means such as the abuse of control over newsprint and radio broadcasting (Art.74). However, under Article 75 prior censorship is allowed to protect the ethical and cultural values of society and the rights of individuals, especially young people.

	Data	Year
Population	4,168,900	1988
Life expectancy	65.0	1987
GNP (US$ per capita)	850	1988
Main religion(s)	Christianity	
Official language(s)	Spanish	
Illiteracy %	26.9	1990
(M/F)	24.5/29.4	1990
Daily newspapers	7	1986
Radio sets	1,760,000	1987
TV sets	315,000	1987
ICCPR:	YES	1981

The authorities have compromised freedom of expression by a variety of legal and extra-legal means, especially in relation to human rights abuses or drug-trafficking by the military. The libel laws, which allow the state to sue individuals for offending public institutions, have been used to stifle critics, and there has been violence and threats against media workers and others.

Freedom of Political Expression Opponents of the government are continually harassed and many receive death threats. Pressure is brought to bear in a number of ways, including poster campaigns by the military-linked AAA death squad accusing named leaders of human rights, trade union and popular movements of being communists, subversives or of being in league with the Nicaraguan Sandinistas. The Honduran Commission for the Defence of Human Rights (CODEH) believes that these methods are used by the military to condition popular opinion against those targeted and to create a climate of fear. The military have also attended regional workshops run by CODEH, their presence effectively intimidating those participating and preventing freedom of expression.

Elections Only four parties are legally registered to participate in elections: the Liberal Party (PL), Nationalist Party (PN), Innovation and Unity Party (PINU-SD) and Christian Democratic Party (PDC). Presidential elections on November 26 1989, marred by complaints of irregularities, were won by Rafael Callejas of the PN.

State of Emergency On April 8 1988, the then President, José Azcona del Hoyo, issued a decree suspending certain constitutional rights for 15 days in response to the burning of the US Consulate by students protesting an extradition. The decree did not explicitly deny freedom of the media, but the government employed indirect censorship by such means as placing the state-regulated radio and television stations on a national network playing only music for about 36 hours.

On April 7, Radio América reporter David Romero broadcast the names of five military officers allegedly involved in drug trafficking. On the following day he was arrested without warrant by security police and interrogated about his sources. He described the events on air on April 10, when an attempt was made to rearrest him and a threat was allegedly made by army intelligence through an intermediary. His wife was repeatedly threatened, his credentials for covering the presidential palace were revoked, and the owner of his station was called and asked to fire him. On April 8, the newspaper *El Tiempo* also named the five officers; it received an illegal directive from presidential staff to suspend publication for one day, but succeeded in having the order countermanded.

Government Libel Action The government has used the libel and slander laws (Arts.162-169 and 345 of the Penal Code) to suppress criticism of the military. On January 12 1989, the Attorney General issued a writ against the editor of *El Tiempo* alleging that a December editorial libelled the military by accusing it of insubordination, an offence under the Military Code. The paper's defence stated that the editorial did not allege criminal conduct by any individual.

The Attorney General had earlier, on October 14 1988, accused the president of CODEH of "abusing freedom of expression" by calling the then-Armed Forces Chief of Staff a "cynic" after the latter alleged that CODEH was engaged in a campaign to discredit the military. The Attorney General said that he was demonstrating "tolerance" by not prosecuting under the libel laws, or under Article 345 of the Penal Code which provides a prison sentence of up to two years for anyone who "threatens, insults, or in any other way offends the dignity of a public official acting in an official capacity" (or three years if the offended party is the president or another high officer of state).

The Media

Newspapers Most news organs are owned by individuals with strong ties to the government or the military. Carlos Flores Facusse, a former PL government minister, owns the centre-right *La Tribuna* (circulation 50,000). The far-right papers, *La Prensa* (40,000) and *El Heraldo*, are owned by Jorge Larach, linked with the PN and the military. *El Tiempo* (30,000) is considered the most independent newspaper with a tradition of reporting human rights abuses; it is owned by former vice-president Jaime Rosenthal.

Broadcasting Radio is the primary source of news, especially in rural areas. Three television stations and the largest radio network are owned by Manuel Villeda Toledo and José Rafael Ferrari, both close to the military. The government's control of licensing and broadcast frequencies enables it to influence not only the content but also the range of radio news. CODEH is expanding its radio access throughout the country, buying space on private radio stations to broadcast advice on constitutional rights.

Licensing of Journalists Journalists are subject to the Press Law which requires them to belong to a professional guild. This law has been employed in an effort to harass and silence domestic and foreign journalists. A newspaper found to employ a non-licensed journalist may be subject to heavy fines, and its editors risk losing accreditation.

Physical Attacks A reporter for Radio América was shot and wounded in late 1989 while covering Nicaraguan-Honduran relations. He was said to have received telephoned death threats accusing him of being pro-Sandinista.

The church-operated Radio San Miguel in La Paz department, which carried CODEH programmes, was disabled by a bomb on May 2 1990. A worker at the station had reportedly been asked by troops to supply advance copies of the CODEH tapes.

In July 1990, Candelario Reyes García, director of the Central Hibueras Theatre Group in Santa Barbara, received the first of a series of death threats. One of those allegedly responsible for the threats is Colonel Guadalupe Reitel Caballero, Chief of Promitec (Military Intelligence Corps). In addition, a number of unidentified people have fired shots around Sr Reyes García's house. Consequently, he has had to restrict his work to radio broadcasts.

Deportations The authorities have repeatedly expelled or refused entry to critical reporters and human rights monitors. James LeMoyne of the *New York Times* was barred from Honduras in February 1988 after writing on death squad activity by the Honduran military.

José Miguel Vivanco, a Chilean attorney in Honduras for the Inter-American Commission on Human Rights, had his visa revoked in September 1988 because of his alleged "animosity towards the Honduran government and people".

Reverend Joseph Eldridge, a United States consultant to Americas Watch residing in Honduras, had an arrest warrant issued against him on November 1 1988 for "defaming" the Honduran military in a *Los Angeles Times* article on the drugs trade. After publishing an article about death squad activity, *Washington Post* reporter Julia Preston was arrested on arrival at Tegucigalpa airport on November 29. She was detained incommunicado and expelled from the country the next day.

Books Books have frequently been confiscated from people on their return to the country.

Student leader Roberto Zelaya went into exile after he was stabbed by unidentified men on May 19 1990. His house had been searched on numerous occasions by the military and three books by renowned Latin American authors were confiscated. Zelaya had received frequent threats and accusations that he was a Sandinista spy.

Actions

On September 12 1990 ARTICLE 19 wrote to the government expressing concern about the death threats received by Candelario Reyes García. (See text)

Mexico

Freedom of expression, of the press and of information are guaranteed by Articles 6 and 7 of the 1917 Constitution, amended in December 1977; prior censorship is prohibited. These guarantees are qualified by a 1917 Press Law and are subject to the protection of privacy, public health and morals.

The media is further regulated by the Organic Law of Public Education on Illustrated Magazines and Publications concerning Culture and Education (1951); the Law on Advertising; the General Health Act (1984), and the National and Federal District Penal Codes. The Federal Radio and Television Act (1960) and the Cinematographic Industry Act forbid the transmission of "anything that is insulting or

	Data	Year
Population	82,734,000	1988
Life expectancy	69.0	1987
GNP (US$ per capita)	1,820	1988
Main religion(s)	Christianity	
Official language(s)	Spanish	
Illiteracy %	12.7	1990
(M/F)	10.5/14.9	1990
Daily newspapers	308	1986
Non daily newspapers	25	1986
Periodicals	98	1986
Radio sets	20,000,000	1987
TV sets	10,000,000	1987
Press agencies:		
Notimex, Noti-Accion, Notipress,		
Agencia Mexicana de Infomracion		
ICCPR:	YES	1981

offensive to respect for (national) heroes", and the controversial Article 130 of the Constitution prohibits members of the clergy from publishing on national political issues or criticizing national institutions. They also lack the right to vote or to be elected.

Mexico is party to the International Convention on the Repression of the Circulation and Traffic in Obscene Publications (1923) and its Protocol (1948), and ratified the ICCPR and the American Convention on Human Rights in 1981. It has not ratified the Optional Protocol nor those parts of the Convention which accept the competence of the Inter-American Commission to receive inter-state complaints (Art.45) or the jurisdiction of the Inter-American Court (Art.62).

Freedom of Political Expression On December 1 1988, Carlos Salinas de Gortari of the Institutional Revolutionary Party (PRI), which has been in power since 1929, took office as President amid allegations of electoral fraud. Respect for the right to political expression remains an issue of grave concern. During the campaign, opposition parties boycotted sponsors of the main TV news programme, *24 Horas*, accusing the government of limiting access to the media. Meanwhile, 37 episodes of an historical series, *Path to Glory*, were cancelled. The series praised the late president, Lázaro Cárdenas, whose son Cuauhtémoc was a 1988 opposition candidate.

According to Cárdenas' centre-left Party of the Democratic Revolution (PRD), more than 60 of its election workers have been murdered by PRI supporters since July 1988. The government has produced a document detailing investigations of 34 cases, but to date sentence has been passed in only one. Elections continue to be marred by violence, for which only PRD members have been charged, and patent fraud, sometimes forcing the PRI to retract declarations of victory and concede to candidates of the PRD or the conservative National Action Party. The PRI has proposed reforms which would take effect in the 1991 legislative elections.

The independent weekly magazine *Proceso* is one of very few media to have seriously investigated electoral fraud. In January 1990, the left-wing daily *La Jornada* was reportedly threatened with withdrawal of government advertising because of its investigation of ballot rigging in the states of Guerrero and Michoacán and its acceptance of propaganda from small left-wing groupings formerly linked with guerrilla activity. Two security guards at the paper were subsequently shot dead, on April 4, after refusing to accept material from two such groups.

The Media

The Government and the Press Although the change of government brought to light allegations implicating the outgoing Interior Minister, Manuel Bartlett, in cover-ups of the murders of investigative journalist Manuel Buendía in 1984, and political journalist Carlos Loret de Mola in 1986, he was retained in a different post by the new administration. Manuel Becerra Acosta, former editor of the liberal daily *Unomásuno*, claimed in October 1989 that the government had won effective control of his majority shareholding in the paper by invoking an alleged US$2 million debt to the state newsprint monopoly PIPSA, and offering a settlement involving a $1 million payment to him and his emigration to Spain. Restrictive and corrupt actions have long marred the practice of journalism. Newspapers have accepted money for inserting government advertising disguised as editorial matter, but the traditional system of "embutes" (government bribes to individual journalists for favourable coverage) has been condemned by the new President. These subventions were unavailable to the pro-PRD newspaper *6 de Julio*, which folded soon after its launch in 1989.

The Drugs Trade Drug-trafficking has had a major impact on freedom of expression; there have been several, mostly unsolved, murders of journalists investigating the trade and collusion by corrupt state and federal officials, including police officers now indicted in the United States.

Murders of Journalists In October 1988, ARTICLE 19 invited the government to comment on the unsolved killings of almost 50 journalists in less than 20 years, including 33 during the De la Madrid administration (1982-88). These included the murder on May 30 1984 of renowned investigative journalist Manuel Buendía. President Salinas, speaking on the annual "Press Day" on June 7 1989, promised movement on the case, and a week later a former head of the Federal Security Directorate was charged with intellectual responsibility for the murder.

The arrest was one of several dramatic steps in a "clean-up" campaign clearly designed for maximum publicity. For example, although the decision to release poet Israel Gutiérrez Hernández and other imprisoned writers was made during the De la Madrid administration, they were not released until February 1989 after the new President was installed. In what may be the most significant initiative in the campaign, Salinas announced on June 6 1990 the establishment of a National Commission on Human Rights to advise on and monitor protection and abuses.

Attacks on Journalists On April 20 1988, Héctor Félix Miranda, a columnist for *Zeta*, was shot by unknown gunmen. On July 13, Ronay González Reyes, editor of three Chiapas newspapers, was shot dead in what police described as a personal vendetta, and on July 23, Linda Bejarano, of XH13-TV in Ciudad Juárez, was shot dead by drugs police apparently in a case of mistaken identity. Also killed in 1988 was Manuel Burgueño Orduño of Mazatlán, Sinaloa, a columnist for *El Sol del Pacífico*.

On February 22 1989, an investigative journalist and refugee rights activist from Chiapas was arrested and detained for six months; he was freed only after numerous appeals by journalists' organizations, political parties and community groups. On April 12, Humberto Gallegos was killed, and on June 28, Elias Mario Medina Valenzuela, former editor of *El Sol de Durango* and *El Norte*, was shot dead by unknown gunmen. On October 1 in León, Guanajuato, four journalists were beaten and detained by police after intervening on behalf of youths arrested at a PRD rock concert. On protesting to the state government, ARTICLE 19 was told that 12 officers had been charged with abuse of authority, wounding and libel.

On November 3, Joel Herrera Zurita of *El Dictamen* was beaten to death by unidentified men; on December 20, Rodolfo Mendoza Morales was killed, and on December 24, Elvira Marcelo Esquivel of *El Día* died a day after she was shot, and two colleagues were beaten up, in what appeared to be an attempted robbery by five men in police uniform. Also in December, Oscar Treviño of *El Bravo* was kidnapped in Matamoros while investigating police involvement in torture and murder. Another journalist killed in 1989 was A Ruvalcaba Torres. On June 6 1990, Alfredo Cordova Solorzano, editor of the Tapachula daily *Uno Más Dos*, was shot by three unknown gunmen at his home. He died of his injuries three days later.

Radio and Television The broadcast media remain prohibited areas for foreign investment and ownership. Several new subscription cable TV franchises have been granted, but broadcast TV remains dominated by the state company Imevisión and the vast private Televisa network, which is closely identified with the PRI and also owns cable companies such as Cablevisión, Telecable, Cablepelícula and Galavisión, which serves the US Hispanic community. Both Cablevisión and the newer Multivisión recently dropped the United States TVS news programme after government criticism.

Newsprint Monopoly In October 1989, President Salinas announced plans to privatize PIPSA, the newsprint monopoly, to remove "any obstacle [to] the full exercise of freedom of expression", a reference to the past use of its discretion in supply and credit to bring into line newspapers critical of the government. It was ultimately decided that PIPSA would remain under government control but with competition from imports, albeit with a 15 per cent duty and subject to availability of exchange.

Cultural Repression Protests by groups have caused the closure, cancellation or censorship of artistic events, including a show by painter Rolando de la Rosa at the Museum of Modern Art in January 1988, and the satirical play, *Nadie Sabe Nada*, by Vicente Lenero, in June 1988. The rock group Black Sabbath was banned in September 1989, and British singer Rod Stewart was prevented from playing in Mexico City. Tear gas was used at another of his venues, and his band's equipment was temporarily seized for alleged non-payment of taxes.

In January 1989, the Tabasco Institute of Culture withdrew funding, allegedly for political reasons, from Laboratorio de Teatro Campesino e Indígena de Tabasco, an internationally-recognized theatre group promoting indigenous and peasant culture.

Actions

In its 1988 Commentary to the Human Rights Committee ARTICLE 19 raised a number of concerns regarding freedom of expression, in particular the death of almost 50 journalists in less than 20 years. Copies of the Commentary and requests for dialogue were sent to Ambassador Tello in Geneva and Ambassador Navarrette in London. Dialogue was not established.

In July 1989 ARTICLE 19 launched its book, *In the Shadow of Buendía: The Mass Media and Censorship in Mexico*, at the Ninth Consultative meeting of the International and Regional Journalists' Organizations in Mexico City. A copy of the book was given to a member of the Salinas Government, Manuel Camacho Solís.

A report documenting the deaths of 29 journalists during the De la Madrid administration was given to the Mexican Ambassador in London. On October 9 1989 ARTICLE 19 was informed by Ambassador Sepúlveda that copies of the report had been sent to the appropriate authorities in Mexico City for reply. To date, ARTICLE 19 has received no further information on the status of investigations into the deaths.

In October 1989 ARTICLE 19 wrote to the government and the local authorities protesting the beating and detention of four journalists who had intervened on behalf of youths arrested at a rock concert in support of the opposition PRD. In March 1990 ARTICLE 19 received a reply from the state government saying that 12 officers had been charged with abuse of authority, wounding and libel.

Nicaragua

After the revolutionary victory of 1979 Nicaragua was governed by a junta led by the left-wing Sandinista National Liberation Front (FSLN), under constant attack from US-funded "contra" rebel armies. By 1990 the war had cost more than 30,000 lives, mainly civilian. In November 1984 FSLN leader Daniel Ortega was elected President and the FSLN won a majority in the National Assembly. Elections brought forward to February 25 1990 in the context of the Central American peace process were won by the National Opposition Union (UNO) coalition led by Violeta Chamorro, who took office on April 25.

	Data	Year
Population	3,384,000	1988
Life expectancy (M/F)	58.7/61.0	1985
GNP (US$ per capita)	830	1988
Main religion(s)	Christianity	
Official language(s)	Spanish	
Illiteracy %	42.5	1971
(M/F)	42.0/42.9	1971
Daily newspapers	5	1986
Radio sets	830,000	1987
TV sets	210,000	1987
Press agencies:		
Agencia Nicaraguese de Noticias		
ICCPR:	YES	1980

A State of Emergency, declared in March 1982, had suspended many rights including freedom of expression. Under peace accords signed in August 1987, the emergency was lifted in January 1988, and these rights were restored in the terms of a new Constitution introduced on January 9 1987. Article 30 guarantees "the right to express ... beliefs freely in public or private, individually or collectively, in oral, written or any other form". Article 68 states that public, corporate or private means of communication may operate within the law, and with no prior censorship; it adds that "the mass media are at the service of the national interest", and authorizes the state to "promote access for the public and its organizations to the media, and prevent the media from being controlled by foreign interests or by any economic monopoly". Articles 29, 54 and 55 protect freedom of thought, assembly and organization.

Laws Affecting Freedom of Expression The General Law on the Media and Public Communications (Law 57), passed by the National Assembly in April 1989 and amended on September 27, replaced the General Law for Social Communications Media (Decree 48) of August 16 1979. Law 57 established freedom from censorship and guaranteed access to paid air-time for different social and political groups. It obliged the media to "promote respect for the forgers of the Nicaraguan nationhood, patriotic symbols, and (national) Heroes and Martyrs" and forbade the use of women as commercial or sexual objects.

The Ministry of the Interior was responsible for enforcement, including compulsory registration and the processing of permits and licences. "Broadcasts contrary to state security, national integrity, peace or law and order" were illegal, and the issuing of "injurious, defamatory or false news" was subject to the right of individuals or government offices to obtain "clarification or reply and rectification", or to a warning for minor offences. The maximum punishment for repeating or refusing to rectify an offence was suspension for up to three editions for print media, four days for radio and three days for TV.

Law 57 was more liberal than Decree 48 which defined the social, economic and political responsibilities of the media, with heavier penalties including indefinite suspension. However, Law 57 was criticized for the range of offences defined and the powers it gave the Ministry, appeals against whose rulings were to the minister rather than to a judicial body.

There was a wide spread of opinion and ownership in radio and print media under the FSLN, but TV was entirely state-run. Requests for permission to open a private channel were refused, and state responsibility for TV was written into both the 1979 and 1989 media laws "because the government of Nicaragua could not compete with the resources of the CIA" (Interior Minister, 1988). Shortly after the Sandinista defeat in the 1990 elections, Law 57 was abolished, thereby allowing the establishment of private TV stations (although the Chamorro government may retain some of the Law's other regulatory features).

The Media

Print Media Since 1980 there have been three national daily newspapers and a number of other periodicals. The dailies are *La Prensa* (circulation 75,000), *Barricada* (95,000) and *El Nuevo Diario* (45,000), all edited by members of the Chamorro family but from markedly different political standpoints. *Barricada* is the official organ of the FSLN, to which *El Nuevo Diario* is also sympathetic, while *La Prensa* was a vociferous critic of it and was owned by Violeta Chamorro, now the President.

According to a report by a UN Observer Mission (ONUVEN) in December 1989, there were then 25 current periodicals, including party and trade union organs.

Radio In late 1989 Nicaragua had 44 radio stations; 24 were privately owned, while the state owned three national and 17 regional stations, the latter via a People's Broadcasting Company (Coradep). A 1988 poll in Managua showed that 34 per cent of the population used radio as their main source of news, compared with 18 per cent for TV and just 10 per cent for print media. A 1989 poll found that the state-owned stations had three times the audience of the private stations. Some 74 foreign radio stations reached Nicaragua, including the US government-run Voice of America and Radio Martí. The Chamorro government has renamed the main state station, Voz de Nicaragua, Radio Nicaragua, and may privatize some or all of Coradep.

Television Under the FSLN, TV was entirely state-owned by the Sistema Sandin-ista de Televisión (SSTV) with two channels, Canal 2 and Canal 6. The Atlantic Coast was served by Channel 9, also state-owned. Some 17 foreign TV stations could be received. Apart from electoral campaigns, opposition voices were largely excluded from TV. The Chamorro administration is to permit private TV stations (the first to be launched shortly by the Telenica consortium), and has renamed SSTV as the Sistema Nacional de Televisión.

Censorship

Print Media During the 1982-1987 State of Emergency all print media had to register with the interior ministry and submit to prior censorship. Censorship and suspension of publication were used to restrict discussion of a range of topics, but especially the war and military conscription.

Several periodicals were closed down for alleged improper registration including *Solidaridad*, bulletin of the opposition CUS trade union confederation, and *Iglesia*, a Catholic journal. The opposition press nevertheless showed few signs of self-censorship.

In October 1987, as part of the peace process, prior censorship was ended, and several opposition periodicals reappeared. Thereafter, only post-publication sanctions were applied under the 1979 and 1989 media laws. *El Nuevo Diario* and the satirical *Semana Cómica* were both temporarily suspended in 1988, the latter for publishing obscene photographs purporting to be of members of a Sandinista women's organization.

La Prensa Throughout the Sandinista era, *La Prensa* was in frequent conflict with the authorities. Owned by the Chamorro family, historically linked to the Nicaraguan Conservative Party, *La Prensa* played a leading opposition role before 1979 and suffered heavy censorship, culminating in the assassination of its editor, Pedro Joaquín Chamorro, in 1978 at the behest of the military ruler, Anastasio Somoza. *La Prensa* welcomed the FSLN victory but within months it reverted to opposition when Violeta Chamorro, widow of Pedro Joaquín, resigned from the ruling junta.

Before March 1982, *La Prensa* was closed down on five occasions for one or two days under Decrees 511, 512 and 513 relating to publication of information that compromised national security, or was alarmist or misleading economic information. (Decree 511 was abolished just before the 1990 change of government.) During the State of Emergency *La Prensa* was heavily censored; according to its staff, 30-40 per cent of copy was cut. After the imposition of more severe emergency regulations in October 1985, staff claimed that average censorship rose to 60 per cent, but the human rights group Americas Watch has said that "what *La Prensa* was actually allowed to publish was the harshest criticism of its own government that could be read in any newspaper in Central America in 1985".

On June 27 1986, the day after the US Congress approved a $100 million aid package to the contras, President Ortega announced the indefinite suspension of *La Prensa* for accepting a grant from the US government-funded National Endowment for Democracy and "becoming a party to (US) aggression against Nicaragua". It was allowed to reopen in October 1987 but, on July 11 1988, was closed for 15 days for "distorted and provocative" reporting of riots in Nandaime.

La Prensa accused the government of limiting its quota of newsprint to that of the other major dailies in order to restrict its circulation. In April 1988, shortage of paper forced it to suspend publication for a week.

Radio Censorship of radio, while less severe than in print media, did occur during the State of Emergency, mainly by temporary or indefinite closures. In March 1982, 22 news programmes were suspended; when the emergency was lifted in January

1988, all those news programmes which requested permission to re-open had it granted.

The best-known case of radio censorship is that of Radio Católica, an anti-Sandinista station run by the Catholic Church. On January 1 1986, it was closed down indefinitely for failing to broadcast President Ortega's end-of-year speech, although another possible reason was that it had encouraged youths to enter seminaries or emigrate to avoid compulsory military service. It was permitted to reopen in late September 1987, but along with two other stations it was closed for periods of up to 10 days in April, May and June 1988 for violations of Decree 48. In July it was closed for three weeks for alleging police brutality in Nandaime, and it was not permitted to resume news broadcasts until March 1989.

Radio provided a greater variety of independent political opinions than either the print media or TV. Of 30 news programmes broadcast during 1988, only one was state-run. In July 1988, the pro-FSLN Radio Sandino morning news programme was cut for two days for broadcasting an obscene insult to the editor of *La Prensa*. On one occasion government harassment took a very direct form: in mid-1988 interior minister Tomás Borge reportedly punched Radio Corporación's director during an argument over news coverage.

Television Because all TV was state controlled, the question of government censorship did not arise. The problem was rather one of lack of access to air time for a range of political opinion. To date, broad access to TV has only occurred during election campaigns.

The 1989-90 Election Campaign

Electoral Law Following an amendment to Law 57 in August 1989, supervision of election coverage passed from the interior ministry to the Supreme Electoral Council (CSE). The Consolidated Electoral Law of June 27 1989 guaranteed access for all political parties or alliances to an equal portion of 30 minutes paid air-time daily on each SSTV channel and 45 minutes on each state-owned radio station (Art.109), irrespective of party size or electoral prospects. Parties were allowed to buy unlimited time on private radio stations which also had to give five minutes free to each group. Similar rules applied to elections for municipalities and the Atlantic Coast Autonomous Region. Religious radio stations were banned from carrying out political campaigns (Art.116).

Television The CSE granted opposition parties free air-time in addition to their statutory but under-used right to paid air-time. Between August 25 and December 2, opposition parties took turns for a daily half-hour programme on Canal 2, divided into three 10-minute slots. In mid-November, following opposition and foreign criticisms that Canal 2 only reached Managua, the government made air-time available free on the more powerful Canal 6 for *Elecciones 1990*, a prime-time one-hour debate (daily from January 12).

Successive ONUVEN reports criticized both state-run and private media for bias and intemperate language, including SSTV's news coverage. Its December report said "not only is there less coverage of the opposition, but (it is) distorted to present opponents in the worst light". However, it subsequently reported that coverage of opposition activities had been increased to equal that allotted to the FSLN, and credited *Elecciones 1990* with a "high level of impartiality".

Print Media ONUVEN reported that in the written press "violence in the messages and distortion of the news continue to predominate". It credited *Barricada* with "a more professional approach" than *El Nuevo Diario* which was guilty of "offensive stances" towards the opposition. All three dailies were warned by the CSE for abusive language, especially *El Nuevo Diario* which refused to drop the term GN-UNO, linking UNO with Somoza's National Guard.

Radio Allocated radio time was underused by most parties. Radio Católica was warned by the CSE for violating the ban on religious radio stations conducting political campaigns.

Freedom for Journalists to Practise ARTICLE 19 is not aware of the death of any journalist for having practised the profession since the revolution of 1979. Staff at *La Prensa* have accused FSLN supporters of issuing death threats. Foreign journalists are subject to the same visa requirements as other visitors, and must also obtain a government press pass. Some journalists have been refused entry for alleged links with the contras, but in most cases, following protests, they were allowed in.

Actions

In its 1990 Commentary to the Human Rights Committee ARTICLE 19 documented a number of violations concerning freedom of expression. Copies were sent to government representatives.

Panama

The constitutional rights to freedom of expression and opinion, already threatened by government action, were further undermined by the political crisis between June 1987 and December 1989. The crisis arose when General Manuel Antonio Noriega, head of the Panama Defence Force and de facto ruler of Panama, was publicly accused of crimes including drugs and arms trafficking.

This led to violent street demonstrations for and against Noriega; many participants and several journalists were beaten, fined or imprisoned, and some

	Data	Year
Population	2,322,000	1988
Life expectancy (M/F)	69.2/72.8	1985
GNP (US$ per capita)	2,240	1988
Main religion(s)	Christianity	
Official language(s)	Spanish	
Illiteracy %	11.9	1990
(M/F)	11.9/11.8	1990
Daily newspapers	9	1986
Radio sets	500,000	1987
TV sets	370,000	1987
ICCPR:	YES	1977

were murdered. Media outlets identified with the opposition were closed down by the government, the successor of that installed by a 1968 coup d'état. Public demonstrations and the free expression of opposition opinion were suppressed.

United States forces invaded Panama on December 20 1989, overthrew Noriega and installed a civilian government which claims legitimacy on the basis of its apparent victory in the annulled elections of May 1989. Observers have noted with concern the sparse reporting of casualty statistics in the United States, where public opinion favoured the invasion; a June 1990 estimation by the human rights group Americas Watch claimed that some 50 Panamanian and 23 US military personnel were killed and that some 300 Panamanian civilians were also killed. Alternative figures range from 1,000 (a group of Panamanian victims' relatives) to 523 (the Pentagon). In January 1990, an Independent Commission on the US Invasion of Panama stated that as many as 4,000 people may have been killed. The Panamanian Committee for Human Rights states that there were 556 civilian and military personnel killed as a result of the invasion. This figure was confirmed by the Panamanian government on October 15 1990.

The institutional, legal and political framework of the new administration of President Guillermo Endara is still evolving, but it has undertaken a substantial revision of media law.

Article 37 of the present Constitution states: "All individuals may freely express their thoughts, in writing or through any other medium, without subjection to prior censorship." Article 38 protects peaceful demonstration. Article 85 defines the mass media as "instruments of information, education, recreation and cultural and scientific exchange", and states that their advertising and propaganda activities must not be harmful to health, morality, education, the cultural makeup of society or national consciousness.

Emergency Measures The Constitution permits the declaration of a state of emergency suspending the freedoms of expression and assembly (Art. 51). The Noriega government did so on several occasions, notably from June 11-21 1987, when there was a ban on independent radio broadcasts, TV news was restricted and prior censorship was introduced for the print media. Similar declarations were in force for a few days in March 1988, and for three days after the annulled elections of May 7 1989, when permission for opposition demonstrations was withheld. On May 10, a pro-government militia (the Dignity Battalions) violently assaulted opposition demonstrators including the presidential candidate. Several journalists were also injured, including a TV cameraman shot in the chest. Although a curfew was imposed in the weeks following the 1989 invasion, the new government has not so far invoked Article 51.

Slander and Libel The right to protection against libel is guaranteed in Article 37 of the Constitution. The 1982 penal code defines slander and libel in nine articles and lays down penalties, while Law 11 of 1978 prohibits the publication of "false news reports, and documents which are forged, altered or wrongly attributed to specific sources", as well as "facts relating to the private life of an individual which may result in moral prejudice towards that person, and commentaries, suggestions or allusions to the physical defects of a particular person".

The Media

Before the 1989 invasion most media were effectively controlled by the military-led government, which enacted a number of laws restricting freedom of expression. These included Law 11 of 1978, prescribing penalties including fines, imprisonment, withdrawal of journalists' licences and even the closure of print and broadcast media, not by the courts but by the Ministry of Government and Justice. The constitutionality of the Law, used against both local and foreign media, was upheld by a 6-3 majority decision of the Supreme Court.

The role of the National Censorship Board, responsible for the classification and censorship of films and some other media, is being re-examined as part of the current review of media law.

Newspapers *La Estrella de Panamá* is the oldest newspaper (founded 1853), and is owned by the Duque family, which has managed to remain on friendly terms with governments of varying tendencies; the current publisher, Tomás Altamirano Duque, was an elected representative of the pro-Noriega Democratic Revolutionary Party (PRD), but after the invasion simply altered the editorial line.

La Prensa is the only newspaper which does not have a single owner. Among its most important shareholders are the current Vice-President, the comptroller-general of Panama and the general manager of the Banco Nacional. These three have reportedly been asked to withdraw from an active role in the affairs of the newspaper to maintain its independence from the government.

El Siglo, a tabloid, is owned by the Padilla family, in opposition to Noriega from 1987 but also critical of the current government. Panamá América SA, a company founded in 1938 and still owned by the politically-prominent Arias family, publishes a newspaper of the same name and another daily, *Crítica Libre*. The company was taken over by the government of General Torrijos in 1968, and its name was changed to ERSA, but it was returned to the family after the invasion.

The Noriega government allowed unhindered publication only for the dailies and one weekly belonging to ERSA. The weekly publication of the Panama-based US military Southern Command, the *Tropic Times*, responded by printing news of a more general nature than before, but the Panamanian authorities regarded it as illegal and clandestine. From May 1989 the *Tropic Times* began to publish articles critical of Noriega and of his annulment of the elections (on the grounds that there had been "foreign interference"). Most of these articles were taken from international press agencies, but had not been used by the local media.

On February 26 1988, after a speech by then-president Eric Delvalle in which he purported to dismiss Noriega as head of the PDF, the opposition newspapers *La Prensa*, *El Siglo* and *El Extra*, along with two weeklies, *Quiubo* and *La Gazeta Financiera*, were closed down. The first four had already been closed for six months from July 1987 for "inciting rebellion". The new closure was not based on a formal written order, but was enforced by the military.

Radio and Television Radio and TV frequencies are subject to government licensing. There are some 96 radio and five TV stations, but up to 700 radio frequencies were allocated under questionable procedures to associates of the former government. On June 7 1990, Decree 229 of the Endara government replaced a 1987 decree, which prevented changes in radio stations' boards of directors without prior government consent, with a new regime under which changes had merely to be notified to the government. A media law currently being drafted may establish formal criteria for licensing.

In early 1988 the then government closed down Radio Mundial, KW Continente, Radio Exitosa and Radio Noticias, all for allegedly violating state security contrary to Law 11; Exitosa was allowed back on air a few months later, but was closed again after it was used in an October 3 coup attempt. Executive Decree 21 of March 11 1988 obliged radio stations to join a national network from 11.45am to 12 noon, to broadcast the government's "national information bulletin". Subsequently, Channel 4 TV and the Corporación Panameña de Radiodifusión, belonging to the Eleta Alvarán family and regarded as open to opposition viewpoints, were taken over by the government for alleged tax debts and their news editors were changed (a PDF spokesman was appointed to Channel 4).

The Foreign Press The former government put pressure on distributors to restrict the importation and sale of foreign publications, and resident foreign correspondents were attacked in pro-government radio programmes. In the first three months of 1988, five were expelled or barred from the country, as were others in later months, mostly for allegedly spreading false information with intent to defame the Panamanian authorities. The correspondent of Spain's *El País* was deported after writing on the private life of Gen Noriega, and writers for the *Washington Post* and *Miami Herald* were each barred twice from entering the country.

Sometimes physical force was used against the foreign press, as on March 28 1988, when police raided an opposition press conference, beating and arresting a number of journalists and confiscating tapes.

After the Invasion

Newspapers and radio and TV stations closed by the Noriega regime have reopened, and according to the justice ministry there is unrestricted freedom of expression. A government-appointed commission consisting of, among others, the

National Journalists' Association and the Journalists' Union of Panama is reviewing media law; no opposition representatives were appointed to it. The aim, as stated by President Endara, is to limit the government's role in media affairs to the minimum required to protect society and the rights of the individual.

A number of concerns arose in the weeks after the invasion. One was the way in which the ERSA group was taken back by the Arias Guardia family on December 26 with no apparent authority other than an alleged verbal agreement with President Endara. Almost 300 ERSA employees were made redundant, and petitioned the Ministry of Labour for compensation or reinstatement. Reconstituted as Panamá América SA, ERSA was made the subject of a sequestration writ by the Ministry; it is being vigorously contested by the family, who present it as a freedom of expression issue.

After the invasion at least 22 ERSA journalists had been detained by US troops, including the then manager Escolástico Calvo, who remains in detention. Several were held for allegedly carrying or firing weapons, and others for questioning on their relationship with Noriega; the authorities maintain that none were held because of their journalistic work.

A group of TV and radio stations controlled by Noriega associates were placed in government custody in December while their legal ownership was investigated. They included Channel 2 and Channel 5 television and Radios América, Verbo, Soberana, Monumental, Millonaria and Ritmo. The move was said to have been made to "guarantee jobs" and "normal news reports". On February 10 1990, Channel 2 filed for bankruptcy and 11 days later it closed down and paid off its workers. The ownership of Channel 5 remains unclear. Channel 11, a state educational and cultural channel, went off the air from December 20 to January 5, but the privately owned Channels 4 and 13 have been broadcasting normally.

Radio Soberana has been returned to its former owner, a supporter of the new government. Most stations broadcast phone-in shows on which criticism of the new government can be heard.

A College of Journalists has been granted the legal status denied it by the Noriega administration, which recognized only the pro-government Journalists' Union (SPP). Baltazar Aizpurua, leader of the SPP, fled to Nicaragua on March 4, but said he would return to "fight for the country's sovereignty". The SPP claims that all media now follow the Endara line and that workers are no longer permitted to freely express their opinions. There have been reports of threats against both pro-government publishers and opposition paper vendors.

Although the attorney-general has authorized an investigation into past crimes against freedom of expression, some concern has been expressed that such a potential "witch-hunt" could hinder the process of national reconciliation.

Most of the local press welcomed the invasion, giving little space to statements from groups who opposed it such as the (communist) People's Party, the Socialist Workers' Party or the SPP. On January 27, however, a pro-PRD newspaper (now called *El Periódico*) was launched to oppose the Endara government and what it terms the US occupation.

Covering the Invasion Foreign journalists experienced hostility from both sides in seeking to cover the invasion. Several were briefly taken hostage by the pro-Noriega Dignity Battalions. Photographers from Reuters and other companies were detained and intimidated by US military personel, as was a crew from the US Cable News

Network. Juantxu Rodriguez of Spain's *El País* was killed and two others wounded in crossfire. US military personnel were criticized for their reticence in explaining these incidents.

Around 200 journalists who landed immediately after the invasion were told their safety could not be guaranteed if they left the US Air Force base; most left Panama without ever reporting the invasion at first hand and some expressed the belief that they had been deliberately misled. Among events they were unable to cover was the destruction by US forces of the government station Radio Nacional.

The University Concern has been expressed about the attitude of Panamanian and US authorities towards the University of Panama, where students and staff complained in February 1990 of harassment by US troops and discrimination against anti-Endara students and pre-invasion staff members.

Actions

On March 22 1989 ARTICLE 19 wrote to the government protesting the arrest on March 20 of five jounalists and the continued detention of one of them, Alfredo Jimenez Valez, who was preparing *La Estrella Civilista*, a new publication funded by the Christian Democratic Party. (He was released on bail on March 30.)

On May 10 1989 ARTICLE 19 wrote to the government expressing concern at the shooting of cameraman Fernando Arauz while he was covering a demonstration against alleged electoral fraud in the May 7 elections. ARTICLE 19 also protested injuries to journalists when soldiers fired bird shot into the air to disperse crowds at a similar demonstration; and foreign journalists' lack of access to the official count at the polling stations.

On August 15 1989 ARTICLE 19 wrote to the government expressing concern at the continued repression of the press, especially the arbitrary detention and beating of journalists.

On November 30 1989 ARTICLE 19 wrote to the government urging the release of Jaime Padilla Beliz, owner of banned newspaper *El Siglo*, who was arrested on September 15 and believed to have been mistreated in custody. He was later deported to Venezuela.

In its 1990 Commentary to the Human Rights Committee, ARTICLE 19 raised a number of concerns including the lack of access to official information about the number of civilian casualties during the US invasion. The report recommended that all journalists should be permitted to gather news without harassment and sought assurance from the Panamanian and US authorities that all materials seized from journalists during this period be returned to their owners.

Paraguay

A coup on February 2 1989 overthrew General Alfredo Stroessner, who had ruled Paraguay for more than 34 years. His successor, General Andrés Rodríguez, had been prominent in the Stroessner government, one of the most authoritarian in the Americas. There were innumerable and gross violations of human rights including arbitrary arrest, imprisonment, torture and "disappearances". Civil and political rights were severely circumscribed and, despite elections held regularly to give a semblance of democracy, Gen Stroessner's Colorado Party (ANR-PC) ran an effective one-party state. From

	Data	Year
Population	4,039,000	1988
Life expectancy	67.0	1988
GNP (US$ per capita)	1,180	1988
Main religion(s)	Christianity	
Official language(s)	Spanish	
Illiteracy %	9.9	1990
(M/F)	7.9/11.9	1990
Daily newspapers	6	1986
Periodicals	4	
Radio sets	645,000	1987
TV sets	92,000	1987
ICCPR:	NO	

the mid-1980s, however, critical factions emerged within the Party, culminating in the coup.

Laws 209 and 294 The culture of fear engendered by Gen Stroessner had a deep impact on freedom of opinion and expression, which was circumscribed by a virtually permanent state of siege and two instruments of repressive legislation. Law 294, "For the Defence of Democracy", was passed in 1955, and made membership of the Communist Party or adhesion to communist ideology a criminal offence. No public institution, or any private enterprise dealing with the public sector, could employ "ostensible or secret" communists, and the government was empowered to close down any teaching institution employing such people. Employees failing to inform on communist colleagues faced dismissal or imprisonment.

Under Law 209, "For the Defence of Public Peace and the Liberty of Persons" (1970), anyone who "preaches hatred among Paraguayans or the destruction of social classes" was liable from one to six years' imprisonment. Any form of critical thought was liable to be subject to its all-inclusive provisions, which encouraged self-censorship within all media.

These laws were used extensively to detain and silence leaders of emerging social protest movements, whether trade unionists, politicians, students, church social workers or those in the media.

The Media

At the end of 1988 no opposition newspaper or magazine circulated legally. The main daily paper, *ABC Color*, had been closed down since 1984, and *El Pueblo*, weekly organ of the social democratic Febrerista Party, since August 1987. The two private television stations, Canal 9 and Canal 13, belonged to relatives and associates of Stroessner. No coverage was permitted of the National Accord, a broad front of four opposition parties. Despite a plethora of local radio stations, self-censorship ensured that criticism of Stroessner remained muted. This was reinforced by the forcible closure in 1986 of Radio Ñandutí and the compulsory reduction in broadcast power of the church-owned Radio Caritas in early 1989. Caritas was accused of inciting disruption of the peace and providing a platform for subversives. Five of its journalists were among dozens of people arrested on December 10 1988 at a banned march to mark the 40th anniversary of the Universal Declaration of Human Rights.

The new government promised to respect human rights and to repair the strained relations between the state and the Church. It also sought to heal the deep divisions within the Colorado Party, which had adopted Gen Rodríguez as its candidate in presidential elections on May 1 1989. He won with a convincing 73 per cent of the vote.

Reforms In late August 1989, Congress repealed Laws 209 and 294, and the government invited the Inter-American Commission on Human Rights to visit Paraguay after decades of being refused entry. In November the Commission reported that since the coup, freedom of association, assembly, expression and access to the media had become general. Previously illegal political parties, such as the Christian Democrats, had been recognized, but the Communist Party remained proscribed. Free air-time had been offered to opposition parties on the state-controlled Radio Nacional. *ABC Color*, Radio Ñandutí and *El Pueblo* had reopened and restrictions on Radio Caritas had been lifted.

However, the report drew attention to the continuing compulsory affiliation of the 200,000 public-sector employees to the Colorado Party. This practice, which spans the armed forces, civil servants and even rural school-teachers, includes payroll deduction of party dues and a subscription to the Colorado daily *Patria*. There is strong opposition within the party to the abolition of obligatory contributions but the new Health Minister has annouced her intention to end the practice in her ministry, as has the new head of the Rural Welfare Institute, suggesting the tacit support of President Rodríguez.

Media freedom has increased enormously since February 1989. New opposition publications include *Ne-Engatú* and *Liberación*, both previously published in exile and circulated clandestinely. *Adelante*, the organ of the Paraguayan Communist Party, now circulates freely, although it is not handled by commercial distributors. *Nuestro Tiempo*, a monthly current affairs magazine, also circulates freely. Established in 1985, it had been printed in Argentina since 1986 after its Asuncion printers were harassed by the police. Several issues had been confiscated at the border. A new fortnightly current affairs magazine, *La Opinión*, has established a wide readership.

News coverage in the daily press bears little resemblance to the pre-coup period; space devoted to sport and foreign news has declined markedly as editors seek to meet the growing demand for domestic news. Three issues have dominated domestic coverage: human rights violations under the former president, corruption among his associates and conflict within the Colorado Party. The press has published detailed testimonies of torture at the hands of named police officials, reports of the mass exhumation of bodies of disappeared political detainees, and witness accounts of the torture and summary execution of prisoners during the guerrilla uprisings of 1959-1963.

Harassment of Journalists On March 11 1990, journalist Dionicio Enciso of Radio Ñandutí and Radio Arapysandu was detained by the military authorities for two hours and reproached for his coverage of a strike at the dam in Yacyreta.

Limitations on Freedom of Expression There has been a quantum leap in both media freedom and individual freedom of expression since the fall of Gen Stroessner. One glaring exception has been the absence of any public discussion of the collective responsibility of Gen Rodríguez and the military in the human rights abuses and the endemic corruption of the last 30 years.

All leading military figures in the present government similarly occupied high positions under Stroessner to whom they regularly swore allegiance. Only one member of the security forces, the former police chief, has been arrested for human rights violations.

The press and broadcasters, however, have refrained absolutely from criticizing the new head of state, including questions about his role as effectively second-in-command to Alfredo Stroessner.

Freedom of Cultural Expression Since the coup, Paraguay's most famous writers, Augusto Roa Bastos and Rubén Saguier, have returned from exile to be greeted by popular and official acclaim, after decades of vilification as "traitors".

The 17th Festival del Lago Ypacaraí took place in August 1989 after several years during which it had been banned. The foremost expression of the *Nuevo Cancionero*, a musical form combining Paraguay's *guaraní* tradition with incisive social comment, the festival attracted thousands of young people.

In late Feburary 1989, the Municipality of Asunción prohibited the showing of a new play, *Los Tribunales de San Fernando*, by journalist Alcibiades González Delvalle, on the grounds that it was offensive to the memory of the 19th century national hero Marshal Francisco Solano López. Despite a series of legal hearings, the ban remained a year later, although sale of the text was permitted.

Actions

On May 4 1989 ARTICLE 19 wrote to the government expressing concern that the restoration of press freedom and legalization of political organizations did not include the Communist Party.

Peru

Peru enjoys press freedom and open debate on most issues, but two factors are threatening the stability of its democracy. One is the devastating decline in the economy; towards the end of 1988 rampant inflation resulted in looting and street violence. The other is the increase in political violence, particularly the growth of the Sendero Luminoso (Shining Path) insurgency. Between January and April 1990, more than 1,100 people died in political violence. In 1989, the number of killings far exceeded that for any year since the campaign started in 1980. Although Sendero was responsible for most, the number of murders attributed to the security forces also increased in 1989. Significantly, presidential elections in 1990 resulted in the rejection of the traditional parties in favour of an independent candidate, Alberto Fujimori, who has taken office at a time when human rights are in danger of being sidelined by urgent economic and security concerns.

	Data	Year
Population	21,256,000	1988
Life expectancy	63.0	1987
GNP (US$ per capita)	1,440	1988
Main religion(s)	Christianity	
Official language(s)	Spanish	
	Quechua	
	Aymara	
Illiteracy %	14.9	1990
(M/F)	8.5/21.3	1990
Daily newspapers	70	1986
Non daily newspapers	37	1982
Periodicals	507	1982
Radio sets	5,000,000	1987
TV sets	1,750,000	1987
ICCPR:	YES	1978

The Media

Killings of Journalists The worst problem for freedom of expression continues to be violence against journalists. The New York-based Committee to Protect Journalists (CPJ) has recorded at least eight murders since 1988. Attacks come from all sides. Sendero and the smaller Tupac Amarú Revolutionary Movement (MRTA) attack journalists whom they consider spies or enemies, or force them to publish propaganda. The right-wing Rodrigo Franco Commando (CRF), possibly linked with elements of the American Popular Revolutionary Alliance (APRA) party or the army, attacks journalists whom it suspects of links with the insurgents. Ayacucho Department, where Sendero was formed, has been under emergency military rule since 1982 and access for journalists is severely restricted and at the discretion of the local army command.

Hugo Bustios of the Lima magazine *Caretas* was shot dead, and a colleague wounded, on November 24 1988 in Ayacucho. They had been given permission to travel to Erapata village by the local military commander, who had questioned Bustios about his knowledge of a captured Sendero suspect. They were ambushed en route, despite security force patrols. The prosecutor closed the file after a brief and inconclusive investigation. *Caretas* published the testimony of seven witnesses, two of whom were then arrested and threatened by the army; one witness was killed months later by unknown assailants. *Caretas* lawyers trying to investigate were threatened by the CRF and had to return to Lima. Another *Caretas* reporter was detained for two days by the army in Ayachucho in April 1989. A CPJ team investigating the murder was refused access to the area by the military authorities, but in 1990 the CPJ and the International Federation of Journalists filed a complaint with the Inter-American Commission on Human Rights, which called on the government to protect the surviving witnesses.

On January 26 1989, Luis Piccone, a radio journalist in Ica, was shot dead in front of the offices of Radio Independencia. A note left at the site suggested that Sendero was responsible, but a witness claimed that the assailant was linked to the security forces. The investigation was closed without result.

On January 30, Juvenal Farfan was killed with his wife and two children in Ayacucho. His family owned the local monthly, *Ahora*, and he also worked at a radio station. Again, leaflets at the scene implicated Sendero.

On April 19, eight men shot dead Guillermo López Salazar in Tingo María, in the San Martín jungle region where both Sendero and the drug trade operate. He had been working for Radio Tingo Maria and had written occasionally for print media and frequently assisted visiting journalists. In 1988 Sendero had forced him to broadcast a propaganda tape, after which he was threatened by security personnel. In September 1988 his house was attacked by the CRF. He was a local official of the United Left coalition, whose members have been persecuted by Sendero and the armed forces. The subsequent investigation was inconclusive.

On April 30, Manuel Martínez, a correspondent for the Lima daily *Hoy*, was killed in Huancayo, apparently by common criminals.

Barbara d'Achille, a Latvian-born reporter on environmental issues, was beaten to death by Sendero on May 31 while on assignment for *El Comercio* of Lima to visit a Huancavelica rural development project. Two of her companions were also kidnapped; one of them was released, but the other, a government engineer, was shot dead.

On November 21, US journalist Todd Smith of the *Tampa Tribune* was strangled by Sendero in Uchiza. He had been kidnapped four days earlier at Uchiza airport while investigating connections between guerrillas and the drug business.

Marino Meza, correspondent for Panamericana TV and a candidate for Congress, was shot dead in Huanuco on March 18 1990 with three other people, presumably as part of Sendero's campaign to sabotage the elections.

On October 22, Pedro Macedo Figueroa, a correspondent for Channel 4 TV news, was murdered in Huarez. He had previously received threats from Sendero.

Threats Against Journalists The CRF published death threats against two well-known TV presenters in Lima on November 11 1988 after they aired criticism of the government's policies. Odilón Farfan, brother of the late Juvenal and editor of *Ahora*, was threatened by the CRF in April 1989 and left the country. The bureau chief of the Italian news agency ANSA also left, on May 10, after hearing of a plot to murder him, but President Alan García persuaded him to return. Two other journalists left the country briefly at that time, also for security reasons.

In September and October 1989, the CRF issued death threats against at least five Ayacucho journalists. Four were told to leave, and one did so. All had written about violations of human rights by the military. On October 4, the MRTA wounded and kidnapped Héctor Delgado Parker, chairman of Panamericana TV and a former presidential advisor. Despite a media agreement to refuse MRTA messages until his release, on February 11 1990 Channel 4 TV showed an MRTA tape in which he was made to discuss alleged corruption in state arms buying. He was released in April. A reporter on the Lima daily, *La República*, received a death threat after she wrote in December 1989 of links between the CRF and the army in Ayacucho.

On October 15 1990, three MRTA members occupied the Lima office of ANSA. They forced a journalist, at gunpoint, to type out and release a proclamation which they dictated.

Revolutionary Press A formerly independent left-wing newspaper, *El Diario*, has come to be regarded as the mouthpiece of Sendero Luminoso. It is the primary source of information on Sendero's policies and statements of responsibility for particular acts. It has published interviews with Sendero leaders, supplements on Sendero internal decisions, and has been a vehicle for threats to Sendero's enemies. In 1989, while in Europe, its editor, Luis Arce Borja, defended the Sendero policy of attacking foreign aid organizations in the southern Andes.

In 1988, the government proposed legislation to punish those who use the media to make a public "apology for terrorism". On August 19, before Congress had even debated the bill (which was later enacted), the police seized 100,000 copies of an *El Diario* supplement carrying a long interview with Sendero commander Abimael Guzman. On August 23, Arce and two colleagues were detained without warrant for several hours, and Arce was rearrested a few days later on a warrant for defrauding the government through the importation of newsprint. A judge found no case to answer but the prosecutor appealed; Arce remained in custody and *El Diario* suspended publication for several days until his release.

Janet Talavera was acting editor of *El Diario* in June 1989, when it carried an unsigned article supporting the Sendero ambush of a bus carrying the President's bodyguards. She was arrested on June 14 and charged with "apology for terrorism" and remains in prison at the time of writing. On November 3, police raided the paper's offices, confiscated copies of the paper and other documents and arrested several persons. Only one issue has been published since that date, although some copies have circulated clandestinely.

Broadcast Media There are eight TV stations in Peru, four of which broadcast nationally. Ministerio de Educación Pública and Radiodifusión del Perú are government owned, the rest are commercial stations. With 20 per cent illiteracy, radio is an important source of information. There are between 400 and 600 stations broadcasting throughout the country, mostly at regional or local level. The principal government station is Radio Nacional del Perú and the main commercial stations are Radio América, Radio El Sol and Radio Panamericana. Air time is sold to journalists amongst others who use radio to advertise products and promote political, financial or commerical messages. However, pressure from media companies ensures that a level of self-censorship operates among journalists.

Access to Information Access to information by journalists is restricted particularly in emergency zones. Reasons of personal safety are frequently invoked by the military to exclude journalists from areas of conflict where most human rights abuse occurs. Information transmitted from these areas is controlled by the local military command. High levels of government secrecy add to the difficulty in gaining access to official information.

Actions

On August 30 1989 ARTICLE 19 wrote to the government expressing deep concern and asking for an investigation into the detention of a 21-year-old, his 16-year-old brother and an eight-year-old child, requesting that relatives be given details of their whereabouts, and that the boys either be charged with a recognized criminal offence or released.

United States of America

The history of freedom of expression in the United States is a complex mixture of profound theoretical commitment to individual liberty and intolerance of dissent and unorthodox views. Freedom of expression did not fare well in the 1980s and, during Ronald Reagan's presidency, unprecedented steps were taken to narrow the range of public discourse. Since taking office in January 1989, President George Bush has given some indication of being more supportive of free expression than his predecessor, for example, by supporting the independence of the National Endowment for the Arts (NEA) from political pressure. He supports, however, the majority of the previous administration's policies which expanded government interference with free expression.

	Data	Year
Population	246,329,000	1988
Life expectancy (M/F)	71.2/78.2	1984
GNP (US$ per capita)	19,780	1988
Main religion(s)	Christianity	
Official language(s)	English	
Illiteracy %	4	1985
Daily newspapers	1,642	1988
Non daily newspapers	7,464	1984
Periodicals	59,609	1980
Radio sets	515,000,000	1987
TV sets	197,000,000	1987
Press agencies:		
AP, Feature News Service, Singer Media, United Media, Religious News Service		
ICCPR:	NO	

The Constitution

The cornerstone of political freedom in the US is the Constitution's First Amendment, which states: "Congress shall make no law respecting an establishment of religion, or prohibiting the free exercise thereof; or abridging the freedom of speech, or of the press; or the right of the people peaceably to assemble, and to petition the government for a redress of grievances."

The ideal implicit in the First Amendment is that of a citizenry that can participate fully in political and social affairs without fear of government interference. Yet freedom of speech is not an absolute; laws exist regarding libel, obscenity, national security, access to government information, and the regulation of electronic mass communications.

Access to information about the activities of government is an essential part of the country's democratic vision. The President is required to make an annual address on the state of the nation; a decennial census must be taken; information is designed to flow from the Executive Branch to Congress to ensure effective supervision.

The courts play a crucial role in preserving First Amendment principles. One of the most famous instances arose during the civil rights movement of the late 1950s and early 1960s when state authorities in the south tried to exclude the national press through the use of libel laws that exacted stiff penalties for damage to a person's reputation. The Supreme Court, refusing to permit libel to be used as a shield for racism, required public officials suing the press to prove reckless disregard for the truth. This landmark ruling (*New York Times v Sullivan*) was both a product of the social climate of the times and a catalyst for further activism.

The strength of the First Amendment has recently been tested in a controversy over the sanctity of the national flag. Political protestors have traditionally used flag burning or other "abuse" of the national symbol to express disagreement with government policies. Laws of several states, however, made flag desecration a crime. In 1989, the conflict reached the Supreme Court, which ruled that flag burning is a protected form of speech, commenting that, "[we] do not consecrate the flag by punishing its desecration, for in doing so we dilute the freedom that this cherished emblem represents".

President Bush, who made patriotism the centrepiece of his 1988 electoral campaign, denounced the ruling. He called for a constitutional amendment banning desecration of the flag, claiming that a statute alone would likely be struck down by the Supreme Court as a violation of the First Amendment. Congress nonetheless passed the Flag Protection Act of 1989. In June 1990, the Supreme Court held this federal Act to be unconstitutional. In July 1990, congressional efforts to enact a constitutional amendment failed.

Laws Affecting Freedom of Expression

The Freedom of Information Act Prior to 1966, when the Freedom of Information Act (FOIA) was adopted, federal officials had discretion to decide whether or not to release information. The FOIA established a policy in favour of disclosure, except where withholding could be justified based on specific exemptions. The list of exemptions currently includes classified documents, confidential business information, and the operational records of the Central Intelligence Agency (CIA).

The FOIA has enabled writers, historians and others to uncover a wide range of information. Documents released have revealed harassment by the Federal Bureau of Investigation (FBI) of civil rights leader Dr Martin Luther King Jr, illegal CIA and FBI surveillance of domestic political groups and writers, safety problems at nuclear power plants, and lax federal enforcement of environmental and civil rights laws.

The importance of the FOIA has risen and declined in accordance with the attitudes of successive administrations. The FOIA requires agencies to respond to written requests within 10 working days, second requests within 20, and permits final agency denials to be taken to the federal court. During the administration of President Reagan, however, certain agencies, including the Energy Department, the Justice Department, the Defence Department and the CIA, were notorious for long delays or for denying the very existence of information requested. In addition, an executive order issued in 1982 and still in force authorized agencies to classify information retrospectively and eliminated an earlier requirement to balance the government's interest in secrecy against the public's interest in disclosure of the requested materials.

Access to information was also restricted when some government agencies began reclassifying requesters as commercial users. In June 1988, for example, an historian researching the 1985 strike of a meatpackers' union in Austin, Minnesota, submitted an FOIA request to the FBI seeking documents concerning the FBI's monitoring of the strike. The FBI first said that it had found 1,400 documents relevant to the request and that the cost of processing the request would be $130. The writer then waited a full year, only to receive another letter informing him that he had been reclassified as a commercial user (for reasons not specified) and would have to pay $3,500 for the same material. The refusal of many agencies (federal and state) to extend the FOIA to the enormous volume of information stored electronically poses another serious obstacle to access to government documents.

In May 1990, Secret Service agents raided 28 homes in an operation codenamed "Sun Devil", designed to weed out computer "hackers". Over 40 computers were impounded, together with 23,000 diskettes. The overzealous action by agents, resulting in brutal treatment of householders and widespread destruction, prompted the organization, Computer Professionals for Social Responsibility, to file a request under the Freedom of Information Act which revealed that the Secret Service routinely monitors electronic bulletin boards, sets up electronic accounts for agents and informers and even created a false bulletin board to lure "hackers".

The Sunshine Act This law, passed in 1976, declared that "the public is entitled to the fullest practicable information regarding the decision-making process of the federal government" and required that the public be given access to the meetings of some 60 federal agencies. It makes the deliberations of agencies, as well as their final actions, open to public scrutiny. Certain important agencies, such as the Nuclear Regulatory Commission, have sought ways around this law, by redefining the word "meeting" and having commissioners vote over the telephone, or by broadly applying exemptions contained in the law.

The Federal Depository Library Programme Administered by the Government Printing Office since 1902, this programme provides government publications free of charge to approximately 1,400 academic, public and private libraries on the condition that they provide access to the public.

"Whistleblower" Laws The public interest often is significantly served by employee disclosure of unlawful or improper actions of their employers. Federal and state governments have passed laws that protect private sector and government employees who "blow the whistle" on their employers.

The Paperwork Reduction Act of 1980 This law was intended to reduce the amount of paperwork that companies were required to submit to government agencies as part of regulatory activity and to provide direction for automation of government record-keeping. It became, however, a potent tool in the federal government's deregulation campaign of the 1980s, causing drastic reductions in the amount of information collected and distributed by federal agencies, including information useful to public interest groups monitoring environmental and other practices.

The Immigration and Nationality Act of 1952 More commonly known as the McCarran-Walter Act, this law restricts freedom of expression by giving government officials discretion to selectively deny entry to foreigners. The act defines 33 categories of foreigners who can be deported or barred from the country, including people with dangerous communicable diseases and drug-traffickers. In April 1989, the immigration authorities detained and deported a Dutch person with AIDS on the grounds that he had failed to inform his local US consulate that he was suffering from a "dangerous contagious disease". Several other foreigners were subsequently reported as having been refused entry on similar grounds. In May, the Immigration and Naturalization Service issued a policy statement enabling people with HIV to apply for a waiver which would allow them to enter the US for up to 30 days on business, to obtain medical treatment, to visit relatives or to attend conferences. Despite this, a number of leading AIDS organizations withdrew from the Sixth International Conference on AIDS, held in San Francisco in June 1990, in protest at the regulations which could breach the confidentiality of delegates or put them at risk of deportation.

Equally controversial are the ideological criteria such as advocacy of communism or anarchism, and determination by the Attorney General that the visitor's activities would be "prejudicial to the public interest." In early 1990, Congress abolished the ideological criteria for visitors to the US, although they are still applied to those seeking permanent residence.

Successive administrations have made extensive use of the law to exclude a varied list of individuals. "Undesirables" denied visas include Nobel Laureate Gabriel Garcia Marquez, Colombian journalist Patricia Lara, Italian playwrights Dario Fo and Franca Rama, and Hortensia Bussi de Allende, widow of the assassinated Chilean President. In 1988, Palestine Liberation Organization leader Yasser Arafat was denied a visa based on a restrictive reading of the US/UN Headquarters Agreement.

National Security

Some of the greatest dangers to freedom of expression in the US stem from the federal government's concern with national security and terrorism. Under those banners, the executive branch has widened government secrecy, justified surveillance of dissidents and placed broad restrictions on the media.

Controlling the Media Efforts to control the media include the requirement that coverage of overseas military manoeuvres be limited to Pentagon-supervised press pools, a rule adopted after the total press ban imposed during the Grenada invasion in 1983. Although the pool was supposed to facilitate press access to manoeuvres, during the invasion of Panama in December 1989, the pool reporters were again kept far from the fighting. Some 200 journalists who entered Panama immediately after the invasion were told upon landing at Howard Air Force Base that their safety could not be guaranteed if they left the base. In this way, firsthand reporting of critical events was impeded. Photographers from Reuters and a crew from the CNN television network were detained and intimidated by US military personnel. One journalist was killed and two others wounded in crossfire and US military personnel were criticized for their reticence in explaining these incidents. Indeed, the whole question of the total number of deaths resulting from the invasion is controversial. In June 1990 the human rights group Americas Watch claimed that some 50 Panamanian and 23 US military personnel were killed along with 300 Panamanian civilians. Alternative figures range from 1,000 (a group of Panamanian victims' relatives) to 523 (the Pentagon). In January 1990, an Independent Commission on the US Invasion of Panama stated that as many as 4,000 people may have been killed.

In the late 1980s, CIA Director William Casey regularly threatened to bring espionage charges against major news organizations. The threats were taken more seriously after Samuel Loring Morison, a civilian Navy analyst, was convicted of espionage for leaking classified photographs to a London publication. This was the first time in the country's history that an unauthorized disclosure of government information to the press was prosecuted as espionage.

In August 1989 the Justice Department announced that any official who leaked classified information to journalists would be prosecuted for theft of government property. Although the Attorney General hastened to assure reporters that they would not be prosecuted, the potentially grave penalties against sources and the warning that journalists could be subpoenaed to identify those sources has had a chilling effect.

Classification Successive administrations have sought to control the flow of information through more stringent use of classification rules, including the creation of new categories of "sensitive" unclassified materials. Military officials have pressed private information companies to restrict the use of their commercial databases. Stricter controls have been placed on the presentation of certain kinds of scientific and technical information at professional conferences and in scholarly journals.

Nondisclosure Agreements Of all the secrecy edicts announced while Ronald Reagan was in office, perhaps none evoked as much opposition as the 1983 presidential directive (classified in part) which obliged current and former government employees to sign lifetime secrecy contracts forbidding disclosure of classified and "classifiable" information. Such contracts, signed by approximately three and a half million people as of December 1989, serve as gag orders, severely limiting congressional and public access to vital information and reducing the supervisory capacity of Congress. Successive efforts by Congress to halt this practice have been unsuccessful.

Surveillance In 1981, President Reagan issued an order expanding the authority of the CIA and FBI to conduct domestic surveillance. Since then, the intelligence agencies have apparently returned to activities criticized during congressional hearings of the 1970s, including infiltration, phone-tapping and searches of the offices of dissident groups, particularly those engaged in criticizing US policy in Central America.

Recently, in response to a lawsuit, the FBI has admitted its programme of surveillance and harassment of opponents of the government's Central America policy. As a result of this suit, the FBI agreed in November 1989 to purge its files of thousands of names of people and organizations collected during its surveillance activities.

"Library Awareness Programme" It came to public attention in September 1988 that the FBI has pressurized librarians across the country to disclose the names and reading habits of certain library patrons deemed "hostile to the US." In one case in which agents were dissatisfied with the outcome of a library visit, they used phone-taps and hidden cameras on reference desks, followed by a visit to a library staff member's home. Records released in 1989 indicate that the Bureau has done over 250 background searches on librarians and other individuals who had publicly criticized the programme. The American Library Association has campaigned against this practice, but the FBI has indicated that the programme is continuing, at least in the New York City area.

Disinformation National security has been invoked to justify disinformation. In 1986, Defence Department officials admitted that incomplete and misleading information had been given to the media on more than 15 military programmes, ostensibly to impede the transfer of technical data to the Soviet Union. In 1989, the government admitted releasing erroneous reports to the press aimed at convincing Libyan leader Colonel Muammar al-Qaddafi that the US or Israel was planning an attack on a chemical production plant in the Libyan desert.

Iran/contra The Reagan administration's most flagrant disregard of laws requiring disclosure of foreign policy initiative to congressional leaders gave rise to the Iran/contra scandal, the secret use of proceeds from arms sales to Iran to subsidize the Nicaraguan contras during a time when such aid was banned by Congress. When one of the key figures in the scandal, former White House aide Colonel Oliver North, was about to stand trial, the Reagan administration moved to block North's lawyers from using classified documents they said were essential for North's defence. The release of that material, the administration claimed, would be harmful to "national security". As a result, Special Prosecutor Lawrence Walsh felt compelled to withdraw some of the most serious charges although he continued to press 12 lesser felony counts. (North was convicted on three of these.)

The Media

There are some 10,500 radio and 1,400 TV stations, 25 per cent of which are non-commercial. More than half the 90 million TV households are wired for cable, 60 million have video recorders, and more than 2 million have satellite dishes. Unlike most countries, the vast majority of radio and TV stations in the US have always been privately-owned (although the airwaves remain a public resource), with advertising providing the bulk of station revenue. The Communications Act of 1934, still the primary law for electronic communications, made broadcasters public trustees through a licensing system that linked the granting and renewal of licences with a broadcaster's ability to serve "the public interest, convenience and necessity".

Deregulation The Federal Communications Commission's (FCC) regulations and judicial decisions until recently encouraged broadcasters to meet local needs for news, information, and entertainment, to offer a diversity of ideas, to limit the number of commercial minutes per hour, to cover controversial issues in a balanced fashion, and to comply with guidelines for children's programming. Since the late 1970s, however, the media have been progressively deregulated. The one exception to the FCC's deregulation campaign is a policy announced in 1987 that expands FCC enforcement of regulations prohibiting the broadcast of sexually explicit material. FCC regulations ban "patently offensive" materials, depicting graphic "sexual or excretory activities" or sexual organs, from radio or TV from 6am to 8pm. Because of this policy, a significant amount of literature, poetry and music are not allowed on the air. In a letter to poet Allen Ginsberg, notifying him that his poems would no longer be aired, the head of non-commercial Pacifica radio explained: "In this climate, Pacifica cannot risk losing its licence or even the cost of defending ourselves."

In September 1988, Congress passed legislation introduced by Senator Jesse Helms allowing the FCC to extend its indecency rules to programming 24 hours a day. The 24-hour ban was postponed by a federal appeals court in January 1989, until the Commission could provide evidence that children were being exposed to late-night programming. Nonetheless, Alfred Sikes, the FCC chairman appointed by President Bush in 1989, initiated indecency actions against three radio stations in Chicago, Indianapolis and San Jose, California, for language used by announcers. In October 1989, the Commission fined four other radio stations for violating indecency rules and notified several others that they were being investigated.

Concentration of Ownership and Diversity Since 1984, the FCC has eased ownership limitations for broadcasting stations. As a consequence, all three major TV networks are under new management: NBC has been acquired by General Electric, ABC by Capital Cities, and CBS is now largely controlled by financier Laurence Tish. These new owners have reduced broadcast staff, particularly in the news and public affairs departments. Concentration of ownership has occurred throughout the media.

The media are subject to strong corporate pressure to treat publications and broadcasts like any other product. More than ever before, management consultants and financial executives make key decisions, narrowing the diversity of content. Fewer documentaries are carried by the networks. The major book publishers increasingly limit their titles to "safe" genres such as celebrity biographies, diet and self-help books. The director of Pantheon Books was forced to resign when he refused to cut back his list and focus on more profitable titles.

The public's response to such changes has proceeded along two lines. First, they are seeking out available commercial options that provide a greater degree of diversity, including the burgeoning video-cassette business, satellite dishes which provide access to dozens of channels, and thousands of small book and magazine publishers. Second, some people are developing alternative media, including independently produced programmes aired on community access channels provided free of charge by many cable TV systems, as well as hundreds of non-commercial "electronic bulletin boards" and networks. The new technologies, however, involve costs and skills which remain outside the reach of much of the population.

Freedom of Opinion and Expression

Pornography The anti-pornography movement was bolstered by the work of a federal commission on pornography directed by Attorney General Edwin Meese in 1986. Although the Meese Commission was unable to establish a direct link between media images and violent behaviour, it nonetheless recommended a crackdown on the production, distribution and consumption of sexually explicit material.

In 1988, Congress passed a broad pornography law aimed at stopping child pornography. In April 1990, the Supreme Court ruled that states may prohibit citizens from possessing or viewing child pornography, even in the privacy of their own homes, extending the law established in earlier cases which had allowed states to ban the sale and distribution of such materials. Concerned citizens' organizations such as the Parents' Music Resource Center have targetted what they consider to be obscenity in rock music and have pressurized record companies to tone down lyrics. In July 1990, Louisiana became the first state legislature to pass a law requiring warnings on the covers of record albums that contain sexually explicit lyrics and forbidding the sale of such records to minors. The law has since been vetoed by the state governor. Similar legislation is pending in 19 other states.

In Florida, in June 1990, a record by the rap group 2 Live Crew was declared legally obscene by a federal court judge, resulting in attempts by some local authorities to ban the sale and public performance of their work. In October, a record shop owner, Charles Freeman, was convicted on obscenity charges for selling a record by the group, and faced a maximum sentence of a year in prison and a US$1,000 fine. However, in the same month the group itself was acquitted of staging an obscene performance at a nightclub in June.

Arts Funding In 1989, a controversy erupted over the use of funds from the NEA for an exhibition of photographs taken by the late Robert Mapplethorpe, which included a strong homoerotic element. Following the Mapplethorpe exhibition and another that included a photograph by Andres Serrano depicting a plastic crucifix submerged in the artist's urine, Congress approved legislation which prevented the NEA from funding art that was legally obscene and established a commission to review the endowment's grant-making procedures.

The Mapplethorpe controversy continued in April 1990 when the Cincinnati Contemporary Art Center and its director were indicted on obscenity charges for exhibiting the same show which ignited the NEA controversy. In October, a jury cleared the museum's director, Dennis Barrie, of the charges.

Censorship in Schools In the wake of a 1988 Supreme Court ruling which upheld the right of a Hazelwood, Missouri high school principal to delete two pages from a student newspaper containing articles about divorce and student pregnancy, school officials across the country have been making use of their new right to regulate the content of student publications. The Student Press Law Center reported in 1989 that it had received hundreds of complaints about censorship in the 12 months since the Supreme Court handed down its decision.

Shortly after the Hazelwood ruling, a federal district court in Florida used the decision to uphold a county school board's banning of a state-approved humanities textbook. The book was censored because it included Chaucer's "Miller's Tale" from *The Canterbury Tales* and *Lysistrata* by Aristophanes. In 1989, the US Court of Appeals upheld that ruling, again citing the Hazelwood precedent.

Actions

On May 8 1989 ARTICLE 19 wrote to the New York TV station WNYC Channel 31 urging it to reconsider its decision to cancel the documentary *Days of Rage: The Young Palestinians*, believed to have been cancelled due to pressure from pro-Israel viewers.

On July 31 1989 ARTICLE 19 wrote to US Senators asking them not to support a bill which would restrict funding for the National Endowment for Arts.

On May 3 1990 ARTICLE 19 joined 43 other organizations and 16 artists in filing a friend-of-the-court brief. This challenged the Flag Protection Act on the grounds that a ruling that the Act is constitutional would represent a serious retrenchment from long prevailing US law, inconsistent with the spirit of the Universal Declaration of Human Rights.

Uruguay

In 1985 Uruguay brought to a close 12 years of military rule marked by stringent censorship and self-censorship of reporting, books, plays and other media, closures of media and curbs on the foreign press, foreign correspondents and academic and artistic expression. The reopening of the political system started in 1980 with the rejection by plebiscite of a military-approved Constitution. In November 1982, a law regulating political parties was enacted but bans remained against a number of left-wing parties and leaders of the mainstream parties. In 1984, elections were won by the Colorado Party, defeated in 1989 by its

	Data	Year
Population	3,060,000	1988
Life expectancy	70.3	1985
GNP (US$ per capita)	2,470	1988
Main religion(s)	Christianity	
Official language(s)	Spanish	
Illiteracy %	3.8	1990
(M/F)	3.4/4.1	1990
Daily newspapers	33	1986
Non daily newspapers	93	1986
Periodicals	465	1986
Radio sets	1,820,000	1987
TV sets	530,000	1987
ICCPR:	YES	1988

traditional rival, the Blanco or National Party. The return to civilian government restored legal and constitutional guarantees and began the process of investigation and rectification of the legacy of military rule, including torture, disappearances, corruption, arbitrary dismissal of thousands of public officials and, in the economy, the external debt and the drop in salaries.

Legislation The Constitution of 1966, reaffirmed on March 1 1985, guarantees freedom of opinion and expression in Article 29, without prior censorship but subject to legal liability for abuses. The military government set aside this guarantee and imposed strict control of the media. Dozens of publications were closed, premises occupied and presses dismantled; editors and journalists were arrested and imprisoned. These measures affected even those media tolerated by the military, but were applied particularly severely to opposition weeklies after 1980. One of the first initiatives of the Colorado President, Julio Sanguinetti, was a Decree of March 5 1985 which set aside "all closures and prohibitions on press organs".

There is no legal right of access to information, but the government allows access to official information subject to considerations of national security.

The New Press Law In November 1989, a new Press Law (Law 16.099) established freedom of communication, thought and information, and introduced the right of journalists to protect sources, an end to censorship of foreign publications and a right of reply for victims of inaccurate or insulting reports. The new law replaces a 1975 decree and abolishes Article 31 of Decree Law 15.672 (1984), which put the circulation of foreign publications under the control of the Interior Minister and prohibited the circulation of a publication for one to 15 editions if it offended against morality, national security or public order.

Printers and editors are no longer required to inform the Ministry of Education and Culture of the full names of editorial staff, the objectives of the publication and its source of finance, but the obligation to notify the names of the publication, editor and owner is maintained.

Defamation, Libel and Right of Reply The right of reply, established in Law 15.672, is a procedure for protection of the right to reputation and honour, independent of legal action for defamation and the offences of slander and insult in the Penal Code. Under Articles 334 and 335 of the Code, journalists can be fined or imprisoned for defamation or slander. In 1987, a journalist was convicted of making false statements on the business connections of a senator and the director of a state bank, but was not imprisoned. In 1988, another journalist was sentenced to six months in prison for libel. Both were private prosecutions.

Eleuterio Fernández Huidobro, an ex-leader of the Tupamaro guerrillas, was imprisoned for 11 years and released in April 1985. In October 1988, he appeared in a TV discussion of the murder of an army intelligence officer in 1974. He repeated his belief that the murder was ordered by the armed forces, and the Ministry of Defence sued for libel. He was charged with "maliciously spreading false news which could cause public alarm or disturb public order, inciting contempt for the state". The case was dismissed on the grounds that there was no malicious intent and no public alarm. On appeal the Supreme Court ruled in December that Fernández' opinion about past events was not "news", concluding: "If the case were accepted, freedom of the press would be in crisis".

Some media have argued unsuccessfully that the law on the right of reply was unconstitutional. On March 31 1989, the Supreme Court decided a case brought by the Servicio Paz y Justicia organization against the daily *El País*. The paper maintained that the law deprived the media of the right to decide on its content in that a mere non-abusive mention of someone gave them a right of reply, and was against the right of property since the medium had to meet the cost, using up to twice as much space as the original news item. The Court held that there was no "absolute right to transmit news which is false, incoherent, injurious to honour and damaging to a third party simply in the name of a so-called unrestricted freedom". According to the Court, the same applies to the right of property since the loss arises from the action of the paper itself.

A uniquely Uruguayan solution to a libel dispute suggested itself in early 1990 to a police inspector implicated by *La República* in smuggling. He invoked an ancient legal provision and challenged the editor to a duel. Although the editor demurred and the episode was reported internationally as Ruritanian farce, the disturbing subtext is that the Interior Ministry, which authorized the challenge, implicitly endorsed violence as a means of settling the dispute.

The Remedy of Amparo The law of *amparo*, comparable to habeus corpus, provides an important judicial safeguard for media freedom. Article 36 of Law 15.672 explicitly establishes a remedy of *amparo* for communications media.

Freedom of Political Opinion Positive measures have now been introduced to restore the right to freedom of thought and opinion, and a system of reparation seeks to rectify injustices committed during the *de facto* government period. Law 15.783 of November 28 1985 led, by the end of 1987, to the reinstatement or compensation of 14,836 officials unfairly dismissed under military rule, and Law 15.739 of March 25 1985, overturning military decrees on educational texts, guaranteed respect for "pupils' independent moral and civic conscience" and requires that "education is dispensed in an atmosphere of tolerance and respect for ideas".

The Media

The Press The press operates freely and covers a wide spectrum of opinion. Political organizations such as the Tupamaros may publish their own newspaper and have access to their own radio station. There are seven national dailies and three evening papers. Journalists, despite the dangers which faced them in the years of de facto rule, now provide adequate coverage of matters concerning the armed forces and human rights abuses. Journalists' unions and professional organizations exist, but membership is not compulsory.

Demand for Reparation Two of the main daily papers, *El Día* and *El País*, have called for government aid for the press because of its oppression and economic losses under the de facto government. An alternative view was that the difficulties of *El Día*, which was not distinguished by its resistance to military rule, and *El País* arose from the same factors affecting non-media enterprises, and in any event the appeals for assistance were not successful.

Radio There is a well-developed local and national service, with, in 1984, 35 medium and short-wave and four FM stations in the capital and 65 provincial stations. In January 1987 Radio CX40 reported that the Army High Command had called for a tape of a programme criticizing the record of the director of the public TV Channel 5 during the de facto government.

Television There are three private national TV stations and one government channel. In 1983 there were 16 private stations outside the capital. It has been claimed that Carlos Maggi, appointed in April 1985 to head public broadcasting, was forced to resign by pressure from private channels when he tried to introduce a news programme seen as a challenge to them.

Access According to a study carried out by the ratings company Pro-medios, in the three months prior to the November 1989 general elections the ruling Colorado Party received 42 per cent of political news coverage on TV, the centrist Blancos were given 28 per cent, the leftist Broad Front 18 per cent and the centre-left Party of Government for the People 11 per cent.

On December 22 1986, an amnesty law (the Law of Expiration or Law 15.848) ended prosecutions of human rights abuses in the period of de facto government (1973-85). In April 1989, the three private TV channels in Montevideo and the national Red Televisora Color network refused to broadcast messages from campaigners for and against the extension of the amnesty, then the subject of a referendum; it was reported that the messages were regarded as over-emotional. The government prevented a referendum campaign group from having access to the state networks.

In April 1990, TV companies, apparently acting independently of the government, refused an advertisement from the PIT-CNT trade union confederation which satirized the new President, Luis Alberto Lacalle.

Harassment of the Press Since early 1985 there have been no serious violations of press freedom by executive or judiciary. However, there have been disturbing reports, even in 1989, of pressure on the media from government officials via the allocation of state advertising and *de facto* reporting restrictions imposed on TV operators.

At a police funeral in August 1989, seven photographers were harassed and threatened by policemen, who also destroyed their equipment. In two other incidents on the following day police officers allegedly insulted, threatened and beat press photographers.

On November 26, *El Día* was shut down for one day by the Electoral Court for violating a rule against the publication of political information in the days preceding elections. The newspaper has challenged the legality of the action.

Protection of Sources In February 1989, the newspaper *La República* published communiques from an Argentinian guerrilla group. This was condemned by the Education Minister as an "abuse of press freedom". Senior staff of the paper were questioned by police but refused to divulge details of their contact with the group. Most of the press backed *La República*, and the government has not taken any official action against the paper.

In August 1989, a journalist from CX 16 Radio Carve was called in for questioning after broadcasting a statement by police officers demanding better working conditions. Police chiefs justified the interrogation as necessary for maintaining police discipline.

Actions

In its 1989 Commentary to the Human Rights Committee ARTICLE 19 welcomed evidence of the government's determination to restore all democratic freedoms. However, concern was expressed at the 1986 Ley de Caducidad (Law of Expiration), which ended prosecutions of police and soldiers accused of human rights abuses during the de facto government. This could result in "censorship of the past" and a denial to the victims, including journalists, of the right to expose those responsible. It was recommended that the right to seek information should be enshrined in law.

Asia

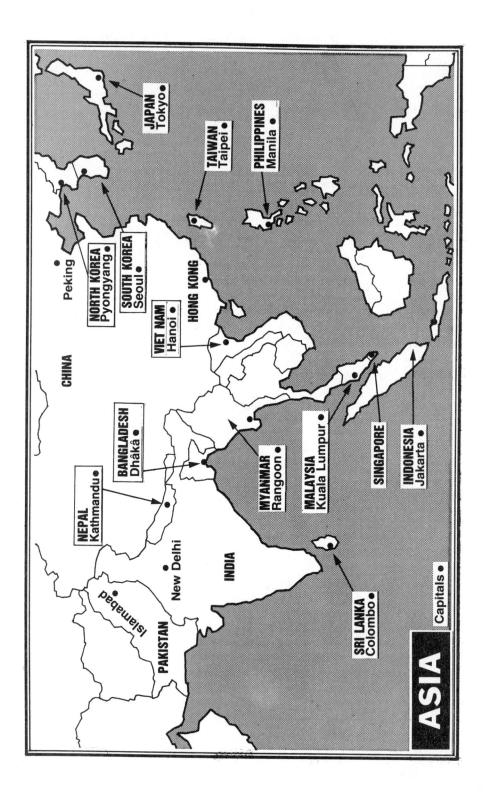

Bangladesh

Bangladesh achieved independence in December 1971 following a bitter war with West Pakistan. The present government, headed by General Hossain Mohammed Ershad, came to power following a coup on March 24 1982 and immediately imposed martial law. Political activities were banned and constitutional rights guaranteeing freedom of expression and freedom from arbitrary arrest and detention were suspended.

Martial law was lifted in November 1986. Parliament adopted the Constitution (Seventh Amendment) Act, known as the Indemnity Bill, which provided for the restoration of some of the fundamental rights guaranteed in the Constitution, but it also legalized those actions taken by the martial law regime since March 1982 including sentences passed by the military courts.

	Data	Year
Population	104,532,000	1988
Life expectancy (M/F)	55.3/54.4	1981
GNP (US$ per capita)	170	1988
Main religion(s)	Islam	
Official language(s)	Bengali	
Illiteracy %	64.7	1990
(M/F)	52.9/78.0	1990
Daily newspapers	59	1987
Non daily newspapers	155	1986
Periodicals	41	1986
Radio sets	4,250,000	1987
TV sets	426,000	1987
Press agencies:		
Bangladesh Sang-bad Sangstha,		
Eastern News Agency		
ICCPR	NO	

A State of Emergency was again imposed on November 27 1987, following widespread demonstrations against army participation in district councils: all political activities and media coverage of opposition parties were banned, and the universities were closed. Thousands of people were detained as opposition activities intensified. On December 6 1987, President Ershad dissolved Parliament after the mass resignation of opposition MPs whose demand that more than 6,000 political prisoners awaiting trial should be released was not met. General elections took place on March 3 1988 and were marked by violence. There were allegations of fraud and vote-rigging which, according to the UK *Daily Telegraph*, was admitted by President Ershad during a visit to London in February 1990. There was growing opposition, led by students, to President Ershad's government towards the end of 1990 and several people were killed during demonstrations. The government's measures to quash the pro-democracy student movement included closing all educational institutions in Dhaka city.

The Constitution

The 1972 Constitution guarantees fundamental rights including freedom of conscience, speech, the press, religious worship and freedom from arbitrary arrest. A range of amendments to the Constitution have curtailed some of these rights including the Second Amendment of 1973, which provided for the declaration of a State of Emergency, suspension of fundamental rights and paved the way for the adoption of the Special Powers Act in 1974. The Fifth Amendment under President

Ziaur Rahman in 1979 legalized all the arbitrary measures taken by the government during the martial law period between 1975 and 1979 and endorsed the promotion of Islamic, rather than secular, ideas.

Special Powers Act Successive governments in Bangladesh have often used the Special Powers Act (SPA) of 1974 which empowers the government to take "measures for the prevention of certain prejudicial activities". It covers any activities "intended to prejudice" the sovereignty, defence or security of the country, its friendly relations with other states, the maintenance of public order, maintenance of supplies and services essential to the community and the economic or financial interests of the state. The Act allows the police and other law enforcing agencies to detain people without charge or trial. Bangladeshi lawyers, opposition groups and international human rights organizations have criticized the act for its broadly formulated definitions that override fundamental constitutional rights. People detained under this Act include writers, journalists and politicians.

The government may consider a news item, book, tape, film or a performance to be a "prejudicial document". Anyone involved in the production, distribution or sale of that document, is liable to punishment of up to five years' imprisonment with or without a fine. Newspapers, periodicals, plays and television series can be banned if they are considered "prejudicial". The Act empowers the government to order pre-censorship of media items; to ban political parties and trade union activities considered "prejudicial to the maintenance of public order", for a period of up to six months; and to confiscate a banned organization's belongings or freeze its assets. No salaries or dues can be paid. The only legal requirement is that the order to ban the organization should be published in the official gazette.

An announcement made on June 8 1989 by the Bangladesh Interior Minister, Major General Mahmudul Hasan, put the total number of political prisoners held without trial under the SPA at 2,157, of which he said 19 people had been in detention for more than three years without trial. In September 1990, the government announced that it would repeal the SPA but no further action had been taken as this report went to press.

The Media

Press Commission In March 1982, the government appointed a press commission to enquire into the state of the press in terms of growth, ownership, management structures, wage and salary patterns and legal provisions affecting freedom of information. A report was submitted in March 1984 with 102 recommendations to the Minister of Information. As of September 1989, this report had not been officially published nor had any measures been taken by the government towards implementing its recommendations.

The report recommends that the provisions in the SPA which affect freedom of the media should be repealed. The commission expressed concern that sections 500, 501 and 502 of the Bangladeshi Penal Code, dealing with libel and defamation, have been used by government officials against journalists who have filed reports critical of them. The maximum penalty under these laws is two years' imprisonment. It is at the discretion of the magistrate who has received a complaint against a journalist whether to summon the accused or issue an arrest warrant and, in most cases, magistrates issue the arrest warrant, thus allowing the police to detain an accused journalist for 24 hours or more until the court is ready to hear the case. The procedure therefore amounts to instant punishment by imprisonment of a journalist who has criticized a government official. The report also calls for a thorough review of the Foreign Relations Act of 1932 and the Foreign Recruiting Act of 1974 whose provisions deter press reports critical of Bangladesh's foreign policy. While the press has a greater degree of freedom than in previous years, newspapers are dependent on government advertising for survival. The press commission recommends that advertising should not be used by the government as a lever to obtain influence and that the government should not own any newspapers.

News Coverage The authorities have frequently banned media coverage of anti-government demonstrations. In October 1987, a new ban was imposed on reporting anti-Ershad protests. No detailed report was printed or broadcast about the arrests of more than 200 opposition leaders after the opposition had announced plans for November demonstrations. Nor did the media carry direct news about two persons who died and the scores who were injured on November 10-11 1987 in Dhaka after police fired at demonstrators demanding the resignation of President Ershad.

The bans led to the closure of dailies, weeklies and periodicals. In February 1987, 18 periodicals were banned for publishing "objectionable, immoral and obscene articles and pictures". A Dhaka-based weekly *Amar Desh* was banned because it alleged government corruption. The leading opposition paper *Banglar Bani*, belonging to members of the Awami League party, was closed because of an article alleging that the government supplied arms to ruling party militias for use against the opposition during the three-day general strike in July 1987.

By February 1988, a total of seven newspapers were unable to operate. The Bengali daily *Khabar* was banned for publishing a map that showed Bangladesh as part of India. The authorities closed down the weekly *Jai Jatra* for "printing objectionable reports". Among other weeklies banned was *Bichinta* whose editor, Minar Mahmud, was released on bail after two and a half months in detention.

The Communist Party of Bangladesh's weekly *Ekota* was only allowed to resume publication after it had been closed for over 10 months. In April 1988, the ban on *Khabar* was also lifted. The Information Minister said the decision reflected President Ershad's respect for the freedom of the press.

The weekly *Robbar* was banned on June 16 1988 for the second time in six months, because it published a commentary, entitled "Dhaka siege", criticizing the government's alleged policy of appointing armed forces personnel to civilian posts. A case was filed under the SPA against *Robbar*'s publisher and printer Saju Hossain, its editor Abdul Hafiz, its acting editor Rafiq Azad and its assistant editor Tapash Majumder.

The daily *Inquilab* was banned in September 1988 because it had published "objectionable" reports. The paper had said that some honest officials, who in the past detected gold smuggling worth millions of dollars, were being phased out by corrupt bureaucrats. Arrest warrants were issued against the editor, the general editor and the publisher of the daily as the state minister for finance filed a defamation suit against the newspaper under the Penal Code.

Fewer newspapers were banned in 1989, due to the fact that bans imposed in previous years remained largely in force throughout 1989. In September, however, the government banned the Bengali weekly *Ashe Din Jai* for printing a satirical piece about the Islamic party, Jamaat-e-Islami. The ban, under the SPA, was imposed after the party attacked the article for ridiculing Islam.

Arrests Although fewer papers were closed in 1989 than in previous years, editors and journalists continued to be detained under the SPA. In April 1989, B M Mahbubul Islam, executive editor of *Dainik Purabi* and general secretary of the Jessore Union of Journalists, was arrested and assaulted by police. He was told a case had been filed against him by the paper's management, but the Bangladesh Federal Union of Journalists believed Islam's arrest was due to his exercise of the right to freedom of information which clashed with government policies.

On June 29 1989, A Q M Zainul Abedin, editor of the daily *Shakti* and general secretary of the Bangladesh Editor's Council, was detained for one night while a case was registered against him on charges of defamation. Prominent journalists condemned his detention saying it was retaliation for Abedin's criticism of the government. An arrest warrant against four journalists, Faruque Ahmed, Zahed Chowdhury, Humayun Kabir Bulbul and Mahbubul Alam, was issued by the Rajshahi city magistrate in July 1989 for their "unauthorized" launch of the newspaper *Jogajog*.

Newsprint The government also brings pressure to bear on recalcitrant publishers through the issue of permits for the procurement of newsprint. Papers may lose their quota of newsprint if they displease the authorities. There is also a practice of telephone calls to editors from officials about items the government may not wish to see in print.

Radio and Television In Bangladesh, one of the poorest countries in the world, where nearly 65 per cent of the people are illiterate, radio and TV inevitably play a significant role. However, both radio and TV are owned and strictly controlled by the government.

Protests The government's actions against the media have been condemned by Bangladesh opposition parties, professional bodies, media associations and international organizations. In November 1987, all newspapers in the country published a four inch blank space on the front page in protest against restrictions on news reporting and increased printing costs. At a protest rally held by the Bangladesh Federal Union of Journalists on June 25 1988, the participants demanded withdrawal of the ban on *Robbar* and *Banglar Bani*, an end to the government harassment of *Inquilab* and the repeal of all legislation that was being used against journalists.

The government invoked the SPA to impose bans on a wide range of subjects. In early September 1988, journalists in Bangladesh criticized the government for effectively curbing free reporting of the flood. This followed a clampdown on newspaper reports of deaths from starvation and cholera, and the coverage of statements by opposition parties accusing the government of corruption and mismanagement. Rallies and protests against bans on news coverage continued throughout 1989. According to press reports, the Prime Minister, who is also in charge of the Ministry of Information, gave assurances that the problems facing journalists, including wage increases and other benefits, would be solved. In response, the union leaders agreed to postpone their planned one-day strike which was due to be held on August 23.

Chittagong Hill Tracts There is a tacit ban on the reporting of operations carried out by the security forces in the Chittagong Hill Tracts and when such reports are published or broadcast they tend to reflect only the government's view. Following the assassination of a local Bengali politician by unknown assassins in Langadu on May 4 1989, settlers attacked the tribal villages in the area, killing over 30 men, women and children and burning hundreds of tribal homes. This incident did not receive any media coverage for several days.

The media, on the other hand, is under pressure to give full coverage to the operations of the Shanti Bahini, a tribal insurgent group. This has created an imbalance in the reporting of events in the Chittagong Hill Tracts and correspondents have found themselves targets of government pressure and of death threats from the Shanti Bahini. The editor of the weekly *Parbatya Barta*, Abdur Rashid, who was assassinated in June 1989, was one of five journalists to receive warnings from the Shanti Bahini not to publish reports critical of them. Abdur Rashid was thought to have been pressurized by the government to adopt a harsher line against the insurgent group.

Foreign Media Under the State of Emergency imposed in November 1987, media reporting of Bangladesh was limited to news releases issued by the government enabling it to exercise strict control over the domestic media. During the year, the authorities attempted to impose restrictions on the foreign media also. In April, the magazine *India Today* was banned from sale and distribution in Bangladesh for publishing "objectionable articles" alleging that the Chakmas in the Chittagong Hill Tracts were persecuted by the Bangladeshi army. In the same month, two more Indian newspapers, *The Telegraph* and *Anand Bazaar Patrika*, were banned under the provisions of the SPA. A month earlier, the Calcutta-based *Weekly Sunday* had been banned for publishing "objectionable articles".

Ataus Samad, the BBC's Dhaka stringer, was arrested on November 12 1987 under the SPA and detained for 16 days. No formal charges were made against him. On December 1 1987, the authorities protested strongly against a BBC report that the US ambassador had advised President Ershad to punish those who killed Bangladesh's first president, Sheikh Mujibur Rahman, in 1975. Such a move would have involved a right-wing Freedom Party leader, Lieutenant-Colonel Sayed Farook Rahman, who had publicly claimed responsibility for the assassination but was protected by a constitutional amendment in 1976 which exonerated him. Both the government and the US embassy denied that any meeting had taken place. On December 11 1987, the government shut down the BBC's operations and its correspondent Phil Jones had his passport confiscated. It was returned an hour later with a stamp saying that he had to leave the country that day. Following a meeting between the then Information Minister, Mahbubur Rahman, and the BBC's Head of Eastern Service, William Crawley, the government lifted the ban on the BBC in May 1988.

In late December 1987, the government refused entry to Robin Pauley, Asia editor of the UK daily, *Financial Times*. He was believed to be the first foreign journalist to be refused entry to the country while in possession of a full entry visa. No reason was given for the move.

Violence erupted in Dhaka when a crowd of about 10,000 people, calling for the execution of the author Salman Rushdie, clashed with the police in March 1989. Later, copies of the April 3 issue of *Newsweek* were seized by the government and the magazine's entry into Bangladesh or its publication there were banned because, according to Interior Ministry officials, a depiction of the prophet Mohammed had appeared in the issue.

Actions

On April 24 1989 ARTICLE 19 wrote to the government calling for the release of Saiful Islam Dildar, chief executive of the Institute of Rural Journalism and a human rights activist, who was arrested on March 31 under the Special Powers Act.

China

Freedom of expression, assembly, association and demonstration are enshrined in the 1982 Constitution of the People's Republic of China, but other provisions can be read as contradicting these rights. According to Article 51, "the exercise of citizens of the People's Republic of China of their freedoms and rights ... may not infringe upon the interests of the state, of society, and of the collective, or upon the lawful freedoms and rights of other citizens". Furthermore, "it is the duty of citizens to safeguard the security, honour, and interests of the motherland; they must not commit acts detrimental to ... the motherland" (Art.54). Other constitutional provisions limiting rights and freedoms include protection of the citizens from libel, insult and false charge (Art.38). Moreover, "citizens must ... keep state secrets, protect public property, observe labour discipline and public order, and respect social ethics" (Art.53).

	Data	Year
Population	1,096,140,000	1988
Life expectancy (M/F)	66.7/68.9	1985
GNP (US$ per capita)	330	1988
Main religion(s)	Confucianism	
	Buddhism	
	Taoism	
Official language(s)	Mandarin	
Illiteracy %	26.7	1990
(M/F)	15.9/38.2	1990
Daily newspapers	73	1986
Non daily newspapers	224	1982
Periodicals	5,687	1988
Radio sets	200,000,000	1987
TV sets	18,000,000	1987
Press agencies:		
Xinhua, Zhongguo Xinwen She		
ICCPR	NO	

The Constitution was invoked to justify both the bid for democracy and its brutal suppression by the government in 1989. The series of demonstrations that culminated in the occupation of Tiananmen Square began in April with the death of Hu Yaobang, former General Secretary, ousted in 1987 for his opposition to the more orthodox elements in the Central Committee. On April 26 1989, an editorial in the Chinese Communist Party (CCP) paper, *Renmin Ribao*, forbidding further demonstrations and making accusations of an "organized conspiracy to sow chaos" orchestrated by "people with ulterior motives", prompted tens of thousands of students, supported by workers, to step up demonstrations, quoting Article 35 of the Constitution which guarantees the right to demonstrate. A hunger strike in Tiananmen Square followed, generating unprecedented support from the media amongst other groups, and led to the declaration of martial law on May 20. Dramatic confrontations with troops, repelled by makeshift barricades, led to a final assault on the night of June 3-4 in which soldiers, armed with assault rifles, supported by tanks and armoured personnel carriers, dispersed the crowds in the Square and the surrounding areas of Beijing. Amnesty International reported that at least 1,000 were killed and thousands more were injured. There followed disappearances, arrests, televised trials, heavy sentences and executions.

Article 35 of the current Constitution promises "freedom of speech, of the press, of assembly, and of association". The inviolability of person (Art.37), home (Art.39) and even of mail (Art.40) receive similar constitutional protection. But Article 51 was the constitutional basis for the new 1989 laws on demonstrations. This law, passed after the suppression of the democracy movement under martial law, forbade all unsanctioned demonstrations and placed Tiananmen Square off limits. The Constitution also empowers the National People's Congress (NPC) and, under certain conditions, the State Council, to use the military to enforce the law. This provision was first used in Lhasa, Tibet, in March 1989 and then in Beijing in May.

Criminal Codes The Criminal Code and Criminal Procedure Law of 1980 defines the crime of counter-revolution as including agitation to break laws, decrees, or orders, and/or simply publishing pamphlets or using slogans deemed to "advocate the overthrow of the proletarian dictatorship or the socialist system." This broad category of offences can lead to sentences of less than five years' imprisonment or, "in aggravated cases", more than five years, a life term, or even the death sentence. A distinction is made between counter-revolutionary agitation and counter-revolutionary activities in the statute, but, in practice, this distinction is not always observed. The counter-revolution statute was the basis for warrants issued against dissident astrophysicist Fang Lizhi, his wife and 21 student leaders in the wake of the 1989 Spring Democracy Movement.

Other Legal Instruments 1989 saw the widespread use of libel charges by local officials against both investigative reporters and writers, as in the case of Tang Min. Two Shanghai writers were disciplined for writing a book called *Sexual Customs* which offended Muslims. The book was pulped, and the authors were deemed guilty of "undermining the unity of nationalities".

There is virtually no independent legal profession (a few independent lawyers are now available, principally for overseas clients, in the major cities). The practice of "sentencing before trial" (*xian pan hou shen*) is common; verdicts in important cases are referred to party cells within the legal system before trial. There is no assumption of innocence before conviction. Some judicial authorities have a legal provision that a lawyer wishing to present a not guilty plea requires prior permission of the local party organization. The Chinese legal press reported the case of two lawyers imprisoned for six months for aiding and abetting a client to enter a not guilty plea and for appealing against the subsequent guilty verdict. There is even a provision for "re-education through labour" (*laodong jiaoyang*); incarceration without trial for up to three years for "counter-revolutionary elements and anti-party/anti-socialist elements whose crimes are minor and do not warrant criminal ... sanction, and also those who incite disturbances and disrupt social order".

The Media

Newspapers fall into four categories, depending on their ownership. First, there are party papers; these include national papers like *Renmin Ribao* and *Guangming Ribao* and at the other end of the scale a few papers put out by county committees (approximately 100 out of a total of 2,000 counties nationwide). Second are the governmental papers, including ministerial organs like *Keji Ribao* and *Jiaoyu Bao*. Third are newspapers run by the various organizations set up by the party for non-party individuals in certain sectors: women, youth, trade unions, and intellectuals. The final category is those papers run by the People's Liberation Army (PLA), including their national daily *Jiefang Junbao*, as well as those run by the military regions which have a restricted circulation. In addition to the official papers, almost every work unit of any size keeps a "wall newspaper", generally on a chalkboard. The content may be decided by the local party committee or the Communist Youth League, or it may simply be copied from the printed dailies. Hygiene, courtesy, and birth control are common topics.

Restrictions on Journalists In March 1989, two British journalists were expelled from Lhasa, Tibet (throughout the Cultural Revolution only two foreign journalists were expelled from China) and in May 1989, foreign journalists were handed guidelines which would have severely handicapped any who observed them. Most did not, and several were beaten and expelled as a result. Even more restrictive "points for attention" directed at journalists from Hong Kong and Macao were released by the State Council on October 27 1989; these demanded that all journalistic activities receive prior clearance from the State Council and that applications for such clearance include precise timetables; they also forbade telephone interviews and the setting up of bureaux inside China. In February 1990, 100 foreign correspondents in Beijing complained about these conditions and constant police harassment; in March, the Ministry of Foreign Affairs construed the complaint as a "smokescreen" for illegal actions.

Media Limitations To manage day-to-day affairs, the CCP maintains "party cells" in all administrative organs of any importance, which includes the media and broadcasting. Important censorship issues are decided by these "party cells" or their "party working groups", which include the top directors of the media. This system has eliminated the necessity for a formal censorship body. To publish anything in China it is necessary to obtain a publishing permit from the level of government concerned, whether national, provincial, or local. The publication must also be registered with the Department of Press, the *Xinwen Bu*. Although local and even provincial government protection can often be bought, the State Council occasionally orders campaigns against "illegal publications" and "re-registrations".

In the campaign against "bourgeois liberalization" of 1987, more than 3,000 people were arrested, and 16 million books, 4.7 million periodicals, 6.5 million newspapers, 1.1 million tapes and 18 million videos were confiscated (according to the *Zhongguo Baike* of 1988); 5,314 periodicals (out of a total of 5,687) were investigated and 594, or 11 per cent, were shut down. The current purge is even more far-reaching.

An interesting footnote to the 1987 campaign surfaced in the July 1989 issue of *Xinwen Jizhe*, intended as an indirect comment on the renewed banning efforts of the government. A government survey was conducted among 1,380 university students to try to ascertain the effectiveness, if any, of the 1987 crackdown. Significantly, the results of the survey were not released, but its general conclusions were: "The old style of propaganda and the new communciation environment would appear to be in sharp contradiction. The continuation of the old policies and directions in propaganda can only bring about a fundamental injury to the prestige of the media and a serious crisis of confidence."

On April 24 1989, the then Shanghai First Secretary, Jiang Zemin, impounded an issue of the *Shijie Jingji Daobao* deemed to be too laudatory of the late Hu Yaobang and the student movement. The August 1989 issue of *Xinwenzhe* reports an incident in the city of Wuwei in Gansu province in which a representative to the Municipal People's Congress made a speech criticizing the municipal authorities and was quoted in *Wuwei Bao*, the local newspaper. The relevant city authorities seized and destroyed all remaining copies of the paper on newsstands throughout the city.

In the purge which occurred in late 1989, under the slogans "sweep out yellow literature" (the Chinese term for pornography) and "combat bourgeois liberalization", large numbers of books by intellectuals involved in the democracy movement were pulped or burned, including Liu Binyan's *Stories of Chinese Who Do Not Tell Lies*, Bo Yang's *The Ugly Chinese*, and the script for the popular TV series *He Shang* (*The River Elegy*). Other *jinshu* (proscribed works) include those by the former head of the Marxism-Leninism Institute, Su Shaozhi, history books by Yan Jiaqi and Su Xiaokang, plays by Wu Zuguang, reportage by former *Guangming Ribao* star reporter Dai Qing, poetry by Bei Dao, and large quantities of pornography and erotica. According to a report in the November 15 1989 issue of *Xinwen Chuban Gao*, more than 30 million books and 400,000 audio and videotapes had been "sealed" (closed with paper seals until the authorities decide whether or how to dispose of them or until the political climate changes again).

Newsprint There was a severe lack of newsprint in China between 1988 and 1990. This was not, as is the case in many other countries, a censorship measure on the part of the government. The new economic policies made paper mills responsible for their gains and losses, and mills soon calculated that there were more gains to be made in selling newsprint to private fiction and romance publishers than to the government. First to be affected were textbooks, with many schools unable to open because of a lack of books. By mid-1988, even the major party papers were forced to import newsprint to continue publishing and there was serious talk of them closing down or cutting the number of pages.

Magazines Many of the best selling "literary" magazines have rather sensational contents based on crime, sex or kung-fu adventures, but others specialize in *baogao wenxue* (a kind of investigative reporting). Recent and successful *baogao wenxue* have spotlighted tobacco smuggling between provinces, bureaucratic incompetence which led to the disastrous forest fire at Daxi'anling in the Northeast in 1988 and prostitution. Another popular form of magazine, still widely on sale in China, specializes in contemporary history, particularly the Cultural Revolution, the Anti-Rightist Campaign of the 1950s, and party abuse of power in other periods. One of the best of these magazines, *Hainan Shiji*, was forced to close in September 1989 with a terse editorial announcement that "magazines like ours have grown too numerous" as the only explanation. After the democracy movement, a large number of magazines devoted to the "crushing of the counter-revolutionary rebellion" were produced, featuring extremely detailed descriptions of events which kept just within the official version, and ended with an affirmation of the authorities' actions.

Dazibaos Wall posters or *dazibaos*, written in big, bold characters, are a traditional form of airing public grievances. After the right to put up *dazibaos* was removed from the Constitution on Deng Xiao Ping's initiative in 1980, Article 45 of the Criminal Code made it illegal to put them up, although the government continued to do so. To circumvent the prohibition, students began to write posters with smaller characters, called *xiaozibaos*. *Dazibaos* can be extremely short, (many after the June 4 1989 events consisted of the single character "sorrow"), or they may contain a whole political treatise. During the democracy movement, many early posters had a poetic quality, but others were written in direct response to speeches by major leaders, often within hours, answering them point by point. Posters, copied by hand or sometimes read aloud onto cassette tape, played a very important role in the 1986-87 student movement and an even more important one in 1989, disseminating news and rumours, issuing strike orders, announcing demonstrations, and engaging in polemics with the authorities and with each other.

Another favoured tactic was the pasting of rhyming eight or twelve character couplets in imitation of the New Year's couplets which peasants hang on their doors. After the death of Hu Yaobang, a popular couplet ran: "Some who have died should not have; some who have not died should". During martial law in 1989, another couplet in Tiananmen Square read "If Li Peng won't step down, we'll stick around; if he won't go away, we'll come every day." After the June 4 massacre: "Blood debts are to be paid in blood".

Photocopying and Fax Machines Photocopying machines are now widely available in China, many privately run. Shortly after the killings in Beijing, reports from Hong Kong newspapers, including graphic photographs, were photocopied and pasted up all over Guangzhou, Chengdu, Shanghai and many other towns. One person was arrested and sentenced to prison for putting up a photocopy in his office in Chengdu; another Hong Kong man was arrested and subsequently expelled for putting up photocopies in Shaoguan city, Guangdong.

Several Hong Kong newspapers, including the *Hong Kong Standard*, published special articles in Chinese to be faxed into the mainland in order to circumvent the news blackout. In October 1989, the Front for a Democratic China, an exile organization based in Paris which includes many former employees of *Renmin Ribao*, began to fax their own commentaries into the People's Republic, using a format similar to that of *Renmin Ribao*, who, in turn, accused the exiles of "stealing" their masthead.

Radio All radio broadcasting in China, which in 1985 reached an estimated 68 per cent of the population, is under the auspices of the Central Television, Radio and Film Administration or under a local branch of government, with the exception of *Haixia Zhi Sheng* (The Voice of the Taiwan Straits, formerly Radio Fujian Frontline) which broadcasts to Taiwan under the control of the PLA.

Many of the more local broadcasting units are in fact converted jamming stations, such as Yangzhou Broadcasting Service in Jiangsu Province. China ceased jamming foreign shortwave broadcasts in the early 1980s, but resumed, despite foreign protests, after May 22 1989, with particular attention to Voice Of America (VOA) and the BBC. The VOA continued broadcasting on medium wave from Taiwan. News broadcasts from both sources and especially from Radio Television Hong Kong were very important in the democracy movement and the content of the news bulletins were often recorded by student activists for replay over campus loudspeakers, or at the sites of sit-ins.

In the spring of 1989, broadcasting was affected by the divisions in the party which resulted in the dramatic but short-lived week of press freedom between May 12-19. The English Service of Radio Beijing carried remarkable live coverage of the hunger strike from Tiananmen Square. This ended on June 4, when a Radio Beijing broadcaster denounced the military action of the previous night as "barbaric suppression of the people" and reported that thousands of people had died, including many of his colleagues. (The broadcast was interrupted and it is believed that the broadcaster was shot.)

Radio has continued to assist the democracy movement in exile. In late March 1990, a ship, "The Goddess of Democracy", chartered by supporters of the democracy movement, embarked from the French port of La Rochelle to begin pirate radio broadcasts to China from the high seas, but the ship was not allowed to load its transmitter in Taiwan.

Television China boasts over 200 million TV sets and it is estimated that over 68 per cent of the population has access to TV. Zhongyang Dianshitai (China Central Television or CCTV) services the whole country and can be picked up virtually anywhere in the People's Republic. Most provinces also have their own TV studios and stations, as do large cities and virtually every provincial capital.

Although more centrally controlled than other media, TV was equally affected by the split which divided Chinese society in the spring of 1989. CCTV staff members not only participated in demonstrations, but filmed their own contingent and broadcast it on the evening news. When Premier Li Peng finally agreed to hold a brief "meeting" with student representatives on May 18, CCTV tried unsuccessfully to broadcast their own tapes of the proceedings. They eventually acquired an amateur videotape and this was repeatedly broadcast, including a shot in which a student, Wu'erkaixi, collapsed and had to be revived by doctors with oxygen while Li Peng apparently looked idly in another direction.

The declaration of martial law, on May 20 1989, was read with evident disapproval by a newsreader who refused to meet the camera's eye, and news of the "glorious victory in crushing the counter-revolutionary rebellion" on June 4 was read by sombre, black-clad newsreaders speaking in hushed voices which flatly contradicted the tenor of the message. Even in the days of harsh news blackout, CCTV, like the newspapers, adopted the practice of using foreign items to provide an indirect comment on events. On June 5, they broadcast an old story from the archives in which the Israeli Prime Minister admitted that it was impossible to crush the (Palestinian) uprising by force.

Freedom of Expression and the Democracy Movement of Spring 1989

Between 1988 and 1989, price and enterprise reforms created dramatic inflation in the economy, bureaucratic speculation and corruption. Unproductive profiteering and the formidable social pressures this created all over the country generated a mass movement which, from April to June 1989, united students, intellectuals and workers, and carried the demand for freedom of expression high on its banner.

The demand was raised in a petition on the day of the funeral of Hu Yaobang on April 22 1989. Spontaneous mourning for Hu was coupled with the demand for a full explanation of his abrupt dismissal in 1987. Student indignation at the complete lack of attention to their demands by the media and the state led to the formation of the first autonomous student organization in Beijing on April 20. On April 24, Shanghai's *Shijie Jingji Daobao* published a special issue on Hu Yaobang and the student protests, only to have it seized by municipal authorities although the paper was not formally under party or even government jurisdiction. Then, on April 26, a strong condemnation of the protests as "a premeditated, planned conspiracy to stir up political turmoil by a small handful of people" appeared as an editorial in *Renmin Ribao*.

Student leaders, well aware of the use of counter-revolution statutes to supress dissent, saw the editorial as an attempt by the government to discredit the protest. They were not alone; a million Beijing citizens came out on a 14 hour march, the largest since Liberation. Party Secretary Zhao Ziyang argued inside the Politburo for the retraction of the editorial and said he would take responsibility for its printing. Externally, Zhao's speeches were conciliatory and on May 4 he said that the students' aims were quite consistent with those of the party. However, no retraction was published.

On May 9, nearly 1,000 well-known journalists and media personalities presented a petition to the National Association of Journalists, asking for discussion on the seizure of *Shijie Jingji Daobao*, greater press freedom, and an increase in the authority of editors with respect to party secretaries. These demands were taken up by the student movement. On May 13, shortly before Tiananmen Square was to be closed off in preparation for the arrival of Soviet Premier Mikhail Gorbachev, students began their hunger strike, hoping for fair coverage from at least the foreign correspondents arriving to cover the state visit.

During his discussions with Gorbachev on May 16, Zhao Ziyang hinted that it was Deng Xiaoping who remained adamant about the banning of the protest demonstrations following the April 26 *Renmin Ribao* editorial, when he said that all major matters of policy had to be discussed with Deng Xiaoping, although Deng was not actually a member of the Politburo. Three days later, Li Peng and several other cadres finally met with the hunger strikers. Li Peng, however, refused to discuss retraction of the editorial. Although students called off the hunger strike to prevent "unnecessary sacrifices", "martial law" was declared two days later.

The attempt to impose "martial law" without bloodshed was a spectacular failure. Papers such as *Keji Bao* and *Zhongguo Funu Bao* began to report the demonstrations sympathetically and even the major party papers defied the ban by publishing pictures. Other less direct acts of defiance included the significant inclusion of foreign stories. Shortly after the declaration of "martial law" the May 20 issue of *Renmin Ribao* featured a prominent quotation by the late premier of Hungary, Imre Nagy: "No matter what disturbances and turmoil face Hungary, the army may not be used to resolve internal problems."

When the army was brought in, one of its first tasks was to occupy the TV stations and then the offices of the major papers. A virtual blackout was followed by a trickle of selective disinformation, and these were enforced with outright bans and purges. More than 1,000 media workers at *Renmin Ribao* took part in the demonstrations, and 1,500 have since been purged; the ruthless purge of the paper's staff became a "model" for all other media. According to the Hong Kong Journalists' Association, many journalists openly defied the ban in going to Tiananmen Square as late as June 4, and some did not return. *Jingjixue Zhoubao* was closed down permanently for sympathetic reporting of the protests and *Xin Guancha* was shut for similar reasons, and its editor Ge Yang forced into exile. *Shekou Tongxun* sent a large sum of money to the Beijing hunger-strikers and it has been shut ever since.

Lin Zixing, the former editor of *Keji Ribao*, has been replaced; his paper was the very first to sympathetically report student demonstrations following the death of

Hu Yaobang. During the hunger strike, *Beijing Qingnian Bao* published the results of a survey which demonstrated that the vast majority of citizens were in sympathy with the student movement; it was severely criticized and many staff lost their jobs. Replacements have also been found for the general editors of *Guangming Ribao*, *Renmin Ribao* and *Hainan Ribao*. Many journalists have simply disappeared, including Gao Yu, editor of *Jingjixue Zhoubao*, who was arrested despite having been in hospital during the whole of the democracy movement.

Fang Lizhi and his wife, Li Shuxian, who had sought refuge for 13 months in the US Embassy in Beijing, were permitted to travel to the UK in late June 1990. However, there is evidence that the repression is continuing, with an Asia Watch report published in September 1990 listing more than 1,000 people still under arrest for their political or religious activities. Many arrests took place in May and June during the anniversary of the 1989 protests. In addition, more than 500 people were executed in the first eight months of 1990 as part of a "crackdown on crime"; more than 40 offences carry the death penalty.

Actions

On May 4 1989 ARTICLE 19 wrote to the government protesting the dismissal of Qin Benli, editor-in-chief of the Shanghai-based *Shijie Jingji Daobao*, the banning of the most recent issue and its distribution with an "offending" article removed.

On June 1 1989 ARTICLE 19 wrote to the government expressing concern at reports that the daily *Renmin Ribao* has to submit the final page proofs to the government for approval.

On June 7 1989 ARTICLE 19 wrote to the government protesting attacks by the army on pro-democracy demonstrators, and reiterating its protest regarding the *Shijie Jingji Daobao*.

On June 12 1989 ARTICLE 19 wrote to the government protesting the treatment by the Chinese police of a BBC film crew which was assaulted, had its equipment smashed and its videotape confiscated.

On July 7 1989 ARTICLE 19 wrote to the government calling for the release of Taiwanese journalist Huang Debei of the *Independent Evening Post* who was arrested after meeting a student leader of the recent demonstrations.

On July 12 1989 ARTICLE 19 wrote to the government protesting the killing of demonstrators, arrests and dismissal of prominent editors, and requesting that all peaceful protestors be released, journalists be reinstated, and impartial accounts of recent events be made available.

On July 18 1989 ARTICLE 19 wrote to the government protesting the dismissal of Li Zisong, editor of *Wen Wei Po*, and the banning of all foreign newspapers from stores in Beijing.

In August 1989 ARTICLE 19 published a censorship report on China, *The Year Of The Lie: Censorship And Disinformation In The People's Republic of China*, providing a detailed account of the democracy movement and focusing on the withholding of information by the Chinese authorities. In the same month an appeal letter was sent to ARTICLE 19 members urging them to protest to the Chinese government.

In May 1990 ARTICLE 19 launched an appeal on behalf of 12 people, including Tang Min, who were victimized for exercising their right to freedom of expression. Four of them, Bao Tong, Cao Siyuan, Dai Qing and Li Honglin, have been released.

Hong Kong

Hong Kong, a United Kingdom "crown territory" which has no political parties and no representative government has, after Japan, the highest newspaper readership in Asia. Prior to 1988 and 1989, years which saw the rapid politicization of the Hong Kong population, the emphasis was largely on financial reporting. Hong Kong is one of the great banking hubs of the world, Asia's leading financial centre after Tokyo, with a trade volume three times the size of its GDP.

Until 1997, power in Hong Kong is vested in the Governor appointed by the UK. He is advised by an Executive Council, and there is also a Legislative Council (Legco). All of these institu-

	Data	Year
Population	5,681,000	1988
Life expectancy (M/F)	73.8/79.1	1985
GNP (US$ per capita)	9,230	1988
Main religion(s)	Buddhism	
Official language(s)	English	
	Chinese	
Illiteracy %	12.0	1985
Newspapers	67	1989
Periodicals	495	1984
Radio sets	3,550,000	1987
TV sets	1,350,000	1987
Press agencies:		
International News Service		
ICCPR: Bound by UK until 1997		

tions will be subject to change in the period to 1997. The judicial system is based on British Common Law.

In 1997, the People's Republic of China will resume sovereignty over Hong Kong which then will become a "Special Administrative Region" with its own executive, legislative and independent judicial power. China has undertaken to protect "the current social and economic systems in Hong Kong ... and the life-style". A similar guarantee concerning "rights and freedoms of person, travel, movement, correspondence, strike, choice of occupation, academic research and religious belief" was undertaken. An annex to the Sino British Joint Declaration of 1984 declares that the provisions of the International Covenant on Civil and Political Rights and the International Covenant on Economic, Social and Cultural Rights "shall remain in force." Recent events on the mainland, however, have cast a long shadow over these undertakings. The committment to uphold the UN covenants can have little meaning in any event since China has not ratified them.

The Joint Liaison Group

The Joint Liaison Group, charged with overseeing the implementation of the Joint Declaration, has been paralysed with acrimony since the crushing of the democracy movement in June 1989, although talks did finally resume in the following December. Two Hong Kong members were expelled in October 1989 from the "Basic Law" drafting committee for "activities incompatible with membership", that is, activities in support of the Chinese democracy movement. Two Hong Kong magazines, *The Contemporary* and *Pai Shing*, were excluded from covering "Basic Law" meetings in China.

Freedom of Expression Issues

The Hong Kong government has the power to enact restrictions on free expression, and has felt free to do so. In March 1987, it was made an offence, punishable by a HK$100,000 (US$12,800) fine or imprisonment for two years, to "publish false news which is likely to cause alarm to the public". After strong protests from the media, this was repealed in 1989. A Film Censorship Ordinance was enacted in 1988, in an attempt to legitimise what, unknown to the public, had been a standard practice, the banning or cutting of films deemed incompatible with public morals, racist, or (of particular importance) likely to damage good relations with neighbouring countries. Of the 20 films estimated by the *Asian Wall Street Journal* to have been banned on political grounds between 1973 and 1987, 11 had China as the subject. The censorship guidelines under which the Authority acts includes an injunction to "consider" Article 19 of the International Covenant on Civil and Political Rights (which guarantees free expression). However, the International Covenant does not allow limitation of expression on the grounds that a film is likely to "seriously damage good relations with other territories". The Film Censorship Authority is advised by 140 members of the public, who are intended to provide a representative sampling of views on public morals.

The Basic Law The Basic Law was adopted in April 1990 by China's National People's Congress as the "mini-constitution" for 1997. It guarantees free expression, a free press, and states that the provisions of the International Covenants will "remain in force", even though they do not have legal force at present. A draft Bill of Rights based on the Civil and Political Covenant was published in 1990 with the expectation that Legco would enact it by the end of that year. Such legal guarantees might have been reassuring but for the fact that 1989 saw the most violent and gross abuse of the rights to free expression, free press, and free assembly enshrined in the full-sized constitution of the People's Republic, using the constitutional provision for martial law (see People's Republic of China). For this reason, some Hong Kong leaders have unsuccessfully sought assurances that the People's Republic would not station units of the People's Liberation Army in Hong Kong. The mainland response has been that under the Joint Agreement they have the right to station troops, and they intend to exercise it.

The Chinese government does not permit dual nationality. It therefore does not recognize citizens of Hong Kong as British subjects, and while on Chinese territory they are treated as Chinese citizens; thus it is possible that Hong Kong citizens who supported the democracy movement may be charged with counter-revolutionary crimes when the territory reverts to Chinese sovereignty. In the aftermath of the severe repression on the mainland, pressure was brought to bear on the British government to offer some form of refuge to the people of Hong Kong (other than its immediate circle of civil servants) should similar events befall the territory after 1997. In May 1990, a Bill granting such refuge to 50,000 Hong Kong business and government personnel was accepted by a majority of the British House of Commons.

The Media

The Television Ordinance, though seldom used, permits the prior censorship and banning of programmes and the revocation of TV licences in cases of "emergency". There have been calls for the removal, prior to 1997, of these and other restrictions on radio and TV which have been on the statute books for many years. Observers in Hong Kong have expressed concern at the growing trend of self-censorship in the media in anticipation of 1997.

Newspapers There are 67 newspapers registered with the Company Registry and the Newspaper Registration Unit, the bulk in Chinese. The Hong Kong Journalists' Association, which unites some 400 local journalists, recently produced a volume on the Chinese democracy movement, in which many of its members took part. Hong Kong also has three management associations: the Newspaper Society of Hong Kong, the Hong Kong Chinese Press Association and the News Executive Association.

Radio Hong Kong has three radio stations and 10 channels; five are operated by the government-run Radio-Television Hong Kong (RTHK), three are run by the Hong Kong Commercial Broadcasting Company, and two by the British Forces Broadcasting Services, the British Army broadcasting network. An estimated 76 per cent of the population over the age of nine listens to the radio. Hong Kong radio, much of which is broadcast in Cantonese, is widely available in China's Guangdong province, where Cantonese is also spoken, and provided a major source of news during the news blackout of May and June 1989.

Television According to government estimates, 96 per cent of Hong Kong households own one or more TV sets. The four available TV stations are operated by two franchised commercial broadcasting firms, TV Broadcasting Ltd (TVB) and Asia TV Ltd (ATV). Each firm has a Chinese channel and an English channel, and in addition RTHK produces about 12 hours a week of programming using the transmission services of the two commercial stations. The successful launch of the communications satellite, Asiaset, in early 1990, has laid the groundwork for an Asia-wide six-channel satellite TV network scheduled for 1991.

Many in Hong Kong can receive the broadcasts of the People's Republic and Teledifusao Macau, the radio and TV broadcasting service of Macau. The latter has created some friction, since Macau has been able to flout censorship guidelines and restrictions on tobacco advertising, at the expense of Hong Kong advertising interests. In September 1988, the government began taking bids to install cable TV in Hong Kong.

Films Hong Kong as a film producing centre is traditionally held in awe for the quantity rather than the quality of its output. Movie moguls such as Jackie Chan preside over film factories pouring out kung-fu adventure stories and sentimental romances; stars such as Chow Yuen-fat boast that they can act in 200 films in three years. In 1988, some 139 films were produced and enthusiastically consumed and Hong Kong's 133 cinemas packed in more than 66 million customers. All films intended for public exhibition must be submitted to a Film Censorship Authority. In December 1989, the Hong Kong Arts Centre attempted to show a documentary film, *Mainland China 1989*, which included some 16 minutes of interviews with the

Chinese dissidents Wu'erkaixi and Fang Lizhi. The authorities banned the film. When it was re-released, the interviews had been cut. The Film Censorship Authority declared the content of the interviews "propagandistic" and liable to offend a neighbouring country.

The Aftermath of Tiananmen Square

In 1989, Hong Kong saw the first mass demonstrations since the Hong Kong General Strike of 1925-26. More than a million people marched on two separate occasions to express solidarity with the democracy movement on the mainland and their horror at its suppression. In addition, some Hong Kong people went to the mainland to contribute to the movement by marching in Guangzhou, making financial contributions, or providing a crucial communications link; a number of Hong Kong citizens were arrested in China, and some, such as Yao Yongzhan, a student at Fudan University in Shanghai who was arrested while being accompanied to an aeroplane by a representative of the British Consulate, were detained until June 1990.

Events on the mainland had repercussions for the Hong Kong media. Two Hong Kong papers with links to the mainland, *Ta Kung Pao* and *Wen Wei Po*, split with the Beijing authorities over the declaration of martial law and the bloody suppression in early June. Their graphic and well-documented coverage was widely available inside China, since both papers are normally distributed there. It was not until July 14 that distribution of the two papers in China was banned. The next day, officials from the Hong Kong branch of *Xinhua*, which acts as China's unofficial embassy in Hong Kong, sacked Li Zisong, the director of *Wen Wei Po*, prompting a mass resignation at the paper. After a similar struggle, *Ta Kung Pao* was also brought in line.

Illegal Immigrants In late September 1989, mainland influence manifested itself in another form. The Chinese student activist, Yang Yang, who was a member of the illegal Autonomous Federation of Qinghua University Students and who had ties to the Chinese Alliance for Democracy, was arrested by the Hong Kong government for overstaying his visa. He had been visiting Hong Kong since before the June events. Normally, all "illegal immigrants" or those guilty of overstaying visas are automatically handed to the Chinese authorities, under an agreement negotiated in 1981. Yang Yang, however, clearly had good reason to fear political persecution if he returned to the mainland. When the Hong Kong government finally allowed Yang Yang to proceed to the United States on October 4, the Chinese government retaliated by refusing to accept "illegal immigrants" for much of the month of October (the Hong Kong border police normally pick up more than 50 such "illegals" a day). The Hong Kong government adviser William Erhman assured the Chinese government that the British government would apply the law to those who broke it which apparently defused the situation.

At an official function on October 1 1989 to celebrate the 40th anniversary of the founding of the People's Republic of China, Hong Kong police arrested a number of counter-demonstrators from the April Fifth Action Group, an organization professing solidarity with the mainland democracy movement. The charges were disorderly conduct, and it was said that they had assaulted police. On October 3, Hong Kong police confiscated several videotapes belonging to ATV and TVB TV studios in Hong Kong of footage of demonstrators clashing with police. The confiscations, which were the target of strong protests, were upheld by the Hong Kong government as legal. The demonstrators, however, were later acquitted.

On July 27 1990, five leading pro-democracy activists were fined HK$188 (US$25) each for using loudhailers in a peaceful demonstration. Ho Chun Yan, Yeung Sum, Wong Pik Wan, Lee Wing Tat and Lau Chin Shek are all senior members of the United Democrats of Hong Kong (UDHK) and in February took part in a lawful and peaceful protest, which they had helped to organize, against the constitutional proposals contained in the Basic Law. The prosecution was brought against the advice of the police who regarded the offence as trivial; it falls under a virtually defunct ordinance which also bans the shoeing of horses in public. That such prominent democracy campaigners were so selectively targetted for what are trivial offences under a rarely enforced clause, seems an ominous fulfilment of William Erhman's pledge. The five members of the UDHK immediately said they would refuse to pay the fine and were prepared to go to prison, although an appeal was expected which could go to the privy council in London.

Hong Kong Alliance In this light, concern has been expressed that the government has chosen to investigate the Hong Kong Alliance, an organization of Hong Kong citizens which supports the exiled democracy movement. The purpose of the investigation is said to be to see if it should be de-registered as a legal organization.

Actions

In its 1988 Commentary to the Human Rights Committee ARTICLE 19 drew attention to the uncertain status of the ICCPR in domestic law when China resumes sovereignty in 1997. It also expressed concern over the offence of "false news" and the criteria for censoring films which include political considerations.

India

The period under review was an eventful one for India. The Congress Party, which had ruled the country almost without interruption since independence in 1947, lost its parliamentary majority in the general elections in November 1989. A new National Front government assumed office in December with Vishwanath Pratap Singh as Prime Minister.

While the new government promised welcome reforms in the functioning of the mass media, especially radio and television, those reforms have, in large part, not yet been initiated. Restrictions remain in special laws passed in previous years by state and central governments to deal with political and communal violence, and government interference with the media, while reduced under the new administration, has only been thwarted through protest and court actions. The courts, however, were not involved in what rapidly became a world-wide freedom of expression controversy which began in India in 1988 over the publication of the novel *The Satanic Verses*.

	Data	Year
Population	800,000,000	1989
Life expectancy (M/F)	55.6/55.2	1985
GNP (US$ per capita)	330	1988
Main religion(s)	Hinduism	
	Islam	
Official language(s)	Hindi	
	English	
Illiteracy %	51.8	1990
(M/F)	38.2/66.3	1990
Daily newspapers	2,151	1987
Non daily newspapers	&	
Periodicals	22,478	1987
Radio sets	62,000,000	1987
TV sets	17,300,000	1988
Press agencies:		
	Press Trust of India,	
	United News of India	
ICCPR:	YES	1979

Threats to Press Freedom

The Defamation Bill Among the major legislative moves to control the media was an attempt by the central government in July 1988 to introduce far-reaching changes to the criminal law of defamation. The Defamation Bill 1988 sought, *inter alia*, to create a new offence of "criminal imputation", punishable by imprisonment of between three months and two years, coupled with a fine of up to 5,000 rupees (US$300). The Bill, introduced against a backdrop of press exposure of corruption involving prominent members of the Congress Party arising from defence contracts with the Swedish armaments manufacturer Bofors, also proposed to make "scurrilous writings" the subject of criminal sanctions.

The contents of the Bill and the attempts to rush it through parliament elicited strong protests, especially from the press. A highly sucessful one-day nationwide strike by the newspaper industry and increasingly strident protests finally forced the then Prime Minister Rajiv Gandhi to withdraw the Bill in September.

Press Registration Bill The Press and Registration of Books (Amendment) Bill 1988, introduced in parliament on December 5, met with a similar fate. The Bill sought, among other things, to broaden the range and volume of information that the

Registrar of Newspapers could seek from the press: elaborate employment statistics, financial data such as the amount of capital invested and the production capacity of the machinery used, the volume of advertisments published and the monetary value thereof, and "such other techno-economic information about printing and other particulars as may be prescribed". The Bill also sought to confer extensive powers on district magistrates to enter newspapers' premises, copy documents and records and ask investigative questions. Professional and trade opposition was so strong that the government was compelled to withdraw the Bill within weeks of its introduction.

Government Pressure Between 1988 and 1990 there was an intensification of government pressure on newspapers critical of the ruling party and its leaders. The *Indian Express* was a prime target following publication of a series of investigative articles on corrupt defence deals involving Rajiv Gandhi and his associates. As well as launching some 200 prosecutions against the paper and its executives for alleged violation of various economic and tax laws, Gandhi's administration, through the Company Law Board, ordered a wide-ranging investigation into the affairs of the newspaper group. This move was promptly stayed by the Bombay High Court on a petition filed by the newspaper. Other intimidatory actions initiated by the government against the *Indian Express* included a move to cancel the lease on its Delhi offices, denial of permission to the group's chairman, Ramnath Goenka, to travel abroad, termination of government and public sector advertising in the group's papers, and denial of working capital and loans previously sanctioned by the government-owned State Bank of India. In April 1988, the Gandhi government also disrupted publication from Bangalore of three of the group's dailies by repeatedly failing to commission facsimile transmission facilities that had earlier been approved by the authorities. After the *Indian Express* challenged the government's action in the Karnataka High Court, the facilities were restored.

The Statesman, known for its independence, also suffered harassment from official quarters. A long-standing proposal by the paper to construct a multi-storeyed building to replace its ageing offices in New Delhi failed to gain necessary approval from the authorities despite the Delhi High Court ordering expeditious grant of approval in an April 1989 judgement. The government's appeal against that judgement resulted in an interim order of the Supreme Court allowing *The Statesman* to commence construction at its own risk. Cushrow Irani, *The Statesman*'s managing director, alleged in a press conference held in August 1989 that both he and his paper were subjected to several other forms of harassment at the behest of a Congress politician close to Rajiv Gandhi, whose alleged wrongdoings the paper had exposed. These included the reopening of Irani's personal income tax assessments for several previous years, detailed scrutiny of his travels outside India with a view to establishing infringements of foreign exchange regulations, and an investigation into the ownership of The Statesman Limited, publishers of the paper.

In October 1989, H K Dua, editor of the Delhi-based *Hindustan Times*, threatened to resign following alleged attempts by the Prime Minister's Office to dictate the newspaper's editorial coverage of events surrounding corruption charges levelled by members of the Congress against the US-based son of Vishwanath Pratap Singh, then a prominent opposition politician. A few days later, the newspaper's cartoonist, Sudhir Dar, tendered his resignation alleging similar interference by the management in his work. The charges against Singh were eventually dropped.

The print media also came under pressure from several state governments. In August 1989, the government of the disputed territories of Jammu and Kashmir introduced legislation pre-censoring newspapers on grounds as wide-ranging as the prevention of "any activity prejudicial to the maintenance of public order" or the "smooth and peaceful running of business establishments". The measure also allowed the state government to prohibit "circulation in any newspaper ... of any matter relating to any particular subject or class of subjects". The ruling drew strong protests from newspapers all over the country, as a result of which the chief minister of Jammu and Kashmir, Farooq Abdullah, withdrew it a few weeks later.

Attacks on Journalists

Journalists were subjected to physical attacks, often at the behest of local politicians, including state chief ministers. In the industrial town of Dhanbad (in the state of Bihar, ruled by Rajiv Gandhi's Congress Party), Brahmdeo Narayan Singh Sharma, the octogenarian and ailing editor of a Hindi daily, *Awaz*, was reportedly dragged from his residence on July 13 1989, arrested on charges of failing to appear before a district court in a defamation case filed against his paper some years ago, and kept in a police cell for several hours. The chief judicial magistrate later ordered his release on bail. Sharma's arrest and mistreatment had, it is believed, been sanctioned by a local police officer reportedly unhappy with *Awaz*'s coverage of the alleged molestation of a tribal girl by members of his force. On several occasions, the government has attempted to censor *Newstrack*, a privately produced video news magazine published in New Delhi, most recently over an item critical of the Delhi police. In Bombay in June 1989, Rahul Singh, editor of *The Sunday Observer*, and five journalists attached to the paper sought anticipatory bail from the state high court after being threatened with arrest on a criminal complaint filed by the local police following the publication of a controversial interview with a senior police officer. In the interview, conducted soon after the police had fired on a group of Muslim activists demonstrating against Salman Rushdie's novel *The Satanic Verses* in central Bombay, the officer was reported to have made certain provocative statements which he later denied. The criminal complaint against the six journalists was later withdrawn.

Other forms of harassment of journalists included the refusal of a visa to P L Lakhanpal, a Stockholm-based author and journalist of Indian origin, who applied to visit India in August 1988. The refusal was widely seen as a retaliatory measure against Lakhanpal for his investigative reporting from Sweden on the Bofors arms scandal in which Rajiv Gandhi and several of his colleagues had been implicated.

In October 1989, staff of *The Independent*, a new daily published in Bombay, were threatened with violence after publishing a report suggesting a former prominent cabinet minister from Maharashtra, now deceased, may have been a paid informer for the American Central Intelligence Agency in the late 1960s. Local politicians and admirers of the minister demonstrated outside the paper's offices for several days and threatened to burn down the building. The editor, Vinod Mehta, who received personal threats of violence, resigned because he felt that the pressure threatened his editorial freedom.

Newsprint Policy For several years the production, import and distribution of newsprint has been tightly controlled by the government. In June 1989, the government raised the prices of both domestic and imported newsprint so sharply as to threaten the survival of many newspapers. The State Trading Corporation of India has a monopoly over newsprint imports and there were allegations that the state was profiteering in an essential commodity. Repeated demands by newspapers for permission to import newsprint directly have been consistently rejected by the government.

Positive Developments

The newly-elected National Front government gave a commitment to ease state control over radio and television and initiated steps towards granting a measure of autonomy to these media. Several court rulings in different states effectively expanded the scope of the constitutional right to freedom of speech and expression, with new limits on phone tapping and interference with the mail.

Court Decisions In a case involving the refusal by the state of permission to show a Tamil feature film *Oré Oru Gramathilé* on the grounds that it was likely to lead to demonstrations and threats of violence by sections of the community, the Supreme Court, in a landmark judgement delivered on March 30 1989, reaffirmed the paramount importance of freedom of expression under the Indian Constitution. That freedom, said the court, "cannot be held to ransom by an intolerant group of people". Any restrictions had to be reasonable and "justified on the anvil of necessity and not (on) the quicksand of convenience or expediency. Open criticism of government policies and operations is not a ground for restricting expression."

The court reached a similar conclusion in a case involving a highly acclaimed TV serial *Tamas*, based on the traumatic events surrounding the partition of India in 1947. On a petition filed by a citizen seeking to prevent transmission of the serial on the grounds that the communal violence depicted was likely to inflame the viewers and consequently affect public order, the court, after weighing such a risk against the constitutional right to freedom of speech and expression, refused to prevent transmission.

In a case where the state refused to allow a Delhi-based journalist access to a police report in a criminal complaint involving allegations of corruption against a cabinet minister, former district judge Jaspal Singh (now Justice of the Delhi High Court) upheld the journalist's right to inspect the document. He overruled the government's plea that such disclosure might jeopardize national security, subvert public order and damage India's relations with friendly countries. The decision was seen as a small, but significant, step towards strengthening the right to information in matters involving the contents of public documents.

Privacy of Communciation The newly-elected National Front government announced on April 9 1990 that it intended to amend the law and prohibit phone tapping for political purposes. A controversial amendment to the Indian Post Office Act, which would have given wide powers to both central and state governments to "intercept, detain or dispose of" postal articles, was dropped.

Radio and Television There has long been discontent over the manner in which governments exercise control over radio and TV. In the last months of the outgoing Congress Administration, there were allegations concerning the disproportionate exposure given to the ruling party, excessive projection of the popularity of then Prime Minister Rajiv Gandhi, distortion of news coverage to the ruling party's advantage and manipulation of the media to spread disinformation about members of opposition parties.

In keeping with a key promise made in its election manifesto, the new government initiated steps to grant a measure of autonomy to All India Radio (AIR) and Doordarshan India, the TV network. The Prasar Bharati (Broadcasting Corporation of India) Bill, introduced in parliament on December 29 1989, envisaged the setting up of a government corporation modelled on the BBC to run radio and TV, which would have an independent board of governors drawn from media professionals, whose appointment would be insulated from government interference. A Broadcasting Council would examine complaints of unfairness or bias in programmes and the corporation. The corporation would be accountable to parliament. Pending consideration and passage of the Bill, the government established a five-member board of distinguished persons from the mass media to oversee the functioning of AIR and Doordarshan.

While the proposals have generally been welcomed, there was criticism that they did not go far enough. In particular, the absence of provisions to allow competition from private sources was seen by some as an impediment to the healthy growth and development of fully independent radio and TV.

Efforts by individuals and groups to seek judicial intervention in loosening the government's control over radio and TV have continued. In July 1989, the Supreme Court admitted a petition by Common Cause, a public interest pressure group, which sought to compel the government to submit "a precise statement of policy regarding the matter of dissemination of news and views" and to give "all political parties and persons broadcasting time which is reasonable both as to the number of broadcasts and their duration". The petition, which cited several instances of bias by AIR and Doordarshan, awaits hearing in the court, along with an earlier petition filed in 1988 by the late journalist Romesh Thapar.

Kashmir

The Indian Government has been criticized by the international press for its severe handling of the growing Muslim protest in the disputed territories of Jammu and Kashmir. Scores have been administratively detained and there are numerous reports of maltreatment during interrogation. In mid-January 1990, foreign journalists were prevented from entering Kashmir although many have since been allowed admittance. On April 17, the government banned eight Kashmiri militant organizations and closed down three Urdu-language newspapers for publishing what the authorities considered to be subversive articles. On May 21, security forces fired at thousands of civilian mourners at the funeral of the assassinated moderate Muslim leader Moulvi Mohammed Farooq. Over 50 people were killed. It is reported that Farooq was murdered by non-Kashmiris despite the government's insistence that it was perpetrated by a rival fundamentalist group.

In March 1990, Indian human rights groups investigated incidents. The separate reports of the Committee of Initiative on Kashmir and the People's Union for Civil Liberties, which provide solid evidence of many abuses by the security forces, have been angrily criticized in the Indian press.

On June 2, a well-known local journalist, Yusuf Jameel, was taken from his home by men in army uniform and driving military vehicles, and interrogated for 30 hours in an army camp before being released. The government originally said that he was kidnapped by Kashmiri militants, a story maintained by most of the Indian press apart from the *Calcutta Telegraph*. Later, the government accepted that Jameel was taken by the army and ordered an inquiry into the matter.

On July 7, the government announced that Amnesty International observers could visit India "to see for themselves" conditions there, especially in Punjab and Jammu and Kashmir. However, after Rajiv Gandhi had condemned the government for planning to co-operate with foreign intervention in India's internal affairs and threatened to organize opposition to the visit, the government told Amnesty that it would not be able to go to Kashmir and Punjab. Accordingly, Amnesty cancelled its visit.

The Satanic Verses In September 1988, *India Today* and *Sunday* published interviews with Salman Rushdie, the Indian-born British author about his forthcoming novel *The Satanic Verses*. Muslim opposition MPs, Khurshid Alam Khan and Syed Shahabuddin, began a vigorous campaign to ban the book. Aslam Ejaz of the Islamic Foundation in Madras wrote to Faiyazuddin Ahmad in Leicester, England, suggesting that a similar campaign be launched in Britain.

On October 5 1988, the Indian Finance Ministry announced the banning of *The Satanic Verses* under Section 11 of the Indian Customs Act adding that the ban did not detract from the literary and artistic merit of Rushdie's work.

Virtually every leading Indian newspaper and magazine deplored the ban; *The Hindu*'s editorial called it "a philistine decision", and *The Indian Express*'s leader called it "thought control".

In an open letter to Prime Minister Gandhi (published in the *Indian Express* October 13) Salman Rushdie expressed his concern that the government of India had banned his book and accused its detractors of extremism and political manipulation. *The Economic and Political Weekly* of October 22 stated that the ban was a political decision and accused Gandhi of capitulating because of the impending November elections.

Also in October, writers, editors and publishers protested the ban in a letter to the Prime Minister, calling it ill-conceived and hastily executed. Others pointed out that only a small section of the English-speaking public in India would read the book if it was available.

Early in 1989, there were several demonstrations against the novel and Salman Rushdie in India. On February 13, one person was killed and over 100 were injured during a riot in Kashmir.

On February 14, Iran's late Ayatollah Khomeini issued a *fatwa*, declaring a death sentence on Rushdie and the following day, a bounty of US$3 million was placed on his head. On February 24, in Bombay, 12 Muslim rioters were shot dead by police and about 50 were injured.

Actions

On June 13 1989 ARTICLE 19 wrote to the government and Vijpayat Singhania, owner of the *Indian Post*, expressing concern about Mr Singhania's request to vet all articles about eight government and business figures, including Prime Minister Rajiv Gandhi, prior to publication. ARTICLE 19 urged that the newspaper be published without such prior censorship.

On February 2 1990 ARTICLE 19 wrote to the government expressing concern about restrictions imposed on the media covering unrest in Jammu and Kashmir state, including confining journalists to their hotel and expelling some foreign correspondents. ARTICLE 19 called on the government to lift these restrictions. A reply from the High Commission in London said that foreign journalists had not been banned from Jammu and Kashmir but "their entry has been temporarily regulated in view of the law and order situation there, based on the assessment of local authorities and motivated by a concern for the safety of the foreign journalists themselves."

On April 18 1990 ARTICLE 19 wrote to the government again protesting the restrictions on the movements and reporting of journalists in Jammu and Kashmir, the expulsion of foreign correspondents, and the closing down of three Urdu-language newspapers based in Srinagar. A reply from the High Commission said that there was no interference with transmission of reports, and that foreign correspondents had not been barred from visiting Kashmir but were advised to leave because "terrorist elements in Kashmir were planning to use the presence of the foreign media to mount a political show".

Indonesia

President Raden Suharto has ruled Indonesia, with the backing of the military, since 1966. Emergency power was transferred to the then General Suharto after an abortive coup in which the Indonesian Communist Party (PKI) was heavily implicated. The death toll of army and army-incited killings between 1965 and 1967 is estimated to be as high as 500,000. In February 1990, four men charged with being involved in the 1965 coup attempt were executed after having been imprisoned for almost 25 years. Six others remain on death row in Jakarta.

Recent years have seen increasing opposition to President Suharto's rule. In August 1990, 58 prominent Indonesians, including former cabinet ministers, published a petition calling on the President to step down when his fifth five-year term ends in 1993. This was followed by the country's leading human rights group, the Legal Aid Foundation, declaring that the right to democracy enshrined in the Constitution is not reflected in real life.

	Data	Year
Population	170,178,528	1987
Life expectancy (M/F)	52.2/54.9	1988
GNP (US$ per capita)	430	1988
Main religion(s)	Islam	
	Christianity	
Official language(s)		
	Bahasa Indonesia	
Illiteracy %	23.0	1990
(M/F)	15.9/32.0	1990
Daily newspapers	61	1986
Non daily newspapers	93	1987
Periodicals	1,436	1987
Radio sets	25,000,000	1987
TV sets	6,800,000	1987
Press agencies:		
	Antara, Kantorberita	
	Nasional Indonesia	
ICCPR:	NO	

Partly in response to the increasing criticism, the authorities announced in September that they were lifting censorship of foreign newspapers, and ending their practice of telephoning local editors to tell them what can and cannot be printed.

In the same month, President Suharto released one of his most prominent critics, Hartona Rekso Dharsono, two years before the end of a seven-year jail sentence for "subversion".

However, freedom of expression remains severely curtailed, with the continued imposition of the Anti-Subversion Law and Article 154 of the Criminal Code which punishes peaceful dissent. Curbs on freedom of expression take many other forms, such as bans on books, warnings to editors, abrupt cancellation of theatre performances and other methods of harassment and intimidation. The opposition is denied access to the media and prevented from voicing criticisms abroad. A principal opponent, General Abdul Haris Nasution, has been prevented from accepting official invitations in Australia and Malaysia.

The Media

The Press According to the Indonesian Press Council, the press must follow a *Pancasila* approach to news. *Pancasila* is a set of five broad social and political principles, monotheism, humanitarianism, nationalism, democracy and social justice, elevated by President Raden Suharto to a state ideology. Although some elements of *Pancasila* appear to be consistent with political tolerance and pluralism, the government has used the ideology to justify restrictions on freedom of expression. Thus, defamation of public officials carries a penalty of up to six years' imprisonment. Insulting such officials is also punishable.

The 1966 Press Act, amended in 1982, requires that each "press enterprise" has a publication permit (SIUPP). It also establishes a Press Council to assist the government in drafting regulations and reaching decisions regarding the press and defines the functions and duties of the national press. These duties include obligations to "fan the spirit of dedication to the nation's struggle", to "strengthen national unity and integrity", and to "exercise social control which is constructive". The Act provides severe sanctions including imprisonment for those who violate its provisions.

The government forbids the publication of material which could be construed as seditious, insinuating, sensational, speculative or likely to antagonize ethnic, religious or racial tensions. Articles and news items are often restricted or forbidden by *budaya telpon*, a practice whereby the Information Ministry telephones editors to tell them what (and what not) to print. A written warning may be issued and the last resort is withdrawal of the SIUPP permit, which is a powerful tool for controlling the press. No licences were withdrawn in 1989 but, in October 1990, *Monitor*, a popular tabloid, had its licence revoked for running a poll of "most admired persons" which rated the Prophet Mohammed in 11th place and thus insulted Islam. The paper was closed after pressure from Muslim leaders and clashes between troops and young Muslims.

At the end of 1988, Major General (retd) Soegeng Widjaja took over as head of the Indonesian Journalists' Association (PWI). Under its new leadership, the PWI controls the issuing of press cards which accredit journalists.

Warnings and Blackouts Soegeng Widjaja instructed PWI members not to hesitate in responding to summonses from the authorities whenever ordered to answer for their professional activities. Widjaja later announced that moves to "clean up" the press by removing politically undesirable elements must be intensified, and said that "bringing order" to the press was now an integral part of the PWI's programme. The daily *Merdeka* received an official warning from the Ministry of Information in October 1988 after an editorial suggested that the facts about the 1965 coup attempt (as a result of which President Suharto came to power) were, more than 20 years later, not yet entirely clear.

On April 25 1989, Information Minister Harmoko verbally warned editors from six leading newspapers and magazines (*Kompas, Terbit, Media Indonesia, Tempo, Editor* and *Jakarta Jakarta*) not to publish information on student demonstrations. *Media Indonesia* also received a written warning that its publication permit could be revoked. A week later, the Ministry of Information issued a statement that a number of newspapers had apologized for violating the "Journalistic Code of Ethics" by reporting on the demonstrations.

At the same time, a Surabaya newspaper, *Jawa Pos*, was warned for revealing the details of a meeting between General Try Soetrisno, the military commander-in-chief, and the editors of all major print and electronic media in the country. At the meeting, Gen Soetrisno asked editors to avoid too much coverage of defence lawyers in prominent trials concerning government corruption. *Jawa Pos* reported the whole meeting although the General had left it to the editors to decide which remarks should "for security reasons" remain "off the record".

In September, the magazine *Jakarta Jakarta* was again strongly reprimanded by the Department of Information, this time for a photograph which appeared in its September 17 issue that "tended toward the pornographic and could cause lust in readers". A similar photograph in the September 24 issue provoked a written "final" warning.

In October, the Ministry of Justice banned reporters of the daily *Terbit* from reporting on the work of any ministry office. The paper had published articles which Judge Djazuli, the head of the district court in Subang, West Java, found "insulting". The articles, about possible corruption in his court, suggested that Judge Djazuli had demanded Rp15 million (US$840,000) from one party in a debt case in Subang and that illegal levies were imposed on defendants by the court. *Terbit* had also been prohibited from reporting on Ministry of Justice activities early in the year, following a cartoon depicting miserable prison conditions.

Following a briefing by the provincial prosecutor in the southern Sumatra province of Lampung, the *Lampung Post* carried an editorial urging the press to observe the "nuances" of trial proceedings in a major case concerning Muslim fundamentalism and to refrain from reporting anything which might cause social unrest.

In April 1990, Gen Soetrisno warned *Tempo* and *Editor* for publishing reports which he regarded as "subversive", about unrest in Aceh. A month earlier, he told the press not to publish reports which would "discourage public participation in development programmes", or "disturb national unity and discourage discipline".

Another intervention by a military officer led to the dismissal of Aunur Rochim from the central Java daily *Wawasan* after he had reported on attacks on Chinese shops in Pekalongan. The officer in charge of information at the provincial military command said that the article was likely to provoke racial or religious tensions.

In April, Rusli Desa, editor-in-chief of the Banjarmasin newspaper *Gawi Manuntung*, was expelled from the PWI for writing about a network of corruption in local government. His article was attached to a complaint submitted by a colleague to the vice-president's official complaints system, which is supposed to be confidential. It is unlikely that Rusli Desa will be able to work as a journalist without a PWI press card.

The Foreign Press Under the 1966 Press Act, no foreign press corporation may be established in Indonesia, although foreign correspondents can apply for one-year work permits which may or may not be granted (and once granted may or may not be extended). A 1972 Information Ministry decision regulates the circulation of foreign publications within Indonesia. Circulation permits may be granted by the Ministry of Information to foreign publications which do not contain concepts "contrary to *Pancasila* principles". Imported foreign publications are scanned for "unpleasant" items. Most foreign coverage of Indonesia, as well as any material deemed offensive, is censored with black ink. Items can be removed before distribution and entire issues can be banned.

Five pages were removed from the November 6 1989 issue of *Newsweek*. It contained two articles which the government found offensive, one by Melinda Liu reporting growing opposition to the possibility of Suharto continuing for a sixth term, and the other by Ron Nordland on East Timor which referred to captured Fretilin guerrillas as "prisoners of war". Indonesia invaded East Timor in 1975, since when, up to 200,000 East Timorese have been killed.

East Timor was accorded "open territory status" in late December 1988 after military analysts declared that the Fretilin separatist group was no longer a major security threat. In line with East Timor's new status, foreign journalists (including two from *The Guardian* and the *Toronto Post*) were allowed to visit in early 1990. Although permitted to travel widely, the journalists reported that a continued heavy military presence restricted access to indigenous Timorese.

Radio and Television The government-owned radio station Radio Republik Indonesia is the largest and most powerful, broadcasting throughout the country and offering national, provincial and district programming. There are many "independent" commercial stations which play mainly popular music and are not allowed to produce their own news programmes.

While the print media reaches only a small percentage of the population, Indonesian TV reaches over 100 million viewers daily. Until 1989, there was only one TV station, the government-owned and operated Yayasan Televisi Republik Indonesia, whose stated goals are to "stimulate the process of nation and character building ... support and promote development programmes (and) play an educational role". In mid-1989, a permit was issued for the first private and commercial channel, Rajawali Citra Televisi Indonesia, which is owned by the president's second son. It broadcasts mainly foreign programmes and transmits only in Jakarta but is expected to expand to other major cities. Viewers, however, need a satellite dish and decoder which only the elite can afford.

Books and Journals Book-banning is commonplace in Indonesia, with certain topics such as communism, the 1965 coup attempt, alleged corruption amongst members of the Suharto family, and dissident movements almost guaranteed to result in banning. Books dealing with liberation theology and Islamic fundamentalism are most likely to be banned. A long-standing example of the use of banning orders to stifle freedom of expression is the complete prohibition on the sale, distribution or possession of all writings by Pramoedya Ananta Toer, the celebrated Indonesian writer and former political prisoner. In October 1990, Bonar Tigor Naipospos, a central Javanese student, was sentenced to eight years' imprisonment for "spreading communism" after having been arrested for distributing "subversive" literature which included several of Pramoedya Ananta Toer's banned books. In 1989, two other Javanese students were jailed for seven and eight years respectively on similar charges.

At the beginning of 1989, the Attorney-General banned a book entitled *Adik Baru* (New Baby) under the country's stringent anti-subversion laws, claiming that it bordered on the pornographic. *Adik Baru* is a translation of a Swedish children's book telling of a father's attempts to explain the process of reproduction and birth to his young son and daughter. On March 14 1989, *The Satanic Verses* by Salman Rushdie was banned because of its "possible impact on Muslim believers in particular and Indonesian society in general". President Suharto had already made it clear that Indonesia would ban the entry and circulation of the book because, in his view, it constituted blasphemy.

On May 5 1989, the Attorney-General banned six more books on the grounds that they might disrupt public order. They included *Tan Malaka: Pergulatan Menuju*

Republik Vol.1 (Tan Malaka: The Struggle Towards a Republic) by Harry A Poeze. (Tan Malaka was one of Indonesia's most important nationalist figures and an early leader of the banned PKI.) It was ruled that the book, which had sold 2,700 copies by the time it was banned, could result in the spread of Marxist-Leninist teachings. The following were also banned: *Pembinaan Usroh, Usroh: Pedoman dan Pelaksanaan,* and *Tentang Usroh,* edited by Abi Harun, which contained guidelines for a stricter observance of Islamic teachings in daily life, and the Attorney-General noted that they contained material which might persuade the public to pursue the ideals of "a certain political group", a reference to fundamentalist Muslim activities; and *Demi Demokrasi,* a journal published by Indonesian intellectuals exiled in the Netherlands, which regularly contained articles critical of the economic and political system in Indonesia.

On August 14, *Peristiwa Lampung dan Gerakan Sempalan Islam* (The Lampung Incident and Islamic Splinter Movements), by Bambang Siswoyo, was banned. The book refers to a conflict in the Sumatran province of central Lampung in February 1989 when up to 100 people died following clashes between Indonesian troops and a previously unknown fundamentalist Islamic group. The provincial prosecutor of central Java ordered the publisher to withdraw the book from circulation but 3,500 copies had already been sold or distributed since the book's publication in April. The book was largely a compilation of previously published material but the ban came just as the first round of trials in the case were underway.

In January 1990, schools in central Java were instructed to stop using three English-language encyclopaedias (including an encyclopaedia of the Third World) on the grounds that "they contain items viewed as offending the Indonesian state".

Public Performances In April 1989, the Fu Hsing Academy of Dramatic Arts in Taipei was about to perform a section of a Chinese opera entitled *Meeting in the Old City* when the performance was abruptly cancelled. The ban came in a letter from the Commission to Evaluate and Investigate Foreign Artists, composed of members from BAKIN (the National Intelligence Co-ordinating Board), the Attorney General's office, the police, the Ministry of Home Affairs and the Department of Information. According to the letter, the opera would disrupt the current programme of assimilation which encourages the Chinese to adopt Indonesian citizenship and names. The ethnic Chinese population has long been a target of discrimination exacerbated by the Suharto government's belief that the ethnic Chinese constitute a security risk due to their support for the PKI in the 1960s.

On May 20 in Medan, a scheduled theatrical performance of a 300-year-old Chinese love story, *Sam Pek Eng Tay,* which had already played for 18 nights in Jakarta, was abruptly cancelled by north Sumatra's local government on the grounds that it contained "cultural and artistic values contrary to *Pancasila*". The theatrical company, Teater Koma, had received permission on May 1 to stage it for four nights at the Tiara Convention Centre in Medan.

In October 1990, the authorities closed down another play being performed by Teater Koma, *Suksesi,* a political satire by Nano Riantiarno, three days before the end of a two-week run. The police were initially reluctant to give reasons for the ban but later cited one actor's departure from the submitted script, the play's lack of educational content and its potential to incite people to irresponsible acts.

Japan

The Japanese Constitution of 1949 guarantees freedom of expression, but over the years the courts have endorsed limitations in cases where free expression has come into conflict with the government. In such cases, courts often make reference to the Constitutions's direction to have regard for the "public welfare". This term has been criticized as allowing greater restriction than is permissible under the international standards to which Japan is committed. Although Article 21 states that no censorship shall be maintained, the Supreme Court has approved censorship of materials imported into Japan and a comprehensive system for the censorship of school textbooks by the Ministry of Education. On several occa-

	Data	Year
Population	122,783,000	1988
Life expectancy (M/F)	74.8/80.4	1985
GNP (US$ per capita)	21,040	1988
Main religion(s)	Shintoism	
	Buddhism	
Official language(s)	Japanese	
Illiteracy %	1	1985
Daily newspapers	124	1986
Periodicals	2,138	1984
Radio sets	105,000,000	1987
TV sets	71,500,000	1987
Press agencies:		
Jiji Tsushin-Sha, Sun Zelephoto,		
Kyodo Tsushin, Radiopress Inc,		
ICCPR:	YES	1979

sions, however, decisions by the Supreme Court have expanded the concept of freedom of expression to include freedom to receive information and to gather news in the public interest.

The Media

There is no press law in Japan and the media is largely self-regulating. Internal codes declare that it is the media's responsibility to keep the public informed about political, economic and social life and to uphold the role of watch-dog, but these standards appear increasingly difficult to maintain. The objectivity of newspapers has been tainted by controversial involvement in political and economic scandals.

There is widespread self-censorship due to a variety of informal pressures: the traditions of the Japanese people; influence exerted by owners, advertisers and government officials; and occasional violence against journalists and others targetted by extreme political groups. The most notable recent examples of such violence include the killing of a reporter employed by the daily newspaper *Asahi Shimbun* and the shooting of the current mayor of Nagasaki.

Taboos Criticism of the Emperor and his relationship to the indigenous Shinto religion are taboo. Following the long terminal illness of Emperor Hirohito, there was no critical analysis in the media of his reign. In December 1988, Mayor H Motoshima of Nagasaki stated that Emperor Hirohito bore some responsibility for World War II and was immediately subjected to numerous death threats. Members of right-wing paramilitary groups, some in uniform, demonstrated against him in Nagasaki. He was threatened with expulsion by the ruling Liberal Democratic Party (LDP) but thousands of Nagasaki citizens signed petitions in his support.

On January 18 1990, he was shot and seriously injured by a member of *Seki-Juku*, a tiny extremist group in Nagasaki. Other politicians, as well as publishers and writers, who debated the behaviour and actions of the late Emperor have also been threatened by extremist groups.

Another taboo subject is the relationship between organized crime, the police and politicians. A recent best-selling book on *Yakuza* (gangsters operating in Japan) has failed to be published there, and the authors have alleged censorship motivated by fear of retaliation from political figures. Until recently it was impossible to criticize the United States military but this has gradually changed. However, there is still no discussion in the media on the subject of discrimination against minorities such as the Burakumin, the Ainu or Koreans living in Japan.

Newspapers There are many newspapers on sale in Japan, generally of a similar standard. Japan has the highest ratio of newspapers sold per capita in the world with 584 for every 1,000 of the population. National newspapers include *Asahi Shimbun*, which has the largest circulation (13 million), *Mainichi Shimbun*, *Yomiuri Shimbun* and *Sankei Shimbun*. A large number of weekly periodicals is also published. In the 1980s, an average of 200 new magazines were published each year.

Japanese newspapers operate a code of practice adopted by the Newspaper Publishers' and Editors' Association which comprises 168 newspaper companies, news agencies and broadcasting companies, including all major daily newspapers and key broadcasting companies. There is no ombudsman or press council but the code of practice advocates public criticism by other media as a means of regulation.

Radio and Television There are more than 180 broadcasting and radio companies in Japan but only one, the Nihhon Hoso Kyokai (NHK), is owned and operated by a government agency. In theory, NHK is editorially independent of government control. However, NHK's budget requires parliamentary consent and a management committee selected by government exercises a strong influence. On May 1 1987, Godo Shiro, a director of NHK, committed suicide, apparently to warn the public about censorship and interference in NHK.

All private TV companies belong to at least one of five major networks centred in Tokyo and Osaka. All are partly financed by newspaper interests which give the newspapers a direct influence on TV.

Film There are four large Japanese film companies but imported films have become more popular than Japanese ones. While censorship of films made in Japan is rare, imported films have been censored under the Customs Standard Law of 1910 and such censorship has been judged constitutional by the Supreme Court. In 1986, a BBC drama, *The Insurance Man*, which showed frontal nudity, was ordered to be cut by the Customs Bureau before being shown at an international TV film festival.

Japanese film-makers exercise great care when confronting taboo subjects. When foreign film-makers address such themes, Japanese distributors often seek to censor the end product or to prevent such films from being shown in Japan. In 1985, sufficient pressure was exerted upon the producers of a film on the life of the controversial novelist Yukio Mishima to persuade them to withdraw it from the first Tokyo International Film Festival and the film was not shown in Japan. Mishima advocated the revival of militarism and lamented the decay of traditional Japanese martial values.

In 1988, Japanese distributors removed 30 seconds from the Bernardo Bertolucci film, *The Last Emperor*, which depicted atrocities committed by Japanese troops in Nanjing, China, during World War II. This treatment of the Oscar-winning film is similar to the Ministry of Education censorship of school textbooks designed to eliminate or tone down descriptions of the activities of Japan's armed forces during World War II.

Media Ownership Cross-media conglomerates are rare in Japan. The best known is the Fuji Sankei Communication Group which owns Fuji TV (a key station), *Sankei* (a daily national newspaper), a local radio station and several evening newspapers. The Fuji Sankei Group invited former US President Ronald Reagan to Japan in 1989 and paid him a multi-million dollar fee.

There is no foreign capital investment in Japanese newspaper companies. It is impossible to buy into Japanese newspapers via the stock market as all shares are unlisted stocks and usually sold only to members of the newspaper companies or banks. There are no financial links between the national newspapers but there are links between national and local newspapers. In many provincial areas, despite a variety of newspapers, the range of views is limited because of the structure of ownership. Shares in broadcast companies, however, are open to both Japanese and foreign investors.

Press and Politics In mid-1989, the LDP was defeated in a general election by the Japanese Socialist Party, its first defeat since 1949. One cause was evidence of government corruption uncovered by a national newspaper, *Asahi Shimbun*, and taken up by many others. An investigation into the Recruit Cosmos Company exposed a number of influential politicians and other senior government officials who were lent money by the company to buy stocks. *Asahi Shimbun* brought to light the involvement of national newspaper executives such as president K Morita of *Nihon Keizai Shimbun*, vice-president I Maruyama of *Yomiuri Shimbun* and chief editor R Utagawa of *Mainichi Shimbun*. Prime Minister Noboru Takeshita and several cabinet ministers and state officers resigned, as did senior newspaper executives. All the politicians involved in the scandal were re-elected to the national Diet (parliament) by their constituencies in February 1990, but none of them has been appointed to a cabinet position.

The uncovering of other scandals exposed large-scale collusion between media executives and public officials. The model of a press free from political affiliation was shown to be far from the reality. It emerged, for example, that local newspapers *Sanyo Shimbun* and *Shizuoka Shimbun*, and local broadcasting companies Shizuokakenmin Hoso, Shizuoka Hoso and TV Shizuoka sponsored candidates of the LDP, thereby breaching the impartiality rules of the broadcasting laws.

It was also revealed that senior staff of all national and most local newspapers belonged to committees organized by the government to help develop LDP policies. For example, Yosoji Kobayashi, president of *Yomiuri Shimbun*, is chairman of a committee which in theory is independent, but in practice supports LDP policy.

Press Clubs There are many press clubs in Japan (some 30 national and 400 local clubs) which provide a privileged and close relationship with sources of information. Press club facilities are provided by government and business sponsors, making the media vulnerable to government and business pressure. These clubs exercise exclusive rights over many news sources, barring non-establishment journalists such as free-lancers and foreign correspondents. The leading press clubs are accredited to different government ministries, courts and major companies, and briefings and news conferences are for members only.

In a Supreme Court judgement on March 8 1989, the court ruled that spectators, as well as courthouse press club members, had the right to take notes in court. The case was taken by Lawrence Repeta, a lawyer, who was ordered by a trial judge not to take handwritten notes at a trial he was observing even though press club members were free to do so.

Invasion of Privacy The newspapers' code of practice is not enforced by law. Under Japan's Civil code, aggrieved persons are able to demand compensation for injury to reputation, but compensation awards are low and of little deterrence. On occasions, the media infringes individual privacy or injures a person's honour, an example being the "Los Angeles scandal", currently the most famous libel case in Japan. On September 11 1985, the Japanese police arrested K Miura on suspicion of attempting to murder his wife in Los Angeles in August 1981. He had been the centre of media attention ever since a magazine article, written two years before his arrest, claimed that he had organized his wife's murder to obtain insurance money. The media kept him under surveillance and, in general, covered the story as though he had already been tried and convicted. His private life was widely reported before his trial, which started in 1986 and is continuing. (Contested criminal trials often last for many years in Japan.)

For the past five years there have been wide-ranging debates, both inside and outside the media, about how to write and report on criminal proceedings. Some newspapers and magazines have harassed suspects' families and friends for information and have published details not relevant to the crime itself. However, the only concrete outcome of this debate is a short-term agreement to use the title *yogisha* (suspect) in any reports prior to conviction.

In recent years, Japan has seen a rapid rise in photo-journalism with, at its peak, over five million copies of photo-journals sold each week. The media and the public labelled these competing magazines "3FET War", from the initials of the five most popular magazines; *Focus, Friday, Flash, Emma* and *Touch*. They often use intrusive methods such as photographing people through windows of their homes.

Other Restrictions on Freedom of Expression

Official Secrecy Article 100 of the National Public Service Law obliges public servants not to disclose information obtained in the course of their employment. Article 3 of the same law makes it an offence, punishable by imprisonment with forced labour, for anyone to induce a public servant to disclose such information. In 1978, Nishiyama Takishi, a reporter with *Mainichi Shinbun*, was convicted of inducing a public servant to commit a crime, following publication in 1972 of a report which revealed that the government had secretly agreed to pay compensation to inhabitants of Okinawa although it had publicly stated that no such deals were made. His source was also convicted for divulging secrets acquired in the course of employment and both were dismissed from their posts.

Censorship of Textbooks The government selects and approves all school textbooks. The Ministry of Education's powers extend to directing that textbooks be amended to remove information or ideas which are considered unacceptable; many changes are usually made. Topics liable to be censored include Shintoism and armed forces atrocities including wartime aggression against China and South East Asian countries. In the 1980s, revised Ministry of Education guidelines for history textbook writers drew domestic criticism as well as condemnation from neighbouring countries about the coverage of World War II in Japanese textbooks.

In three law suits, the historian, Professor Ienega, challenged the Ministry of Education's powers as unconstitutional interference with his freedom of expression, academic freedom and children's rights to education, as well as challenging changes to his textbook recommended or required by the Ministry. In the many court judgements since Professor Ienega's first lawsuit was filed in 1965, there have been victories and defeats for both sides. The latest judgement, by the District Court in October 1989, upheld the Ministry's powers of review as "necessary and appropriate", but found in favour of Professor Ienega on one point: that a reference to an incident involving the Imperial Army over 100 years ago should not be deleted. Professor Ienega intends to appeal the decision.

The Satanic Verses On February 16 1990, the Japanese translation of Salman Rushdie's novel *The Satanic Verses* was published by a small Japanese publishing house, Sinsen-Sha; the large publishing companies were reluctant to take the responsibility for printing it. The publisher, however, was attacked with a microphone stand by a leader of an extremist Muslim group during a news conference. The book has sold well but is not displayed by major bookshops.

Actions

In its 1988 Commentary to the Human Rights Committee ARTICLE 19 raised the practices of press clubs and their effect on restricting access to information including to foreign journalists. ARTICLE 19 also expressed concern over the operation of self-censorship, the position of minorities in Japan including, foreign residents, and government censorship of textbooks.

North Korea

The Democratic People's Republic of Korea (DPRK) was officially proclaimed in the north in 1948. It has been ruled throughout its existence by Kim Il Sung, now the world's longest-serving political leader. State power is exercised through the Korean Workers' Party (KWP), headed by Kim Il Sung since its formation in 1949. It bases its policies on the speeches and writings of the party leader, in particular his philosophy of *Juche* (self-reliance). The whole population is expected to show loyalty to party policies and to Kim Il Sung.

North Korea is not a member of the

	Data	Year
Population	21,902,000	1988
Life expectancy (M/F)	64.6/71.0	1985
GNP (US$ per capita)	767	1988
Main religion(s)	Buddhism	
Official language(s)	Korean	
Illiteracy %	10	1985
Daily newspapers	11	1986
Radio sets	3,750,000	1988
TV sets	260,000	1987
Press agencies:		
Korean Central News Agency		
ICCPR:	YES	1981

United Nations. It has, however, ratified the International Covenant on Economic, Social and Cultural Rights and the International Covenant on Civil and Political Rights. Under the 1972 Constitution the citizens of North Korea are guaranteed "freedom of speech, the press, assembly, association and demonstration" (Art.53) and of "scientific, literary and artistic pursuits" (Art.60). These guarantees have little meaning in practice. The rights formally extended under Articles 53 and 60 are cancelled by the implications of other articles, notably Article 2 which states that North Korea relies on the "politico-ideological unity of the entire people", and Article 21 which declares that "citizens must heighten their revolutionary vigilance against ... all hostile elements who are opposed to our country's socialist system".

The KWP places extreme emphasis on secrecy and the maintenance of national security, due to its hostile relationship with South Korea and the United States in particular. All citizens have been compelled to wear a badge of Kim Il Sung on their lapel, and every living room has his portrait (and now, also that of his son and heir Kim Jong Il) displayed on a wall bare of any other decoration.

Despite nominal adherence to Marxism-Leninism, North Korea has a secret but rigid system of social stratification. Every individual falls into one of three broad classes: core, hostile, or wavering (with a total of 51 sub-classes). The criteria are a mix of family background, birthplace, skills and loyalty. The categorization wholly determines an individual's life, place of residence, occupation, and rewards. Within the core class, an elite of some 200,000, living mainly in the showpiece capital Pyongyang, have special privileges.

The Media and Freedom of Expression

All forms of media in North Korea are state-owned and in practice controlled by the KWP. The KWP defines what and how subjects are to be treated. Party officials lay down policies for different groups of media workers, who are obliged to produce according to planned quotas. Quotas apply to novelists as well much as to radio script writers, and all writers and other media personnel are state-employed.

The press, literary production, broadcasting services, films and drama are all strictly monitored. The media devotes the majority of its time to praising Kim Il Sung and Kim Jong Il, as well as uncritically upholding current party policies. South Korea is always portrayed as a US-dominated state where starvation is rife. (North Korea is still officially at war with the South; only an armistice was signed in 1953.) All arts and media have been restricted by the KWP for so long that independent expression has disappeared.

Newspapers All news is filtered through the Korean Central News Agency (KCNA). International news is minimal, apart from reports of foreign praise of Kim Il Sung, who is the main subject of most articles. The press did not report the political upheavals in Czechoslovakia, Hungary, Poland and East Germany in 1989, although it noted the elections of new officials in those countries. There were a number of articles about Romania in late November and early December praising its allegiance to socialism; however, Ceausescu's overthrow was announced immediately.

One study showed that in one six-page issue of the party paper *Rodong Shinmun* in 1981 there were over 200 references to Kim Il Sung and Kim Jong Il.

In the past, the North Korean authorities often placed advertisements in papers like *The Times* and the *New York Times*, and then reported them in the North Korean media as if they were straightforward news or feature items. The North Korean press has also been known to fabricate writings by well-known journalists and visitors to the country.

The only foreign news bureaux in North Korea are TASS and APN, both from the Soviet Union. In May 1990, the authorities expelled one of two TASS correspondents, Alexander Shebin, who had been based in Pyongyang for seven years. He had written articles critical of Kim Il Sung's rule, including one describing the difficulties of being a correspondent in Pyongyang.

One sign of a change in policy was a directive issued in February 1990 which indicated that European journalists would be allowed to visit North Korea freely.

No foreign newspapers are publicly available, but an elite has access to a restricted digest of world press reports, as well as to foreign broadcasts. No underground press has come to light, nor any literature that can be construed as having a double meaning or conveying covert criticism of the authorities.

Books and Publications The estimated 350 writers in the Union of Writers and Artists produce, among other writings, 20 novels and 450-500 short stories each year. Their chief role is to promote the personality cult of the party leader. Publications are censored on a number of levels, beginning with numerous criticism sessions at the workplace and continuing through a series of higher authorities, with the most crucial stage being political censorship by KWP officials.

Radio and Television South Korea broadcasts to North Korea (and vice versa), but it is doubtful whether North Koreans are able to listen. Most North Korean households, workplaces and hotel rooms are equipped not with radios but with installed speakers, which are tuned to the national and local networks. Radios brought in from Japan have their dials fixed to prevent reception of external broadcasting; those on sale in department stores have fixed dials. All radios are reported to be inspected annually.

The North Korean government broadcasts in Chinese, Russian, English, French, German, Japanese, Spanish and Arabic through its broadcasting body, the Korean Central Broadcasting Service (KCBS). KCBS's total foreign language broadcasting hours rival those of the BBC World Service.

On July 7 1989, the government reportedly censored a TV broadcast of the opening ceremony of the 13th World Festival of Youth and Students in Pyongyang, cutting out footage of delegates carrying signs such as "Solidarity with the Chinese students" and "Let Amnesty (International) in". TV allocates an estimated 50 per cent of its broadcasting time to films about Kim Il Sung.

Telephone and Letters The postal services are unreliable, although some citizens correspond with relatives in Japan. Such letters are censored. Telephone services, both inland and international, are poor. Resident foreign embassies cannot routinely obtain telephone numbers of government ministries. There is only one telephone line between North and South Korea, that between the two Red Cross offices. In 1989, however, direct dialling was introduced from Hong Kong to North Korea.

Travel A virtual ban on travel is another factor hindering access to information. Private transport systems do not exist and even visits to relatives in other parts of the country are carefully controlled. However, in his 1990 New Year's Day address Kim Il Sung mentioned a proposal for Korean citizens to travel between North and South Korea. The movement of goods vehicles in and out of Pyongyang and around the country is carefully planned. These and railway journeys take place chiefly under cover of darkness, ostensibly because of the fear of invasion by South Korea.

Contact with Foreigners Contact between North Koreans and foreigners is very limited. Only officially approved people are sent abroad, and very few students study overseas. Tourism has been minimal, but there seemed to be a new attitude towards group tourism in 1990. At the beginning of the year, the first charter flight from Hong Kong visited Pyongyang. Tourist offices also opened in Beijing, Hong Kong and Nagoya (Japan). However, visitors are not permitted to meet privately with North Koreans.

A Polish film director, Andrzej Fidyk, was allowed to produce a film to mark North Korea's 40th anniversary in 1988. The only commentary used was read from tourist guides and literature provided to the film makers by officials. It received worldwide acclaim as a study in the effects of totalitarianism, which contributed to North Korea's subsequent refusal to co-operate with foreign journalists and film makers.

Youth Festival A rare moment of exposure to the outside world was furnished by the World Festival of Youth and Students held in Pyongyang in July 1989, for which an unprecedented 15,000-20,000 foreigners travelled to North Korea. Amnesty International delegates were due to attend, but their visas were delayed.

Freedom of Opinion and Expression

During its 37-year rule, the KWP has made use of an all-embracing control apparatus: periodic purges of its membership and leadership; extensive investigation and detailed classification of the ideological beliefs of every individual citizen; torture and secret trials and convictions; the death penalty; concentration camps which are said to contain some 150,000 inmates; an education system heavily weighted towards ideological indoctrination; and a neighbourhood surveillance system of groups of five families which meet twice-weekly. Even trivial remarks construed as disrespectful to Kim Il Sung or critical of the government can lead to long prison sentences.

Political Parties and Religious Groups Political parties are permitted under the Constitution (Art.53) and freedom of religion is guaranteed (Art.54). However, such political parties and religious organizations as do exist seem to be little more than committees set up by the KWP, apparently to act as links with international organizations not open to the KWP itself. The other political parties, the Korean Social Democratic Party and the Chondoist Chongu Party, do not constitute any kind of active political opposition.

Freedom of Religion Freedom of religion is centrally controlled by two organizations, the Korean Christians Federation (Protestant) and the Korean Catholics Association. Both have a church in Pyongyang built before the 1989 Youth Festival. It is reported that the 10,000 Christians in North Korea mainly worship in "house churches". Religious bodies may not oppose party or state policies, or act on behalf of the people. Although the government may and does spread anti-religious propaganda, it does not permit religious organizations to proselytize.

Current Detainees Current political prisoners may include Li Gun Mo, Prime Minister until December 1988 when he retired (ostensibly on health grounds), who has subsequently disappeared from public view.

South Korea

Press freedom was a key demand in nationwide disturbances which led to presidential elections in late 1987 won by Roh Tae-woo of the ruling Democratic Justice Party. Hopes ran high that greater freedom would follow. There were new constitutional guarantees and significant changes to previously restrictive legislation on freedom of expression, especially concerning relations with North Korea. But the changes were short-lived. Since April 1989, the government has carried out a campaign of suppression of freedom of expression. In June and July 1989, several thousand people were arrested and 700 charged under the National Security Law (NSL). One notable case was that of former freelance journalist Kim Hyon-chang and his wife Kim Hyon-ae, the Wonju bureau chief of the *Hankyoreh Shinmun*. They were each sentenced on February 22 1990 to seven years' imprisonment on charges of violating the NSL. Kim Hyon-chang was accused of sending a fax message containing details of a meeting to the Council of Korean People in Europe. His wife was found guilty of meeting members of the Council during a visit to West Germany. On her return to Korea she sent newspaper clippings and publications, freely available in Seoul, to the Council. She has been released on bail pending appeal after the appeal judge ruled that she may not have known that the groups in Germany were pro-North Korean. During her six months' detention before trial, Kim Hyon-ae was brutally interrogated on several occasions, with the result that she suffered a miscarriage.

	Data	Year
Population	41,975,000	1988
Life expectancy	70.0	1987
GNP (US$ per capita)	3,530	1988
Main religion(s)	Buddhism	
	Christianity	
Official language(s)	Korean	
Illiteracy %	3.7	1990
(M/F)	0.9/6.5	1990
Daily newspapers	35	1986
Radio sets	41,575,000	1987
TV sets	8,700,000	1988
Press agencies:		
	Naewoe Press,	
	Yonhap News Agency	
ICCPR:	YES	1990

Despite two amnesties for political prisoners in December 1989 and March 1990, under which 27 and 22 prisoners respectively were released, freedom of expression remains severely curtailed.

In 1990, the government no longer issued daily guidelines instructing the press exactly what and how to report but maintained limited press access to government departments and officials dealing with sensitive issues such as security, defence and relations with North Korea.

New guidelines from the Ministry of Information restrict what can be reported about North Korea and Eastern European countries. The government no longer places security agents in the offices of newspapers and periodicals, but everyone knows that they are only a phone call away. Fewer books are officially banned than under the previous government, but book banning continues. Books are confiscated and authors, editors, publishers and booksellers are all liable to imprisonment for breach of "national security".

In early 1989, the "Joint Public Security Investigation Headquarters" was formed, composed of officials from the prosecutor's office, the Agency for National Security Planning (ANSP), the police and the Defence Security Command. In its first 10 weeks the agency arrested some 530 people, including dissidents, publishers, writers, artists and bookshop owners, and seized tens of thousands of "leftist-leaning" publications from bookshops.

The government portrays the victims of its suppression as being on the fringes of South Korean society, and claims that the majority of the population welcomes action to restore law and order, despite the restrictions on freedom of expression. However, the boundaries, atlhough ill-defined, of what can be expressed and published, are broader now than under the previous government.

Legal Restraints on Opinion and Expression

The National Security Law The NSL prohibits activities deemed "anti-state" or of benefit to "anti-state organizations". These activities are vaguely defined and include such non-violent acts of expression as: "praising, encouraging, or siding with anti-state organizations", and "publishing or distributing publications deemed beneficial to the enemy". Violation can result in long prison sentences. In April 1990, the Constitution Court ruled that these two clauses were constitutional, but acknowledged that the wording was "too loose and the scope too broadly defined, allowing them to be misused or abused to suppress anti-government groups and infringe upon freedom of expression in ways irrelevant to national security". The ruling recommended "that the clauses be limited in application to cases where there is explicit harm to national security, existence, or the basic order of free democracy".

According to the National Police Headquarters, by August 1989, 53,116 people had been convicted of violating the NSL since it came into force in 1981. Furthermore, prisoners convicted under the NSL or other security-related laws are required to sign statements "renouncing" their "leftist beliefs" before they are considered for release under government amnesty, although this violates the right to freedom of conscience as guaranteed by the Constitution (Art.19).

Agency for National Security Planning With the ushering in of a new "era of democracy" in June 1987, ANSP agents were no longer placed in newsrooms and magazine editorial offices. Some journalists have stated, however, that security agents continue to exercise influence on editorial content and reporting. On February 12 1990, two labour activists, Ann Min-kyu and Park Ja-ho, were arrested and charged by the ANSP for printing and disseminating "impulsive and subversive materials".

The ANSP continues to engage in widespread domestic surveillance. According to the National Police Headquarters, some 10,000 people previously convicted of violating the NSL were under ANSP surveillance in August 1989. Surveillance of opposition figures was believed to have been ended when Roh Tae-woo came to power but, in October 1990, a Defence Security Command agent revealed that the army had continued to spy illegally on opposition politicians, religious leaders, journalists, dissidents and others. In response, President Roh fired his defence minister and the chief of military intelligence, the men held responsible for the surveillance.

The Social Surveillance Law Enacted in September 1989, the Social Surveillance Law allows "security offenders" to be placed under surveillance and reimprisoned without trial.

Criminal Code The Criminal Code provides for a penalty of up to seven years' imprisonment (in addition to a concurrent suspension of civil rights for up to 10 years) for a Korean national who insults or defames the Republic of Korea outside the country (Art.104). In early June 1987, a student leader was charged with violating this Article for having compared South Korea to Nazi Germany in a *New York Times* interview. In June 1988, the new government announced that it would repeal the provision, but there has been no official action.

The Constitution protects citizens against libel and the Criminal Code provides for both civil and criminal penalties for libel. In 1988, Son Chung-mu, a journalist, was held in jail for about four months while facing libel charges. His book contained unflattering information about the family of the founder of the Samsung Corporation, South Korea's third largest business conglomerate. The author contended that he was being harassed for having accused the Samsung Corporation of corrupt business practices and profiteering. He was released in October 1988 after an out-of-court settlement.

Law on Assembly and Demonstration Sponsors of demonstrations are required to provide the police with 48 hours notice of assemblies and demonstrations (Art.4) and to describe the nature of the assembly. The government continues to block many demonstrations organized by student activists and dissidents, arguing that they may cause "social unrest".

Basic Guidelines Concerning Co-operation for Exchanges with Northern Countries Issued in September 1988, these guidelines outline what can and cannot be reported about North Korea and Eastern European countries. For example, it is prohibited to commit "any acts that benefit either North Korea or an anti-state organization; or any acts that create opinions that run counter to the government's policy on North Korea". The phrases "anti-state organizations" and "anti-state activities" are sufficiently vague as to penalize peaceful exercise of the right to freedom of expression.

In April 1989, the editor of *Hankyoreh Shinmun*, an opposition daily paper, and three of his colleagues were arrested under the NSL and charged with planning to send reporters to North Korea. Staff reporters were also questioned and the newsroom was raided by security agents, backed by 800 riot police. The four detainees were eventually released, although one was given a suspended sentence of 18 months.

Lee Yung-hee, a professor, spent six months in prison for writing to President Kim Il-sung of North Korea without prior permission.

In Feburary 1990, the government allowed news organizations to make contact with North Korea in order to plan a visit. In the same month Im Su-kyong, a student, and Moon Kyu-hyun, a Catholic priest, were sentenced to 10 and eight years' imprisonment respectively for travelling illegally to North Korea.

All exchanges with or visits to North Korea must first be approved by the government. However, in July 1990, Roh Tae-woo declared that for five days in August the border between North and South Korea would be opened allowing citizens of both countries to travel freely from one to the other. At the end of the year the respective prime ministers held a series of meetings to try and reduce tension between the two countries and to discuss cultural and humanitarian exchanges. In what was regarded as a conciliatory move, the South Korean government also announced the release of Moon Ik-hwan, 72, a Presbyterian pastor jailed in 1989 for 10 years for illegally visiting North Korea.

The Media

Press and Periodicals In November 1987, the National Assembly repealed the repressive Basic Press Law of 1980 and replaced it with two new laws on periodicals and broadcasting. Since the beginning of 1988, the media has repeatedly demonstrated in support of editorial independence and unionization; these demonstrations have often been brutally broken up by the authorities, with many arrests. The government has increased the size of major dailies from eight to 12 pages. However, journalists still have no access to government bodies responsible for links with North Korea or other communist countries. Liaison between the official press and senior government officials is close which undoubtedly influences the way in which news is reported.

Although there has been a great surge in periodicals since the liberalizing of the publication laws, progressive magazines have come under attack. In November 1989, Lee Shi-young, a poet and member of the editorial committee of *Creation and Criticism* magazine, was arrested under the NSL for publishing the novelist Hwang Suk-young's account of his trip to North Korea. He was released on February 3 1990. In January 1990, police and ANSP agents raided the publishing company, Labour Literature History Co, and seized nearly 46,000 copies of books, magazines, original writings and address books of labour organizations.

On June 19 1990, police arrested Jang Myung-guk, a leading labour activist. He had not been charged with any offence by September but was apparently being interrogated about his work with unions and articles he had written about the labour situation for *Dawn*, a monthly magazine published by his wife.

The Law on Registration of Periodicals still requires periodicals to register, but the Ministry of Information must now obtain a court order before revoking a magazine's registration. The registration requirement, according to the International Commission of Jurists, has discouraged many from continuing to publish. Officials may cancel a company's registration for several reasons including lack of full disclosure of the officers of the company; four companies have had their registration cancelled for this reason.

Broadcast Media The Broadcast Law of 1987 guarantees that broadcasting stations may serve the public interest without government interference. However, "private enterprises" are banned from running broadcasting companies. The government indirectly owns the two Korean television networks, the Korean Broadcasting System (KBS) and the Munhwa Broadcasting System.

The Broadcast Law empowers the President to appoint the heads of broadcast networks and the members of the Korean Broadcasting Commission. The new law appears to strengthen the role of the Commission in programming and management decisions. The networks are required to submit details of daily broadcasts to the Commission and the Minister of Culture and Information, and the Commission is authorized to consider basic programming issues and to approve the contents of programmes.

On April 9 1990, President Roh Tae-woo appointed Soh Ki-won as president of the KBS. The KBS trade union demanded the resignation of Soh, a former presidential press secretary and editor of the pro-government daily *Seoul Shinmun*, asserting that his appointment was an attempt by the government to control the broadcast media. The union staged a sit-in outside Soh's office and, after the police arrested 117 protesting workers, over 3,000 KBS employees joined the protest, bringing the network to a halt. On April 23 the government declared the collective action illegal and a challenge to the government's right to manage personnel and, at midnight, about 2,000 riot police stormed the KBS headquarters arresting 333 journalists, producers and other workers.

In July, KBS workers again went on strike along with members of two private radio stations, Christian Broadcasting System and Peace Broadcasting, in protest at Bills to restructure the broadcasting industry. On July 23, all 80 opposition MPs resigned over the legislation which they claimed was forced through the National Assembly by the government.

Drama and Films In January 1988, the government abolished prior censorship of all drama scripts. In April, the official censor announced that it would no longer preview "adult" films and dramas. 1988 was heralded by some as the year of the flowering of drama but police raided university campuses to prevent students staging a "revolutionary" North Korean play, *Pibada*.

President Roh's July 1988 "nordpolitik", in which he advocated increased contact with North Korea and Eastern European countries, made it possible for films from communist countries to be shown in South Korea. Soviet and Chinese films were screened for the first time, as were films from around the world about the suppression of human rights. In February 1990, officials announced that "art-orientated" films from North Korea would be screened but "revolutionary films" would still be excluded.

Arts Artists have benefited from the liberalization, but they are also subject to restrictions on works considered "pro-North" or "leftist". The most stark example is that of Hong Song-dam, painter and co-chairman of the dissident painters group *Minminyon*. In January 1990, he was sentenced to seven years' imprisonment for sending slides of a painting to North Korea to be displayed at the World Youth Festival held in Pyongyang in July 1989. Hong had been arrested in July 1989 along with three other artists who had collaborated on the painting. At Hong's trial, a forensic pathologist supported Hong's claim that he had been tortured by the ANSP. The other artists were released on suspended sentences in December. Another painter, Shin Han-chini, was arrested in July 1989 for having a painting reproduced on a calendar in North Korea.

Books In September 1989, the Seoul district court ruled against the Ministry of Culture and Information which had forbidden the second printing of a book on a former Korean Central Intelligence Agency director. However, books continue to be banned and confiscated. On November 29 1989, the prosecutor's office released a list of 138 banned books.

On February 21 1990, Oh Pong-ok was arrested for writing a poem, allegedly praising North Korea, published in May 1989 in a book of poems by the Silchon

Munhak publishing company. The managing editor of the company, Song Ki-won, and the publisher, Lee Mun-ku, were also arrested. The three face up to seven years in jail under the NSL.

On March 24 1990, Kim Yon-in of The Him Publication Company was arrested under the NSL for publishing material sympathetic to North Korea. He was accused of having published over 1,000 copies of a North Korean book, *Dawn of the Revolution*.

Actions

On August 5 1988 ARTICLE 19 wrote to the government asking that it release all writers, publishers, poets and journalists imprisoned for the peaceful expression of their beliefs; remove the regulations that require foreign publications to be licensed; speed the process of reviewing the banning of more than 1,000 pop songs; and end the confiscation of books and the censorship of plays.

On November 27 1989 ARTICLE 19 wrote to the government about Yoon Jai-kol and Cha Il-hwan. Yoon Jai-kol, a reporter with *Hankyoreh Shinmun*, was issued with an arrest warrant because of a proposed visit to North Korea. Cha Il-hwan, an art gallery owner, was arrested after a photograph of one of his paintings had been reproduced at the 13th World Festival of Youth and Students in North Korea.

In 1990 ARTICLE 19, along with Amnesty International, the Catholic Institute for International Relations, the British Council of Churches and a UK Labour MP, twice met with the South Korean ambassador to the UK. Cases concerning freedom of expression were raised, particularly those of Hong Song-dam, Cha Il-hwan and Oh Pong-ok.

Malaysia

The issues that are causing grave concern in Malaysian politics today are electoral gerrymandering on an unheard of scale; the powerlessness of the mainstream print and broadcasting media; and the furore over an independent election monitoring group in which the Commonwealth Secretariat is now embroiled. All these are serving to derail fundamental liberties in the country. The formation of a powerful, multiracial, united opposition, for the first time in 33 years, forced Prime Minister Dr Mahathir Mohamed to call a general election a year ahead of schedule. In October 1990, his ruling Barisan Nasional coalition won 127 seats in parliament against 48 for the nine-party opposition alliance and four for the independents.

	Data	Year
Population	16,921,000	1988
Life expectancy (M/F)	67.6/72.7	1984
GNP (US$ per capita)	1,870	1988
Main religion(s)	Islam	
	Buddhism	
Official language(s)		
	Bahasa-Malaysia	
Illiteracy %	21.6	1990
(M/F)	13.5/29.6	1990
Daily newspapers	40	1986
Non daily newspapers	20	1984
Periodicals	1,631	1984
Radio sets	7,100,000	1989
TV sets	2,270,000	1987
Press agencies:		
	Bernama	
ICCPR:	NO	

Malaysia is a multi-ethnic, multi-lingual and multi-religious society. Some 53 per cent of the population of 17 million are Malays, 35 per cent are Chinese, 10 per cent are Indian and two per cent are of other ethnic origin. The national language is Bahasa Malaysia (based on Malay). In addition, Mandarin and other Chinese dialects, Tamil, Punjabi, Hindi, Urdu and a number of aboriginal and East Malaysian tongues are spoken. Almost all ethnic Malays are Muslims and Islam is the dominant and national religion.

The political, economic, social and religious differences between the ethnic communities have created a constant source of tension, sometimes resulting in open conflict. In 1969, there were violent ethnic riots during which a reported 200 lives were lost and 117 people were arrested in the biggest crackdown since the passing of the 1960 Internal Security Act (ISA). As a result, political rallies have been banned since 1969, although the dominant United Malays National Organization (UMNO) and Dr Mahathir Mohamad, (leader of UMNO and also Minister of Home Affairs and Justice) have been allowed to organize such demonstrations.

On October 28 1987, the ISA was invoked, allegedly to prevent violent racially-motivated riots between the majority Malay and minority Chinese communities over politically sensitive issues. As a result, 119 leaders and activists from a broad spectrum of political parties and other organizations were detained, including 10 members of Parliament and the opposition leader Lim Kit Siang, and newspapers were closed by the government.

Government critics, however, believe that the reason behind this last crackdown was the political crisis within the Barisan Nasional coalition, following a series of infighting and financial scandals which had resulted in a split in the coalition and a reduced majority after the election for the Sarawak State Assembly. The Barisan

Nasional includes UMNO, the Malaysian Chinese Association (MCA), Malaysian Indian Congress (MIC) and about 10 other smaller parties.

In February 1988, Dr Mahathir Mohamad formed a new party, UMNO Baru, and announced that members of the original party would have to re-register in order to join; dissident members of UMNO were excluded from membership. Amendments to a number of existing laws increased the power of the executive. These included amendments to the Printing Presses and Publications Act, the Societies Act and the Police Act. Most important of all was the March 1988 amendment of the Federal Constitution, which made the judiciary subservient to the executive. Between May and August 1988, the President of the Supreme Court, Tun Salleh Abas, and five other independent Supreme Court judges were suspended for "gross behaviour" because of their resistance to government pressure. In August, following an investigative tribunal chaired by Malaysia's acting head of judiciary, Abdul Hamid Omar, Salleh and two of the five were dismissed from office. In a subsequent book on the subject, Tun Salleh has written: "Judges in Malaysia have been deprived of their independence ... without an independent judiciary, all our freedoms are in jeopardy".

The Media

The Malaysian Constitution does not expressly guarantee freedom of the press but does provide for it in the "Fundamental Liberties" section (Art.10), which allows citizens the right to free speech and expression. Proposals for a freedom of information act have been unsuccessful. Following the October 1987 invocation of the ISA, the closure of newspapers and the increased powers of the Minister of Information, the government gave clear indications that it intended to use every legal constraint at its disposal to curb the media.

Newspapers All major English and Bahasa Malaysia dailies are owned by one or other of the political parties of the ruling Barisan Nasional and are expected to co-operate with the government in promoting official policy and campaigns.

The English-language daily, the *New Straits Times*, is the organ of UMNO, the other English-language daily, the *Star*, is controlled by the MCA, and the largest Malay-language daily newspapers *Utusan Malaysia* and *Berita Harian* are owned and controlled by supporters of UMNO.

In October 1987, the government closed down the *Star*, *Sin Chew Chit Poh*, a Chinese-language daily, and *Watan*, a Malay-language bi-weekly, for actions said to be "prejudicial to public order and national security". The *Star* had published the names and photos of those detained on October 27 under the ISA. In November, the government introduced legislation imposing stringent penalties on editors and publishers for publishing "false news".

In March 1988, the newspapers had their licences restored but, in the case of the *Star*, the threat of losing its licence has profoundly affected its domestic news coverage to the extent that one Malaysian social organization recently accused its editor of blatantly fabricating the facts to support the government.

On July 12 1988, after the Australian media had criticized Malaysia's domestic policies, the Ministry of Information issued a directive to all editors, asking them to discredit those foreign countries whose newspapers carried negative reports on the Malaysian government.

News Agencies The government-controlled national news agency, Bernama, was established by the 1967 Bernama Act and began operating as the sole national news agency providing local news and information to the press and media. Since May 1984, it has also become the sole distributor of news and features from foreign news agencies. Its stated aims are to strengthen the national news service, to combat the problem of "news flow imbalance" between developed nations and developing nations such as Malaysia, and to correct the "inaccurate and biased" reporting of events in the Third World. Malaysia was one of the most vigorous proponents of the New World Information and Communication Order (NWICO) during the debates on the media at UNESCO in the 1970s.

In June 1990, the Parliament approved an amendment to the 1967 Bernama Act, which gives Bernama exclusive rights to distribute news photographs, economic and financial data, and features on "other material in whatever form or manner". It will also allow Bernama, currently a non-profit-making statutory body, to pursue profits and to cease being guided by the UN international conventions protecting freedom of information.

Restrictions on the Press On December 2 1987, the amended Printing Presses and Publications Act was introduced proscribing the malicious publishing of false news (defined as "not taking reasonable measures to verify the truth"). Faced with such a charge, journalists may be forced to expose their sources. On conviction, reporters, editors, publishers, printers and distributors may be sentenced to three years' imprisonment or fined M$20,000 (US$8,000) or both. Under the Act, the Home Affairs Minister can ban the publication, import and circulation of any manuscript or publication deemed prejudicial to bilateral relations, public morality, security, public order, national interests, or which may alarm public opinion. Proscribed publications have no right of access to the courts.

The Act prescribes that printers, distributors and publishers must apply annually for a licence (which may be revoked for breaching any licensing conditions). Furthermore, the Act ends the right to a court appeal against a ministerial refusal, suspension or revocation of a licence. Aliran, the Penang-based pressure group concerned with social, economic and political issues, had its application to publish a Bahasa Malaysia-language monthly, in addition to its current English edition, turned down three times.

The Official Secrets Act, amended in December 1986, expands the classification of government documents and places the onus on journalists to prove information is not secret before it is published. If published information is found to be classified, reporters can be charged and, if convicted, face mandatory prison terms of a minimum of one-year. The Act deters journalists from investigating alleged malpractices within the public sector.

Radio and Television Under the Broadcasting Act of 1987, the Minister of Information is empowered to control and monitor all radio and television broadcasts and to revoke the licence of any private company broadcasting material conflicting with "Malaysian values".

Critics have accused Radio Television Malaysia (RTM) and TV3 (a private station but controlled by UMNO) of reporting fabrications. In February 1990, both stations broadcast a report that Tunku Abdul Rahman (the first prime minister of Malaysia and a prominent critic of the present administration) had been re-admitted to hospital and advised by doctors to refrain from speaking and other activities. The report was intended to create an impression among the public that he was in a critical condition and totally incapacitated. Although the stations were advised that their reports had no foundation, they refused to broadcast a correction when requested.

Prohibited Publications Prohibited publications include offending articles and any "extract, precis or paraphrase thereof". Offending articles include those which counsel "disobedience to the law", or which promote "ill-will, hostility, hatred, disharmony or disunity". The word "publication" encompasses "anything which by its form, shape or in any manner is capable of suggesting words or ideas". It includes "audio recording", whether voice or music.

Oppressors and Apologists, by Fan Yew Teng (then secretary-general of the opposition Social Democratic Party which is now defunct), was banned because it contained a prohibited article written in 1983. Fan was fined M$2,000 (US$900) and imprisoned for one day in July 1987. His publisher was also fined M$1,500 (US$675). Earlier, in March 1985, Haji Suhaimi Said, legal adviser to the opposition Islamic Party (PAS), was arrested in Pahang state for publishing pamphlets giving an account of clashes between supporters of PAS and UMNO in Lubuk Merbau. Haji Said was detained for trying to "split the country's Malay and Muslim community" and "threaten public order and national security". His office was raided by the police and a number of documents were confiscated.

In July 1986, Kassim Ahmed was banned from giving sermons or lectures on Islam because of his book *Hadis: A Re-evaluation*, in which he argued that the *Hadis* (the sayings of the prophet Mohamed) should not be a source of Islamic law, a common argument among some Islamic scholars. The book was banned and those found in possession of it could be fined up to M$500 (US$225).

Foreign Publications The Control of Imported Publications Act regulates foreign publications circulating in the country (the Official Secrets Act is also used). The Minister of Information has absolute discretion to ban any foreign publications deemed prejudicial to public order, morality or the security of Malaysia. Magazines such as *Playboy* and *Penthouse* are banned. Political and financial publications such as the Hong Kong-based *Far Eastern Economic Review* and the *Asian Wall Street Journal* are occasionally banned, especially when their coverage of Malaysia features sensitive subjects such as ethnic problems or financial scandals among members of the government.

In September 1986, the *Asian Wall Street Journal* was banned for nine months and its correspondents, John Berthelsen and Raphael Pura, were expelled. The Malaysian authorities gave no specific reasons for their action. Deputy Home Affairs Minister Datuk Megat Junid declared that the paper had created "feelings of uncertainty among the people ... in a way there is a sabotage of the economic development of this country". According to the *Far Eastern Economic Review*, the move against the *Asian Wall Street Journal* came after an escalating campaign against the foreign press in Malaysia, a campaign identified closely with the Prime Minister. One of the Prime Minister's favourite themes is that major American newspapers are controlled by "Zionist forces". He is believed to view criticism of Malaysia from these newspapers as an attempt to sabotage his country because of his government's support for the Palestine Liberation Organization.

The Internal Security Act

The Internal Security Act (ISA) of 1960 is regarded as repressive of press freedom and freedom of expression, association and assembly. A relic of British colonial emergency legislation which allowed detention without trial for long periods, the ISA has often been used to suppress opposition views and political opponents. The Act gives the government unlimited powers in the name of state security and is used by the Malaysian Special Branch whose activities include monitoring, surveillance, telephone tapping and harassment of suspected "subversives".

Under Section 73 of the Act, the Home Affairs Minister can order the detention for 60 days for interrogation by the Special Branch of any person, on the suspicion that "he or she acted or is about to act in any manner prejudicial to the security of Malaysia or any part thereof". In July 1988 and June 1989, the Act was amended to limit the right of detainees to challenge the legality of their detentions in the courts. As a result of the amendments, ISA detainees alleged to be a threat to national security may now turn to the courts on procedural matters only.

In October and November 1987, the government, using the ISA, ordered the arrest and detention of 119 leaders and activists of a number of political parties and social and religious organizations. All but 49 detainees, who had been served with detention orders, were released after 60 days. Most of those detained were released by the end of 1988 except the opposition leader of the Democratic Action Party, Lim Kit Siang, and his son Lim Guan Eng, who were released in April 1989.

The government also uses the Police Act to curtail the right of assembly and the Societies Act to limit the right of association. Eleven people were arrested under the Police Act on November 6 1988 whilst taking part in a peaceful candlelight vigil at Lake Gardens Park in Kuala Lumpa, in protest against the continued detention of those arrested in October 1987. Both Acts have been used to harass members of Aliran and another social reform group INSAN. Aliran leader, Chandra Muzaffar, was among those detained during the October 1987 crackdown.

Actions

On January 19 1990 ARTICLE 19 wrote to the government expressing concern that two lawyers, Encik Mohideen Abdul Kader and Meenaksh Raman, were fined M$5,000 (US$1,850) on December 16 1989 for contempt of court committed more than two years previously. ARTICLE 19 believes they were punished for exercising their right to free expression.

On February 9 1990 ARTICLE 19 wrote to the government urging it to reverse its decision denying *Aliran* the right to publish in Mayalsia's national language, Bahasa Malaysia. (See text)

On March 8 1990 ARTICLE 19 wrote to the government urging it to abandon a Bill which would give the Bernama News Agency sole rights to news distribution. (See text)

Myanmar

Myanmar has remained in a state of political and social crisis since the summer of 1988 when over 3,000 civilians were reportedly killed by security forces during the student-led democracy protests. These were quashed by an army coup, on September 18, led by Myanmar's new military leader, General Saw Maung. In the aftermath, a further 10,000 students and civilian activists fled into borderlands controlled by various ethnic and communist insurgent forces which have been at war with the central government virtually since independence in 1948.

	Data	Year
Population	38,541,000	1988
Life expectancy (M/F)	55.8/59.3	1985
GNP (US$ per capita)	200	1988
Main religion(s)	Buddhism	
Official language(s)	Burmese	
Illiteracy %	19.4	1990
(M/F)	10.9/27.7	1990
Daily newspapers	7	1986
Radio sets	3,100,000	1987
TV sets	50,000	1987
Press agencies:		
News Agency of Myanmar		
ICCPR:	NO	

The State Law and Order Restoration Council (SLORC), brought to power by the coup, promised that multi-party democracy would be restored, ending 26 years of one-party rule by the Burma Socialist Programme Party (BSPP), once law and order had been established. However, political repression continued and in the following months thousands of political activists were arrested.

Nonetheless, by February 1989, 233 new political parties had formed. Primary schools reopened in June, high schools in September but universities have remained closed. May 27 1990 was set for elections to a new People's Assembly which, Saw Maung pledged, would have sole responsibility for drafting a new Constitution.

The election result, despite severe restrictions on freedom of speech and assembly and the continued arrest of political leaders, resulted in an overwhelming victory for the country's largest and most outspoken pro-democracy party, the National League for Democracy (NLD). The result was a crushing defeat for the National Unity Party (NUP), the former BSPP, which the SLORC had backed.

Immediately following the polls, however, army leaders declared a protracted transitional period, setting pre-conditions to any changes in government.

Myanmar's ageing military strongman, General Ne Win, (who instituted authoritarian control after staging a military coup in 1962 and who officially resigned from office in July 1988) has continued to manipulate events from behind the scenes.

The 1974 Constitution, which is now being revised, enshrines the principle that Burma become a one-party state (Art.11). Although there are clear guarantees for the basic rights of all citizens before the law "regardless of race, religion, status or sex" (Art.22), the exercise of such rights must not be "to the detriment of national solidarity and the socialist social order" (Art.153b). Press laws are similarly restricted; Article 157 declares: "Every citizen shall have the freedom of speech, expression and publications to the extent that the enjoyment of such freedom is not contrary to the interests of the working people and socialism."

The NLD has announced its intention to base Myanmar's new constitution on the "independence" Constitution of 1947. But Saw Maung has publicly stated that the army will want to designate certain areas, including "national security", "national sovereignty" and the "unity of races" as its exclusive preserve and will feel duty-bound to interfere in the political process whenever and wherever it appears that those interests are threatened. The SLORC has also demanded that the proposed constitution must be approved by the military before being submitted to a national vote.

Legacy of Ne Win Following Ne Win's 1962 military coup, Burma became one of the most secretive and isolated countries in the world. Foreign journalists and publications were banned, and the few foreign visitors were restricted to Rangoon, Mandalay and a handful of other government-controlled towns. As the one-party rule of the army-dominated BSPP was instituted, thousands of politicians and trade unionists from the parliamentary era of the 1950s were imprisoned without trial.

Ne Win and the Media In the 1950s, Burma's press was one of the most free in Asia, with more than 30 daily papers, including three in English, six in Chinese and several in Indian languages. A month after Ne Win seized power, journalists established the Burma Press Council to preserve press freedom through a voluntary code of ethics. However, in 1963 several prominent newspaper editors were arrested, and the Ministry of Information began publication of *Forward Weekly* and *Working People's Daily* as the official voice of the BSPP. Finally, in September 1964, Ne Win nationalized the country's principal newspapers, allowing those that reopened "freedom of expression within the accepted limits of the Burmese way to socialism". By 1988, just six papers remained, all of them state-owned and virtually indistinguishable.

Since 1962, the main instrument of government control of publications has been the Printers and Publishers Registration Law, which established "Publications" or "Press Scrutiny Boards" to monitor and censor every aspect of the written word, including lyrics and film scripts. These boards govern the text, language and subject of all publications and the numbers printed. With paper always in chronically short supply, print-runs of only 2,000-3,000 copies have been permitted.

Given these tight restrictions on books, newspapers and news information, periodicals have become very popular. Several monthly literary/fiction magazines are government-published, (*Myawaddy*, *Ngwetayi* and *Shwei-thwei* (children's cartoons)), but some 20-30 are privately-owned. All are purely for entertainment.

Burmanization Policy Following the nationalization of schools under the BSPP, successive administrations have embarked on what minority leaders allege is a straightforward policy of "Burmanization" (Burmans form the largest ethnic group). Minority languages are rarely taught or used beyond fourth grade and ethnic minority writers, struggling to promote their little-published languages, have repeatedly run foul of the Press Scrutiny Boards. Minority literature has been restricted to little more than folksy magazines such as *Our Home* and *Go Forward*. Distribution of religious literature, including the Bible, has also been restricted. Licences to publish the country's remaining Indian and Chinese language newspapers were discontinued in January 1966.

Another casualty of the BSPP's promotion of Burmese has been the English language whose continued usage was guaranteed, after Burmese, in the 1947

Constitution, partly to placate minority fears of Burman cultural domination. In 1966, the Chair of English at Rangoon University was abolished and English was reduced to the status of a minority subject in schools.

Literacy Myanmar has long prided itself on its high literacy levels and under the BSPP twice won UNESCO prizes for special literacy campaigns. But in 1987 the previously reported adult literacy rate of 78.6 per cent dropped to 18.7 per cent (apparently to conform with the strict requirement of less than 20 per cent literacy in order to be granted Least Developed Country (LDC) status).

The State Law and Order Restoration Council

Despite the promise by SLORC Chairman Saw Maung to restore Myanmar to multi-party democracy, the military government has employed a number of legal devices to restrict freedom of speech and assembly. These include the 1950 Emergency Measures Act, which allowed for up to seven years' imprisonment for anyone spreading news or stories "disloyal to the state" and the 1975 State Protection Law under which the authorities can order the detention for up to three years without trial of anyone they believe "endangers" the "security and sovereignty of the State".

Since September 1988, the SLORC has also issued a number of martial law decrees. Order 2/88, on the day of the military coup, imposed a night-time curfew and a ban on public gatherings of more than five people. This was further refined by Order 8/88 which banned all activities, literature, speeches and propaganda "aimed at dividing the Defence Forces".

Under these laws, hundreds of civilians were imprisoned in the months following the coup. Thousands of others fearing arrest, such as the famous *Myawaddy* magazine writer U Ye Gaung, escaped into the hills where an estimated 2,000-2,500 students, monks and democracy activists still remain. Another 1,000 fled to the State of Kachin, 2,000 went to Bangkok and some escaped to India. The SLORC has only intermittently acknowledged the large numbers of arrests, but in April 1989 announced that 721 people, including 183 students, arrested after the coup were still in detention. Opposition groups claim far higher numbers and there have been consistent allegations, documented by Amnesty International, of the torture, ill-treatment and killings of detainees. Few of those arrested have ever been charged or brought to trial.

The SLORC also abolished all existing legal institutions but, on September 26 1988, a judicial law re-established courts at various levels and a number of legal principles, including the right of appeal, public trial and self-defence. However, in July 1989, as the anniversary of the democracy uprising approached, a second wave of mass arrests began. Against a background of growing tension and student-organized street protests, the SLORC announced Martial Law Orders 1/89 and 2/89, which established military tribunals across the country. Details of those tried or arrested were only spasmodically released but, in October 1989, the SLORC announced that, since July, 100 people had been sentenced to death by military tribunals.

In July, foreign diplomats in Rangoon estimated that between 3,000 and 6,000 civilians were arrested under these new provisions, including the leadership of the NLD which, with a claimed 2 million members, most observers believed would convincingly win any freely-held election. The NLD leadership, built around the personality of Daw Aung San Suu Kyi, daughter of the engineer of Myanmar's independence and former Defence Minister U Tin Oo, contains many prominent writers, journalists and artists, including U Win Tin, U Aung Lwin, Tharrawaddy San San Nwe and Ma Theingi, all of whom were arrested.

On June 18, Saw Maung declared Law 16/89, increasing maximum sentences under the 1962 Printers and Publishers Registration Law to seven years' imprisonment and/or a 30,000 kyat (US$4,620) fine. On June 27, the head of the Military Intelligence Service (MIS), Brigadier-General Khin Nyunt, issued Martial Law Order 3/89, announcing that martial law regulations would be used against political parties, publishers and organizations illegally printing and publishing documents without registering with the Ministry of Home and Religious Affairs.

Many parties publicly objected to these draconian orders and the NLD leadership, stressing non-violence, called for a campaign of non-compliance with all martial law regulations restricting civil liberties. Aung San Suu Kyi described the NLD's campaign as "no more violent than is necessary in banging the keys of a typewriter". On July 20 1989, she was placed under house arrest, under the 1975 State Protection Law, for allegedly "endangering the State", and the SLORC announced she could be held incommunicado for up to one year. Many NLD leaders arrested then have never been charged but, in December 1989, the NLD's 65 year-old Chairman, Tin Oo, was sentenced by a special military tribunal to three years' hard labour on a number of charges, including "contacting, writing and sending false anti-government reports to foreign organizations and leaders".

In December 1989, the SLORC moved against the country's second largest opposition party, the League for Democracy and Peace (LDP), headed by the country's last democratically elected Prime Minister, U Nu, a prolific writer and Buddhist lecturer. He refused an order by the SLORC to renounce a provisional "parallel" government he had declared during the 1988 uprising, and on December 29 the LDP's senior leadership was arrested.

The May 1990 Elections A five-man civilian General Election Commission, headed by U Ba Htay, was ostensibly responsible for monitoring the conduct of the polls, but privately admitted they had to endorse the SLORC orders; these included barring several NLD leaders from the polls. A number of objections were raised against Aung San Suu Kyi's candidacy but, despite her detention, the NLD continued to hold rallies and openly challenged the government and the army. Aung San Suu Kyi was eventually banned in January 1990, allegedly for having "unlawful association with insurgent organizations".

The Election Commission also endorsed the army's banning of a number of parties accused of pro-communist sympathies, notably the People's Progressive Party, and its three leaders, U Hla Shwe, U Khin Maung Myint and U Nyo Win were arrested. The leaderships of the All Burma Federation of Students' Unions and the legally registered Democratic Party for New Society, were decimated by arrests and the figure-head of the student movement, Min Ko Naing, has been detained since March 1989.

Eventually, 93 mostly small parties were left to put up 2,311 candidates for the 485 available seats. All political campaigning had to be conducted under the conditions of Martial Law Order 3/90 issued on February 23 1990 which decreed that all speeches and publications had to be approved by the local township authorities.

Nationally, the parties were confined to one carefully-censored 10-minute statement on state television and 15 minutes on state radio. The Ministry of Information then further edited these speeches for publication in the state-controlled press.

An unknown number of candidates were arrested in the run-up to the elections, including 82 year-old U Oo Tha Tun, a respected ethnic Rakhine historian who was standing for the Arakan League for Democracy in Kyauktaw constituency: he was detained on May 7 1990 and reportedly later sentenced to three years' in jail. The only serious contender besides the NUP which escaped army harassment was the Union Nationals Democracy Party (UNDP), headed by Ne Win's former deputy, Aung Gyi, with 270 candidates. Opponents alleged the UNDP was simply a stalking horse candidacy to be admitted to the government with the NUP to give the appearance of multi-party reform.

Nonetheless, the NLD put up 425 candidates and won 396 seats. The NUP won just 10; most of the other 79 seats went to ethnic minority candidates, many of whom are affiliated with the NLD.

Despite the public's endorsement of their party, no NLD leaders were released in the aftermath of the polls. The SLORC, having taken a month to announce the results, began a series of delaying tactics with the carefully floated suggestion that it could take two years for the new People's Assembly to draw up and institute the right kind of reforms under the army's guidance and mooted that a further election or referendum might yet be needed.

In September, another round of political detentions began with the arrest of the NLD's acting leader, ex-Colonel Kyi Maung, who had led the party to victory in the absence of Aung San Suu Kyi and the first-line leaders. Kyi Maung, who had called on the SLORC to hand over power to the NLD, faced treason charges of "passing state evidence to unconcerned persons". Then, in October, dozens of monks were arrested and Buddhist monasteries were raided and threatened with closure after monks organized a boycott of religious services for military personnel and their families until the SLORC released all political prisoners and honoured the result of the polls. As a result of the arrests of another 14 members of the NLD later that month, most NLD leaders were either under house arrest or in jail.

The Insurgent Press In many insurgent-controlled areas of Myanmar there is a lively underground press. Circulation of these news sheets and magazines is irregular, but amongst the best-known publications are *Than Noo Htoo* (in Karen), its English-language equivalent, the *Karen National Union Bulletin*, the English-language *Dawn News Bulletin* of the All Burma Students' Democratic Front, and the *Baknoi Bat Shiga* (in Jinghpaw) of the Kachin Independence Organization. The Communist Party of Burma (CPB) ran an illegal radio station, the Voice of the People of Burma, broadcasting virtually uninterrupted in several indigenous languages from secret locations close to the China frontier from 1971 until 1989. Subsequently, a breakaway ethnic organization, the United Wa State Army, has broadcast propaganda on the same frequencies. In December 1989, the Democratic Alliance of Burma opened a broadcasting station in south-east Myanmar, but reception is generally poor.

The Official Media Since 1988 During the brief democracy summer, dozens of news sheets and newspapers sprang up and even state-controlled media, including the *Guardian* and *Working People's Daily* (*WPD*) began reporting news more accurately and questioning government policies. Following the Saw Maung coup, the

SLORC closed down all new publications and the six state-run newspapers. Only the *WPD*, in Burmese and English editions, was allowed to reopen. Printed in Rangoon, only limited numbers reach towns such as Moulmein and Mandalay. Although references to socialism have been dropped, changes in the *WPD* are virtually undetectable and reporting still consists largely of military news releases (prepared by the SLORC) and eulogies of the defence services and army leaders. State-run radio and TV echo word for word reports in the *WPD*.

Music, Films and Videos Words of songs have to be submitted to the Press Scrutiny Boards and film-scripts are closely checked before permission to film is granted. A thriving trade in recycled video tapes has developed. Private TV ownership remains low but, in remote communities, many villagers have clubbed together to buy video recorders. A video law, enacted in November 1985, requires official registration of all aspects of the video business. Those failing to comply face prison terms of up to five years and 40,000 kyat (US$6,160) fines. Since 1988, foreign news reports of the democracy uprising and home-produced videos of NLD and LDP rallies have become much sought-after. In response, in May 1989, security officials began raids on the estimated 400 private video rental shops in Myanmar and many subsequently closed. The *WPD* reported that those arrested faced three years' imprisonment. Nonetheless, in many areas, illegal video films and reports remain a popular source of information and entertainment.

The Foreign Press Foreign journalists, with the exception of local Tass and Xinhua correspondents, were for the most part banned from Myanmar during Ne Win's long reign. Since January 1989, they have been briefly and selectively readmitted as the SLORC (virtually ostracized in the international community) has periodically tried to gain political respectability. All foreign journalists were again banned from the country in the months preceding the 1990 election. David Storey of Reuters, the only foreign reporter in Myanmar at the time, was summarily deported in July 1989, the eve of the arrest of the NLD leaders. International telephone and telex lines were then shut down for two weeks. Applications from international human rights organizations to observe the 1990 elections were refused but, at the last minute, a number of carefully vetted Western journalists were allowed to witness the conduct of the polls before the ban was reimposed.

Most Burmese nationals are understandably cautious about giving information to the foreign media. U Sein Win, of Associated Press and a former *Guardian* editor, was arrested and held for nearly one month without trial in July 1988. Ironically, Sein Win is a close associate of Ne Win's former deputy, Aung Gyi, and is himself regarded as sympathetic to the military.

The SLORC has unleashed a sustained propaganda attack on foreign news organizations, culminating in the publication in late 1989 of two books by MIS Chief Khin Nyunt, *The Conspiracy of Treasonous Minions Within the Myanmar Naingngan and Traitorous Cohorts Abroad* and *A Sky Full of Lies*, which claimed the 1988 uprising was the work of right-wing groups and foreign sympathizers in the media. These charges are reinforced by photographs and biographical details of a number of Western journalists, politicians and academics. The names of Burmese citizens working abroad for foreign news organizations, including the BBC, are prominently published in these books and the *WPD* along with their parents' names in what appears to be deliberate intimidation.

Current Detainees U Nay Min, a 42 year-old lawyer, sentenced to 14 years' hard labour in October 1989 by a Military Tribunal under Section 5-E/J of the 1950 Emergency Measures Act for sending "false news and rumours" to the BBC, is believed to be seriously ill in prison; U Ba Thaw (alias Maung Thaw Ka), ex-naval officer and popular writer, sentenced to 20 years' hard labour in October 1989 under Section 5 A/B of the same law, on the charge of trying "to cause the navy to secede from the defence services"; U Win Tin, former editor of the *Hanthawaddy* newspaper and vice-chairman of the Writers' Association, sentenced to three years' hard labour in October 1989 on trumped-up charges; Ma Theingi, a writer and painter, arrested on July 20 1989, now held in Insein prison; U Aung Lwin, actor and chairman of the Film Society, arrested on June 28 1989 and reportedly tortured, is now believed to have been sentenced to five years' hard labour. The latter four are all senior leaders of the NLD.

Win Myint, video cameraman, sentenced to death on October 19 1989, under the 1908 Illegal Associations Act and 1878 Amended Weapons Act, on explosives charges and for filming crowd scenes during the 1988 uprising. Zargana, a popular satirist, was arrested after the 1988 demonstration and detained from October to April 1989; he was re-arrested on May 19 1990 and sentenced to five years' imprisonment.

Nepal

On April 9 1990, following a popular movement for democracy, King Birendra of Nepal announced the abolition of the party-less *Panchayat* system, in force since 1960, and the introduction of multi-party democracy. For the first time in 30 years the Nepali press can openly question the involvement of its royal family and senior officials in corruption and discuss Nepal's trade conflict with India. Even more astonishing, in this, the only Hindu kingdom in the world, the press can and does debate the merits of a secular state.

On February 18 1990, the Movement for the Restoration of Democracy

	Data	Year
Population	17,131,000	1988
Life expectancy (M/F)	50.8/48.1	1981
GNP (US$ per capita)	170	1988
Main religion(s)	Hinduism	
Official language(s)	Nepali	
Illiteracy %	74.4	1990
(M/F)	62.4/86.8	1990
Daily newspapers	28	1986
Radio sets	550,000	1987
TV sets	24,000	1987
Press agencies:		
Rastriya Samachar Samiti		
ICCPR:	NO	

(MRD), established in late 1989 in response to mounting popular discontent at the inefficiency, corruption, abuse of human rights and poor economic performance of the *Panchayat* system, launched its public campaign. Despite intense police and army repression and the arrest of tens of thousands of demonstrators, the movement gathered force resulting in many towns in the Kathmandu Valley becoming "no-go" areas for the security forces. On April 6, the largest protest demonstration ever held in Nepalese history, composed almost exclusively of young men, marched on the Royal Palace in the centre of Kathmandu. The army opened fire on the unarmed protesters, killing between 50 and 100 people.

In a vain attempt to control dissent and reporting during the MRD, many newspapers were closed down and some 50 members of the Nepal Journalists' Association (NJA) were arrested. Several issues of foreign weeklies such as *Time*, *Newsweek*, and *Asiaweek* were banned. Although the government-controlled media ignored clashes between security forces and demonstrators, middle-class Nepalis, who owned TVs, saw live coverage of the clashes by satellite from India. This contradiction between official and foreign versions of events shifted influential opinion in the weeks leading up to April 9. Owners of FM radios listened to the communications between security forces who regularly reported numbers of casualties and the security situation from flash points around the city. These also sharply differed from official versions of events. The Acting Deputy Inspector General of Police, Achut Kharel, achieved such widespread notoriety for the coarseness and brutality of his commands over the air that after April 9 he was forced into hiding.

The Media

During the *Panchayat* years, the media was crucial for instilling in the population a respect for monarchy and the virtues of the "party-less democratic system". The national news agency, Rastriya Samachar Samiti, established in 1962 and employing over 120 journalists, was a key institution for delivering the "official version of news", under the close control of the Press Secretariat of the Royal Palace. The state-owned Gorkhapatra Corporation is still the largest publishing organization in Nepal, with two daily newspapers, *Gorkhapatra* in Nepali, and *The Rising Nepal* in English, and a new English-language weekly *Sunday Dispatch*. The failure of the state-controlled media to reflect the mood of the country during the MRD, coupled with the banning of independent newspapers, sharply highlighted the extent of media control in Nepal, and led to widespread demands for the privatization of both the Gorkhapatra Corporation and Radio Nepal.

The Press Before the overthrow of the 104-year Rana regime in 1951 there were virtually no newspapers in Nepal. Despite the proliferation of papers since then, most journalists work only part-time and professional skills are low. In the 1970s the government amended press regulations obliging editors to hold a minimum of educational qualifications and training in journalism from a recognized institution.

There are four major newspapers, each with a circulation of between 20,000-40,000; *Gorkhapatra*, the government-owned daily, *Bimarsha*, an independent weekly, *Nepali Awaj*, a weekly identified with Lok Bahadur Chand, a leader of the new National Democratic Party which is composed of ex-members of the *Panchayat* system, and *Dristi*, a weekly published by the Nepal Communist Party, a member of the United Left Front. The Nepal Congress Party, which heads the interim government, does not have a large circulation newspaper, although its members have been appointed to leading positions in the Gorkhapatra Corporation.

The vast majority of newspapers have a limited (less than 5,000) circulation. Many papers which identified with the *Panchayat* system have closed down because their owners can no longer compel public sector bodies to buy bulk subscriptions and provide advertising revenue. Most of the new papers are identified with the many strands of the leftist political movement, which were prohibited under the *Panchayat* system.

Radio and Television The sole radio station, Radio Nepal, was commissioned in 1951 and Nepal TV began broadcasting only in 1985. Radio Nepal has a monopoly on the airwaves, as the government has consistently refused to allow private radio stations to operate. Throughout the *Panchayat* period, headline radio news broadcasts always referred to activities of the royal family. Neither a major football stadium tragedy in March 1988 nor a major earthquake which destroyed large parts of eastern Nepal in August 1988 was headlined. This distortion of relative news value reached absurd limits during the MRD, when major clashes in Nepal, reported as headline news by foreign radio stations, were totally ignored by Radio Nepal. Since April 9, there have been some changes in programme content, with a current affairs programme and an educational programme about multi-party democracy, called *Shero Phero*. Radio Nepal has also broadcast, simultaneously with the BBC Nepali Service, five "Debates on Democracy" which involved politicians of all parties, civil servants and journalists. Songs praising the King and the *Panchayat* system have been banned and there are still no programmes broadcast in national languages other than Nepali.

Press Laws Laws dating from 1948 defined in detail the limits to freedom of publication and spelt out the sanctions if those limits were transgressed. The 1976 Press and Publication Act introduced compulsory registration fees for new publications and prohibited any journalism which led to "an increase in party politics".

The Press and Publication Act of 1982 (Art.23) introduced a system of evaluation of newspapers for which large cash prizes and financial co-operation would be awarded annually by the government. The criteria included the contribution of the paper to promoting the honour of the royal family or to the spirit of nationalism and sovereignty. Article 7 of this Act also ruled that publishers of newspapers or journals should be Nepalese citizens.

Several general laws restricting freedom of expression serve to reinforce the Press Acts such as the State (Offence and Punishment) Act of 1962 which provides for imprisonment and fines or both for the creation of hatred, enmity or disrespect of the Crown or royal family by writing, speech, or signs.

Journalists have also been restricted by the Libel and Defamation Act of 1959. Although Section 4 of the Act gives certain safeguards to media professionals, many journalists were silenced by use of this legislation during the *Panchayat* years. A new Press Act is now under consideration and the Nepal Press Institute has submitted proposals for the reform of the existing 1982 Press Law.

Freedom of Expression

The Constitution (which was largely suspended during the MRD) was promulgated in 1962 and guaranteed the "right to freedom" (Art.11), including "freedom of speech and expression". Article 17 restricted these rights under the need for: the preservation of the security of Nepal; the maintenance of law and order; the maintenance of good relations among people of different classes or professions or between people of different areas; the prevention of internal disturbances or external invasion; and the prevention of contempt of court or contempt of the National *Panchayat*. There was also the right to "freedom to form associations and unions", but no political party or any other organization, union or association motivated by party politics could be formed.

In October 1990, a nine-member committee completed a draft constitution, designed to limit the King's powers, guarantee fundamental rights and bring parliamentary democracy to Nepal, which was promulgated on November 9. However, it had not been published as this report went to press.

Attacks on the Press In 1989, several newspapers were censored, some had their registrations cancelled and 14 journalists were arrested. The period of the MRD (February 18 to April 9 1990) saw a marked deterioration in freedom of expression in Nepal and intensified harassment of the media began days before the formal inauguration of the MRD.

In protest against the censorship and confiscation of newspapers, a number of weeklies, *Matribhumi, Saptahik, Bimarsha, Yugantar, Gatividhi*, and *Swastik*, decided not to publish their next issues. The February 12 issue of *Swastik* was confiscated from the printing press, while seven other weeklies voluntarily ceased publishing due to the limitations imposed by the government. In response, the Zonal Commissioner of Kathmandu, Narendra Kumar Chaudhary, summoned editors and publishers to his office and asked them to publish their newspapers under official guidance, and not to publish anything on the MRD or issues likely to foment party politics.

The NJA issued a statement describing the censorship and banning of newspapers and arrest of journalists as "illegal, unconstitutional and undemocratic" and demanded an immediate end to such actions and the release of all arrested journalists. On February 10, the Minister of Communication, Kamal Thapa, told a protest delegation from the NJA that the government would lift censorship if newspapers promised not to publish material that might "incite the public". The delegation asked the minister either to declare a state of emergency or to publicly announce the existence of press censorship and threatened to withhold publications in which censorship had been imposed. In response, the government issued a statement to the effect that it did not have a policy of censoring the press and the NJA called on its members to end their action.

During the following month many newspapers were confiscated, journalists were arrested, including a representative of Associated Press who was briefly detained, and plainclothes police were posted outside newspaper offices, private courier services and public post offices in order to restrict the mass circulation of the press.

Arrests of Writers On March 17, 138 writers, artists and poets were arrested when they staged a protest demonstration in Kathmandu for freedom of expression, wearing black bands tied around their mouths. On March 21, police arrested over 500 intellectuals attending a symposium at Tribhuvan University on "Our Responsibility in the Present Situation". By March 23, nine editors and 24 reporters were under arrest, including Govinda Biyogi, the president of the NJA, and eight more papers had issues seized.

Foreign media coverage of lightning protests such as these, which were a feature of the MRD, had earlier provoked the Minister of Communications, Kamal Thapa, in a speech at Hetauda on March 10, to blame the foreign press for what was happening in Nepal: "The unnecessary propaganda resorted to by foreign communications media has clearly indicated how much of foreign interest is involved in bringing instability to the country by inciting the so-called movement".

By the time that the *Panchayat* system was finally overthrown on April 9, some 50 journalists were under arrest, most newspapers in Nepal had effectively been silenced, and of those which remained, only the government newspapers *Gorkhapatra* and *Rising Nepal* were allowed to circulate outside the Kathmandu Valley. As protest over press censorship grew, there were attempts to disrupt the circulation of both newspapers and, in several instances, copies were burned *en masse*.

Religious Expression In June 1990, all jail sentences in force for religious offences were withdrawn, as were those pending in connection with such offences. At the time, according to the Home Ministry, 11 Christians and one Muslim were in jail on charges of religious conversion. There were also 20 other detainees against whom legal action was underway. Despite the long-standing presence in the country of over 500 foreign Christian missionaries of the United Mission of Nepal, and a long-established Muslim community, neither Christian nor Muslim religious bookshops are permitted, nor is literature of either faith sold in general bookshops.

Recent Developments

Since the introduction of multi-party democracy on April 9 1990, there has been a noticeable improvement in media freedom in Nepal. Subjects on which no media dissent was tolerated, the royal family, the *Panchayat* system and foreign policy, are now widely debated. On April 12, all restrictions imposed on newspapers and journals were lifted and cases pending against them were withdrawn. Restrictions on the entry of some foreign newspapers and magazines were also lifted. Treason cases filed against editor Ang Dorje Lama of the *Rajdhani* weekly and its columnist Bhairav Risal were also withdrawn. On May 16, the government announced that government offices could subscribe to private newspapers and not solely to the government newspapers, *Gorkhapatra* and *Rising Nepal*, as before.

The Press Council was re-constituted in May with a mandate to propose revisions to the existing press laws in order to improve media freedom. On June 4, the government stated: "Official communication media will not be allowed to be influenced by the government or by any political party. The question of making corporations in the communications sector autonomous will be studied. Full press and academic freedom will be guaranteed. A policy of including regional languages, besides the Nepali language, in official communication programmes will also be formulated."

Pakistan

President Zia ul-Haq was killed in an, as yet unexplained, air crash on August 17 1988. General elections took place as scheduled in December 1988 and Benazir Bhutto of the Pakistan People's Party (PPP) was elected Prime Minister. On August 6 1990, Ms Bhutto and her government were dismissed by President Ghulam Ishaq Khan with the backing of the military. Former PPP member Ghulam Mustafa Jatoi was appointed Prime Minister to lead a seven-man interim administration until a general election on October 24. The Islamic Democratic Alliance won the election, gaining two thirds of the seats in the National Assembly. An international observer group from the National Democratic Institute in the

	Data	Year
Population	105,409,000	1988
Life expectancy (M/F)	59.0/59.2	1978
GNP (US$ per capita)	350	1988
Main religion(s)	Islam	
Official language(s)	Urdu	
Illiteracy %	65.2	1990
(M/F)	62.7/78.9	1990
Daily newspapers	177	1988
Radio sets	9,800,000	1988
TV sets	1,504,000	1987
Press agencies:		
Associated Press of Pakistan,		
Pakistan Press International,		
United Press of Pakistan Ltd.		
ICCPR:	NO	

United States said that it had received no evidence to substantiate Ms Bhutto's allegations of vote-rigging. However, it criticized the caretaker government for giving advantage to one side, and said that the state-controlled television coverage was not balanced.

When Benazir Bhutto came to power, the two most significant changes on the political horizon were the restoration of the independence of the judiciary and moves towards a free press. In her first address to the nation, Benazir Bhutto promised to repeal all press laws restricting the freedom of the press, dissolve the government-controlled National Press Trust (see ARTICLE 19 World Report 1988), grant full autonomy to state-owned television and radio, discontinue the press advice system, and ensure full protection of the rights of working journalists.

Within days of assuming power she removed the ban on student and labour unions and abolished the black-list of intellectuals, writers, poets, and journalists denied access to the media during the previous 11 years. She declared an amnesty for political prisoners from the years of martial law. The amnesty brought about the release of about 1,000 prisoners convicted by special military courts and the commutation of over 2,000 death sentences passed by various courts.

The Media

The Press By the end of 1989, the promise to abolish the National Press Trust had not materialized. A number of government measures, however, were welcomed by the press, including the appointment of two veteran journalists, I A Rehman and Aziz Seddiqi, as the editor-in-chief and editor of the government-run *Pakistan Times*. Both journalists were opponents of the martial law regime. The paper gained a degree of credibility by reflecting the views not only of the government, as in the past, but of the opposition.

The government abolished all the previous conditions required for licensing of new newspapers, which resulted in a rapid growth of new dailies and periodicals in all the regional languages, as well in Urdu and English. Between January and June 1989, 1,031 new licences were issued, 108 of them for dailies. This boom in the newspaper industry has created a problem because of a paucity of experienced journalists. Between 1966 and 1986, only 96 new licences were granted and few young people were trained.

Most newspapers and periodicals were believed to have functioned free of government censorship during 1989. In 1990, the National Assembly was hearing a proposed Freedom of the Press Act which would give journalists the right to inspect federal and provincial government files, except sensitive defence files.

Violence and ethnic clashes spread throughout the province of Sind, and the offices of some newspapers were occupied by supporters of political parties demanding sympathetic coverage of their activities. Journalists were assaulted and threatened. The Federal Interior Minister met the president of the Pakistan Newspaper Society in January 1990 and assured him that the government would act to protect journalists against such attacks. In February, at least two more offices were attacked and several journalists and photographers were injured.

Pressure on journalists also comes from some newspaper owners who want to impose their own views. Maleeha Ludhi, editor of one of Pakistan's leading English-language dailies, *The Muslim*, together with four of the paper's senior journalists, resigned in January 1990 after attempts by the owner, Agha Pooya, to turn the paper into a mouthpiece for Islamic opposition parties.

In September 1989, Christina Lamb, Islamabad correspondent for the *Financial Times*, was told by the Interior Ministry that her visa would not be renewed, after she filed a report on an alleged coup attempt.

Television   The Pakistan Broadcasting Corporation is controlled by the state. General Zia's control over news coverage was almost absolute and he imposed censorship on all aspects of TV production. In keeping with his policy of "Islamicization", all programmes had to conform to strict religious rules and regulations.

Under Benazir Bhutto, media workers sacked during the rule of General Zia regained their jobs. Censorship of opposition views and activities is believed to have been greatly reduced, but there are indications of dissatisfaction with the amount of broadcasting allocated to the government. Coverage of the Prime Minister is given 10 minutes in the main half-hour news bulletin and this is often followed by the activities of federal and provincial ministers. Only then is the foreign news broadcast.

In January 1990, a group of 79 opposition parliamentarians took to the streets, protesting that TV was biased against the opposition. Despite a government ban on political rallies in the capital, the police did not interfere.

Performing Arts   Theatre groups, mostly of writers and performers banned under General Zia's rule, have flourished. No ban on theatre production was imposed by the government but theatre groups' freedom to experiment with new ideas is constrained. Fundamentalist Muslims would not hesitate to disrupt a performance if they considered it to be "un-Islamic" and the Dramatic Performance Control Act of

1876, designed by the colonial British administration to control the growth of indigenous culture, provides for a ban on performances with a political overtone.

Banned Publications The type and nature of bans on publications varies from province to province. In one case, the ban imposed by the federal government was defied by two provincial governments. The federal government banned the book *Dr Abdul Qadeer Khan and the Islamic Bomb* for divulging "defence secrets", but the provincial governments of Punjab and Baluchistan refused to ban it. The Urdu translation of Dostoevsky's novel *The Idiot* was banned in late 1988 because it contained "objectionable material".

The Satanic Verses Salman Rushdie's novel, *The Satanic Verses*, was banned by the National Assembly on February 8 1989. The ban was followed by a demonstration on February 12, when some 2,000 rioters tried to storm the US Embassy in protest at the forthcoming publication of the book in the US. In response to attacks by stones and bricks, police opened fire at the crowd, killing five people and injuring more than 100. The incident marked the beginning of a new wave of Muslim protest against the publication of *The Satanic Verses*. The federal government acted swiftly and confiscated all copies of the Urdu weekly *Takbeer* for publishing extracts from *The Satanic Verses*, and a case was registered against *Takbeer*'s publisher and printer for reproducing the content of a proscribed book. An issue of *Time* magazine was banned for reviewing the novel and copies of the UK *Times*, which contained excerpts, were confiscated. On February 28, a Pakistani security guard was killed in a bomb attack on the British Council Library in Karachi.

The Judiciary

The reassertion of the independence of the judiciary has been of enormous significance. The High Courts and the Supreme Court have shown a marked degree of impartiality when hearing petitions challenging laws and regulations curbing civil liberties. In October 1988, the Supreme Court ruled that political parties would be allowed to campaign during the elections. On another occasion, when the newly-restored democracy underwent a serious crisis due to the unexpected dissolution of the Baluchistan Assembly by the province's governor, the High Court of Baluchistan ruled that the move was illegal; the ruling, in effect, brought the crisis to an end.

Freedom of Expression

Arrests Under the government of Benazir Bhutto, the number of people arrested for exercising their right to freedom of information and association has been far fewer than before, although some political arrests have been carried out. On August 6 1989, Zahid Malik, editor of the evening paper *Pakistan Observer* and the Urdu weekly *Hurmat*, was detained under the Official Secrets Act after officials confiscated hundreds of copies of his book *Dr Abdul Qadeer Khan and the Islamic Bomb*. The Chairman of the Council of Pakistan Newspaper Editors stated that Zahid Malik's detention had serious implications for the freedom of the press and called for his release. On August 21 he was released on bail.

The Sind correspondent of *Dawn*, Iqbal Khwaja, was arrested in April 1989 for allegedly misquoting a provincial chief minister about a controversial dam project. He was released on bail the next day. Baluchistan police arrested a correspondent of an Urdu daily for filing a report which alleged that an hotel was being run during the fasting month of Ramadan, "with the help of the local police".

In October 1989, G M Syed, the leader of Sind National Alliance (SNA), was placed under house arrest following an incident at Sukkur airport in which a Pakistani flag was alleged to have been burnt by his Sindhi nationalist followers. About two dozen SNA leaders had already been arrested on charges of desecrating the national flag.

In Punjab, where the PPP was in opposition, members of the party claimed to have been harassed and detained for short periods. A veteran human rights activist and Deputy Leader of the opposition in Punjab's provincial assembly, Salman Taseer, was detained in August 1989 for 24 hours because he had criticized provincial government policies in January that year.

Religious Expression Since its creation as an Islamic state in 1947, Pakistan has been a nation of Muslims with two distinct approaches to religion. The fundamentalist approach calls for strict adherence to rules and regulations dating from the seventh century AD. The more liberal approach regards Islam as a matter of national identity, capable of responding to the social and cultural demands of modern times.

In mid-1990, the National Assembly was hearing an Islamic Shari'a Bill which had been passed by the upper house. This Bill called for all legislative, judicial and bureaucratic decisions to conform to the Koran, and for the full Islamicization of education and the media. The law would establish a special commission to scrutinize the government for un-Islamic practices. It was expected that the Bill would be passed.

The Constitution discriminates against religious minorities. Members of the Ahmadiyya community, who regard themselves as Muslim, continue to be arrested for practising their faith. According to an ordinance decreed by General Zia, it is an offence punishable by imprisonment or even death for Ahmadis to call themselves Muslim or offer Muslim prayers. Dozens of Ahmadis have been arrested under this law. The ordinance has rendered the Ahmadiyya community defenceless in the face of violent attacks by angry crowds, usually at the instigation of fundamentalist religious leaders. One such attack took place in July 1989 at Chak Sekander in Punjab. Three Ahmadis and one of the attackers were shot dead.

Women An important component of General Zia's policy of Islamicization was the Hudood Ordinance which deals with the sexual offence of zina (adultery), punishable by imprisonment or death by stoning. In the majority of cases women are not allowed to give testimony; when they are, the testimony of a woman is not equal to that of a man. Women have been sentenced to three years' imprisonment for reporting rape, since their report is considered a "confession" to zina. According to the UK *Guardian*, in May 1990 some 3,000 women were in jail on Hudood charges.

Two women's organizations, the Committee for the Repeal of the Hudood Ordinance and the Women's Action Forum, have been campaigning against this Ordinance since its inception. When Benazir Bhutto took office she created the Federal Ministry for Women's Development (FMWD) and promised that all laws discriminating against women would be repealed. In December 1989, the FMWD Minister described the Hudood Ordinance as undemocratic, un-Islamic and inhuman and promised that it would be amended, but by mid-1990 no action had been taken.

Philippines

On February 25 1986, Corazon Aquino took office as President of the Philippines. The 14-year administration of Ferdinand Marcos, responsible for widespread violation of freedom of expression, had been brought to an end by a peaceful "people power" revolution. Despite assurances by President Aquino that she would respect human rights and guarantee press freedom, conditions in the Philippines (the continuing challenge in the countryside by communist rebels and the attempted *coup d'etats* of October 1987 and December 1989 by military personnel) have resulted in a clampdown on the press equal to that experienced under Marcos.

	Data	Year
Population	58,721,000	1988
Life expectancy (M/F)	60.2/63.7	1985
GNP (US$ per capita)	630	1988
Main religion(s)	Christianity	
	Islam	
Official language(s)	Filipino	
Illiteracy %	10.3	1990
(M/F)	10.0/10.5	1990
Daily newspapers	30	1988
Radio sets	7,800,000	1987
TV sets	2,100,000	1987
Press agencies:		
Philippines News Agency		
ICCPR:	YES	1986

Constitutional Provisions Freedom of expression and information are guaranteed by the new Constitution promulgated on February 2 1987. Article III provides that "no law shall be passed abridging the freedom of speech, of expression or of the press" and guarantees the "right of the people to information on matters of public concern". This right includes access to official information subject to the limitations provided by law.

Access to Information Foreign and local journalists now require accreditation from the International Press Center under the Office of the President (IPC-OPS) in order to gain access to vital government offices and special activities. Limits have been imposed on the number of accredited journalists working for the same publication and some government offices require journalists to obtain special ID for specific coverage in addition to their IPC-OPS card. Critics have emphasized a dearth of information about matters of public concern, such as the negotiations over US military bases, as well as lack of access to the President. "Ambush journalism" (where the President replies to hurried questions with half sentences) or "quiz journalism" (where reporters submit written questions) are fast replacing the more formal press conferences.

Physical restrictions have also been imposed on journalists. Memorandum 211 of December 20 1988 restricts reporters' access at Manila international airport to a media centre there "unless they are actually engaged in coverage of specific events". Previously, journalists could only be prevented from entering an area on grounds of national security.

Defamation Articles 353 and 354 of the Revised Penal Code refer to defamation. Multi-million peso libel suits have been filed by private citizens against media organizations and personnel such as that filed by logger José Alvarez against the *Far*

Eastern Economic Review for its article on deforestation in Palawan. The President has also filed a libel suit against a columnist for claiming she hid under her bed during Gregorio Honasan's coup attempt in October 1987.

On December 18 1989, four senators filed a Bill seeking, among other things, to increase to a maximum of 10 years the imprisonment of persons who incite sedition through "libellous writing, cartoons, and speeches".

Emergency Legislation Article VII of the Constitution permits the derogation of certain rights, including freedom of expression, on grounds of "invasion", "rebellion" or "public safety". There have, however, been occasions when restrictions on free expression were imposed without invoking emergency legislation. On October 8 1987, Radio DZME was closed down by an undated order from José Alcuaz, Chairman of the National Telecommunications Commission (NTC), who invoked a provision from the 1931 Radio Code. The station remained off the air for seven days for allegedly broadcasting a recorded speech by Ferdinand Marcos during a coup attempt led by Gregorio Honasan. A complaint filed by Capitol Broadcasting Corporation's owner-manager, José Luison, citing the absence of an officially proclaimed State of Emergency, resulted in the NTC conceding that the case against DZME was one of mistaken identity. The NTC lifted the closure before the High Court could pronounce a verdict.

In April 1988, Radio DZXL withdrew its exclusive interview with Gregorio Honasan (who had escaped from a prison ship) following a government threat to revoke its licence if the broadcast went ahead.

Freedom of Expression in a State of Emergency On December 6 1989, a State of Emergency was declared following an attempted coup by military personnel and Congress passed a memorandum introduced by Chief of Staff General Renato de Villa urging strong government action. On December 20, the Republic Act 6826 (also known as the National Emergency Act) was passed by Congress.

The tenor of the National Emergency Act has led to expressions of disquiet by media workers since provisions within the Act could have negative repercussions on freedom of expression. The provision permitting the President to "temporarily take over or direct the operation of any privately-owned public utility or business affected with public interest that violates the herein declared national policy" could apply to the media. The provision empowering the President "to undertake such measures as may be reasonable and necessary to enable ... [her] ... to carry out the declared national policy subject to the Bill of Rights and other constitutional guarantees" is deemed to be a sweeping measure to cover the media and freedom of expression.

The Military Members of the military have been central in shaping the guidelines for media operation during crises. A number of draconian measures curbing press freedom, recommended by Gen De Villa for incorporation into the National Emergency Act, were excluded only after vigorous protests by the media, legislators and others. Most of his other recommendations were accepted.

Commentators have expressed concern about the readiness of the military to intervene in civilian affairs and noted threats made to journalists by both the military and government in an effort to control the press. On December 6 1989, Gen De Villa summoned *Daily Globe* reporters Philip Lustre and Dionisio Pelayo and lectured them on how to write their stories about the coup attempt. De Villa warned Pelayo: "I did not call you here to detain you, although I can do that anytime."

The General also disclosed that he had recommended to Executive Secretary Catalino Macaraig Jr the closure of the *Philippine Daily Inquirer* for alleged anti-military stories and erroneous reporting on the coup. Earlier, Gen De Villa was reported to have said at a press conference that if he had his way he would close down all media companies.

More importantly, the media have received warnings from the President. On December 19, the *Daily Globe* reported President Aquino as saying: "The broadcast media operate under franchises. They will have to operate within the terms and conditions imposed by these franchises. If they violate these terms and conditions they will be closed and their franchises will be taken away."

Proposed Guidelines for the Press in Times of Emergency Other guidelines for the press include: defining the boundaries of reporting during an emergency and endorsing a proposal from the University of the Philippines College of Mass Communication for a "national emergency broadcast system" ensuring that information coming from "official channels" can reach even the people residing in remote places.

Alice Villadolid of the Philippines Press Institute supported the proposal saying that "Congress' focus should be on how to enable the state to practise its right to self-defence." However, Andre Kahn, president of the Association of Broadcasters in the Philippines (KBP) (a self-regulatory organization of the broadcast industry founded during the Marcos government) and some radio stations protested the proposed measures which they said would infringe on the right of those in the broadcast industry to cover coups.

Pending bills, filed by Congressmen Abdullah Dimaporo and Rodolfo del Rosario, seek the establishment of guidelines on radio and TV reporting during "abnormal" times.

The NTC has also asked Congress to speed up the passage of a Bill giving the NTC extra powers. During the December coup attempt, the NTC closed down Manila radio stations DZEC and DZME, and the Cebu-based DYLA which had broadcast rebel statements. The NTC move for new guidelines came in the wake of the reported statement of the President that the government would close down stations which broadcast rebel propaganda and would file charges against publications which incite rebellion. The then Justice Secretary Sedfrey Ordoñez said that media organizations which broadcast or publish "distorted reports" could be summarily closed down by the President.

The Media

Newspapers Since the change of government in 1986 the newspaper industry has expanded fourfold. There are currently 31 daily newspapers published in Manila, reflecting a broad spectrum of opinion. Newspapers are published in Filipino, English and the vernacular. There are a further 240 (mainly weekly) newspapers published in the provinces.

Radio and Television The broadcast industry is divided between government-operated and privately-owned stations. TV broadcasting, especially in metropolitan Manila, is dominated by government; there is no substantial TV broadcasting outside the capital region. Programmes are regulated by the Cinema and TV Review and Classification Board. In May 1987, the censor prohibited the showing of an episode of *Filipino Mind*, a programme depicting the life of urban slum dwellers. Protests against the ban resulted in the episode being screened after the congressional elections held on May 11.

Radio stations are effectively controlled by the NTC and to a lesser degree by the KBP and the Standards Authority.

Journalists There are approximately 4,000 journalists in the Philippines, some 50 per cent of these working in the capital. Low wages and poor working conditions have led to widespread corruption and unethical practices in the profession. Attempts by journalists' unions to combat poor conditions have been repelled by newspaper publishers and managers. Complaints lodged by the unions with the government labour agencies have been largely unsuccessful. One case where a complaint was accepted, and the employer was ordered by the Secretary of Labour to reinstate workers, resulted in the publisher closing down the paper, *Business Day*, and starting a new one, *Business World*. Political bias and business interests of publishers have strongly affected editorial policy and act as a tool for self-censorship among journalists.

There has been an alarming increase in the deaths of Filipino journalists since 1986. Under the Marcos administration, 30 journalists were killed, an average of two per year. Under President Aquino, 20 journalists had been murdered by 1990, an average of five per year. Most of those killed were provincial journalists, victims of the military, paramilitaries and private militia.

Protection of Sources Republic Act 53 (October 5 1946) exempts the publisher, editor or reporter of any publication from being compelled to reveal the source of published news or information obtained in confidence "unless the courts or a House or Committee of Congress finds that such revelation is demanded by the interest of the state". This law was amended by Republic Act 1477 (June 15 1956) to narrow the exception clause to "unless the courts or a House or Committee of Congress finds that such revelation is demanded by the security of the state".

In June 1988, Ramon Tulfo, a columnist for the *Inquirer*, was jailed for five hours by Olongapo City Judge Ester Robles Bans who invoked the amended law on sources. Tulfo refused to reveal the source of his allegations about a "corrupt lady judge of the Olongapo Regional Trial Court" published in his column on March 21 and March 28 that year. The judge directed Tulfo to appear before her again for a "clarification hearing" but the journalist filed a petition in the Supreme Court to restrain Judge Robles Bans from further hearing of the case after it was revealed that the "corrupt lady judge" referred to Robles Bans herself. The High Court granted the petition, but did not rule on the judge's earlier claim that she could invoke the exception clause of Republic Act 1477.

Films The Cinema and TV Review and Classification Board has extensive censorship powers. Established by presidential decree in October 1985, the Board may ban or censor portions of a film which, in its view, tends to "undermine the faith and confidence of the people in their government". *The Last Temptation of Christ* was banned without being viewed. The Board also exercises political censorship, proscribing material which "incites subversion, insurrection, rebellion or sedition against the state".

Singapore

Singapore is an economic success story, with one of the highest per capita incomes in Asia. Since its independence from the British in 1959, it has emerged from a Third World economy to the status of a newly industrialised nation.

The government reiterates its openness when under attack from the foreign media for lack of press freedom and freedom of expression and claims that there are over 3,000 foreign publications circulating in the island city state. The BBC World Service is available 24 hours a day and Singapore has more than 90 accredited journalists, working for over 60 foreign news organizations. The government statistics are beyond dispute, but they do not guarantee freedom of the press or of expression. Since the country's independence, the ruling People's Action Party (PAP) has been in power under the leadership of Prime Minister Lee Kuan Yew. The government is well-known for its intolerance of criticism in the domestic or foreign press and has used laws which allow indefinite detention without trial and the restriction or closure of publications to silence its critics.

	Data	Year
Population	2,647,000	1988
Life expectancy (M/F)	68.7/74.0	1980
GNP (US$ per capita)	9,100	1988
Main religion(s)	Daoism,	
	Buddhism, Islam,	
	Christianity,Hinduism	
Official language(s)	Malay,	
	Mandarin, Tamil, English	
Illiteracy %	14.0	1985
Daily newspapers	10	1986
Non daily newspapers	7	1984
Periodicals	1,786	1984
Radio sets	800,000	1987
TV sets	421,000	1975
ICCPR:	NO	

During the 1988 election campaign, a number of opposition figures who might have contested local seats were detained without trial; others were subjected to politically motivated criminal proceedings. There were also arbitrary restrictions on the rights of opposition groups to assemble freely.

The Media

Newspapers All newspaper enterprises must be public companies. The government has directly and indirectly controlled the privately-owned press and compulsory government scrutiny of newspaper management has been in operation since 1974. Opposition journalists are liable to be arrested and imprisoned or exiled abroad. Critical foreign correspondents are simply expelled without explanation.

Restrictions on the Press The Newspaper and Printing Presses (Amendment) Act 1986 (NPPA) empowers the Minister of Communications and Information to restrict the circulation of foreign publications which have "engaged in the domestic politics of Singapore". Once a foreign publication is deemed guilty of such an offence, it is declared a "gazetted publication" and circulation is restricted to a number decided by the Minister and copies can only be sold by authorized outlets.

The Singapore authorities search people entering the country for copies of "gazetted publications"; they also search the mail. Postal subscriptions to such publications are prohibited and unofficial distribution carries maximum penalties of S$10,000 (US$5,050) or two years' imprisonment.

Since early 1987, Singapore has severely restricted the circulations of *Asiaweek*, *The Asian Wall Street Journal* and the *Far Eastern Economic Review*. These publications, all Hong Kong-based, constitute the most influential English-language news publications in the region.

In December 1987, the *Far Eastern Economic Review* had its Singapore circulation reduced from 9,000 to 500 copies after covering the detention of 22 alleged "Marxist conspirators". Prime Minister Lee Kuan Yew filed libel writs against the *Far Eastern Economic Review*, its editor, publisher and printer and, in November 1989, a Singapore High Court found the magazine guilty and ordered it to pay damages of S$230,000 (US$116,000) plus interest and costs. The *Far Eastern Economic Review* no longer sells copies in Singapore but (under a 1988 law which permits gazetted publications to be photocopied without penalty) 10,000 officially-sanctioned counterfeit copies (minus advertising) are published each week. The government claims this is proof that it is not restricting the free flow of information but is simply depriving the errant publishers of their unjust financial gain. This is a violation of international copyright law.

In a related case, the Attorney General brought a contempt of court action against the *Asian Wall Street Journal* in December 1989, for an article concerning the High Court's libel judgment against the *Far Eastern Economic Review*.

During 1989, the government wrote letters about articles on Singapore to the three Hong Kong-based publications and demanded that the letters be printed unaltered and in full; they declared that compliance with the demand would determine whether the publications would be allowed back into the country. *Asiaweek* published two letters which it had previously declined to print, an action which had resulted in its restriction, and was then allowed to keep a staff reporter in Singapore as well as having its circulation partially restored. In September 1990, the government announced that it would allow *Asia Week* to raise its local circulation to 7,500 copies from a current ceiling of 500 copies.

The circulation of the US *Time* magazine was cut from 18,000 to 2,000 copies in early 1987 but was restored after it published a letter from the government.

On July 26 1990, the *Far Eastern Economic Review* published a report that an amendment to the Newspaper and Printing Press Act, introduced in parliament on July 18, will require any foreign publication selling more than 300 copies in Singapore "whose contents and editorial policy are determined outside Singapore" and which covers the politics and current affairs of South-East Asia, to obtain a licence, renewable annually. The licence may limit the number of copies sold and require the deposit of security against possible legal proceedings involving the publication. Permits can be refused or revoked without any reason given.

In October 1990, Dow-Jones and Co, owners of the *Asian Wall Street Journal*, announced that they could not agree to the new restrictions on overseas publications and were suspending sales in Singapore.

Restrictions on Correspondents Foreign correspondents based in Singapore who write critical articles about Singapore are often expelled or refused extended visas. During the past 12 years, five correspondents of the *Far Eastern Economic Review* have been expelled and, during the 1988 general election, two of its journalists were refused temporary entry visas to cover the elections. In October 1989, Simon Elegant of AP-Dow Jones was refused an extended work permit and was ordered to leave the country. In November 1989, AP-Dow Jones was advised that no work permit would be issued for a new correspondent.

Applications by *The Asian Wall Street Journal* and the *Far Eastern Economic Review* to cover the second Asia-Pacific Economic Co-operation conference, held in Singapore on July 30-31 1990, were refused by the government despite diplomatic interventions from other member nations.

Radio and Television The government-run Singapore Broadcasting Corporation (SBC) operates Singapore's three TV channels and five radio stations. During the 1988 general election, opposition candidates had little access to the broadcast media.

In 1987, after the arrest of 22 church and community workers accused of involvement in a "Marxist conspiracy", the SBC broadcast a series of interviews, recorded while the detainees were in custody. These broadcasts, which were edited to appear as confessions, were reportedly instigated by the Internal Security Department (ISD); SBC employees, including interviewers, worked closely with ISD officers in their preparation.

Laws Restricting Freedom of Expression

The Internal Security Act The Internal Security Act (ISA), which derives from the British colonial government's Preservation of Public Security Ordinance 1955, and which was extended to Singapore when it became part of the Federation of Malaysia in 1963, empowers the Minister of Home Affairs to prohibit any publication deemed to be "prejudicial to the national interest, public order, or security of Singapore" and to order the indefinite detention without trial of critics of the government. The provisions of the Act include restricting comment on race, language, religion or culture.

Since 1971, the government has used the ISA, closing newspapers and arresting their staff members. Further clampdowns on the press occurred in 1976 and 1977 when a number of journalists working for local and foreign publications were accused of taking part in "communist conspiracies".

The Act was used in May and June 1987, when 22 young professionals belonging to the Justice and Peace Commission of the Catholic Church, Catholic welfare organizations, the opposition Workers' Party and theatre groups were arrested for alleged "involvement in a clandestine communist network". Vincent Cheng, Executive Secretary of the Justice and Peace Commission, was accused of being a key figure in a "Marxist conspiracy".

After being held for 30 days, a two-year detention order was imposed on Vincent Cheng, and one-year detention orders were served on 14 others. The rest were released a month later, subject to restriction orders. All had been released by the end of 1987, except Vincent Cheng, who was released on June 18 1990 after agreeing to abide by six conditions including restrictions on travel, association with other former detaines and issuing public statements.

On April 19 1988, eight of the 22 were re-arrested, a day after issuing a statement to newspapers and human rights groups abroad in which they denied that they had been involved in any conspiracy and alleged that they had been ill-treated in prison.

On May 6, Francis Seow, former Solicitor General, submitted *habeas corpus* applications for the release of Patrick Seong and Teo Soh Lung, two lawyers among those arrested. That evening, Francis Seow was himself arrested under the ISA.

Two days later, Chew Kheng Chuan, one of the original 22 detainees, was arrested for helping produce the joint statement, even though he was not a signatory.

By the beginning of 1989, all had been released except Teo Soh Lung. In March 1989, her counsel, British human rights lawyer Anthony Lester QC, who was applying for a writ of *habeas corpus*, was barred from practising in Singapore on the grounds that he had engaged in Singapore's domestic policies. The bar provoked strong protests from the British Foreign Office and the Singapore government threatened to ban all British Queen's Counsel from appearing in Singapore unless the British Foreign Office withdrew its protest. Teo Soh Long's application for *habeas corpus* was dismissed by the High Court and, on June 17 1989, she was served with a further one-year detention order. In June 1990, Teo Soh Lung was released on three conditions, one of which prohibits her from participating in politics.

Chia Thye Poh, who was an MP for the opposition Bartsan Sosialis at the time of his arrest in October 1966, was detained without trial under the ISA and released, conditionally, on May 17 1989. He was arrested for allegedly engaging in activities aimed at destabilizing the government amd detained because of his refusal to renounce violence and sever his alleged ties with the Communist Party of Malaya. The government has acknowledged that Chia has refused such a renunciation and has released him on condition that he does not leave the island of Sentosa, associate with ex-detainees, address public meetings, or engage in any political activity.

In January 1989, the government amended the ISA explicitly to deny courts the power to review the government's reasons for detentions under the ISA. In addition, the amendment denies detainees the right to appeal to the Judicial Committee of the Privy Council.

The Criminal Law (Temporary Provisions) Act   Under this law, a person suspected of criminal activities can be detained without trial, indefinitely, with virtually no means of redress. In August 1989, the Minister for Home Affairs disclosed that there were 1,228 people detained without trial in prisons under this Act, 740 of whom were said to be drug traffickers and the rest were said to be involved in secret societies and criminal activities. None has ever been allowed to challenge their arrest and detention in a court of law.

Maintenance of Religious Harmony Bill   On January 15 1990, the government proposed the Maintenance of Religious Harmony Bill. When the Bill becomes law, it will empower the Minister of Home Affairs to restrict any individual judged to be engaged in political causes or subversive activities under a religious guise, or those who propagate ideas which may incite conflict between religious groups. The law will prohibit any individual judged to be engaged in such activities from addressing congregations, publishing articles or from being a member of the editorial boards of publications.

People found guilty of engaging in such activities after an initial warning could be imprisoned for two years or fined a maximum of S$10,000 (US$5,050), or both. Second offences will carry a sentence of three years' imprisonment or fines of S$20,000, or both. Singapore will be the first country in the world to have such legislation. It appears that the accused will have no right of appeal.

Actions

In July 1989 ARTICLE 19 wrote to the Singapore government protesting the detention of Vincent Cheng and Teo Soh Lung. A reply was received from the High Commission in London denying that either the arrests or the implementation of the ISA infringed freedom of expression.

On January 12 1990 ARTICLE 19 wrote to the Singapore government urging it not to pursue legal action against the *Asian Wall Street Journal*, its editor, publisher, printer and distributor for allegedly claiming that a judge in a libel case was biased in favour of the plaintiff, Prime Minister Lee Kuan Yew.

On January 31 1990 ARTICLE 19 wrote to the Singapore Democratic Party expressing concern over its response to the Maintenance of Religious Harmony Bill. The SDP had indicated that it did not want religious groups to form political parties or to ally themselves to any party.

On June 4 1990 ARTICLE 19 wrote to the government welcoming Teo Soh Lung's release from detention and requesting that Vincent Cheng also be released. (See text)

Sri Lanka

Sri Lanka operated a Westminster-style Constitution from its independence in 1948 until 1978 and during this period government alternated between the Sri Lanka Freedom Party (SLFP) and the United National Party (UNP). The UNP has governed since 1977, and in September 1978 adopted a Gaullist-style Constitution which recognizes freedom of speech, expression, publication, peaceful assembly and association.

These freedoms are subject to restrictions prescribed by law "in the interests of national security, public order and protection of public health or morals or for the purpose of securing due recognition and respect for the rights and freedoms of others or for meeting the requirements of the general welfare of a democratic society" (Art.15(7)). Further restrictions relating to parliamentary privilege, contempt of court, defamation or incitement to an offence, racial and religious harmony, and the national economy are also prescribed by Article 15.

	Data	Year
Population	16,587,000	1988
Life expectancy (M/F)	67.7/71.6	1981
GNP (US$ per capita)	420	1988
Main religion(s)	Buddhism	
	Hinduism	
Official language(s)	Sinhala	
	Tamil	
Illiteracy %	11.6	1990
(M/F)	6.6/16.5	1990
Daily newspapers	17	1986
Non daily newspapers	12	1986
Periodicals	170	1986
Radio sets	3,100,000	1987
TV sets	520,000	1987
Press agencies:	Lankapuvath,	
Cesmos Economic News Agency,		
Press Trust of Ceylon.,		
Sandesa News Agency		
ICCPR:	YES	1980

The President has almost unlimited power to invoke emergency regulations overriding the rule of law (Art.155(2)), and Sri Lanka has had long periods of emergency rule. Sirimavo Bandaranaike's SLFP administration imposed a state of emergency in 1971 which lasted six years. The current government imposed a state of emergency in May 1983 which lasted until January 1989, was reimposed in June 1989 and is still in force.

Emergency regulations, at different times, have included the prohibition of affixing posters or distributing leaflets without the permission of the Inspector General of Police, prohibition of public meetings and processions, banning of newspapers and sealing of printing presses, censorship of all publications and broadcasts, and proscription of political parties. Emergency regulations, the wordings of which can be changed without notice, are not always well publicized and the Civil Rights Movement of Sri Lanka has complained of the lack of public access to these regulations.

Under the Prevention of Terrorism Act (PTA), which was introduced as a temporary measure in 1979 and made permanent in 1982, people can be detained without charge or trial for 18 months. The Act also prohibits political or public activities of any person for up to 18 months, empowers the imposition of censorship of news and prohibits the distribution of foreign journals. On past occasions when individuals subject to the PTA have made successful fundamental rights petitions to the courts, the government has paid scant regard to the judgements.

The Ethnic Conflict The two largest ethnic groups are the Sinhalese who comprise 70 per cent of the population and the Tamils, who make up almost 18 per cent. Tension between them has been aggravated by continual chauvinistic election campaigning by the UNP and SLFP, and by the gradual erosion of democratic and civil rights of Tamils. In 1956, Sinhala was adopted as the official language and in 1972 this was incorporated into the Constitution, along with the ruling that Buddhism should have "the foremost place" among religions. (The Sinhalese are largely Buddhist, Tamils are largely Hindu but there is also a small group of Muslim Tamils.) In response to the changes in the Constitution, the Tamil parties formed the Tamil United Front which, in 1976, became the Tamil United Liberation Front (TULF) and called for a separate Tamil state in Eelam. This demand was incorporated into the TULF election manifesto in 1977 and, by claiming a popular mandate for separatism, it became the largest party in opposition. The Constitution, however, was amended by the majority Sinhalese government to exclude from parliament any person supporting the demand for a separate Tamil state. This ended the parliamentary phase of the ethnic conflict and marked the beginning of full-scale ethnic war in which Tamil groups advocating armed struggle gained ascendency.

The predominant armed Tamil group is the Liberation Tigers of Tamil Eelam (LTTE), who established control of the Jaffna peninsula. There are also several smaller groups. Between 1983 and 1987 more than 6,000 people were killed in outbreaks of violence between the Sinhalese and Tamil communities. Early in 1987, the LTTE tried to declare unilateral independence and the government retaliated with a military offensive in which they regained control of the whole of the north and east except the Jaffna peninsula.

The Indian government intervened to negotiate on behalf of the Tamils, but without a clear and explicit mandate from them, and, on July 29 1987, the Indo-Sri Lanka Peace Accord was signed. LTTE leader Velupillai Prabakharan was under virtual house arrest in Delhi when the Accord was signed. India was opposed to secession in Sri Lanka and sought to negotiate provincial autonomy in the Accord. The LTTE initially made a partial surrender to the Indian Peace Keeping Force (IPKF) but did not renounce secession.

In October 1987, the IPKF launched an offensive in order to disarm the LTTE. The Jaffna press stopped publishing, and telephone links were cut; there has been no direct telephone communication with Jaffna since. The LTTE had held the peninsula for some months during which there was relative stability although they dealt ruthlessly with members and supporters of other Tamil groups. There were heavy casualties on both sides and appalling atrocities were committed by all sides. Countless numbers of people became refugees and rapes, beatings, and killings of civilians were widespread.

On November 14 1987, the 13th Amendment was introduced under the Indo-Sri Lankan Accord designating Sinhala and Tamil as the official languages of Sri Lanka with English as the link language.

The withdrawal of the IPKF in the early months of 1990 allowed the LTTE to reclaim its former territory, and those Tamils who had co-operated with other Tamil groups or with the IPKF became extremely vulnerable to attacks by the LTTE.

Developments in the South As a part of the Accord, provincial council elections were held which, along with the general elections of February 1989, were boycotted by supporters of several armed groups. The Janatha Vimukthi Peramuna (JVP), an armed Sinhalese group which was banned in 1983 but legalized in 1988, was widely believed to be responsible for hundreds of deaths in the south. Their victims included election candidates, members of the ruling UNP, security forces personnel, senior public officials, broadcasters and opposition activists, including some Buddhist monks. Government reaction was ruthless; security forces killed many Sinhalese youths and thousands more disappeared. As well as the actions of the security forces and the JVP, unidentified armed gangs, believed by many to be connected with the security forces and/or government ministers, also carried out many killings.

The Media

The Press The adult literacy rate is 88 per cent and newspapers are widely read. There are four main newspaper publishing groups which publish in Sinhala, Tamil and English.

Associated Newspapers of Ceylon Ltd (Lake House Group) was nationalized in 1983 and publishes five dailies, three Sunday newspapers and 11 periodicals. Express Newspapers (Ceylon) Ltd publishes two dailies and two Sunday newspapers. Independent Newspapers Ltd is under private ownership and publishes three dailies, four weeklies and one monthly. Upali Newspapers Ltd publishes two dailies, two Sundays and five weekly magazines and one which is sold abroad only, *The Island International*.

Section 16 of the 1973 Press Council Law makes it an offence for newspapers to publish details of Cabinet proceedings or decisions without prior authority or to publish false reports about issues under consideration by any Minister or Ministry. As a result of an item in a regular *Sunday Times* column in early 1990, the government announced its intention of enforcing Section 16. This effectively reduces political reporting to a reproduction of government press statements. People are aware of the deterioration of news reporting but an atmosphere of fear curtails even the word of mouth reporting that used to be widespread.

In 1989, the government banned the direct importation of newsprint and newspapers now have to apply to the Government Newspapers Quota Committee for further supplies. This has led to a reduction in the pagination of some national papers which published condemnations of the prohibition.

News Agencies Newspapers rely on Lankapuvath (National News Agency of Sri Lanka) for information or reprints from the international press, carefully attributing their stories to international news agencies. There are three other Sri Lankan news agencies, Cesmos Economic News Agency, Press Trust of Ceylon, and Sandesa News Agency. The Press Association of Ceylon and the Sri Lanka Foreign Correspondents' Association both operate from Colombo. There are several foreign bureaux including Deutsche Presse-Agentur, IPS, Reuters, UPI and Xinhua.

Radio and Television In 1987 there were 3.1 million radios and an estimated 520,000 TV sets in use. The government-run radio, Sri Lankan Broadcasting Corporation (SLBC), broadcasts in Sinhala, Tamil and English and has regional stations throughout the island. A small religious radio station, Trans World Radio, broadcasts for a few hours each day to the Indian subcontinent. Both Sri Lankan TV stations are government-controlled. Sri Lanka Rupavahini Corporation (SLRC) has five transmitting stations and transmits throughout Sri Lanka. Independent Television Network transmits within a 50 kilometre radius of Colombo.

The Ministry of State for Broadcasting and Information controls programme content on both radio and TV but does not provide any financial assistance. Opposition views are broadcast only immediately prior to an election when the law requires that all contesting political parties be granted equal time on radio and TV. However, news items filed by reporters are carefully vetted and nothing detrimental to the government is broadcast. The public is increasingly frustrated by the lack of hard news and some have refused to license their radio sets in protest.

In 1987, a bomb exploded in a busy area of Colombo, killing hundreds of people. The SLBC, situated less than a mile away, received the news via the BBC but did not broadcast it until it had been confirmed by Lankapuvath several hours later.

On July 31 1989, a popular TV and radio announcer, Premakeerthi de Alwis, was abducted from his home and killed. Within a week, Kulasiri Ameratunge, chief news editor of SLRC, was shot in his home by unidentified gunmen. The JVP is believed to be responsible for both killings.

Censorship and Repression

Other censorship in Sri Lanka is enforced through intimidation by armed groups. In July 1987, the JVP called for a boycott of all Lake House newspapers and *Aththa* newspaper, published by the Communist Party of Sri Lanka. Drivers of newspaper vans were attacked and killed, as were newsagents. Individuals buying or reading these papers, or listening to the radio or viewing TV during JVP bans, were threatened with death. In June 1988, the police confiscated two cameras belonging to a Reuters photographer who was taking photographs of them forcing open shops that had been closed by order of the JVP.

On September 21 1989, the Tamil group Eelam People's Revolutionary Liberation Front (EPRLF) took control of and stopped publication of the three Tamil daily newspapers, *Eelanadu, Murasoli* and *Uthayan*. It also stopped the distribution of the southern Tamil newspaper *Virakesari* and all English newspapers in the north-east. The EPRLF began publishing its own paper, *Viduthalai*, on October 9, giving it absolute control over the press in the north.

When the LTTE reoccupied Jaffna after the IPKF left in March 1990 they took over the press and offices of the *Saturday Review*, which had a history of bannings and censorship. Its editor, Gamini Navaratne, issued a press release on May 25 stating: "Though the LTTE's intolerance of criticism is well known, the Tigers, even during the worst period earlier, never interfered in our publication." He also said that he had recently turned down a request from the Tigers to edit an English paper for them because he was not willing to work under editorial interference.

The Chairman and Director General of the SLBC, Thevis Guruge, was shot dead on his morning walk on July 24 1989. On July 5, the government had appointed him chief censor of the press and it was widely speculated that this was the reason for his killing, allegedly by the JVP. Further censorship provisions, which had been imposed on July 5 under the Emergency Regulations, were immediately lifted but many Sri Lankans, who would have welcomed this move in other circumstances, were dismayed that it appeared to be in response to his assassination. However, on

July 26 1989, it was announced that the security forces had been vested with powers to control radio, TV and the Lake House press.

Attacks on Journalists Several journalists and broadcasters have been assassinated. On October 8 1988, Edwin Rajapakse, a reporter, was killed in Matara. Nelson Karunaratna was killed in Galewala on November 23 and H E Dayanda was shot dead in Colombo in December. A printer, P D Wimalasena, was gunned down at the printing press he managed in Colombo in May 1989. The *Divayina* reported the abduction of their Vavuniya correspondent, Jinasena Rathugamage, by unknown persons, wearing army-style uniforms, in August 1989. The editor of *Murasoli* escaped assassination in Jaffna but his 17-year-old son was killed, allegedly by the LTTE.

On February 19 1990, the bullet-ridden, mutilated body of Richard de Zoysa, one of Sri Lanka's leading journalists, was found washed up on the beach south of Colombo. He had been abducted from his mother's house two days earlier by six gunmen led by a man in police uniform. His killing has attracted the attention of the world's press. He has been posthumously named "Outstanding Journalist of the Year" by IPS, the news agency for whom he worked. Richard de Zoysa's mother, Dr Manorani Saravanamuttu, in an affidavit, named a police chief superintendent as one of the men she saw abduct her son. On August 30, the Attorney General dismissed the case against the chief superintendent due to lack of evidence.

In September 1990, despite both receiving anonymous death threats, Dr Saravanamuttu and her lawyer called on parliament to demand an independent inquiry which can be appointed only by the president.

Freedom of Expression

Since 1983, many thousands of Sri Lankans have lost their lives in the violent and brutal ethnic conflicts which continue to devastate the island. Western diplomats estimate that 30,000 died during 1989 and Sri Lankan activists put the death toll for the last two years at 75,000. The true figure will never be known.

Human Rights Organizations The Citizens' Committee played an extremely important role in reporting incidents and publishing reports of infringements of civil and human rights. The President of the Citizens' Committee of Kalmunai, Paul Nallanayagam, was arrested in 1985 and charged under the Emergency Regulations with making "rumours or false statements" designed to bring the authorities into disrepute, after he had reported irregularities, including the secret killing of 23 young men. He was subsequently acquitted in the High Court.

M S Kandasamy, a former secretary of the Sri Lanka section of Amnesty International, who had worked with Tamils both in London and Sri Lanka and who refused to identify with any one Tamil group, was abducted on June 19 1988. He was reportedly executed by Tamil militants.

In July 1988, human rights organizations met under the chairmanship of Mahinda Rajapakse MP and condemned the proposed Indemnity Act, which provides indemnity from prosecution for government and security force members provided that their actions were done "in good faith". The Act applies from August 1977 to December 1988, almost the entire term of the last government. A few days after the meeting, Rajapakse's house and car were damaged by fire.

The University Teachers for Human Rights (UTHR), based at Jaffna University, published three reports giving precise details of incidents that occurred while the IPKF were stationed in the area and criticizing the IPKF, the EPRLF and the LTTE. On September 21 1989, just before the publication of the third report, Dr Rajani Thiranagama, Professor of Anatomy at the university and the driving force behind the UTHR, was shot dead. It is widely believed that the LTTE were responsible. A book, *The Broken Palmyra*, containing writings by Dr Thiranagama and other UTHR members about the October 1987 IPFK offensive on Jaffna, has been published.

The wife and son of Sam Tambimuttu, an MP from the Eastern Province and a member of the Parliamentary Human Rights Committee, were abducted by the LTTE for two days in December 1989. Tambimuttu continued with his political and human rights work. In May 1990, he and his wife were gunned down in Colombo outside the Canadian Embassy after applying for a visa for a lecture tour in Canada. Tambimuttu died immediately and his wife some days later. The deaths are widely believed to be the work of the LTTE.

Attacks on Lawyers On September 4 1988, human rights lawyer Wijedasa Liyanarachichi, who had filed over 100 *habeas corpus* petitions on behalf of disappeared Sinhalese youths, died in police custody. The post mortem stated that he had died of shock and haemorrhage caused by multiple internal injuries. In April 1989, there was an attempt on the life of Ian Wickramanayake, a lawyer representing the police officer accused of Liyanarachichi's death. According to Amnesty International, Charitha Lankapura and Kanchana Abhayapala, who had both filed many *habeas corpus* cases, were killed by unknown armed men, the former in July, the latter in August, and at least 20 other lawyers were reportedly threatened with death. Very few *habeas corpus* petitions were filed after Lankapura's death because lawyers feared reprisals. Several leading lawyers have sought refuge in Europe and the Sri Lanka Bar Association protested the situation to the President late in 1989.

Academic Freedom Universities closed in the south of Sri Lanka in mid-1987 following student demonstrations and JVP activity on campuses. Many students were arrested and held without trial, killed or disappeared, and student unions were banned.

In March 1989, Professor Stanley Wijesundera, the vice-chancellor, was shot dead at Colombo University, a murder widely attributed to the JVP. Later in the year, Professor Patuvathawithana, vice-chancellor of Moratuwa University in the north, was gunned down. He had encouraged an independent student body and resisted pressure from the military authorities and political groups alike. At Peradeniya University, the decapitated heads of some 15 youths were placed around the pond during the night following the murder of an assistant registrar. This atrocity was attributed to the army.

By December 1989, 221 students from six universities had been reported missing according to the committee monitoring the arrest of university students. They reported that a further 156 students had been detained. In January 1990, the government announced further emergency regulations which forbid any form of political activity or gathering at universities and workplaces.

Political Expression Political expression is further restricted and manipulated by the actions of armed groups or by those who hire guns for protection or intimidation.

On July 29 1988, in the north-east, the LTTE forced people on to the streets at gun-point, during a curfew, to demonstrate against the presence of the IPKF. More than 100 of these people were shot dead by Sri Lankan forces. In response to public condemnation, the Defence Minister stated that if those killed were innocent they should have opposed the LTTE.

The LTTE has been responsible for the deaths of several prominent Tamil leaders, inluding Uma Maheswaren of the People's Liberation Organization of Tamil Eelam, who was shot dead in Colombo on July 16 1989, and Appapillai Amirthalingam of TULF who was killed two days later.

Retaliation was taken in the north against those co-operating in the 1989 elections which the LTTE boycotted. Their many victims included a Tamil parliamentary candidate and the government agent of Jaffna.

Trade Unions Emergency regulations of July 1990 prohibit workers meeting and effectively stop trade unions functioning within the law. These regulations are allegedly to combat the strikes which paralysed workplaces in 1989. However, these were not organized by the recognized trade unions but were part of the activities enforced by the JVP. Therefore, the regulations would have had no effect on the disruptions of 1989 but will restrict the actions of organized, democratic, established trade unions.

The Secretary of the LSSP Trade Union Federation, P D Wimalasena, was shot by gunmen who stormed the Federation headquarters and set fire to the press there in the summer of 1989.

On October 27 1989, Herath Mudiyanselage Ranjith, a machine operator, and Madurappulige Lionel, an advice worker at the Katunayaka Legal Advice Centre, disappeared in the Free Trade Zone where trade union activities are greatly restricted. They had been to an internal inquiry at Floral Greens Ltd who had suspended Ranjith after he had protested about dangerous machinery . The same evening, two men were seen being knocked off a bicycle and detained by men, believed to be police; the bicycle belonged to Ranjith. The next day, two bodies were found nearby, burned beyond recognition but believed to be those of Herath Mudiyanselage Ranjith and Madurappulige Lionel.

Actions

On August 21 1989 ARTICLE 19 wrote to the government expressing concern at a series of attacks on media personnel.

On December 5 1989 ARTICLE 19 launched a campaign to counteract censorship in Sri Lanka by providing a means for information to leave the country.

On February 19 1990 ARTICLE 19 wrote to the government expressing concern at the abduction of journalist Richard de Zoysa (see text).

On May 18 1990 ARTICLE 19 wrote to the government expressing concern at the murder of Sam Tambimuttu, MP, lawyer and human rights activist, and his wife, and calling for an inquiry into the killings (see text).

On July 31 1990 ARTICLE 19 launched an appeal, "Three Women Speak Out", focusing on three Sri Lankan women (including Richard de Zoysa's mother, Dr Manorani Saravanamuttu) who are campaigning against violence and repression in their country.

On September 3 1990 ARTICLE 19 wrote to the government expressing concern at the Attorney General's decision to dismiss the evidence brought by Dr Manorani Saravanamuttu about the murder of Richard de Zoysa. ARTICLE 19 called for an independent commission of inquiry to examine the evidence.

On September 18 an ARTICLE 19 video about the "Three Women" was shown at the UN during the IPS presentation of the posthumous award of "Outstanding Journalist of the Year" to Richard de Zoysa.

Taiwan

Taiwan has been governed since 1945 by the *Kuomintang* (KMT), or Nationalist Party which lost control of mainland China to the Chinese Communist Party in 1949. The KMT claims the right to rule the "Republic of China", which includes the mainland and Taiwan, and refuses to recognize the Communist government of the People's Republic of China. The continued claim to the mainland is a central anachronism of Taiwan's political life. Calls to repudiate the pretension and to begin negotiations with the mainland over independence are considered criminal. The Legislative Yuan Council is packed with ageing legislators elected from mainland constituencies before 1949. A large student sit-in in March 1990, which became known as Taiwan's Tiananmen, called for the elderly mainland representatives to retire and for direct presidential elections. In July 1990, the Constitutional Court, called the Council of Grand Justices, declared that the mainland representatives must retire by July 1991.

	Data	Year
Population	19,903,812	1988
Life expectancy	68.2	1985
GNP (US$ per capita)	6,053	1988
Main religion(s)	Buddhism	
Official language(s)	Mandarin	
Daily newspapers	26	1989
Radio sets	16,000,000	1988
TV sets	5,200,000	1988
Press agencies:		
Central News Agency, Chiao Kwang News Agency, China Youth News Agency		
ICCPR:	NO	

The Constitution guarantees "freedom of speech, teaching, writing and publication", but also contains provisions which have allowed the government to declare martial law, denying these rights and imposing censorship. The KMT ruled Taiwan by martial law from 1949 until July 1987. In 1986, an opposition party, the Democratic Progressive Party (DPP), was formed. Since the end of martial law, censorship has eased but the National Security Law, which unduly restricts freedom of expression, remains in force. Many prominent opposition politicians have been imprisoned on political charges, deprived of certain civil rights and thereby prevented from standing in elections. Since the end of martial law the atmosphere has been more open and the print media has been able to criticize the authorities and publish information that would previously have led to confiscation. The military has, however, made renewed efforts to press charges against opposition publications. The KMT retains control of all radio and television broadcasting.

In May 1990, President Lee Teng-hui appointed General Hau Pei-tsun, former Minister of Defence, as Prime Minister. The appointment was bitterly opposed by the DPP, students and intellectuals: as Taiwan's longest serving Chief-of-Staff, Hau had been in power during the years of martial law. On the day he was officially appointed, fights broke out in parliament and there were riots in the streets.

Sedition In April 1988, an amnesty was declared releasing or reducing the sentences of more than 22,000 prisoners. Those released included the chairman and vice-chairman of the DPP and some two dozen other political opponents of the KMT who had been convicted in 1979 of sedition in what was called the

Kaohsiungor Formosa case. Others released included Pai Ya-Tsan, sentenced in 1975 to life imprisonment for distributing "Twenty-nine Questions" to the then prime minister, and Chang Hua-min, sentenced to 10 years' imprisonment in January 1980 for suggesting negotiations with China. Tsai Yu-chuan and Hsu Tsao-teh, sentenced to 11 and 10 years' imprisonment respectively in January 1988 for advocating Taiwan's independence, had their sentences reduced. Tsai Keh-tang, sentenced to eight years' imprisonment in December 1987 on charges of spreading propaganda for China, was released in November 1989. In August 1988, Chuang Kuo-ming and Huang Kuang-hsiung were sentenced to 10 and five years' imprisonment for being members of the World United Formosans for Independence. Their sentences were reduced by one-third.

President Lee Teng-hui was re-elected to a six-year term in March 1990 and in May he released virtually all prisoners charged with political crimes such as sedition. However, political activists continue to be convicted and imprisoned for advocating independence, and many convicted of common crimes, such as incitement to public disorder, were not included in the amnesty.

In April 1990, Luo I-shih, a Canadian national of Taiwanese origin, was indicted for advocating independence at the World Federation of Taiwanese Associations conference. In October, a court ruled that the facts of the case did not support a charge of sedition, which carries a maximum sentence of life imprisonment. Instead, he may be tried for advocacy of illegal conduct, which carries a maximum sentence of two years' imprisonment and/or a fine of NT$6,000 (US$200).

Demonstrations In January 1988, a ban on demonstrations, which had been in force for 38 years, was relaxed. Demonstrations were permitted if authorized by the police and provided they did not advocate either communism or Taiwan's independence. The number of demonstrations has greatly increased. Several people have been arrested for holding demonstrations without police authorization and the authorities have held organizers of demonstrations criminally liable for any violence. In October 1989, Hong Chi-chang was sentenced to 15 months' imprisonment for organizing a demonstration in June 1987 to protest against the National Security Law. In the same month Hsu Hsin-liang was indicted on sedition charges for violence that occurred during a demonstration in December 1979 in Kaohsiung, even though he was not in Taiwan at the time.

Political Parties In January 1989, the new Civic Organizations Law allowed political parties to be formed, provided that they advocated neither communism nor division of the national territory, and that they registered formally; by 1990 more than 40 parties had registered. The law also required all non-governmental organizations to apply for licences. In August 1989, the Ministry of the Interior ruled that all organizations using "Taiwan" in their names must add "Republic of China". More than 100 organizations have refused to change their names and many have refused to apply for licences but, as of 1990, none had been prosecuted for operating without a licence.

The 1989 Election There was much criticism of the government and the ruling party during the elections campaign in late December 1989. In November, 32 DPP candidates formed an alliance to campaign for Taiwan's independence. The government threatened to prosecute them for sedition. The alliance alleged vote-rigging, bribery and intimidatory filming of opposition rallies by government agents. Television and radio coverage was heavily biased in favour of the KMT.

Denial of Entry Visas Dozens of Taiwanese dissidents abroad have been denied entry visas to return home. In July 1989, Chen Wan-chen, an opposition journalist, was sentenced to five months' imprisonment for entering Taiwan illegally. In August 1989, the World Federation of Taiwanese Associations, the major umbrella organization for Taiwanese abroad, held its annual conference in Kaohsiung. The authorities had attempted to prevent the meeting by refusing permission to overseas Taiwanese to enter the country.

Access to Information Access to government information is restricted, often arbitrarily. A Freedom of Information Bill modelled on the United States Freedom of Information Act has been pending before the Legislative Yuan since mid-1989. Information withheld on grounds of national security includes the number of pigs on the island, information which environmentalists are seeking because of the impact of pigs on pollution. The number of pigs, believed to be around seven million, is considered classified because it relates to the amount of food on the island, which could be relevant to a country planning an invasion.

Pornography On March 27 1990, authorities confiscated some 450 copies of a new Chinese-language Taiwanese edition of *Playboy* magazine on the grounds that it "offended public morality" and that it had not been properly registered.

The Media

The Government Information Office works closely with the KMT's Cultural Affairs Department and the National Press Council (NPC) in issuing guidance to the media on sensitive issues. The NPC produces a weekly 10-minute prime-time TV programme, *News Bridge*, which, in its own words, "is intended to strengthen self-discipline among the local press, so that the authorities will not be forced to take the necessary control measures".

The Press From January 1 1988, restrictions on the press were considerably relaxed. The government allowed existing newspapers to expand from a maximum of 12 to 24 pages and one year later lifted the 24-page limit. The 36-year-old ban on new newspapers ended. The principal beneficiaries of the relaxation of press laws were the two dominant morning papers, the *United Daily News* and the more liberal *China Times*, both owned by KMT Central Committee members. Many reporters and editors also belong to the KMT and, as a result, overt censorship is rarely necessary. Numerous journalists have described how before major events the government or the KMT will call with "suggestions" on how a story should be handled. Such interference has decreased but not ceased since the lifting of martial law. The government can acquire a controlling share in a newspaper if it becomes "unco-operative".

In June 1989, Kang Ning-hsian, a DPP legislator, started the *Capital Morning Post*, the first opposition daily newspaper. In October, the military asked the Taiwan High Court to charge its publisher and chairman with sedition for a report, later corrected, that there had been an explosion at a new Memorial Hall, a building under military control. The charges were dropped but, in August 1990, the paper went out of business, mainly due to its inability to attract advertising, a problem that has plagued most of the non-KMT papers.

In September 1987, two journalists from the *Independence Evening Post* defied a 38-year ban on travel to the mainland by going to Beijing. Both faced charges which were later dropped but a two-year travel ban was enforced. In April 1989, the government lifted the ban on journalists and film-makers from working on the mainland, but Taiwanese journalists were forbidden to co-operate with their mainland counterparts and only allowed to stay for up to six months, and media organizations were not to be allowed to open offices on the mainland. Despite this, the *Independence Evening Post* announced in May 1989 that it planned to open bureaux in Beijing, Shanghai and Canton. In November 1989, the prominent dissident, Lin Yi-hsiung, returned from four years' self-imposed exile with draft basic laws of "the Republic of Taiwan", which were printed in the *Independence Evening Post*. The chief prosecutor of the Taiwan High Court is considering sedition charges against Lin and the newspaper.

Attacks on the Press Suspensions and bannings of opposition publications have decreased but not disappeared. In October 1988, the Kaohsiung City authorities suspended the publishing licence of the monthly magazine *Taiwan Culture* for one year for "disseminating separatist sentiment". In February 1989, the Taipei City authorities ordered *The Movement* magazine to suspend publication for one year on similar grounds. When the magazine ignored the order its staff were harassed and issues of the magazine were confiscated. The most heavily censored magazines since martial law ended have been *Freedom Era Weekly* and *Democratic Progressive Weekly*. Twenty-two successive titles of *Freedom Era* have been suspended for a year, while 16 individual issues have been banned. According to its publisher, several thousand copies of the magazine have been confiscated at newsstands. Early in 1989, Cheng Nan-jung, editor-in-chief of *Freedom Era Weekly*, was charged with treason for publishing a new draft constitution of Taiwan. On April 7, he set himself on fire during a police raid on his office. The staff published a special memorial issue, which was then banned. In November, its management decided to close the paper because of financial problems caused in part by the many suspensions and confiscations.

In December 1988, Chen Wei-tu, editor of the *Democratic Progressive Weekly*, and its publisher were sentenced to seven months' imprisonment on libel charges for publishing an allegation that a military police officer had abused his position. In April 1989, Chen was sentenced to eight years' imprisonment on sedition charges for producing a pamphlet warning of a military plot to overthrow the government, but was released as part of the May 1990 amnesty. In July 1989, police confiscated 3,500 copies of the magazine on the order of the Taiwan Garrison Command. In October, the magazine's former publisher and former editor were charged with sedition for publishing an article about an alleged attempted mutiny by troops on Kinmen island. Between January and November 1989, the authorities banned at least 31 issues and suspended 16 licences among the six opposition weeklies. Issues of overseas Taiwanese publications critical of the KMT authorities, such as the Los Angeles-based *Taiwan Tribune*, have been confiscated and, in August 1989, three books by the Taiwanese-American Chen Fang-ming were banned.

Radio and Television The KMT, the military, and the Taiwan provincial government control and own majority shares of the three TV stations. Radio is also effectively under KMT control. News coverage has been strongly biased in favour of the
KMT, especially during elections, and stations have refused to broadcast opposition
campaign advertisements, despite the Civic Organizations Law's requirement that
"political parties have equal access to the use of public buildings and the publicly-
owned mass media". The government has denied opposition requests to set up independent radio and TV stations.

The KMT is considering legislation that would establish a public TV station. Advocates of media freedom consider the proposal a way to justify continued denial of
a licence to the DPP especially because, as the proposal stands, the public TV station would be primarily devoted to arts and intellectual programmes, and would not
be bound by an impartiality doctrine, requiring balanced coverage of major candidates, or a requirement of community or alternative programming.

In July 1988, a well-known radio programme was discontinued after the broadcaster, Wu Le-tien, criticized the government. In May 1989, the GIO issued regulations restricting TV programmes and films relating to the mainland. In June, Chen
Sheng-man was sentenced to seven-and-a-half years' imprisonment for showing
publicly a videotape of a Communist Chinese military parade. In November, the
GIO refused to approve video recordings of the elections made by the *Journalist*
magazine.

Viet Nam

The Socialist Republic of Viet Nam was formally proclaimed on July 2 1976 following the collapse of the former Republic of (South) Viet Nam at the end of a 30-year revolutionary war led by the Communist Party against French and US forces.

The media in Viet Nam are tightly controlled by the government, but in the past two years journalists and intellectuals have been increasingly outspoken. "Renovation, openness and democracy" were the watchwords of official government policy established by the Communist Party in 1986, a policy whose limits have been tested by writers and journalists. The recent reassertion of Communist Party control has led to the closure of numerous periodicals and the dismissal of several editors and a leading Communist Party official who apparently supported liberalization.

	Data	Year
Population	64,412,000	1988
Life expectancy (M/F)	56.7/61.1	1985
GNP (US$ per capita)	109	1988
Main religion(s)	Buddhism	
Official language(s)	Vietnamese	
Illiteracy %	12.4	1990
(M/F)	8.0/16.4	1990
Daily newspapers	4	1986
Radio sets	6,600,000	1988
TV sets	2,200,000	1988
Press agencies:		
	Viet-Nam News Agency	
ICCPR:	YES	1982

Freedom of Expression

At least eight provincial periodicals were closed down during 1989 ostensibly for violating publishing laws, and the editor of one of the most widely-read newspapers in Ho Chi Minh City, *Saigon Giai Phong*, and the editor of *Lao Dong*, a popular weekly, were reported to have been dismissed. Several other provincial publications underwent major changes. In the central highlands city of Da Lat the editor-in-chief of the journal *Lang Bian* was dismissed and subsequently expelled from the Communist Party. At a hastily organized Communist Party Plenum in August 1989 Lieutenant- General Tran Do, director of the Communist Party Central Committee's Department of Culture and Arts, was dismissed for what appears to have been his frequent support of demands for greater liberalization for writers and artists.

In April 1989, Information Minister Tran Hoan issued an order barring the unauthorized use of printing presses, banning the reprinting or distribution of any book printed before 1975, and ordering the closure of any newspaper failing to submit pre-publication copies to the government. In September 1989, the Ministry of Information reported some success in controlling the publication of "special issues" of newspapers, after it had revoked the permits granted to a number of publishers.

In mid-May 1989, alarmed by the proliferation of "decadent" books and video tapes over the past two years, the government "temporarily suspended" the circulation of half-a-dozen books in Ho Chi Minh City and restricted the showing of video tapes. However, video shows had become a lucrative business, and of the more than 40,000 video recorders nationally, only 20,000 had been registered. In July alone, a crackdown on illegal video shows in Ha Noi revealed that more than 1,000 video re-corders had not been registered, and that even the Police Department and units of the Ministry of Interior had shown banned videos.

In a series of short stories in January 1987 in the weekly magazine of the Vietnamese Writers' Association, *Van Nghe*, Nguyen Huy Thiep challenged con-ventional wisdom about two prominent Vietnamese historical figures, prompting an uproar in literary circles. The subsequest dismissal in December 1988 of Nguyen Ngoc, editor-in-chief of *Van Nghe*, led to a widely publicized controversy and open criticism of his dismissal by Viet Nam's journalists' and writers' associations.

Perhaps the most serious challenge to the Communist Party's monopoly over the media was launched in September 1988. A group of opposition figures with im-peccable revolutionary credentials who, two years earlier, had set up the Club of Former Resistance Fighters in Ho Chi Minh City, clandestinely published *Truyen Thong Khang Chien* (Tradition of Resistance). Its first issue was confiscated but at least four subsequent issues have circulated secretly: the reports criticize the Com-munist Party leadership for incompetence, corruption, economic mismanagement, the prevailing secrecy surrounding party meetings and decisions, and abuses of human rights including freedom of expression. On May 31 1990, the *Far Eastern Economic Review* reported that Nguyen Ho and Ta Ba Tang had been ousted from their leadership positions in the Club of Former Resistance Fighters and are under house arrest.

Encouraged by the official "renovation" rhetoric, the past two years also saw the first public demonstrations in post-war Viet Nam. In late 1988, frustrated southern farmers, who had lost their fields during the collectivization campaign in the late 1970s, held public demonstrations in provincial and district towns of the Mekong Delta. In May, in a spill over effect from Beijing's student demonstrations, students of two colleges in Ha Noi mounted protests in demand of better living conditions. The authorities responded almost immediately by increasing their living allowances.

A new Constitution was formally adopted by the National Assembly in Decem-ber 1980. Articles 67 and 68 specify the right to "enjoy" freedom of speech, free-dom of the press, of assembly, and of worship. Articles 44 and 45 define the scope of literature, the arts and the mass media, which are to be "developed on the basis of the perspective of Marxism-Leninism" with the express objective "of guiding public opinion" and mobilizing "the entire population to participate in socialist emulation". The basic rights granted to Vietnamese citizens have to be seen in the context of Articles 76, 77 and 78, which oblige citizens to be "loyal to the homeland".

Legal Restrictions on Freedom of Expression

Criminal Code The first Criminal Code was adopted by the National Assembly in June 1985. Its stated purpose is to serve as an "effective tool of the state to protect the gains of the revolution and to protect the socialist system". Among the offences defined as crimes against national security are the following: actions aimed at over-throwing the people's government (Art.73), actions that undermine the policy of national unity (Art.81), spreading propaganda against the socialist government (Art.82) and actions that disrupt public security (Art.83). These provisions forbid the establishment of any organization aimed at overthrowing the government or causing divisions among the people. They also prohibit disseminating anti-socialist literature or cultural material.

Press Laws In December 1989, the National Assembly adopted a new Press Law by a majority vote, after heated debates. The new law reasserts that the press and other media are organs of the Communist Party and the state while also serving as a "forum of the people" (Art.1). Article 6 stipulates that the media have the duty to "propagandize and disseminate the Communist Party's lines and policies" while Article 10 prohibits the media from "inciting people to oppose the state" or disclosing "state, military, security, economic and diplomatic secrets". One entire chapter of the new law is devoted to "state management of the media". The Council of Ministers and provincial people's committees are given a "guiding and controlling function in the implementation of media orientation". The media can only operate with a permit issued by these state bodies and printed newspapers have to submit copies to the responsible state bodies before they can be distributed. The new Press Law appears to have placed strict limitations on the Communist Party-initiated "anti-negativism campaign", which for three years had allowed the press unusual licence in revealing mismanagement, corruption, incompetence and human rights abuses.

The Media

There are no privately-owned newspapers in Viet Nam. The main dailies *Nhan Dan* and *Quan Doi Nhan Dan*, with a combined circulation of nearly half a million copies, are the offical organs of the Communist Party and the armed forces respectively. There are two additional dailies, *Ha Noi Moi* and *Saigon Giai Phong*, with an estimated circulation in 1987 of 91,000 for both Vietnamese and Chinese-language editions. In addition, a number of periodicals are published with varying frequency in the capital and with different editions in the provinces.

An article in the offical daily *Quan Doi Nhan Dan* in August 1989 lamented that there were more illegal newspapers published in Viet Nam than newspapers with legal permits, and that they were more popular than the official publications due to their over-indulgence in "love stories", "beautiful women" and "court cases". The result was a 14 per cent decline in the circulation of the two main dailies between June 1988 and June 1989.

Social organizations under the umbrella of the Vietnamese Fatherland Front publish their own periodicals under the control of the Ministry of Information. The Fatherland Front publishes the weekly *Dai Doan Ket* while the Federation of Trade Unions, the Committee for Solidarity of Patriotic Vietnamese Catholics, the Association of Writers, the Association of Women and the Communist Youth Union all publish their own periodicals.

The official Viet Nam News Agency disseminates daily news summaries to newspapers and periodicals, while Communist Party and government cadres have access to a restricted news bulletin with in-depth analyses of national and international events. Most foreign news agencies allowed to operate are those of fraternal socialist countries, though Agence France Presse and Kyodo News Service also operate bureaux in Ha Noi. No foreign newspapers, journals or periodicals are distributed apart from a limited number of publications from countries of the Council for Mutual Economic Assistance.

Books The Communist Party carefully screens all book manuscripts before publication. Any author wishing to submit a manuscript for publication must first obtain permission from his "Unit Head" and must append to the manuscript observations by his "leadership organization". Sometimes publications have been approved by local authorities but subsequently censored by higher officials, resulting in all copies being withdrawn from bookshops within days of release.

Arrest and Detention of Writers

Doan Quoc Sy and Hoang Hai Thuy were tried with four others in April 1988 after nearly four years in detention and, on appealing to the Supreme Court, were sentenced to eight and six years' imprisonment respectively on charges of counter-revolutionary propaganda. Both had earlier spent several years in "re-education" camps without trial and before their arrest had been publicly described as "psychological warfare cadets of the USA". Hoang Hai Thuy was released on February 2 1990, three months before the end of his term. Two other writers arrested with them in 1984 died in custody in 1986 and 1987 before being tried. The circumstances surrounding their deaths are not clear.

In September 1988, two leading Buddhist scholars, Thich Tue Sy and Thich Tri Sieu, who had for several years worked to compile a Vietnamese Buddhist Encyclopaedia, were brought to trial together with 19 other defendants charged with "activities aimed at overthrowing the people's government". During their trial, they were publicly labelled in the media as "reactionaries under the cloak of Buddhism". Both monks were sentenced to death but had their sentences commuted to 20 years' imprisonment at an appeal hearing in November. All the other defendants were also convicted and given long prison terms.

During 1987 and 1988, the government released large numbers of prisoners who had been detained without trial in "re-education" camps, including some 1,500 persons who had been so detained since 1975. It is not clear how many remain in detention. The government puts the figure at about 130 while Amnesty International has received reports that about 400 people detained in "re-education" camps are unaccounted for and may still be in detention.

At least two prisoners held without trial for exercising their freedom of expression are believed to remain in prison. Nguyen Chi Thien is a 58-year-old poet who was first arrested in 1958 for his involvement in the "Hundred Flowers" campaign which criticized the Communist Party land reform in the mid-1950's. He has spent half his life in various "re-education" camps, interrupted by only brief periods of freedom. He was last re-arrested in April 1979 after handing a manuscript of his poems to a British diplomat and has remained in detention since. To Huy Co, an academic from Ha Noi, who spent several years in "re-education" between 1969 and 1976 for alleged "counter-revolutionary offences", was re-arrested in 1982 for his involvement in founding a "free literature movement" which translated banned literature and circulated manuscripts of unpublished works among its members. The reasons for the continuing detention of Nguyen Chi Thien and To Huy Co are unclear, especially given that in February 1988 the Vietnamese Writers' Association re-admitted five members of the "Hundred Flowers" campaign after 30 years.

Europe

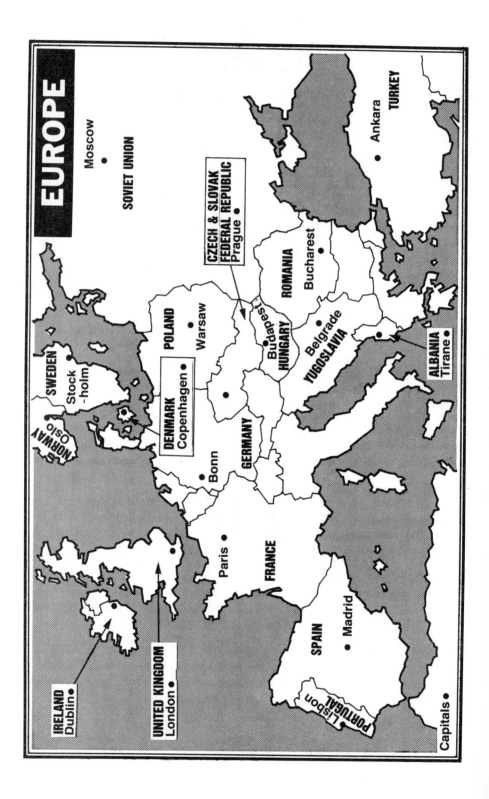

EUROPE

Capitals ●

IRELAND
Dublin ●

UNITED KINGDOM
London ●

NORWAY
Oslo

SWEDEN
Stock
-holm ●

DENMARK
Copenhagen ●

POLAND
Warsaw ●

CZECH & SLOVAK
FEDERAL REPUBLIC
Prague ●

SOVIET UNION
Moscow ●

GERMANY
Bonn ●

FRANCE
Paris ●

SPAIN
Madrid ●

PORTUGAL
Lisbon ●

HUNGARY
Budapest ●

ROMANIA
Bucharest ●

YUGOSLAVIA
Belgrade ●

ALBANIA
Tirane ●

TURKEY
Ankara ●

Albania

The People's Republic of Albania was proclaimed on January 11 1946, led by Enver Hoxha, head of the Albanian Communist Party, later the Party of Labour of Albania (PLA). Albania became increasingly isolated as it turned against its allies: Yugoslavia in 1948, the Soviet Union in 1961, and China in 1972. It withdrew from the Council for Mutual Economic Assistance in 1962 and from the Warsaw Pact in 1968, following the invasion of Czechoslovakia. A new Constitution was adopted in December 1976, declaring Albania a People's Socialist Republic, and reaffirming its policy of self- reliance.

	Data	Year
Population	3,182,417	1989
Life expectancy (M/F)	68.5/73.7	1985
GNP (US$ per capita)	740	1988
Main religion(s)	Islam	
Official language(s)	Albanian	
Illiteracy %	15	1985
Daily newspapers	2	1987
Non daily newspapers	21	1985
Radio sets	514,000	1987
TV sets	255,000	1987
Press agencies:		
Albanian Telegrapghic Agency		
ICCPR:	NO	

In April 1985, Enver Hoxha died. His successor, Ramiz Alia, had been engaged in a gradual change of policy long before the effects of the 1989 revolutions in Eastern Europe began to have repercussions in Albania. The result has been an acceleration in reforms although not sufficient to convince the thousands of Albanians who occupied foreign embassies in Tiranë in July 1990 and who were ultimately allowed to leave the country.

Albania was the only European country not to join the Conference on Security and Co-operation in Europe (CSCE) in 1975, but hoped to do so at the Paris summit in November 1990. At the CSCE Conference on the Human Dimension in Copenhagen in July, Albania was granted observer status.

Diplomatic relations have now been established with a wide range of countries, including the Soviet Union. In October 1990, Albania hosted a meeting of Balkan foreign ministers, only the second such gathering since World War II, and the highest-level international meeting in the country in decades.

Significant internal economic and legal reforms were announced at the People's Assembly session on May 7-8 1990. Agitation and propaganda against the state have been redefined: only those forms of agitation and propaganda that are "aimed at overthrowing the social and state order" are to be considered crimes. Criticism of the authorities voiced in private is no longer punishable, but if made in public will be treated as an appeal to overthrow the government by violence. This measure is believed to be aimed at preventing any public demonstrations. On July 7, President Alia dismissed several Politburo members and announced that new legislation on parliamentary elections was being drafted.

There has been little relaxation of censorship: the authorities continue to restrict freedom of expression and the government controls the media and its journalists, writers and artists.

Dissent and Repression

The 1976 Constitution mentions "freedom of speech, press, organization, association, assembly and public demonstration" (Art.53), "freedom of scientific work, and literary and artistic creativity" (Art.51), and declares that citizens hold the right to "unite in various organizations operating in the political, economic, cultural, and any other area of the country's life" (Art.54). In practice, these rights have had little meaning. Foreign sources estimate that the authorities are detaining between 20,000 and 40,000 political prisoners, figures denied by the government.

The government has long used police surveillance and informants to inhibit expressions of dissent and even exiles hesitated to criticize the government for fear that relatives in Albania might suffer retribution in the form of internal exile. The Sigurimi (secret police) is highly effective in instilling fear; Albanians had to obtain a pass from the local Sigurimi agent to travel from one administrative district to another. Citizens tend to reserve the most prominent position in their homes for a picture of the Party leadership, or risk being informed on by visitors.

In 1989, the novel, *Thikat* (Knives) by Neshat Tozaj, a former Interior Ministry official, sharply criticizing the Sigurimi, was published in Tiranë and sold out within days. A review of the book, written by Ismail Kadare, the country's most successful official writer, condemned violations of human rights and law in Albania and praised the book as an important literary work.

There were reports of anti-government demonstrations in Shkoder, Albania's fourth largest city, in December 1989 and January 1990, and in Tiranë in February 1990. On December 19 1989, the Albanian government denied Yugoslav reports that mass deportations to labour camps had followed the crushing of anti-communist demonstrations in Shkoder. On January 11 1990, the Yugoslav newspaper *Politika* reported that a State of Emergency had been imposed in Shkoder, that demonstrators had been arrested, and that five young Albanian printers who had been distributing leaflets were immediately sentenced to death. Four demonstrators who escaped arrest later testified that arrests had been made and that another demonstration of 6,000-7,000 people on January 14 had been broken up by the police using tear gas and truncheons. According to students at Tiranë University, silent demonstrations took place in early February 1990 when 2,000 students and workers gathered in Tiranë's Skanderbeg Square, despite some intimidation from the Sigurimi.

The Media

When rumours of serious unrest in Albania circulated in December 1989, the Albanian media reacted swiftly, reporting that the situation was stable. However, on January 22 1990, the Ninth Plenum of the Central Committee of the PLA called on the press to replace its "general phraseology and slogans with persuasive and understandable arguments". The media has improved and the public is receiving more comprehensive and up-to-date information.

Newspapers The press is controlled through the Albanian Telegraphic Agency (ATA). There are two major daily newspapers, *Bashkimi*, published by the Democratic Front, an organization controlled by party members and sympathizers, and *Zeri i Popullit*, published by the PLA. They have a combined circulation of

145,000. In 1990, Albanian newspapers began sending journalists abroad for on-the-spot reporting. Two *Zeri i Popullit* reporters attended a meeting of Balkan journalists in Sofia and reported their colleagues' curiosity about current developments in Albania, specifically about the speed with which the country was trying to adjust to the changing situation in Europe.

Foreign journalists have long been banned from Albania unless accompanying offical guests, but it is progressively easier for them to enter as tourists and some have obtained interviews with leading politicians. Some 18 foreign journalists went to Tiranë and interviewed President Alia during the visit of UN Secretary-General Javier Perez de Cuellar in May 1990.

Radio and Television Radio Tiranë has many powerful Chinese-built transmitters and broadcasts daily to other countries in 21 languages. Since 1971, government-supported TV has transmitted for five or six hours a day in the late afternoons and evenings. Although viewing or listening to foreign broadcasts was once prohibited, both activities are now legal. Many tune in to Italian radio, the BBC World Service or Voice of America or watch Yugoslav, Greek or Italian TV. Albanian TV has been transmitting a nightly Italian news show which tends to dwell on sensational stories. It seems that the Albanian authorities have now abandoned the practice of modifying home-built TV sets to make them incapable of receiving foreign broadcasts. Nevertheless, Albanians tend to watch or listen to foreign broadcasts alone or only with close friends for fear of being reported to the authorities.

Artistic Expression

To enter the Academy of Art in Tiranë, one must first pass a highly selective entrance exam. A PLA representative instructs professors and gives orders to the director of the Academy. Artistic training focuses on the Socialist-Realist school and includes regular classes on Marxism and political economy. After graduation, works are commissioned solely by the government and the price is set by an offical commission. Artists not adhering to Socialist-Realism risk offical censorship or even imprisonment, sometimes of long duration. The artists' dependency on government commissions encourages some to report on others in order to get ahead. Those who find favour with the government commissions have access to subsidized foreign art supplies and perks such as studios, academic and government posts and paid leave during which they can paint full-time.

Contact with Foreigners It is doubtful that contact with foreigners is any longer an indictable offence but the Albanian authorities tamper with mail from abroad and cheques or clothing from exiles have been returned. From mid-1990, telephone access to and from Albania has been easier and a direct-dial service to 56 countries has been opened.

Religious Expression

The 1976 Constitution was unique in that it expressly outlawed religion, believed to be a divisive force. Article 55 of the 1977 Criminal Code supports the constitutional restrictions: "fascist, anti-democratic, religious, warmongering or anti-socialist propaganda, as well as the preparation, distribution or the possession for distribution of literature with such a content in order to weaken or undermine the State of the Dictatorship of the Proletariat are punishable by imprisonment of between three and 10 years".

Decree 4236 in 1967 authorized local executive committees and co- operatives to expropriate all fixed assets and possessions of religious institutions without compensation. In September 1967, the government announced that it had closed all religious buildings, including 2,169 churches, mosques, monasteries and other institutions. Of these, 630 major Orthodox churches were razed to the ground and an equal number were converted to other uses.

Religious holidays and, for a time, private religious practice were also suppressed. During the anti-religion campaign, authorities confiscated religious artefacts from individuals, including personal crucifixes, icons and prayer-books. Religious leaders, both Christian and Muslim, were publicly denounced, shaven, defrocked, imprisoned or killed.

President Alia has eased the government's harsh policies, opening the way for the resumption, albeit small-scale and monitored, of overt religious practice. Since May 1990, "religious propaganda" is no longer a crime against the state. Now it is merely decreed that "the state is separated from religion and the question of religious belief is a matter of conscience for every individual". However, the then Deputy Prime Minister, Manush Myftiu, said that the state would continue to promote "atheistic propaganda". Agence France Presse was told that Albania had no intention of allowing the reopening of mosques and Catholic and Orthodox churches closed down in 1967. Nevertheless, according to visitors in 1990, extensive restoration of churches and mosques as cultural relics and tourist sights is taking place.

The Greek Minority Greece has often complained about human rights violations against the ethnic Greek minority in Albania (numbering about 250,000 people). The Albanian authorities claim that the Constitution guarantees "all rights for the Greek minority in Albania". In 1984 Amnesty International reported several complaints that ethnic Greeks were expressly forbidden to use the Greek language when visiting relatives in Albanian prisons. However, there is now a bi-weekly Greek-language newspaper *Laiko Vima*, some publications and radio broadcasts in Greek, and many observers anticipate further concessions to the Greek minority as Albania's reform programme proceeds. On February 22 1990, the then Interior Minister Simon Stefani, commenting on foreign reports on the thousands of ethnic Greek prisoners, said that the total number of prisoners was 35 and that "not one of them has been sentenced for grave political crimes".

The Name-changing Campaign In 1975, the Albanian government mandated name-changes for "citizens who have inappropriate names and offensive surnames from a political, ideological, and moral standpoint". Local civil affairs offices were supplied with lists of government-approved names. Although the Albanian government's name-changing programme has affected the whole country, it appears to have been particularly imposed on the ethnic Greek minority.

Reform

The People's Assembly session of May 7-8 1990 was a major event and produced a package of human rights and economic reforms. Penal reforms include the creation of a new Ministry of Justice (the old one was abolished in the mid-1960s at the height of Albania's Cultural Revolution); the establishment of rehabilitation centres; the early release of convicts (prisoners who have served over half their sentences and behaved well are now eligible for early conditional release, a measure abolished in 1981); and the right to a speedy trial, legal defence, and appeal. Furthermore, the number of crimes punishable by death has been reduced from 34 to 11.

While attempting to defect remains an offence, it is no longer considered an act of betrayal (punishable by 10-25 years' imprisonment or death) but rather "illegal border trespassing", punishable by a maximum of five years' imprisonment. Early in December 1989, the Archbishop of Athens alleged that four brothers of the ethnic Greek Prassos family had been brutally killed in public following their attempt to flee from Albania to Greece in October. On December 16 1989, the government denied Yugoslav reports of the same case which claimed that they had been tortured to death. Amnesty International has expressed concern that Ilir (31) and Agim Zari (27) may have been killed by border guards on February 1 or 2 1990 while trying to cross to Greece without official permission.

Another offence struck from the list of treasonable crimes was "the creation of companies and other foreign or joint economic and financial institutions with capitalist, bourgeois or revisionist monopolies or states, and acceptance of credits from them".

Additionally, all Albanian nationals would receive a passport for travel abroad on request. In the past, passports were issued on a very limited and selective basis. As of July 1990, 6,000 passports had already been issued, but there were many complaints about the prohibitive charges.

Embassy Refugees Between July and August 1990, some 5,000 Albanians sought refuge in Western embassies in Tiranë, hoping to obtain asylum. There were more than 2,000 refugees in the West German embassy compound alone. These incidents began on July 2 following a demonstration in Tiranë sparked off by disappointed hopes that the government would relax restrictions on travel abroad. The demonstration was met with force by the police and foreign diplomats estimated that up to 50 people were killed. Scores of Albanians surged into embassies under a hail of police gunfire, confronting the Albanian government with a rare display of public dissent. Those who entered the Chinese and Cuban embassies were promptly returned to the Albanian authorities. The ATA broke with tradition by reporting the events on July 3, stating that between 300 and 400 people, including "vagabonds, former prisoners, as well as some deceived adolescents" tried to enter a foreign embassy in Tiranë on the night of July 2. The authorities blamed hostile foreign forces for these events. In an effort to stem the flood of refugees, Ramiz Alia assured Albanians that anyone could obtain a passport but few seemed willing to leave the embassies for fear of reprisals and people continued to climb into embassies, encountering no more opposition from the security forces until July 8 when the diplomatic quarter was sealed off.

In December, diplomats reported demonstrations in Tiranë on an "unprecented" scale in support of reform and an end to dictatorship.

Czech and Slovak Federal Republic

On October 24 1989, the Federal Prime Minister of Czechoslovakia, Ladislav Adamec, on a visit to Vienna to sign a human rights accord, declared that the two leading Czechoslovak dissidents, playwright Václav Havel and the 1968 Foreign Minister Jirí Hájek, were "nobodies" or "zeros". On December 29, Václav Havel was inaugurated as President, Adamec having resigned earlier that month.

Before the Revolution 1988 was a year of important anniversaries for the Czech and Slovak people. Czechoslovakia (renamed the Czech and Slovak Federal Republic (CSFR) on April 20 1990) was 70 years-old; it was 50 years since the Munich agreement gave Hitler's Germany large and important areas of the country's terri-

	Data	Year
Population	15,624,254	1988
Life expectancy (M/F)	67.1/74.3	1984
GNP (US$ per capita)	5,820	1988
Main religion(s)	Christianity	
Official language(s)	Czech	
	Slovak	
Illiteracy %	2	
Daily newspapers	30	1986
Non daily newspapers	115	1986
Periodicals	935	1986
Radio sets	3,966,000	1987
TV sets	4,985,000	1975
Press agencies:		
Ceskoslovenska Tiskova		
Kancelar, Orbis Press Agency		
ICCPR:	YES	1975

tory; the people also recalled the Communist Party takeover of 1948, the Prague Spring of 1968 and the August Warsaw Pact invasion which crushed it. On several of these anniversaries there were large demonstrations tackled by police with varying degrees of violence. However, on December 10 1988, an unofficial demonstration in Prague, called by independent, illegal groups to mark the 40th Anniversary of the Universal Declaration of Human Rights, was allowed by the authorities who used the occasion to launch their own official human rights committee. It was attended by Václav Havel who was cheered by the crowd of some 3,000 people. The demonstration encouraged a feeling among the growing number of independent activists that a more relaxed relationship with the state might gradually develop.

Wenceslas Square At the beginning of 1989, any hopes of a possible thaw in Czechoslovakia were crushed. As Foreign Minister Jaromír Johanes visited Vienna to sign the final document of the Helsinki follow-up meeting which contained extensive passages on human and civic rights, Prague saw unprecedented police brutality and the repression of dissent intensified. Independent groups had gathered in Wenceslas Square, Prague's main boulevard, on January 16, to commemorate the 20th anniversary of the death of Jan Palach, a student who immolated himself there to protest against the consequences of the 1968 invasion, in particular the renewal of censorship. Police used water cannon, tear-gas, batons and dogs to disperse the crowd, but people returned for demonstrations on five consecutive days. Many activists were arrested, among them Václav Havel, subsequently sentenced to nine months' imprisonment. The sentence was later reduced to eight months and he was released on parole in May, half-way through his term.

During the 1970s and early 1980s, harassment and punishment of dissidents and their associates deterred the majority of people from involvement in unofficial political activity. Dissidents, especially those associated with the Charter 77 human rights movement, were generally treated with apathy by the population who viewed their activities as futile. The state media constantly disparaged the movement and was particularly successful in rural areas where contact with unofficially sanctioned ideas was difficult.

The imprisonment of Václav Havel mobilized popular support. The artistic community, which had not previously been active in his defence, launched petitions for his release. In early Autumn 1989, Communist Party leader Milos Jakes told party officials that it was a mistake to keep harassing Havel because he was too well-known and it caused too many ripples in public opinion and embarrassment abroad. He suggested that the authorities concentrate on less well-known members of the growing dissident movement. His speech was leaked in a secretly-made recording and broadcast on Radio Free Europe.

"A Few Sentences" In June 1989, a petition began to circulate and soon attracted tens of thousands of signatures among people from all walks of life. Called "A Few Sentences", the document demanded greater democracy and freedom in the country. It became a target of persistent attacks in the official media which described it as an anti-state pamphlet created with the aid of subversive centres in the West, aiming to undermine the Czechoslovak way of life. Far from deterring people, the propaganda campaign encouraged them to enquire about the manifesto and demand that its full text be printed in the state press. It gained further attention by the harassment meted out to public figures in the artistic community who signed the document. Actors, relying on television and film work to supplement their generally meagre theatre wages, were banned from TV appearances and the public missed them. In protest, the prestigious Czech Philharmonic Orchestra, led by chief conductor Václav Neumann, refused further co-operation with Czechoslovak radio and TV.

The Media: Before the Revolution

In theory, the most important sections of the media (radio, TV, party newspapers and magazines, official state publications, books) were controlled directly by the state and the rest indirectly through their publishers' membership of the National Front, but in practice there was not a great difference between the two. Although censorship was officially removed in 1968, it was exercised through *Útisk* (the Office for the Press and Information) and through editors personally responsible for the content of their publications. Despite the great variety of newspapers and periodicals, in general, all reflected or repeated the party line. The Communist Party daily *Rudé Právo* enjoyed a privileged position, selling over one million copies per day, largely through block subscriptions with institutions and factories. Other party dailies, such as the Socialist Party's *Svobodné Slovo* and the People's Party's *Lidová Demokracie*, had circulations in the region of 200,000.

Once the leadership had embarked on *prestavba*, its own version of *perestroika*, new attention was paid to the media. In early 1989, the Prognostic Institute of the

Czechoslovak Academy of Sciences produced an outline of the country's immediate prospects which were so bleak that the document was kept secret, only to be leaked to the dissident movement and foreign media. In August, a leading economic forecaster, Milos Zeman, wrote an unusually open article in *Technical Magazine* about the country's economic prospects, directly blaming the leadership for the country's difficulties. In his article, Zeman compared Czechoslovakia to a marathon runner whose rivals had disappeared over the horizon and who is therefore convinced that he is leading the race. All issues sold out instantly and when Zeman returned from an official visit to the Soviet Union he was dismissed and his entire department was closed.

On the officially designated "Day of the Press, Radio and Television" (September 21 1989) Karel Horák, the editor of the party's ideology weekly *Tribuna*, wrote that "it is precisely the media which have a decisive significance in securing one of the key parts of restructuring, and that is informing the public". He stressed that keeping silent about important facts or events could undermine confidence towards journalists and politics in general. However, trust in the Czechoslovak media was very low. "Open discussion" on the letters pages of newspapers was, in fact, very one-sided and selective with no material supportive of dissent. Problems of the economy and the environment were covered half-heartedly.

In autumn 1989, journalists in the official media finally made a defiant stand prompted by the arrests on October 12 of Jirí Ruml and Rudolf Zeman who since 1987 had published a *samizdat* monthly called *Lidové Noviny*. Several hundred journalists signed a petition demanding their release and the legalization of the monthly.

The Church   A further impetus to the reform process came from the Roman Catholic Church; some 60 per cent of the public are thought to be Catholic. By law, anyone might profess religious faith but, in practice, religious believers were harassed and persecuted. The Catholic Church endured bureaucratic obstacles including the authorities' refusal over a number of years to agree to new appointments of bishops. The state also encouraged priests, whose salaries it paid, to join its own organization called *Pacem in Terris* which the Vatican refused to recognize.

The first large-scale demonstration in 20 years took place in the Slovak capital, Bratislava, in March 1988. A crowd had gathered to protest the state's obstruction of the filling of vacant bishoprics and was dispersed by police using extreme violence. A few months later, a Catholic layman, Augustin Navrátil, conceived a 31-point petition for greater religious freedom and the separation of the Church from the state. Signed by over 600,000 people, it had the support of Czechoslovakia's most senior spiritual leader, Cardinal Frantisek Tomásek, who, like Václav Havel, became a symbol for the people's hopes and demands.

Other Political Parties   In the years after 1948, with a brief period of limited independence in 1968, the parties of the National Front umbrella organization were completely subservient to the Communist Party, achieving little real power. Two of the smaller political parties, tolerated by the ruling Communists as proof that pluralism was already well-established in Czechoslovakia, were an important part of the revolutionary process: the Socialist Party, with some 16,000 members, and the People's Party, with about 50,000 members.

The Revolution

On November 17 1989 in Prague, students took part in a legal gathering in memory of Jan Opletal, a student killed by the Nazis in November 1939. The demonstration gave the long-dissatisfied students an opportunity to voice their discontent with the government, peacefully and with good humour. The authorities deployed a previously unused special police unit, the "Red Berets", which surrounded and brutally beat the demonstrators. Although no deaths occured, there were many serious injuries. Most of those attacked by the special unit were young and the population was incensed. First to respond were students led by those at the DAMU drama school who called a protest strike and were almost instantly joined by actors. The impact of the theatre strike, which called for political reforms, was immediate as people were more prepared to listen to the striking actors whose faces they knew rather than to unfamiliar personalities.

Civic Forum On November 19, Civic Forum was formed, soon to grow into a movement with mass support. The new group's impromptu leadership was, for the most part, comprised of former dissidents like Václav Havel and other Charter 77 members. Mass demonstrations took place daily in Wenceslas Square, interspersed by two general strikes on November 20 and 27. On November 29 , the Federal Assembly voted unanimously to abolish the constitutional guarantee of the Communist Party's "leading role" in society. On December 3, Prime Minister Ladislav Adamec, the first communist leader to begin negotiating with Civic Forum, presented a new cabinet which was rejected by the people because it was still communist-dominated. A week later, a new government led by Marián Calfa was formed; the Communist Party was in a minority for the first time in over four decades. Since then, Calfa and Deputy Premiers Valtr Komárek and Vladimír Dlouh have handed back their Communist Party cards. Václav Havel was elected President and inaugurated on December 29.

Freedom of Expression since the Revolution

The Media Attempts by the Communist leadership and apparatus to block the reporting of developments in the country led media workers to impose their own demands. Once the revolution was in full swing, some official newspapers such as *Svobodné Slovo* began to report freely. Families would sometimes buy up to five newspapers and take turns to listen to the radio and watch TV in order not to miss any news. Radio and TV were particularly important in rural areas because, at the start of the revolution, the authorities had tried to prevent newspapers leaving the cities. Students tried to bypass this blockade by delivering newspapers in private cars or taxis whose drivers supported the revolution.

Reporting gradually became open and factual, although there was very little comment. This remained the case some weeks after the revolution was formally over, so that people still tuned into foreign radio stations like Radio Free Europe, Voice of America or the BBC to obtain an outside view of the situation. All three stations were suddenly mentioned in positive terms and people admitted they had listened to them for years as the only source of truthful information.

Legal Provisions In March 1990, the Czechoslovak Parliament approved amendments to the Press Law of 1966, allowing all citizens aged 18 and over the right to publish periodicals (previously only organizations had enjoyed that right). The amended press law is intended to remove legal barriers obstructing media freedom and the emergence of new publications. It forbids censorship (which *de facto* ceased to exist in November 1989). Responsibility for the truth of published information is now borne by editors. The press law leaves intact the article in the Czechoslovak Constitution which declares radio, TV and cinematography to be national property. It also allows foreign companies and citizens to launch or purchase newspapers and other mass media.

The Press Since the revolution, Czechoslovakia has witnessed a press expansion. Between December 1 1989 and mid-January 1990, 25 new newspapers and magazines were registered, while five titles were suspended, among them the Communist Party's ideological weekly *Tribuna*.

Jirí Ruml and Rudolf Zeman were released on November 26 1989 and given premises to start publishing legally. Their *Lidové Noviny* converted to a daily paper in April 1990 with a print-run of 280,000 and is rapidly establishing itself as a major independent newspaper.

The most outspoken and radical newspaper is *Respekt*, a weekly review of politics and the arts which covers taboo subjects such as racism and discrimination against the Gypsy and Vietnamese minorities. According to Petr Janyska, one of *Respekt*'s editors, lacking experience as journalists is actually an advantage for his staff because most of the official journalists "were very close to communist ideology, and that is very difficult for a journalist to get rid of. What we want is a different editorial approach: more fresh, more rude, more open".

Czechoslovakia has little or no libel legislation; under the communist government none was needed. There are likely to be many libel cases in the near future testing the country's antiquated defamation laws. The need to have these laws amended to encourage greater responsibility among journalists is now generally acknowledged.

Paper shortage and a chaotic state-run distribution network are major problems faced by all publications in Czechoslovakia. (According to *Lidové Noviny* senior editor Jaroslav Veis, their circulation could reach 350,000 but for paper rationing.) *Rudé Právo* has reduced its circulation by half to 500,000 because demand had fallen and to make more paper available to the market. With its current subscription terms lapsing in July 1990 and in January 1991, the supremacy of *Rudé Právo* will be further reduced.

Some incidents in the media give cause for concern. During President Havel's visit to Bratislava during the election campaign there were protests against him from some Slovak nationalists. These were shown on state TV and, as a result, the head of the department was sacked. With the exception of *Lidové Noviny* and *Respekt*, the media tend towards deferential treatment of President Havel.

Journalists' Unions The Czechoslovak Union of Journalists was officially disbanded on January 6 1990 and new bodies, the Syndicate of Czech and Moravian Journalists and the Slovak Syndicate of Journalists, have been founded. Journalists sacked and persecuted after the 1968 invasion have been reinstated in unions and many have started reviving old publications or founding new ones. Many have been invited to help train the younger generation which has virtually no experience of a free press.

Political Parties Towards the end of 1989, a large number of political parties were either newly-established or reformed from some National Front parties. Some parties suppressed by the communists after the 1948 coup were also revived. Around 50 political parties were registered by spring 1990 including a Green party and others such as the Independent Erotic Initiative, the Friends of Beer Party and the Gay Initiative.

Elections On June 8 and 9 1990, the first free parliamentary elections in 44 years were held, contested by 22 political parties. Foreign observers were unanimous in describing the elections as fair and democratic. The coalition of Civic Forum and its Slovak counterpart, Public Against Violence, won a convincing victory. Campaign rules were relatively strict with each party having four hours of airtime on TV and radio. Civic Forum was criticized for breaking the rules, once by broadcasting live on TV a rally described as a commemoration of the first six months since the revolution and, secondly, for broadcasting a documentary of the revolution which again seemed to boost Civic Forum.

The most controversial issue during the election campaign concerned Josef Bartoncík, the leader of the People's Party, who was accused of having been a paid agent of the former State Security (StB) (secret police). These accusations first appeared in May 1990 in the Austrian magazine *Profil*. Further investigation by Jan Ruml, head of the new Office for the Protection of the Constitution and Deputy Interior Minister, found that Bartoncík was involved with the StB for 17 years. Ruml announced his findings a few days before the elections but full details were given immediately after the polling stations had closed. The affair influenced the election results of the People's Party which was running with two other Christian Democratic parties in an electoral coalition. The three parties obtained five per cent less than had been predicted before the scandal. Jan Budaj, a leader of Public Against Violence, revealed after the elections that he, too, had contacts with the StB when he was a "dissident", and resigned. These affairs touched on the problem of people's involvement with the former government. The StB is estimated to have had a network of around 140,000 agents and informers, a large number in a population of 15 million, and explains why some parties requested screening of their candidates for the elections by the Interior Ministry who had access to StB files. As a result, a number of candidates withdrew, although the parties tried to mask their identities by various means. Civic Forum, for example, asked a number of people untarnished by the findings to step down, hoping to protect those who failed to pass the screening process from any problems in the future.

The Church For the first time in decades, all Roman Catholic dioceses in Czechoslovakia have a resident bishop and old religious orders are being re-established but there are still problems concerning the restoration of former Church property. Many people now openly acknowledge and practise their religion.

Actions

In November 1988 ARTICLE 19 sent an appeal letter to its members urging them to write to the government on behalf of Václav Havel, who had his computer and discs confiscated, and of those still in detention after an unofficial celebration in October of the 70th anniversary of Czechoslovak independence.

On April 17 1989 ARTICLE 19 wrote to the government protesting the detention of Stanislav Devaty, a journalist with Charter 77 publication *Infoch*, who was charged with incitement for allegedly organizing signatories to two open letters sent to the government calling for the release of political prisoners. Concern was also expressed for the health of Mr Devaty who had been on hunger strike since his arrest on March 16.

On October 20 1989 ARTICLE 19 wrote to the government calling for the release of Jirí Ruml, editor, and Rudolf Zeman, administrative officer of *Lidové Noviny* and for legal recognition of their newspaper. On October 27 1989, an appeal was sent to ARTICLE 19 members asking them to write to the government on behalf of Jirí Ruml and Rudolf Zeman. They were released on November 26 1989. (See text)

Denmark

The 1953 Danish Constitution states that "any person shall be entitled to publish their thoughts in printing, in writing, and in speech, provided that they may be held answerable in a court of justice. Censorship and other preventive measures shall never again be reintroduced" (Art.77). Traditionally, this provision has been seen as guaranteeing only freedom from prior restraint ("formal protection") and not freedom from subsequent civil or criminal sanctions ("substantive protection" of free speech). However, the Danish courts do in fact provide substantive protection in matters concerning the public interest.

	Data	Year
Population	5,129,778	1989
Life expectancy (M/F)	71.6/77.5	1985
GNP (US$ per capita)	18,470	1988
Main religion(s)	Christianity	
Official language(s)	Danish	
Illiteracy %	1	1985
Daily newspapers	47	1986
Non daily newspapers	11	1986
Periodicals	220	1986
Radio sets	4,500,000	1980
TV sets	1,900,000	1988
Press agencies:		
	Ritzaus Bureau	
ICCPR:	YES	1972

Recent Cases In 1989, the Supreme Court decided three cases concerning substantive protection of free speech. The first concerned two television journalists employed by Danmarks Radio who had broadcast an interview with a racist group called the Green Jackets. The Supreme Court held by a majority that the broadcast did not involve a matter of public interest which could outweigh the concern of protecting the rights and reputation of others and upheld the journalists' convictions for aiding and abetting racist speech.

In 1985, the tabloid newspaper *Ekstra Bladet* ran a series of articles on hospital conditions for psychiatric patients. One article carried a picture of a young female patient, who was named, tied to her bed at a psychiatric hospital in Copenhagen. The caption read: "They tie her up 23 hours a day". A later article had a picture which showed the journalist with another female patient who was tied to a chair. The local authority obtained a court injunction against the further use of the pictures and against using the name of the young patient on the ground of invasion of privacy. The newspaper claimed that it had obtained consent to take and use the pictures from one patient's mother and from the other patient herself. The Supreme Court held that the consent could not be considered valid. However, the injunction was lifted on the grounds that the articles and the pictures had been published in co-operation with the doctors at the hospital as part of a factual report on a subject which was in the interest of the public. Freedom of expression on this occasion was found to outweigh the protection of privacy.

In a case decided by the Supreme Court in November 1989, a particular form of investigative journalism was said not to justify breaking the law. Martin Breum, a journalist from the monthly magazine *Press*, was held to have violated the Penal Code by showing a false Iranian identity card to the police. The case arose from extensive public disquiet over the treatment of refugees and asylum seekers. Breum disguised himself as an Iranian asylum seeker at Copenhagen airport intending to write about how asylum seekers were treated by the Danish police on arrival. When asked to identify himself he presented a false Iranian identity card to the airport police. He was convicted of forgery. The Supreme Court ruled that while the issue of the authorities' treatment of asylum seekers was a matter of public interest, it could not excuse the use of a false document in breach of the Penal Code. In a subsequent article, Breum described his experiences of racism and negligence by the police at the airport reception point and, as a result, the chief of police wrote to the Retsudvalget (Parliamentary Committee for Legal Matters) stating that he had enjoined police officers to treat all asylum seekers properly.

Freedom of Information Legislation defining this right, "Offentlighedsloven" (Access to Information Act) and "Forvaltningsloven" (Public Administration Act), came into force in October 1987. The former Act confirms that everyone has the right of access to documents received or produced by an administrative authority; the latter governs professional secrecy of employees in the public sector.

Exceptions to the right of access to official information include: working documents for internal use; letters circulated within an agency; documents concerning affairs of state; correspondence between ministries concerning legislation; documents concerning proposed European Community (EC) legislation; and data for statistical use. Access to documents can also be limited to the extent necessary for the protection of the state, foreign policy, the investigation of crime, public order or the protection of private and public economic interests. The law is considered by journalists to be good in principle but most find that the exceptions are interpreted too widely by officials thus undermining the spirit of the Act. The exception for EC-related documents is to be amended to reduce secrecy following severe criticism in the Folketing (parliament).

In February 1990, the Ombudsman decided that the right of access extends to documents produced by *ad hoc* committees whose members are civil servants from different ministries. Such a committee, with two sub-committees, was established in 1987 to plan a follow-up to the recommendations of the so-called Brundtland report. A journalist was refused access to documents produced by the committees on the grounds that they were internal documents and exempt. The Ombudsman determined that documents which were not prepared specifically for ministerial meetings, but rather for the use of civil servants, should not be exempt from public access.

Publishing Leaks Article 152 of the Criminal Code makes it a crime to publish confidential material obtained from a civil servant who has disclosed it contrary to the obligation of professional secrecy. A defence exists when the disclosure concerns a matter of obvious public interest. Controversy over this offence arose following publication of a confidential document, containing an account of a cabinet meeting, in the newspaper *Berlingske Tidende* on July 20 1989. The meeting concerned the construction of a bridge over the Great Belt (a sea passage in Danish waters) which had led to legal procceedings against Denmark by the EC Commission. The document contained highly controversial remarks by the Foreign Minister. Subsequently, a civil servant was charged with disclosing confidential information and a journalist, Michael Ulveman, and the editor of *Berlingske Tidende*, Hans Dam, were charged with violating Article 152. The case led to an important amendment of the law following a report from the Commission on Media Responsibility. It is no longer an offence to publish confidential information once leaked except where the information concerns the defence of the realm or matters of state security. The charges against the journalists were expected to be dropped in late 1990.

Data Protection Computers have made it possible to gather large amounts of information in private or public databases, information that is often of a sensitive nature such as personal IQ ratings, personal solvency and political affiliation. The Act on Public and Private Registers has been passed to ensure protection for such data. A board supervises the management of the registers and ensures that information stored is not abused, for example, that it is not accessed for advertising purposes. However, the board has been criticized because it allows cross-referencing of personal information on individuals and the merging of registers.

The Media

Television and Radio The Law on Radio and TV allows Danmarks Radio and TV2 the right to broadcast. Danmarks Radio is an independent public institution, financed by licence; it is not allowed to obtain funding from advertisements. The board consists of 11 members, the chairman of which is appointed by the Minister for Communication; nine members are appointed by parliament and the other by employees of Danmarks Radio. In October 1988, the monopoly of Danmarks Radio on broadcasting national TV was broken by the establishment of the independent TV2, which is funded by licence and advertisements. Its five board members are appointed by the Minister for Communication. Approximately 30 local, privately-owned TV stations, funded by advertisements, operate in many parts of the country with permission from local authorities. There is free access to German and Swedish TV and satellite TV can be received.

Danmarks Radio operates the only national radio station. There are approximately 300 local radio stations licensed by local authorities which obtain funding through advertisements.

Newspapers In Denmark there is no censorship of the press, which is privately owned. Press freedom was first written into the law in 1849. There are no registration or licensing requirements. There are no restrictions of any kind on foreign journalists. Most major daily newspapers are published from Copenhagen with the exception of *Jyllands Posten*. The other main papers are the tabloids, *Ekstra Bladet* and *B.T.*, and the quality dailies, *Berlingske Tidende*, *Politiken* and *Information. Det Fri Aktuelt*, owned by the trade unions, has been seeking to attract a wider readership by following a more independent editorial line.

Protection of Sources Article 172 of the Administration of Justice Act ensures the right of editors and journalists of periodicals and newspapers to protect their sources. These rights can be overruled by a court if the case concerns an offence which can lead to a defendant's imprisonment, or if the case concerns leaks by civil servants who are obliged to maintain confidentiality. However, the enforced revealing of sources must also be considered absolutely necessary to the investigation by the court.

In 1986, the Supreme Court ruled that Article 172 does not protect journalists who work in radio or TV. Kurt Madsen of Radio Aarhus was taken to court following an interview broadcast in January 1985 in which an unnamed spokesman explained why a group had destroyed a McDonald's burger bar two days earlier. Madsen refused to comply with police requests to name the perpetrators. A ruling by the High Court, confirmed by the Supreme Court, held that Madsen must go to jail for a maximum period of six months unless he supplied the information. The law protecting journalists' sources was held not to extend to the electronic media. The Danish Journalists' Union, representing more than 5,000 active journalists, protested and stated that it was prepared to call for international support. On December 4 1986, the Chief Constable of Aarhus decided not to take Madsen into custody, apparently considering it futile to try to make him reveal his sources.

In September 1987, the Supreme Court ruled that the editor of *Information*, Peter Wivel, had to reveal information which could help identify the person responsible for writing an article (published May 20 1987) in which responsibility for a fire at a Shell petrol station was claimed on behalf of an anti-apartheid group. The court ruled that it was in the interest of justice to require Wivel to give information about the case in order to investigate the crime. In this case it was said that the reasons for granting the press a right to protect its sources could not outweigh the interest of justice.

Wivel refused to reveal the identity of the writer and was ordered to pay a daily fine of Dkr500 (US$60) as a means of compulsion until he did so. After a month, this was doubled by the court to Dkr1,000. This latter order was reversed in the Supreme Court in 1988: Wivel still had to pay Dkr500 a day. When the fines reached a total of Dkr60,000 (US$7,200), the court decided to suspend the daily fines, but it can reopen the case at any time. Wivel, who was unable to pay the fines at once, has reached an agreement to pay Dkr3,000 (US$360) a month.

In 1990, a new journalists' group, Forning for Undersoegende Journalistik, dedicated to investigative journalism, was established.

Media Ownership Most major newspapers are run as limited companies, owned by foundations established for this purpose. The boards of the foundations generally do not interfere with the editorial policy of the newspaper. One small business-orientated newspaper, *Borsen*, is owned by a foreign company, Bonniers. The legal structure of foundations makes it difficult for one person or company to take over the control of the major newspapers. None of the foundations control a majority of the printed press.

Local TV stations and radio channels are owned by private individuals or companies, but no one individual has control over a majority of the stations. Trade unions are involved in running 38 radio channels and seven TV stations.

Films Film and video distributors must submit films and videos that are to be viewed by children under 16 for approval by state advisors on film. Films of all kinds may not receive state distribution subsidies unless they are approved by the state advisors on films. This has been criticized as a form of government censorship through refusal to approve a film for subsidy.

Advertising

The Danish Consumer Ombudsman ensures that advertisements are in accordance with the Law on Marketing. The Ombudsman can prohibit the intended publication of "misleading" or "improper" advertisements. This form of prior restraint is assumed to be in accordance with Article 77 of the Constitution. There are also many examples where a publisher has been fined after an advertisement has been published.

The Radio and TV Advertisements Board is responsible for reviewing advertisements according to guidelines. It is prohibited to advertise for religious or political motives and advertisements by economic interest groups are also banned.

AIDS In February 1990, the Board rejected a TV advertisement on AIDS because it overstepped the limit of "prevailing morals" in society. The advertisement was aimed at male homosexuals and was produced by a group defending gay and lesbian rights, Landsforeningen for Bosser og Lesbiske, in co-operation with the Department of Health. It showed two men kissing and a packet of condoms in the back pocket of the trousers of one of them. The decision to reject the advertisement has been widely criticized and condemned by doctors.

Freedom of Opinion and Expression

Racism and Free Speech It is a criminal offence (Art.266(b) of the Penal Code) to make derogatory remarks directed at a person's racial or ethnic background. This offence implements Denmark's commitment to prohibit racist speech under the UN Convention on the Elimination of All Forms of Racial Discrimination.

In the summer of 1985, a racist youth group, Groenjakkerne, (Green Jackets) was shown on a news programme, *TV Avisen*, during which racially offensive remarks were made by members of the group. Several Green Jackets were later convicted under Article 266(b). Journalist Jens Olaf Jersild and the responsible editor, Lasse Jensen, from Danmarks Radio were convicted of aiding and abetting the spread of racist propaganda; the Supreme Court upheld the convictions. In 1985, the phenomenon of violent racism in Denmark was unknown to the general public and the journalists claimed that it was in the public interest to alert the public to the existence of the group. The programme revealed that the police had not taken effective measures to prevent attacks and harassment of immigrants. It was pointed out that the TV feature had followed a story in *Information*, which had directly quoted racial slurs made by the Green Jackets. The newspaper was not prosecuted. In October 1989, Jens Olaf Jersild filed an application with the European Commission of Human Rights, alleging a violation of his right to freedom of expression, as guaranteed by Article 10 of the European Convention on Human Rights.

France

In 1989, France celebrated the bi-centenary of its revolution and the adoption of the Declaration of the Rights of Man and the Citizen, one of the most important early texts guaranteeing human rights, particularly freedom of expression. The French Constitution of 1958, based in part on the text of this Declaration, proclaims: " ... the free communication of thoughts and opinions is one of the most precious rights of mankind. Each citizen may therefore speak, write and print in liberty, except in abusing this freedom in cases set forth by the law".

Despite this provision, freedom of information remained under constant threat. Until 1978, there was no legal instrument guaranteeing the right to information. The need for this right was further exacerbated by changes

	Data	Year
Population	55,874,000	1988
Life expectancy (M/F)	71.0/75.0	1985
GNP (US$ per capita)	16,080	1988
Main religion(s)	Christianity	
Official language(s)	French	
Illiteracy %	1	1985
Daily newspapers	92	1986
Non daily newspapers	526	1982
Periodicals	22,443	1982
Radio sets	49,500,000	1987
TV sets	22,000,000	1986
Press agencies:		
Agence France-Presse,		
Agence Parisienne de Presse,		
Agence Republicaine		
d'Information Presse Services,		
Science Service-Agence Barnier		
ICCPR:	YES	1980

such as the technological revolution and its effect on the media, the increasing development of broadcasting since the privatization of television in 1986, and the increasing control of the flow of information by a few multi-media groups. France also confronts an upsurge in racist and anti-semitic speech which in 1990 provoked the French legislature to introduce a law prohibiting the expression of ideas prejudicial to members of racial, religious or national groups, or which deny the existence of crimes against humanity during World War II.

The Media

The Print Media The 1881 Press Law guarantees the right to publish newspapers without any prior authorization and also ended the *délit d'opinion* (crime of opinion). The law, however, prohibits other offences, such as incitement to crime, publication of false information that disturbs the peace, defamation, publication of material offensive to the President and disclosure of official secrets.

Newspapers In 1988, there were 11 daily newspapers published in Paris with a national circulation of three million and 65 regional dailies with a circulation of seven million. Circulation has declined since 1946, when 28 Parisian dailies had a circulation of six million and 175 regional dailies totalled nine million.

Television and Radio There are six national TV channels: Antenne 2 and FR3 are state-owned, and TF1, Canal Plus, La Cinq and M6 are privately-owned. RFO is a public channel which broadcasts to the Overseas Territories and Departments (DOM-TOM). Antenne Réunion is the only private overseas TV. Tele-Toulouse, 8 Mont-Blanc and Tele-Lyon Metropole are private local channels created in 1988 and 1989. TF1, which was privatized in 1986, is the most popular, claiming 42 per cent of the viewers and receiving 50 per cent of all French TV advertising revenue.

French radio networks include five national radio stations, one station in Paris and 47 local FM stations, all state-owned. The private network includes four national radio stations and 1,800 local stations, of which 300 are non-commercial, community stations subsidized by the government.

Broadcasting Control and Regulation On January 30 1989, the Conseil Supérieur de l'Audiovisuel (CSA) replaced the Commission National de la Communication et des Libertés (CNCL). The latter, established by the Chirac government, had been discredited by fraud scandals and accusations that its members were politically associated with the previous government.

The CSA authorizes radio and TV stations, including cable TV; regulates children's and youth TV programmes; controls advertising; and appoints the heads of state TV and radio stations. The CSA also ensures that political parties and trade unions have access to TV and radio, particularly during election campaigns. It also ensures that the government, the majority and the opposition in the National Assembly have equal allocation of broadcasting time. This system, known as the *Régle des Trois*, excludes political parties which have no representation in either of the two chambers of the National Assembly, such as the Green Party. The CSA recognizes the discriminatory nature of this rule and is working for its reform.

Media Ownership and Concentration Hachette, Havas, Hersant, Groupe de la Cité and Filipacchi are among the major media groups. In the 1970s, individual owners sought dominance in particular sectors: Hersant in the press, Havas in advertising and Hachette in publishing. But by the 1980s, multi-media corporations were established combining press, radio, TV, records, cinema, printing, telecommunications, publishing and advertising. The Hersant group, for example, in addition to its press holdings of 28 dailies, 13 periodicals and seven monthlies, owns 87 private radio stations and a 25 per cent share in La Cinq TV. In 1988, Hachette controlled six regional dailies, nine weeklies, 16 national monthlies and 11 international monthlies, seven of which are in the USA. In May 1990, Hachette increased its shareholding in La Cinq to 22 per cent.

Since 1988, European groups have also entered the French media and communications market. The German Bertelsmann group owns shares in the monthly magazine *France-Loisirs* and launched a new consumer magazine *Prima*. It has also purchased shares in the publisher and distributor, la Société Générale d'Edition and Diffusion. The Italian Berlusconi group has acquired 25 per cent interest in la Cinq TV and 3.9 per cent in TF1. The British Maxwell Corporation owns 10 per cent of TF1 and 67 per cent of François Imprimerie which prints the magazine *Paris Match*. News International, owned by Rupert Murdoch, has acquired shares in the financial newspaper *Les Echos*.

Ownership Laws On October 23 1984, the socialist government adopted a law to prevent the concentration of newspaper and magazine ownership in the hands of a small number of press conglomerates. The law established the National Commission for Transparency and Pluralism in the Press and provided that a press group could own only 15 per cent of national dailies, 15 per cent of regional dailies, or 10 per cent of the combined circulation of national and regional dailies. The law made it compulsory for newspapers to publish the names of their shareholders and their annual accounts. This law was abrogated in June 1986 by the new government of Jacques Chirac and replaced on August 1 1986 by the Act on Reforming the Legal System Governing the Press. The Act introduced a new system of regulation and control which takes into consideration the combined ownership in all media, and limits newspaper ownership to 30 per cent of the total circulation of national dailies or 10 per cent if the owner controls a 25 per cent share in other media. The Act does not take non-dailies and periodicals into consideration.

In its 1989 report, the CSA recognized that the mechanism provided by the Act to prevent excessive concentration was inadequate because of difficulties in interpretation and the lack of a statistical apparatus capable of collecting and evaluating the necessary data.

Protection of Sources A number of legal provisions oblige journalists to reveal sources. In order to avoid a libel conviction, a journalist must prove that the statements were either true or in good faith. This almost always requires that the source be revealed and a refusal automatically leads to conviction. In July 1989, Isabelle Horlans, a journalist with *Union de Reims* was arrested by the police and required to name her informant in the context of the Affaire Boutboul-Dassac. She refused and was detained for 24 hours while her home was searched and her note-book was confiscated.

Restrictions on Journalists On January 20 1988, Robert Edmé, a French photographer with *Egin*, the Spanish Basque Independent Movement newspaper, was arrested on suspicion of being a "letter box" for the separatist organization ETA. On March 9, an *Egin* correspondent in Saint Jean de Luz was arrested for the same reason. Both were released without charge. In June, the director of the Basque magazine *Abil* received a 20-month suspended prison term and a fine of FF30,000 (US$4,700) for incitement to violence. He had published a press communiqué from the Basque organization Ipparetarrak, which accused the police of responsibility for the killing of some of its militants.

In Corsica, some journalists working for the regional TV station FR3 have been subjected to harassment and arrest or have been dismissed due to perceived sympathy with separatist organizations. Editor-in- Chief Sampiero Sanguinetti was dismissed by FR3's authorities. Others have had their films confiscated. On August 10 1988, commandos of the former Front de Liberation Nationale de la Corse (FLNC) raided the studios of Radio Corse Internationale (RCI) and forced staff to broadcast a message.

Since its launch in 1987, *Globe*, which has published several investigative reports about the activities of extreme right-wing groups in France, has received regular threats. On July 30 1988, its offices were destroyed by a bomb. In January 1990, the police arrested four police officers suspected of involvement in the attack.

Foreign Publications The 1939 law on foreign publications authorizes the Interior Minister to ban the circulation, distribution or sale of any foreign publication or any publication written in a foreign language which may harm public order or national interests. On April 23 1988, the Interior Minister Charles Pasqua, invoking the 1939 law, banned the publication and distribution in France of the Algerian opposition monthly magazine *al-Miqlaa*, as "harmful to French diplomatic interests". The socialist government of François Mitterand also banned the magazine when it reappeared under the title *al-Badil Démocratique*. The book *Euskuda Gaduan*, about the history of the Basque struggle for independence, published in the Basque region in Spain, is also banned on the grounds that the book threatens public order.

Information in the French Overseas Territories In New Caledonia, in accordance with a 1922 decree, publications in local or foreign languages require prior authorization. If no authorization is requested or obtained, the publication may be seized by the administrative authorities (without recourse to the courts) and the authors and printers can be sentenced to heavy prison sentences. This legal exception has no parallel in metropolitan France, where it is possible to publish in any language.

Robert Hersant owns the newspapers *France-Antilles Martinique*, *France-Antilles Guadeloup*, *Les Nouvelles Caledoniennes*, *La Dépëche de Tahiti*, and also has interests in the *Journal de l'Ile de Réunion*. The news pages of these papers are facsimile copies of articles from the Hersant press in France.

In French Guiana, the only daily paper is owned, edited and printed by the local authority, which severely limits criticism of official policies.

Protection and Access to Information

The slow development of French law relating to the right of access to information reflects the context of secrecy within which governments have traditionally functioned. Between 1978 and 1979 a series of laws were promulgated with the aim of establishing the individual's right to seek and receive information from the government. They include the January 1978 law on Informatics and Liberty, dealing principally with the individual's access to manual and computerized data; the law of July 1978 concerning Access to Administrative Documents; the law of January 1979 ensuring the right of access to public archives, and the law of July 1979 requiring the administration to justify decisions refusing access to information.

Data Protection In 1974, French public opinion was alerted when the press reported that a government project named SAFARI planned to use the social security number of each citizen for all other individual files held by the government. Following public protests, the government designated a commission to draft proposals for the protection of personal data. As a result, a law on data protection and liberties was passed in January 1978.

This law provided for the establishment of a National Commission on Informatics and Liberties (CNIL), mandated to promote Article 1 of the law which declares that: "computer science has to be at the service of each citizen; its development has to operate within the framework of international co-operation; it should not damage the human identity, nor human rights, private life or individual and public liberties".

The CNIL supervises the creation of public or private data banks and ensures the individual's right of access to his or her files. The law stipulates that recorded personal information must be pertinent, exact, and should not contain unwarranted information such as political opinions or religious beliefs. Names and addresses should not be sold to companies for marketing purposes. It also ensures that individuals are informed if they are registered on computerized index cards and that they are allowed the right to add to or correct false information. Prior authorization by the CNIL is a prerequisite for the creation of data banks. In 1989, the CNIL received 29,875 declarations or requests for advice on setting up data banks and 522 requests for the removal of personal information held by companies specializing in direct mail. In 1989, the CNIL filed an action against the Front National (FN) and the National Committee of French Jewry because both organizations had sent propaganda leaflets to French Jews during the 1988 legislative and presidential elections. The CNIL demanded to know where the organizations had obtained their mailing lists but, as at August 1990, they have refused to reveal their sources. The CNIL has also warned the local council of Ajaccio City that the establishment of an index file of people in Ajaccio who abstain from voting in elections is in violation of the ban on recording and storing individuals' political opinions.

French human rights groups have expressed criticism of the 1978 law concerning the provision justifying non-communication of information on the grounds of national defence or state security. The law, however, provides that any person whose name is likely to be on the Ministry of Interior or Ministry of Defence files can have only indirect access through a legal officer appointed by the CNIL. There were 65 requests for indirect access in 1989, which required 206 interventions by the CNIL, of which 182 concerned the Ministry of the Interior and 24 concerned the Ministry of Defence. The majority of the cases concerned individuals who had been refused jobs or who had been rehabilitated after criminal convictions.

Access to Administrative Documents The law of July 7 1978 on Access to Administrative Documents provides for the publication of non-personal documents such as government circulars, directives, reports and statistics. On July 11 1979, the law was extended to personal documents, restricting access to the person concerned. In 1978, the Commission of Access to Administrative Documents (CADA) was established to arbitrate between the public and the administration.

Article 6 limits access to information to protect both industrial and commercial secrets and this has created a conflict of interest between consumer and environmental groups. Thus, information on the toxicity of a product or the effects of various pollutants has been withheld. Other restrictions on freedom of information concern national security, public order, judicial proceedings and international relations.

Two major limitations give the administration the power to withhold information, the excessive delay in proceedings (which can take a minimum of five months) and the fact that CADA has no legal power to oblige the administration to furnish an individual with the required documents. In its 1989 report, CADA stated that it had received 2,018 demands for access to information. The government administration responded to 43 per cent of the demands but refused to communicate information in 8.5 per cent of those cases. The other applications were rejected.

Freedom of Opinion and Expression

Racist Speech Racist and anti-semitic speech has recently become a major issue in French political debate. The rise of Jean-Marie Le Pen's FN party and its impact on French politics is believed to have been a contributing factor. There has been an alarming increase in physical attacks on Arab and African communities living in France and, recently, in the desecration of Jewish graves.

Muslim protests against the publication of the French translation of *The Satanic Verses* by Salman Rushdie, and issues such as the wearing of head scarfs by Muslims in schools, have polarized French politics on the immigration issue. In 1989 in Creil, three Muslim school girls from North African families were denied access to classes unless they removed their scarves. According to the headmaster, the scarf is a religious symbol which contradicts the spirit of secular public education. It is believed that this case helped the extreme right-wing FN to win its only seat in the National Assembly following a by-election in the town of Dreux in December 1989.

The rise in anti-semitism is of equal concern to public authorities and human rights activists. The attack on the Jewish cemetry in Carpentaras in May 1990 is one of many incidents which have occurred in the last two years.

Despite a 1972 law proscribing the publication or utterance of words liable to incite racial hatred, the practice has continued. Some newspapers such as the weekly *National Hebdo* and the monthly magazine *Révision* have close connections with the FN. On May 14 1990, Alain Guionnet director of *Révision* was sentenced to three months' imprisonment and a fine of FF75,000 (US$11,800) for writing and distributing three successive issues containing "delirious and obsessional" anti-semitic statements.

On February 28 1990, the Law Faculty Council in the Jean-Moulin University (Lyon III) suspended Bernard Notin's seminars following an article in the *Revue Economies et Sociétés* in which he denied the existence of the gas chambers during World War II. The article was described as "scandalously anti-semitic". On July 18 1990, he was suspended from his teaching post at the Institut d'Administration des Entreprises for one year by the University Council.

On December 14 1989, a court in Strasbourg ordered the FN and Robert Spieler, one of its officers, to pay the French Human Rights League a FF3,000 (US$470) fine for an election poster, used by the FN during the 1986 local and national elections, which depicted one or more French women wearing a Muslim veil. The court stated that the "mixture of symbols" in this poster "inevitably created a feeling of repulsion *vis à vis* foreigners and especially North Africans".

A French government survey in March 1990 revealed that half the population endorsed the view that campaigning politicians should be allowed to claim that "blacks and North African Arabs are racially inferior to Europeans". In June 1990, the National Assembly adopted, by 308 to 265 votes, a new law allowing judges to punish any racist, anti-semitic or xenophobic speech. The text provides that any public official found guilty of incitement to racial hatred be deprived of civic rights for up to five years. The law also established a new offence of public denial of the existence of the crimes against humanity as defined by the International Court of Nuremberg which is punishable by up to two years' imprisonment and a heavy fine. The French section of Reporters Sans Frontières described the law as circumstantial and opportunistic, and directed against Le Pen and the FN Party.

Actions

In its 1988 Commentary to the Human Rights Committee ARTICLE 19 drew attention to issues affecting freedom of expression, particularly: the extensive interpretation of an act to control literature to protect young people; government powers to control and ban foreign publications; and questions the independence of La Commission Nationale de la Communication et des Libertés.

On March 20 1989 ARTICLE 19 wrote to the government protesting the banning of a demonstration in Lyon by five Muslim associations against *The Satanic Verses*, on the grounds that it might disturb public order.

Germany

The accession of the German Democratic Republic to the Federal Republic of Germany required the former East German state and its newly-created five Länd (regional states) to accept the West German Constitution (the Basic Law) in its entirety. Freedom of the press and freedom of opinion as guaranteed in the Basic Law have thus become fundamental human rights for the 16 million former GDR citizens.

There is, however, no general federal press law and press legislation is a matter for the Länd which are, therefore, expected to introduce press laws compatible with the Constitution for their respective regions.

	Data	Year
Population	61,077,042	1987
Life expectancy (M/F)	71.1/78.0	1985
GNP (US$ per capita)	18,530	1988
Main religion(s)	Christianity	
Official language(s)	German	
Illiteracy %	1	1985
Daily newspapers	358	1989
Non daily newspapers	38	1986
Periodicals	6,908	1986
Radio sets	58,000,000	1987
TV sets	23,378,000	1987
Press agencies:		
Deutsche Presse Agentur, VWD		
ICCPR:	YES	1973

The Constitution

Under the Constitution, the press is free and all forms of censorship, whether pre or post-publication, are forbidden: "Everyone has the right to freely express and disseminate his opinion in words, writings and images and to inform himself unhampered by means of generally accessible sources. Freedom of the press and freedom of reporting by broadcasting and film are guaranteed. Censorship shall not take place." (Art.5)

The Federal Constitutional Court (FCC) has ruled that freedom of the press is a sub-division of freedom of opinion and is, therefore, a basic individual right. However, "these rights are only limited by the regulations of general law, legal regulations on the protection of juveniles and by the right of inviolability of personal honour" (Art.5(2)). Article 5 can also be restricted by other basic rights, but any decision to limit that freedom can be challenged by any citizen in the courts.

The press and the general public are equally bound by these limitations, but the FCC has ruled that in the event of conflict, freedom of the press is paramount except in cases in which general laws, of higher priority than that freedom, must be safeguarded.

Under the West German Länd press laws, journalists have to work within the general framework of the law, but they enjoy special protection such as the right to protect sources and to refuse to give evidence. Similarly, there is a ban on confiscation of material or search of press premises if such action could lead to the identification of a source or the discovery of facts which were withheld because of the right to withhold evidence.

Defamation Freedom of the press and freedom of expression are restricted by the basic right to personal honour. Defamation of character is a serious constitutional offence. A false statement discovered prior to publication can be stopped by applying for a temporary court injuction. However, the newspaper or magazine has the opportunity to provide the necessary evidence to have the injunction revoked. In most cases of libel or defamation of character, the aggrieved party will use the right to reply guaranteed under the press laws of the respective Länd, as happened repeatedly when the late Bavarian politician Franz Joseph Strauss was in continuous conflict with the Hamburg news magazine *Der Spiegel*. The courts can be asked to rule that an article is libellous and the aggrieved party can apply for compensation, although damages are minimal. It is considered more important to restore honour than to award a person compensation for the assumed loss of reputation.

It is a criminal offence to slander the Federal President. However, the public prosecutor can only initiate proceedings if he is authorized to do so by the President and, thus far, no President has considered it necessary to "defend his honour and integrity in a court of law". Similarly, it is against the law to slander "foreign signs of sovereignty"; a German flag can be legally burnt but not those of the United States or United Kingdom. During the Viet Nam war, however, many US flags were burnt but there were no prosecutions.

Protection of Youth Pornographic material as well as literature inciting crime, violence, racial hatred or which glorifies war must not be made available to persons under the age of 18 years. However, such publications are widely available. Retailers are usually only required to keep them under the counter for sale to adult readers. The interpretation of the law differs from one Länd to the other and also within the same Länd. The decision as to whether a publication contravenes the law for the protection of juveniles or the law of public decency (which covers everyone regardless of age) rests with the public prosecutor, who can ban certain printed material and can also confiscate offending publications. However, the Prosecutor's ruling is limited to a specific local area. As a result, what is permitted in one area may be prohibited in another. Contrary to widespread belief, there is no federal index of prohibited publications.

Subversion There are other controversial laws limiting freedom of the press. The so-called political criminal law, enshrined in the Criminal Code, protects government and state from subversion and treason. Any publication furthering the activities of persons or groups aiming to abolish the democratic order, as laid down in the Basic Law, can be declared illegal and local public prosecutors are empowered to confiscate relevant publications.

Minorities Paragraph 131 of the Criminal Code outlaws anti-semitism and any other forms of racism and provides that: "anyone who disseminates literature which recounts violence against persons in a lurid or other inhuman manner, thus expressing glorification or minimization of such acts of violence or incites racial hatred" is liable to prosecution. However, the law is rarely used and anti-semitic papers and magazines have been freely published by extreme groups for many years. Furthermore, it is not uncommon for bars or restaurants to display signs barring "Gypsies and Turks".

Terrorism Anti-terrorist laws introduced in the 1970s, in response to terrorist groups such as the Red Army Faction, impinged on freedom of the press. Such groups published their manifestos and declarations underground, but the press (which wanted to inform readers about the activities of terrorists without condoning their acts) found themselves in a grey area and were repeatedly threatened with prosecution under the anti-terrorism laws. Most editors chose to avoid confrontation with the authorities and relinquished their rights to publish without waiting for a court order. Press freedom was seriously infringed for a period and the law still applies, in principle, today.

Blasphemy Blasphemy as a criminal offence has been abolished, but disturbing a religious service is still punishable by law. Books such as Salman Rushdie's *The Satanic Verses* can, therefore, freely be published. In order to pre-empt any threats of violence to the publishers of *The Satanic Verses*, a consortium of publishers established a new publishing house, Artikel 19, which, in October 1989, published the novel in association with a number of leading German authors.

Freedom of Information There is no freedom of information act, but the FCC has ruled that the press can invoke a right of access to information under the press laws of the Länd. Public authorities are obliged to provide journalists with any kind of information they may possess, and such information can only be refused if it is classified as secret or if an overriding public or private interest would be infringed. The press can apply to the courts for a ruling in the event of a refusal.

Data Protection Act On January 1 1988, the Data Protection Act came into force. Data collection on individuals remains legal as long as the individual rights of the person are not infringed. Every German can demand to see any data about him or her which is stored by any private organization or state authority but, in the case of state authorities, the right to demand correction or the erasure of data is strictly limited. Furthermore, state bodies can refuse access to such data on the grounds of national security, the overriding public interest or in the interest of law and order. However, the aggrieved person can appeal to an independent commissioner for data protection who can order a state authority to make the data available or carry out necessary corrections.

Freedom of Expression

Political Restrictions Political parties must comply with the democratic order as laid down in the Basic Law. The National Socialist Party (Nazi party) is a proscribed organization under the Constitution and cannot be resurrected. Similarly, any political party aimed at overthrowing the democratic order can be proscribed under Article 21 of the Basic Law. In 1952, the Socialist Reichs Party was banned as a neo-Nazi party and, in 1956, the Communist Party of Germany was declared unconstitutional on the grounds that its programme called for the introduction of the dictatorship of the proletariat. In practice, the proscription of political parties is no longer invoked. Until reunification, West Germany had nine neo-Nazi parties and four communist parties, all of which were, strictly speaking, unconstitutional but allowed to operate legally. Political parties operating against the Constitution can only be banned if the government or parliament apply to the FCC to rule on their constitutionality.

Radicals' Decree There are regulations which limit the freedom of expression of individuals who belong to a political party which has not been declared unconstitutional but which is nevertheless regarded by the authorities as an anti-democratic organization. The so-called "Radicals' Decree" directs that members of supposedly anti-democratic parties of the extreme left and right may not be employed as civil servants. Civil servants include post office workers, railway workers and teachers, all of whom are covered by the ban. The Federal and all the Länd governments argued that since civil servants enjoyed special rights, such as tenure for life and a higher than average pension, they have a special duty towards the state as employer. The "Radicals' Decree" is officially still in force but it is no longer applied at the federal level. No post office worker or train driver is prevented from carrying out his job if he belongs to the Communist Party or to one of the neo-Nazi parties. However, the decree is still used at regional level; for instance, in the conservative-run state of Bavaria, both communists and left-wing Social Democrats are precluded from public office. It remains to be seen what happens to the "Radicals' Decree" during the months following German reunification. If applied to the former GDR, there would hardly be anyone eligible for public sector employment.

The Media

Newspapers The media landscape has changed considerably since the post-war ruling by the allied forces that all newspapers had to be licensed by the government. Since licences were granted on a strictly regional or local basis it was difficult to expand existing newspapers or establish new ones to achieve a national circulation.

Gradually, small independent newspapers were taken over by larger ones and the popular press entered the market, with the *Bild Zeitung* becoming Europe's biggest-selling daily.

Today, there are four daily quality newspapers which claim a national circulation: *Die Welt, Frankfurter Allgemeine Zeitung, Sueddeutsche Zeitung*, and *Frankfurter Rundschau*.

Media Concentration In spite of the fact that there are about 300 newspaper publishing companies today, the question of press concentration was a major issue in the 1960s and 1970s. The Axel Springer publishing company became the target of sometimes violent student demonstrations as it took control of the newspaper market in major cities such as Berlin and Hamburg. The editorial policy of its late owner, Axel Springer, demanded a strong conservative line, extremely critical of East Germany and also the Social Democrat-led governments of Willy Brandt and Helmut Schmidt.

Today, Germany has five important newspaper magnates: Bertelsmann, Holtzbrink, Springer, Bauer and Burda. Complaints about press concentration have been disregarded by successive governments, with the argument that every German still has the opportunity to choose between the four nationals and many regional papers. Since there is no specific law in Germany restricting press concentration, journalists have taken the initiative. Editorial statutes were negotiated which gave them the right not only to determine editorial policy independently from the owner but also to have a voice in the appointment of the chief editor. This system has been adopted by a few "liberal" newspapers, but not by the major newspaper owners.

The influence of the popular press on opinion forming is thought to be over-estimated; research has shown that readers of the politically conservative mass circulation *Bild Zeitung* vote Social Democrat rather than for the conservative Christian Democrats.

Broadcasting For many years broadcasting was restricted to nine public broadcast-ing companies run by the regional states. They had sole responsibility for radio pro-grammes, but their television stations were incorporated into a national network (First Programme) with each regional station contributing to the national output. Broadcasting law stipulates that programmes have to be unbiased, that the output should reflect all strands of opinion, and that supervisory boards or broadcasting councils have to be created to guarantee the independence of the stations from any party-political or government influence.

Broadcasting Councils As the right to reply applies only to press and not to the electronic media, Broadcasting Councils are asked to defend the rights of the in-dividual as well as the interests of the public. They are either elected by the regional parliaments or appointed by political parties, churches, trade unions, employers' federations and other relevant groups. The Broadcasting Council elects the Adminis-trative Council which authorizes budget proposals, supervises management, ensures that broadcasting guidelines on impartiality are observed, and also elects the presi-dent of the station who must be confirmed by the Broadcasting Council. However, regional governments frequently pack the Broadcasting Councils with persons of their own political persuasion and stations are strongly politically biased towards the party in government. Bavarian TV, which is part of the First Programme network, repeatedly cut off Bavarian viewers from the national output, substituting allegedly left-wing programmes with local Bavarian entertainment programmes.

Zweites Deutsches Fernsehen Attempts by the former Federal Chancellor Konrad Adenauer to create a second TV channel under federal control were thwarted when, on February 28 1961, the FCC banned government-owned TV broadcasting as un-constitutional. The gap was filled by an inter-state agreement to establish Zweites Deutsches Fernsehen (ZDF) which is a centrally-operated corporation under public law. The major difference from the first channel can be seen in the composition of its Television Council. In addition to major public organizations, seats are held by representatives of the Länder, political parties at federal level and, importantly, rep-resentatives of the federal government. As with the national radio stations, Deutschlandfunk and Deutsche Welle, whose broadcasting councils also include representatives of the federal government, central government exercises a much stronger influence on these stations than on the regional broadcasting stations.

In 1966, after many years of political and legal controversy, the FCC gave the go-ahead for a regulated co-existence of public and private broadcasting stations which cleared the way for an inter-state broadcasting agreement on a dual broadcast-ing system. There are four private TV channels in Germany (Sat 1, RTL-Plus, Tele 5, Pro 7) as well as numerous private radio stations. Licensing and supervision of private broadcasting are controlled by nine regional authorities. Private stations are required to observe the relevant broadcasting laws but, in contrast to the public cor-porations, their programme content does not have to be balanced and, under the present regulations, it is possible for a political party to take a share in a private broadcasting company. There have been few complaints regarding political bias or of attempts of government interference, but there are growing fears that the quality of public broadcasting will suffer as a result of private competition.

East Germany

Following the abolition of all travel restrictions and the opening of the Berlin Wall on November 9 1989, relations between the two German states became appreciably closer. On March 18 1990, East Germans voted overwhelmingly for the Christian Democrats in the Volkskammer elections and for accession to the Federal Republic. In July, the constitution was suspended and on August 31 a German unification treaty was signed in Berlin. East Germany availed itself of Article 23 of the West German Constitution to join West Germany on October 3 when West Germany's Constitution took effect on the whole of Germany.

	Data	Year
Population	16,666,340	1988
Life expectancy (M/F)	69.5/75.4	1985
GNP (US$ per capita)	7,180	1988
Main religion(s)	Christianity	
Official language(s)	German	
Illiteracy %	1	1985
Daily newspapers	39	1986
Non daily newspapers	30	1986
Periodicals	1,203	1986
Radio sets	11,000,000	1987
TV sets	12,500,000	1987
Press agencies:		
Allgemeiner Deutscher Nachrichtendienst		
ICCPR:	YES	1973

The former German Democratic Republic (GDR) under Walter Ulbricht (1949-1971) and Erich Honecker (1971-1989) was regarded as one of the most conservative Eastern European countries. One major factor was that East Germans could receive external radio and television programmes including West German and West Berlin stations, the BBC World Service and the Voice of America. Access to Western electronic media, however, strengthened the resolve of the Communist Party (SED or Socialist Unity Party) to maintain strict control over the media and the arts.

The Censorship System In the GDR's 1968 Constitution "freedom of the press, radio and television is guaranteed" (Art.27). According to the official commentary on the Constitution, guaranteeing this freedom meant, foremost, to ensure that the media promoted Marxist-Leninist ideology, and that it was not abused for the purpose of spreading bourgeois ideologies.

Although there were no formal censorship laws, the system ensured a great deal of restrictions on freedom in the media. The press was licensed and printing and distribution of papers were state monopolies. The importation of printed or written material was strictly censored. The mass media were controlled centrally by the Politbureau. The responsible Central Committee Secretary during the last years of the GDR's existence was Joachim Herrmann (1978-1989), a former editor of the party's daily *Neues Deutschland*. Directives on a weekly or sometimes daily basis came via the press and radio/TV offices within the Central Committee Department for Agitation and Propaganda. Every Thursday, the chief editors of newspapers and magazines went to the government press office (*Presseamt*) to be told what was new. Radio and TV editors were subordinate to a state committee. The state news and photography agency, Allgemeiner Deutscher Nachrichtendienst, was run directly by the head of government. At the district level, the *Bezirksleitungen* (district governments) and parties were responsible for passing on instructions.

Church papers were the only media not directly controlled. However, before printing anything in the GDR, permission had to be obtained: printers had to show the authorities copies of all newspapers before distribution. In 1988, a large number of newspapers could not be published because the authorities refused to allow distribution. This had not happened since the 1950s. Some newspapers left blank spaces where articles deemed unsuitable by the authorities should have been; others did not appear.

The Cultural Ministry's Department of Literature and Publishing Affairs was in control of all books published. Similar departments existed for film, theatre and the fine arts. A publishing house had to send an annual list of books intended for publication and this was then "refined"; each book had to be individually assessed.

Despite the lack of formal censorship, the party made sure that the right people were put into the right positions (*Kaderpolitik*). In addition, self-censorship by authors, editors and publishers ensured that the whole system worked smoothly.

The Honecker Era

When Erich Honecker became party leader in 1971 he proclaimed that there were no taboos in the arts and literature as long as the common basis was socialism. This led to a "blossoming of a thousand flowers". Books relating to sensitive issues were published, critical plays were staged and films previously censored were shown. There was even the suggestion that the party could come to terms with dissidents like Wolf Biermann and Robert Havemann. This was a short-lived affair; after censorship was strictly tightened during 1974-1975, Wolf Biermann was expelled from the GDR in 1976.

During Erich Honecker's leadership, artists and intellectuals began to resist the party's monopoly on publishing. Open letters of dissent (in 1976 in protest against the Biermann expulsion and in 1979 against the disciplinary action taken against critical writers) were published in the Western media. One-sided campaigns by the party in the GDR's media followed. The stage was set for a continuous battle between dissident forces and the authorities via the media in both Germanies.

The Churches On March 6 1978, relations between the party and the Protestant Churches became more liberal. Erich Honecker, in a meeting with Bishop Albrecht Schonherr, conceded that the Churches could act as autonomous institutions with their own views and publish their opinions, provided that they acted within the framework of the Constitution. This was an historic step, allowing a broader view of religious freedom than in most other Eastern Bloc countries. The Churches strove to end discrimination against Christians by the party and this led to them providing a rallying point for the opposition. Klaus Gysi, State Secretary for Church Affairs, was responsible for regulating these developments. He took as liberal a view as possible.

Environmental and Human Rights Groups In the mid-1980s, environmental and human rights groups became the centre of dissident activities. The Initiative for Peace and Human Rights group in East Berlin was the first which tried to loosen connections with the Churches. There was growing awareness that the Churches could be of only limited use for promoting political goals. Using church facilities, these groups began publishing magazines and news sheets. Leading members were imprisoned or forced to leave the country. The Luxemburg-Liebknecht demonstration of January 17 1988 was a crucial event in this process. A number of dissidents (more than 60 from East Berlin) were imprisoned and six were sent abroad for between six months and two years. However, the party could not sustain its attacks on these groups and concessions were made; most of those temporarily expelled were allowed back.

Increasing friction between the SED and the Soviet leadership over ideological questions and growing internal opposition then led to open challenges to the Party. Parties and national organizations were established which, generally, were founded by members of the Initiative for Peace and Human Rights or sympathizers.

Democratic Changes

The Exodus On November 9 1989, the GDR lifted travel restrictions in a desperate attempt to halt the exodus of East Germans which began on September 11 when Hungary opened its border to Austria. Thousands of East Germans had crossed the border and besieged the West German embassies in Prague and Warsaw. Their departure represented a grave loss for the East German economy; the present and the next generation of skilled workers.

The mass exodus was particularly embarrassing because it started as the GDR was preparing for its 40th anniversary. The exodus sparked off protests in most major towns and cities, such as in Leipzig, where tens of thousands demanded greater democracy. On October 18, Erich Honecker and several other Politbureau members were ousted. His successor, Egon Krenz, initiated a rapid transition to a more democratic society but refused to legalize the opposition group New Forum; the exodus and mass demonstrations continued. (By January 1990, the number of refugees had reached 400,000 since September.)

Role of West German Journalists The changes brought about in East Germany since October 1989 encouraged a freer press which was aided by West German journalists working in the GDR who risked expulsion by reporting on the opposition activities. This was a crucial factor in breaking down the tight media controls of the party. East Germans could receive Western radio and television but, without precise information on the situation in the GDR, Western media reports would not have been so interesting. The opposition urged better reporting on its own activities and, by the end of 1989, critical reports of the party and government were to be found in most media.

Temporary Media Law In February 1990, the GDR adopted a transitional law on press and audiovisual communications. The law guaranteeing "freedom of opinion, information and of the media" breaks with the Marxist-Leninist principles as stated in the Constitution (total submission to the leading role of the SED and democratic centralism). This law abolished all forms of censorship (Art.5), the licence system which controlled the press (Art.9) and the monopoly of distribution of newspapers (Art.10). Radio and TV were declared to be public property (Art.11).

Media Control Council On February 13, the *Medienkontrollrat* (Media Control Council) (MCC) was formed, composed of representatives of the People's Chamber and the Runder Tisch (Round Table of Opposition Movements). It will continue until a new press law is adopted. Its principal roles are to guarantee freedom of opinion and information and the independence of the media.

Media Competition The encouragement of new enterprise and the increasingly free influx of Western papers has meant that the media face stern competition. Since April 1990, state subsidies to the press have stopped, resulting in price increases and a drastic drop in circulation. The exceptions to this rule were the district papers which fall neatly into the category of traditional papers, a market gap which they were quick to exploit. New papers were established, most of which have since folded.

Most East German publishers (whether in the media sector or in literature) have found a Western partner. Some of the most notable exceptions are the enterprises belonging to the Party of Democratic Socialism (PDS), which changed its name from the SED in early 1990. Their flagship *Neues Deutschland* and also some of the other papers like *Junge Weit* (the youth daily) still hold rather rigid views. While it quickly became fashionable even for these papers (and radio and TV) to be very critical of the old leadership, they maintain their strong anti-Western attitude.

West German media companies have moved in quickly; Springer, Gruner & Jahr, Burda, Bertelsmann and also Frankfurter Allgemeine Zeitung have a stake in one of the big East German publishing houses. Robert Maxwell, the UK publisher, has bought a share in an East Berlin daily paper and a weekly magazine. On the question of foreign investment in the media, the MCC has recommended a foreign capital share of less than 50 per cent and also demanded that the relevant partnership agreements refer to the People's Chamber resolutions on the media to secure the right of media employees to participate in decision-making.

Distribution Prior to October 1989, the Post Office was responsible for the distribution of all papers and magazines. The Post Office could not cope with the upsurge in demand yet wanted to retain its monopolistic position. A compromise has been reached: after a lengthy argument between the smaller East and West German publishers and the East German authorities, the four big West German publishing houses started their own regionally-divided distribution networks. However, the East German sales system is in danger of coming under the control of a few large Western publishers. The most pertinent sign of this is the struggle for the distribution network. The MCC has recommended that the distribution system should be independent of the publishers, not swayed by companies which dominate the market and should take the interests of the local press into account.

Radio and Television On April 1 1990, the MCC authorized advertising on radio and TV. Regulations are less restrictive than those in the FRG, which should enhance foreign currency earnings and will help East German audiovisual media in the fierce competition it faces. The president of East German TV, Hans Benzien, has said that additional revenues will be invested in modernizing equipment.

Some journalists who used to promote the party's "truths" now project themselves as former dissidents, with stories about the corruption of the former leadership. In fact, few real corruption cases have so far been unravelled, although misappropriation of funds has undoubtedly occurred (such as the cases of former trade union leader Harry Tisch and politbureau member Werner Krolikowski). Most accusations levelled against the leadership fall into the category of "abuse of office", which is more difficult to prove in the criminal courts.

The electronic media are still run by the "old forces", despite their modern-day image. The pending restructuring of radio and TV on a regional basis will be the first opportunity to change the system.

Actions

On October 3 1988 ARTICLE 19 wrote to the Senator for Internal Affairs concerning attacks by West Berlin police on reporters and photographers covering a demonstration during an IMF/World Bank meeting, and over his statement that press freedom has to take a back seat in such situations.

On November 11 1988 ARTICLE 19 wrote to the East German government calling on it to lift the ban on the Soviet monthly *Sputnik*.

Hungary

Officially, censorship did not exist under the recently deposed Hungarian Socialist Workers' Party (HSWP): however, the government issued weekly guidelines to the press on what to write and telephone calls to editors offering "advice" were common. Editors were answerable to The Party's Agitation and Propaganda Department (AgitProp) which controlled all editorial appointments. The Party no longer has such powers and the media have changed beyond recognition.

In the 1980s, the government's policy of diverting attention from politics by offering material benefits and limited freedom of expression was undermined by the rapid decline of the

	Data	Year
Population	10,588,600	1989
Life expectancy (M/F)	65.6/73.5	1985
GNP (US$ per capita)	2,460	1988
Main religion(s)	Christianity	
Official language(s)	Hungarian	
Illiteracy %	2	1985
Daily newspapers	29	1988
Non daily newspapers	95	1986
Periodicals	1,559	1986
Radio sets	6,200,000	1987
TV sets	4,260,000	1987
Press agencies:		
	Magyar Tavirati Iroda	
ICCPR:	YES	1974

economy and of living standards. By repeatedly rejecting changes that it was subsequently unable to resist, the HSWP encouraged opposition and undermined its own authority.

The partial relaxation of controls gathered speed in the late 1980s, spreading from the economic sphere to other fields: travel regulations were liberalized, a law on assembly and association was passed allowing independent groups to form. The emerging opposition had support from the journalists; the HSWP's effort to conceal economic collapse exacerbated frustrations with party control and journalists gave increasing coverage to criticisms of the party. In June 1989, the HSWP agreed to hold talks with nine opposition groups and the agreement reached in September laid the legal framework for the transition to democracy. At the October 1989 Congress the HSWP changed its name to the Hungarian Socialist Party (HSP).

On March 25 and April 8 1990, Hungary held its first free elections since 1947. The HSP's political role was reduced to that of one Party of the opposition in parliament, having come in fourth. The Hungarian Democratic Forum (HDF) emerged as the victor followed by the Alliance of Free Democrats (AFD).

Legal Provisions

Article 64 of the 1949 Constitution guaranteed freedom of speech, freedom of the press and freedom of assembly "in a manner conforming to the interests of socialism and the people." This guarantee meant nothing in practice, since its interpretation was defined by the people's sole "legitimate" representative, the HSWP. In the early 1950s, party policy held true to the Stalinist spirit of the Constitution. By the 1960s and 1970s, the party adopted a more lenient interpretation as part of its depoliticization of society, playing down its role, avoiding a personality cult of the leader and limiting open interference in people's daily lives. There was no central office of censorship and greater freedom of social and economic activity was permitted. Some criticism was allowed but the limit was drawn at political subjects and citizens were encouraged by the authorities not to take risks. *Samizdat* publishers endured constant harassment but dissent was permitted, so long as it was confined to intellectual circles. Members were prosecuted for "unauthorized trading" rather than for their ideas or political activity. This meant they could be summarily fined. Hungary was thus not embarrassed by trials of its dissidents.

The 1986 Press Law   This Act sought to define the relationship between the government and the press and also the role of the press and the individual's right to information. It left the system of censorship and self-censorship untouched and offered no clarification of the limits to party power. Janos Berecz, a leading party ideologist, then said that socialist achievements could not be questioned under the pretext of freedom of the press. Greater freedom of speech since 1986 is due less to the Press Law than to the weakening of party power.

In January 1989, a new law gave private individuals the right to launch periodicals and operate TV and radio stations, despite the terms of the 1986 Media Law which granted this right to public bodies only. In May, the HSWP relinquished control over editorial appointments of publications and in June the 1986 law was modified so that newspapers had to be registered but only as a formality. Only publications that "violate national interests or racial sensibilities or are considered indecent" were forbidden.

The Amended Constitution of 1989   Talks between government and the opposition in the summer of 1989 resulted in amendments to the Constitution and the drafting of several other key laws. The new Constitution has lost all mention of the leading role of the party and socialist state, and emphasizes the rights of the individual. Article 61 guarantees freedom of expression and states: "The Hungarian Republic recognizes and protects the freedom of the press". A Constitutional Court has been created and the law now provides that judges cannot be members of political parties.

Other Media Laws   Further laws are being drafted to ensure a media free from political control, with ownership of the media open to all and an end to the Post Office's monopoly over distribution and radio transmission. The first signs of monopoly regulations to limit media ownership have appeared in drafts of a press law, but so far these have only referred to television and radio. Measures to protect privacy and offer libel victims some means of protection are also under discussion. Libel suits are by no means new to Hungary, but for 40 years the ruling Party had a decisive influence over what could be said about whom. Journalists are now thriving on their new freedom and libel cases are taking up to two years to be heard. There is support for the restoration of the notion that damages should be paid to those who suffer at the hands of the mass media, as featured in the 1914 Press Law. But there remains the fear that the main drift of the proposals so far presented by the Ministry of Justice, whereby the state, rather than the victim would initiate proceedings and be paid the fine, would restore the state's control over the press.

The Media

The Press A more openly political press emerged in late 1989 as opposition groups gained confidence and free elections approached. *Beszelo*, once the hounded *samizdat* journal of the democratic opposition, was launched as a weekly in October 1989 under the aegis of the AFD. All the main political parties now boast a weekly publication but a flood of magazines was available far earlier and covers a wide range. Sex magazines, long forbidden, are a growth industry; *Playboy* has started a Hungarian version. *Reform*, a brash colour tabloid weekly, launched in May 1988, immediately drew a large readership with its diet of gossip, sex and politics. Although *Reform* calls itself "independent", the HSWP holds a 15 per cent share. Between June and October 1989, 220 new publications were registered, adversely affecting the sales of more established papers.

Provincial Newspapers The first independent daily, *Datum*, was launched in May 1989 in Szekszard, southern Hungary, followed by other provincial papers. Problems facing new provincial papers are due less to open censorship than to indirect interference: struggling with party monopolies of paper supplies, printing and distribution, pressure on journalists, and police action against vendors. These new papers threaten a strong local interest: the media monopoly of the county committee of the HSWP, who have controlled the 20 county papers for 40 years. Regional papers carry considerable weight in the provinces, with a wider readership locally than the national press and were an important tool for the party's local committees, which have been reluctant to end their monopoly. In several cases journalists and local groups have established committees to supervise the papers, effectively removing them from party control.

Foreign Investment Bargain-rate privatization makes Hungary an attractive market for foreign investment and its press is no exception. Rupert Murdoch has bought 50 per cent of the shares of *Reform* and its sister tabloid, the evening paper *Mai Nap*. Robert Maxwell has bought 40 per cent of *Magyar Hirlap* (with an agreement that any major decision requires 66 per cent shareholder approval, but with safeguards to prevent the imposition of an editor). In March 1990, West German Axel Springer tried to buy up most of the local press, producing an immediate outcry from opposition parties. Although the advantages of privatization (such as proper investment, huge losses being paid off and new technology) are widely perceived there are also fears that jobs will be lost and that the newly found independence will be limited by foreign interests.

In July 1990, a parliamentary committee investigating privatization of the media reported that papers had been taken over in a legal and administrative vacuum in which properties were under-valued or simply expropriated. The committee, dominated by the ruling conservative coalition, called on the government to take control of media privatization. The report has prompted opposition fears that the HDF, the leading party of the government, is trying to control the press. (The previous month the government stopped the sale of *Magyar Nemzet*, a leading daily newspaper, which party leaders had accused of being hostile to the Forum.)

Books Censorship of books no longer exists. Books by authors such as George Konrad, George Orwell, Milan Kundera and Arthur Koestler who have been banned or whose books were only available in limited editions for party members ("official *samizdat*" as the opposition dubbed it) are now openly sold. The ending of party control has offered new opportunities for profit: one publisher, Uj Ido, was recently taken to court by Solzhenitsyn's Paris publishers for infringement of copyright. The fine imposed was extremely heavy to deter others.

Television and Radio Until 1989, all branches of TV and radio were state-owned. The heads of Hungarian Radio, Hungarian TV (MTV) and the News Agency MTI had previously served at party headquarters. The state's decision to abandon its monopoly was influenced by three factors: the need to build-up the tourist industry, attract foreign investment, and the growing availability of satellite TV.

At the first session of the newly-elected parliament on May 2-3 1990, the HDF and AFD reached an accord on the media. In future, the heads of TV, radio, and MTI would be proposed by the prime minister and candidates would be interviewed by a parliamentary committee, with elected members of staff from these three institutions and delegates from the relevant professional institutions.

A fourth national radio station, Radio Danubius, was launched in 1986 and a second TV channel was established in early 1989. In summer 1989, two independent TV channels began broadcasting: one, a temporary channel serving the tourist region of Lake Balaton, the other as breakfast TV on the first national channel. The government has received a large number of applications for new radio stations and TV channels and the opportunities have aroused great interest among foreign media magnates such as Axel Springer, Rupert Murdoch and Robert Maxwell. In July, the government announced that the allocation of the limited number of frequencies available would be postponed until after relevant laws had been passed. At the time of the moratorium there were 29 radio and 32 TV applications under consideration, some with teams and studios already set up.

Reception of satellite broadcasts has been permitted since 1987. Estimates of the numbers receiving satellite and cable TV vary from 300,000 to 1,800,000 people. The number is certainly rising, as this gives immediate access to much desired Western TV channels. A prospering business has started in installing cable TV, particularly in large housing estates. Official estimates calculate that 400,000 homes were connected to cable systems by 1990.

Foreign Media The policy of the Janos Kadar years allowed selective access to foreign media and generally welcomed foreign journalists. It remained hostile to certain foreign radio stations such as Radio Free Europe, but accepted the fact that many people tuned in to their broadcasts. Change came in June 1988 when a discussion programme was jointly broadcast by Hungarian Radio and Voice of America, involving Hungarian emigrees and the writer George Konrad. In 1989 Radio Free Europe opened a bureau in Budapest.

Freedom of Opinion and Expression

Until spring 1989, the party issued weekly guidelines to radio and TV on what topics could or should be covered, and in what manner. The removal of this control, combined with the drive for scoops and revelations, has led to over-zealous reporting and sensationalism. TV and radio have had to broadcast apologies for libellous statements. Editors are now looking abroad for guidance on how to draft guidelines to curb these excesses. Concern has been voiced at the spread of pornography in shops and the content of a 1989 New Year's Eve show on TV caused a storm of complaint. Other undesirable features of the more open media are the expressions of anti-semitism and anti-gypsy sentiment. Since May 1990, there have been regular religious programmes on MTV.

The new freedom has its dangers. Death threats have frequently been issued to leaders of opposition groups and journalists uncovering the corruption of the past. At the foot of a recent article revealing corruption in the Interior Ministry, a note recorded that the author had received a threatening anonymous phone call.

Ireland

The Irish Constitution guarantees freedom of expression and specifically refers to the freedom of the press to criticize government policy. However, it is qualified by the duty of the state to ensure that the media are not used to undermine "public order or morality or the authority of the state". In conjunction with the teachings of the Roman Catholic Church, this has led to widespread censorship, particularly on issues of morality.

Sexual morality has been a long-term preoccupation. State censorship machinery, Customs and Excise officers and Catholic lay militants have pursued the indecent and obscene

	Data	Year
Population	3,515,000	1989
Life expectancy (M/F)	70.1/75.6	1982
GNP (US$ per capita)	7,480	1988
Main religion(s)	Christianity	
Official language(s)	Irish	
	English	
Illiteracy %	1	1985
Daily newspapers	8	1988
Non daily newspapers	59	1984
Periodicals	257	1984
Radio sets	2,100,000	1987
TV sets	826,000	1987
ICCPR:	YES	1990

through the years with vigour. Much has changed; Ireland has the youngest population in Europe and has a choice of 16 TV channels, 10 via satellite. Only the most lurid of publications is today likely to be failed by the censor.

The new battleground is over abortion which is illegal in Ireland. Court decisions in the past two years have led to the closure of clinics involved in abortion counselling, and students who provided abortion information in welfare handbooks have been pursued relentlessly through the courts by anti-abortion pressure groups.

Considerable restrictions are also imposed on the sale and advertising of contraceptives. The government campaign against AIDS has done little to promote the use of condoms and teachers have complained that an educational booklet on AIDS has been suppressed by the government because of the Catholic Church's resistance to the promotion of the use of condoms. In May 1990, the state prosecuted the Irish Family Planning Association (IFPA) for selling condoms at a retail outlet, contrary to a law which confines their sale to "medical" outlets. The IFPA was convicted and fined IR£400 (US$570). It intends to appeal and to mount a campaign for a change in the law.

Emergency Laws

The Offences Against the State Act 1939 contains wide powers to proscribe unlawful organizations and to prohibit or seize publications. While organizations such as the Irish Republican Army (IRA) remain banned, its publications are sold openly in both the Republic and Northern Ireland. In 1988, however, a *Sinn Féin* councillor was sentenced to five years' imprisonment for incitement to join the IRA. In the same year, a Cork man received a similar sentence for possession of a pro-IRA poster, even though it had been on open sale for some years.

The Media

Newspapers Ireland has a strong independent newspaper tradition. There are no formalities in starting up a newspaper. Every week over 90 per cent of the adult population read at least one of the national dailies: principally *The Cork Examiner*, *The Irish Press*, *The Irish Independent* and *The Irish Times*. In 1988, a new tabloid *The Star* was launched. Over 80 per cent read one of the four established Sunday papers: *The Sunday Independent*, *The Sunday Press*, *The Sunday Tribune* and *The Sunday World*. A new business paper, *The Sunday Business Post*, was launched in late November 1989.

In April 1989, all the national newspapers appointed Readers' Representatives in an attempt to improve their relationship with the public. Irish papers are concerned at the inroads being made by the cheaper British tabloids which sell approximately 150,000 copies daily. Newspapers' circulation has been declining and advertising revenue is low by international standards.

The libel laws also weigh heavily on the press as politicians and public figures regularly gain high awards in libel suits that would not succeed in other countries. The government has admitted that it underwrites the legal costs of civil servants who sue newspapers for defamation. The law of defamation is being reviewed by the Law Reform Commission.

Radio and Television The past two years have seen major changes. In 1988, legislation was passed allowing independent commercial broadcasting stations. Existing "pirate" stations were outlawed from the end of 1988 but allowed to apply for licences. To date, some 15 of 24 local stations have begun broadcasting; the remainder, together with the new third national TV station, TV 3, were expected to be on air in 1990. A number of community and special interest radio stations will be licensed and an Irish-language TV station is proposed. Local newspapers are prominent in commercial radio ownership, as are the churches.

Before 1988, the national broadcasting service, RTE, enjoyed a virtual monopoly of the airways. RTE operates at "arm's length" from government, on the model of the BBC. Government interference, both formal and informal, has always been a problem in that it leads to self-censorship. RTE's position is particularly vulnerable given its dependence on government for its income from licence fees and the competition it now faces from commercial stations. Proposed legislation to cap advertising further threatens RTE's position.

Most of the country receives all the British TV channels via an extensive cable network. In 1990, Ireland is set to become the first European country to introduce a Multipoint Microwave Distribution System (MMDS). It will carry up to 11 additional TV channels to areas of the country difficult to connect up to the cable system.

Books Following a rather inactive phase when many had forgotten its existence, the Censorship of Publications Board hit the headlines with the decisions in early 1987 to ban two books, *The Erotic Art of India*, out of print for some years, and *The Joy of Sex*, which provoked considerable protest from doctors and clinics who have used the book widely in counselling. Over 1,000 copies had been sold by the IFPA. The ban was finally revoked by the Censorship Appeal Board in September 1989.

Irish book publishers are, for the most part, small family concerns whose very existence has been threatened in recent years by the enormity of libel awards against them. They are, therefore, becoming unwilling to publish books that might involve such a risk and distributors are also unwilling to handle sometimes major but risky titles. The Irish Book Publishers' Association is actively seeking changes in the libel laws.

Film and Video A Video Recordings Act became law in 1989 in response to the increasingly widespread use of video recorders and concern over "video nasties" and sexually explicit films. The law provides for the banning of any film likely to incite crime, racial or religious hatred, or to deprave or corrupt. It also introduces a classification system designed to provide guidance for parents.

Access to Information The High Court in Dublin in December 1986 granted an injunction to prevent two Dublin organizations (the Well Woman clinic and Open Line Counselling) from offering non-directive counselling and referral information on abortion facilities in Britain. (Abortion is unlawful in Ireland and it has been estimated that each year between 5,000 and 10,000 Irish women travel to Britain for terminations.) The decision was upheld by the Irish Supreme Court in March 1988. The organizations complained to the European Commission of Human Rights in Strasbourg, arguing that their right to know was being denied and, in May 1990, the European Commission of Human Rights referred the case to the European Court in Strasbourg.

The Society for the Protection of the Unborn Child (SPUC) have moved against a number of students' unions who had, since the 1970s, included information on abortion services in Britain in their welfare booklets. The Irish High Court decided to refer to the European Court of Justice in Luxembourg the question of whether the Treaty of Rome's guarantee of the right to travel and to obtain abortion services in another member state carried with it a corollary right to information about those services. Thus the issue of the censorship of information about abortion in Ireland appeared simultaneously before the two highest courts in Europe.

Meanwhile, students' unions have continued to defy a temporary ban pending the European court decision. A newsletter with abortion information printed in Northern Ireland was circulated on campuses in November 1989 and police visited two students' union offices in Dublin following complaints that they were "corrupting public morals".

In September 1989, the Censorship of Publications Board gave the British women's magazine *Cosmopolitan* an ultimatum: withdraw its abortion advertisements or be banned in Ireland. In January 1990, the magazine carried a full-page apology to its readers explaining that it was no longer able to print advertisements in Ireland "providing abortion advice and help". In February 1990, *Company*, a British magazine for young women, removed an eight-page supplement on abortion from copies circulating in Ireland.

In consequence, FBAS, the national training and employment authority, decided to have all references to abortion referral services deleted from a guide to help young people emigrating to Britain and the ethics committee of a large Dublin hospital cancelled a lecture on a new treatment for Parkinson's Disease because it involved the use of foetal tissue.

A new Data Protection Act came into force in January 1989, providing rights of access, rectification and erasure and outlining the powers of the Protection Commissioner with regard to registration and the investigation and handling of complaints.

The Official Secrets Act of 1963 remains in force and, although rarely invoked, it is as broad as the much criticized British legislation. Combined with the lack of any freedom of information legislation, its effect is to inhibit the flow of information from official sources. In 1988, An Foras Forbartha, the quasi-independent national environmental agency, was replaced by an Environmental Research Unit within the Department of the Environment. This means that its staff are now required to abide by the Official Secrets Act.

In 1987, two leading political journalists were awarded damages in the High Court as a result of the tapping of their telephones, but no legislation to outlaw telephone tapping has been introduced. In recent years attempts to achieve freedom of information legislation by means of Private Member's Bills have failed.

Freedom of Political Opinion and Expression

Much controversy has been generated over the years by Section 31 of the Broadcasting Act which, since 1976, has banned the IRA's political wing, *Sinn Féin*, from appearing on television and radio. One of the most disturbing aspects of the broadcasting ban has been the self-censorship it has generated. However, self- censorship is not a recent development. In 1964, RTE withheld a documentary which dealt with discrimination against Catholics in Northern Ireland on the grounds that it would be "unhelpful" to show it when the then prime minister was engaged in a rapprochement with the Unionist government of Northern Ireland. The documentary was finally shown in September 1989.

In March 1988, an RTE reporter had her contract terminated when her radio report of the funerals of three IRA members shot in Gibraltar by British security forces contained a statement to mourners by a member of *Sinn Féin*. There have been other instances of government pressure on RTE: in one case, when members of *Sinn Féin* spoke from the audience in a live TV show, and in another when they contributed to a phone-in on mushroom growing. The ban excludes members of *Sinn Féin* from being interviewed on any topic. Unlike its British counterpart, the Irish ban remained in force during the national elections of June 1989.

The Prohibition of Incitement to Racial, Religious or National Hatred Act was passed in 1989. The law extends to other minority groups including travellers and homosexuals.

Blasphemy The Constitution prohibits blasphemy; blasphemous libel is covered by the 1961 Defamation Act (with fine of up to IR£500 (US$712) or up to seven years' imprisonment). There have been no prosecutions for the offence.

The film *Last Temptation of Christ* was approved for those over 18 on the unusual condition that no-one would be admitted after the start of the film when a statement would be shown to the effect that the film was based not on the Bible but on a Greek novel.

Actions

In August 1989 the National Union of Journalists and the Federated Workers' Union of Ireland, with the assistance of ARTICLE 19, lodged a challenge to the Irish broadcasting ban with the European Commission of Human Rights. No decision is expected before late 1990.

On October 9 1989 ARTICLE 19 published a report, *No Comment: Censorship, Secrecy and the Irish Troubles*, scrutinizing the operation of the Irish broadcasting ban as well as that imposed in 1988 by the British government.

Norway

A rticle 100 of the Norwegian Constitution of 1814 guarantees freedom of expression and freedom of the press in what, for its time, was remarkably clear language. However, the article made exceptions for incitement and acts of disobedience to the laws, contempt of religion, morality or the constitutional powers, resistance to their orders, and defamation of individuals. Over the years, several laws and court interpretations have served to narrow the range of freedom of information in various ways.

In January 1989, the Norwegian government resolved to work towards incorporating the international human rights treaties to which it is a party into Norwegian law in the form of a Bill of Rights. As a result, it is expected that greater importance will be accorded to

	Data	Year
Population	4,196,000	1988
Life expectancy (M/F)	72.8/79.5	1985
GNP (US$ per capita)	20,020	1988
Main religion(s)	Christianity	
Official language(s)	Bokmal	
	Nynorsk	
Illiteracy %	1	1985
Daily newspapers	61	1988
Non daily newspapers	77	1986
Periodicals	3,887	1986
Radio sets	3,300,000	1987
TV sets	1,454,000	1987
Press agencies:		
	Bulls Presse-tjeneste,	
	Norsk Presse Service,	
	Norsk Telegrambyra	
ICCPR:	YES	1972

freedom of expression. In deciding a private libel case in favour of a newspaper, the *Rogalands Avis*, the Supreme Court, on March 7 1990, for the first time referred directly to Article 10 of the European Convention on Human Rights (ECHR), the freedom of expression guarantee, and justified its decision, in part, by reference to the *Lingens* case (see Themes & Issues section ECHR entry).

Prior Censorship Article 100 is generally interpreted as an absolute prohibition of prior censorship. No established procedures for such censorship exist, but in individual cases publishing has been halted through the courts and the threat of prosecution for defamation has been used to deter writers and publishers.

People who consider themselves defamed can apply to have the publication of a film, newspaper or book halted, prior to publication. In 1989, a Court of Attachment (*Namsretten*) halted publication of a film on Norwegian sealing, in response to a complaint by sealers, who claimed that the film defamed them.

Privacy The reputation and private lives of individuals enjoy a high degree of formal protection under Norwegian law. In February 1990, the Ministry of Justice published a Bill which would extend legal constraints to the use of information from taped conversations in which one of the participants is unaware of the recording. The Bill was a response to a highly publicized incident in 1989 where a private individual phoned prominent Norwegian politicians and recorded the conversations unknown to the politicians. In the autumn of 1989, a book was published from the transcribed tapes which included stories of political intrigue and confidences. Prime Minister Gro Harlem Brundtland initiated a study with a view to amending the law (Ms Brundtland was a conspicuous subject of discussion on some of the tapes).

Two of those whose conversations were taped, a former cabinet minister and a former chairman of the Norwegian Trades Union Congress, reported the author to the police for infringing privacy. In spite of the argument that the conversations were intellectual property which should not be reproduced without the consent of all contributing parties, the Director General of Public Prosecutions decided that no offence had been committed.

Access to Information

The Public Access Act The Administrative Procedures Act 1967 provided for access to public records for anyone who was a party to the relevant decisions. Broader access is provided by the Public Access Act (1970), which decrees a general right for any person to inspect documents held by state and municipal administrations. Exceptions to this basic right are limited by the law and, where documents are withheld, the reason must be given. Refusal may be appealed to higher administrative authority or the courts. Even when there is a legal ground under which disclosure may be denied, it is the duty of the authorities to decide whether the information in question should nevertheless be made available.

The Public Access Act applies only to post 1970 documents. However, in practice, most agencies deal with earlier documents on the same terms and new archival legislation is promised. The Public Access Act is defective in that it does not cover records from the Storting (parliament) which has proved very reluctant to let even qualified historians examine its archives.

The main complaints are not about the legislation but the fact that many civil servants are still unfamiliar with it and tend towards restrictive interpretation particularly in national security cases. Other laws limit access to official information. For instance, the Planning and Building Act 1985 exempts military agencies from the control of local authorities in the process of obtaining building permission. Public debate on the establishment of military installations which are potentially controversial in local communities is thereby blocked.

Defamation Protection of a person's reputation enjoys a secure position in the Norwegian Penal Code. In recent years there has been concern that these provisions are being used to unduly restrict freedom of expression.

In 1987, the Supreme Court convicted *Fredrikstad Blad*, a local newspaper in Fredrikstad, of defamation over an article claiming that a local council tax collector had been paid twice for carrying out one job. The allegation was not disputed and the conviction was based on the size of the caption, its place on the front page, and the picture of the official in what the court called "the accompanying circumstances".

In another noteworthy decision in 1988, the Supreme Court upheld the conviction of a journalist from the Norwegian Broadcasting Authority (NRK) of defaming a lawyer. The journalist had reported on a radio news programme that the lawyer, who was unnamed, in selling a house for his wife demanded that one third of the price be paid "under the counter". The journalist characterised this as tax evasion. The lawyer claimed in court that he only sought to evade the fee on the transaction, not the taxation of the profits. The Supreme Court interpreted the journalist's statement to be an accusation of tax evasion, which he had the onus to prove. The decision aroused strong reactions in press circles and a complaint challenging the conviction has been filed with the European Commission of Human Rights in Strasbourg.

The Media

Norwegian media have lacked a tradition of investigative journalism, and have traditionally exercised considerable self-restraint. In part, this has shielded public figures from intrusion into their personal lives, but it has also limited serious investigation into important issues such as corruption. In the national security field, the restraint of the mass media has bordered on self-censorship. However, there are signs of change.

Press Subsidies The state subsidises most Norwegian newspapers in order to maintain an independent and politically differentiated press. The state has no control of the content of newspapers and the subsidy is given on the condition that the newspaper has free and independent editors. The state also subsidises book publishing and film production, without exerting any influence on what is published.

Professional Ethics The Norwegian press operates under a code of ethics established by the press itself. The Press Council deals with complaints from the public over the conduct of the press and rules on specific complaints and issues public statements. The rules of professional ethics stipulate that the press correct and apologise for mistakes which have been published. Anyone subjected to strong criticism in the press has a right of reply. If purely factual errors have been published the person directly concerned is entitled to publication of a correction. If the editor refuses, he/she may be fined (Section 430 of the Civil Penal Code).

Protection of Sources Journalists and editors have a qualified right not to answer questions concerning their sources' identity. The court may, nevertheless, order an editor to disclose a source if the court considers it particularly important. The right to protect the source is significantly less pronounced in Norway than in Sweden and journalists and editors are regularly fined for refusing to reveal their sources. In 1988, a public committee suggested that the right to protect sources should be made statutory but, so far, no action has been taken.

Broadcasting During the 1980s, the traditional Norwegian broadcasting monopoly was gradually relaxed to permit local radio broadcasting. In 1989, it also became legal to broadcast advertising under certain restricted conditions. The NRK operates one TV channel and two radio channels. However, anyone with a dish aerial or connected to a cable network is free to receive any transmission from another country. NRK was reorganized in 1989 to become a self-owned foundation. NRK's transmissions are independent and advertisement-free "public service" transmissions. It is expected that Norway will soon ratify the 1989 Convention on Transfrontier Television of the Council of Europe.

Freedom of Opinion and Expression

National Security Security classification is regulated in the Security Instruction, an executive order largely consonant with similar rules in other NATO countries.

Researchers have been given access to classified and other non-public documents on a case-by-case basis. In October 1988, the Security Instruction was amended to introduce a 30-year rule for declassification, with broadly formulated exceptions for defence plans, military facilities, and security and intelligence matters.

A Council for Declassification, representing various agencies and users and chaired by a civilian official in the Ministry of Defence, was established in November 1989. The Council will monitor the declassification procedures in the executive branch and implement standards of practice in classification and declassification. It is too early to say how this institution will work in practice but a number of important documents have been declassified in accordance with the 30-year limit.

Destruction of Documents The Norwegian National Archives has uncovered massive destruction of documents in the archives of many defence agencies. Norway has inadequate archival legislation to prevent this and to permit the National Archives to fulfil its role in recording and making available to the public official records in the defence area. This problem applies in many areas but is particularly acute in the area of defence where the value of historical records is enhanced by the shortage of accurate current information. The new archival legislation will help to prevent similar destruction in the future.

National Security in the Courts A common conflict between national security and freedom of expression concerns the collection and dissemination of information. Norwegian law contains a large number of specific secrecy requirements.

These provisions have led to a number of actions against journalists, researchers and members of the general public. In 1989, two students on a journalism course at the District College in Bodo were charged under the Law on Defence Secrets for taking pictures of a satellite ground station in Fauske, but the charges were later dropped. At about the same time, the Defence Staff released its own pictures of the very same installation, in a complete reversal of its previous policy. The Ministry of Defence is currently considering the relaxation of the ban on photography from aircraft in the light of photographic capabilities of surveillance satellites.

Journalists have been fined for violating the ban on photography in reporting incidents on the Norwegian-Soviet border. The military and civilian defence authorities have exercised pre-publication censorship in relation to maps, books and even postcards. Military and intelligence officials have been threatened with prosecution for publishing their memoirs and, in 1977, a former military officer was convicted for revealing secrets which were about 25 years old.

"Spy Paragraphs" Until 1977, the national security paragraphs in the Civil Penal Code (popularly called the "spy paragraphs") had only been used in espionage cases. Since then, there have been a number of actual and attempted prosecutions of journalists, researchers and political activists. The legislation refers to "the revelation" of information detrimental to national security and the clauses apply regardless of the number of people to whom the secrets have been revealed and regardless of the means chosen to reveal them. However, the law prescribes stricter punishment in cases where information has been revealed to a foreign power. The prosecution claimed in one case that public exposure was equivalent to revealing information to a foreign power, but this argument was rejected by the Supreme Court. A public committee is to be appointed by the Ministry of Justice to consider the "spy paragraphs".

Fewer prosecutions after 1987, the introduction of the 30-year rule for declassification, the increasing openness of the military authorities, and the declassification programmes of the ministries of defence and foreign affairs suggest a lessening of the conflict between national security and freedom of information. Because of archival weeding and slow de-classification, Norwegian historians will still have to rely to a large extent on US archival sources in their work on Norwegian security topics. The news media will have to readjust from a long period of self-censorship on national security issues inspired by a mixture of patriotism and fear of official sanctions. These developments are likely to be reinforced by *glasnost* in the USSR and a new political climate.

Blasphemy Norwegian legislation on blasphemy protects all religions. In practice, most attempts to invoke the law have been made by Lutheran groups, inside or outside the dominant Evangelical Lutheran Church. However, in 1989 a Norwegian Muslim group sued publishers H Aschenhoug and Co for defamation, discrimination and blasphemy after they published the Norwegian translation of Salman Rushdie's novel, *The Satanic Verses*. The case is still pending in the courts. The book is sold openly in leading bookstores and, just before the court proceedings started, a paperback edition was issued.

Actions

In its 1988 Commentary to the Human Rights Committee ARTICLE 19 requested a review of the laws which affect media freedom, particularly the defamation law and those governing access to official information.

Poland

The historic "Round-Table" discussions between Solidarity and the government opened on February 6 1989 and concluded on April 5 with an agreement to overhaul the legislative system, legalize Solidarity and hold free parliamentary elections. The elections took place on June 4 with Solidarity overwhelmingly defeating the ruling Communist Party. On August 24, the *Sejm*, the lower house of the National Assembly, approved Solidarity candidate Tadeusz Mazowiecki as Prime Minister. At the beginning of December, the government introduced a programme to create a market economy with sharp cuts in state spending and subsidies. On December 29, the parliament changed the country's name from the Polish People's Republic to the Republic of Poland and eliminated a clause in the Constitution which guaranteed a leading role to the Polish United Workers' Party, as the Communist Party was officially called. One month later, at its final Congress, delegates voted to dissolve the party which had ruled Poland since 1948. A few days later the Communist Party's main daily, *Trybuna Ludu*, along with numerous other papers and journals ceased publication.

	Data	Year
Population	37,862,000	1988
Life expectancy (M/F)	66.5/74.8	1985
GNP (US$ per capita)	1,850	1988
Main religion(s)	Christianity	
Official language(s)	Polish	
Illiteracy %	2	1985
Daily newspapers	45	1988
Non daily newspapers	52	1986
Periodicals	2,986	1986
Radio sets	11,084,000	1988
TV sets	10,031,000	1988
Press agencies:		
Polska Agencia Interpress,		
PAP, CAF, KAW, MAW		
ICCPR:	YES	1977

On March 22 1990, a law was passed abolishing the party's publishing house Prasa-Ksiazka-Ruch (RSW), Eastern Europe's largest publishing and distribution concern, which had owned the majority of Polish papers and periodicals. In October 1990, the government approved the sale of RSW, and announced the auction over a period of six months of 118 newspapers; a further 70 were to be taken over by journalists' co-operatives. The state would take nine printing works, five would be leased to the new newspaper co-operatives, eleven others would be sold. Western newspaper publishers, including Robert Maxwell and Rupert Murdoch, had expressed interest in the sale.

One of the main problems, common to all Poles, is the economy. In the six months after the government introduced its programme for a transition to a market economy on January 1 1990, real wages and industrial output fell by a third and 400,000 people lost their jobs. Among the unemployed are an estimated 1,000 journalists. Sharp cuts in state spending and subsidies have hit the film industry and all branches of publishing. In January 1990, the price of newsprint rose nearly 500 per cent and newspapers are losing their readers as they raise prices to compensate.

On November 26 1990, Prime Minister Mazowiecka and his goverment resigned following his defeat by Lech Walesa and Stanislaw Tyminski in the first round of presidential elections.

Background Censorship in post-war Poland was introduced in the 1946 Decree on the Establishment of the Central Office for the Control of Publications and Public Performances. This law underwent many changes, but retained institutionalized censorship of all forms of public expression and of the dissemination of information and ideas. No free press existed in Poland for over 30 years but, with the beginning of organized opposition and the growth of Solidarity, attempts were made to revive freedom of expression. For several months in 1981, a relatively liberal Press Law was in force, but this came to an abrupt end with the imposition of martial law in December 1981. The state's formal censorship powers were then largely restored, although not always applied in practice.

A licence to publish a newspaper or periodical had to be sought from the Central Office for the Control of Publications and Public Performances. The applicant had, among other things, to provide evidence concerning the source of newsprint and availabilty of printing facilities. Newsprint, however, was distributed solely by the government and the Communist Party-owned RSW Prasa which had provided 90 per cent of the country's printing facilities. The authorities frequently blocked publications simply by using this monopoly.

Underground Publications Although publishing without a licence was a punishable offence known as "second circulation", independent, underground publishing thrived in Poland. The authorities tried strenuously to suppress it, with the result that publishers, printers and distributors of independent publications constituted the majority of political cases in the courts. In recent years, however, there had been no trials of authors for publishing articles in either the Polish emigré or underground press. Instead, in their last year of power, the Communist authorities harassed "underground" printers. At the beginning of 1988, for instance, Solidarity activist Hanna Lukowska-Karniej was sentenced to 90 days' imprisonment for printing *samizdat* publications. Ryszard Szpryngwald from Warsaw was fined 50,000 zlotys when police found book-binding equipment and *samizdat* papers in his flat.

Censorship Official statistics, published in January 1990 by the independent daily *Gazeta Wyborcza*, showed that in 1988 there were 2,528 interventions by the censors. The true number was higher because censors also had indirect ways of using their power. For instance, in the case of dailies, the censor had the right to hold on to a disputed text for 12 hours for closer scrutiny, thus destroying the article's topicality.

In 1988, the government attempted to prevent even the foreign press from reporting the true situation in Poland. The Foreign Ministry warned a group of journalists who had entered the Gdansk shipyard during the strike in May 1988 that they would be denied permission to work in Poland if any similar incident occurred again. On the same day, the authorities ordered the expulsion of seven Belgians accused of having contact with an "illegal peace group". Solidarity spokesman Janusz Onyszkiewicz was sentenced on May 7 1988 to six weeks' imprisonment on charges of supplying false information to foreign journalists. His sentence was later reduced to 20 hours' manual labour.

Signs of Liberalization A letter signed by 151 writers and intellectuals appeared in the paper *Rzeczpospolita* in June 1988 demanding the reinstatement of the Polish PEN Club, which had been suspended under martial law and dissolved in 1983.

The petition was supported by the main board of the Writers Union. In August, the Polish PEN Club was granted official permission to reconvene.

In November 1988, George Orwell's banned novel *1984*, which previously had been printed underground, suddenly appeared, published by one of the state publishing houses.

In the same month, the Supreme Court took the unusual step of interpreting more liberally the Customs law which bans the importation of publications "harmful to the interests of the Polish People's Republic". The Supreme Court referred to the constitutional provision of freedom of speech and publication and ruled that Customs law did not apply to foreign publications imported by libraries.

In February 1989, Andrzej Wajda's film, *Man of Iron*, about the 1980 Gdansk shipyard strike and the birth of Solidarity, which was banned shortly after its première in 1981, was again screened in Warsaw. Tadeusz Konwicki's novel *A Minor Apocalypse*, widely translated around the world but previously available in Poland only from the independent press, was officially published.

These outward signs of liberalization, however, were not the whole story. As late as April 12 1989, Miroslaw Jasinski, an activist from the Polish-Czechoslovak Solidarity group, was sentenced in Wroclaw to a fine of 30,000 zlotys and the confiscation of 105 books "published by hostile foreign centres". The books were single copies of foreign language publications, many of them by leading Czech writers.

The situation in the film industry was not very different. In March 1989, Janusz Majewski, Chairman of the Association of Polish Film-makers, complained of government intervention during the production and distribution of certain films. He stated that four feature and 31 documentary films had been banned.

Dismantling Censorship

Four independent journalists and an independent video crew were officially accredited to the "Round Table" talks in February 1989. However, they were asked not to mention publicly the titles of the underground publications they worked for, but merely to say they were from the "Round Table" press office. Access to information from these crucial discussions was still limited, and the Journalists' Association issued a statement on February 16 protesting against "journalists being barred from places where significant events are taking place" and against attempts to "limit the information transmitted".

Opposition Newspapers In March 1989, the sub-committees of the "Round Table" dealing with the media and censorship reached agreement on granting Solidarity the right to print and distribute its own daily and weekly newspapers, and on guaranteeing Solidarity access to the state-controlled media in the run-up to the free elections set for June 1989. The first opposition daily newspaper in a country ruled by a Communist party, *Gazeta Wyborcza*, appeared in Warsaw on May 8 1989. After only four months, it reached a print run of more than 500,000. By the end of May, *Tygodnik Solidarnosc* was also published legally for the first time since the imposition of martial law in December 1981. The editorial board was led by its original editor, Tadeusz Mazowiecki. Solidarity had published 37 editions of its weekly before December 1981. When most of its staff were interned under martial law it continued to be published underground. The first legal edition in 1989 had a print run of 500,000.

On May 29 1989, the *Sejm* passed amendments to the Press Law which abolished the licensing of newspapers and replaced it with a system of registration. In order to publish a paper it was no longer necessary to obtain permission from the Central Office for the Control of Publications and Public Performances. Notification was enough. The amendment also deleted the clause prohibiting "the dissemination of texts of a clearly criminal nature", which had been used to ban any mention of Solidarity in print.

State Secrets There has also been a growing openness in official information. A 1981 law on the Protection of State Secrets had classified information on such topics as public health, pollution and foreign debt as official secrets. By the end of April 1989, the main Statistical Office had decided to declassify 7,000 secret publications and papers published since 1950. In June, it made public 4,000 statistical records covering several decades. The data included previously withheld information on housing, accidents, industrial pollution, work efficiency, the standard of living and technological progress. There remain 39 areas which are still subject to secrecy.

Radio and Television On September 23 1989, the Prime Minister, Tadeusz Mazowiecki, appointed a Solidarity journalist and academic, Andrzej Drawicz, to chair the State Committee for Radio and TV. This body oversees Poland's two state-run TV and four radio channels. Andrzej Drawicz clearly stated his intentions: "TV should not be what it has been until now, the ideological instrument of one party. It should be an instrument of political freedom which will speak to the people and on behalf of the people in a language familiar to them."

On February 22 1990, proposals were published to transform the administration of radio and TV. There would be an end to the state's monopoly on production and dissemination of broadcasts and a new nine-member "national broadcasting council" appointed by parliament and the prime minister.

In the same month, Echo, the first private TV station, began broadcasting in Wroclaw. The programmes were partly locally-produced, partly retransmissions from satellite stations. The owners announced that the next private radio and TV station would be launched in Lublin. The first Polish commercial radio station began broadcasting in November 1989.

Despite these changes, in 1989 there were 1,164 interventions in the press by the censors, 11 in the theatre, two at exhibitions, 19 in small print-run publications, 30 in radio and TV and 10 in cinematography. Calls for the true abolition of censorship intensified.

Member of parliament Jan Rokita appealed in the *Gazeta Wyborcza* on January 2 1990 for the censors' offices to be closed down. He pointed out the difficulties of many theatres and periodicals, and concluded that given the state of the economy, "in this situation, plain decency does not permit us to channel from the state budget millions of zloties to keep 465 censors who prevent free speech ... ".

Three months later, on April 11, the *Sejm* voted to abolish the censorship law and the Central Office for the Control of Publications and Public Performances was dissolved.

Whilst no censorship laws remain in Poland, there are continuing barriers to freedom of expression. This is due, in part, to the fear engendered in people during 40 years of suppression of free speech.

Actions

In its 1987 Commentary to the Human Rights Committee ARTICLE 19 urged the Polish government to abolish the legislation and machinery which combines to impose control and censorship on all forms of expression.

Portugal

Since the 1974 overthrow of the Estado Nova (which had been in power since 1926) Portugal has gradually achieved political stability based on democracy. In particular, media freedom has been enhanced by the increasing confidence of journalists, together with rules to emphasize the importance of their role.

The 1976 Constitution, which has been amended twice, guarantees freedom of expression through the media. Prior censorship is forbidden (Art.37.2) and any infringements committed by the media are dealt with by the ordinary courts (Art.37.3). Access to sources of information, professional secrecy and participation in the media are recognized rights (Art.38.2). There is freedom to found newspapers (Art.38.2) as

	Data	Year
Population	10,250,000	1988
Life expectancy (M/F)	68.3/75.2	1982
GNP (US$ per capita)	3,670	1988
Main religion(s)	Christianity	
Official language(s)	Portuguese	
Illiteracy %	15.0	1990
(M/F)	11.2/18.5	1990
Daily newspapers	28	1989
Non daily newspapers	288	1988
Periodicals	1,300	1989
Radio sets	2,173,000	1988
TV sets	1,660,000	1988
Press agencies:		
AEI, ADS, Unipress,		
Agencia Lusa de Informacao		
ICCPR:	YES	1978

well as radio and television stations through the granting of licences by public franchise (Art.38.7). Political parties and trade unions are entitled to radio and TV airtime even outside elections (Art.40).

The Media

Television   TV is the most powerful means of communication in Portugal, with Channel 1 of the state-owned Radio TV Portuguesa (RTP) reaching more than 70 per cent of the population over the age of 12. State monopoly of TV, which began in 1956, will end in 1991 when two private channels are due to begin broadcasting alongside the two RTP channels. Ownership of the new channels, through a public franchise, will be decided by the government on the advice of the High Authority for Social Communication.

The end of the state monopoly has widespread support although some of the implications have caused concern. The most controversial issue has been the allocation of broadcasting time to the Roman Catholic Church and other religious organizations. This decision, which has been criticized by the socialist parties, was not, for a variety of reasons, approved of by the Church.

Another decision which raised public concern was the fact that there will be no local or regional channels. Many viewers currently watch Spanish channels and, in some parts of the country, illegal TV stations have formed as a means of protesting against RTP which is perceived as pro-government and city-orientated. The illegal channels may be tolerated by the government, if the example of pirate radio stations operating between 1984 and 1988 is to be followed, at least until franchise decisions are made.

It is hoped that more freedom and pluralism will be achieved in programming by granting licences to privately-owned channels, a departure from the traditionally strong role the government has played. The current practice of the government selecting the governors, who then appoint directors, is known to have resulted in people being chosen for their political credentials rather than their professional suitability.

In the autonomous regions, Azores and Madeira, the RTP manager has to be approved by the respective regional governments. The control which the regional government of Madeira exerts on freedom of information was shown in January 1990, when the region's President, Alberto João Jardim, tried to stop the screening of news of a crude oil leak which had reached the island of Porto Santo. The government stated that access to information could be restricted when disclosure conflicted with other interests and, in this case, the adverse image for Madeira's tourist trade was cited. Madeira's TV was unable to report the incident with total freedom although mainland RTP, despite some difficulties, broadcast the story.

Other issues have been raised by the prospect of competition between two publicly-owned and two private channels. A substantial amount of RTP's income has come from advertising, particularly so since 1985, and from the licence fee which TV owners pay every year. However, that may no longer be the case once RTP ceases to enjoy a monopoly over publicity and the licence fee has been abolished.

In February 1988, four TV journalists were acquitted in what was regarded as a test case for press freedom in Portugal. They were charged with fomenting terrorism by filming a clandestine interview with hooded, left-wing guerrillas of the FP-25 group. However, the judge said that the charges, which would have carried jail sentences of up to two years, were unfounded because the journalists, Caros Fino, Manola Belo, Solano de Almeida and Fernando Balsinha, were merely doing their jobs in informing the public.

Radio Radio's position in Portugal underwent changes when approximately 30 local pirate stations were legalized. The new stations, with increasing audiences, are becoming rivals to the two main national stations: the publicly-owned Radiodifusão Portuguesa and the Catholic Radio Renascenca, the most popular radio station in Portugal. The increase in popularity of private radio stations, particularly in Lisbon and Oporto, does not reflect their financial status. Many stations struggle to survive and depend almost exclusively on advertising from local businesses. A request for a subsidy, similar to that given to the regional press in 1979, has been refused by the government which stated that the future of private radio stations should be decided by the market without government involvement.

The government, however, refused permission for the broadcast of news through a chain of radio stations. TSF, the best-known local station in Lisbon, started a system whereby news was transmitted to 20 local stations around the country which would then broadcast it to their audiences. This system helped win higher audiences and increased advertising revenue, generating enough resources to employ correspondents in various parts of the world. The government's refusal was, allegedly, based on the premise that the new system was unfair to other national radio stations, including those of the state and Church, whose survival depended on advertising. This prohibition was followed by threats of fines and the withdrawal of TSF's broadcast licence. The local radio stations are appealing against the government's decision.

Press The Portuguese newspapers, in particular the dailies, have a very low readership for reasons ranging from the power of TV and radio and the traditional lack of reading skills, to the unsatisfactory distribution system.

The two most widely read papers are the weekly *Expresso*, an independent paper owned by ex-prime minister Pinto Balsemao, and *A Bola*, a sports paper published four times a week. Each paper has a circulation of 160,000. Despite the relatively high number of daily papers in Portugal (seven in Lisbon, three of which are afternoon papers, and three in Oporto) nearly all of them rely on bank loans for their survival.

Since 1989 the events that have characterized the press in Portugal are twofold: on the one hand, the government proceeded with the privatization of newspapers particularly those nationalized in 1975. This was not opposed and did not result in major changes in the papers. On the other hand, many recently established daily and weekly newspapers closed down, a sign of the limits of the newspaper market and the conservative nature of readers.

Despite this, a new daily, the *Publico*, linked to the financial group SONAE, is to be established. SONAE is owned by Belmiro Azevedo, an industrialist who also owns Radio Nova, Oporto's most popular local radio, and is a candidate for ownership of a new TV channel. The *Publico* venture is considered the biggest media investment ever made in Portugal. It will be the first time that a newspaper has been published simultaneously in Lisbon and Oporto, Portugal's biggest cities. The team behind the venture intends establishing a high quality independent newspaper modelled on the Spanish *El País*.

Defamation Defamation is a crime according to Article 164 of the 1983 Penal Code. However, an offender is not punishable if an allegation is made "in order to pursue a legitimate public interest" or if the allegation is proved to be true or "there is reason to believe in good faith" that the allegation is true.

It has been characteristic over the last decade for public figures to sue newspapers that have offended them and two independent newspapers have been particularly affected. *O Diabo*, a satirical weekly, was sued over 150 times in the 1980s. Its editor, Vera Lagoa, was found guilty in 1981 of defaming President Ramalho Eanes because of an editorial criticizing him for not speaking out on behalf of dissidents in Poland. Since 1980, at least 200 actions under the defamation law have been taken against Miguel Urbano Rodrigues, editor and founder of the daily *O Diário*. He has won more than 95 per cent of the cases. In one case, he was prosecuted because of articles claiming illicit financial transactions by the late Prime Minister, Sá Carneiro. Rodrigues was banned from all foreign travel for up to two years between 1984 and 1986, government subsidies were withdrawn from his paper during 1985-1988 and he was banned from directing his paper or any other publication.

High Authority for Social Communication

Following a constitutional amendment, a new body entitled the High Authority for Social Communication is to be created. The Authority is to play a wide-ranging role to secure the right to information, freedom of the press, independence of the media from political and economic power and the right of reply. In addition, the Authority is to take charge of monitoring the co-existence of different currents of opinion and the right of opposition parties to airtime.

According to law and the Constitution, the High Authority is also empowered "to give its opinion regarding the government's allocation of television licences to the private sector" and to make a public statement, which is fair but not binding, on the appointment and dismissal of directors of publicly or partially state-owned media.

The role of this body, inspired by the French model, is already a subject of controversy concerning how the four representatives of "public opinion, media and culture" are to be elected. The government proposed that they should be chosen by individuals appointed by the government and parliament. The opposition, supported by the Union of Journalists, claimed that the government will, in this way, increase its control over the running of the High Authority. This, the opposition pointed out, would greatly undermine the independence of that body and proposed that members of the public should be chosen from among actors, journalists, consumers' associations and universities. Despite this dispute, the government's proposal was approved.

The High Authority replaced the Council on Social Communication which was regarded as being ineffective in monitoring the level of independence. The power to appoint and dismiss the governors of radio and TV lay solely with the government and the governors were responsible for appointing the directors. Successive governments took advantage of these powers and sometimes journalists were forced to resign because of political pressure from the government. In 1988, press reports questioned the political integrity of the then president of RTP, Coelho Ribeiro, who had allegedly served as a member of the censorship board for theatre under the dictatorial administration of the Estado Novo.

In September 1989, journalist Estevão Gago da Camara was asked to resign from the RTP in the Azores following protests by the government about the way a political meeting was covered by TV.

Dissolution of the Press Council The government has justified its controversial decision to abolish the Press Council by stating that it would allow only one body to deal with the media, the High Authority, so resulting in less bureaucracy. The government also claimed that, unlike press councils in other countries, the Portuguese Press Council was created by decree and not through an initiative of the press. However, the government has offered to allocate funds, if necessary, to the establishment of a new council if required by the majority of journalists and newspaper owners.

The opposition argued that the Press Council had done some excellent work in areas that will not be covered by the High Authority, namely the protection of the rights of journalists, including the right to privacy, the indexing of publications and access to the deliberations of the Union of Journalists (on matters such as the attribution of press cards and the right of reply). The Press Council has succeeded in formulating new guidelines as well as filling obvious gaps in the Press Law. Once it ceases to exist, complaints about the press will cease to be referred to a body able to exercise the role of "moral tribunal" and whose main task in remedying a situation was to request publication of its opinion on the pages of publications considered to be "guilty".

Given the weak tradition of association in Portugal, it is very doubtful that organizations representing journalists and newspaper proprietors will, in the near future, come to an agreement on the creation of a new press council.

The Right of Reply The right of reply has been progressively undermined despite the efforts of the Press Council. Most papers do not publish the reply in the same column in which the offending article appeared, nor do they use the same size print. Replies tend to appear on the letters page and easily pass unnoticed.

Media Concentration The 1975 Press Law ruled that anti-monopoly laws should have been approved within three months of the Press Law coming into effect but no action has yet been taken on this and no-one has protested about the lack of action. There are several reasons why there is no great concern about concentration of ownership. Until recently, the state was the major media owner in Portugal and this had positive effects in terms of the pluralistic and objective style of journalism that developed (the negative effects concerned radio and TV). One of the major Portuguese media owners, Pinto Balsemao, did not stop his paper from criticizing him when he was prime minister and Belmiro de Azevedo, a Conservative industrialist and owner of SONAE, chose a team of journalists considered politically independent to run his papers. Finally, concentration of ownership does not seem, so far, to have resulted in a lack of pluralism and objectivity for the consumers.

Actions

In its 1989 Commentary to the Human Rights Committee ARTICLE 19 expressed concern over government interference in the media, particularly broadcasting; and over the use of the defamation laws which have involved a large number of prosecutions against several independent newspapers.

Romania

At the XIVth Party Congress on November 24 1989, Nicolae Ceausescu was unanimously re-elected General Secretary of the Romanian Communist Party (RCP) and President of the Socialist Republic of Romania. While other countries in Eastern Europe were moving swiftly and dramatically towards democratic free elections and the dismantling of communist control, the power structure in Romania seemed unshakable.

During 1988 and 1989, a few individuals had striven to alert people abroad to the true nature of the Ceausescu regime and the impoverishment, both material and spiritual, imposed on its citizens. In March 1989, the poet, Mircea Dinescu, had an exceed-

	Data	Year
Population	22,940,000	1988
Life expectancy (M/F)	66.9/72.6	1984
GNP (US$ per capita)	2,540	1988
Main religion(s)	Christianity	
Official language(s)	Romanian	
Illiteracy %	4	1985
Daily newspapers	36	1987
Non daily newspapers	24	1986
Periodicals	435	1987
Radio sets	6,600,000	1987
TV sets	3,879,000	1988
Press agencies:		
	Rompres	
ICCPR:		
	YES	1974

ingly frank and critical interview published in the French daily *Liberation*. Following this, he was placed under house arrest, kept under constant guard by the Securitate (secret police) and harassed.

The persecution of a Hungarian pastor, Laszlo Tokes, in Timisoara, provoked massive popular demonstrations against the regime throughout the country. These, initially, were brutally suppressed with many hundreds killed, but culminated in the uprising in Bucharest and the flight of Nicolae and Elena Ceausescu from the capital on December 22 1989. Their execution on December 25 and subsequent events were followed by millions throughout the world in dramatic televison coverage, the first uncensored TV news broadcasts from Romania.

The National Salvation Front (FSN), initially an eclectic group with representatives from the military, intelligentsia and "reform" politicians under the leadership of Ion Iliescu, rapidly proclaimed that it would fill the power vacuum and steer the country to democratic elections by the early spring. The most hated restrictions imposed by the previous regime were soon abrogated, including the lifting of travel restrictions, the depoliticization of the school curriculum and an amnesty for political prisoners. The anti-abortion laws of 1964 and 1985 were repealed and restrictions were imposed on the export of food.

Romanians were no longer limited in their choice of place of residence, were free to make contact with foreigners and to marry foreigners, and no longer had to report conversations with strangers to the police.

Decrees issued on December 28 indicated the future political course of the country and included the following clauses: "In order to achieve a genuinely democratic society in our country and to ensure and defend the basic rights of man and citizen, the programme of the FSN Council envisages: abandoning the leading role of a single party and establishing a pluralistic democratic government system; ...

freedom of press, radio and television and their transition into the hands of the people; ... observing the rights and freedoms of national minorities and ensuring the full equality of their rights with those of Romanians; ... freedom of the cults, guaranteeing the free practice of religious creeds".

On January 4 1990, a further decree guaranteed the right of repatriation of Romanian citizens living abroad, ensuring they would benefit from all political, economic and social rights granted by law to Romanian citizens.

In the following weeks, the "historic" political parties were re-established: the National Liberal Party, under the leadership of the former head of the Young Liberals, Radu Campeanu, who returned from exile in Paris; and the National Christian Peasant Party, which brought back the head of the Union of Free Romanians, Ion Ratiu, from exile in London. Scores of other parties were formed representing ethnic minorities and other interest groups.

Freedom of Expression and Information

After the fall of Ceausescu, a succession of uncensored stories revealed the façade his regime had maintained. These related particularly to the degree of pollution and its effect on people's health; the plight of women, subjected to humiliating gynaecological examinations with a view to ensuring a rapid increase in the birthrate; the suffering of children in orphanages and hospitals and the extent of HIV infection; and corruption and mismanagement at every level of the economy.

The press contributed greatly to the awakening and development of political and social awareness in the general public. Out of this was born the Timisoara Proclamation of March 12 1990, issued by a coalition of organizations and explaining why they had supported and fought in the December revolution. The Proclamation is a crucial document in the process of Romania's democratization. Clause 8 calls for an amendment to the electoral law to prevent former communist activists and Securitate officers from running as candidates for the parliament or for president in the first three consecutive legislatures. The Proclamation circulated throughout the country, gaining some four million signatures. Significantly, in view of the terror which existed in Romania during the past 40 years, the signatories added their addresses and ID card numbers.

Ensuring that full freedom of expression is established in Romania is one of the many tasks facing the new FSN government and President Iliescu, both elected with overwhelming majorities, as they draft a new constitution for the country.

Political Expression

The FSN's announcement in January 1990 that it would stand as a party in the forthcoming elections (which it was supposed to be supervising), caused widespread fear that members of the old RCP were trying to regain power. In protest, veteran dissident Doina Cornea and the poet Ana Blandiana resigned from the FSN along with First Deputy President Dumitru Mazilu. Alexandru Paleologu, appointed ambassador to France, was fired because of his criticism of the government.

During protests against the FSN decision to contest the election, FSN supporters stormed the headquarters of the main opposition parties, the National Peasants'

Party and the National Liberal Party, destroying posters and assaulting people. Simultaneously, organized attacks on the headquarters of the Peasants' Party in Iasi, Notosani, Pitesti, Bacau, Onesti, Slatina and Rimnicu Vilcea and the National Liberal Party in Galati, Bacau, Suceava, Focsani, Pertosani, Ploiesti and other cities were carried out. It is unclear what role the government played in the co-ordination of such attacks. The animosity held by workers toward the Peasants' and National Liberal parties may not have been manufactured entirely by the FSN; prior to World War II, these parties represented the landed and bourgeois classes and mistrust of them has not abated.

On February 23, the Provisional Council passed a law limiting protests to public parks and protecting buildings from public demonstrations, with strict penalties for violations. On August 28, demonstrations in Bucharest's six main squares were outlawed after several days of anti-government rallies.

Electoral Abuse In the weeks preceding the elections there was increasing violence directed at parties and independent groups opposing the FSN. Some parties, especially in smaller towns and villages, were reportedly afraid to conduct campaigns for fear of threats of violence. In some villages people were unaware that there was more than one party, partly due to the shortage of campaign time. The heads of opposition parties received death threats as did reporters from *Romania Libera*.

The most common electoral abuse was the destruction of party posters and campaign materials, which is illegal under Article 84 of the Electoral Law. Attacks on the headquarters of various parties were a common occurrence, including the Peasants' Party and the Liberal Party in Golesti and in Gostuleni. There were no reports of such violence against the FSN. Foreign observers reported that the government manipulated events throughout the election campaign, using exclusive TV coverage, with extremely limited airtime allowed to other parties, and then at times of minimum viewing.

By the end of April, a continuous anti-government protest had been established at University Square (in support of the freeing of Romanian TV from government control) which continued throughout and after the elections. At 4am on June 13, the Square was violently cleared by police armed with batons and electric prods. There were sporadic protests and fighting throughout the day and in the evening some 4,000 protestors stormed the TV building. The government made a radio appeal to factory workers to come to the TV station to "save the democracy" and fighting ensued between protestors and workers. The national TV channel went off the air for more than an hour. Unconvinced that the army would fight the protesters, President Iliescu twice appeared on TV, declaring a state of emergency and calling on miners to come and support the government. (Miners' salaries had recently been doubled by the government.) Transport was provided, as well as accommodation and food, and the miners, armed with iron bars, axes and truncheons, attacked people at random and apprehended anyone they thought might be critical of the government. A group including miners and workers from the Printers' Union, allegedly led by Securitate officer Nicolae Camarasescu, forced its way onto the premises of *Romania Libera*, attacked staff and ransacked its offices. They also attacked the opposition parties' headquarters and the offices of the newspapers *Dreptatea* and *22*, and the "21 December" Association.

Romania Libera did not appear on June 15, 16 and 18, and *22* and *Dreptatea* also stopped printing for a time. Government newspapers demanded that all citizens denounce the protesters at University Square. The printing presses of the National Peasants' Party were destroyed, its leader Ion Ratiu was briefly held and his home ransacked. Radu Campeanu, head of the National Liberal Party, went into hiding. Groups of miners wrecked the School of Architecture and "detained" students including Marin Teodora, Andrea Morarescu and Dinu Marin, who was violently beaten. The president of the Students' League, Marian Munteanu, was forcibly removed from the University, brutally beaten and taken to a prison hospital where he was detained without charge until August 3 when he was released. By 6pm on June 15, according to medical sources, there were 462 injured, six deaths and at least 1,000 people were arrested on suspicion of harbouring anti-government attitudes.

At the first sitting of parliament, Geza Szocs, President of the Democratic Union of Hungarians in Romania, was prevented by the speaker from putting forward a motion asking about the violent suppression of the demonstration and its consequences for the country.

Neither the TV nor the press reported the international condemnation of President Iliescu's actions and no report was made of the USA's decision to withhold economic aid. Instead, the President was shown congratulating the miners for restoring order to the capital. However, in his inauguration speech a week later, he dissociated himself from the miners' "excesses" but criticized elements of the press for inciting protest by their critical articles and promised a tight control on what is published in the future. He also accused the army of not taking a stand against the demonstrators and announced the formation of a special group, loyal to the government, for use in similar circumstances.

The Media

Although the FSN guaranteed the freedom of the media, it did not dismantle the totalitarian apparatus it had inherited. All new political parties (over 80) were allotted equal TV airtime in the run-up to the elections but the FSN retained a tight control on scheduling using 50 per cent of all such available airtime, with the remainder divided amongst the other contending parties.

In August, a proposed new press law, which allegedly contained clauses from Ceaucescu's 1974 press law, was rejected by the opposition press as repressive. In an editorial of August 23, *Romania Libera* proposed that the press law should be completely re-written so as to eliminate its totally vague character, and suggested it should be accompanied by an article to protect copyright. A new version was expected to come before parliament prior to 1991.

Radio and Television Prior to the revolution, people in the west of Romania, including Timisoara, had clandestine access to Radio Free Europe, Voice of America and Yugoslavian TV. This access, combined with the number of immigrants in the region, resulted in this area being more informed than the rest of Romania about events in other Eastern European countries.

Since the revolution, the government has maintained full control of radio and TV. In response to accusations of bias, Aurel Dragos Munteanu resigned as President of Radioteleviziunez Româna Libera, and a non-FSN person was appointed president, but concerns remain about its partiality. During anti-government demonstrations at University Square in Bucharest, Romanian TV showed only those protests occurring during the day when there were fewer people in the Square and not those in the evening when several thousand were present, and only broadcast during the afternoon when the audience was minimal. In this way, news of the protests in Bucharest, Timisoara and Cluj did not reach the provinces. In May, it was announced that a parliamentary commission and not the President would monitor TV and radio.

Radiotelevisiounea Romania transmits on only two of its available frequencies. Channel 1 broadcasts nationwide for 17 hours daily and Channel 2 broadcasts to approximately 13 per cent of households for 10 hours per day. Ion Ratiu, the National Peasants Party leader who wishes to establish an independent television station, had his request denied on the grounds that independent television could not be considered until a media law had been ratified by parliament. On September 3, the Romanian Society for a National Independent Television Company was established with the backing of the independent press.

The Press There has clearly been a change in press freedom since the December revolution and, within days of the overthrow of Ceausescu, a plethora of new titles was launched throughout the country. However, since the FSN retained control over the supply of paper, printworks and distribution, accusations of partiality are frequently expressed.

The Group for Social Dialogue, formed by intellectuals at the end of December 1989, launched a weekly entitled *22* under the editorship of Stelian Tanase which rapidly established itself as an important forum for debate. Newspapers such as the independent *Romania Libera*, *22*, *Dreptatea* (owned by the Peasants' Party), *Express* and *Timisoara* publish articles differing from government opinion. The government has not banned the publication of any newspaper nor engaged in overt discrimination against particular newpapers, although *Romania Libera*, *22* and *Dreptatea* were all prevented from printing for a few days in June when miners raided their offices and destroyed equipment during violence in Bucharest.

The main difficulties these papers have encountered are the lack of independent printing facilities, access to the state-run printing houses which do not have the capacity to cater for the proliferation of titles, chronic newsprint shortages and disruption in distribution. On July 1, a new law stipulated that the independent press must pay quarterly income taxes in advance, based on state-controlled estimates of their future income. On August 1, the government announced a 200 per cent increase in production costs for the independent press and, since September 1, the independent press have been obliged to pay in advance of printing.

In May, 80 leading journalists formed the Democratic Journalists' Union, for "independent and democratic journalists" which will compete with the Union for Professional Romanian Journalists (UPRJ) established in April. The UPRJ was accused by the new union of admitting incompetent and corrupt journalists.

Ethnic Minorities After the overthrow of Ceausescu, the Hungarian minority in Romania demanded more cultural rights including the reopening of Bolyai University and the re-establishment of Hungarian-language schools. Tense relations between Hungarians and Romanians in Transylvania erupted into violence in Tirgu Mures on March 19-20 1990; five people died and over 300 were injured. During the clashes, the UDMR headquarters was ransacked and its contents destroyed.

Investigation of the violence by local officials seems to have focused almost exclusively on Gypsies who supported the Hungarians on March 20 and it appears that the authorities in Tirgu Mures are attempting to make Gypsies the scapegoat. By May, all those convicted and sentenced were Gypsies; of a further 31 under investigation two are Romanian, five Hungarian and 24 are Gypsies. By most accounts, Gypsies represented only a small percentage of those in the vicinity of the trouble and were not implicated to any significant extent in violence. The Gypsies were tried under Decree 153 of April 13 1970 which is directed against those who are "parasites" of the socialist order. Apparently, this decree was intended to apply to those who were unemployed, but the Gypsies convicted had jobs.

Decree 153 does not allow an appeal to a higher court but does allow a retrial by the same court with two judges instead of one. At the retrial of some of the Gypsies, their lawyer requested that one of the judges be Hungarian but her request was refused. It was also reported that the judges ordered a Romanian substitute for a Hungarian prosecutor who happened to be assigned to the court for that day.

After the December revolution, Decree 153 was identified as an extremely abusive tool of the Ceausescu regime. Although it was targetted to be abolished, it remains in force.

Securitate It is not clear what happened to the members of the Securitate which, at its peak, numbered between 10,000 and 20,000, with many more informers. Defence Minister General Victor Stanculescu stated that members of the secret police "directly involved" in the repression of demonstrations in December had been arrested, but gave no figures as to how many were killed, arrested or under investigation. According to Ion Pacepa, Romania's former head of foreign intelligence, fewer than 4,000 members of the Securitate have been sacked.

The government claims to have stopped the bugging of telephones and warrantless searches but former dissidents claim their telephones are still bugged and that they are harassed by telephone calls from the Securitate. On February 21, General Stanculescu stated that the Securitate had been disbanded, but that the army would establish a new internal security group, the Romanian Intelligence Service, who would not bug phones or have powers of arrest, detention, confiscation, search, or of criminal investigation. Although the Minister said that the new organization would be composed of army officers "who have proven their loyalty to the state", he added that its role was to protect the government "from those who would destabilize society", the stated goal of the Securitate during the Ceausescu regime.

Actions

In its 1987 Commentary to the Human Rights Committee ARTICLE 19 called on the Government to end censorship of political expression and to allow freedom to playwrights, writers and poets to independently pursue their art; and to consider the abolition of certain sections of the Press Law, the Decrees on typewriters and copying machines and the Decree on access to foreign visitors.

On July 28 1989 ARTICLE 19 wrote to the Government calling for the release of three Romanian journalists arrested in January for alleged propaganda against the "socialist society".

On November 22 1989 ARTICLE 19 wrote to the Government expressing concern over the expulsion of a number of foreign journalists and the refusal to allow two *Le Monde* reporters into the country.

Soviet Union

Censorship was officially abolished in the Soviet Union on August 1 1990, when the new Law on the Press came into force. The extension of freedom of expression to a degree unimagined only a few years ago is a striking illustration of the dramatic change now taking place in the USSR. Sweeping constitutional and political reforms have led to the creation of new political institutions and fundamentally transformed the political climate. There is a hesitant but growing recognition that pluralism and opposition are natural aspects of the development of civil society. However, the attempt to reform an unwieldy and inefficient system has led to an accumulation of seemingly intractable problems: a collapsing economy, the proliferation of crime,

	Data	Year
Population	286,717,000	1988
Life expectancy (M/F)	62.8/72.7	1985
GNP (US$ per capita)	4,550	1988
Main religion(s)	Christianity	
	Judaism	
	Islam	
Official language(s)	Russian	
Illiteracy %	1	1985
Daily newspapers	723	1986
Non daily newspapers	7,792	1986
Periodicals	5,275	1986
Radio sets	192,100,000	1987
TV sets	88,000,000	1987
Press agencies:		
APN, TASS, Postfactum		
ICCPR:	YES	1973

widespread ethnic unrest, and the advancing paralysis of central authority. In the course of 1989-1990, national front movements gathered strength with the result that toward the end of 1990 all the Union republics of the Soviet Union have proclaimed their national sovereignty as have some of the subordinate autonomous republics and regions. Although the Soviet Constitution always proclaimed the right of the Union republics to secede from the Soviet Union (Art.72), it provides no mechanism for the exercise of that right. In April 1990, shortly after the Lithuanian unilateral declaration of independence, the Supreme Soviet passed a law on secession which envisaged a lengthy and unwieldy process that made independence a virtual impossibility. Although the contents of the declarations of sovereignty vary considerably, most proclaim the supremacy of republican over all-Union laws and republican ownership of natural resources. The much-publicized confrontation between President Mikhail Gorbachev and Boris Yeltsin (President of the Russian Republic) is only the apex of an ongoing power struggle unlikely to be resolved by the new draft Union Treaty published in November. The Treaty reserves the right to determine defence, foreign and overall economic policy for the Union and retains a "coordinating" or "regulating" role in almost all other areas. The three Baltic republics and Georgia have already stated that they will not sign the Union Treaty, whatever its provisions, because they want full independence, even from a new union of sovereign soviet republics.

The resurgence of traditional ethnic animosities has resulted in thousands of deaths in violent clashes between Kirghiz and Uzbeks, Georgians and Abkhazians, Azeris and Armenians. In many republics the Russians are blamed for widespread poverty and ecological disaster. In Russia, the national-religious renaissance has fostered a virulent anti-semitism that is perceived to be a serious threat by Soviet

Jews who are emigrating in large numbers. Vulnerable groups fear that minority rights will be sacrificed on the altar of self-determination. There are now more than one million internal refugees from ethnic violence, with over 40,000 in the Moscow area alone. These displaced persons lack basic rights as well as bare necessities and little is being done to help them.

Constitutional Change On March 13 1990, the Congress of People's Deputies voted to abolish the Communist Party's constitutionally guaranteed monopoly on power (Art.6), thus radically transforming the political foundation of the Soviet system.

As part of a package of sweeping constitutional changes, deputies also voted for the creation of a presidential system and endowed the new executive president with extensive political prerogatives. Within weeks, Mikhail Gorbachev's personally-appointed Presidential Council replaced the Politburo of the Communist Party as the central policy-making body of the country. Less than a year later, however, in an atmosphere of developing crisis, new structures were devised. An up-graded Council of the Federation is intended to involve republican presidents in policy-making while a "modern-minded" Council of Ministers is to be under the direct control of the President rather than the Prime Minister; the President is also to head a new Security Council in charge of law and order.

The Communist Party itself is in disarray. The rebellion of republican parties against Moscow, the departure of Boris Yeltsin at the 28th Party Congress, the resignations of many prominent radical figures (including the mayors of Moscow and Leningrad, Gavriil Popov and Anatoly Sobchak), and the downgrading of the Politburo, all reflect an increasingly acrimonious conflict about fundamental issues, as well as about property and power.

New Parties New parties have been forming at a rapid rate: Constitutional Democrats, Christian Democrats, Liberal Democrats, Social Democrats, and also Monarchists and Greens. A United Workers Front of Russia opposes *perestroika* from a conservative and nationalist standpoint. The bloc of Russian Public-Patriotic Movements serves as an umbrella organization for a number of conservative and ultra-nationalist groups. The Democratic Russia Bloc which won control of Moscow, Leningrad and other large cities in the 1990 local elections includes people of diverse and often contradictory views, from social democrats of the Communist Party of the Soviet Union (CPSU) to liberals who reject the socialist idea in its entirety, all united by a belief in democracy.

In October 1990, the USSR Supreme Soviet passed a law granting equal status to all political parties, thus providing the legal framework for a multi-party system. The most contentiously debated aspect of the new law concerns the role of political activity in the army and law enforcement agencies. A compromise provision was adopted calling for military and law enforcement personnel to be guided by law rather than the decisions of any party. However, the Communist Party's extensive organizational structure in the armed forces has been left intact.

The "Law Governed" State At the Nineteenth Party Conference in June 1988, President Gorbachev announced his intention to transform the Soviet Union into a "law governed" state. A major review of the entire legal system is currently under way and, in November 1989, a commission was appointed to draft a new constitution. The debate about ideal models of legal systems focuses on three main areas of concern: the limitation of government, protection of the individual, and economic arrangements (the legal system still reflects the dynamics of a planned economy). Because of the present weakness of legal institutions and the low level of legal culture, bureaucratic regulation and "telephone justice" (courts subject to political interference) are still characteristic aspects of Soviet life.

In September 1990, however, the Committee for Constitutional Supervision did suspend a presidential decree transferring control of demonstrations and public events in central Moscow from the city soviet to the USSR Council of Ministers. Although there is as yet no guarantee that legislation judged to be unconstitutional will be repealed, the Committee's affirmation that the head of state is not above the law is an important step toward the establishment of the rule of law in the Soviet Union.

In the past, the legal codes of all the republics were centrally drafted and virtually identical. Republican soviets now demand the power to legislate independently on a wide variety of issues. In October 1990, the USSR Supreme Soviet passed a law establishing the precedence of all-Union laws throughout the Soviet Union until a new Union treaty is agreed upon. Within hours, the RSFSR (Russia) Supreme Soviet adopted a law declaring that all acts and laws of the all-Union authorities, including presidential decrees, would take effect in the RSFSR only after they have been ratified by the RSFSR Supreme Soviet. The precedence of republican over all-Union legislation has also been asserted by Ukraine and Byelorussia.

Freedom of Expression

Glasnost It is generally agreed that *glasnost* is the one clear success story among President Gorbachev's reforms. During 1990, the evolution of *glasnost* has reached the point where even the most outspoken articles are no longer regarded as a sensation. Virtually all remaining taboos have been broken, from the question of party privileges to the role of the KGB; even Lenin is no longer beyond criticism. The current debate deals with the very fundamentals of the Soviet system and is, to all intents and purposes, unrestrained. One striking aspect of the new "openness" is what Andre Fontaine has called the "reunification of the language". Words and concepts (democracy, justice, law) once again have the same meaning East and West after years of hollow "newspeak" rhetoric. It is now accepted that there are "universal human values" that transcend the interests of social class.

Yuri Afanasiev, who was appointed Rector of the Moscow State Historical Archive Institute in 1986 and who has become an increasingly radical critic of the Soviet system, maintains that "there is no people and no country with a history as falsified as Soviet history". Soviet society is now undergoing a painful process of learning about itself and reclaiming its collective memory.

The first revelations of *glasnost* treated Stalin and Stalinism as a phenomenon *sui generis*, without historical antecedents. Only later did it become possible to ask questions about roots and causes, blasphemous questions directed at the most sacred taboos of Soviet culture. Critical assessments of Lenin's legacy, including terror, forced labour and a Marxist class approach that "justifies any form of violence", first appeared in the work of scholars and journalists (Tsipko, Selyunin, Klyamkin) and in two long-suppressed novels that were published in 1989, Solzhenitsyn's *Gulag Archipelago* and Grossman's *Forever Flowing*.

During 1990, further disclosures about more recent events aroused great interest both within the Soviet Union and abroad: the Hitler- Stalin Pact, the Katyn murders, the invasion of Czechoslovakia, and the war in Afghanistan (although there is still little information available about the devestation inflicted on that country by Soviet forces). Details of the Ukrainian famine of 1932-1933 are to be published after more than 50 years of silence and denial.

Glasnost has had a considerable impact on the arts as well as the media. A major "restructuring" took place within the film and theatre unions leading to the screening of films which had been banned for years and to greater independence for theatre directors in choosing more adventurous repertoires.

The loosening of ideological control has opened the way for the expression of freer sexual attitudes; the sexual act was portrayed on the screen for the first time in a 1989 film called *Little Vera*, to the consternation of many older Soviet citizens who complained to the press in large numbers. The sensation of 1990 was Stanislav Govorukhin's bitter film, *We Can't Live Like This*, which represents the Soviet system itself as founded on crime, from the murder of Nicholas II and his family to Stalin's mass murders and beyond. Nikolai Gubenko, a popular actor and director and also the new Minister of Culture, has pledged that the government will not impose limits or guidelines upon the arts as in the past.

The Limits of Glasnost Although by 1989-1990 overt censorship rarely took place, there were regular examples of interference by party authorities in the coverage of politically sensitive issues and events.

Lithuania Reports in the Soviet media on the first crisis in Lithuania almost entirely reverted to the one-sided polemical style that was usual in the pre-glasnost era. During the period of blockade, Lithuania was closed to foreign correspondents with the exception of shepherded tours under the auspices of the Foreign Ministry.

Chernobyl For almost four years responsible officials were able to conceal information about the true scale of the Chernobyl disaster and only recently has the cover-up been exposed. People were kept in ignorance and not evacuated from territory where dangerously high levels of radiation have caused an alarming number of health problems, birth deformities and deaths. Farms near the arbitrary 18.5 mile exclusion zone have, reportedly, produced contaminated food which was distributed throughout the Soviet Union.

AIDS Officially imposed silence about AIDS, which until recently was dismissed as a disease of Western decadence and not a problem in the Soviet Union, has left the country ill-prepared to combat the spread of the virus or treat its victims. There is widespread ignorance about the disease as well as a basic lack of sterile facilities, disposable syringes and reliable condoms. In April, the leading liberal magazine *Ogonek* published a plea for an end to the criminal prosecution of homosexuals (who still face five years' imprisonment if charged). Although largely ignored in big cities, the law is still enforced in the provinces and is seriously hampering the anti-AIDS campaign since homosexuals are understandably reluctant to come forward for testing.

Abuses Under Brezhnev Despite a general policy of filling in the blank spots of Soviet history, there are, apparently, still constraints on the exposure of "justice" under Leonid Brezhnev. Many take the view, and President Gorbachev is among them, that society is too unstable to risk exposure to a possible "witch hunt". People sent to labour camps and psychiatric hospitals for criticizing the system were "pardoned" or released in a haphazard fashion without rehabilitation or compensation. A presidential decree in August 1990, restoring Soviet citizenship to those who were exiled between 1966 and 1988, was described by the radical deputy of Moscow, Sergei Stankevich, as "only the first step in the right direction for settling old debts". In October 1990, the Chairman of the KGB, Vladimir Kryuchkov, said on Radio Moscow that all persons convicted for anti-soviet agitation and propaganda in the 1960s and 1970s should be rehabilitated, although he made no mention of compensation for years of unjust imprisonment. However, Lev Timofeev, a former political prisoner and editor of the *samizdat* journal *Referendum*, won a libel suit against the newspaper *Sotsialisticheskaya Industriya*, which had stated that Timofeev, along with three other former prisoners of conscience, had engaged in "anti-socialist activities". The Moscow court ruled that the article was slanderous and that the newspaper must publish an apology.

During 1989, as part of the government's campaign to gain respectability before the World Psychiatric Association meeting in Athens, certain publications were permitted, even encouraged to publish material about the abuse of psychiatry for political purposes. A number of articles appeared exposing the unethical practices of certain psychiatrists. Nevertheless, the long-discredited official leadership of the profession remained unchanged, including Dr Georgy Morozov, head of the Serbsky Institute (who retired in August 1990) and Dr Marat Vartanyan, head of the Soviet Centre for Psychiatric Health. Thus, the same men who dominated the profession for two decades and were responsible for the internment of dissidents in psychiatric hospitals are still in a position to obstruct reform (including more effective legislation on psychiatric procedures and patients' rights) and to deny the fact that the political abuse of psychiatry ever took place. No doctors have been punished, nor have their victims received compensation.

Access to the Media During March 1990 local elections, independent candidates found it extremely difficult to gain access to the press or television. The official media rarely reported incidents of police dispersal of pre-election rallies or cases where the authorities refused to register independent candidates. The overwhelming victory of democratic activists in Moscow and Leningrad was achieved with the help of home-made posters (a ruling against them in Moscow was widely ignored) and *samizdat* publications.

May Day Coverage of the 1990 May Day celebration in Red Square was distorted by the media. Although *Izvestia* reported the premature departure of President Gorbachev and his party from the scene when faced with hostile demonstrators, most newspapers published glowing accounts with only passing reference to "extremists" and "provocateurs" who attempted to spoil the holiday. *Vremya*, the main evening news programme, concentrated on the official part of the proceedings and showed only brief and carefully selected shots of the second parade organized by the pro-democracy Moscow Voters' Association.

Insult of the President In May 1990, the Supreme Soviet enacted a law to protect "the honour and dignity" of the President. Under this statute, public utterances "insulting or slandering" the President are punishable by a fine of up to 3,000 roubles or up to three years' imprisonment (six years if the offending remarks were published or broadcast). During the parliamentary debate, one deputy wondered whether jokes could be grounds for legal action, while others expressed concern that the new measures could be used to stifle criticism and restrict freedom of speech.

Samizdat In the first half of 1990, distributors of *samizdat* materials still experienced sporadic harassment, detention and the confiscation of their "illegal" (unregistered) publications. On the whole, registration has become more straightforward under the new press law (see below), although there have been examples of obstacles encountered by independent publishers, notably former political prisoner, Sergei Grigoryanis, the editor of *Glasnost*.

New Legislation In 1989, the two offences that explicitly circumscribed freedom of expression (Article 70 on anti-Soviet propaganda and Article 190-1 on slandering the Soviet state) were removed from the Criminal Code. It was under these Articles that thousands of innocent people were imprisoned during the Brezhnev years. An attempt to introduce a new Article which made it a crime to "insult or discredit state organs or public organizations" was rejected by the Congress of People's Deputies. Finally, a law "On Criminal Responsibility for Crimes Against the State", which outlaws only calls for the use of violence, was approved by the Supreme Soviet in July 1989.

On June 12 1990, following a prolonged and heated dispute, the Supreme Soviet adopted a Law on the Press that guarantees a degree of freedom of expression unprecedented in Soviet history, including the abolition of censorship. The provision of the law which aroused the most controversy gives individuals as well as associations the right to found a publication by means of a simple registration procedure with few grounds on which registration can be refused. Journalists are promised access to information and their guaranteed rights include the possibility of refusing to prepare material that runs counter to their convictions. Restrictions on freedom of the press are limited to the publication of state secrets, calls for violent political action, the dissemination of pornography and the propagation of racial, national or religious intolerance.

In August, *Glavlit* (the former censorship body) was transformed into the Main Administration for the Preservation of State Secrets in the Mass Media (GUOT) and instructed to function as a consultative organ. Misgivings about this new body were expressed in an *Izvestiya* article which claimed that GUOT has already issued a secret list of forbidden topics which included non-military matters such as cattle viruses. Critics have also pointed to the law's failure to deal with the CPSU's near monopoly of publishing facilities and control over access to paper. During 1990, *Novy Mir* did not appear for several months in succession because paper was not made available. In the autumn of 1990, a number of popular Soviet publications took advantage of provisions of the press law that allowed them to form collectives and become independent of their former "founders". Thus, the conservative Writers' Union can no longer exercise broad rights to close down liberal periodicals or dismiss their editors and will also be deprived of an important source of income.

On September 26, the Soviet parliament approved in principle a Bill on freedom of conscience and religion which will allow citizens to propagate their beliefs. Previously, the laws decreed that a person could not undermine the Communist state by "spreading religion". The new law also allows religious activity in the armed forces where atheism was always strictly enforced.

Ethnic Hatred In a situation of escalating ethnic tension, the press law's prohibition of the propagation of racial intolerance will pose difficult tests for the principle of freedom of expression. Pro-democracy demonstrators in Moscow have protested about the "growth of fascism" and urged the authorities to take action against the anti-semitic activity of extremist groups. There has been extensive criticism of an apparent official reluctance to institute proceedings under Article 74 of the Criminal Code which forbids the propagation of ethnic hatred or intolerance. In early 1990, however, a case initiated by the Procurator General against Konstantin Smirnov-Ostashvili, a member of the extreme right-wing Pamyat group who led a violent raid by Pamyat members on a meeting of the independent writers' organization, Aprel, screaming anti-semitic slogans. In October, a Moscow court sentenced him to two years in a strict regime labour camp.

Radio and Television On July 15 1990, on Soviet TV, President Gorbachev called for "cardinal changes" in the state broadcasting monopoly, including a considerable degree of decentralization and the elimination of party control. In his statement, he urged the Supreme Soviet to approve a new law prescribing the rights and responsibilities of radio and TV, appropriate to the new conditions of political pluralism. Although the statement suggests a federal approach to broadcast control and recommends that provision be made for independent studios and TV centres to compete for broadcasting contracts, it nevertheless reserves licensing rights to Gostelradio and the Ministry of Communications.

At present, one government body, the State Committee for TV and Radio Broadcasting (Gostelradio), headed by Mikhail Nenashev, oversees both radio and TV. It is a centralized organization controlled by President Gorbachev's allies within the party apparatus and remains one of the strongest levers of his personal power. There are two national networks, both originating from the Central TV Studios in Moscow. Local TV stations have their own limited broadcasting schedules which are not allowed to conflict with important social or political broadcasts from the central stations. The technical base of Gostelradio satellite telecommunications is controlled by the Ministry of Communications which is part of the military-industrial complex and is as secretive as other defence sector ministries.

Under conditions of *glasnost*, Soviet TV has been able to deal with issues of genuine public concern: ethnic problems, the economic crisis, disputes in the Supreme Soviet, corruption; subjects which until quite recently could not have been touched. The presentation of news on TV was transformed by newly-appointed editors whose fresh approach considerably increased its variety and reliability. Party control, however, has been most evident in the reporting of international news, where TV, much more than the press, tends to reflect the policies and views of the government. Party authorities have also been able to ban individual programmes.

Eduard Sagalayev, editor-in-chief of the evening news programme *Vremya*, has publicly discussed the pressures which compelled him to present an unbalanced picture as events unfolded in Lithuania. Critics of Central TV claim that its reluctance to provide in-depth coverage of ethnic conflicts, even if motivated by fear of making the situation worse, has resulted in a damaging loss of public trust.

A major challenge to the control of Central Television has been launched as part of the political struggle now under way between the central and republican authorities. Rejecting the central government's proposal to allot a "Russian channel" at Gostelradio, the Russian Federation proclaimed television to be an issue of sovereignty and announced the creation of the All Russian Radio and Television Company, to be serviced by three of its own telecommunications satellites. Support has been found among some of the young journalists of Gostelradio (notably the makers of the popular programme Yzglyad) who have become more radical than the first generation of reformers.

In May 1990, authorization was given for the reception of satellite TV channels. Its prohibitive cost will restrict the number of Soviet citizens able to buy or import a satellite dish, but even limited availability of Cable News Network TV or European transmissions is bound to have an effect on the Soviet media. As the struggle for control intensifies, Soviet TV, which has played such an important role in the development of *glasnost*, could be on the threshhold of momentous change.

Actions

In its 1989 commentary to the Human Rights Committee ARTICLE 19 discussed the limitations of *glasnost* and urged the Soviet Union to enact and enforce legislation that would guarantee freedom of expression and information.

Spain

Media and communications in Spain expanded considerably in 1989. Two national daily newspapers were launched, three private television licences and a substantial number of radio licences were granted. These developments in the electronic media are causing a debate familiar elsewhere in Europe over state versus private involvement in communications. Plans to privatize TV and restructure radio have led to predictions that the new commercial ownership will dominate these media and that local community stations will be eliminated.

Article 20 of the 1978 Spanish Constitution guarantees "the right to communicate freely or receive any accurate information by any means of dissemination whatsoever". In addition, "the exercise of these rights cannot be restricted by any form of prior censorship". The article adds, however, that these rights are limited by "the right to honour, privacy, personal reputation, and the protection of youth and children". Further limits are contained in Organic Law 8/84 (the "anti-terrorist law") and by Organic Law 1/82 concerning the right to honour, personal and family intimacy and personal reputation (*proprio imagen*). Article 55 of the Constitution further states that the right to free expression may be suspended by the proclamation of a State of Emergency or state of siege.

There is ambiguity over the term "accurate information", which is used in the Constitution again in Organic Law 2/84. This enables individuals to request the media to publicly correct inaccurate information published about them and to appeal to the courts if the media refuse such a request. A similar protection is afforded by Organic Law 1/82.

Spain is now a party to the European Convention on Human Rights and the Constitutional Tribunal tends to interpret the Constitution in line with the European law on human rights.

	Data	Year
Population	38,832,000	1988
Life expectancy (M/F)	72.5/78.5	1980
GNP (US$ per capita)	7,740	1988
Main religion(s)	Christianity	
Official language(s)	Spanish	
Illiteracy %	4.6	1990
(M/F)	2.6/6.6	1990
Daily newspapers	105	1986
Non daily newspapers	85	1986
Periodicals	1,998	1986
Radio sets	11,473,000	1987
TV sets	14,900,000	1989
Press agencies:	EFE, Colpisa, Agencia de Informacion, Europa Press, Multipress, Iberia Press	
ICCPR:	YES	1977

The Media

Newspapers Only 80 newspapers are sold for every 1,000 inhabitants (108 on Sundays), but there are indications that sales are slowly increasing, with a rise of 13 per cent between 1982 and 1987. The General Director of Social and Communications Media decided in 1988 that this increase was substantial enough to end direct subsidies for newsprint and distribution given to the press since 1977. The grants had encouraged the modernization of an industry that had been ailing under Franco, but the decision to end them was also required by European Community law. Economic support will now be indirect, such as reduced postal rates and no value added tax. It is doubtful that this will compensate for the loss of direct subsidies.

Advertising revenue is substantial but the loss of government subsidies, along with low sales figures, will lead to even greater dependency on advertising for survival. In 1988, of all the media, newspapers received the greatest share of advertising expenditure, 35 per cent, or 143,100 million pesetas (US$1,431 million); in 1989 this increased by 28 per cent. The government invests significant sums in advertising and there have been allegations that it exerts control over the media by discriminating in favour of newspapers offering favourable rates.

In 1989, two national quality daily newspapers were launched, *El Mundo del Siglo XXI* and *El Independiente*. *El País*, a politically liberal newspaper, is Spain's best seller with a daily circulation of 376,230 (819,112 on Sundays).

Concentration of ownership is accelerating, with 33 proprietors owning over 60 per cent of the press. Sixteen per cent of newspapers account for 60 per cent of sales.

Magazines General interest magazines which focus on scandals and the private lives of personalities are very popular; the so-called "heart-throb" press sell three times more than *El País*. *Pronto*, a weekly TV magazine, had a circulation of 924,216 copies in 1988.

Since the law for "the protection of honour, privacy and personal reputation" came into force in 1982, these magazines have frequently been charged with violating its principles. The most famous case in 1989 was that of celebrity Marta Chavarri. She brought lawsuits for slander and invasion of privacy against *Interviú* over photographs taken of her while in a discotheque which she claimed showed "her most intimate sexual characteristics". Such cases occur quite frequently; in 1987, there were 330 court cases. As a result, the law has been criticized for excessively impeding press freedom.

Radio With an average weekly audience of 18 million, radio is a powerful instrument for dissemination of information. Sociedad Española de Radiodifusión (SER) and Radio Nacional de España (RNE) are the two biggest and most popular radio networks. RNE is a public broadcasting service and only began to accept advertising in 1990.

At the beginning of 1988, the Ley de Ordenación de Telecomunicaciones came into force following opposition in parliament from the private sector. A year later the Plan Técnico was approved. Both laws granted substantial powers to the government in deciding which private broadcasters are eligible for licences. In 1989, the authorities offered 153 new FM licences, to be awarded through a "public" competition as previously determined by the Plan Técnico which regulates radio and TV transmissions.

Only two of these licences were awarded to existing unlicensed or "free" radio stations (community radio stations whose aims are, in general, social and cultural rather than commercial). About 100 such stations have formed a committee to try and gain legal recognition and the right to broadcast. Without the financial resources of advertising, the community stations are unable to meet costs for improved technical equipment or supply the basic capital which the government has declared necessary to compete for a licence.

Television There are two new government-owned channels based in Madrid, TV1 and TV2, broadcast by Radio TV Española (RTVE). The Basque region, Catalonia and Galicia have their own TV stations which broadcast in the local language. In the Basque region, residents have a choice of two channels besides TV1 and TV2: ETB1, which broadcasts in Euskera, and ETB2 in Castilian. Catalonia also has two stations, TV3 and TV33 which began regular transmission in April 1989, and the majority of programmes are in Catalan. Opinion polls show that two-thirds of the population use TV as a primary source of information.

Channel 33 recently began broadcasting to the Valencian region in response to popular requests there. The authorities protested that this was illegal and halted transmissions, arguing that the number of channels in each community has to be limited to ensure the survival of each. The decision has led to widespread protest that Catalans are being denied the right to receive and impart information in their own language.

In 1990, private TV began broadcasting in Spain. Licences were awarded in August 1989 to three of seven applicants in a competition under the Plan Técnico; the licences are limited to a 10-year period and only three were available. Minimum capital of 1,000 million pesetas (US$10 million) and a monthly rental fee of 305 million pesetas (US$3 million) is charged for airspace. Critics of the licensing procedure claim that all but the most powerful aspirants, who have access to large amounts of capital and technical expertise, have been excluded.

Antena 3 is owned by banks, businesses and newspapers, and will be financed by advertising. Unlike any existing channels, the private TV companies plan to give their programming a specific focus; for example, Antena 3 will broadcast news and sport. Telecinco is also owned by a large conglomerate; the Italian media baron, Silvio Berlusconi, owns 25 per cent of the shareholding. Telecinco plans to allocate 80 per cent of its programming to shows and competitions. Canal Plus will be a pay-TV, with 10 per cent of its income coming from advertising and the rest from a fixed charge of about 3,000 pesetas (US$30) per month for each subscriber. Canal Plus will devote 55-60 per cent of its programming to films and the rest to music, theatre and sport.

Satellite TV is gaining popularity quickly. By 1988 there were 25,000 antennae installed in Spain and at least 20 channels are now received.

Attacks on Journalists The attitude of private security guards and the police often presents serious problems for the press. In 1988, Ricard Cugat, a photographer for *El Periódico*, was assaulted by a private security guard when he attempted to take photographs during a rock concert in Barcelona. The victim made a formal complaint but nothing resulted from it. Also in Barcelona, a photographer for *Avui* was beaten by a policeman during the general strike on December 14 1988, despite wearing visible identification. Kim Manresa, working for *La Vanguardia*, was taking photographs of police evicting tenants when he was arrested. Officers tried to take his camera but he gave it to a passer-by who later handed it in to *La Vanguardia*. The photographer was escorted away handcuffed and it is alleged that he was insulted and threatened during the journey to the police station. *La Vanguardia* said that the police chief had attempted to persuade its editor to minimize the incident in return for Kim Manresa's freedom.

Freedom of Opinion and Expression

Organic Law (1/82) on Protection of Reputation has been a source of complaint by all media. It is claimed that the main newspapers follow a tradition compatible with the law and rarely censure the armed forces or government ministers.

The authorities appear particularly sensitive over press representation of the monarchy and leading political figures. In December 1987, the political cartoonist Jesús Francisco Zulet was charged with contempt for drawing an unflattering cartoon of Prime Minister Felipe González. The charges were later dropped. In November 1987, journalist Juan José Fernández Pérez was sentenced to six years' imprisonment for insulting King Juan Carlos in *Punto y Hora* magazine. Satirizing the Pope can also be restricted.

In November 1989, Jesús Fabo Legarda was acquitted of slandering the King. The previous February, while the King was visiting the Basque region, Jesús Fabo hosted a live phone-in public debate on the free radio, Eguski Irratia, in Pamplona, about the King's visit. Fabo claimed that although people insulted the King, there were also others who supported him, and he had not actually expressed his own opinion on the King.

The law on "right to honour and personal reputation" was invoked in June 1990 in a celebrated case involving José María García (Butanito), a popular radio journalist. He was convicted of slander arising from calling the Spanish Football Federation President, José Luis Roca, "little pebble", and for revealing that he had falsified travel expenses. The court accepted that this accusation was true but decided he had violated the law by words which made fun of someone's height and name. The court upheld a four-month prison sentence which included an earlier suspended sentence for calling a government minister a "clown". However, the government finally intervened and his sentence was commuted to a fine of 600,000 pesetas (US$5,500).

The Co-ordinadora Lurraldea, a group comprising ecologists and others concerned by plans for a new motorway between Navarra and Gizpuzkoa, protested in 1990 against what they saw as a clear breach of their right to freedom of expression through the mass media. The group criticized the refusal of RTVE to accept publicity for a video which explained their project for an alternative to the motorway. Basque Television and two newspapers, *El Diario Basque* and *El Correo Español*, also refused to accept publicity for the video. A spokesperson for Co-ordinadora Lurraldea reported that RTVE would not accept the advertisement because of its supposedly political content. However, RTVE have broadcast publicity for the county council which sets out the advantages of the construction of a motorway in the area.

Basque Region The Basque region is particularly aware of restrictions on freedom of expression resulting from the central government's efforts to suppress the violence of the Basque separatist organization ETA. *Egin*, the daily paper reflecting ETA views and which is linked to the separatist party, Herri Batasuna, is under constant vigilance and criticism from the authorities; state subsidies have been withheld and state-owned companies have refused to advertise in *Egin*. The government's view is that *Egin*, whose circulation in the Basque region is 42,000, is little more than a front for terrorism. The current director has frequently appeared in court to answer charges over articles but no convictions have been sustained against the paper. Basque radio stations which operate without licences are continually suppressed and their equipment confiscated.

During the general elections in October 1989, Herri Batasuna was denied TV and radio election airtime. In November 1989, four Herri Batasuna elected representatives were ordered to leave parliament after they refused to promise to uphold the Constitution in the usual manner. They stated that they did not recognize the jurisdiction of the Spanish Constitution over the Basque nation and were forced to abide by its principles "by legal imperative". In June 1990, the Constitutional Court ruled that the Basque representatives could add the qualifying "by legal imperative" when being sworn in, and so take their seats in parliament.

Censorship of Basque Publications Abroad In France, in April 1988, the Minister of the Interior prohibited the book *Euskadi Gaduan* which was written and published in the Basque region, claiming the book threatened public order. In Switzerland, all copies of the magazine *Euskadi Information*, printed in Freiburg, West Germany, were confiscated by the public prosecutor on August 4 1989.

Actions

On November 22 1989 ARTICLE 19 wrote to the government condemning the murder of Josu Muguruza and the serious wounding of Inaki Esnaola, both members of parliament for the Basque Herri Batasuna Party, by an extreme right-wing group. ARTICLE 19 requested the government to do everything necessary to find those responsible.

In its 1990 Commentary to the Human Rights Committee, ARTICLE 19, among other points, called for a review of the long prison sentences awarded in libel cases, and asked the government to do everything in its power to ensure that journalists are free to work unimpeded in accordance with the rights guaranteed in Article 19 of the Covenant.

Sweden

In 1766, the Swedish parliament adopted a Freedom of the Press Act, the earliest legislation of its kind. The emerging press was given the right to act as a watchdog. The present Freedom of the Press Act dates from 1949 and is specially protected by being part of the Constitution. The Swedish press, radio and television operate in a rare climate of freedom but, paradoxically, by the standards of countries less fortunate, the media are considered less forceful and enterprising in reporting on public affairs.

Freedom of Information The principle of free access to public documents dates back to the Act of 1766, and is regarded as a vital part of Swedish democracy. This principle gives anyone

	Data	Year
Population	8,436,000	1988
Life expectancy (M/F)	73.7/79.6	1985
GNP (US$ per capita)	19,150	1988
Main religion(s)	Christianity	
Official language(s)	Swedish	
Illiteracy %	1	1985
Daily newspapers	114	1986
Non daily newspapers	72	1986
Periodicals	46	1986
Radio sets	7,300,000	1987
TV sets	3,314,000	1988
Press agencies:		
Svenska Nyhetsbyran, SIP,		
Tidningarnas Telegrambyra		
ICCPR:	YES	1971

the right to go to a state or municipal agency and ask to be shown any documents in the files, regardless of whether the document concerns them personally or not. Officials are legally required to comply and even to supply copies of the document if requested. In most cases the officials may not ask the applicant for identification or the reason for the request. As soon as any letter or document arrives at a public authority's office, anyone has the right to read it, regardless of whether the addressee has read it or not. It is not only mail to the authorities that is public, but so too are most documents written by the authorities themselves.

The computer storage of information by the authorities caused initial problems. In 1974, the law recognized computerized material as public documents, although citizens themselves were not entitled to search for information. After much debate, an amendment was adopted in 1982 which permits anyone to use a computer terminal provided by the authorities to find out what is stored. Concern has been expressed, however, over the failure to address issues of personal privacy alongside open access to computer data.

The difficulty of extracting usable information is the concern voiced by the press. Only about five per cent of government agencies have computer systems that separate open and secret information. Furthermore, it is almost impossible to obtain new (but not secret) information from government databases which are not programmed to supply such information.

Exempt Documents Documents that may be withheld from public scrutiny are those dealing with national security, foreign policy and foreign affairs. Other documents relating to criminal investigations and the personal integrity or financial circumstances of individuals are also restricted to prevent criminal misuse. Exceptions to the general rule of accessibility are spelled out in the Official Secrets Act.

Any type of document not explicitly listed in this Act is by definition available to the public.

Anyone who is refused a public document is immediately entitled to a written statement quoting the legal authority for withholding the document. Information must also be given about a right to appeal, ultimately to the Supreme Administrative Court. The only cases in which there can be no appeal are those in which secret decisions are made by the Cabinet, Parliament, the Supreme Court and the *justitieombudsman* (parliamentary ombudsman). One of the duties of the latter, however, is to ensure the right of access to public documents.

Private Sector In 1988, the government caused a storm of protest by proposing a law that would make it a criminal offence for employees to reveal secrets about the company they worked for. The goal was to protect companies from illegal competition, but it was seen by critics as a way to silence employees and diminish their rights to protest against working conditions, environmental pollution or illegal acts by companies.

The most famous "whistle-blower" in Sweden is civil engineer Ingvar Bratt. When he worked for the arms manufacturer Bofors in 1985 he leaked documents to the media about illegal arms sales. He became a symbol of resistance to the proposed law which became widely known as *Lex Bratt*. The legal establishment was divided in its views as to whether Bratt would have been sent to jail had the proposed law been in effect.

The proposed law was amended to allow serious or illegal misdeeds to be revealed, and was passed by a majority in Parliament. At the same time the government appointed a parliamentary committee to consider ways to introduce freedom of information in the private sector. One member of this committee is Ingvar Bratt, who represents the Green Party.

The Media

Censorship Censorship of the press is explicitly forbidden. Anyone has the right to establish a newspaper or magazine and the Freedom of the Press Act prevents the authorities from raising obstacles to printing, publication and distribution.

By protecting those who communicate information to the media, the law also encourages the supply of information. Responsibility for the content of newspapers, magazines and other periodicals is vested in a single person, known as the "responsible publisher", who is usually the editor-in-chief. The Act protects all other editorial staff and third parties from prosecution or liability on account of their contribution to the publication.

Protection of Sources The law explicitly prohibits the investigation or disclosure of a journalist's sources. This protection is extended to state and municipal employees, who are thus free to give information to the media without fear of legal repercussions or intimidation.

It is not regarded as a problem in Sweden that immunity of informants might induce some of them to leak irresponsible, harmful or even untruthful statements to the media. The law may protect the informant but does not exonerate the crime. The "responsible publisher" can be prosecuted for publishing matter actionable by law.

There are some exceptions to the general rule of anonymity of sources. If state employees, including military personnel, inform the media of matters that could jeopardize state security, they could face legal action. The same applies if a doctor violates professional secrecy by disclosing information given in confidence by a patient. The protection of anonymity may also be overruled in a criminal case which does not involve the freedom of the press, and where the court finds that the disclosure of a source is justified by an overriding public or private interest.

In 1988, a court ordered a reporter on *Dagens Nyheter* (the largest morning paper) to reveal her source for conversations obtained by the police in secret recordings of telephone calls. (Such material appears excluded from protection of sources.) The reporter did not test the limits of the law, and told the court her source.

Legal Safeguards The media are protected from legal harassment by the Freedom of the Press Act. A decision to prosecute must be made by the Chancellor of Justice not an ordinary local prosecutor, and the consent of the Cabinet must be obtained in cases with political ramifications.

Trial regulations are also modified when press cases are heard. Cases are tried by jury, an institution otherwise alien to the Swedish judicial system. At least six of the nine jurors must be in agreement for a conviction. The judges may acquit a person, despite a jury verdict of proven, but may not overrule a finding of not proven.

Investigative Journalism The Freedom of the Press Act does not give the Swedish media access to everything. The private sector is protected and has no obligation to give journalists the information they seek. Many journalists gather stories from the easiest sources, where the law gives them automatic access to information. So state and local authorities are scrutinized, while private companies and other privately-run bodies often have a comparatively easy ride. But there has been a reaction within the Swedish press after several notable failures in which non-journalists exposed stories in the foreign press. These were the early stages of the Palme murder-hunt; the Bofors arms affair; and the Fermenta scandal, involving the sudden collapse of one of Sweden's leading enterprises. Inspired by the 3,000-member US organization, Investigative Reporters and Editors, Gravande Journalister (digging journalists) was launched in 1989. Their aim is to increase in-depth reporting by sharing experiences and by arguing for more space and greater resources for investigative journalism.

Code of Ethics As distinctive as Sweden's formal guarantee of press freedom, is the discipline achieved by the journalists' own ethical code and procedure. In 1916, the Press Council was founded to function as a tribunal for reviewing the practices of the press. A Code of Ethics was adopted to guide the press and serve as a basis for the Council's work. In the 1960s, in response to increasing criticism of press behaviour and to avoid a threat to the Freedom of the Press Act, the National Press Club, the Newspaper Publishers' Association and the Union of Journalists volunteered a number of reforms. The most important of these were lay representation on the Press Council and the creation of the Press Ombudsman. The system is voluntary, and is financed entirely by the press, including the journalists' union.

Press Ombudsman The task of the Press Ombudsman is to mediate between the general public and newspapers and to help individuals assert their rights by ordering the publication of corrections and rejoinders. For example, if a complaint concerns a minor breach of the Code of Ethics, the Press Ombudsman can issue a censuring opinion. Other complaints are transferred to the Press Council for judgement.

If the Press Council censures a newspaper, the paper has to print the decision and pay a fine to the Council. The complainant is also free to sue the newspaper for damages in court in accordance with rules of the special court system for press cases. Damages are low, rarely more than the equivalent of a few thousand US dollars.

The annual number of complaints is approximately 400 and only one quarter of these are transferred to the Press Council. About 20 per cent of the complaints result in a censuring opinion, either by the Press Ombudsman or by the Press Council.

Defamation Actions for libel are infrequent. In May 1990, Stockholm City Court ruled that an article in the magazine Z libelled former tennis player Bjorn Borg and ordered it to pay substantial damages. Z had published an article in which Borg's former lover said that he had used cocaine. The court ruled that the article was "unjustifiable", whether it was true or not. The judgement has been heavily criticized because Z was not allowed to offer evidence as to the truth of the statement, and because truth was no defence. Among others, the Press Ombudsman has asked whether the law should be changed on this point. An appeal was lodged with the Supreme Court.

Open Justice It is generally considered unethical in Sweden to mention the names of defendants in court cases, unless they are public figures, although justice is otherwise public and open to the media. Considerations of the defendant's future rehabilitation in society and of the family's embarrassment are taken to override those of the public's right to know.

Films Films intended for public viewing are previewed by the National Board of Film Censorship which can delete certain sequences or ban the film altogether. There have been attempts through the years to have film censorship abolished, but they have all been defeated.

Turkey

The legal maze surrounding publishing in Turkey is such that Fatma Yazici, one-time editor of the left-wing *2000'e Dogru*, said she spent more time in court than at her desk. That was before she left the country in 1989, unable to withstand the pressures of dozens of cases against her under several Turkish laws restricting freedom of expression.

Although the military handed back power to civilians after general elections in 1983, from which most shades of civilian opinions were barred, mass trials in martial law courts continued in 1990. The 1982 Constitution and associated legislation introduced by the military, such as the Law on Political Parties, the Associations Law, and the Press Law, continue to function and reflect the military's desire to maintain strict curbs on political activities of which they disapprove.

	Data	Year
Population	50,664,000	1988
Life expectancy (M/F)	60.0/63.3	1985
GNP (US$ per capita)	1,280	1988
Main religion(s)	Islam	
Official language(s)	Turkish	
Illiteracy %	19.3	1990
(M/F)	10.3/28.9	1990
Daily newspapers	24	1986
Non daily newspapers	519	1986
Periodicals	2,670	1986
Radio sets	8,400,000	1987
TV sets	9,000,000	1987
Press agencies:	Akajans	
Anatolian News Agency, EBA,		
ANKA Ajansi, IKA, Tuba,		
Hurriyet Haber Ajansi, UBA		
ICCPR:	NO	

A whirlwind of economic and social change in Turkey following the 1980 coup did not include reform of penal code articles taken from Mussolini's Italy in 1926 nor an end to what Amnesty International in January 1989 called "brutal and systematic abuse of human rights". In October 1990, the government was discussing the possibility of executing political prisoners as part of measures needed to combat political violence.

Eleven mainly Kurdish-speaking provinces in south-east Turkey, soon to be divided into 13 provinces, make up a "State of Emergency Region" where a local Regional Governor has wide powers which, in some cases, cannot be appealed.

The government is dominated by Turgut Ozal, elected President by parliament in November 1989 after six years as Prime Minister. The 1989 presidential election was boycotted by all opposition parties, a significant protest since in March 1989 the ruling Motherland Party came a poor third in local elections with only 21 per cent of the popular vote. President Ozal frequently states that he believes freedom of thought and religion will solve Turkey's conflicts, but his critics say that he has not made headway against the establishment view that such freedoms should be kept under strict control.

Freedom of Expression

There are a wide variety of statistics cataloguing state prosecutions under laws curtailing freedom of expression. Turkey's non-partisan Press Council, founded on

February 6 1988 to campaign for a better and freer Turkish press, documented 118 cases in 1989, mostly against left-wing or pro-Kurdish publications. ANKA news agency counted 183 cases against 16 Istanbul publications alone. Turkish reports quoted by Helsinki Watch, the New York-based human rights group, said a total of 400 journalists were prosecuted in 1989.

The 1982 Constitution, drawn up and approved by referendum during the 1980-1983 military takeover, is the Turkish Republic's third, and in important ways much more authoritarian and less liberal than the previous 1960 Constitution. Article 2 of the Constitution provides for a democratic, secular state "within the concepts of public peace, national solidarity and justice". Article 12 states that "everyone possesses inherent fundamental rights and freedoms" but Article 13 cautions: "Fundamental rights and liberties may be restricted with the aim of safeguarding the state, comprising its territory and the nation, national sovereignty, the Republic, national security, public order, general tranquillity, public morals and public health and also for special reasons designated in the relevant articles of the Constitution."

Article 14 continues in the same vein, saying that none of these rights may be used to violate Turkey's territorial integrity (for example, Kurdish separatism); establish the hegemony of one social class over others (for example, Communism); or "create discrimination on the basis of language, race, religion or sect".

There are provisions in the Constitution against "anyone who writes or prints any news or articles which threaten the internal or external security of the state ... or which tend to incite offence, riot or insurrection". Under other articles, opposition and minority opinions may be silenced, foreign publications may be prohibited and any publication may be confiscated or suspended temporarily.

The instruments used to curb dissent are penal code Articles 141 and 142 (added to the 1926 penal code in 1936), which aim to keep communism and Kurdish or any other kind of separatism at bay, and Article 163, which is aimed against religious (particularly Islamic) extremism. Most of Turkey's political prisoners are convicted under Articles 141 and 142. In April 1990, more than 200 intellectuals, journalists and singers called for "the immediate lifting of Articles 141, 142 and 163 and an end to all arrests and detention for 'thought' crimes".

Other articles in frequent use against non-violent dissent are 140 (damaging Turkey's reputation abroad), 158 (insulting the president), 159 (insulting the authorities), 311 (inciting others to commit a crime) and 312 (praising a crime).

Lawsuits and criminal investigations are a form of punishment in themselves. A trial may last many years, with a hearing only once a month or less often. Political trials lasting nearly a decade are not uncommon. During the trial period, the accused person is not allowed to travel abroad and may be imprisoned and released at intervals by the court pending the final verdict.

The Kurds In April 1990, the government issued Decree 413, among whose 13 points was the threat to close printing presses that undermined its fight against Kurdish rebels if their reports were false, "excited the population" or "disturbed public order". Initially aimed at the mainly Kurdish-speaking provinces, the edict was quickly extended to cover the whole country.

Turkey's "State of Emergency Region" was formed in July 1987 to help crush a Kurdish insurgency that started in 1984 and had claimed over 2,000 lives by March 1990. The State of Emergency in the south-east has never been debated or approved by parliament. The rebel Kurdish Workers' Party (PKK) demand autonomy leading to possible full independence for Turkey's 10 million Kurds. The PKK carry out acts of terrorism in pursuit of their aims and their violence is cited by officials as a reason not to allow cultural or language rights to Kurds.

Kurdish rights are not proscribed by name, only by implication. For instance, Law 2932 of October 1983 bans any "expression or publication of thoughts in banned languages that aim to divide the state or upset public order" and goes on to define banned languages as "any other than the first languages of any state recognized by the Turkish government". The ban is extended in Article 3 to cassette tapes, records, posters and even money-changers' signs.

There are a number of prominent cases such as that of the former mayor of Diyarbakir, Mehdi Zana, who refuses to speak Turkish in court. He has now served nearly 10 years of a 24-year sentence imposed because of his Kurdish views. The bans have been gradually relaxed in recent years: Kurdish villagers can and do get translators in court, Kurdish tapes are freely available and, despite occasional harassment, Kurdish songs can be heard in south-eastern nightclubs.

Government ministers admit that there are many places where people do not speak Turkish and officials close to President Turgut Ozal have frequently promised a new approach to the laws. But anti-Kurdish laws remain and can be invoked at will.

Current Detainees Some 3,000 people are in jail or detention awaiting trial under laws restricting freedom of expression. According to *Cumhuriyet* newspaper on November 23 1989, about 85,000 people had been tried since the 1980 coup under Articles 141, 142 and 163. The newspaper estimated that 15,000 Turks live abroad for fear of prosecution at home. At any one time, about two dozen journalists or writers are in jail or awaiting trial under these or similar laws restricting freedom of expression.

The Media

Newspapers Istanbul is the home of most major Turkish newspapers. The major dailies are *Cumhuriyet, Milliyet, Tercuman, Turkiye, Sabah, Hurriyet,* and *Gunes,* most of which are also printed in Ankara, Izmir and other regional centres. Total circulation is under three million copies a day, low for a population of 51 million, despite some of the most modern colour printing technology in the world. Editors blame low rates of literacy, high prices and, to some extent, low quality of content.

The Turkish press has had an uneasy relationship with government for over 100 years with recurrent episodes of censorship, imprisonment, court cases and murders of journalists. A system of governmental press regulations and privileges, including the use of press cards to license journalists (who may be refused them), curbs many potential critics. These pressures, combined with a population which is largely only semi-literate and keen for sensationalist stories featuring blood, nudity and political scandal, produce a national press of extremely low quality. This is compounded by Turkey's legal system which allows newspapers to publish with impunity libellous and untrue allegations about individuals while making the expression of many types of political opinion a criminal offence.

The press barons of Turkey also retain a high degree of control. Asil Nadir, an Anglo-Turkish Cypriot industrialist, who bought several leading newspapers and magazines in Turkey in 1988 and 1989, was criticized by the independent Press Council for instructing his editors early in 1990 that all reports about Cyprus should be vetted by his office before publication. A number of reputable *Gunes* journalists resigned from the Press Council in protest.

As martial law gradually diminished through the 1980s, newspapers experienced more freedom to cover political debate, to publish accounts of human rights abuses and to print the words "Kurds" and "Kurdish" in reference to the country's largest but officially unrecognized minority ethnic group; the word *Kurdistan*, however, remains strictly taboo. Journalists report that they use considerable self-censorship when writing about such taboo subjects which also include the Armenian question and the army.

Since there is no mechanism for formal censorship in Turkey, new curbs on the press in Decree 413 of April 1990 rely heavily on self-censorship. This decree followed President Ozal's unsuccessful attempts to put a stiff new press law through parliament to legislate against "false news". The law, which faced great resistance from the Istanbul press, would have added to current restrictions in the 1986 Harmful Publications Law (usually used against pornography), the 1982 Constitution and 153 other pieces of legislation relative to the press dating back to the 1920s.

Up until 1990, the government has only taken action according to the law; it prevented the distribution of newspapers it found offensive 50 times in 1989, according to the Press Council's February 1990 report. In April 1990, however, even before Decree 413 was implemented, political police entered the offices of three major newspapers to order that articles about a new witness in the June 1988 assassination attempt on President Ozal should not be published. The justice minister later said that such action was illegal.

Interior Minister Abdulkadir Aksu took this approach one stage further after Hurriyet Holding, the publishers of *Hurriyet*, decided in April to break its contract to print the pro-Kurdish *2000'e Dogru* because it was too risky under Decree 413. Speaking while the contents of the publication were unknown, Mr Aksu told deputies: "If Hurriyet had published *2000'e Dogru*, we would have closed them down." A further 16 journals are suffering similar difficulties in finding printers because of the risk of closure under the decree. In addition, the national press now employs severe self-censorship when reporting events or disturbances in Kurdish areas, sometimes simply failing to mention them.

In an unusually strong condemnation, Nezih Demirkent, president of the Turkish Journalists' Association, said of the decree: "The government may defend the supremacy of the law, but the way it has put itself above the law has breached all human rights, not just those of the press. From now on it is impossible to speak of the rule of law or a democratic society."

In June, *2,000'e Dogru* was closed down following its detailed coverage of Kurdish unrest. On August 7, its publishing director, Dogu Perincek, was arrested in connection with speeches he had made referring to the Kurdish issue. He was charged under Article 142 with dissemination of separatist propaganda, and the state prosecutor is demanding a 25 year prison sentence.

President Ozal has been vigorous in bringing libel charges against his critics, and schoolchildren have even been prosecuted for criticizing him in their homework. In 1989, a member of parliament was prosecuted and fined for insulting Ozal in a parliamentary question which alleged corruption in the Ozal family. After two national newspapers, *Sabah* and *Bugun*, were banned from printing a hard-hitting series hinting at widespread corruption in Ozal's family circle, the Press Council said in a statement on May 23 1989: "We must all see that today in Turkey the biggest obstacle to press freedom is Turgut Ozal."

In a case still pending appeal, *Tercuman* columnist Nazli Ilicak has been ordered to pay 300 million Turkish lira (US$130,000) to over 100 deputies from the ruling Motherland Party for referring to them as Ozal's "Pavlovian dogs".

Attacks on the Press Perhaps more serious than the legal trial of strength between press and government is a worrying tendency of physical attacks on journalists: 48 attacks by state employees, almost all police, and 23 other attacks by readers or others were recorded by the Press Council in 1989. The Council again blamed President Ozal for encouraging an aggressive police attitude in his speeches attacking the press. In the nine months to March 1990, five people were killed in attacks on the press, four of them journalists. Kurdish rebels are believed to be responsible for the killing of a *Hurriyet* reporter in south east Turkey. Two more were separately shot dead by readers who felt their honour was besmirched by reports in *Gazete*, a sensationalist Hurriyet Holding newspaper that has since folded, and Cetin Emec, a senior *Hurriyet* columnist and board member, was shot dead with his chauffeur by unknown assailants. On September 4 1990 Turan Dursum, a columnist with *Yuzyil* and its predecessor *2,000'e Drogu*, who had written articles critical of Islam and the Koran, was shot dead. The journal had requested police protection for him but this had been refused.

Foreign Press A number of foreign journalists operate in Turkey and there are occasional conflicts between them and the Turkish authorities. In January 1990, the Ministry of the Interior ordered the expulsion of a British freelance journalist, apparently because he was a Jehovah's Witness, but the order was later withdrawn. In April, the elected Mayor of Nusaybin, in south east Turkey, was removed from office after allegedly telling Reuters and BBC correspondents about support among the local population for the PKK guerrillas. In June 1990, the Director General of Press and Information warned the Ankara correspondent of the UK *Sunday Telegraph* that she could be expelled or prosecuted if she continued to write unfavourable articles such as a recent profile of President Ozal's wife.

There have been more serious clashes in the past. In 1984, the Turkish Foreign Ministry made a formal complaint to the editor of the UK *Financial Times* about the activities of David Barchard, then the paper's Ankara correspondent. Earlier in the 1980s there was an attempt to place the previous *FT* correspondent, Metin Munir, on trial for a news item by him on the BBC Turkish Service. He was also periodically summoned for questioning by the military on other matters. In 1983, the then Turkey correspondent of UPI, a Turkish national, who had written a string of hard-hitting human rights articles, was beaten by Istanbul police when applying for a passport and accused of working against the country. Months of police harassment followed including an abortive attempt to frame him for murder. Seven years later, although no longer facing legal charges, he is still not allowed to travel abroad. His case is periodically quoted by Turkish employees of the foreign press to discourage their younger colleagues from going too far.

Books In December 1986, 39 tonnes of books, periodicals and newspapers were pulped. Among the publications were *The Penguin Map of the World, National*

Geographic Atlas of the World, the Turkish edition of the *Encyclopaedia Britannica* and the *Nouveau Petit Larousse Illustré*. All had been declared "means of separatist propaganda" by the Turkish authorities for containing articles or maps related to the history of the Armenians and Kurds. A new Turkish edition of the *Encyclopaedia Britannica* ran into immediate problems with the authorities in 1987 because its view of history conflicted with theirs. An independent editorial committee is now in charge of the edition.

Cumhuriyet newspaper reported on July 30 1989 that the Turkish Armed Forces had banned 96 writers and 280 books as reading matter for its personnel, including all works by Turkey's best-known writer, Yasar Kemal, and other books by writers from Tolstoy to Hemingway. The report added that 356 books had been investigated, forbidden or seized since the 1980 coup.

Book bannings, a hallmark of the early to mid-1980s, have diminished. In April 1990, publisher Suleyman Ege won an Administrative Court decision that the state should pay him damages and interest for 133,000 copies of 30 books destroyed by martial law authorities in December 1982. The destruction had been carried out despite the fact that the books had been approved by the courts.

Overall, a huge variety of books is being published in Turkey. Some have met with great success despite government disapproval, such as *Where is Turgut Running From?*, a tendentious, racy account of President Ozal's career by *Hurriyet* columnist Emin Colasan, which sold over 100,000 copies. Mr Colasan is now on trial for defaming the President, but his case has turned into something of an embarrassment for the government with opposition politicians and national celebrities giving evidence in his defence.

Radio and Television All Turkish electronic broadcast media is controlled by the state, and radio and TV stations come under the aegis of the state-run Turkiye Radyo Televizyon Kurumu (TRT). However, satellite dishes are selling throughout Turkey and municipalities are testing legal limits by plans to re-broadcast foreign satellite transmissions in Turkish towns and cities.

Repeated government promises of private commercial TV have so far come to nothing, but three colour channels are now available in major cities and many rural areas. A January 1990 study for the State Planning Organization noted that more people had colour TVs than running water.

An international service is being prepared for satellite transmission to the *gastarbeiter* (guest worker) Turks in Europe and in April 1990 was already available in major Turkish city centres.

One ex-TRT director has been in Germany to establish a rival TV station to TRT. Known as Magic Box, and rumoured in the press to be backed by relatives of the President, it started satellite transmission in mid-1990.

Evening news bulletins usually reflect state protocol priorities rather than news values. The opposition frequently complains of bias, but coverage of opposition points of view has been given since political rights were restored to pre-1980 coup politicians in September 1987.

There have recently been increasing restrictions on the right of opposition leaders to appear on TV. In July 1990, Suleyman Demirel and Deniz Baykal were banned at the last moment from giving TV interviews on the grounds that they would infringe laws on local elections. Several opposition leaders have now begun giving interviews to the satellite channel Magic Box as the only alternative available.

Film Censorship A new film law of February 1986 transferred chairmanship of the Upper Censorship Committee from the Ministry of the Interior to the Ministry of Culture and Tourism, which has brought greater tolerance. The other committee members are a military representative, two state bureaucrats and one person each from the music and cinema industries.

None of the 107 films made in Turkey in 1989 suffered stringent censorship and no films in the 1990 Istanbul Film Festival were censored. However, erotic scenes from the wide variety of international films now shown in Istanbul tend to be cut, sometimes so heavily as to make understanding the plot difficult.

In February 1990, the film *Umut*, directed by the late Yilmaz Guney, the country's most famous film-maker who was stripped of his nationality in 1982, was screened for the first time in nine years under a temporary import permit. All Guney's works had been banned since 1982.

A proposed new law to "simplify" censorship, placing it completely in the hands of film producers, was being discussed in mid-1990. The main criteria for censorship were to be pornographic content and offences against the unity of the Turkish Republic, meaning Kurdish separatism.

Actions

On March 23 1990 ARTICLE 19 wrote to the government protesting the detention of Tunca Arslan, director of *2000'e Dogru*, and the banning of two issues of the magazine after it argued that Kurds should be allowed an independent state within Turkey. ARTICLE 19 also protested the arrest and detention of Ismail Besikci, author of a banned book on the Kurdish question, and called for the release of both men and a lifting of the ban on their publications. Besikci was released on bail in July and was due to stand trial on charges of making separatist Kurdish propaganda.

United Kingdom

The United Kingdom has no written constitution, only a series of constitutional principles and conventions, the most fundamental of which is the sovereignty of Parliament. There is no constitutionally significant protection of freedom of expression or of information. Any protection there is depends upon conventions of restraint on the part of the law-making and law-enforcement authorities. Restraint does exist but has become increasingly superficial. This has been amply demonstrated in recent years as former Prime Minister Margaret Thatcher sought to re-assert secrecy as a central principle of government, and the courts have set novel and far-reaching precedents of prior restraint on the press, radio and television.

	Data	Year
Population	57,077,000	1988
Life expectancy (M/F)	71.4/77.2	1984
GNP (US$ per capita)	12,800	1988
Main religion(s)	Christianity	
Official language(s)	English	
Illiteracy %	1	1985
Daily newspapers	124	1989
Non daily newspapers	882	1984
Periodicals	6,408	1984
Radio sets	65,000,000	1987
TV sets	24,650,000	1987
Press agencies:		
Associated Press Limited,		
Exchange Telegraph Co Ltd,		
Press Association, Reuters, UPI		
ICCPR:	YES	1976

If 1988 was dominated by the book *Spycatcher* and the world-wide efforts of the British government to suppress it, 1989 was dominated by the novel *The Satanic Verses*, published on September 26 1988 in London. After initial hesitation, following the *fatwa* (religious edict) pronounced on Salman Rushdie by the late Ayatollah Khomeini, which called for the author's murder (see Iran entry), the UK authorities acted in defence of the book and its author while acknowledging that the novel offended Muslims. *The Satanic Verses* has resurrected a debate in Britain long thought to be over, about the law of blasphemous libel and whether it should be abolished. The larger question of Salman Rushdie's personal security remains unresolved with the author under the protection of the police and in hiding.

Otherwise, the debate in the UK over freedom of expression continues to circle inconclusively around four issues: government secrecy, executive interference, pressure on and manipulation of the media, and what to do about the collapse in journalistic standards in the tabloid newspapers.

Although the UK has no written constitution, it has acquired two sets of external constitutional laws: the treaties establishing the European Community (EC), and the European Convention on Human Rights. While Community treaties do not contain any principles relating to freedom of expression, Community law is beginning to move into relevant areas, such as TV broadcasting, telecommunications and copyright.

Article 8 of the Council of Europe's European Convention on Human Rights protects privacy, and Article 10 protects freedom of expression and information. The UK has accepted the right of individual petition and the compulsory jurisdiction of the European Court of Human Rights and has defended several Article 10 cases before the Court, winning some, such as *Handyside*, and losing others, such as *The*

Sunday Times case. Unlike many other contracting states, the UK has not incorporated the Convention into its domestic law. Several initiatives to adopt it as a Bill of Rights have failed. Article 10 therefore cannot be applied by the courts, although legislation has been changed as a result of the Convention; *The Sunday Times* case led to the Contempt of Court Act 1981 and *Malone* led to the Interception of Communications Act 1985, introducing safeguards on phone tapping. Several of the most significant freedom of expression issues in the UK are pending before the European Commission of Human Rights (see below).

Laws Restraining Expression

Libel In February 1990, a government review of defamation law proposed changes aimed at curbing excessive libel damages awards by juries. The main change would give the Court of Appeal power to reduce or increase a jury award it considers inappropriate. The present law has been attacked as a serious constraint on freedom of the press and, from the public's point of view, the cost of suing newspapers is prohibitive. There have been several large awards by libel juries, particularly against newspapers. The *Star* had to pay £500,000 (US$900,000) to Jeffrey Archer, the former deputy chairman of the Conservative Party, after it alleged that he had visited a prostitute, and in May 1989, *Private Eye* was ordered to pay £600,000 to Sonia Sutcliffe, wife of a convicted mass murderer, after claiming that she had sold her story to a daily newspaper. The amount was reduced to £60,000 in a settlement. However, the highest award was made against a private individual, Nikolai Tolstoy, who had written a pamphlet about the forcible repatriation of Cossacks and Yugoslavs at the end of World War II. In November 1989, he was ordered to pay £1.5 million damages to Lord Aldington.

Two Private Member's Bills seeking to protect people from press intrusion into their private lives failed to pass through Parliament in 1989: a Bill to provide a right of reply, and a Protection of Privacy Bill which would have enabled an individual to sue anyone who published private information without consent. The Bills were unsuccessful largely because of the announcement of a government inquiry under David Calcutt QC to consider the adequacy of the law on newspaper breach of privacy.

Contempt of Court The courts have powers to postpone or ban the publication of information which, in their view, might threaten the administration of justice. A breach of such an order is contempt of court.

In December 1987, the Court of Appeal prevented Channel 4 Television from broadcasting a contemporaneous re-enactment, using actors, of highlights of the "Birmingham Six" appeal against their 1974 convictions for Irish Republican Army (IRA) bombings in Birmingham. The Lord Chief Justice held that the broadcast "was likely to undermine public confidence in the administration of justice" and would therefore amount to contempt of court. A similar order was made against Channel 4 during the Clive Ponting Official Secrets trial in 1985. In June 1990, Ulster Television failed to relay a four-hour drama-documentary, which was carried in other regions, on the alleged shoot-to-kill policy of the security forces in Northern Ireland in the early 1980s. The station cited fear of the law on contempt of court as justification for its decision. In 1988, the government introduced a right of appeal against a court's decision to exclude the press after losing a case before the European Commission of Human Rights.

In July 1990, the Court of Appeal fined the editor of *Private Eye* and its publishers £10,000 each for serious contempt. *Private Eye* had published two articles on Sonia Sutcliffe while her libel action against the magazine was pending.

Protection of Sources On April 10 1990, William Goodwin, a trainee journalist on *The Engineer* magazine, was fined £5,000 for refusing to comply with a court order to reveal the source of confidential information he had been given about a company's financial affairs. The company, citing potential financial loss, sought disclosure to identify the source whom they believed to be from within the company. The House of Lords ruled that the administration of justice required disclosure, although the company had already won an injunction to stop publication by Mr Goodwin of an article based on the information and a court order to maintain its anonymity.

Journalists have the right under the Contempt of Court Act to protect their sources except where disclosure is "necessary in the interests of justice or national security, or for the prevention of disorder or crime". The decision against Goodwin is regarded by journalists as rendering this limited statutory protection effectively valueless. Mr Goodwin is taking his case to the European Commission of Human Rights.

Police and Criminal Evidence Act (PACE) 1984 Journalists, particularly photographers, are increasingly at risk when covering demonstrations. In the past four years, several have been injured by demonstrators or by police, their equipment has been damaged and some have been arrested on charges of obstruction or incitement to riot. There is increasing use of the PACE to compel photographers and media organizations to hand over unpublished material leading journalists to fear that they are being used to collect police evidence. Some journalists have destroyed material or sent it to the International Federation of Journalists in Brussels rather then accede to court orders.

The poll tax riots of March 31 1990 led to the biggest round-up by British police of unpublished pictures and film. Within days, the Metropolitan Police applied for court orders to compel 29 news organizations to surrender unpublished pictures and untransmitted film of the event. Most media organizations unsuccessfully contested the applications. When challenged as to whether the confiscated material would be used in police investigations, the judge stated that until he had seen the material, he could not tell if it was relevant. Some newspapers published photographs which led to arrests. As a result, TV camera crews and press photographers were the target of physical and verbal abuse from angry crowds during another poll tax demonstration held on October 20; leaflets had been distributed which stated that all photographers, TV crews and journalists were "legitimate targets".

Spycatcher From 1986 to 1990, a series of contempt of court proceedings, arising from injunctions prohibiting publication of extracts from *Spycatcher*, written by former government intelligence agent Peter Wright, were pursued against national newspapers.

The central question raised during the course of conflicting legal decisions by the courts concerned the extension of the laws of confidence and contempt to silence all other media organizations through an injunction issued against only one. Thus, the

Spycatcher case has shown that a single injunction for breach of confidence can bind everyone in the UK.

In June 1986, the government obtained an injunction against *The Observer* and *The Guardian* which had published some of the allegations made in the then forthcoming book. In April 1987, *The Independent* and several other papers carried reports based on the book and, in July, *The Sunday Times*, which had obtained serialization rights, printed extracts. The newspapers argued that they were not affected by the initial injunction. However, the government obtained a ruling from the House of Lords banning all media in Britain from reporting on the book's allegations pending the outcome of the legal action against *The Observer* and *The Guardian*.

In December 1987, Mr Justice Scott set aside the original injunction, rejecting the government claim that national security must always have priority over freedom of the press. On May 8 1989, *The Independent*, *The Sunday Times* and the *News on Sunday* were each fined £50,000 (US$90,000) on the ground that they intended to prejudice legal proceedings between the government and *The Observer* and *The Guardian*. The fines were waived by the Court of Appeal on February 27 1990.

On October 25 1990, the European Commission of Human Rights ruled that the government was in breach of Article 10 of the European Convention on Human Rights in its injunctions against *The Guardian* and *The Observer*. The decision will now be considered by the European Court of Human Rights.

Privacy There is no privacy law as such in the UK, except for the Data Protection Act 1984 which applies privacy principles to computerized databases.

The Calcutt Committee on Privacy reported in June 1990 and among its recommendations, which have been accepted by the government, are the replacing of the existing Press Council by a Press Complaints Commission on a non-statutory basis. Unlike the Press Council, the new body, to be established and funded by the newspapers themselves, will not be concerned with promoting press freedom but would concentrate on giving redress to those who complain of unfair treatment and invasion of privacy by the press. Significantly, the new Commission would also have a specific responsibility to initiate enquiries, thus acting as both judge and jury. The proposals in the Calcutt report were presented as a last opportunity for self-regulation, failing which, legislation would be introduced.

The Committee recommended new criminal offences: entering or planting a bugging device on property without permission in order to obtain information for publication; and taking a photograph or tape-recording on private property with the intention of identifying the subject for publication. The report also suggests that the courts should be given power to make an anonymity order, where necessary, to protect the mental or physical health or personal safety of a victim of crime.

The reaction of the newspapers to the proposals has been broadly hostile, tempered by the fact that their own efforts to raise standards have failed. In joint declarations in November 1989, the editors of most national newspapers agreed on a code of acceptable behaviour and pledged to appoint readers' representatives or ombudsmen to deal with readers' complaints. The signatories to the declaration included mass-market tabloid papers which attract the most serious complaints. This was followed in December 1989 by a more detailed code of practice issued by the Press Council. Both codes stressed the need to protect privacy, publish corrections, give readers the opportunity to reply, and to avoid racial slurs. The new press ombudsmen system has been criticized because the majority of the appointments have been internal.

Secrecy

The Official Secrets Act On March 1 1990, a new Official Secrets Act came into force replacing section 2 of the Official Secrets Act of 1911. This law followed an attempt to introduce alternative legislation by Richard Shepherd MP in January 1988. Mr Shepherd's Protection of Official Information Bill had allowed for a "public interest defence" for unauthorized disclosure of information where the existence of crime, abuse of authority or other misconduct was revealed. That Bill was defeated by 37 votes. The new Act does not provide for any form of "public interest defence" and created four absolutely protected categories of information: information the government considers damaging to defence; information entrusted in confidence to other states or international organizations; information concerning the activities of the security and intelligence services, and international relations.

A lifelong duty of confidentiality is imposed upon Crown Servants which includes members of the intelligence and security services.

Inside Intelligence Temporary injuctions taken out against *The Scotsman* in late 1987, and *The Observer* and *The Sunday Times* on New Year's Day 1988, prohibited the papers from publishing extracts from the memoirs of a former intelligence agent, Anthony Cavendish, entitled *Inside Intelligence*. Cavendish was deemed to have broken the lifelong duty of confidentiality in publishing personal memoirs of activities concerning World War II. On November 18 1988, the government warned the US monthly magazine *Harper's*, not to distribute in the UK copies of its December 1988 issue which carried extracts from the banned memoirs.

Shortly before, *Granta* magazine had been forced to comply with the terms of the same injunction in both its British and US editions, printing only those extracts from the memoirs approved by the Attorney General, Sir Patrick Mayhew.

Colin Wallace Colin Wallace, a former senior information officer at British Army Headquarters in Northern Ireland, has repeatedly claimed that in the 1970s he was instructed to spread disinformation to denigrate elected politicians, including former Prime Ministers Edward Heath and Harold Wilson, through an operation codenamed Clockwork Orange. Wallace claimed that this had been organized by MI5, the domestic branch of the Intelligence Service, with the approval of Army Intelligence in Northern Ireland. Wallace also claims to have been unfairly dismissed from his post when he refused to continue with Clockwork Orange and to have been "framed" for manslaughter.

In May 1987, the government issued statements denying Wallace's allegations but refused to carry out a full public inquiry into the matter on the ground that there was insufficient evidence to suggest that such illegal operations had taken place. In Feburary 1990, new documentary evidence was finally brought to public attention. The Prime Minister told the House of Commons that she and Parliament had been "misled", and an inquiry, limited to the circumstances of Wallace's dismissal, was ordered. In September 1990, he was paid £30,000 for unfair dismissal.

Under the new Official Secrets Act it is doubtful whether Colin Wallace would now be able to make his allegations, nor would it be possible for the media to report on them.

Security Service Act The 1989 Security Service Act placed the security service on a statutory footing for the first time. The Act gives power to the Home Secretary to issue warrants for "entry on, or interference with, property" to obtain substantial information for the protection of national security.

The government resisted attempts to amend the Bill including the introduction of either parliamentary supervision of the service or a Security Service Commission which would report annually to the Home Secretary, thus providing an external check on MI5. MI6, the intelligence service which collects information from abroad, continues to operate without any statutory authority or official acknowledgement that it exists.

Access to Information The UK has no general freedom of information legislation, and its secrecy code, the Official Secrets Act, is widely regarded as too extensive. Government papers are made accessible after a 30-year period which can be extended for up to 100 years for materials considered sensitive.

For more than a decade, the Campaign for Freedom of Information, a broad alliance of groups and individuals, has sought new legislation to open up government and to reform the Official Secrets Act. The need for freedom of information laws was highlighted when, under the 30-year rule, records released for 1957 disclosed that the then Prime Minister, Harold Macmillan, had ordered the suppression of information on an accident at the Windscale (renamed Sellafield) nuclear plant. The release of radioactivity reached levels 600 times those of the Three Mile Island accident in the United States, making it the worst known nuclear accident before Chernobyl. These facts had been suppressed until the release of government papers in January 1988.

Some limited advances have been made. The Local Government (Access to Information) Act 1985 provides for greater access to local council meetings, agendas, reports and documents. The Access to Personal Files Act 1987 gives an individual the right of access to files on themselves, but at present only those relating to housing and social services records. The Bill initially covered a wide range of records but was eviscerated in its passage through Parliament. The government has promised to extend the principle to educational records under separate legislation.

In July 1990, an Access to Health Records Bill was before Parliament and was expected to be passed. The Bill gives people the right to see their written medical records; they already have access to computerized records by virtue of the Data Protection Act.

The Satanic Verses

In official protest over the *fatwa* on Salman Rushdie (see Iran entry) the British government recalled its diplomats from Tehran. Ayatollah Khomeini's action was also condemned by the United States, Australia, Sweden, Norway and Brazil. On February 20, the EC recalled their ambassadors from Iran and UN Secretary General Javier Perez de Cuellar appealed for the death threat to be lifted. On February 21, Iran recalled its envoys from the 12 EC countries.

The *fatwa*, which forced Salman Rushdie into hiding, also gave rise to protest and indignation among writers worldwide. On February 20, in an initiative co-ordinated by ARTICLE 19, the International Committee for the Defence of Salman Rushdie and his Publishers was formed. A World Statement in support of Salman Rushdie's right to publish "free from censorship, intimidation and violence" was signed by 1,000 eminent writers and carried without charge in 62 newspapers and periodicals in 23 countries. Subsequently, some 12,000 writers and other concerned people from over 60 countries signed the declaration.

Blasphemy Laws In Britain, one by-product of the Rushdie affair was a heated debate over the exclusion of Islam and other faiths from the protection afforded Christian beliefs under the country's blasphemy laws. The division of opinion concerned whether or not the blasphemy law should be extended to cover other religions or whether it should be abolished altogether as being incompatible with freedom of expression. On March 13 1989, in a test case, the Chief Metropolitan Magistrate refused to grant Abdul Hussain Choudhury summonses against Salman Rushdie and his publishers, Viking/Penguin, alleging "blasphemous libel and seditious libel at the common law". The ruling that the law of blasphemy in England and Wales protected only the Christian religion was later upheld by the High Court.

In April 1989, a group of MPs introduced a "Bill to abolish prosecutions for the expression of opinion on matters of religion"; it was not debated in the House of Commons and was dropped. On May 27, some 30,000 Muslims demonstrated in London and, carrying placards, portraits of Ayatollah Khomeini and effigies of Salman Rushdie, marched to Parliament Square. The march ended in violence with a dozen police injured and over 100 arrests. There were numerous threats to bookshops displaying *The Satanic Verses* and several were fire-bombed. On June 27, applications to a magistrate for summonses against Salman Rushdie and Viking/ Penguin for offences against Section 4 (1) of the Public Order Act 1986 were dismissed. Leave to appeal this decision was later given by the High Court.

On January 29 1990, the Director of Public Prosecutions decided there was insufficient evidence to justify a prosecution over a speech given by Dr Kalim Siddiqui, Director of the London-based Muslim Institute, in Manchester in October 1989. Dr Siddiqui had been alleged to have solicited or incited the murder of Salman Rushdie.

In June 1990, the British Board of Film Classification (BBFC) refused the video *International Guerrillas* a distribution classification on the grounds that the video, which depicted Salman Rushdie as immoral and suffering retribution from God, might constitute criminal libel against the author. There was a public outcry at what was considered to be an act of prior restraint. The Appeals Committee reversed the ruling, justifying its decision mainly by reference to Salman Rushdie's objection to the ban and his pledge not to prosecute.

In October 1989, alleged blasphemy caused the BBFC to refuse a certificate to the video *Visions of Ecstasy*. Without a certificate the video cannot be released for public distribution. The BBFC ruled that the film, which depicts St Theresa of Avila's visions of Christ in an erotic manner, was at risk of prosecution and that "public distribution would enrage and insult the feelings of believing Christians". The decision was upheld by the Appeals Committee. It was the first film in the BBFC's 77-year history to be rejected on grounds of blasphemy. The case is to be taken to the European Commission of Human Rights.

The Media

Broadcasting Act 1990 Broadcasting is a state monopoly under the Wireless and Telegraphy Acts and requires a special licence from the Home Secretary. Such a licence is granted to the BBC and the Independent Broadcasting Authority (IBA). However, under the terms of the new Broadcasting Act of November 1 1990, the IBA together with the Cable Authority will be replaced in January 1991 by the Independent Television Commission (ITC), a "light touch" regulatory body, in a major restructuring of commercial broadcasting. The government will directly appoint the majority of the ITC's members and remaining appointees will require government approval. Non-EC citizens are barred from controlling interests in the new Channel 3, the proposed Channel 5 and UK-based satellite TV. Companies based in other EC countries could own franchises if quality thresholds were reached and takeovers were allowed.

Ten-year franchises will be issued by the ITC to the highest bidder who passes a quality threshold unless "exceptional circumstances" prevail. The Home Secretary could refuse to grant a franchise if he believes the funding arrangements to be suspect or feels "it would not be in the public interest".

Throughout 1990, Parliamentary debate on the Broadcasting Bill centred on the financing of a new "consumer-driven" independent television network and the effects of extending existing legislation, notably the Obscene Publications Act and public order offence relating to racial hatred, to the broadcast media.

Sky TV's November 2 1990 merger with British Satellite Broadcasting (BSB), to form British Sky Broadcasting, exposed serious flaws in the Broadcasting Act. Provisions, promised in May 1989, to prevent newspaper companies, owning more than twenty per cent of a UK-based television franchise, with similar limitations on cross-interests between national radio stations, commercial TV and satellite TV, have not yet been incorporated into secondary legislation amplifying the Act.

But for the merger, Rupert Murdoch's ownership of five national newspapers and four channels of Sky TV would have been unaffected by these provisions because Sky is transmitted on Astra, the Luxembourg-based satellite service, which is defined as a non-domestic service and thus exempt from any ownership restrictions. However, through the merger, Murdoch has effectively taken control of the five UK-based BSB television channels; the merger appears to violate the terms of the Act on the grounds that he is a non-EC national.

Broadcasting Standards Council The Broadcasting Act places the Broadcasting Standards Council (BSC) on a statutory basis, replacing the former system of self-regulation by broadcasters. The Council was established in May 1988 to draw up a code "giving guidance on violence, sex" and "standards of taste and decency". Responsible for all viewers' and listeners' complaints, the Council will also monitor programmes broadcast from abroad but received in the UK. There is widespread unease in the broadcasting industry over the powers the BSC will have, particularly since the government will again appoint its senior members.

The Radio Authority A new government-appointed body, the Radio Authority, will allocate three new national radio licences by competitive tender, subject to a diversity requirement. In the next three years, a further 300 local radio stations could be established.

The Radio Authority will have power to "give directions with respect to the exclusion of any programmes from a licensed service". Fears have been expressed that this will enable the Radio Authority to act as a "state censor".

While ownership of the new radio stations by an individual or institution will be restricted to one national station and six local stations, the latter may account for 49 per cent of independent local radio audiences. Regional newspaper publishers will not be able to own local radio and TV stations broadcasting within their circulation areas although there are no such constraints for national newspaper publishers.

Government Interference There is now more direct interference in BBC decisions by government ministers, compromising the Corporation's traditional independence. Its much admired and imitated philosophy of public broadcasting requires the government to be kept at arm's length. Both BBC and ITV have been accused of bias and have suffered government criticism of programmes and court injunctions. The questionable independence of the new broadcasting authorities established by the Broadcasting Act, together with the lack of any positive formulation in that law of the importance of freedom of expression and editorial independence, have caused concern.

Death On The Rock A major controversy over the legitimacy of investigative television journalism erupted over Thames TV's programme, *Death on The Rock*, on the Special Air Service (SAS) shooting of three IRA members in Gibraltar on March 6 1988. The documentary, broadcast on April 28 1989, four months before the official inquest into the killings, contained interviews with key witnesses who were to appear at the inquest. It was vehemently criticized by senior government ministers and some sectors of the press who claimed that the documentary prejudiced the legal process.

On January 26 1989, an independent report by Lord Windlesham concluded that although there were two notable lapses in the making of the programme, it had not prejudiced the inquest into the killings. The inquiry also declared that Thames TV and the IBA were correct not to bow to government pressure to ban the programme.

Broadcasting Ban On October 19 1988, the then Home Secretary, Douglas Hurd, issued a directive banning for an unlimited period the broadcasting of words spoken by representatives of Sinn Féin, Republican Sinn Féin and the Ulster Defence Association and any organization proscribed under the Prevention of Terrorism (Temporary Provisions) Act of 1984.

Sinn Féin, against whom the ban was widely interpreted as being directed, is a legal political party in Northern Ireland with around 35 per cent of the nationalist vote, one elected MP (Gerry Adams), and some 60 local councillors. The party has elected members in 11 of 26 local government councils.

The directive required that the broadcasters refrain from broadcasting any matter which includes: any words spoken, whether in the course of an interview or discussion or otherwise, by a person who appears or is heard on the programme in which the matter is broadcast where, (a) the person speaking the words represents or purports to represent [a proscribed organization] or (b) the words support or solicit or invite support for such an organization unless the words spoken were during parliamentary proceedings or in support of a candidate at a local, general or European election.

Douglas Hurd stated that the ban was designed to bring UK legislation in line with broadcasting restrictions in the Republic of Ireland. Justifying the ban, then Prime Minister Thatcher said on October 26 1988: "To beat off your enemy in a war, you have to suspend some of your civil liberties for a time". The ban met with widespread disapproval from broadcasters who claimed that it would make their reporting of Northern Ireland affairs incomplete. They also sought a clear interpretation of the directive after several incidents following the ban outlined the extensive sweep of the directive. One of the first victims was Channel 4's 52-minute video *Mother Ireland*, on contemporary history. The channel's legal services division stated that the ban "would cover any such material recorded at any time in the past, such as newsreel footage shot before the creation of the Republic of Ireland".

On November 20 1988, the IBA banned a record *Streets of Sorrow/Birmingham Six* by the Irish rock band The Pogues, which supported claims of miscarriage of justice over the convictions of Irish defendents (the "Guildford Four" and the "Birmingham Six"). The IBA explained that the song "indicates a general disagreement with the way the government responds to and the courts deal with the terrorist threat".

The Home Office said that the ban applied to direct statements but not to reported speech, so permitting a film "of the initiator with a voice-over account (of what was said), whether in paraphrase or verbatim". Actors are therefore allowed to read out the words of representatives of proscribed groups. The ban does not apply to genuine works of fiction, although no definition of a genuine work of fiction has been given, but it does apply to archive material.

On December 19 1988, six journalists and an employee of the National Union of Journalists lodged a challenge in the British courts on the grounds that the directive was in breach of Article 10 of the European Convention on Human Rights. The High Court refused to overturn the restrictions and the Court of Appeal upheld the ruling on December 6 1989, rejecting additional arguments that the ban conflicted with the duty of the broadcasters to preserve "due impartiality". A further appeal to the House of Lords is pending and, if unsuccessful, the issue will be brought to the European Commission of Human Rights in Strasbourg.

Constitutional Reform In 1988, a new initiative seeking wide-ranging reforms was launched by Charter 88 in a public statement signed by people representing a variety of opinion. In its continuing campaign for a new written constitution for the UK the group has criticized the extension of censorship and has called *inter alia* for a Bill of Rights and a Freedom of Information Act.

Actions

ARTICLE 19 chairs and co-ordinates the International Committee for the Defence of Salman Rushdie and his Publishers which was founded on February 20 1989. The Committee, representing writers, publishers, booksellers, journalists, trade unionists and human rights groups, has campaigned worldwide for the repeal of the *fatwa*, lobbying governments, the UN Security Council, UNESCO and the Commonwealth Secretariat.

On November 23 1989 ARTICLE 19 issued a statement supporting William Goodwin of *The Engineer* in his refusal to disclose confidential sources of information (see text). On April 9 1990 the organization condemned the fine imposed on Mr

Goodwin and called on the government to comply with the Article 10 of the European Convention on Human Rights.

On December 14 1989 ARTICLE 19 protested the British Board of Film Classification's refusal to grant a certificate to the video *Visions of Ecstasy* on grounds of blasphemy.

In 1990 ARTICLE 19 successfully campaigned to have clauses 144 and 145 of the Broadcasting Bill modified. These clauses would have given police officers the power to seize films before transmission on the suspicion of an infringement of the law; the changes stipulate that the Secretary of State must obtain a court order to allow an officer to take a copy of the material in question.

On June 1 1990 ARTICLE 19 wrote to the government protesting the deportation on grounds of "national security" of two Kuwaiti nationals who had peacefully lobbied for democracy in Kuwait. ARTICLE 19 expressed a concern that when "national security" is cited, there is no obligation upon the government to provide any further reason for expulsion.

On July 25 1990, ARTICLE 19 protested the British Board of Film Classification's refusal to grant a certificate to the film *International Guerrillas*. The Board reversed its decision on August 17 (see text).

On November 6 1990 ARTICLE 19 joined the National Union of Journalists in supporting the journalists who are challenging the Broacasting Ban. The involvement includes generating publicity about the case, co-ordinating arguments with the lawyers, providing legal research and assisting in decisions regarding the approach to the European Commission and Court of Human Rights in Strasbourg in the event that the Law Lords rule against the journalists.

Yugoslavia

For over 40 years, Yugoslavia has been a one-party state with the League of Communists of Yugoslavia enshrined in the Constitution as "the leading force in the society". Alternative political groups were unheard of until recent years, the first ones being formed only in 1988. At its 14th Congress in January 1990, the Communist Party managed to agree upon only one resolution, to end its monopoly of power enshrined in the 1974 Constitution.

The country's six republics (Slovenia, Serbia, Croatia, Montenegro, Bosnia-Herzegovina, and Macedonia) and two autonomous provinces (Kosovo and Vojvodnia, both within Serbia), have enjoyed a high degree of self-government and independence. However, in October 1988, Serbia took control of Kosovo, effectively removing all freedom of expression from the majority ethnic Albanian population and, in September 1989, Slovenia introduced radical changes to its Constitution, which strengthened the republic's autonomy and included the right of secession.

	Data	Year
Population	23,559,000	1988
Life expectancy (M/F)	67.6/73.2	1981
GNP (US$ per capita)	2,680	1988
Main religion(s)	Christianity	
	Islam	
Official language(s)	Serbo-Croat	
	Macedonian	
	Slovenian	
Illiteracy %	7.3	1990
(M/F)	2.6/11.9	1990
Daily newspapers	28	1986
Non daily newspapers {AND}		
Periodicals	1,450	1987
Radio sets	4,735,000	1988
TV sets	4,092,000	1988
Press agencies:		
	Novinska Agencija Tanjug	
ICCPR:	YES	1971

As communism has waned in the country, the political vacuum has been filled by resurgent nationalism. Ethnic tensions have increased, threatening to lead to a breakdown of the federation.

In April 1990, Slovenia held its first multi-party elections which were won by Demos, a centre-right democratic coalition. A month later, the Communists lost power in Croatia for the first time in 50 years when the Croation Democratic Union, a right of centre nationalist party, won a two-thirds majority in the three-chamber parliament. In May 1990, Borisav Jovic, the new Yugoslav president, condemned the elections in the two republics, saying that they violated constitutional law, and warned against the introduction of a multi-party system for the country as a whole.

Elections were scheduled for Bosnia-Herzegovina on November 18 1990 and are planned for the other three republics.

The Media

Yugoslavia has an abundance of publishing houses, radio and television stations, newspapers and periodicals because of its historical and multi-ethnic background. The Federal Law on Public Information explicitly forbids censorship and the Constitution guarantees freedom of expression. However, there are ample and vaguely-worded laws which enable the authorities to impose censorship. The Federal Law on the Prevention of the Abuse of Freedom of the Press and Media states that books or publications can be banned if they include "criminal acts against society or the security of the state, army, state or military secrets, incite aggression or other acts against humanity and international law, hinder friendly relationships between Yugoslavia and other countries, harm the honour and reputation of Yugoslavia, its Presidency or foreign heads of state."

Self-censorship (which is difficult to identify) has until recently been extremely widespread. Self-censorship is now used less in the interests of the Pan-Yugoslav state and more in the interests of ethnic nationalism. The media are free to criticize events in other republics, but not necessarily in their home republic.

Recent changes in the law allow private ownership of newspapers, radio and TV stations.

The Press For all its new-found freedoms, the press is still very much in the hands of local republican leaders especially in Serbia where, in 1987-1988, several independent-minded editors lost their jobs to supporters of the Serbian leader Slobodan Milosevic.

Newspapers are founded by political organizations (usually the Socialist Alliance of the Working People, a group dominated by the Communist Party). The founder appoints the editor-in-chief and an editorial board (one third of the members from the newspaper itself, the rest from all parts of society). The editorial board analyzes editorial policy and content of the paper and, in the past, disciplined "independent" editors. The publisher of any book, magazine or newspaper is obliged to send two copies of any printed text (before the text is bound) to the public prosecutor.

Books and Periodicals The office of the Belgrade Public Prosecutor receives about 40 books and other publications daily but, since it barely has time to glance at them, the office is generally alerted to specific items for scrutiny. There have also been cases where "conscientious printing workers" refused to publish a magazine which contained "offending" articles. Many books have remained unpublished, without any explanation. It was only in 1988 that privately-owned magazines were established.

Films Only one film, *Grad* (The City), has been banned. However, at least a dozen other films have simply never been screened, with no explanation given. A number of plays have been cancelled just before opening, without any official explanation from the public prosecutor.

Foreign Media Foreign media are not restricted in any way. There is no jamming of radio or TV programmes, and foreign newspapers are on sale throughout the country. Foreign journalists are free to travel in and report from Yugoslavia.

Attacks on the Media In March 1989, Ismail Smakaj was fired from TV Pristina in Kosovo for "spreading false information" about the miners' strike in Kosovo. A month later, ethnic Albanian journalist Zenun Celaj of *Rilindija* was arrested by the state security police for "spreading false information" about the strike and interrogated for two weeks.

On April 10, the Slovene weekly news magazine *Mladina* was temporarily banned by the authorities in Ljubljana for articles that "offended Yugoslavians".

Distribution was postponed until April 28, when the prosecutor's appeal was dismissed.

On June 19, *Grafit*, a youth paper from Serbia, was permanently banned and all copies destroyed because an article "caused offence" to a member of the Yugoslav Federal Presidium.

In mid-1989, author Svetislav Basara was sentenced to 45 days' imprisonment for "abusing the patriotic feelings of working people and citizens". The sentence is under appeal.

In April 1990 news editors at TV Novi Sad (an autonomous region of Vojvodina) were demoted for giving priority to international news and featuring a nationalist rally only in the third slot. In the same month, Dodeja Tot-Isakova, Biljana Vorkapic and several other journalists on *Politika*, the main daily paper in Belgrade, were demoted, while Blerim Shalla, a journalist in Pristina and correspondent for *Mladina*, was arrested and held for two weeks without charge.

Access to the Media In September 1990, oposition groups at a mass rally in Belgrade demanded an end to disinformation from the state-run media and called for three months' notice before Serbia's first post-World War II elections, with equal access to the media for all parties. In October, regular nightly television slots were given over to the various parties.

Positive Changes For decades, journalists were taught that they were "socio-political workers" and, as such, they had a duty to protect the party, the state, the system and what subjects were appropriate to cover. A phone call from the local party leader was until very recently enough to stop an item from being published or broadcast, and party membership was a prerequisite for top editorial posts. In the last two years, journalists' associations have begun to abandon their "socio-political role".

Since 1989, many "blacklisted" authors, journalists and dissidents, absent from the media for years, have been able to express their views openly in the press. These include the most famous Yugoslav dissident, Milovan Djilas. At the end of 1989 he received an official prize for a translation he made during his prison years. Another leading dissident, Mihajlo Mihajlov, had his passport and citizenship revoked in 1988. By the end of 1989 he was being interviewed on developments in Eastern Europe.

On December 6, the Belgrade Communist Party Committee called for the prohibition of a new series of books by two prominent Serbian pre-war politicians, Slobodan Jovanovic and Dragisa Vasic. The Writers' Association and many others reacted angrily and the books were published in late spring 1990.

Freedom of Expression

There are a number of penal provisions associated with *delikt misljenja* (the "crime of thought"). In December 1989, the federal government announced the abolition of the infamous Article 133 of the Federal Penal Code, which had in recent years been frequently used to punish dissidents by imprisonment from one to 10 years for "hostile propaganda".

In April 1989, Sima Dubajic was prosecuted under Article 133 for a public speech and for interviews in *Vijesnik* newspaper and *NIN* news magazine. However, neither publication was banned.

Also in 1989, Serbian police withheld the passport of Milan Mihajlovic because of a speech he made to the Assembly of the Association of Serbian Authors in which he criticized the political work of the late President Tito. A special law protecting the name and legacy of President Tito, introduced after his death, is currently under review.

Political Expression The alternative political groups have little or no funds, limited access to the media and are divided, especially along ethnic lines.

The first trial of a leading politician in Yugoslavia since the 1950s was held in 1989. One-time Tito favourite and ex-party leader in Kosovo, Azem Vilasi, was arrested in the spring and went on trial for "counter-revolutionary activities". The beginning of his trial sparked off further demonstrations that left at least two people dead. All charges against Azem Vilasi and the rest of the Albanian leadership from Kosovo were eventually dropped.

Kosovo The 1.8 million population of Kosovo is 85 per cent ethnic Albanian, the remainder being predominantly Serbs. Nationalist uprisings in 1981 led to the banning of all forms of mass assembly including funerals, which may only be attended by close relatives of the deceased. In the seven years to 1988, over 350,000 ethnic Albanians had undergone police interrogation and 2,000 had been sentenced for political offences.

In January 1990, demonstrators called for free elections, the release of all political prisoners and the reinstatement of autonomy. Kosovo police used water cannons, tear gas dropped from helicopters, batons and, finally, bullets to suppress the largely peaceful protests. By the end of January, the death toll had reached 48 of whom 47 were ethnic Albanians.

In March, further protests against curbs on self-rule left 28 ethnic Albanians dead and Serbia imposed emergency regulations which included a ban on demonstrations. In April, 108 political prisoners were released and the ban on political protests was lifted. However, later that month, demonstrations by ethnic Albanian nationalists ended with over two dozen deaths. A State of Emergency was imposed and special riot police units were deployed in the province. A large number of people were detained in "isolation", without legal assistance or visits from their families.

In July, the Kosovo parliament broadcast a declaration on Radio-TV Pristina, that the province was an "independent unit with equal status to other such units in Yugoslavia". In a swift reprisal, the Serbian authorities dissolved the Kosovo parliament and police occupied the TV and radio stations.

Widespread strikes, the only legitimate form of political protest remaining, led to tens of thousands of workers being sacked. Journalists refused to work under police occupation and, by August, 1,800 media workers had been dismissed, leaving screens blank and radios silent. On August 5, the Serbian parliament "suspended" publication of *Rilindja*, the only Albanian-language daily newspaper.

On September 27, Zenun Celaj, a journalist with *Rilindja* and a human rights activist, was arrested and charged with attending a meeting on September 14. He was released from detention on October 27 1990, but it is not known whether the charges against him have been dropped. Members of the dissolved Kosovo Assembly who were at the meeting have also been arrested.

On September 29, the last vestiges of autonomy were removed with Serbia's proclamation of its new Constitution giving it total control over Kosovo.

Middle East
and
North Africa

MIDDLE EAST & NORTH AFRICA

Algeria

In October 1988, Algeria was shaken by the most violent riots since independence. In many cities people took to the street protesting over economic conditions and the lack of political freedom. The riots were suppressed by the army and police leaving several hundred dead and many more injured. Martial law was imposed and over 4,000 people, most of them young, were arrested. By November 1 1988, after public order was restored, all detainees were released.

The Algerian media were prohibited from reporting freely on the riots. Television and radio were later accused by journalists of having engaged in a campaign of disinformation and distortion and of having supported the repression. Newspapers kept silent. Some journalists were arrested at the riots, including Youssef Dahbiya of the Algérie Presse Service (APS). Sidi Ali Benmiche, chief editor at APS, was accidently killed by the army while covering the riots in Bab el-Oued in Algiers.

The Algerian public depended heavily on foreign media for news about the riots, listening to foreign radio stations and circulating photocopies of articles published in the foreign press.

The authorities tried to prevent the foreign press from covering the riots. A number of journalists were detained for several hours on October 8 and 9, including British TV reporter Paul Davis and American cameraman Hassio Nocco. Film crews had video cassettes confiscated and were routinely prevented from sending footage via satellite. Many correspondents were refused visas to enter Algeria and some with visas, such as Agence France Presse photographer Jacques Demarthon, were expelled on arrival.

	Data	Year
Population	22,971,558	1987
Life expectancy (M/F)	58.5/61.3	1982
GNP (US$ per capita)	2,450	1988
Main religion(s)	Islam	
Official language(s)	Arabic	
Illiteracy %	42.6	1990
(M/F)	30.2/54.5	
Daily newspapers	6	
Non daily newspapers	15	1982
Periodicals	27	1982
Radio sets	5,250,000	1987
TV sets	1,607,000	1987
Press agencies:		
	Algérie Press Service	
ICCPR:	YES	1989

Reforms

As a result of the riots the Algerian government took steps towards liberalizing the political system and advancing human rights. On February 23 1989, a new Constitution was adopted by national referendum. Algeria constitutionally converted from a state with political power in the hands of a single party, the Front de Libération Nationale (FLN), to a multi-party system, allowing 25 political organizations and many more independent civic associations. Many opposition leaders returned from exile.

The new Constitution guarantees freedom of conscience and opinion (Art.35) and freedom of expression, association, and the right to hold meetings (Art.39).

Political Parties The revolutionary change is contained in Article 40 of the new Constitution and the July 5 1989 law on political associations which guarantees the right to establish political parties. Of the new political parties, four were formerly clandestine, including the Front des Forces Socialistes (FFS) (whose leader, Hocine Ait Ahmed, returned from 27 years' exile in France) and the party of Ahmed Ben Bella, the Mouvement pour la Démocratie en Algérie (MDA). Only le Parti du Peuple Algerien has been refused recognition on the grounds that it is the heir to the Mouvement National Algerien which did not play an acceptable part during the liberation struggle.

Among the new political groups are le Front Islamique du Salut (FIS), chaired by Abassi Madani, which is campaigning for the institution of an Islamic state and the implementation of Shari'a (Islamic law), and the Rassemblement pour la Démocratie et la Culture (RCD), a Berberist movement whose leader, Dr Said Saadi, is calling for the establishment of a secular state and the recognition of Berber culture and language.

A new political consciousness which has reached many social and professional categories, particularly women, students, white collar workers, professionals and entrepreneurs, has resulted in mass organizations previously controlled by the FLN losing their influence. Women's associations (14 operate legally) have demonstrated against the Family Code which considers women to be subordinate. Other women's associations, controlled by Muslim activists, have demonstrated for the enforcement of *Shari'a* through the maintenance of the Family Code, the separation of men and women, and the right of women to have passport photographs wearing the veil.

Elections On June 12 1990, Algerians took part in the first free elections in the country. Eleven out of 25 political organizations competed for 1,539 seats in local and regional authorities. To the surprise of many observers, the FIS won 853 seats (55 per cent) and took control of the four major cities, including Algiers and also Annaba. The ruling FLN came second with 487 seats (31 per cent). The rest was shared between three other organizations and independent candidates. The authorities governing the state TV are reported to have decided not to report the election campaign so as not to be accused of bias vis à vis the FLN.

The Media

The 1982 Information Code, which established total government and party control over the media, and made the Information Ministry the editor of all publications and broadcasting operations, came under severe criticism in 1989. According to the Code, "information is a domain of national sovereignty". Article 12 provided that "publication of newspapers is an exclusive prerogative of the party and the state". Since 1965, there has been no independent press in Algeria. The Ministry controls four radio stations, one TV channel, four daily papers and an estimated 40 periodicals. The FLN controls three weekly newspapers and four periodicals. Directors of these publications are nominated by presidential decree.

Journalists Following the events of October 1988, journalists became the most outspoken professional group in the country. Many have left the official Union of Journalists, Writers and Interpreters and have joined the newly created Mouvement des Journalistes Algériens (MJA).

Prior to the October riots, journalists had released a document which revealed the scale of censorship imposed on the media over many years as well as the self-censorship that was practised. The document disclosed a blacklist of journalists prevented from writing or travelling in Algeria or abroad, and listed journalists who had been arbitrarily suspended or dismissed.

Journalists on the weekly *Révolution Africaine* issued a declaration denouncing the practice of systematic censorship, threats of redundancy, intimidation and pressure on journalists, and the "totalitarian attitude" of the editor-in-chief for refusing to publish articles dealing with subjects such as the use of torture by police during the riots.

Journalists have also protested over the excessive powers of the government-appointed editors and directors and have called for journalists to be included on editorial committees. The directors and editors-in-chief, they say, implement guidelines from the party or the government without considering journalists' ideas and opinions.

The New Information Code Following protests against censorship by the MJA and the Algerian Human Rights League, the government submitted a new Information Code to the National Assembly. Journalists were not involved although they had demanded consultation.

A clause that attracted most criticism forbade the use in new publications of any language other than Arabic. This contradicted the law on political associations which allowed political parties to issue publications in foreign languages (provided the first and main one is in Arabic). The code also reaffirmed that the importation and distribution of foreign publications remain under state control; and proposed a "clause of conscience", which would allow journalists to refuse to write anything contrary to their political, moral, or religious convictions.

In May 1989, the MJA condemned the code, stating that it "does not guarantee freedom, independence and pluralism of the press and does not regulate the ownership and management of the media, or mention the question of government and party monopoly of the media".

On May 30, the MJA organized demonstrations by journalists in Algiers and Oran against the Bill. In spite of journalists' opposition, in December 1989, a new draft code was sent to the National Assembly and was approved on March 19 1990. It contains many restrictions on the exercise of freedom of expression. Independent publishers must now use Arabic for newspapers of general information and local circulation; specialized magazines and newsletters distributed abroad can be published in a foreign language, but only with the approval of the Supreme Council of Information. It is an offence, punishable by five to 10 years' imprisonment, to publish or distribute information which could harm state security or national unity. Opinions which attack Islamic or national values are forbidden. The code does not guarantee the protection of journalists' sources, especially concerning economic or military secrets.

The New Journalism The new atmosphere of open debate and criticism of government policies by the public, and journalists in particular, has encouraged editors and
directors of newspapers to be less acquiescent on official directives. Many have
started publishing investigative reports about the political and social situation in the
country, official corruption and abuse of power, and opened their columns to the
public or their own journalists to freely express their opinions. This new journalism
has not escaped official harassment.

On January 31 1989, the director of the Arabic-language daily *al-Joumhouria*,
Habib Rachidine and his reporters Laila Ghazat and Kheira Tarra were arrested and
questioned by the Algerian security police and charged with defamation and libel.
They had reported the existence of large-scale corruption, speculation and illegal
sales of properties in the town of Mostaganem involving the Prefect and other influential people close to the Chadli Benjedid family. After protests organized by the
MJA, they were released.

In August 1989, Mohamed Hamdi, editor-in-chief of the FLN-owned weekly
Révolution Africaine, was dismissed because he wrote an article criticizing the in-
fluence of Muslim groups on members of the FLN. He later became an editor with
Algérie Actualités.

Publications of the Political Parties and the Independent Press Many political
parties now produce their own publications. On October 4 1989, the FIS published
the first issue of *al-Mounqid*, an Arabic-language bi-monthly. Two weeks later, the
Parti d'Avant Garde Socialiste launched *Sout Ech Chaab*, which was followed by
l'Avenir Ettajamou and *Asalu*, produced by the RCD. *Alger Républicain* (a daily
paper created in 1938 and banned in 1965) is now published in Arabic and French.
Le Progrés is the organ of the Parti Social-Démocrate (PSD) and *Libre Algérie* represents the views of the FFS. *Tribune d'Octobre* is the organ of the Mouvement pour
la Démocratie en Algérie and is printed in France.

The newly created political press has to overcome huge problems; lack of printing facilities, premises, qualified staff and, above all, the cost of paper.

At the end of February 1990, the Algerian Government agreed to a financial contribution of 120 million dinars (US$15m) for the work of opposition parties. The
money was intended for the 1990 regional and local elections and to support publications. Journalists working in the public sector may now join political organizations, and their salaries will be secured by the state for two years. According to observers, these subsidies have been allocated in order to stop the parties receiving
money from abroad.

The magazine *At-Tabyine* was created by the Association Culturelle, and novelist
Tahar Attar launched *Djahidia* magazine.

Berber Culture and Language

One positive development in Algerian society is the prospect now offered for the
Berber population to express its cultural identity and language. Berbers, representing
more than 30 per cent of the population, have since independence been denied official recognition of their specific cultural and linguistic identity. Soon after independence, the University Chair of the Berber language at the University of Algiers
was abolished, Berber-language radio programmes were reduced to a strict min-

imum and most Berber publications were stifled. Almost all cultural expression was discouraged except for their folklore, promoted for tourism. In November 1988, the director of the French-language radio station blocked the airing of the second part of an interview prepared by journalist Laila Boutaleb with the Algerian writer Kateb Yacine in which he pleaded the cause of the Berber language.

In January 1990, the Algerian government announced its decision to establish the first Berber Language Institute since independence in 1962. The Berber Cultural Movement reacted to the government decision by stating that the Berber language should be taught at all universities.

Literary and Artistic Expression

In the past, in order to be published, any work of literature had to reflect the ideological and patriotic stance of the FLN, and any work which diminished patriotic sentiment was considered by the authorities to be a product of the neo-colonial cultural dependency and therefore seditious.

Many Algerian writers operated within the framework of the paradigm of the War of Liberation, patriotism, the FLN, and Martyrs of the War of Liberation. Writers who explored and experimented with different types of literature were officially rejected and ended up being published in the many unofficial and sometimes clandestine presses, or in France.

For many years, the work of Rachid Boujedra, published by Denoel in Paris and critical essays on Algeria by Algerian historian Mohamed Harbi have been banned.

Since the October 1988 riots, the prohibition on importation and circulation of previously banned books has been lifted. One sign of the new tolerance was the publication in October 1989, by a state printing house, of a book by the National Committee Against Torture on police torture during the October 1988 riots.

Actions

On October 10 1988 ARTICLE 19 wrote to the government protesting the attempts to prevent foreign journalists from covering the riots, including expelling reporters, refusing them entry and confiscating equipment. (see text)

On August 10 1989 ARTICLE 19 wrote to the government expressing concern over the proposed Information Code (see text) especially the provisions that would forbid the use in new publications of any language other than Arabic, and that would keep the importation and distribution of foreign publications under state control.

On November 15 1989 ARTICLE 19 wrote to the government protesting its decision not to legalize the National Committee Against Torture.

Egypt

On October 5 1987, Hosni Mubarak was appointed to a second six-year term as President in a single-candidate referendum. He had been nominated earlier in the year by the Majlis Ash-Sha'ab (parliament) in which the ruling National Democratic Party (NDP) holds a commanding majority. Since the beginning of President Mubarak's previous term in 1981, the constitutional guarantees of freedom of opinion, expression and publication, which include a prohibition on censorship, have been suspended. Emergency law together with many legal provisions give the state wide powers to censor all publications and to restrict freedom of assembly and movement.

	Data	Year
Population	51,897,000	1988
Life expectancy (M/F)	56.8/59.5	1985
GNP (US$ per capita)	650	1988
Main religion(s)	Islam	
Official language(s)	Arabic	
Illiteracy %	51.6	1990
(M/F)	37.1/66.2	1990
Daily newspapers	12	1986
Non daily newspapers	29	1985
Periodicals	277	1985
Radio sets	15,500,000	1987
TV sets	4,150,000	1987
Press agencies:		
Middle East News Agency		
ICCPR	YES	1982

In May 1990, the Supreme Constitutional Court ruled that the Assembly had been elected under unconstitutional electoral laws which had discriminated against independent candidates. A referendum, called by President Mubarak and held on October 10, resulted in 94 per cent of voters in favour of the dissolution of the Assembly. New elections were due be held on November 29 but the opposition planned to boycott them on the ground that the referendum was unconstitutional.

Legal Restrictions The Egyptian Penal Code contains 41 provisions criminalizing the expression of opinions including those that instigate hatred of the ruling system, humiliate the civil authorities, the army or parliament, or excite public opinion by propaganda and transmitting false news. Speech in favour of atheism and comment which reflects adversely on monotheistic religions are prohibited.

A series of exceptional measures, the 1977 law on political parties, the 1978 law protecting the internal order and social peace, the law protecting social and moral values and the Press Law, both passed in 1980, confine criticism of the government within certain limits rather than totally suppress it. In 1987, the editors of *al-Ahali* and *Sawt al-Arab* newspapers were investigated because of criticisms of the Saudi King Fahd and in 1988 copies of *Sawt al-Arab* were confiscated and the newspaper was suspended. However, criticism of other presidents did not attract the attention of the censors.

The Media

Ownership of the mass media is, to a large extent, concentrated in the hands of the state which owns the radio and television services, the sole news agency, major newspapers, and publication and distribution institutions.

The Press Advisory Council The Advisory Council, which owns a controlling interest in national newspapers and dominates the press in Egypt, has one-third of its members appointed by the president, and two-thirds elected through a system named the "exclusive list". This has resulted, in practice and through direct interference of state authorities, in the ruling party winning all the elective seats in all the elections that have been held. The Press Law authorizes the Advisory Council to appoint editors-in-chief of national newspapers. This power is the government's method of ensuring control of the three main Cairo dailies, *al-Ahram, al-Akhbar, al-Gomhouriga*, and several other important publications.

The Supreme Press Council A constitutional amendment, approved by referendum in May 1980, established a Supreme Press Council (SPC) to safeguard press freedom, check government censorship and protect the rights of journalists. However, the SPC is also dominated by the ruling party and has the authority to allow or refuse the publication of newspapers.

The Press Bureau The Press Bureau is an office within the Ministry of Information that provides national newspapers with daily guidance on what to publish.

Newspapers There are three kinds of newspapers. The "national" titles, which are published by state-owned institutions and controlled by the Advisory Council, are required to mobilize public opinion in support of government policies. They have a dominant position in the Egyptian press because they enjoy subsidies and a regular flow of information from the state. The amount of opposition views allowed in these newspapers is limited. There are also political party newspapers which first appeared in 1976 when political pluralism was permitted in Egypt. With the exception of the daily *Wafd* (organ of the New Wafd Party), these are published weekly. All suffer financial problems owing to lack of access to information and advertising revenue. Finally, there are a number of newspapers published by trade unions and associations. They enjoy little influence and low circulation.

Periodicals While the 1980 press law permits private ownership of newspapers and periodicals, a large financial deposit is a precondition. As a result, few independent newspapers have been launched in the past decade. During the second half of the 1980s, groups of young novelists, poets and artists began a cottage industry publishing magazines at irregular intervals to avoid payment of a deposit. At one point there were 35 such magazines. However, in the spring of 1987, the SPC decided to ban the publication of unlicensed non-periodical printings. Another device is to rent newspaper licences from political parties allowed to publish more than one newspaper. A third possibility for those aspiring to publish newspapers is publication through licences issued in European capitals (London, Paris and Nicosia). These newspapers are regarded as foreign publications and are subject to Customs regulations, although their editorial material is produced in Cairo.

In March 1989, the SPC refused authorization to the Arab Women's Solidarity Association, a legal association with consultative status with ECOSOC, to sell its quarterly journal *Noun*, because it had refused to place a large deposit in a national bank before printing the magazine. The decision is arbitrary since it contradicts Article 19 of the 1980 Press Code which requires a deposit for publication of daily or weekly newspapers only.

The newspapers of opposition parties are not subject to direct censorship but political pressure helps prevent the press from crossing the line and risking the danger of confiscation. Under President Mubarak, the opposition newspaper *al-Ahali* was threatened with confiscation over three issues if specific items were published. On one occasion the newspaper had to destroy 40,000 copies.

1988 saw the first confiscation and suspension of a newspaper. On August 27, security forces raided the printing plant of *al-Ahram* and confiscated issue 108 of the *Sawt al-Arab* newspaper, the organ of the Nasserite trend, forbidden to form a political party. Police then raided the headquarters of the newspaper and arrested the editor, Abdel Azim Manaf. He was released two days later following the intercession of the Journalists' Union.

Television and Radio Political pluralism is not reflected in radio or TV which are state monopolies. News bulletins on TV are, in essence, propaganda about the activities of senior state officials. News concerning the *Intifada* receives negligible coverage due to a concern that Egyptian public opinion might be influenced. Several demonstrations of solidarity with the uprising were suppressed in Egyptian cities following the outbreak of the *Intifada*.

Access to Information During the period 1984-1988, 48 decisions were made banning publication of news about some of the most important cases under criminal investigation. Most dealt with issues of public interest, such as the rebellion of the Central Security Forces, political assassinations and, more recently, cases of official corruption. The law imposes secrecy on sensitive official documents for 50 years and also bans publishing statistics from sources other than the Central Agency for Public Mobilization and Statistics even if they are not related to national security.

Attacks on Journalists In 1988 and 1989, a number of writers and journalists faced arrest, detention, beating, torture and imprisonment under emergency law. Journalists have also been subjected to abuse at airports and prevented from travelling abroad. Ten journalists were detained at Cairo International Airport either on leaving or on return. These included Hussein Abdel Razek, editor of *al-Ahali*, in March 1988, and Dr Ghali Shukri, of *al-Ahram* in March 1989. Between September and November 1989, Dr Mahgoub Omar of *al-Shaab* and Abdel Aziz Manaf, editor of *Sawt al-Arab*, were prevented from travelling abroad and Saber Mohey El-Din and Daoud Talhamy, Palestinian editors of *al-Hadaf* and *al-Houriyya* magazines, were refused entry to Egypt after being invited by Cairo University.

In June 1988, the house of Medhat El Zahed, specialist legal and human rights editor of *al-Ahali* newspaper, was searched and his books and notes were confiscated. A year later, he was arrested and accused of belonging to a banned communist organization. Thirteen other journalists were detained briefly by the police at different events they were reporting and their equipment and note books were confiscated. Among those arrested in April 1988 were Sayed Abdel Aty, Mahmoud Shaker and photographer Abdel Wahab el Seheity, all with the *Wafd* daily newspaper. They were detained in police custody for several hours. Essam Abdel Rahman of *al-Shaab* was arrested in May 1989 while covering a by-election to the People's Assembly in Cairo. He was held in police custody for five days.

On August 24 1989, State Security Intelligence mounted a wide-ranging campaign in which 62 people were arrested, including 10 journalists and writers, for allegedly forming a secret communist organization, the Egyptian Workers Communist Party.

Foreign Journalists Visas are easily obtained and no foreign correspondents have been expelled in recent years. Dispatches and footage are transmitted without interference.

Censorship of Artistic Expression

Book Censorship There are two main bodies authorized to censor publications in Egypt, the Council of Ministers and the Ministry of the Interior. According to the 1980 Press Code, both have the authority to confiscate "sexually stimulating" publications or those dealing with religion in a way that can "upset public peace".

The Islamic Research Academy (IRA) in al-Azhar (a Mosque-University enjoying a great deal of influence in religio-juridical matters) censors religious books, but recent years have seen an increase in the role of al-Azhar and the rising Islamic movement. The Islamic movement exercises strong pressure, successful in many instances, on al-Azhar and the civil authorities, through its several forums. The most prominent example was its success in preventing the lifting of the ban on Nobel Prize winner Naguib Mahfouz's novel *Children of Gabalawy* whose publication has been banned since 1959.

Although Act 102 of 1985 confines the role of the IRA to censoring books related to the Koran and Sunna only, this role has expanded in practice to include books discussing historical and intellectual issues in Islam from viewpoints differing from those of the Academy.

In February 1988, the IRA confiscated six books from the Cairo International Book Fair on the grounds that they denied Islamic teaching and methods. In March 1988, the Academy ordered the confiscation and banning of *Letters of Gahiman El Etaiby*, by Dr Refaat Sayed Ahmed. The book was later unbanned, but it is believed that the confiscation was requested by the Saudi embassy which alleged that the book attacked the Saudi royal family.

In October 1989, the Council of al-Azhar University referred Dr Hamed Abou Ahmed, professor at the Faculty of Languages and Translation, to a disciplinary council for his translation of the Peruvian novelist Mario Vargas Llosa's novel *Who Killed Palomino Molero?* because the novel contains sexual language.

On March 12 1990, novelist and civil servant Alaa Hamed was arrested on the basis of a letter sent by the Islamic Research Academy of al-Azhar to the Public Prosecution Office. If charged, Alaa Hamed faces a maximum punishment of five years in prison or a fine of 1,000 Egyptian pounds for contempt of religion. On the same day, his novel *A Distance in a Man's Mind*, published in 1988, was confiscated on the grounds that it contains subversive opinions in contempt of religion in general and Islam in particular. He has also been referred to a disciplinary tribunal on the grounds that his novel contradicts the ethics of his job as a state official.

Naguib Mahfouz Soon after Naguib Mahfouz won the Nobel Prize in 1988, intellectuals campaigned to lift the ban imposed in 1959 on his novel *Children of Gabalawy*, regarded by al-Azhar as blasphemous. In 1989, the *al-Masaa* newspaper attempted to publish it in serial form, but the Islamic press and al-Azhar stopped its publication. The campaign reached its climax when, in April 1989, Dr Omar Abdel

Rahman, a Muslim leader of an illegal political group, declared a *fatwa* (religious edict), calling for the killing of Naguib Mahfouz unless he repented. On May 3 1989, the Mufti (the leading religious official, based at al-Azhar) condemned the *fatwa* and the government offered Naguib Mahfouz protection which he refused.

Foreign Publications The Council of Ministers uses Customs regulations to ban the import of foreign publications (including newspapers) if they endanger public order. The law was invoked in 1989 to ban an issue of the British magazine *The Economist* which featured "The Richest of the Rich in Egypt". It is an offence to import or circulate banned publications.

Banning decisions reflect state policy. The *Green Book*, by Libyan leader Colonel Muammar al-Qaddafi, was long prohibited in Egypt; when diplomatic relations were restored between the two countries in 1989, an Egyptian edition of the book was issued and distributed by a state publishing house.

Film and Theatre Cinema and theatre are subject to censorship by a department in the Ministry of Culture which censors a work twice: when it is still in script form and before it is shown to the public. Appeals are heard by a 12-member board established by the Ministry. The former director of censorship, Hamdy Sorour, has defended the Ministry's role: "art should not clash with the supreme interests of the state or its political achievements", he has said.

The censor has also defended the practice of taking a second opinion from the Ministry of the Interior and Defence before artistic works are performed or shown to the public. This is known to have happened with two films, *Wife of an Important Man* and *The Innocent*, whose director was forced to cut some scenes and make changes in order to allow their screening. A change in the title of the play *The Day of Killing the Leader*, taken from a novel by Naguib Mahfouz, was also ordered. The play was retitled *Cairo 80*. It deals with life in Egypt before the assassination of President Sadat. In March 1988, the censor also stopped the play *King of the Beggars*, written by the late Naguib Sourour. At least 2,000 songs have fallen foul of the censor, according to official figures.

Television Films When plays and films are shown on TV, they are re-censored by a specialist committee in the Ministry of Information. This can mean that an artistic work may be censored four times: when published as a book, another time if adapted for theatre or cinema, a third time before public performance or screening and a final time when it is shown on TV.

Actions

On September 28 1988 ARTICLE 19 wrote to the government protesting the confiscation and closure of the Cairo-based *Sawt al-Arab*.

On October 9 1989 ARTICLE 19 wrote to the government protesting the arrest and detention of Mohamed El-Kabahy, a journalist on the National Progressive Party's weekly *Al-Ahali*.

In February 1990 ARTICLE 19 sent an appeal to its members urging them to protest the SPC's refusal to allow the Arab Women's Solidarity Association to publish and sell a quarterly magazine. (See text)

On September 5 1990 ARTICLE 19 expressed its deep concern at the arrest, detention and torture of Khalid Sherif, journalist with the newspaper *al-Hakika*.

Iran

Iran ratified the International Covenant on Civil and Political Rights in 1975. However, its stipulations on human rights had been ignored by the Shah, who was overthrown in January 1979, as they have been under the Islamic Republic which followed.

The Constitution of the Islamic Republic proclaims freedom of thought: no-one can be questioned or persecuted because of his or her beliefs (Art.23). Nevertheless, Azizollah Golshani was condemned to death by public hanging in Mashad in May 1982 on a charge of propaganda on behalf of the Bahai religion and for writing an article, "Why am I a Bahai?".

Since 1979, at least 50 writers, 13 teachers, thousands of high school and university students, 27 doctors and nurses and countless lawyers have been executed, many during the latest wave of executions of political prisoners between 1988 and 1989, when over a thousand political executions took place.

	Data	Year
Population	49,857,384	1986
Life expectancy (M/F)	55.7/55.0	1976
GNP (US$ per capita)	3,766	1988
Main religion(s)	Islam	
Official language(s)	Farsi	
Illiteracy %	46.0	1990
(M/F)	35.5/56.7	1990
Daily newspapers	11	1986
Non daily newspapers	41	1982
Periodicals	180	1982
Radio sets	12,000,000	1987
TV sets	2,700,000	1987
Press agencies:		
Islamic Republic News Agency		
ICCPR:	YES	1975

Recognized religious minorities are allowed to worship and to practise their own religions, but are not allowed to propagate or promote them. Others whose beliefs are not recognized are forbidden to express, promote or propagate their faith. Ideas opposed to Islam are not tolerated.

The Media

Articles 24 and 25 of the Constitution guarantee the right of free expression in publications and the press unless it is contrary to Islamic law and the public good. For radio and television, the Constitution as modified in 1989 declares that freedom of expression and propagation of ideas is ensured if Islamic principles are observed and the interest of the country is taken into account. These clauses provide the legal basis for censorship. A commission, comprising two representatives of the President, two representatives from the Islamic Assembly and two from the judiciary, supervises the state media. Appointment and dismissal of the head of the state media is vested in the authority of the religious leader.

Newspapers In August 1979, the Ministry of Guidance introduced a press law to the Revolutionary Council which was passed with unusual speed. Forty newspapers were banned and the law required a new permit for the publication of any newspaper. It has been estimated that, as a result of the new countrywide controls, 1,000 publications were banned between 1979 and 1987.

An Islamic Committee took control of the newspaper *Kayhan*, dismissing its most prominent journalists and typographers and causing other *Kayhan* employees to strike in protest. The strike lasted two months, during which 10 issues of *Kayhan-e Azad* were published before the Revolutionary Guards stopped publication. The purged employees continued to publish a monthly magazine, *Victory*, which was suppressed after six issues. Rahman Hatefi, editor of *Kayhan*, was arrested and executed soon after.

On August 8 1979, the daily *Ettela'at* was closed on a charge of "collaboration with Zionism", and its editors and writers were imprisoned. The newspaper *Peygham-e Emrouz* and the satirical weekly *Ahangar* were closed down. On August 20, two other newspapers were forced to close; *Omid-e Iran*, on a charge of supporting Bakhtiar, the last Prime Minister of the Shah, and *Tehran-Mossavar*, on a charge of promoting liberalism.

Since 1981, banned political parties and organizations have found it impossible to publish or distribute any literature even on an underground basis because of the serious and lethal consequences of being caught. *Samizdat* literature is either copied by hand and passed from person to person, or sent by post anonymously (known as "red post").

Recently, a number of weekly publications have appeared which present a more "liberal" and varied choice to readers. One such is *Adineh*, dealing with literary and artistic themes. A violent campaign against these weeklies began in May 1990, led by the official daily *Kayhan*. The attacks are particularly directed against the theme of "democracy".

Radio and Television Blatant censorship manifested itself on radio and TV immediately after the Islamic Republic came to power. Ayatollah Khomeini entrusted this important institution to Sadegh Qotbzadeh (later executed for treason). Qotbzadeh, in his first meeting with directors and employees of radio and TV, announced a policy of systematic censorship to be implemented in order to prevent "counter-revolutionary" influences in the mass media. All secular employees were purged, despite a public outcry.

On Qotbzadeh's instructions, pre-revolution documentaries underwent a transformation. Scenes in which unveiled women appeared were cut and, later, all evidence that intellectuals and academics had participated in the revolution disappeared. The archives of Iranian Radio and TV were destroyed, with the exception of certain revolutionary marches, and invaluable historical material was lost. Music was eliminated from all programmes. The Olympic Games held in 1980 were not shown on TV.

In recent years, paraliamentary debates have been broadcast live. In October 1990, a broadcast of a debate on forthcoming elections for the Assembley of Experts was abruptly halted when hardliners and moderates clashed and violence erupted.

Book Censorship Soon after the 1979 revolution, thousands of books were burned by setting fire to bookshops and private collections. By the end of 1984, virtually all independent publishing houses had closed in Tehran.

Today, the Central Office of Press and Publications (under the supervision of the Ministry of Islamic Orientation) controls book publication. Two of its most active departments are the "Assessment Department" (AD) and the "Inspection Department" (ID). All printing houses are inspected by the ID and their current work is checked. ID agents check and record the numbers on the meters of printing presses, assessing the precise number of copies printed of each book under publication. The AD controls prose, children's literature, poetry, history, science, religious literature, art and any material in foreign languages. Some specialized books are sent to other Ministry of Guidance-affiliated offices.

When printing is permitted, a proof of the book is taken to the AD for an "exit licence". Only on receipt of this may the printing house allow the galleys to leave the premises or go for page-setting. The examination of a manuscript may take from a few days to several months. If the book is judged to be anti-government, it is pulped. If alterations are required, the modifications to the proofs must be made so that censorship cannot be detected. The rejected proofs are destroyed in the presence of AD agents and new proofs must be taken to the Ministry of Guidance.

The evaluation section of the Ministry of Guidance controls the sale price of each book. The "agreed" price must be specified on its cover before the book can be sent to the AD for final approval for publication. Pricing books is a formidable instrument of censorship. Favoured publishers of the government or government-appointed publishers, are given numerous advantages, receiving prior allocation of official paper and other facilities, and they are allowed a cover price which does not reflect their own cost but the market average. Publishers of religious texts or government publications obtain "fair" prices and make a considerable profit. Less trusted publishers publish at a loss. All independent publishers now accept that first editions are a loss-making business and are reluctant to publish new titles as long as they can find suitable second editions.

Paper Allocation of imported paper is a further effective censorship mechanism. The bulk of available paper is distributed to government organizations for official publications and propaganda. Pro-government daily newspapers receive a regular quota. The remaining publishers obtain paper rations from the Ministry of Guidance. Private sector access to imported paper is generally restricted. Paper is available in the "free" black market at exorbitant prices. If a book has been approved by the censors then it is publishable provided it gets an allocation of paper from the Ministry of Guidance, or it can be published with paper available on the black market. However, the book is priced by the Ministry of Guidance according to how much it will cost at official prices (including government-allocated paper). Publishers who buy paper from the black market risk bankruptcy or must sell their book "under the counter" at several times the cover price. Frequently, people share the cost of purchasing a book. Given the general rate of inflation, some customers may be prepared to pay above the cover price, but the publisher or the bookshop is liable to prosecution on charges of profiteering.

Theatre As soon as the Shah's censorship was abolished, theatrical groups began to flourish. A union of theatre actors was formed. After the revolution, theatres were appropriated and used for speeches by government officials. In 1980, Sa'id Soltanpour produced a documentary play he had written about the life of a worker in an automobile factory. Revolutionary guards attacked the performances and beat the actors. Soltanpour was seized on his wedding night and summarily executed without trial on July 26 1981. He was a member of the executive board of the Iranian Writers' Association. A seven-stage censorship was imposed for every play, each stage controlled by a different official. Gradually, theatrical performances were eliminated altogether.

Films New restrictive rules for film production went into effect that were even harsher than for the theatre. Government appointees controlled every stage of production, from the writing of the script to the framing of the scenes and the editing. Films produced by well-known film directors were confiscated. The situation became particularly intolerable for female actors.

Academic Freedom

In September 1979, the Minister of Education, declared that academic freedom was a colonial ploy to corrupt Islamic youth. At primary and secondary schools, textbooks were changed to conform to the views of the government, and Islamic committees were established in all schools to approve reading materials. Total segregation of boys from girls and the obligatory wearing of "Islamic garments" by all female pupils and staff was imposed. Private schools were closed or taken over. Women were deprived of many branches of study, including mathematics courses, the natural sciences and the humanities.

The universities, traditionally a stronghold of secular thought and of opposition to the Shah, were purged of a large number of academics. They were later executed on the indictment that they had resisted the Islamic drive in the universities. Intellectual curiosity, scientific research and independent thinking were therefore restricted to limits permitted by theologians.

Imprisonment and Execution of Political Opponents

Since 1979, the prisons of Iran have held hundreds of thousands of opponents of the government. In August 1986, Amnesty International reported that it had recorded 6,627 executions, but believed that the total number was much higher. Iranian opposition groups put the figure at about 40,000.

Following the end of the Iran-Iraq war in 1988, a major wave of killings of political prisoners, estimated at over 1200, took place in virtually every town and city of the country. Among known victims are at least five prominent writers.

Recent events in Eastern Europe and other parts of the world have given momentum to the increasingly vocal demands for democracy. In May 1990, 90 leading liberal figures of the Iranian revolution signed an open letter to President Rafsanjani, condemning the "new tyranny" in Iran and deploring the denial of elementary human rights and political, judicial and economic freedoms as guaranteed by the Constitution. They demanded "freedom for political parties, associations and publications which have legal and open activity". The signatories included Mehdi Bazargan (post-revolution prime minister between February to November 1979), 14 of his cabinet ministers, a former police chief, former chief-of-staff General Nasser Farbod, Ayatollah Zanjani, a senior clergyman, and Hendi Khomeini, a nephew of the late revolutionary leader. Some prominent signatories were arrested on June 12 and accused of having secret contacts with "foreign circles".

On June 17, *Abrar*, an Islamic newspaper demanded that a "revolutionary verdict" (death penalty) be applied to those arrested. The organ of the Islamic Republic, *Joumhouri Eslami*, added that the government should have no mercy for "those who attempted to reinstate a diabolical regime in Iran".

The Satanic Verses

After a series of violent protests against Salman Rushdie and his novel *The Satanic Verses* in Bombay, Kashmir and Dacca, on February 12 1989 some 2,000 protesters tried to storm the US Embassy in Islamabad. Police opened fire on them, killing at least five people and injuring more than 100. This confrontation was televised world-wide including in Tehran. On February 14, the late Ayatollah Khomeini declared a *fatwa* (religious edict) calling on Muslims everywhere to kill Salman Rushdie and his publishers for apostasy.

On February 15, thousands of anti-Rushdie protesters stoned the British Embassy in Tehran (reopened in November 1988 after a closure of eight years). A senior Iranian cleric, Hassani Sanei, through his charity, the June 5th Foundation, offered a US$3 million reward to any Iranian and US$1 million to any foreigner who killed Rushdie.

On February 17, in Tehran, President Ali Khamenei suggested Salman Rushdie might be pardoned if he repented. The following day, the author issued a statement of regret which was rejected in Iran as falling short of the public repentance required for a pardon. On February 19, Ayatollah Khomeini renewed the death sentence, declaring it every Muslim's duty to send Salman Rushdie to hell. In protest, the United Kingdom recalled its diplomats from Tehran and requested Iran to recall its UK diplomats.

On February 20, the member states of the European Community recalled their ambassadors from Iran and the following day Iran recalled its envoys from EC countries. The *fatwa* has since been reiterated by the religious leaders of Iran.

In October 1990, Iran renewed diplomatic relations with the United Kingdom. Salman Rushdie remained in hiding despite fresh initiatives by Iranian and UK politicians to resolve the issue.

Actions

On March 20 1989 ARTICLE 19 wrote to the government expressing its concern at the detention, since 1983, without charge or trial, of Malakeh Mohammadi, who had been a journalist for *Nameh Mardom* and *Donya*, and Mariam Firooz, who was editor-in-chief of *Jahan-e-Zanan*. ARTICLE 19 requested the unconditional release of the women.

Iraq

On August 2 1990, Iraq invaded Kuwait and, as this report went to press, was still in control of the country. Since then, the Iraqi authorities have attempted to jam broadcasts in Arabic by the BBC World Service and Voice of America by use of a powerful transmitter south of Baghdad. The following is an account of the situation prior to the invasion.

Between September 1980 and August 1988, Iraq engaged with Iran in one of the longest and most savage armed conflicts of modern history. Casualties in both countries were estimated at 1.5 million dead and injured. The Iraqi government took advantage of the conflict to implement a vigorous policy of repression against members

	Data	Year
Population	17,250,000	1988
Life expectancy (M/F)	61.5/63.3	1985
GNP (US$ per capita)	2,942	1988
Main religion(s)	Islam	
Official language(s)	Arabic	
Illiteracy %	40.3	
(M/F)	30.2/50.7	1990
Daily newspapers	6	1986
Non daily newspapers	22	1986
Periodicals	807	1986
Radio sets	3,400,000	1987
TV sets	1,100,000	1987
Press agencies:		
	Iraqi News Agency	
ICCPR:	YES	1971

of opposition political groups (Shiites, Kurds and their sympathizers). Thousands of people were jailed, tortured, executed or simply disappeared. Many others were expelled across the Iranian border. These abuses have continued since the end of the war and the Iraqi government has escalated repression against its population by using chemical weapons to crush resistance and by the destruction of hundreds of Kurdish villages and the forced relocation of their inhabitants.

Despite National Assembly elections in 1989 and promises that a new, more liberal constitution is nearing approval, there is no optimism that freedom of expression or respect for a multi-party political system can take root after nearly 12 years of President Saddam Hussein's rule.

In theory, Article 26 of the Interim Constitution of 1968 guarantees "freedom of opinion, publication, meeting, demonstration, and forming political parties, unions and societies". In practice, censorship is total and enforced by terror. All political groupings other than the Ba'th Party are banned, as are their newspapers. No public meeting or demonstration is permitted unless organized by the authorities. No independent trade unions or professional, cultural and religious associations are allowed. A Revolutionary Command Council (RCC) resolution of April 1989 has declared that to hold office in any association, the individual must have participated in "the sacred battle against Iranian aggression".

The Media

The Press Information is tightly controlled; nothing appears in the media that is in any way critical of prevailing policy or the leadership. Although there are at least three dailies published, *al-Jumhuriya*, *Baghdad Observer* and *al-Thawra*, the news content is the same in each because it is taken directly from the state news agency INA. The authorities view the press, first and foremost, as a means of controlling public opinion and promoting the authorities' views. The entire press is dedicated to extolling President Saddam Hussein.

Nothing in the Iraqi Constitution specifically affirms the freedom of the press. Newspapers are staffed by members of the ruling Ba'th Party and the school of journalism is open only to members of the Ba'th youth organization.

In 1978, following the implementation of the RCC decree of April 12 1978 "restructuring media personnel", hundreds of writers and journalists employed in the Ministry of Information and Culture, radio and television broadcasting and state publishing houses were made redundant, retired or transferred to clerical posts in the civil service. Among them were writer Su'ad Khairi and journalists Fatima Muhsin and Burhan el-Shawi. Over 300 others were detained, interrogated and subjected to physical and psychological torture to force them to renounce their political affiliations. Many others went into exile. The Journalists' Union was reorganized and scores of its members were transferred or detained. Some later disappeared, among them Abdu Salam al-Nasiri, director of *al-Thqafa al-Jadida*, arrested in May 1979, and Dr Hussain Qassim El-Aziz, editor of *al-Fikr al-Jadid*, arrested in 1980.

The Press Code The 1968 Press Code lists 12 subjects that the censor cannot allow to be published. These include: criticism of the president, members of the RCC or those who act on their behalf; defamation or criticism of the state and its administration; or news which may cause the devaluation of the national currency. Seven other subjects require the approval of the censors prior to publication including any words or statement attributed to the president or members of the RCC; discussions or decisions of the Council of Ministers or other officials; and agreements and treaties concluded by the government of Iraq.

Censorship of the Law Iraqi law itself may be subject to censorship. Certain laws and decrees are given only restricted circulation and others remain unpublished. According to Law 78 (1977), "the President of the Republic may decide on the publication of laws, resolutions, texts of treaties, agreements or instructions in special issues of *al-Waqai al-Iraqiya* (the Official Gazette) if the supreme interests of the state require so ... the President of the Republic may decide on the non-publication of laws, resolutions and regulations which concern the security of the state or which have nothing of public interest in their provisions".

Insult In November 1986, the RCC decreed a new law (840) stipulating that the penalty for publicly insulting the president or the authorities would be imprisonment for life and confiscation of all property. The decree provides for the death penalty "if the insult was flagrant and aimed to stir public opinion against the authorities". In May 1987, a theology lecturer and three doctors were executed for "insulting the president". With such laws, freedom of political speech has disappeared.

Foreign Correspondents Reports by foreign news organizations are seen as a threat to the information system the government has erected. Local journalists working with foreign news agencies must exercise extreme caution.

The issue of visas and invitations is the chief means of controlling foreign correspondents. Journalists are escorted from one government official to another. Telephones and telex lines are tapped and correspondents are unable to use telex or fax machines personally, only through an operator. Film is inspected and a licence, which is rarely given, is needed for typewriters and photocopiers. Some foreign journalists entering Iraq have claimed that the model numbers of their typewriters, recording equipment and short-wave radios are written in their passports; they must have all the equipment when they leave. In May 1990, a BBC TV crew visiting Iraq during an Arab summit had their video tapes confiscated.

Farzad Bazoft Many news agencies no longer send journalists to Iraq since their coverage may be compromised and the journalists may be arrested. On September 15 1989, Farzad Bazoft, a reporter for the UK *Observer* newspaper was arrested after investigating an explosion at an Iraqi military installation. Bazoft had been invited by the Iraqi government to cover elections in Kurdistan. In a summary trial, Bazoft was found guilty of spying for Israel, a charge he denied. Despite international appeals for clemency, he was hanged on March 15 1990.

The Arab Press Abroad The Iraqi government owns and heavily subsidizes a range of magazines and newspapers published in London, Paris and Cyprus. These are produced for the Arab community abroad and for circulation in Arab countries to promote the government's views, but they do not circulate freely inside Iraq.

Foreign Publications Publications from outside Iraq are forbidden, even those from Arab countries supporting Iraq. Iraqis, even government officials, may not subscribe to any non-Iraqi publication without prior permission.

Radio and Television The Ministry of Culture and Information controls these media through the State Organization for Broadcasting and TV. Radio and TV stations are staffed solely by government employees and are subject to rigid political and ideologial control. Iraqis are closely watched to ensure that they do not listen to "hostile" (Syrian, Iranian) radio stations and there are reports that some have been arrested and questioned for doing so. Military personnel are provided with radio sets that receive Baghdad radio only.

Freedom of Opinion and Expression

In 1980, the authorities dissolved all cultural and literary groups and societies and replaced them with a "General Federation of the Literate and Writers".

Arts Artists must belong to the state-controlled Artists' Union and their work is dictated by the Committee of the Union. No non-Union artist has the right to work. The rules of the Union provide that its activities must conform to Ba'th Party principles. Since the war with Iran, art has been exclusively directed to the service of the Ba'th Party and Saddam Hussein. Every town has large murals of Saddam Hussein. Artists who painted his portrait with their own blood were specially praised by the President.

Film Films are censored by a committee representing the Ministries of Culture, Information, Defence and the Interior, and the Ba'th Party. Films and videos are prohibited "if they propagate atheism or affect public order or internal security, have anti-masses objectives, interests and aspirations or are of low intellectual and artistic standards and not dealing with useful subjects". Films made before the Ba'th Party assumed power are banned.

Independent film makers require licences from the Ministry of Culture and to ensure that their work is not banned they produce films which avoid depicting the present situation in the country. Most films screened by state-run TV or at cinemas are of a military nature.

Songs Iraqi and non-Iraqi singers who refuse to co-operate with the government by lauding it have their songs banned. A list exists containing more than 200 prohibited Iraqi and foreign songs, including all the works of the Egyptian Mohamed Abdelwahab, the Spaniard Julio Iglesias and the Iraqi Mohamed Masoud.

Books The number of banned books in Iraq is believed to exceed 100,000. The banned list is sent to all sections of police intelligence who then inspect libraries and bookshops and ensure that prohibited titles are seized and burned. The list is also available at airports. Many banned books are about Islam and Islamic subjects. Books written in Iraq are produced under the control of state publishing houses and no Iraqi writer can publish a book if the Ministry of Information and Culture has not scrutinized the draft and checked the book after printing. No Iraqi citizen or foreign resident can open a bookshop without a licence and no bookshop can sell a book without the authorization of the Censorship Department.

Actions

In its 1987 Commentary to the Committee on Human Rights ARTICLE 19 called on the government to provide full information on the whereabouts of arrested journalists and for the release of those in detention; to allow freedom of political association and publication; amend or abolish those laws that impose systematic censorship on Iraqi citizens; to restore freedom of association and permit artists, writers and intellectuals to pursue independently their professions; to abolish the death penalty and life imprisonment sentences for crimes of speech and association.

ARTICLE 19 took concerted action on behalf of Farzad Bazoft, the Iranian-born reporter for the UK *Observer*. (See text)

On October 5 1989 ARTICLE 19 wrote to the government calling for the release of Mr Bazoft, detained without charge or trial and being investigated for alleged espionage.

On October 23 1989 ARTICLE 19 sent an appeal letter to its members urging them to write to the Iraqi government on behalf of Mr Bazoft.

On November 2 1989 ARTICLE 19 wrote to the government protesting the continued detention of Mr Bazoft and his "trial by TV".

On November 23 1989 ARTICLE 19 wrote to the government protesting the detention without charge or trial of Daphne Parish, a British nurse. (She was held in connection with the alleged offences of Farzad Bazoft, and later sentenced to 15 years. She was released on July 16 1990.)

On February 19 1990 ARTICLE 19 wrote to the government asking that Farzad Bazoft receive an open and fair trial. In the same month an appeal letter was sent to its members urging them to write letters of protest on behalf of Mr Bazoft.

On March 2 1990 ARTICLE 19 wrote to the government asking that an independent legal observer be allowed to attend Mr Bazoft's trial. A reply from the Iraqi under-secretary for foreign affairs, Nizar Hamdoon, promised a "fair and just trial for Mrs Parish and Farzad Bazoft".

On March 14 1990 ARTICLE 19 met with the Iraqi Ambassador to the UK to plead for clemency for Farzad Bazoft. On the same day, in reply to a telex condemning the death sentence on Mr Bazoft, Nizar Hamdoon sent a telex to ARTICLE 19 saying that "investigative reporting" is not an absolute human right.

On March 15 1990 ARTICLE 19 sent a telex to Nizar Hamdoon condemning the execution of Farzad Bazoft.

On May 3 1990 ARTICLE 19 organized a seminar in London on censorship in Iraq.

Israel and the Occupied Territories

Israel has no written constitution and its laws do not provide any formal guarantee of freedom of expression. Although the country's courts have stated that the principle of free expression is an integral part of the legal system, they have upheld censorship of the Hebrew and Arabic media to highly differing degrees.

Censorship within Israel is based on the Press Ordinance of 1933 and the Defence (Emergency) Regulations of 1945. Under the regulations, the military censor or the Minister of the Interior has draconian powers of censorship. The censor may prohibit the publication of matters deemed to be prejudicial to the defence of the state, public safety or public order, or the import or export of any publication for the same reason. These restrictions also apply to the Palestinian press.

	Data	Year
Population	4,431,000	1988
Life expectancy (M/F)	73.1/76.6	1984
GNP (US$ per capita)	8,650	1988
Main religion(s)	Judaism	
	Islam	
Official language(s)	Hebrew	
Illiteracy %	8.2	1983
(M/F)	5.0/11.3	1983
Daily newspapers	27	1986
Non daily newspapers	83	1985
Periodicals	890	1985
Radio sets	2,050,000	1987
TV sets	1,150,000	1987
Press agencies:		
Jewish Telegraphic Agency,		
ITIM, Palestine Press Service		
ICCPR:	NO	

Newspapers and publications require a permit which may be suspended or revoked at any time. The censor may order copy to be submitted before publication. It is forbidden to print any matter from which "it may be inferred" that an alteration has been made by the censor.

The Media

Newspapers While the Hebrew-language press enjoys a fair degree of freedom of expression, the Arabic papers within the country's 1948 borders face more restrictions. Israel has eight major Hebrew daily newspapers. Four of these, *Ha'aretz*, *Ma'ariv*, *Yedioth Ahronoth* and *Hadashot*, are independent. The others are aligned to various political groups. *Davar* is owned by the Histadrut, Israel's labour federation; *al Hamishmar* by the Mapam Party and *Hatsofeh* by the National Religious Party. The English-language daily *The Jerusalem Post*, is partially owned by the Histadrut. The one major Arabic daily, *al-Ittihad*, is aligned to the Communist Party. There are also numerous weekly, bi-weekly and monthly journals.

Censorship of the Hebrew Press The effects of the emergency regulations have been mitigated through the Editors' Committee, formed in 1948, in which the mainstream Israeli press participates. The Committee reached an agreement with the military to exercise self-censorship on certain "sensitive" subjects, primarily those that could be harmful to national security. Editors are trusted to submit material relating to security issues. Although the agreement specifies that censorship does not apply to political matters, opinions, commentary, assessments or any other matter except for security information, the list of sensitive subjects has included Israeli purchases of petroleum, international loans, information about Jewish immigration, Jewish communities abroad and the activities of the Shin Bet secret service. More recently, such topics as Israel's nuclear capability and the meeting of the Palestinian National Council (PNC) in Algeria in November 1988, and Soviet-Jewish immigration have also been subject to restrictions under the agreement.

Disagreements between editors and the military over censorship can be taken before a special three-member panel rather than the courts. This panel, consisting of a representative of the Editors' Committee, and of the General Staff, with an independent chairperson, can also hear appeals against the censor's decision or the censor's complaints over press violations.

All Israel's Hebrew-language dailies, except *Hadashot*, participate in the Editors' Committee. Those newspapers not represented, including non-daily publications and the Arabic-language press, are subject to the full force of the press regulations. The censors may demand to see any or all copy and the authorities may close these publications at any time.

Reporting the Intifada Since the start of the *Intifada* in December 1987, the Israeli authorities have on many occasions expressed their disquiet over international and national coverage. Newspaper and television reports of the anti-occupation strikes and demonstrations, especially shootings and beatings of Palestinians by security forces, have been attacked. Prime Minister Yizthak Shamir's spokesman, Avi Pazner, went on Israeli TV to accuse a cameraman for the United States ABC network of paying Palestinians to riot for the cameras. On another occasion, Prime Minister Shamir told a delegation of Jewish organizations that "journalists refuse to listen to us and always seek Arab sources for their information". Of equal concern to the authorities has been the growing "credibility problem", the disparity between the official version of events and what the public read and see on TV. As a result, increasingly harsh measures have been adopted to control media coverage of the *Intifada*.

Harassment of Journalists Many Israeli journalists have found themselves on the front line. When Makram Houri Manoul published an article in the Hebrew-language publication *Ha'ir*, on December 18 1987, he found himself under intense pressure and threats of prosecution for libel. The article described how a Palestinian youth was shot dead in a hospital courtyard, how a child was shot in the same place, and how an Israeli soldier was captured by a crowd who released him wearing only his trousers. On December 24 1987, an Israeli correspondent for the army radio station Galei Zahal was arrested by order of the military commander of the West Bank Central Region, General Mitzna. Two weeks earlier, the general had ordered the correspondent, Zohar Melamed, to be dismissed from the radio station. At the beginning of 1988, an Israeli camera crew working for CBS network in Gaza was beaten by soldiers while filming troops beating a Palestinian youth. On October 25, British journalists Paul Taylor and Steve Weizman of Reuters news agency, and Andrew Whitley of the *Financial Times* were stripped of their press credentials for failing to submit reports to the military censors about alleged under-cover army "death squads" engaged in killing Palestinian militants in the Occupied Territories. All three have been denied government information services. In June 1989, Paul Taylor, Reuters' bureau chief, was warned by the Israeli military censor that if Reuters violated censorship regulations during the next year, the authorities would withdraw his permit to operate in Israel.

Derech Hanitzotz The Jerusalem-based Derech Hanitzotz/Tariq al-Sharara collective published a joint Hebrew and Arabic bi-weekly newspaper which was critical of the Israeli occupation. On February 18 1988, the paper's licence was cancelled by the Jerusalem District Commissioner, on the grounds that it was linked to the Democratic Front for the Liberation of Palestine (DFLP). Five of the paper's Israeli-Jewish editors, Yaacov Ben-Efrat, Roni Ben-Efrat, Michal Schwartz, Asaf Adiv and Hadas Lahav, were arrested. In January 1989, four of the editors were convicted by the Jerusalem District Court of membership of a terrorist organization, membership of an illegal organization and of providing a service for an illegal organization. All were sentenced to terms of imprisonment ranging from nine to 30 months.

The Alternative Information Centre (AIC) The AIC is a joint Israeli-Palestinian enterprise which aims to "cover events that do not receive the attention they deserve". The Centre, which publishes a licensed newsletter, *News from Within*, was closed for six months in February 1987 under the 1948 Prevention of Terrorism Act. This Act, amended by the Knesset in 1980, makes it a criminal offence for anyone to "publish, in writing or orally, words of praise or sympathy for ... or support of, a terrorist organization". The AIC was charged with having links with the Popular Front for the Liberation of Palestine (PFLP); its equipment was confiscated and its six staff members were arrested. All except its director were released within 48 hours and the Centre was allowed to re-open in August 1987.

In November 1989, the Centre's director, Michel Warshawsky, was convicted and imprisoned for publishing a leaflet for a "terrorist organization" which contained information on how to withstand Israeli methods of interrogation. It was said to have been written by the PFLP. The AIC was fined IS10,000 (US$5,000).

Radio and Television These media are also subject to government censorship and, as with the written press, there is consensual censorship on military and security matters. Israel has, at present, one TV channel broadcasting in Hebrew and Arabic, with a second undergoing trials. Its four civilian radio stations are controlled by the Israel Broadcasting Authority (IBA), while the army radio station, Galei Zahal, comes under the Ministry of Defence. Although the Israeli broadcast media have carried extensive coverage of the *Intifada*, there have also been attempts by the authorities to restrict journalists.

On November 15 1988, the director of the IBA, Uri Porat, announced a series of restrictions on the radio and TV coverage of the PNC meeting in Algiers that month. According to the instructions, speeches could only be summarized indirectly; no interviews or commentaries should be aired unless made by persons in official positions; and no studio panel discussion or debates should be held.

Following these restrictons and Uri Porat's remarks that "radio journalists serve the PLO and enemy propaganda", journalist David Grossman resigned from the Voice of Israel news service. Reporter Uri Goldstein, who had previously been banned from covering the Occupied Territories, also resigned. Reacting to Porat's statement, Voice of Israel journalists sent a petition to the IBA, informing them of their decision to sue for libel.

In September 1990, the IBA instructed journalists to use Hebrew instead of Arabic names for places in Israel and the Occupied Territories.

Books Unlike the occupied territories, few books are banned in Israel. Books which contain "sensitive" information must be submitted to the military censor for approval.

In September 1990, the military censor permitted the publication of *Let My People Go To Hell*, by Zohar, after the deletion of several paragraphs on the grounds they may endanger certain persons' lives or harm Israel's relations with other countries. The book claims that the Israeli government could have saved hundreds of Argentine Jews who were murdered or disappeared in Argentina between 1976 and 1982 but refrained from processing immigration applications from Jews with left-wing backgrounds.

On September 14, Israel dropped attempts to ban publication in Canada of *By Way of Deception: The Making and Unmaking of a Mossad Officer*, by former Mossad officer Victor Ostrovsky. A United States ban was overruled in New York's Appeals Court on September 13. This was the first time that a foreign state had sought or obtained a prior restraint against the publication of a book in the United States. One revelation in the book which aroused controversy is that Mossad allegedly had forwarning of the Shiite terrorist attack on the US marines' headquarters in Beirut in 1983 but failed to notify Washington. Since then, imported copies of the book have sold out immediately in Israel.

Music Censorship A Hebrew song, *After the Deluge*, by the popular singer Nurit Gairon, was banned in May 1989 for being "sympathetic to the *Intifada*". Si Hyman's song, *Shooting and Crying*, which condemned the practices of the army in the Occupied Territories, was also banned.

Closure of Arab Papers Two Nazareth-based Arabic periodicals, *al-Rai'a* and *al-Jamaheer*, were closed down. The licence of the bi-weekly *al-Jamaheer* was revoked without explanation and the closure order was upheld by the High Court of Justice in December 1987. The weekly organ of the Abna' al-Balad Palestinian movement, *al-Rai'a*, within the "green line", was accused of having links with the PFLP and on January 15 1989 was informed that its licence would be withdrawn.

On January 11 1988, an *al-Ittihad* journalist was arrested for two days, while the newspaper was ordered to close for a week from March 24 on the grounds that "the paper has been publishing items which could encourage acts and deeds likely to endanger public security". One of these was an article by Tawfiq Zayyad, the Mayor of Nazareth and Knesset member, who wrote that "the Palestinian Arab population of Israel not only blesses the uprising in the territories and identifies with it, but also has to draw lessons from it".

Nuclear Secrecy and the Vanunu Affair Mordechai Vanunu was put on trial in the summer of 1987, charged with treason and espionage for revealing to the UK paper *The Sunday Times* that Israel had developed 100-200 nuclear bombs. On March 27 1988, Vanunu was sentenced to 18 years' imprisonment; no details of the trial or judgement were revealed since the court proceedings were held in camera. The secrecy surrounding his case was reinforced by a ban on the Israeli press from reporting the affair except by quoting foreign newspapers. Previous allegations that Vanunu was illegally abducted abroad and smuggled into Israel by Israeli agents were also banned from publication by the military censor.

In May 1990, the Supreme Court rejected Vanunu's appeal after an in camera hearing and banned publication of their 89-page verdict. In September 1990, the Supreme Court partially lifted the ban on publication and released 60 pages of the ruling.

Foreign Funding A proposed amendment to the 1948 Prevention of Terrorism Act will prevent Palestinian welfare organizations inside the "green line" from receiving funding from foreign sources if such sources are suspected of links with the PLO. Non-profit organizations, which are regulated by the law of corporations and must apply for registration, may, under the Bill, be refused registration or shut down. A broad-based coalition against the amendment claims that the legislation "would cause grave damage to Arab voluntary organizations working in such fields as education, sport, health, women's rights and religion, which are mainly funded by overseas philanthropic and charitable organizations".

West Bank and Gaza Strip

Since 1967, Palestinians in the Occupied Territories have been under military rule in which military commanders have legislative and administrative power of government. Over 1,100 military orders have been issued for the West Bank and over 800 for Gaza, four of which govern the press. Order 50 (1967) forbids the importation of newspapers into the West Bank or their distribution without a permit from the local military authorities. Order 101 (1967), amended in 1977 and 1981, creates the offence of inciting readers to violate the "security and public order" of the area and prohibits publication in the West Bank of any matter "with political significance" except under a licence from a military commander. Order 379 (1970) permits the confiscation of any publication that lacks a permit, or of a publication that has a permit and has passed the censor, if it is considered a threat to "security or public order". In addition to the Defence Regulations and the military orders, the chief military censor sends an annual directive to the Palestinian press "in order to clarify any ambiguity" regarding censorship.

Censorship Regulations Since the major Palestinian newspapers, magazines and press agencies are located in East Jerusalem, which Israel annexed in 1967, they are theoretically subject to the same press laws as the Israeli press. However, the Palestinian press is clearly treated differently.

The Palestinian Press As of October 1989, the Palestinian press consisted of 14 publications including the daily newspapers *al-Quds*, *al-Fajr*, *al-Shaab*, and *al-Nahar*. There are also four weeklies, *al-Tali'a*, *al-Bayader al-Siyyasi*, *al-Usbu' al-Jadeed* and *al-Awdeh*, one Arabic monthly, *al-Katib* and one Hebrew bi-weekly, *Ha-Gesher*.

The Arab Journalists' Association (AJA), affiliated since 1990 to the International Federation of Journalists, represents Palestinian journalists in the Occupied Territories. It has 200 members of which 80 are full-time.

Censorship of the Palestinian press has increased since the start of the *Intifada*. Between July and December 1987, six Palestinian press offices were closed down. Practically every Palestinian newspaper has suffered restrictions since December 1987.

The Israeli authorities have justified restrictions on media coverage of the *Intifada* by claiming that the press was behind the unrest. In June 1988, Israeli President Haim Herzog accused the foreign press of distorting coverage of the *Intifada*.

Licensing Publications All publications require a licence from the Ministry of the Interior. Many applications are refused or granted only after drawn-out legal battles. Licences may be suspended or revoked at any time without explanation and have been permanently revoked or suspended for periods ranging from several days to a month. Al-Awdeh, which publishes Arabic and English weekly magazines, had its licences revoked on May 2 1988 and the *Monday Report*, a weekly English-language newsletter distributed to foreign journalists and diplomats, was banned in May 1989.

Licensing Distribution All publications require additional licences from the military government to distribute in the Occupied Territories. Under the regulations, such licences may be suspended or revoked at any time. Possession of an unlicensed publication has resulted in heavy sentences (one Palestinian was sentenced to a month's imprisonment, one-year suspended sentence and a fine of IS600 (US$1,200)).

Censorship in Action During the first nine months of the *Intifada*, the distribution permits of East Jerusalem publications were suspended at least 10 times. *Al-Fajr* was banned five times for a total of about 100 days, the first instance being on December 10 1987, when it carried news of the Gaza military truck that killed four Palestinians, an incident which is regarded as having sparked off the *Intifada*. The article was regarded by the censor as "incitement". On December 15 1988, *al-Shaab* newspaper was banned for one week for publishing a translation of an article on the *Intifada* from the Hebrew press without first submitting it to the censor.

Since the Palestinian press is required by the chief military censor to submit practically all written material, and because the threat of closure has increased during the *Intifada*, editors include pictures, cartoons, statements, translations from the Hebrew press, reports from Israel radio, advertisements, news of demonstrations in Europe in support of the *Intifada*, even crossword puzzles and sports reports. This has resulted in overload at the censorship office and a request not to send so much material. This in turn has led to an impossible situation where the papers never know what is and what is not permissible. *Al-Quds* newspaper was banned from the Occupied Territories for 18 days in December 1987 for reproducing a photograph that was published in the Hebrew press of an armed Israeli soldier retreating before a demonstration in Gaza. Similarly, *al-Fajr* and *al-Nahar* were banned for publishing a photograph of two Palestinians suspected of dropping a rock which killed an Israeli soldier in Nablus, even though it was reprinted from *Hadashot*.

Although most material taken or translated from the Hebrew press passes the censor, Palestinian journalists estimate that about 60 per cent of original material sent to the censor, including editorials, is totally or partially cut. This, they claim, means that in order to issue a 12-page newspaper, at least 30 pages must be prepared to allow for deletions.

Restrictions on Journalists In addition to curfews and the declaration of closed areas, the movement of individual Palestinian journalists is further restricted by house and town arrests, travel bans, short-term arrests, intentional delays at military checkpoints and at interrogation sessions, and deportation.

It is estimated that about 30 per cent of members of the AJA have been detained or placed under administrative restrictions (without charge or trial) during the *Intifada*. *The Jerusalem Post* (May 21 1989) reported that during 1988, 30 Palestinian journalists were in prison. During the uprising, 39 journalists have been placed under administrative detention (extended from six months to one year in August 1989). Sama'an Khoury, AJA member and journalist for Agence France Presse, was placed under six months' administrative detention in Janaury 1988; Mutawakil Taha, president of the Union of Palestinian Writers (UPW) and editor of *Abeer* women's magazine, was also given six months in February 1988. At least 10 journalists have served more than six months' detention under renewal orders. Journalists have also been detained for periods from 48 hours to 18 days under "preventive" detention.

Deportations of Journalists Deportations of Palestinians from the Occupied Territories have been condemned by the international community as a violation of the Fourth Geneva Convention: a total of 56 Palestinians have been expelled since the *Intifada* began. On January 3 1988, the expulsion of nine Palestinians was ordered for allegedly inciting unrest. Among them was Jibril Mahmud Rajab, deputy editor of *Abeer*. He was described as a "major operative in the Judea and Samaria region". Like many other deportees, Rajab withdrew his appeal to the Israeli High Court (which has never overturned a military-ordered deportation order) after the Court ruled that evidence against him should not be revealed to him or his lawyer.

Attacks on Journalists Palestinian journalists have been attacked in the field, in their offices and at their homes by soldiers and by Israeli civilians. In March 1988, 60 bullets were fired into the house of the editor of *al-Bayader al-Siyyasi*, while the editor of *al-Quds* has had his house raided on over 10 occasions. In March 1989, a freelance Palestinian journalist accompanying a foreign TV crew through Shati refugee camp in Gaza was beaten and then shot twice by soldiers. In May, a Palestinian cameraman working for NBC TV was beaten by soldiers while filming in Ramallah and another was shot in the chest. The offices of a number of newspapers and agencies have been raided by the Israeli authorities: in March 1989, documents, photographs and equipment were confiscated from Bethlehem Press Office and, in May, from the Gaza Press Office. A photographic agency in Jerusalem was raided twice, its equipment vandalized and two of its employees were detained, beaten and interrogated. The premises of *al-Fajr*, *al-Shaab* and *al-Tali'a* have all been raided on different occasions.

The Foreign Press There are about 250 correspondents working for the foreign press in the Occupied Territories, as well as visiting journalists. It is estimated that at the beginning of the *Intifada* there were around 1,200 foreign journalists in the area. The situation they faced was summarized in *The Jerusalem Post* (January 28 1988): "First, access to areas of tension is barred, then sources of second-hand information are silenced, and finally, the finished news reports are subject to tightened censorship. Surrounding this system of restrictions, like an outer ring, is a public atmosphere of hostility to the press."

According to the Foreign Press Association, which represents the majority of foreign news agencies in Israel, there have been over 150 incidents since 1987 against foreign journalists by Israeli police, border guards, soldiers, settlers and civilians, including physical attacks, firing, confiscation of news equipment and personal property, short-term detention and the black-listing of particular journalists. One example is that of the CBS TV crew who filmed four Israeli soldiers breaking the limbs of two Palestinian youths with rocks and rifle butts in February 1988. The network had to hire security protection after receiving telephone threats following its transmission of the incident. Whole areas have been designated "military areas" by army officers on the spot and closed to the Palestinian and foreign press for long periods. Correspondents, particularly those with cameras, have been prevented from entering areas open to other traffic. The local press recorded 28 days in June 1989 when one or more West Bank towns was declared a closed military area.

Another disturbing development is that of Israeli military and Shin Bet agents impersonating journalists to obtain information or using press stickers on their vehicles to gain trouble-free entry into areas. Most foreign journalists covering the *Intifada* will now only venture into the Occupied Territories in the company of Palestinian colleagues (known to the local population) as guides or translators.

Palestinian Press Agencies The closure of Palestinian press agencies has further deprived foreign journalists of valuable information from Palestinian sources. The Gaza Press Office was shut for a month in January 1988. The Palestine Press Service (PPS), which had built up a reputation for providing important and accurate information, was closed in March, and in the same month the Bethlehem Press Office was closed for six months. In August, Haya Press Service was shut down for a year and its co-owner, Nabil Joulani, was served with six months' administrative detention. The Gaza Office for Press Services was closed in January 1989 for a year. The Holy Land Press Service was closed for two years from June; its head, Sari Nusseibeh, was said to have "harmed security and disturbed public order", and the press service was described as being a vehicle for certain "ideas" in support of the PLO, promoting the uprising and that its premises were used to plan the *Intifada*.

Censorship of Telecommunications The working conditions of Palestinian journalists have also deteriorated because the authorities banned the use of equipment such as fax machines in the Gaza Strip from August 27 1989. Telephone lines in many towns have frequently been cut for periods of between four days and over one month and lines to individual press offices have also been cut. All telephone lines in the Occupied Territories were cut for seven days during the meeting of the PNC in Algiers in November 1988. During that period, the whole of the Gaza Strip was placed under curfew and the West Bank sealed off.

Censorship of Books It is estimated that more than 10,000 books are banned. Books are banned if their contents, in the opinion of the censor, are liable to damage state security, public safety, or public order. Books targeted for banning include: those containing political information; those not indicating the existence of Israel; those issued by a Palestinian publisher; those carrying poems that express nationalistic feelings; or those displaying on their covers the four colours of the Palestinian flag. Among banned books are *Can the Palestinian Problem be Solved?*, by Alouph Har Even, *Studies in the History of Palestine During the Middle Ages*, by PP Bartholdy and *At the end of the Night*, by Mahmoud Darwish.

Detention of Writers Over 50 Palestinian writers and poets have been detained without charge or trial, and many have been put under town arrest or issued with a green card prohibiting them from entering East Jerusalem. Sami al-Kilani, a writer and poet, spent 1983-1985 confined to the village of his birth and has been under administrative detention since March 1 1989, his third administrative detention since December 1987.

Closure of Universities and Educational Establishments The closure of Palestinian universities and other educational institutions has affected 35,000 students who have lost three years of study since the *Intifada* began. The closures are considered a collective punishment aimed at coercing the population to end the uprising. Popular Education Committees, which organized classes and courses outside the educational institutions, have also been declared illegal. The military authorities refer to the Committees as "cells of illegal teaching" and has made association with them a crime punishable by up to three years' imprisonmment. One example is the closure of the Friends of Najah University in September 1988 and the arrest of two lecturers and dozens of students caught studying science.

According to a briefing issued by Bir Zeit University, students wishing to study abroad must obtain travel documents, which are frequently refused to students who have or have had a member of their family in detention. Palestinians have also been increasingly excluded from Jordanian universities since King Hussein of Jordan severed his country's ties with the West Bank in July 1988.

Actions

In June 1989 ARTICLE 19 sent an appeal to its members urging them to protest the closure of the Holy Land Press Service in East Jerusalem for a period of two years.

On October 5 1989 ARTICLE 19 wrote to the government protesting the six months' prison sentence imposed on Abie Nathan, a peace campaigner and owner of VOP radio station, for contacting a PLO representative. ARTICLE 19 urged the release of Nathan and the repeal of the 1986 law which forbids any Israeli citizen from communicating with any Palestinian organization. A reply from the Israeli government stated that Nathan was a citizen of Israel, tried by an Israeli court and sentenced in accordance with Israeli law.

On November 14 1989 ARTICLE 19 wrote to the government protesting the 30 months' prison sentence imposed on Michel Warshawsky, director of the Alternative Information Centre, for "providing services to a forbidden organization", and urging that the charges be dropped.

On December 12 1989 ARTICLE 19 wrote to the government expressing concern over the censorship measures implemented in the Occupied Territories of the West Bank and Gaza Strip, and requesting the release of Palestinian journalists held under administrative detention.

On March 19 1990 ARTICLE 19 wrote to the government expressing concern over its decision on March 2 to impose military censorship on media reports about the immigration of Soviet Jews to Israel. A reply from the government stated that the only items which may not be reported are the numbers of Jews going to Israel and their routes, because of "threats by some terrorist organizations to hit the new immigrants in order to dissuade others from coming to Israel".

Kuwait

On August 2 1990 Iraq invaded Kuwait and, as this report went to press, was still in control of the country. Some 40 Kuwaiti publications have been closed down by the Iraqis, including eight daily newspapers, six in Arabic and two in English. Many journalists have lost their jobs and the Iraqi forces have confiscated and removed to Baghdad all modern printing equipment. The occupation forces have established a temporary office of the Iraqi News Agency in the Kuwaiti Information Ministry building. The following is an account of the situation prior to the invasion.

Under the 1962 Constitution, executive power is vested in the Emir, the head of state, chosen by and from mem-

	Data	Year
Population	1,958,000	1988
Life expectancy (M/F)	69.6/73.7	1985
GNP (US$ per capita)	13,680	1988
Main religion(s)	Islam	
Official language(s)	Arabic	
Illiteracy %	27.0	1990
(M/F)	22.9/33.3	1990
Daily newspapers	8	1986
Non daily newspapers	3	1982
Periodicals	73	1986
Radio sets	600,000	1987
TV sets	480,000	1987
Press agencies:		
	Kuwait Press Agency	
ICCPR:	NO	

bers of the ruling al-Sabah family and exercised through a Council of Ministers and the National Assembly. Suffrage is confined to citizens proving Kuwaiti ancestry before 1920. In 1981, they comprised only 6.4 per cent of the population (65,000 male Kuwaitis out of a total population of around two million). Women are not permitted to vote or to stand for parliament. The remaining population, considered second-class citizens, are not entitled to vote.

The National Assembly, comprising 50 per cent elected members who may not belong to political parties, was dissolved by an Emir decree in July 1986, after MPs tried to call to account government ministers and members of the ruling family for inefficiency and corruption.

Since early December 1989, demands have increased for the return of parliament and for the removal of censors from the offices of the local press. A series of *diwaniyas* (gatherings of people) at the private houses of prominent Kuwaitis, many of them ex-MPs, were held to exchange views and opinions.

In late 1989 and early 1990, there were unprecedented confrontations between security forces and thousands of demonstrators, some of whom, encouraged by events in Eastern Europe which they had followed from satellite broadcasts, took to the streets, demanding a democratic system but offering no challenge to the ruling al-Sabah family.

Thirty-two former MPs established a Committee for the Restoration of Democracy, calling for the restoration of the National Assembly, a reduction in the excessive powers of the ruling family and an end to corruption and censorship.

On January 22 1990, police used teargas and batons to disperse a crowd of about 6,000 gathered at the *diwaniya* of an opposition figure. A 70-year-old former MP was beaten along with several other leading Kuwaiti politicians including Dr Ahmed Bishara, former vice-rector of the university. Soon after, the authorities announced the banning of such gatherings. On May 8 1990, in defiance of the ban, an estimated 2,000 people gathered at the *diwaniya* of Abdul Mohsen al-Farhane. Police arrested him with seven other prominent Kuwaiti politicians, among them Dr Ahmed al-Khatib and Ahmed al-Naffiss, both former MPs. In June, the authorities arrested nine more opponents, all of whom were released after the Emir waived charges. Elections to a new forum, the Transitional National Council, which would have no legislative powers and whose main brief would be to spend up to four years preparing plans for "seemly revival of parliamentary life", were held on June 12 1990 and were boycotted by the opposition.

The Media

The Press The press is privately-owned although some newspapers and magazines receive financial support from the government. There are seven daily papers, five in Arabic and two in English. The 1986 decree suspended the Press Law of 1961 and imposed prior censorship on the press. Article 35 of the Revised Censorship Regulations requires newspapers to allow two officials from the Censorship Department of the Ministry of the Interior to enter the premises and review each page of the paper. The regulations forbid criticism of the Emir, the ruling family, Islam, or leaders of Arab states. Penalities are severe: criticism expressed by publishers, editors or journalists may warrant a prison sentence of up to three years and a fine of up to KD4,800 (US$17,000). The government is empowered to suspend a newspaper for up to two years or cancel its licence if it publishes anything deemed contrary to the national interest or if it accepts financial assistance from foreign sources without approval of the Information Ministry.

Expulsion of Journalists The government has in recent years expelled several non-Kuwaiti journalists. In 1985, the Kuwait-based Palestinian political cartoonist Naji al-Ali, one of the Arab world's best known satirists, was ordered to leave, apparently because his drawings had offended several Arab governments. (He was assassinated in London two years later). There followed a wave of expulsions and residence permits of some two dozen Arab journalists, including prominent editors and columnists in the local press, were cancelled. Questioned about the expulsions, Kuwait's Crown Prince and Prime Minister remarked that if resident nationals of other Arab states were so keen on free speech "let them practise it in their own countries". Among Arab jounalists expelled were: Sulayman Flihan, a Lebanese; Mahmood al-Dimawi, a Palestinian and M al-Idres, a Yemeni. The well-known Iraqi poet Ahmad Matar was expelled to Britain.

Foreign Correspondents and Publications The "Charter for Honour in Information" adopted by the Gulf states in the 1980s states that any publication attacking any member of the Gulf Co-operation Council (GCC) is subject to a collective ban by these states. Such a ban was imposed on a book about the socio-political issues in the Gulf by Dr Khaldun al-Naqib, Dean of the School of Arts at Kuwait University, which was banned in 1988. Dr Khaldun was arrested and interrogated about his book for six days before he was released uncharged.

Kuwait has an active censorship department which reviews all books, films, videotapes, periodicals and other material brought to Kuwait for commercial or private purposes. In general, the control on foreign publications is as comprehensive as on domestic publications.

An additional list of prohibited topics to those affecting the national press applies to foreign media. It contains five forbidden topics; criticism of the government, its foreign or domestic policy, the ruling al-Sabah family and the Crown Prince.

On February 9 1989, the Ministry of Information ordered all local print and broadcast media not to publish excerpts from the work of Dr Su'ad al-Sabah, a writer and member of the board of the Arab Organization for Human Rights. Soon after, a number of Arab magazines published in Europe were confiscated, including issue 340 of the weekly *Kol al-Arab* and issue 1727 of the weekly *Sabah al-Kheir*. The reason for the ban on Dr Su'ad al-Sabah (a member of the Kuwaiti royal family) was not given, but it has been reported that the authorities were reacting to her involvement in human rights activities.

Radio and Television Kuwait Broadcasting SCE, the state-owned radio station, broadcasts in Arabic, Farsi, English and Urdu. TV of Kuwait, controlled by the Ministry of Information, transmits in Arabic; a second channel opened in 1979. Radio and TV programmes are carefully censored. TV programmes feature the daily activities of the Crown Prince and other members of the ruling family. Scenes of the Palestinian *Intifada* are not screened.

Artistic Expression

Theatre The four official theatre companies are sponsored and supervised by the Ministry of Information and financed by the Ministry of Social Affairs. Private companies receive financial subsidy from the government and are supervised and censored by the Ministry of Information. The script of any new play is scrutinized by the Ministry of Information and a team of officials must be present at rehearsal. An official is present at performances, to ensure that the performance is identical to the approved text.

On October 1989, actors Abdul Hussein Abdul Rida, Saad Faraj, Khalid al-Nafeesi and Mohammed al-Surayib, and director Abdullamir al-Turki were charged with staging a play offensive to Islam after citizens filed a complaint with the state prosecutor, claiming the play was offensive. The play entitled *This is Seif* is a comedy depicting the present conflict between traditionalists and modernists. In March 1990, Mr Rida, who played the role of a Shiite who insults a Sunni Muslim, received a one-year suspended prison sentence.

Films Films are mainly produced for TV or imported by the government-owned cinema company. The Ministry of Information supervises the censorship of locally-produced and imported films. Despite availability of up-to-date technical equipment, the government gives little encouragement to the production of films that tackle social or political issues. Producers do not embark on serious projects because of official restrictions.

Morocco

The 1972 Constitution guarantees "freedom of opinion, expression, assembly and association" (Art.9). However, these guarantees are seriously qualified in law and in practice. Restrictions on freedom of expression have led to the banning and seizure of many publications and the imprisonment of hundreds of critics of the political system.

There are a number of prohibited topics including criticism of the King's person, the monarchial political system, Islam, and state policy on the Western Sahara. According to the Constitution, the person of the King is "inviolable and sacred" (Art.23) and consequently his speeches to parliament and to the nation cannot be judged or debated (Art.28).

	Data	Year
Population	23,920,000	1988
Life expectancy (M/F)	56.6/60.0	1985
GNP (US$ per capita)	750	1988
Main religion(s)	Islam	
Official language(s)	Arabic	
Illiteracy %	50.5	1990
(M/F)	38.7/62.0	1990
Daily newspapers	11	1989
Periodicals	35	1989
Radio sets	4,800,000	1987
TV sets	1,500,000	1989
Press agencies:		
Wikalat al-Maghreb al-Arabi		
ICCPR:	YES	1979

The Media

Legislative Provisions The press is regulated by the November 15 1958 Press Code as modified on May 28 1960 and April 10 1973. Newspapers, including opposition papers, are obliged to publish the King's speeches in full or in part, without comment or criticism. The Press Code provides a sentence of from five to 20 years' imprisonment and/or a fine of from 100,000 to one million dirhams (US$80,000-US$800,000) for anyone who attacks, by any means, including writing and speech, the person of the King (Art.41).

No newspaper or periodical may commence publication without an official declaration to the judicial authorities (Art.5). Two copies of each issue must be sent to the prosecutor's office and the information service of the Ministry of the Interior prior to distribution (Art.8). The Minister of the Interior may order the seizure of any newspaper or periodical which may pose a threat to public order (Art.77). The Prime Minister may decide to prohibit a publication if it "has threatened the institutional, political or religious basis of the Kingdom" (Art.77).

The amendments of 1973 introduced additional provisions authorizing severe penalties for publication of news held to be false, or for articles considered offensive to the King and the royal family, (5-20 years' hard labour and a fine of between 100,000 and one million dhs (US$125,000)) (Art.41).

The Print Media The Moroccan press is linked to about 12 political parties. Each party has one or two publications promoting its political stance and activities. Since 1987, the state has subsidized these papers along with the trade union press.

The independent press, of which there is little, consists of monthly magazines with very low circulation and is heavily dependent on advertising revenue.

Journalism Investigative journalism in Morocco is inhibited by many factors including the absence in some newspapers of professional journalists and the fact that many are party militants who have learned their skills in-house. Editors are reluctant to send reporters on investigative missions because of the financial cost and because of intimidation by the authorities. In 1988, a reporter from the newspaper *al-Ittihad al-Ichtiraki*, working on a prostitution story, was arrested while photographing an hotel alleged to be a brothel. He was detained for two days in police custody. In another case, Zakia al-Hanani, a reporter with the feminist weekly *March 8*, was arrested on June 13 1989 and questioned. She had been recording interviews with people in the streets of Rabat. She was released without charge after one day in custody but her recording equipment was confiscated.

Information concerning important public matters is often suppressed such as diplomatic or military developments affecting the Western Sahara conflict, the impact of AIDS, or as happened on December 18 1989 when the Minister of Interior and Information censored news of an environmental catastrophe on the Moroccan Atlantic coast (caused by the discharge of thousands of tonnes of oil from the damaged Iranian tanker *Kharq*). Ten days elapsed before the Moroccan press and public were informed of the accident and then through the French media.

There is a lack of co-operation between public officials and journalists who complain about secrecy surrounding the activities of the state and officialdom's negative attitude *vis-à-vis* the press.

Public officials often refuse to give interviews, information or comment and sometimes intimidate journalists who seek information about problems in the public services for which the former are responsible. Such an incident occurred in April 1989 when a public official spat in the face of a correspondent of the opposition newspaper *l'Opinion* because of a critical article.

Censorship of Newspapers Pre-distribution censorship, applied to all opposition newspapers for many years, was abolished in 1985. It was then re-imposed for a short period in 1988 on two Arabic-language opposition dailies, *al-Bayan*, organ of the Party of Progress and Socialism (PPS), and *al-Ittihad al-Ichtiraki*, the paper of the Union Socialiste des Forces Populaires (USFP), because they had reported news of a clash between students at the University of Fez and government forces in which two students died and 19 others were injured.

The authorities now exercise an informal and indirect influence on the press by encouraging directors and editors to practise stringent self-censorship. The authorities often summon directors, editors or journalists, force them to justify articles considered objectionable, and issue them with warnings or threaten their publications with seizure. This practice has placed journalists under heavy pressure to conform to government policies.

If unofficial guidelines are ignored, the authorities summon the director and issue him/her with a warning or threaten the publication with seizure. It is difficult to determine what is self-censored, but events like student demonstrations, arrests of suspects, or political prisoners on hunger strike are given little coverage and then only in two or three opposition papers. Pro-government newspapers do not report on stories of this nature. Foreign policy is a domain which even the opposition press dare not criticize. The King, the monarchy, the political system, the Islamic religion, and government policy on the Western Sahara are never criticized. Many social issues, including prostitution and child labour, are considered controversial and rarely investigated. Political cartoons depicting government officials are also banned.

Added to an absence of investigative journalism and hard news is the poor quality of many publications and their low circulation. Owners hesitate to invest money to improve their papers and increase readership because of the absence of legal guarantees to protect against the financial risk since the authorities can intervene at any time without reason to order suspension or closure.

Attacks on the Press

Attacks on the press and harassment of journalists critical of the political and social conditions prevalent in Morocco are a growing trend.

Al-Massar, an opposition weekly paper and organ of a radical wing of the USFP, was ordered on December 13 1988 by the Court of Appeal to cease publication until its director-owner Ahmed Benjelloun paid libel damages of 150,000 dhs (US$18,450) to a local public official. In October 1985, the paper published a letter signed by 12 people in the city of El-Jadida, accusing the official of stealing land belonging to them. He sued the paper for libel and the court awarded him the highest damages in the history of the press in Morocco: 300,000 dhs (US$36,900). The Court of Appeal reduced the amount by half and the director, Ahmed Benjelloun, was sentenced to a two months' suspended prison term and a fine of 1,000 dhs (US$123).

Ahmed Benjelloun later launched a new paper, *al-Tariq*, but within months was arrested and interrogated about an article he published on May 1 1989 criticizing a judgement by a court in the town of Beni-Melal regarding a dispute between an employee and the public administration. The court decided in favour of the public administration. Benjelloun reported the judgement as unjust and cynical and was accused of defamation of the judicial system. In June 1990, Benjelloun was sentenced to four months' imprisonment and a fine of 5,000 dhs (US$615).

The September 13 1989 issue of *l'Opinion* printed a joint statement by two human rights groups alleging that the authorities were responsible for the deaths in detention of four Moroccans. On November 11 1989, Mohamed Idrissi Kaitouni, director of *l'Opinion*, was tried and sentenced to two years' imprisonment and a 2,000 dhs (US$246) fine for publishing "false news likely to disturb public order" (Art.42 of the Press Code). Mohamed Kaitouni, who had won widespread public support during his prosecution, was pardoned by King Hassan II three days later.

Other publications brought to court in 1989 include the weekly *Asrar* on October 10 1989 for "defamation against a pro-government party" and the weekly *al-Ousbue As-Sahafi* on October 17 1989 for "defamation of justice". On May 18 1990, Mustapha Alaoui, director of *al-Ousbue As-Sahafi*, was sentenced to three months' imprisonment and fined 5,000 dhs (US$615).

On October 15 1990, director Mohamed Labrini and editor Abdelkader Himer of the daily newspaper *al-Ittihad al-Ichtiraki* were brought to trial on charges of defaming the courts and tribunals. Their alleged offending article described the poor conditions and corruption under which courts and tribunals in Casablanca function, causing long delays in examination and judgement of cases. In court, 120 lawyers are defending the journalists who claim that they had no intention of defaming the judiciary and that their article was published in the public interest.

Closure of Lamalif The monthly magazine *Lamalif* was obliged to cease publication after its editor, Zakiya Daoud, was repeatedly harassed by the Ministry of Interior for publishing a series of articles describing the poverty-stricken state of large sectors of Moroccan society.

These articles were drawn to the attention of the King who demanded that the magazine be closed. The Interior Minister and other personalities close to the King summoned the editor and advised her to change the magazine's line or cease publication. Zakiya Daoud and her husband Mohamed Loghlam, owner of *Lamalif*, closed down the magazine.

The last issue in June 1988 also marked the 20th anniversary of the magazine. Many observers believe that, with the closure of *Lamalif*, Morocco has lost one of its finest magazines and a pioneering effort in post-independence journalism.

Closure of Kalima The Moroccan authorities seized the March 1989 issue of the French-language *Kalima*, an independent magazine published in Casablanca. Established in February 1986, the magazine regularly published articles discussing socio-cultural issues considered taboo in Morocco, especially issues related to the status of women. The March issue contained feature articles on the Moroccan press and Moroccan writers' statements supporting the British writer Salman Rushdie. After the seizure of the March 1989 issue, the owner decided to close down *Kalima* for reasons of "repetitive seizure causing a great financial loss".

Foreign Media and Journalists Morocco imports European and Arabic newspapers and magazines but there are legal restrictions on their circulation. The Press Code prohibits the importation of foreign papers containing news or information contradicting the political and religious foundation of Moroccan society (the person of the King, Islam and the Western Sahara conflict).

It is believed that a censorship service exists in Casablanca Airport which screens the content of imported papers before their distribution. Those found containing criticism or news which impinge on the limits prescribed by the state are banned. Bans also result from photographs the authorities find offensive to Moroccan moral standards.

In June 1989, the authorities banned, without explanation, issue number 60 of the Paris-based monthly magazine *Jeune Afrique*. The magazine carried an article on child labour in Morocco. *Jeune Afrique Plus* was also banned in the same month because it contained an article about the Sahara conflict, illustrated with a map outlining Morocco and Western Sahara as two separate countries. The Paris-based monthly *Le Monde Diplomatique* has been banned five times since 1988 (in December 1988, March and September 1989, and January and April 1990). These issues contained articles or readers' letters about the human rights situation in the country. The French daily *Liberation* was banned 18 times between 1989 and February 1990.

In the first two weeks of October 1990, many foreign newspapers and periodicals, including *Le Monde*, were unavailable at newsstands. Moroccan sources alleged that the papers had been confiscated. The authorities refused to give any explanation.

Foreign journalists are free to enter the country and move freely, except in the military zone in the Western Sahara, but can sometimes be subjected to harassment and expulsion when their reports anger the authorities. During the urban riots of January 1984, Jean Michel Tondre, AFP, Henry Karm, *New York Times*, and Ramon Ganuza, a reporter with a Spanish radio station, were expelled because of reports they sent to their media about the violent reaction of the army against the rioters.

Television and Radio The state controls the electronic media which expresses only government opinion. Few political parties have access to radio and TV during elections. Nothing is broadcast by televised media without the consent of the Ministry of the Interior which also controls the Information Ministry.

TV is heavily dependent on French, American and Egyptian programmes; local production is poor. Moroccan artists and writers are underused, and sometimes banned because of their political opinions. One example is the popular comic duo Ahmed Snoussi (Bziz) and Houcine (Baz) who have been banned from further appearences on TV after a live comic sketch in which they criticized the criteria used by officials in choosing artists for TV appearances.

Owing to its geographic position, Morocco receives a number of foreign TV channels including those broadcast by satellite. Satellite TV channels which can be received include: TV5 (a consortium of francophone stations); RAI Uno (Italy); Channel 2, 5, 6 and Canal Plus (France); World Net (USA); Swedish TV; RTP2 (Portugal); and TV2 (Spain). Morocco has also inaugurated a subscription-run, private TV channel, MI2, believed to be the first privately-owned channel in Africa or the Arab region. Although privately-owned, MI2 does not escape government control.

Repression of Writers There are few known cases of writers arrested and punished specifically for their writings. The routine form of repression of writers is the banning of their books or of literary magazines in which they publish. Those who have been prosecuted, however, include the poet Abdellah Zrika, arrested in 1978 for "attacking the religious and political foundations of the state" and sentenced to two years' imprisonment. The poet Ali Idrissi Kaitouni was arrested in 1982 for publishing an anthology entitled *As-Sharara* (Sparks). He was sentenced to 15 years' for "insulting the King's dignity" and "publishing falsehoods detrimental to public security". He remains in prison.

Many Moroccan writers have been prosecuted for political offences in connection with "membership of banned political organisations" and activities which "undermine the security of the state" including: Abdellatif Laâbi, sentenced in 1972 to a 10-year prison term, and released nine years later; Abdel Kader El-Chaoui, arrested in 1974, sentenced to 15 years imprisonment and released in an amnesty in 1988; and Abraham Serfaty, who was sentenced in 1974 to life imprisonment.

Many authors have had their work banned including Mohamed Lamrini, writer and director of the opposition newspaper *al-Ittihad al-Ichtiraki*; his collection of poems, *Aghlal al-Madi* (Chains of the Past), was banned in 1976. The novel *al-Khobz al-Hafi* (By Bread Alone), by Mohamed Choukri, was banned in 1983, as was his collection of poems *al-Khaima* (The Tent) in 1985. *Al-Harim As-Siyassi* (The Political Harem), by Moroccan feminist and sociologist Fatima Marnissi, was published in France and describes the political role of the Prophet Mohammed's wives. The Council of Ulema (religious council) pressurized the authorities to ban the book because it portrays the prophet's wife Ayesha as subversive and as mixing with men.

Literary magazines known to have been closed down by the authorities since 1984 include *al-Jusur* edited by Abdel Hamid Akkar, *al-Badil* edited by Ben Salem Hammich, *Attaqafa al-Jadida* edited by Mohamed Benis and *az-Zaman al-Maghrebi* edited by Said Allouch.

Actions

On April 14 1989 ARTICLE 19 wrote to the government requesting information about the arrest and detention, on March 29, of Mahomed Ait Kaddour of the Socialist Union of People's Forces.

On April 28 1989 ARTICLE 19 wrote to the government protesting the banning of the March issue of the monthly *Kalima* (See text).

On July 6 1989 ARTICLE 19 wrote to the government protesting the banning of the June issue of the Paris-based *Jeune Afrique*, reportedly because of an article on child labour in Morocco.

In its 1990 Commentary to the Committee on Human Rights ARTICLE 19 recommended that, among other actions, the government should release all political prisoners, lift the bans on political and cultural associations, books and magazines, and allow the free circulation of foreign newspapers without prior censorship.

Saudi Arabia

The Iraqi invasion of Kuwait on August 2 1990, the deployment of Western troops in Saudi Arabia, and the division which has emerged in the Arab world have compelled the Saudi authorities to admit great numbers of foreign journalists and Saudi newspapers have been permitted to publish comprehensive coverage of the conflict. As yet, no substantial freedom has resulted. The following is an account of the situation prior to the crisis in the Gulf.

The Kingdom of Saudi Arabia has no constitution, parliament or elected bodies of any kind. It is not party to the International Convenant on Civil and Political Rights. Political and social life in the country are controlled by strict laws and rules which do not allow for freedom of expression. The governmental system gives no opportunity for popular participation in the administration of the country.

	Data	Year
Population	14,016,000	1988
Life expectancy (M/F)	59.2/62.7	1985
GNP (US$ per capita)	6,170	1988
Main religion(s)	Islam	
Official language(s)	Arabic	
Illiteracy %	37.6	1990
(M/F)	26.9/51.9	1990
Daily newspapers	13	1986
Non daily newspapers	7	1984
Periodicals	58	1984
Radio sets	4,000,000	1989
TV sets	3,750,000	1989
Press agencies:		
	Islamic Press Agency,	
	Saudi Press Agency	
ICCPR:	NO	

Political organizations and trades unions are prohibited; elections and candidacy for elections are taboo; freedom of the press is totally absent and demonstrations and strikes are strictly prohibited.

The Media

Information policy is determined by a Supreme Council, approved by the Council of Ministers in March 1980, which has appointed members with Prince Nayef Ibn Abdul-Aziz, Minister of Home Affairs, as president and Ali Sharif, Minister of Information as vice-president. The Council controls all newspapers, magazines, radio and television broadcasts and can order the arrest and detention of journalists, editors and any media worker who offends against the rules.

The Press There are three daily newspapers and six weekly or monthly magazines, all subject to careful scrutiny and censorship. The press is privately-owned and most of it is financed by al-Saud princes, but the government has total control of its activities. The Minister for Information appoints chief editors and board members and has the power to dismiss them. A policy statement of 1982 requires all newspaper owners to refrain from criticizing the government, the royal family or the clergy; they must also uphold Islam, oppose atheism, and promote Arab interests. In addition to the policy statement, newspapers receive regular guidelines issued by the Ministers of Information or Interior on government positions on controversial issues. In one example in September 1988, a note by the Minister of Home Affairs was sent to newspaper editors prohibiting them from publishing articles debating the issue of "modernism" versus "traditionalism". As a result, the daily press has become repetitive, expressing only official opinions, praising the royal family and with comment on subjects irrelevant to the political and economic life of the country.

The 1963 Press and Publication Law requires that all newspapers be licensed and establishes a censorship committee comprising officials of the judiciary, the Publications Department of the Ministry of Information and the Department of Education, to review and censor all national and foreign publications according to the policies of the state. The law forbids journalists to criticize or blame government officials or any government body, and they may not criticize monarchs or other heads of state bound by treaties with Saudi Arabia. Editors-in-chief are held responsible for the publication of everything in their newspapers and journalists accused of breach of the regulations are tried by Emergency Courts.

Royal Decree 15 of 1958 defines the censorship functions of the Publications Department as follows: to censor all publications, magazines, leaflets, bulletins, video tapes and imported films; to receive drafts and manuscripts of books intended for publication, whether by Saudi authors or others; to prepare a list of books allowed to be circulated in the Kingdom; to inform newspaper distributors of orders issued by the Censorship Departments; to delete and cut all material that does not conform to state policies; to seize and confiscate all publications brought into the country by travellers or passengers.

In April 1988, the Ministry of Information issued an order prohibiting the importation or distribution of Palestinian national songs.

Foreign Journalists Foreign journalists are allowed to visit Saudi Arabia only in exceptional circumstances. No international agency has an office there and international news services employ local journalists as stringers. Foreign papers critical of Saudi policies, or containing advertisements for alcoholic beverages, or depicting beach scenes, are automatically confiscated. The *International Herald Tribune* has been confiscated on many occasions.

Freedom of Expression

Political organizations and labour unions are prohibited. A few professional associations are permitted, particularly in the civil service, but they are not allowed to affiliate with their recognized international counterparts. Foreign workers, including Arabs, are frequently expelled and deported, usually without notice.

Academic freedom is constrained by very tight guidelines: study of Freud, Marx, Western art, music and philosophy and many other subjects is prohibited. All student activities are closely monitored and no cultural magazines may be circulated on campuses. Some Saudi intellectuals have abandoned all intellectual activity because of restrictions imposed on debate and publication. Recordings of lectures on cultural topics by Arab and foreign intellectuals have been withdrawn from public circulation. People entering the country have their books confiscated regardless of their content.

Public demonstrations as a means of political expression are prohibited and punishment of offenders can be severe. On September 21 1989, following demonstrations at the Holy Haram in Mecca, the Saudi authorities executed 16

Kuwaiti pilgrims and sentenced four others to long periods of imprisonment, ranging from 15 to 20 years, in addition to severe lashings.

During the last three years, over 700 prisoners of conscience have been detained without trial including many hundreds of students and state employees. One known detainee is the poet Fatima Ahmad Yusuf, who is believed to have been paralyzed as a result of torture.

Some 1,300 citizens have, on release from detention, had their passports withdrawn and been denied the right to travel abroad. Government departments refuse to employ any ex-detainee charged with political offences and they are often prevented from taking other employment. Most ex-prisoners of conscience remain unemployed.

Saudi exiles number approximately 4,000, scattered in Europe, Syria, Iran and east Asian countries. The Saudi secret service has kidnapped over 200 opposition activists, including Nasser al-Said, author of *History of al-Saud*, in Beirut in 1979, and Taher al-Tamimi, a Jordanian national.

Discrimination

Religion Islam is the official creed of the state. All Saudi citizens must be Muslims and conversion to another religion is punishable by death. Places of worship other than those for Muslims are non-existent.

The Shia minority of the Eastern Province, totalling over half a million, is subjected to political control and social and economic discrimination. Shia citizens are under constant surveillance and their freedom of travel is restricted. Many have been arrested for observing their religious rites and they are not allowed to settle their internal problems within their own institutions. The government gives no financial support to their religious institutions, nor to Shia religious judges.

Among the many hundreds of Shiites detained without trial in 1989 were the religious figures Sheikh Ja'far al-Mubarak and Sheikh Abd al-Karim al-Habil.

On July 22 1990, Zahra Habib Mansur al-Nasser, a 40-year-old housewife, died in police custody as a result of torture. She had been arrested on July 15 with her husband at the check-point on the Saudi-Jordanian border because she had in her possession a Shia prayer book and a photograph of Ayatollah Khomeini.

Non-Muslims are not allowed to observe their own religious ceremonies nor to possess religious material. In 1987, a number of Ethiopians were expelled when they were discovered reciting Christian prayers in a house. The congregation was interrogated, then deported.

Education is free in Saudi Arabia but few Shia students are admitted to Riyadh University and then only after stringent interviews. Of a total of 93 Shia applicants to the King Faisal University in Damman, only three students were admitted in 1989. It is believed that university authorities reject them for sectarian reasons.

Saudi authorities have also passed laws prohibiting Shiites from employment in some 14 public sectors including the air force and navy, the post of judge, head teacher, governor of a province or mayor of a city or village.

Women Women who wish to be socially or politically active face many obstacles. They are not allowed to drive or travel alone, except in cases where their guardians grant them permission. Female employment in civic administration or the major companies is generally limited to teaching or health care. Women have been arrested for their political views including Widad al-Qamri, a member of the executive committee of the Union of Palestinian Women and Fouziyyah al-Bakri, a lecturer on sociology at Riyadh University and a writer and journalist for *al-Jazira*, a Saudi daily newspaper.

Sudan

Before the military coup on June 30 1989, which overthrew the civilian government of Prime Minister Sadiq al-Mahdi, Sudan enjoyed considerable freedom of expression and freedom of the press. Soon after the coup, Lieutenant-General Omar Hassan al-Bashir, the head of the new military government, announced the formation of a military council with wide legislative and executive powers. The Constitution was suspended and a State of Emergency, which still remains in force, was declared. The security forces were empowered to arrest people without warrants and detain them indefinitely without charge or trial. All newspapers, non-religious organizations and political parties were banned and their properties and assets confiscated. Several hundred people were arrested and detained without trial at the

	Data	Year
Population	23,776,000	1988
Life expectancy (M/F)	46.6/49.0	1985
GNP (US$ per capita)	340	1988
Main religion(s)	Islam	
	Animism	
	Christianity	
Official language(s)	Arabic	
Illiteracy %	72.9	1990
(M/F)	57.3/88.3	1990
Daily newspapers	5	1986
Non daily newspapers	9	1984
Periodicals	25	1984
Radio sets	5,300,000	1987
TV sets	1,200,000	1987
Press agencies:		
	Sudan News Agency,	
	Sudanese Press Agency	
ICCPR:	YES	1986

time of the coup. Many were released but more than 300 are still detained at Kober prison in Khartoum, at Shalla prison in the remote western Darfur province and at a prison in Port Sudan; others are believed to be held in detention at secret locations.

Organizing or calling for a strike became an offence punishable by death. On July 31 1989, a number of trade unions and professional associations presented the government with a memorandum protesting the new restrictions on trade union rights. From August onwards, more than 150 trade union activists and dozens of others, including academics, lawyers and journalists, were arrested and detained. In December, Maamun Mohamed Hussein, a doctor, was sentenced to death for organizing a meeting in preparation for a doctors' strike but was released in May 1990, after a concerted international campaign on his behalf.

During November and December, dozens of intellectuals and professionals were arrested, held in newly established secret detention centres and severely tortured. Some 80 politicians, most of whom served in the previous government, were held at Kober prison but most of them were released in early 1990. The military authorities appear to have ordered the arrest of all those who may be potentially opposed to their policies, and trade union activists have been particularly targetted.

The Media

Under the Sadiq al-Mahdi government (1986-1989), the media experienced a period of new freedom and development. The coup was a major setback for freedom of expression in Sudan and the new authorites have made it clear that the media will be brought under government control. Senior government officials have also repeatedly stated that freedom of the media necessarily leads to anarchy and disorder.

Newspapers Before the coup, there were more than 40 newspapers and magazines in Sudan reflecting the views of a wide range of social, political and cultural groups. Most of these newspapers and magazines were published in Khartoum.

All newspapers and other periodicals have now been banned including the organs of political parties. Among them were *al-Itihadi*, supported by the Democratic Unionist Party (DUP); *al-Hadaf*, the official organ of the Sudanese Ba'th Party; *al-Maidan*, edited by al-Tijani al-Tayeb and, since the early 1950s, the official newspaper of the Sudan Communist Party; *al-Rayah*, the official organ of the National Islamic Front (NIF), *Sawt al-Gamahir* and *Alwan*, newspapers which also reflected the views of the NIF, the only party in Sudan known to have supported the new military government; and *Sawt al-Umma*, the organ of the Umma Party whose leader is Sadiq al-Mahdi, the deposed Prime Minister, now under house arrest.

Other newspapers independent of the major political parties are also banned including *al-Khartoum, al-Ayyam, al-Anbaa, al-Nahar, as-Siyassa* and all the English-language newspapers. *The Sudan Times*, edited by Bona Malwal, a southerner and former minister, was the most popular English-language paper and was regarded as having the best coverage of the civil war in southern Sudan and of human rights issues.

The army weekly, *al-Quwat al-Mussallaha*, is the only newspaper authorized to continue publishing on a daily basis and represents the views of the new government. *Sudanow*, an English-language magazine published by the Ministry of Culture, is still publishing but under strict government control. Focusing on cultural and economic affairs, it has a circulation of less than 7,000.

In early September 1989, the authorities created two daily newspapers, *al-Inqaz al-Watani* and *al-Sudan al-Hadith*. Journalists working for these newspapers have been carefully vetted by the military authorities for loyalty to the government rather than competence and experience. In February 1990, the military government issued a decree which authorized the establishment of three press and publications houses under government control. These institutions will have a monopoly on all press and other publications in the country. In the same month, nine sports newspapers were banned by decree, for which no reason was given. It is believed that the authorities have drafted a new press law, which deals with foreign journalists in Sudan. The draft has not yet been published.

Radio and Television Radio and TV come under the control of the state-owned National Radio and TV Corporation. Radio Omdurman, the national radio station, broadcasts principally in Arabic and also broadcasts programmes in English, French and venacular southern Sudan languages. A number of regional radio stations are also in operation. A joint Sudanese-Egyptian radio station opened in 1982 and broadcasts daily in Arabic.

The single TV channel broadcasts mainly in Arabic but has a daily news bulletin and some programmes in English. Since the military coup, the authorities have appointed military officers to key positions within the Corporation. TV is now openly used as a medium for political propaganda and for encouraging support for government policies from the population.

Banned Publications Despite the ban on all newspapers, a number of leaflets and underground literature have been clandestinely produced and circulated. The banned Ba'th Party and the Communist Party have published newsletters in stencil form. In late December 1989, Idris al-Banna, a member of the Umma Party and a former member of the Supreme Council of State (who was sentenced to 40 years' imprisonment on corruption charges in September 1989 but later had the sentence dropped) was brought to trial with nine others on a charge of "circulating anti-government leaflets". Idriss al-Banna was accused of writing a poem, whilst detained in prison, criticizing the new military government.

Al-Maidan is still published regularly on stencil and distributed secretly. On December 24 1989, its editor, al Tijani al-Tayeb, was visited in prison by a member of the ruling military council who complained about the continuing publication of the paper and threatened him with severe punishment if the Communist Party continued its opposition to the government.

Human rights activists have also gathered and secretly distributed information concerning the conditions of political prisoners and reports of torture.

Successive governments of Sudan have repeatedly suppressed information on a number of issues and the new government is no different. Information concerning famine in various provinces in Sudan has continued to be suppressed and, in October 1990, the government was warned by Western doners that emergency food aid was dependent on acknowledging the "very serious" famine crisis now confronting Sudan. Reports about people infected with the AIDS virus have been, and continue to be, routinely censored. Governments have also systematically prevented reports of massacres carried out by militias and government troops from reaching the media. On July 19 1989, dozens of southerners were indiscriminately killed in Wau by government troops. The authorities refused to disclose any information about the massacre. Following another massacre in Jabalain in December 1989, when an estimated 2,000 people were killed, the government disclosed minimal information, putting the number killed at 200.

Arrests of Journalists In mid-June 1989, following an announcement by Sadiq-al-Mahdi's government that a coup attempt supported by former President Nimeiri had been foiled, Sid Ahmed al-Khalifa, editor of *al-Watan* magazine, and Mohamed Medani Tawfiq, editor and publisher of *al-Ra'ay al-Am*, were arrested. Although their arrests were alleged to be in connection with the coup attempt, it appears that they were arrested following *al-Watan*'s publication of an interview with Nimeiri, in which he said that he would come back to power within a month. They were released immediately after the military took power.

Many other journalists were arrested and detained without charge or trial in 1989. The following are among those believed to be still held: Siddiq al-Zeilai, an investigative journalist working for *al-Maidan*, detained since August 22, now held at Shalla prison, and Mahjoub Osman, co-editor of *al-Ayam*, detained at Kober prison since September 20.

Other journalists were also detained but then released. These include al Tijani al-Tayeb, editor of *al-Maidan*, detained at Kober prison from June 30 to August 1990; Yousuf Salih al-Shanbali, co-owner of the independent weekly *The Telegraph* and a general secretary of the now banned Sudanese Journalists' Union and Taha al-Nu'man, a correspondent of the Abu Dhabi-based official daily newspaper *al-Ittihad*.

Journalists continued to be arrested and detained throughout 1990. In March, Arop Madut Arop, a journalist working with the Sudan Council of Churches, was detained in Kober prison, reportedly in connection with "activities and visits" related to the Sudan Council of Churches. In the same month, Arop Bagat, a radio announcer based in southern Sudan, was also detained in Kober, reportedly in connection with alleged involvement with the SPLA.

In May and June, 46 people associated with the Socialist Arab Ba'th Party in Sudan were arrested and detained including journalist Omar Muhajir Muhammadine and broadcaster Ahmed Abdel Nabi. Neither is known to have been released.

Writers have also been detained since the coup including Kamal al-Gazouli, a lawyer and general secretary of the now banned Sudanese Writers' Union, held at a prison in Port Sudan, and Mahjoub Sharif, a teacher and prominent poet, who is detained at Kober prison.

In June, al-Fatih al-Mardi, executive editor of the now banned business journal *al-Saha al-Tigaria* was arrested and charged with possession of a typewriter and two duplicating machines, along with subversive "Alliance" material. Ibrahim Bakheit, a journalist, was subsequently arrested whilst visiting the al-Mardi home. Abdul Moniem Awad al-Rayah, a journalist employed by the UN Information Centre and a former executive editor of *Sudanow*, who lives in the same house as al-Mardi, was also detained. In July, all three were secretly tried before three military officers at a special court in Khartoum under articles 96, 97 and 123, relating to inciting hatred against the state and working by act or by word to undermine it. Such charges can carry the death penalty.

On July 31, a group of lawyers, led by Sati'i Ahmed al-Haj, was denied authorization to act on behalf of the defendants. However, for the first time since the junta came to power, lawyers for the accused were allowed to address the court directly, to plead on behalf of the defendants and to cross-examine the prosecution witnesses, all of whom were security soldiers. In the past, lawyers were only allowed to attend the trial as a "friend" of the defendants and were not allowed to "talk" to the court. In late August, al-Fatih al-Mardi was sentenced to 14 years' imprisonment. The other defendants were acquitted.

Attacks on the Foreign Press In January 1990, the military government accused the BBC of "conspiracy". In two editorials, one broadcast on the radio on January 26 and the other published on February 4 in the Armed Forces newspaper, the Sudanese authorities claimed that "the BBC has developed the habit of painting the news from Sudan with colours and then putting it in a form which suits the goals of Sudan's enemies". The next move was the arrest and detention or expulsion of journalists working for the BBC, Reuters and British newspapers.

Julian Ozanne, a British journalist working for the *Financial Times* and *Sunday Correspondent*, was arrested on February 21, detained for a week then released uncharged. The day before his arrest he interviewed Colonel Mohamed al-Amin al-Khalifa, a member of the ruling military, who verbally abused him. During the interview the senior military leader complained, among other things, against the press and Western attitudes. Prior to Julian Ozanne's arrest, members of the security service searched his hotel room and confiscated documents.

Hamza Hendawi, an Egyptian national and Reuters correspondent in Khartoum, was detained on March 23 1990 without explanation. After diplomatic pressure from the Egyptain authorities, Mr Hendawi was released and expelled.

Alfred Taban, a Sudanese journalist who works for *Sudanow* and who is a part-time correspondent for Reuters and the BBC, was held from March 31 1990, reportedly accused of dispatching false information to the foreign media and writing an article about a poem that he claimed was written by the former deputy chairman of the State Council, Idris al-Bana. After seven months in detention, he was released on October 19 1990.

Actions

On July 11 1989 ARTICLE 19 wrote to the Sudanese government calling for the release of the people arrested and detained since the June military coup. ARTICLE 19 also asked for the suspension of the Constitution to be lifted and for all political parties, trade unions and newspapers to be unbanned.

On October 5 1989 ARTICLE 19 wrote to the government protesting the detention without charge or trial of more than 40 trade unionists arrested during August and September.

On December 15 1989 ARTICLE 19 wrote to the government protesting the death sentence passed against Dr Mamoun Mohamed Hussein on the grounds that he chaired a meeting calling for a strike. (See text)

On February 22 1990 ARTICLE 19 wrote to the government calling for the release of Julian Ozanne of the *Financial Times* and *Sunday Correspondent* (UK). He was released, uncharged, after a week. (See text)

On March 26 1990 ARTICLE 19 wrote to the government protesting at the continued detention of journalists and ban on newspapers. An appeal letter to ARTICLE 19 members asked them to write to the government on the same matter.

On March 26 1990 ARTICLE 19 sent a letter and telex to the government protesting the detention of Reuters correspondent Hamza Hendawi, and BBC and Reuters journalist Alfred Taban. (See text)

In April 1990 ARTICLE 19 published *Starving in Silence*, a report on the effects of censorship on famine in Sudan, Ethiopia and China. It demonstrated that censorship can prevent or delay famine relief and prolong the effects of famine. It also pointed out that it is highly unlikely that famine would occur in a country with a free press, as even a suggestion of food shortage would become a topic for public debate and, thus, for preventative action.

Tunisia

After 21 years of Habib Bourguiba's presidency, he was deposed on November 7 1987 by his Prime Minister, General Zine al-Abidine Ben Ali, who announced plans to revise the Constitution and ensure more civil and political rights. Public opinion demanded greater freedom after the long era of repression and political trials. Political changes had been gradual throughout the 1980s and were characterized by major conflict between the state and the Muslim opposition who demanded political recognition. In 1981, the one-party system was abandoned; the suspension of the Communist Party was lifted and other political organiza-

	Data	Year
Population	7,809,000	1988
Life expectancy (M/F)	60.1/61.1	1985
GNP (US$ per capita)	1,230	1988
Main religion(s)	Islam	
Official language(s)	Arabic	
Illiteracy %	34.7	1990
(M/F)	25.8/43.7	1990
Daily newspapers	6	1986
Radio sets	1,693,527	1989
TV sets	520,000	1987
Press agencies:		
	Tunis Afrique Presse	
ICCPR:	YES	1969

tions, the Mouvement des Démocrates Socialistes (MDS) and the Mouvement de l'Unité Populaire were tolerated and later legally recognized. Elections in November 1981 saw, for the first time, more than one party running and some opposition groups had access to the media. However, the old pattern of restrictions was gradually restored in full and a major confrontation in 1987 between the government and the Islamic political movement culminated in trials of Muslim activists the following summer during which death sentences were pronounced.

President Ben Ali's Reforms

President Ben Ali's promised policy of national reconciliation began with the abolition in December 1987 of the State Security Court and the release of 3,000 political and non-political prisoners. In February 1988, the ruling party changed its name to the Rassemblement Constitutionnel Démocratique (RCD). In April, a new law of association confirming the multi-party system was passed although to obtain legal recognition, political parties had to confine their aims and activities to the limits set by the Constitution and could not pursue purely religious, racial, regional or linguistic objectives. In July, the president-for-life provision in the Constitution was repealed by the National Assembly.

In the same month, the 1975 Press Code was revised, but not to the extent that journalists wanted. Access to information concerning the government was not mentioned and several previous regulations still forbid this freedom. Civil servants are tied by the obligation of discretion and can be punished by a year's imprisonment if they break this regulation. Special provisions in the Press Code and harsh sentences of up to five years' imprisonment (Arts.44, 48, 52, 54) protect the President and all members of the government against abuse and slander. The new text introduces some reforms: it limits the number of newspapers owned by an individual to "two publications of the same periodicity" (Art.15); it obliges the newspapers to reveal sources of funding (Arts.16, 18); and suspending a newspaper is no longer the responsibility of the Ministry of the Interior but of the courts (Art.73). However, the system of registration of newspapers is still controlled by the Minister of the Interior.

The Media

Radio and Television Radio and TV are run by the state-owned Radio Télévision Tunisienne (RTT) whose directors are appointed by the President. RTT runs three radio stations and one Arabic-language TV channel. The French TV channel Antenne 2 is broadcast directly with the assistance of the French government and the Italian channel RAI Uno is received along the coast and in the north of the country. The wealthier are buying satellite dishes in increasing numbers.

Newspapers The six daily newspapers belong either to the ruling RCD or the government (*al-Hurriya, Le Renouveau, La Presse*), or are privately-owned (*as-Sabah, Le Temps, Echourouk*). Three of the authorized opposition parties have a weekly paper: *al-Moustaqbal* published by the MDS; *al- Maoukif* by the Rassemblement des Socialistes Progressistes and *At-Tariq al-Jadid* by the Parti Communiste Tunisien. In early 1990, the authorities authorized An Nahda (the Islamic Party) and the Parti Ouvrier Communiste Tunisien to issue their weekly newspapers, *al-Fajr* and *al-Badil* respectively, although these organizations are not legally recognized. All weeklies operate under financial difficulties. Newsprint is mostly imported and subsidized by the government and the threat of withdrawal of paper has been used as an effective deterrent against criticism. The most informative weekly magazines, *Le Maghreb* and *Réalités* have often been censored, harassed and occasionally closed down for lengthy periods. Other daily papers or periodicals are either specialist or tabloid papers. The first two independent political periodicals, *Errai* in Arabic and *Démocratie* in French, which played a major role in the first moves towards democracy, have now closed down. The new government maintains the policy of careful surveillance of the press but acts with more sensitivity to public opinion when it intervenes.

Suspensions In January 1988, the independent newspaper *Les Annonces* was seized for publishing a cartoon depicting journalist Mohamed Hedi Triki reading President Ben Ali's November 7 declaration on his accession to power. The paper's two directors, Mr Karmaoui and Mr Azzouz, were fined.

At the end of 1988, the weekly *al-Maoukif* was suspended. The official reason was the publication of a statement from the unrecognized Mouvement de la Tendance Islamique, the main Islamic opposition group, (now An Nahda).

In December 1988, the independent French-language magazine *Le Phare*, which had been a platform for radical writers and journalists, also ceased publication indefinitely. That month, its director and owner, Abdeljelil El Behi, was questioned and detained by the police four times, despite his poor health. Finally, the government's economic department confronted him regarding alleged irregularities in his company which financed the magazine.

Prosecutions An incident that struck public opinion most was the prosecution of well-known Tunisian academic, Hichem Jait, for an article published in December

1988 in the weekly magazine *Réalités*. The author denounced the continuing pattern of human rights violations, observing that, as in the past, any improvements were not the result of better institutional safeguards but relied on the goodwill of the president. The magazine was seized and both Jait and the magazine's director were charged with "defamation of justice". There was a strong campaign in support of the author and the case was finally dropped.

In July and August 1989, the weekly *Le Maghreb* published in successive issues articles on "Sexuality in Islam" by Ziad Krichen and Slim Daoula. Both journalists and the director were prosecuted and accused of undermining Islam and public morals, but these cases were also eventually dropped.

On May 24 1990, the Court of First Instance in Tunis sentenced Professor Moncef Ben Salem to three years' imprisonment for "disseminating false news and defaming the head of the state". The charges relate to an interview he had given to the Algerian Islamic newspaper *al-Munqid* published on April 19. In the interview, Professor Ben Salem criticized the government's "secularism" and harassment of Muslim activists.

The issue of June 20 1990 of the weekly *al-Fajr*, published by the unauthorized An Nahda, was seized from the printer because of an article by Rached Ghannouchi (president of An Nahda) criticizing the government for not serving the people. The authorities declared that the article "might disturb public order by calling for insurrection" and was "harming republican institutions". On June 23, the newspaper was suspended for three months and, on Octber 6 1990, its editor, Hamadi Jebali, received a six months suspended sentence and a fine.

Dismissals   Tensions between journalists and the official news agency Tunis Afrique Presse (TAP) and RTT resulted in the dismissal or suspension of several journalists. Kamel al-Abidi and two other members of the Tunisian Association of Journalists were suspended for opposing the nomination of Mohamed Hedi Triki as deputy director of TAP. Another RTT journalist, Nejib Ben Abdallah, was dismissed from his job in September 1989 for a commentary on "rumour and official information", blaming the quality of the latter for the fact that rumour was flourishing. In October, he was again crticized for a critical commentary about "change and conservative forces". In September, the director of *Renouveau*, organ of the ruling RCD, was dismissed for another journalist's article about the political situation and rumours of a change of prime minister.

On January 22 1990, Mohamed Mahmoud, the managing director of the weekly *Essahafah*, dismissed two journalists, Azza Zarrad and Toufik Ben Brik, because they protested publicly against his decision to censor their articles on the media in Tunisia.

Foreign Publications   Under the Press Code, copies of foreign publications must be submitted to the Ministry of the Interior before they may be distributed. Violation of this law is punishable by confiscation of the issue. In November 1989, the authorities confiscated an issue of the monthly, Paris-based magazine *Jeune Afrique Economie* because of an article which criticized the country's economic situation, citing cases of widespread strikes and protests. The June 14 1990 issue of *Le Monde* was banned from distribution because of an article about the Tunisian people's apathy towards that month's local elections.

Films Cinema production is largely state-controlled although there are also several independent companies. Financial and other constraints result in the few Tunisian producers looking to co-productions with foreign companies. Films are censored most frequently for violence and sexual themes. Very few cases of politically motivated censorship are known.

The film *Fatma 75*, directed by Selma Baccar, was banned because it did not conform to official policy concerning women's issues and, allegedly, for not giving sufficent credit to President Bourguiba for reforms which improved women's conditions. After November 1987, the film continued to be banned for giving too much credit to the former president. The film has been shown, by special authorization, on cultural occasions and at the 1988 Journées Cinématographiques de Carthage.

Nouri Bouzid's film *The Golden Shoes*, which received awards outside the country in 1989, was only authorized for distribution in early 1990. Bouzid was asked by the Censorship Committee to cut 14 minutes which depicted scenes of torture and sex. After considerable negotiations, Bouzid agreed to cut four seconds. Consequently, the film may be shown throughout Tunisia without further restrictions.

Censorship of Books Under President Bourguiba, there had been a number of well-known books banned on the grounds that they harmed public morals, public order or defamed public servants. Most titles were unbanned after the change of government in November 1987.

In July 1990, three books were known to be banned: *Fi al-Maslah al-Watania wa at-Tawajuh al-Dimuqrati* (In the Interest of the Nation and Democracy) by Abdul Rahman Abid, *Misr wal-Hudud* (Egypt and the Borders) by Hichem al-Karoui, banned in September 1989, and *al-Jarima al-Shaklya wa Ekhtilas Amwal al-Sha'b fi Dawlat al-Qanun* (Crimes of Corruption in the State of Law) by Rida al-Jawhari, banned in April 1990.

Freedom of Opinion and Expression

Initiatives are being taken to strengthen resistance against censorship and other forms of human rights violations. A committee against censorship has been launched by the Tunisian League of Human Rights and other associations of journalists, writers, film-producers, actors, and young lawyers. In January 1990, two books, *Abbas Yafqidu as-Sawad* (Abbas Loses His Mind) by Hassan Ben Othman and *Oghniat al-Naqabi al-Fasih* (The Song of the Bright Trade Unionist) by Adam Fathy, were unbanned after the committee began its anti-censorship campaign.

Actions

In its 1987 Commentary to the Human Rights Committeee ARTICLE 19 called on the government to end all suspensions of the press and prohibitions on books, and to abolish the provisions of the Press Code and offences in the Penal Code that enforce censorship.

On October 10 1988 ARTICLE 19 wrote to the government urging it to lift its ban on six books by Tunisian authors.

On April 3 1990 ARTICLE 19 wrote to Mohamed Mahmoud, managing director of *Essahafah*, protesting the dismissal of journalists Azza Zarrad and Toufik Ben Brik (See text).

On July 20 1990 ARTICLE 19 wrote jointly with the Committee to Protect Journalists and Reporters Sans Frontières to the government protesting the suspension of *al Fajr* and the prosecution of its editor Hamadi Jebali (See text).

Oceania

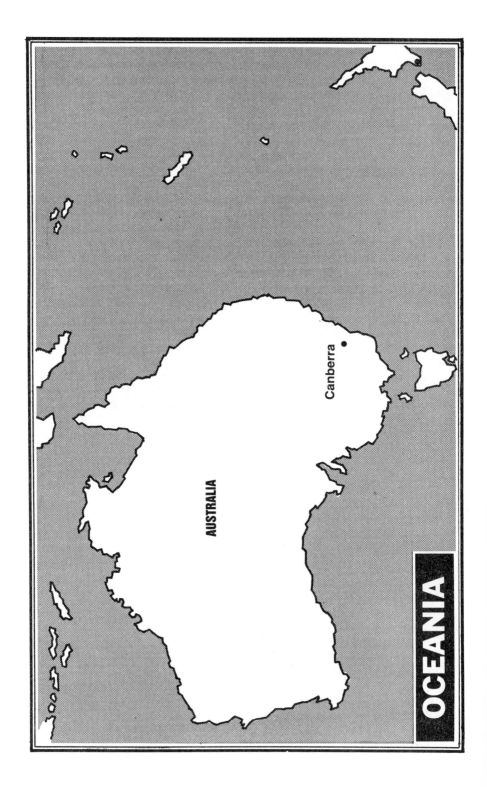

AUSTRALIA

Canberra

OCEANIA

Australia

Neither Australia's federal Constitution, nor any of its state constitutions contain any provision guaranteeing freedom of expression or other human rights, although there is a limited guarantee of religious freedom. Despite the absence of constitutional guarantees, the right to freedom of expression is widely recognized as being essential to the democratic process.

Law-making is dispersed between the Federal Parliament, six state parliaments and two territory assemblies. Most aspects of freedom of expression are governed by the states, which tend to be slow in introducing reform. In broadcasting, telecommunications and implementation of international obligations, the Federal Parliament can override the states.

	Data	Year
Population	16,532,000	1988
Life expectancy	76.0	1987
GNP (US$ per capita)	12,390	1988
Main religion(s)	Christianity	
Official language(s)	English	
Illiteracy %	1	1985
Daily newspapers	62	1986
Non daily newspapers	465	1984
Radio sets	20,500,000	1987
TV sets	7,800,000	1987
Press agencies:		
Australian Associated Press		
ICCPR:	YES	1980

A Constitutional Commission on the revision of the federal Constitution reported to the Federal Parliament in August 1988. It recommended that a new chapter dealing with fundamental rights and freedoms should be inserted in the Australian Constitution to guarantee freedom of expression and other rights. The report has, however, been shelved.

Restrictions on Freedom of Expression

Official Secrets Several federal laws prohibit the publication of material deemed to prejudice Australia's national security. For example, it is a serious criminal offence to disclose the identity of a member of the Australian Security Intelligence Organization (ASIO). In September 1988, the Attorney-General obtained injunctions preventing information about the identity and activities of an ASIO officer being published in *The Eye*, a magazine published by journalist Brian Toohey, and in a book by him and William Pinwill.

As well as laws covering official secrets, there is a voluntary agreement, known as the D-Notice system, between some media proprietors and the Department of Defence not to disclose information which might be prejudicial to national security.

The Committee to Review Commonwealth Criminal Law has proposed strengthening controls on the disclosure of official information. The proposals canvassed by the Committee included: extradition for breach of official secrecy provisions; penalizing unauthorized publication of documents related to the national economy; and making the voluntary D-Notice system legally binding. The proposals have been opposed as a serious threat to the free flow of information to the public about the activities of Australian governments.

Suppression Orders The press can publish "fair and accurate" reports of court proceedings but federal and state courts may issue suppression orders prohibiting the publication of evidence. One coroner issued over 100 suppression orders during a public inquiry into the death of an Assistant Police Commissioner. Suppression orders are also regularly sought by the police over evidence submitted to the Royal Commission into Aboriginal deaths in custody, which has been sitting since 1987.

After widespread complaints that South Australian courts were issuing suppression orders too freely, the state government enacted legislation in 1989 to reduce their availability.

Defamation Australia's defamation laws, which permit injunctions to prevent publication as well as providing for damages after publication, are generally regarded as the main restriction on freedom of expression in Australia. In some states it is not a sufficient defence to prove that the material published was true; the publication must also be "on a matter of public interest" or "for public benefit". The procedural complexities and delays of defamation law, and inconsistencies between states, are a threat to anyone seeking to expose corruption or to criticize powerful people. Public figures, particularly politicians, have used the law to stifle public discussion on matters of public interest. Often "stop writs" which have prevented publication are subsequently lifted by the courts, but the prospect of another writ continues to inhibit public debate.

The sums awarded by juries in defamation actions have grown very large, particularly in New South Wales (NSW). In 1989, two cases attracted wide public attention. The proprietor of a Sydney seafood restaurant was awarded A$100,000 (US$77,750) after a negative review by the food critic of the *Sydney Morning Herald* and a solicitor was awarded A$600,000 (US$466,500) after an article by its legal correspondent. Because of the tendency for increasingly disproportionate damages to be awarded, the NSW government is proposing to let juries determine liability and judges assess damages.

While the large media corporations have the financial resources to absorb adverse judgements, a small publisher often faces bankruptcy if a defamation action is lost. The threat of a defamation suit therefore promotes self-censorship by the media and over-cautious journalism.

The Constitutional Commission recommended that the Federal Parliament should make uniform laws on defamation applicable to all forms of print and electronic media.

The President of The Free Speech Committee, Tony Katsigiannis, is being sued by Michael Hutchinson, an assistant secretary of the Department of Communications, over letters he wrote to *The Age* and *The Newcastle Herald* criticizing the government's communications policies.

Contempt of Court The law of contempt of court prevents the publication of material which risks prejudicing a fair trial or is in breach of a court order.

Radio broadcaster Derryn Hinch was sentenced to 28 days' imprisonment for contempt of court, the first time in Australia that a broadcaster has been imprisoned for a breach of the *sub judice* rule. On a Melbourne radio station, he identified a Catholic priest charged with sexual offences against young men and revealed that the priest had a previous conviction for sexual assault. The Victoria Attorney General filed a motion of contempt against the journalist and the radio station.

Some four months later additional charges were laid against the priest and Derryn Hinch again broadcast the information. The Attorney General filed a second motion of contempt. Derryn Hinch and the radio station were convicted of contempt: Derryn Hinch went to prison and the radio station was fined A$45,000 (US$35,100).

Disclosure of Sources The Code of Ethics of the Australian Journalists' Association (AJA) obliges journalists to protect their sources, but journalists cannot claim professional privilege to avoid disclosing their sources of information if they are called before courts, royal commissions or parliamentary inquiries. In December 1989, a Western Australian journalist, Tony Barrass, was jailed for refusing to identify a source.

Obscenity and Blasphemy Mechanisms to censor written publications remain, and are largely confined to obscenity under various federal and state codes, with protection of children being the main aim.

Blasphemous and terrorist material is also sometimes restricted. The issue of blasphemy was raised recently in NSW by conservative religious groups protesting against the screening of two films, *Hail Mary* and *The Last Temptation of Christ*.

Racial Vilification In October 1989, a new law prohibiting public acts of racial vilification came into operation in NSW as part of the Anti-Discrimination Act. Penalties include damages of up to A$50,000 (US$39,000). Other states and the Federal Parliament are considering similar legislation. The Broadcasting Tribunal penalized a radio announcer for racial vilification in 1989 and is investigating several other cases.

In July 1990, the Jewish Board of Deputies invoked the NSW law over *Your Rights*, a booklet published by John Bennett, the President of the Australian Civil Liberties Union. Among the statements complained about in the pamphlet is the assertion that the extent of the Holocaust had been deliberately exaggerated.

Freedom of Information

The Freedom of Information Act 1982 gives members of the public a right of access to documents held by government departments and agencies. Decisions to refuse access must be accompanied by reasons and appeals can be taken to the Administrative Appeals Tribunal and the Federal Court. The legislation has been criticized on the grounds that it provides only a small improvement in access to information and does not reach far enough into the more controversial decision-making processes of government. Most of the 27,429 requests made under the Act during 1987-1988 were for access to personal files held by the departments of Veterans' Affairs, Social Security and Taxation.

The states have been slow to introduce freedom of information legislation but legislation now exists in the two most populated states, Victoria and NSW.

Developments in the Media

Broadcasting Commercial television is concentrated in the hands of three proprietors, Alan Bond, Christopher Skase and Steve Cosser. There are only three commercial TV licences granted in each of the major cities, which ensures that TV is effectively a government-sanctioned oligopoly. Diversity is increased by two public TV stations run by the Australian Broadcasting Commission (ABC) and the Special Broadcasting Service (SBS), a multicultural and multilingual broadcasting service, but there is no policy to develop low-budget community-based TV.

Concentration of Press Ownership Public access to a wide range of dissimilar sources of printed information has been seriously eroded by the concentration of ownership of the Australian newspaper industry. One corporation, News Limited, which is controlled by Rupert Murdoch, dominates the Australian newspaper market. As of January 1989, newspapers owned by News Limited controlled 61.6 per cent of the total national circulation of metropolitan daily newspapers (the nearest rival, Fairfax, had 18 per cent); 58.5 per cent of Sunday newspapers (the nearest rival, Fairfax, had 23.6 per cent); and 56 per cent of suburban newspapers (the nearest rival, Fairfax, had 18 per cent). Rupert Murdoch also controlled just under 50 per cent of Australian Associated Press news service and 50 per cent of Australian Newspaper Mills.

In Australia, foreign nationals or corporations have to have permission from the Treasurer to acquire control of daily newspapers, and foreign investment in TV or radio stations is strictly limited to 20 per cent. In 1988, the federal government twice used the Foreign Takeovers Act to prevent foreign investment in Australian newspapers: to prevent Robert Maxwell acquiring *The Age* (Melbourne) and to stop a Malaysian company, MUI Australia, from acquiring 49.9 per cent of the *Perth Daily News*.

In an effort to dilute the concentration of media ownership in Australia, the federal government introduced cross-media ownership limitation rules. Under the rules, a newspaper owner is limited to a 5 per cent interest in a TV station in the same market and a proprietor of a TV station to 15 per cent of a newspaper in the same market.

Editorial Independence In February 1988, Chris Anderson, the editor-in-chief of *The Sydney Morning Herald*, and 10 senior editorial executives and journalists resigned in a dispute over the editorial independence of the newspaper, following the takeover by Warwick Fairfax of John Fairfax and Sons Ltd. These resignations were followed by a three-day strike by journalists employed on the paper. The matter was resolved when Chris Anderson was appointed Fairfax group editorial director.

Non-Government Organizations

The main non-government organizations concerned with monitoring freedom of expression are the Press Council, the AJA, the Free Speech Committee, the Australian Society of Authors and the Writers' Guild. Other groups have emerged from time to time such as Friends of the ABC, formed after proposed government changes to funding of the Australian Broadcasting Commission, and Free the Media, formed at the time of Rupert Murdoch's takeover of the *Herald* and *Weekly Times*.

The Press Council is a voluntary body established to correct unfair reporting and censure invasions of privacy. It is composed of an independent chairman and media and citizens' representatives. Journalists' representatives withdrew in 1987 after it refused to oppose further acquisitions of newspapers by Rupert Murdoch.

The AJA has internal disciplinary proceedings to uphold its Code of Ethics. Members of the public may complain to the union about alleged breaches of the code and such complaints are considered by a judicial committee.

The Satanic Verses In 1989 the Free Speech Committee, Australian Society of Authors and the Australian Writers' Guild picketed a number of bookshops which had withdrawn copies of *The Satanic Verses* after threats were received by staff. Many small booksellers continued to stock the book and one, Abbeys, was fire-bombed, resulting in extensive damage.

Actions

In its 1988 Commentary to the Human Rights Committee ARTICLE 19 drew attention to some issues regarding freedom of expression which remain unsatisfactory: the continuing development towards concentration of media ownership despite government efforts to introduce legislation regarding TV ownership; the threat to the freedom of information law through increased charges to users and the inconsistency and difference in defamation laws throughout Australia.

Themes and Issues

This section attempts to classify and annotate the many themes and issues that arise from an examination of international practice concerning freedom of expression and censorship. It provides a ready overview of the principal impediments to the full enjoyment of the free exchange of ideas and information envisaged by the Universal Declaration of Human Rights (UDHR). Theme and issue headings are included in the General Index and are illustrated with references to practices of countries discussed in the Country Reports.

The starting point of any analysis of freedom of expression, opinion and information as global entitlements must be the *International Standards* to which most governments claim commitment. These are set forth in Part 1 of this section, as are the exceptions, restrictions and limitations which they permit. Parts 2, 3 and 4 examine *Censorship: Justifications, Methods* and *Targets*. Part 5 addresses the various organizations, policies and programmes responsible for *Defending Freedom of Expression, Opinion and Information*.

1. International Standards

A major achievement of the United Nations (UN) since its founding in 1945 has been the development of universal standards for the protection of human rights. Although efforts to draft a separate UN-sponsored treaty on freedom of information failed in the 1950s, the UDHR and the major international human rights treaties all include the rights to freedom of expression, opinion and information. Today, the pressing challenge is to persuade states to implement those standards. The major UN bodies engaged in this task are the Commission on Human Rights, its Sub-Commission on Prevention of Discrimination and Protection of Minorities, and the Human Rights Committee, established in 1978 to promote compliance with the International Covenant on Civil and Political Rights (ICCPR). Various regional bodies have been established to promote compliance with regional human rights treaties.

In addition to defining the positive right to freedom of expression, the international texts provide the only grounds a government may invoke to limit that right. Any restrictions on free expression must be authorized by duly enacted laws and must be necessary to preserve public order or other enumerated interests in a democratic society. Their imposition should be judged, if contested, by a court and not by the executive power of the state; independent courts play a crucial role in implementing both national and international legal guarantees of freedom of expression.

Universal Declaration of Human Rights Proclaimed by the UN General Assembly in 1948, the Declaration is still the most powerful statement of the global aspiration of respect for human rights. Although not a treaty, it is now widely regarded as expressing general principles of international law binding on all nations. Its provisions have been incorporated in many constitutions of the world.

Article 19 of the Declaration reads: "Everyone has the right to freedom of opinion and expression; this right includes freedom to hold opinions without interference and to seek, receive and impart information and ideas through any media and regardless of frontiers". Governments may limit enjoyment of Article 19 rights, but only in accordance with Article 29, which requires that any limitation must be "determined by law solely for the purpose of securing due recognition and respect for the rights and freedoms of others and of meeting the just requirements of morality, public order and the general welfare in a democratic society".

International Covenant on Civil and Political Rights The ICCPR came into force in 1976 along with the Covenant on

Economic, Social and Cultural Rights. As of July 1990, 90 countries had become parties to the ICCPR. Those countries are obligated to submit reports to the Human Rights Committee, established under the ICCPR, on their compliance with the requirements of the treaty. States which in addition become party to the Optional Protocol to the ICCPR agree to allow individuals to complain directly to the Committee about human rights violations by the state.

Article 18 of the Covenant guarantees freedom of conscience, religion and belief; Article 19 protects freedom of expression; and Article 20 deals with the duty to prohibit propaganda for war and incitement to national, racial or religious hatred. Article 19 of the Covenant reads:

"1. Everyone shall have the right to hold opinions without interference.

"2. Everyone shall have the right to freedom of expression; this right shall include freedom to seek, receive and impart information and ideas of all kinds, regardless of frontiers, either orally, in writing or in print, in the form of art, or through any other media of his choice.

"3. The exercise of the rights provided for in paragraph 2 of this article carries with it special duties and responsibilities. It may therefore be subject to certain restrictions, but these shall only be such as are provided by law and are necessary: (a) for respect of the rights or reputations of others; (b) for the protection of national security or of public order (*ordre public*), or of public health or morals."

Article 20 of the Covenant reads:

"1. Any propaganda for war shall be prohibited by law."

"2. Any advocacy of national, racial or religious hatred that constitutes incitement to discrimination, hostility or violence shall be prohibited by law."

African Charter on Human and Peoples' Rights The African Charter came into force in 1986 and had been ratified by 35 states as of November 1989. The Charter is distinctive because of its emphasis on group as well as individual rights. The African Human Rights Commission has been established to implement the Charter and individuals have the opportunity to lodge complaints with the Commission. The Charter's text does not protect freedom of opinion nor, at least explicitly, the right to seek and impart information and ideas.

Article 9 of the Charter reads:

"1. Every individual shall have the right to receive information."

"2. Every individual shall have the right to free association provided that he abides by the law."

American Convention on Human Rights Adopted in 1969, this Convention of the Organization of American States (OAS) follows the American Declaration of the Rights and Duties of Man of 1948. Twenty countries from Central and South America have ratified the Convention; it has not been ratified by the United States. Canada, which joined the OAS in 1989, is expected to accept the Convention soon. A Commission and a Human Rights Court have been established. The Convention has an elaborate and strong formulation of the right to freedom of expression set forth in Article 13. In addition to protections similar to those set forth in Articles 19 and 20 of the ICCPR, Article 13 includes the following provisions:

"2. The exercise of the right ... [to freedom of thought and expression] shall not be subject to prior censorship .... "

"3. The right of expression may not be restricted by indirect methods or means, such as the abuse of government or private controls over newsprint, radio broadcasting frequencies, or equipment used in the dissemination of information, or by any other means tending to impede the communication and circulation of ideas and opinions."

"4. Notwithstanding the provisions of paragraph 2 above, public entertainments may be subject by law to prior censorship for the sole purpose of regulating access to them for the moral protection of childhood and adolescence."

The American Convention is unique among international conventions in that it recognizes the right of individuals to reply to offensive statements, set forth in Article 14 as follows:

"1. Anyone injured by inaccurate or offensive statements or ideas disseminated to the public in general by a legally regulated medium of communication has the right to reply or make a correction using the same communications outlet, under such conditions as the law may establish."

"2. The correction or reply shall not in any case remit other legal liabilities that may have been incurred."

"3. For the effective protection of honour and reputation, every publisher, and every newspaper, motion picture, radio, and television company, shall have a person responsible, who is not protected by immunities or special privileges."

European Convention on Human Rights Adopted by the Council of Europe in 1950, the European Convention on Human Rights is embraced by 23 European states. The Convention is enforced by a Commission, a Court and a Committee of Ministers from the member states. The European Court of Human Rights issues binding judgements enforcing the Convention and has developed the most extensive case law of any regional human rights system, with important opinions on freedom of expression. The right to seek information is not expressly recognized in the Convention.

Article 10 of the European Convention states:

"1. Everyone has the right to freedom of expression. This right shall include freedom to hold opinions and to receive and impart information and ideas without interference by public authority and regardless of frontiers. This article shall not prevent states from requiring the licensing of broadcasting, television or cinema enterprises."

"2. The exercise of these freedoms, since it carries with it duties and responsibilities, may be subject to such formalities, conditions, restrictions or penalties as are prescribed by law and are necessary in a democratic society, in the interests of national security, territorial integrity or public safety, for the prevention of disorder or crime, for the protection of health or morals, for the protection of the reputation or rights of others, for preventing the disclosure of information received in confidence, or for maintaining the authority and impartiality of the judiciary."

Arab Charter on Human Rights A project to prepare an Arab Charter on Human Rights was initiated by the Arab League on March 11 1979. Drafted by the permanent Arab Committee for Human Rights, it was submitted to the 20 members of the Arab League for comment in 1983, and was discussed by the Council of Foreign Ministers in 1984 and 1985. As of July 1990, it had not yet been formally adopted by member states of the Arab League. The final draft may contain limited provisions concerning freedom of expression and information.

Helsinki Final Act The Helsinki Final Act is the title given to the accord agreed upon after the Conference on Security and Co-operation in Europe (CSCE) held in Helsinki in 1975. Thirty-five states participated, including all Eastern and Western European states (with the exception of Albania which achieved observer status), the United States and Canada. The accord has been reviewed at follow-up conferences, the latest in Copenhagen in 1990. Although the accord is not a treaty, governments, including the United States and the Soviet Union, have acknowledged its binding character. It includes 10 principles guiding relations between participating states and three "baskets" of more detailed promises including "co-operation in humanitarian and other fields". The pact includes a section on increasing human contact, improving the dissemination of information and improving the working conditions of journalists.

The Helsinki Final Act has been the springboard for the development of a network of non-governmental initiatives to monitor compliance by states. Now gathered in the International Helsinki Federation, they publish regular reports and lobby at CSCE review conferences. In the past, Helsinki monitoring groups in Eastern European countries have suffered harassment and suppression. After the revolutions of 1989, however, the International Helsinki Federation was able to monitor elections in Hungary and Romania without incident. In addition, representatives of Helsinki Watch were permitted by the Bulgarian government to monitor pre-election conditions for the first free elections in nearly 50 years.

2. Censorship: Justifications

Governments invoke a wide variety of reasons for censoring speech and publications, for justifying secrecy, and for taking action against individuals because of their opinions. Many reasons lack justification in the sense that they are not recognized as permissible restrictions under international law, and in fact may have illegitimate aims, such as the suppression of criticism and unorthodox ideas.

While interference with the holding of opinions is never justified, limits may be placed on freedom of expression and the availability of information in certain circumstances. The general guiding principle is that freedom is the rule and its limitation the exception, with the onus of justification resting with those wishing to impose restrictions. It should be possible to contest any restriction through a procedure independent of the executive branch, such as a judicial hearing or the opportunity for judicial review.

Rights of Others

The claim that freedom of expression should be limited in order to protect the rights of others is one of the most common reasons given for censorship.

Defamation and Protection of Reputation
Defamation is the act of damaging another's reputation or honour through words or publication. In many countries, defamation is a criminal as well as a civil offence, and can act as a major constraint on reporting by the media. In *common law* countries (United Kingdom, United States, Canada, Australia and others), awards of money damages for defamation against media defendants can be very large. By contrast, *civil law* countries (continental Europe, Latin America) award relatively modest money damages which do not present a major financial burden to the media.

In 1986 in the *Lingens* case, the European Court of Human Rights ruled that politicians must tolerate stronger comment on their activities than private individuals. With the exception of the United States and Western Europe, however, this distinction is not widely recognized. *See Australia, Canada.* Indeed, the reverse is often the case: people holding high office, such as monarchs, presidents, cabinet ministers, military leaders and judges may be protected by laws that make it a criminal (and sometimes capital) offence to voice criticism. *See Algeria, Chile, Honduras, India, Iraq, Malaysia, Morocco, Singapore, Spain, Tunisia, Zaire.*

Privacy Privacy is recognized by international human rights instruments and some national laws as a fundamental right. The right to privacy is usually specified as the right to respect for a person's private life, home and correspondence. Breach of privacy has a chilling effect on free expression as people often will not write or converse freely if they fear that their communications may be read or overheard by others. With the advent in the 1990s of new technologies which allow automated, undetectable interception of communications, it will be increasingly difficult to ensure privacy of those communications.

In the United Kingdom, concern over media encroachments on privacy led to the formation of the Calcutt Committee on Privacy and Related Matters. In June 1990, the Committee recommended replacing the existing Press Council with a Press Complaints Commission which would concentrate on giving redress to those with complaints against the press involving unfair treatment and invasion of privacy. In addition, the Committee has recommended new criminal offences: entering into private property without permission to obtain information for publication; planting a bugging device on private property to obtain information for publication; and taking a photograph or tape-recording on private property with the intention of identifying the subject for publication.

Recently, privacy has been a major issue in Japan where the practices of *paparazzi* photographers and press smearing of criminal defendants have been widely debated. *See Japan, Spain, United Kingdom.*

National Security

National security may be defined as the safety of a nation from threats by other nations to its political and economic independence, its territorial sovereignty, its cultural heritage and its way of life. National security has been cited, however, to prevent or delay publication of material potentially embarrassing to government officials unrelated to national defence. National security legislation may affect fundamental freedoms. Until recently in the Soviet Union, knowledge of state secrets was used as a pretext to deny exit visas to citizens seeking to emigrate. In some countries, indigenous populations may be prevented from making contact with foreigners (especially journalists) on the ground that they might inadvertently pass on information useful to enemies of the state. National security also has been used as a reason to deport or deny entry to non-nationals because of their political opinions or affiliations.

Some governments have responded to the difficulty of maintaining control of "classified" national security information by implementing highly restrictive classification systems. *See China, India, Israel and the Occupied Territories, Malaysia, Nicaragua, Norway, South Africa, South Korea, Sweden, Taiwan, Turkey, United Kingdom, the United States and also Yugoslavia.*

State Security

In contrast to national security, state security refers to the safety of a particular form of state or government from either internal or external threats.

State security is frequently invoked to justify censoring opinions and maintaining secrecy over information liable to discredit or embarrass members of the government. State security laws, for example, are used to prevent "slander" of the head of state or head of the armed forces. Internal security acts often provide the legal basis for repressing critics of the government. *See Chile, India, Israel and the Occupied Territories, Malaysia, Nicaragua, Romania, Singapore, South Africa, Sweden.*

Sedition

In every country it is a crime to plot the overthrow of the government. There is a distinction, however, between efforts to overthrow a government through violence, and peaceful efforts to advocate change which are recognized as legitimate under international law. In many countries, this distinction is ignored. Anyone who by word or deed propounds reform may be subjected to severe penalties, including detention, imprisonment and death.

Legal definitions of what may or may not be considered seditious are often dangerously vague. Possession of publications deemed seditious may result in imprisonment. A political system violates the rights to freedom of opinion and expression when it denies the possibility of non-violent advocacy for change. *See India, Indonesia, Iraq, Kenya, North Korea, South Korea, Uganda, Viet Nam, Zaire.*

Public Interest

There is no specific reference to "public interest" in international treaties. In general, information which promotes the "public interest" supplies new and important material for public debate. According to the European Court of Human Rights, such information may only be withheld when a "pressing social need" for its suppression is demonstrated (*The Sunday Times* case, 1979).

Information that is simply embarrassing to government officials is often deemed "against the public interest" when disclosure is threatened. A few countries have enacted "whistleblower" statutes to protect public as well as private employees who disclose information about their employer's wrongdoings which may promote the public interest. In the United Kingdom, however, the Official Secrets Act of 1989 disallows a "public interest defence" for civil servants who leak classified information. In the United States, the California legislature took further action by passing a law in May 1990 designed to curb the growing number of lawsuits filed against citizens who speak out publicly on development projects and other issues. These "strategic lawsuits against public participation" have increasingly intimidated people into stifling the exercise of their rights to free speech. *See Australia, Canada, Denmark, Mexico, Sweden, United Kingdom, United States, Zambia.*

Public Health

Laws of many countries permit limitations on the right to freedom of expression and other fundamental rights in order to protect public health. Such restrictions are recognized in international law. Controls on advertising of tobacco and alcohol are well-known examples. In 1990, for instance, France banned alcohol advertising on television. Requirements that manufacturers include compulsory warnings of specific health hazards on their products (such as pharmaceuticals and toys) and provide information concerning the ingredients and secondary effects of drugs, foods and other products, are ways in which states control information in the interest of public health. *See Ireland, Kenya, Rwanda, Turkey;* **see also** **Public Health Information.**

Public Morals

Concern for public morals, morality and *bonnes moeurs* (standards of good behaviour) is accepted in international human rights law as proper justification for restrictions on free expression. According to the European Court of Human Rights, however, restrictions must be "necessary in a democratic society" and "provided by law". No restrictions should be imposed to suppress the freedom of expression of minorities or to "encourage and uphold prejudice against minorities, even if their opinion is insulting or shocking to the majority" (the *Handyside* case, 1976). However, the Court also recognized that states have a wide margin of discretion in matters of public morals and decency.

The protection of youth is a major concern of public morals legislation. Article 13(4) of the American Convention provides that "public entertainments may be subject by law to prior censorship for the sole purpose of regulating access to them for the moral protection of childhood and adolescence". In Mexico in 1989, concert performances by Rod Stewart and Black Sabbath were cancelled by government authorities because of concern about adverse effects such entertainment might have on the morality of the nation's youth. In July-August 1989 in Tunisia, the weekly newspaper *Le Maghreb* was charged with undermining public morals and Islam for publishing articles on "sexuality in Islam", although the prosecution was eventually dropped. In India in 1987, state television banned winking by women in commercials as part of a campaign to "improve the nation's morals".

Governments in many countries refer to public morals to restrict freedom of political expression and opposition views. This is particularly true in countries with strong single political parties, where the distinction between offending public morals and questioning the political system is often vague. In Zaire, the application of *bonnes moeurs* has been used extensively to suppress opposition views and thinking. Reference to public morals is often used to restrict the importation of foreign publications. *See Iran, Iraq, Ireland, Kuwait, Malaysia, Mexico, Pakistan, Singapore, South Africa, Tunisia, Turkey, Yugoslavia, Zaire.*

Obscenity Obscenity includes offensive, indecent or pornographic material. Precise definitions of what is obscene have proved notoriously difficult to formulate. In 1964, United States Supreme Court Justice Stewart confessed his inability to define obscenity but claimed "I know it when I see it".

Definitions of the obscene have also been viewed as legally unworkable. In the United Kingdom, for example, the Williams Committee commented in 1979 that "to specify what we regard as representing the level of offensiveness against which the law should act involves fixing a standard relative to our conception of current reactions. But that standard may no longer be valid when legislation comes to be enacted; and once it is enacted it will become an extremely inflexible standard which will tend to attract even more ridicule and odium to the law". Nevertheless, laws regulating obscene publications continue to exist in the United Kingdom and in 1990 a Broadcasting Bill was introduced in Parliament which for the first time would extend such laws to cover radio and television.

Art is one of the first victims of obscenity law in many societies. In October 1989, the United States Congress passed legislation prohibiting the National Endowment for the Arts (NEA) from funding art projects and exhibitions that are legally obscene and established a commission to review the NEA's grant-making procedures. The law was passed in response to a federally-funded exhibition of photographs by Robert Mapplethorpe which contained a strong homo-erotic theme. In June 1990, a record by the rap group, 2 Live Crew was judged legally obscene by a federal district court in Florida. *See Australia, Canada, India, Ireland, Mexico, Pakistan, South Africa, Turkey, United Kingdom, United States.*

Public Order

"Public order" in the English language means absence of disorder, but the French legal term *ordre public* denotes the wider concept of the principles which underlie an entire social structure. Maintenance of public order is invoked to regulate rioting and civil disturbances but may also be used arbitrarily to block peaceful demonstrations or manifestations of political opinion. Reporting restrictions are often imposed on the media and justified as necessary to protect public order. *See Chile, Israel and Occupied Territories, Kuwait, Malaysia, Nicaragua, Romania, South Africa, South Korea, Spain, Uganda, Zaire.*

Violence

A link is made in many countries between public order, public morals and the depiction of violence. The debate on whether the representation of violence in the media leads to greater violence in society centres on limited statistical studies and conflicting expert reports. Demands to ban violence from the media, including violence depicted in news reporting, often arise in reaction to mass murder, rioting or violent demonstrations. In contrast to this trend, in March 1989, the Indian Supreme Court upheld the right to show a Tamil feature film even though the government believed it was likely to provoke violence by sections of the community, stating that any restrictions must be "justified on the anvil of necessity and not (on) the quicksand of convenience or expediency". In the United Kingdom in 1990, there was public debate over whether media coverage of violent acts by the Irish Republican Army and animal liberation groups was an incentive for such groups to commit further violence to gain publicity for their causes. In South Africa, despite the revocation of media restrictions in February 1990, it is still prohibited to publish a photograph or broadcast a film depicting "unrest situations", without specific authorization from the Minister of Law and Order.

Article 20 of the ICCPR requires countries to prohibit "any advocacy of national, racial or religious hatred that constitutes incitement to ... hostility or violence." In May 1990, the French National Assembly passed a Bill prohibiting for a period of five years the candidacy of any person convicted of advocating racial violence. *See Chile, Colombia, France, India, Singapore, South Africa, United Kingdom, Yugoslavia, Zaire and* **Racism**.

Racism

Racism is regarded in international law as proper justification for restricting freedom of expression because it constitutes an infringement of the fundamental rights of others. Article 20 of the ICCPR requires countries to prohibit "any advocacy of national, racial or religious hatred that constitutes incitement to discrimination, hostility or violence". Some countries, upon ratification, have entered a reservation to this Article because of its conflict with freedom of expression. *See Denmark, Norway, Sweden, UK.*

A more detailed and, some commentators contend, a more powerful prohibition of racist speech is set forth in the International Convention on the Elimination of All Forms of Racial Discrimination, a UN treaty ratified by 129 countries as of July 1990. Article 4 of the Convention requires parties: (a) to "declare an offence ... all dissemination of ideas based on racial superiority and hatred, incitement to racial discrimination, ... and acts of violence or incitement to such acts against any race or group of persons of another colour or ethnic origin"; (b) to "declare illegal and prohibit organizations, ... and all other propaganda activities, which promote and incite racial discrimination, and ... recognize participation in such organizations or activities as an offence"; and (c) to prohibit "public authorities or public institutions, national or local" from promoting racial discrimination.

Although prohibition of racist expression is required by international human rights standards, the debate on the permissibility of racist speech continues. Fresh concern about the rise of xenophobia and racism in Eastern Europe has added fuel to the debate. Rather than engage in prior censorship by denying individuals and groups the right to disseminate racist views through the media, some argue instead for stiff penalties subsequent to the expression.

In 1985, a Danish court convicted a TV reporter and an editor of violating a criminal law based on Article 4 of the Racial Convention, merely for having broadcast an interview with members of a group that espoused extreme racist views. In 1990, the TV reporter petitioned the European Commission of Human Rights to declare his conviction to be in contravention of European law. The case will provide the Commission with its first opportunity to consider the scope of permissible restrictions placed on dissemination of racist speech.

In October 1989, the Australian state of New South Wales passed a law prohibiting public acts of racial vilification as part of an Anti-Discrimination Act. In May 1990, a French court ordered the Front National leader Jean-Marie Le Pen to pay damages for making a public statement that the Nazi death chambers were a mere "detail" in the history of the war. Some universities in the United States have adopted new disciplinary codes prohibiting speech that stigmatizes individuals or groups on the basis of race, ethnicity, religion, sex, sexual preference, or other status, but have run into legal challenges by those who believe such bans violate the First Amendment. *See Australia, Denmark, France, South Africa; and* **Violence**.

Sexism

Sexism may be considered any discriminatory practice against an individual on the basis of sex. The UN Convention on the Elimination of All Forms of Discrimination against Women (1981) seeks "the elimination of prejudices and customs and other practices which are based on the idea of the inferiority or the superiority of either of the sexes or on stereotyped roles for men and women". Of related concern is discrimination based on a person's sexual orientation.

Demeaning depictions in the media of the role of men and women in society may encourage sexual discrimination. Some argue that the elimination of sexist material (including the obscene or pornographic) constitutes a valid ground for censorship or self-regulation by the media. Others contend that such censorship may, in the end, advance the cause of continuing sexism by limiting debate. In an effort to combat sexism, Norway has adopted laws which ban advertisements depicting the subjugation or inequality of either sex, and Nicaragua forbids the use of women as "commercial" or sexual objects. The denial of suffrage and political participation to women in certain countries, such as Kuwait, is a limitation on the free expression of political opinion. *See Canada, Kuwait, Norway.*

Religious Intolerance

The UN Declaration on Religious Intolerance (1981) recognizes that an important aspect of religious freedom is the ability to propagate the dogma, aims or beliefs of a religion. Censorship affects religious, dissenting, and non-religious groups and individuals if they are formally proscribed or otherwise prevented from manifesting their beliefs or objections to beliefs. In Pakistan and several other Islamic countries, the content of teaching materials must conform to political and religious dogma endorsed by the government. In Mexico, members of religious orders are prohibited from criticizing state institutions and government actions, and are not permitted to participate in the electoral process. In Albania, the practice of religion had been prohibited entirely. *See Albania, Cuba, Egypt, Indonesia, Iran, Iraq, Kuwait, Malaysia, Mexico, North Korea, Pakistan, Saudi Arabia.*

Heresy Heresy is a theological opinion or doctrine contrary to the official orthodox tenets of a religious body or church. It is often considered to be a dangerous deviation. In countries where religion and the state are merged, heresy is considered a criminal offence. In Iran, for example, members of the Baha'i religion are considered "heretics", all Baha'i religious activity is banned, shrines have been demolished and some 300 Baha'is reportedly were executed between 1979 and 1987. In Egypt in 1987, 48 adherents of the Baha'i faith were fined and imprisoned on charges of "holding ideas that run counter to the divinely revealed religions on which the system of government in Egypt is based" and of belonging to an "apostate religion".

Blasphemy Blasphemy is any oral or written reproach deemed contemptuous or insulting to God or religion. In many countries blasphemy is a criminal offence which applies only to insults to the dominant belief (Christianity in the United Kingdom, Islam in Pakistan, for example). In February 1989, British novelist Salman Rushdie was condemned to death by Iran's Ayatollah Khomeini because his novel *The Satanic Verses* was viewed as blasphemous and insulting to Islam. Demonstrations, book burnings, bomb threats and public disorder occurred in several countries. In India and Pakistan more than 17 people were killed and hundreds injured. In reaction to the Ayatollah's *fatwa*, writers across the world rallied in support of Salman Rushdie, signing a World Statement in defence of freedom of expression, which was carried free of charge by 62 newspapers and magazines in 23 countries. Since the *fatwa*, the author has been in hiding, unable to lead a normal life. The novel is currently banned in over 25 countries.

In April 1989, Dr Omar Abdel Rahman, leader of an illegal political group, declared a *fatwa* against the Nobel prize-winning Egyptian author, Naguib Mahfouz, for his book *Children of Gabalawy*. Egyptian religious and political authorities condemned the *fatwa* and offered Mahfouz protection, which he refused. In 1988, Martin Scorsese's film *The Last Temptation of Christ* caused offence amongst some Christian groups in Europe and the United States. Many considered its depiction of Christ blasphemous, provoking demonstrations, bomb threats and violence at the cinemas where it was shown. *See Egypt, France, India, Indonesia, Iran, Ireland, Pakistan, South Africa, United Kingdom, Zambia.*

Linguistic and Cultural Hegemony

All forms of cultural oppression contravene Article 27 of the ICCPR which states: "In those states in which ethnic, religious or linguistic minorities exist, persons belonging to such minorities shall not be denied the right, in community with the other members of their group, to enjoy their own culture ... or to use their own language".

In a variety of countries, linguistic and cultural dominance of ethnic or linguistic groups is maintained through censorship and the deprivation of language rights. This can lead to the systematic destruction of a community's linguistic and cultural integrity. In some countries, languages and dialects may be curtailed in school teaching and access to the media denied to certain ethnic groups. In Turkey, for example, use of the Kurdish language is a criminal offence. The Turkish authorities have consistently criticized Bulgaria for enforced "Bulgarization" of Bulgarian Turks through name changes.

Language has been a major issue in Canada; in June 1990, the federation failed to adopt the Meech Lake Accord which would have acknowledged French-speaking Quebec as a "distinct society". After riots in Algeria in 1988, new political parties and civic organizations emerged to fight for the promotion of Berber culture and the recognition of Berber language as a national language equal to Arabic. In Australia in February 1989, the International Federation of Journalists' Sydney Declaration drew attention to the fact that transnational media companies are promoting global integration of language, culture and information and called for new media technologies to promote diversity and recognition of the value of national, cultural and linguistic identities. .

Official histories taught in schools may deny minority groups' own interpretations of events. A study of book censorship in the Occupied Territories by Israeli authorities noted that prohibited titles included those that fostered Palestinian nationalism and celebrated Palestinian history. *See Albania, Algeria, Canada, Iran, Iraq, Israel and the Occupied Territories, Japan, Mexico, Turkey, Yugoslavia.*

Propaganda

Propaganda is the dissemination of news and opinion for the purpose of convincing others to adopt a particular viewpoint. Propaganda informs, albeit selectively.

Government Propaganda Governments have a duty to inform the public about their activities and policies and about matters of general concern such as public health. The term "propaganda" may be used to describe government information which has been supplied in a biased form. Government propaganda usually expresses the official political or religious ideology, and divergent or dissident views are described as "anti-government propaganda", such as the offence of "anti-Soviet agitation, slander and propaganda", contained in Article 70 of the Soviet Criminal Code (the offence was abolished in June 1990). The Ministries of Information of several countries serve primarily to propagate the ideas of the ruling party through the organs of government.

In 1989, Chinese authorities manipulated news footage and carried out disinformation campaigns in an effort to convince the public of the authenticity of the "official" version of the Tiananmen Square student uprising and its suppression. In March 1990, a group of Chinese dissidents embarked from France on a ship named the "Goddess of Democracy" to begin pirate radio broadcasts of "anti-government propaganda" into China from international waters. The mission was foiled in May when Taiwan reneged on a promise to supply the ship with a transmitter and Japan refused to let the ship dock.

Article 20 of the ICCPR states that "any propaganda for war shall be prohibited by law". There is, however, no internationally accepted definition of "war propaganda" and national laws likewise fail to specify what information is prohibited. As the Council of Europe's Committee on Human Rights has commented, legal prohibitions that are not clearly defined can lead to abuse. *See China, Egypt, Iraq, South Africa.*

Disinformation Disinformation, a form of propaganda, is the deliberate dissemination of false or misleading information in order to manipulate or influence people's perceptions of certain situations or events, often to create a climate of fear or mistrust as a pretext for taking certain action. Disinformation techniques are used by governments, opposition groups and others wishing to maintain or change the *status quo*. Some countries have been accused of employing disinformation about the spread of AIDS within their borders. In 1989, United States authorities admitted employing an elaborate disinformation campaign aimed at making Libyan leader Colonel Muammar al-Qaddafi fear a United States or Israeli military attack on a suspected chemical weapons plant in the Libyan desert. In Algeria, journalists accused state television and radio of engaging in disinformation regarding the October 1988 riots. In 1986, French authorities proposed the establishment of a research institute to investigate alleged disinformation strategies in reports by journalists writing on military matters. *See China, Mexico, North Korea, Soviet Union, United States.*

Media Bias

Media bias involves the conscious manipulation of news and information to serve the interests of a government, business, racial group, individual or ideology. Accusations of media bias arise when restrictions are placed on media access, news coverage is unbalanced, or pressure is placed on journalists which jeopardizes impartial reporting. Accusations of bias are frequently levelled at television coverage of events since it is both the most difficult medium to monitor and is perceived as the most powerful means for manipulation of public opinion. Many governments employ their own media bias monitors to ensure that opposition views are not given excessive airtime. *See Taiwan.*

In the United Kingdom, the Independent Broadcasting Authority is required by the 1981 Broadcasting Act to ensure "due impartiality on the part of persons providing the programmes as respects matters of political ... controversy or relating to current public policy". Most media organizations, however, have no statutory obligation to be impartial. There has been recent concern in the United Kingdom about politicians dictating the content of interviews by demanding questions in advance, refusing to appear with members of the opposition and insisting on having the last word. In Ireland and the United Kingdom, *Sinn Fein*, the UDA and other banned organizations are excluded from direct access to the broadcasting media, justified on the grounds that any appearance of a representative would be likely to encourage violence or be offensive to viewers. *See France, Spain.*

Governments often accuse foreign broadcasters of unbalanced reporting. The Malaysian government, for instance, claims that its own news agency, Bernama, the sole distributor of news from foreign agencies, aims to combat the imbalance of news from developed nations and "biased" reporting of events occurring in the Third World. The same rationale lay behind restrictions by Chinese authorities on foreign news publications after the violence in Tiananmen Square in June 1989. *See China, Colombia, El Salvador, Ireland, Malaysia, Mexico, Singapore, United Kingdom.*

Copyright and Intellectual Property

Copyright is an internationally protected legal right, under the International Copyright Convention of 1971, to control copying and other commercially significant exploitation of authors' works (writings, art, music and drama), certain manufactured works (sound recordings, films, published editions of books and other literary works) and electronic phenomena (broadcasts, cable programmes and computer software). Each type of work protected by copyright can usually be used or copied in accordance with laws which tolerate certain forms of "fair dealing" and

unauthorized, non-commercial use of another's work. In the United Kingdom, for example, courts will not restrain an alleged copyright infringement if they find that the public's interest in gaining access to the information outweighs the copyright owner's interest in suppressing unauthorized use. Other forms of intellectual property include patents (which protect inventions) and trade secrets law (a refined branch of the law of breach of confidence). *See Malaysia, Singapore.*

Contractual Obligations to Maintain Secrecy

Contractual obligations to maintain secrecy and confidentiality are frequently imposed on civil servants as well as on certain private sector employees. The obligation not to transmit information to unauthorized bodies may relate to any information obtained in the course of the contractual arrangement about policies, activities, plans, supplies, inventions, contracts under negotiation, finances and personal files. The reasons for requiring contractual secrecy vary depending on the parties involved. Civil servants may be bound for national security reasons or the need to maintain citizens' trust that their personal files and applications will be kept confidential.

The obligation to maintain secrecy sometimes lasts beyond the expiration of the contract. In the United States since 1983, government employees have been required to sign lifetime secrecy contracts forbidding disclosure of classified and "classifiable" information. The need for confidentiality will in some cases conflict with what is claimed to be in the public interest. This was a major theme in the *Spycatcher* case in Australia and the United Kingdom in 1987. Courts in both countries recognized that, in some cases, the public interest in disclosure of crime outweighs the duty of confidentiality. *See Australia, Denmark, Sweden, United Kingdom, United States; see also "Whistleblowing" laws under* **Corruption** .

Protection of Sources

Confidentiality is essential to journalists' research and investigation. Sources of information often will speak to journalists only if they feel secure that their identities will not be revealed. Countries differ in the amount of protection afforded to sources. In Britain, journalists can be compelled by courts to reveal their sources upon a relatively vague showing, whereas in Sweden the journalists' privilege is more rigorously protected. In February 1988, Colombian journalists from the magazine *Voz* were ordered to supply information concerning the location of an interview with a hired killer who had named an army captain as his employer. In 1990, the International Federation of Journalists noted an increase in pressure put upon journalists to reveal their confidential sources, particularly in Belgium, Denmark and the United Kingdom. *See Argentina, Australia, Canada, Colombia, France, Germany, Norway, Sweden, United Kingdom.*

Corruption

Censorship, including death threats, murder, detention, expulsion and filing of spurious defamation charges, is used frequently to prevent journalists from investigating topics which expose corruption, abuse of office, or vested interests in government and business. In January 1989, the director and two journalists from an Algerian daily newspaper, *El Joumhouria*, were arrested for defamation for exposing large-scale corruption, speculation and illegal activities of influential persons close to the president's family. Indonesian authorities expelled two Australian journalists in April 1986 after the *Sydney Morning Herald* published a report on alleged corruption at the highest level and banned three issues of the *Asian Wall Street Journal* in November 1986 which contained a similar analysis.

Drug Trafficking One of the most dangerous forms of corruption to investigate is the involvement of government officials, police, and influential persons in drug trafficking. In 1989, at least 12 reporters were killed in Colombia and Mexico allegedly for exposing drug-related activity. *See Algeria, China, Colombia, India, Indonesia, Japan, Kenya, Mexico, Sweden, Turkey, Zaire; and* **Contractual Obligations to Maintain Secrecy**, **Media Workers**.

Special Situations

States of Emergency and War Freedom of expression and opinion are often among the first rights subjected to special regulations under states of emergency or war. International law recognizes that a state of emergency may justify a country's imposition of censorship, extending not only to control of the media but also to other forms of expression, such as correspondence. Any curtailment of rights, however, must not involve infringement of fundamental rights including the rights to life to be free from torture and cruel, inhuman or degrading treatment, and to freedom of thought, conscience and religion; must be necessary to protect public order or national security; and may not involve discrimination solely on the basis of race, colour, sex, language, religion or social origin. There is serious concern that certain governments declare states of emergency in order to facilitate the taking of repressive measures by censoring independent reporting of their actions.

Journalists face extreme risks during situations of armed conflict. At least 40 of the 53 or more journalists killed during 1989 were killed in countries racked by armed conflict, namely Bangladesh, Colombia, El Salvador, Ethiopia, Guatemala, Pakistan, Panama, Peru, Philippines, Somalia and Sri Lanka. Some appear to have been killed by the military, others by government-linked death squads, some by guerrillas, and still others in crossfire.

States of emergency may continue long after the circumstances that provoked them have abated. In Egypt, the president may still exercise state of emergency powers (including the power to censor letters, publications and drawings, confiscate or close printing facilities, and disperse mass meetings and demonstrations) authorized in 1981 following the assassination of President Anwar Sadat. In South Africa, now-suspended state of emergency regulations allowed for draconian powers of censorship, including detention without trial, the harassment of journalists and a virtual news blackout on matters concerning "unrest situations". Commenting on the expulsion of some foreign correspondents from South Africa, the Foreign Correspondents' Association stated that the government intended to end independent coverage of South Africa's social conflict "because it believes secrecy will help it win". In many countries, states of emergency lead to the creation of "emergency zones" where reporting is restricted or prohibited. In May 1990, Israeli authorities began to require that journalists visiting the Gaza Strip be accompanied by members of the military. In the states of Jammu and Kashmir, Indian security forces denied entry to foreign journalists in January 1990 following demonstrations for independence and self-determination. During its invasion of Panama in December 1989, the United States Military Command restricted the US "press pool" to US bases, attempted to ban all non-pool journalists from entering the country and journalists already in Panama from entering conflict zones, and detained and harassed journalists trying to cover the invasion. *See Egypt, India, Indonesia, Israel and the Occupied Territories, Kenya, Nicaragua, Panama, Peru, Philippines, South Africa, Taiwan, Turkey.*

Election Periods During election periods ruling parties are apt to be especially sensitive to the exercise of the right to free expression by opposition parties. Access to broadcasting and radio stations is often curtailed or denied and a disproportionate amount of time allocated to the ruling party. The European Commission of Human Rights noted that there is "no general and unfettered right" for any particular political party to have access to broadcasting time but also ruled that "the denial of broadcasting time to one or more specific groups or persons may, in particular circumstances, raise an issue ... for instance if one political party was excluded from broadcasting facilities at election time while others were given broadcasting time" (*X and the Association of Y v. United Kingdom* (1971)). During the 1988 presidential campaign in Mexico, allegations were made that television news distorted the views of opposition candidates to manipulate public opinion in favour of the ruling party. *See France, Mexico, Myanmar, Nicaragua, Peru, Romania, South Korea, Spain.*

3. Censorship: Methods

A variety of direct and indirect methods are employed to suppress the rights to freedom of expression and information.

Press Laws

Press laws define the rules regulating the press, the publishing industry and the electronic media. Such laws frequently determine the rights and responsibilities of journalists. They can also serve to dictate content. For instance, in Egypt the 1980 Press Law makes it an offence to challenge the truth of divine teachings or to advocate opposition to or hatred of state institutions.

The existence of press laws does not *per se* constitute infringement of freedom of expression. On June 12 1990, the Soviet Union adopted a new press law which incorporates

recommendations of members of the press and civil rights lawyers, guarantees "freedom of the press", bans government censorship, and gives non-governmental organizations and individuals the right to publish. Unfortunately, the abuse of press laws is common throughout the world. *See Soviet Union, Tunisia, Viet Nam, Zaire.*

Licensing

The mandatory licensing or registration of journalists is a common method by which governments control the media and promote self-censorship. Turkish press laws require that all journalists be licensed, with licences to journalists who have been criminally convicted (often for having freely expressed their opinions) routinely refused. Honduran press laws require all journalists to belong to a professional guild. In Iraq, entry into government journalism courses is mandatory for all journalists but restricted to members of the Ba'th party. In March 1989, Ghana adopted a law requiring all newspapers and magazines in the country to apply for licences annually in order to control "bad taste and cultural pollution". *See Ghana, Honduras, Iraq, Malaysia, Singapore, Turkey.*

Attacks and Restrictions on Journalists

Killings, Death Threats and Beatings Assassination of the writer is the ultimate censorship. Unfortunately, physical attacks on journalists, such as beatings, bomb attacks, and killings are not rare phenomena. Attacks are committed by government-linked death squads, rebel groups and drug-traffickers as well as by government authorities. According to the Committee to Protect Journalists (CPJ), in 1989, 53 journalists were murdered or disappeared in the line of duty, twice the number killed in 1988. Most of the killings took place in Latin America, but 11 countries outside that region also registered deaths, including Pakistan, Sri Lanka, the Philippines and Turkey. In Sri Lanka on July 31 1989, guerrillas abducted and killed Premakeerthi de Alwis, a popular radio and TV announcer. Richard de Zoysa, one of Sri Lanka's best-known journalists, was killed in February 1990 after being abducted by assailants including one who was identified by an eye witness as a chief superintendent of police. On March 15 1990, the Iraqi government hanged Farzad Bazoft, a journalist for the UK *Observer* newspaper, despite an international outcry and unconvincing evidence of his guilt. Iraq had accused Bazoft of spying for Israel after he investigated an explosion at an Iraqi military installation. In Colombia, drug barons have killed journalists who spoke out against cocaine trafficking.

More than 100 journalists were physically assaulted in 1989 and countless numbers were subjected to death threats. These incidents are often intended to serve as warnings not to investigate or expose practices such as government corruption, human rights abuses, or drug trafficking. *See Colombia, Honduras, Iran, Iraq, Japan, Mexico, Sri Lanka, Sudan; and* **States of Emergency and War, Corruption.**

Kidnappings and Disappearances Under various governments journalists may be abducted or they "disappear". In Latin America, the fate of many missing journalists has never been explained. Journalists can also be the target of political opposition groups seeking to attract local and international media attention, and have been used as bargaining tools to gain political concessions. As of July 1990, three journalists were believed to remain hostage in Lebanon after several years in captivity. *See Colombia, Honduras, Peru, Sri Lanka.*

Arrest, Detention and Imprisonment Journalists are arrested for expressing views and reporting events that cast an unfavourable light on the government; reporting on proscribed groups and organizations; and publishing information perceived to be contrary to the interests of national security or likely to incite public disorder or violence. According to the CPJ, more than 325 journalists were arrested in 1989 throughout the world. Some were held for only a few hours, others are still in prison. Reporters Sans Frontiéres lists 140 journalists in detention as of July 1990. Short-term detentions are often used as a means of intimidating journalists and preventing them from reporting on a current crisis. Long-term detention without trial and fear of long-term imprisonment are used to silence dissent within a country.

In China more than 24 journalists were arrested in the last half of 1989, of whom more than half remained in prison as of May 1990. In Kenya, Gitobu Imanyara, editor of a monthly journal, was arrested on July 5 1990 along with 10 others who had called for legalization of opposition parties. Journalists may be arrested in Iraq for publishing statements that "injure" the President, the revolution, its ideology, or the Republic, or that propagate imperialism, separatism or for zionist or racist opinions. Dozens of journalists were arrested and detained without charge following the June 1989 coup in Sudan, of whom at least nine reportedly remain in detention as of April 1990. *See India, Malaysia, Myanmar, Singapore, South Africa; and* **Writers.**

Restrictions on Movement and Expulsions Freedom of movement is essential to journalistic activity. Both domestic and foreign journalists have been barred from or severely restricted within zones of war and emergency. Since May 1990, for example, journalists have been able to visit the West Bank and Gaza Strip only when accompanied by representatives of the Israeli Defence Forces and access to the West Bank has been severely curtailed by the imposition of curfews and other military restrictions in many areas. Israeli authorities have also placed numerous Palestinian journalists under house or town arrest.

Many foreign correspondents are expelled from or denied entry to countries each year. According to the CPJ, in 1989, more than 60 journalists were expelled from countries while attempting to do their jobs, twice as many as in 1987. In China alone, 12 foreign journalists were expelled in 1989. Governments also place restrictions on the freedom of resident journalists to leave the country, exclude journalists from conflict and emergency zones and refuse to issue or renew visas and work permits. South African journalists have routinely been denied passports to travel abroad. *See Cuba, Ethiopia, Indonesia, Iran, Iraq, Israel and the Occupied Territories, Malaysia, Myanmar, North Korea, Singapore, South Africa, Sudan, Zaire; and* **Special Situations.**

Dismissals and Harassment Thousands of journalists have lost their jobs or been subjected to harassment during the last several years for exercising their professional rights and duties. Journalists have been dismissed for expressing views critical of the government, for questioning the official account of events and for engaging in trade union activity. In South Africa between 1975 and 1980, 600 to 700 journalists lost their jobs as a result of their demands for greater press freedom. In Poland in the 1980s, over 1,000 journalists lost their jobs and as many were demoted in the aftermath of the introduction of martial law. In January 1988, Mexican television news anchorman, Guillermo Ochoa, was dismissed for broadcasting an interview which implied links between the government and corrupt oil workers' union officials. In Kosovo province, Yugoslavia, the Albanian-language radio and television station was occupied and closed on July 5 1990 and, by August, all 1,800 employees of the Albanian-language press and broadcast media had been dismissed. Sweden has attempted to build legal safeguards into its Press Act to protect individual journalists from harassment. *See China, France, Mexico, Poland, South Africa, Sweden, Zaire.*

Censorship of Materials

Many governments prohibit or restrict the distribution and possession of newspapers, books, films, videos, and music recordings. Materials so banned often contain pornographic themes or reflect unpopular political views. *See China, Egypt, Iraq, Morocco, Myanmar, Singapore, Viet Nam.*

Prior Restraint Prior restraint covers all procedures, formal and informal, whereby publications are censored prior to distribution, in contrast to post-publication censorship and liability for the content of publications. Government censorship of newspapers prior to publication can substantially delay publication and interfere with distribution deadlines. These delaying tactics of censors cost newspapers (especially dailies) crucial time and money.

In Zaire, press laws require prior authorization to publish all newspapers and periodicals. In response to an offensive by the Farabundo Marti Liberation Front in November 1989, new restrictions were placed on Salvadoran journalists requiring all stories to be submitted to government officials prior to publication.

An important form of prior restraint is the issuing of government guidelines to publishers, editors, and writers. Guidelines vary from mandatory to discretionary, from simple requests to warnings. Official guidelines are issued through bodies such as the "D" Notice Committee which operates in the United Kingdom, Australia and Canada. "D" Notice guidelines usually apply to national security materials. Informal and consultative methods are used in some countries, where members of the government make personal contact with editors to influence content and perspective. *See Egypt, El Salvador, India, Indonesia, Iran, Israel and Occupied Territories, Malaysia, North Korea, Romania, Tunisia, United Kingdom, Zaire.*

Post-publication Censorship Post-publication censorship refers to any censorship action taken after initial publication or broadcast which interferes with dissemination or transmission. It includes any legal or extra-legal action taken against matter already in the public domain leading to the banning, burning, classification or confiscation of books and visual materials (paintings, photographs, films, videos) and the confiscation of the technical means by which any of these are produced (typewriters, photographic and video cameras, sound recording apparatus). It can also include the oppressive or arbitrary application of defamation and other laws against writers, journalists and artists. *See Cameroon, Chile, China, Egypt, Iran, Israel and the Occupied Territories, Malaysia, Nicaragua, Singapore, Taiwan, Tunisia, Turkey, Uganda, Zaire.*

Book Banning The publication, importation and distribution of books may be circumscribed because of political, religious or sexual content. Many countries have an official censorship board or equivalent which reviews new publications for "objectionable" content. The protection of state secrets is often used to justify the screening of books; for example, in the United States and the United Kingdom, current and former secret service personnel and others with access to classified information are required to submit writings concerning their employment for prior approval. Some countries publish lists of banned books. It has been estimated that there are more than 100,000 books banned in Iraq and that thousands of books have been banned by Israeli military authorities in the Occupied Territories.

Book banning often increases the sales of titles. The sales success of Peter Wright's *Spycatcher* (which topped bestseller lists worldwide) and Salman Rushdie's *The Satanic Verses* (which by June 1990 had sold 1.2 million English language hard cover editions) is evidence of this phenomenon. In Ireland book banning can result in illegal importation across the border from Northern Ireland. In Brazil, the re-publication of 500 titles banned under the former military government has contributed to massive growth in the publishing industry since 1985. The same is true in the Soviet Union since the advent of *glasnost*.

In recent years, the public burning of books has occurred in Chile in 1986 with the destruction of 14,000 copies of the Gabriel Garcia Marquez novel, *Clandestine in Chile: The Adventures of Miguel Littin*. In January

1989, the public burning of Salman Rushdie's novel, *The Satanic Verses*, in Bradford, England, by protesting Muslims, was one of a series of incidents worldwide which led to the issuing of the *fatwa* by Iran's late Ayatollah Khomeini.

Less extreme methods of post-publication book censorship are more usual but no less effective. In Turkey in 1986, 39 tonnes of books were destroyed following the publication of a list of books banned by the Minister of Justice. In China in 1986, seven million books and magazines containing martial arts, romantic or erotic themes were seized by authorities as part of the "anti-Bourgeois Liberalization" policy. In Israel in 1986, a book exhibition organized by Palestinians was raided, resulting in the confiscation of 1,000 books and the arrest of three of the exhibition's organizers.

Censorship of textbooks is common in many countries. Following the Islamic Cultural Revolution in Iran, educational books were replaced with Islamic texts. In Poland, 650,000 copies of a history textbook were shredded because it made reference to taboo historical subjects. In 1989 a Japanese court upheld the deletion of references in a history textbook to atrocities committed by Japanese soldiers in other Asian countries. *See Algeria, Brazil, China, Egypt, Honduras, India, Iran, Iraq, Israel and Occupied Territories, Japan, Pakistan, Turkey, Tunisia.*

Foreign Publications In many countries the circulation of foreign publications is restricted. Ministers can prohibit the sale and distribution of such publications without recourse to judicial proceedings. Iraq finances newspapers abroad for circulation in other Arab countries but bans their circulation in Iraq. *See China, Malaysia, Singapore, Taiwan, Vietnam, Zaire.*

Media Concentration

Ownership of print and electronic media is becoming increasingly concentrated. A few powerful individuals and organizations have acquired large shares in both national and international markets. In certain countries, a select number of politicians or influential families own the leading newspapers. The UN Human Rights Committee has commented on the possible effect concentration of ownership may have on freedom of expression. Other human rights monitors have expressed concern about the future of the Eastern European media market which has been besieged by communications conglomerates since the revolutions of 1989.

Media concentration is often defended on the grounds that it is the only viable commercial method that can secure the continuing progress and development of media ventures. The burden of proving that concentration might be against the public interest generally falls on opponents of such concentration.

The possible dangers of concentration of ownership are that a narrower range of opinions may be available to the public, that those opinions may reflect only proprietorial interests, that journalistic values may be compromised by commercial interests, and that general standards might fall in the absence of competition. At greatest risk is the level, range and quality of debate on issues of public concern. All of these dangers were emphasized in a statement of principles adopted by the International Federation of Journalists in Sydney in February 1989. The Sydney Declaration calls for action to regulate the international media through international standards and national legislation requiring transnational media enterprises to disclose the full extent of their global holdings; to promote industrial and professional democracy in the media through the appointment of external independent editors, to limit the concentration of media ownership and to promote alternative publishing and distribution networks. Faced with concentration of media ownership, media workers combined in 1990 to form the International Media Union Forum to demand new rules safeguarding media diversity and guaranteeing workers' rights. Several governments have regulated private ownership of media organizations to allow smaller organizations opportunities to compete.

Dangers similar to those posed by media concentration exist with state or single party ownership of all or the bulk of media outlets. Control varies from subtle "guidance" to the use of media outlets as mouthpieces for ruling individuals or parties. *See Australia, Brazil, Colombia, France, India, Iraq, Mexico, Poland, Soviet Union, Spain, Uganda, United Kingdom, United States.*

Closure of Media Outlets

The forced closure of radio and television stations, printing houses, and newspapers may constitute both prior restraint and post-publication censorship. According to the

Committee to Protect Journalists, in 1989, at least 33 media organs were ordered closed by authorities in 17 countries, either temporarily or permanently. *See China, Israel and the Occupied Territories, Panama, South Africa, Sudan, Turkey, Viet Nam.*

Economic Pressures

Economic pressures on the media exerted by governments and private interests are a serious and persistent form of interference with freedom of expression. Most independent newspapers, radio stations and television stations rely heavily on revenue from advertisers including government agencies for their survival; hence threats to withdraw funding can result in compliance with their demands.

Government monopolies on materials essential to media production and selective subsidies to outlets that espouse government views can be used effectively to force closure of media bodies. *See Colombia, Egypt, Honduras, India, Mexico, Myanmar, Paraguay, Spain, Uganda, Zaire; and* **Restrictions on Equipment**.

Bribery and Corruption Corruption is common in countries where journalists are poorly paid and the acceptance of bribes from politicians and business people has become routine. *See Honduras, El Salvador, Mexico.*

Restrictions on Equipment and Materials

Newsprint Authorities with monopoly control of newsprint and machinery often try to control the raw materials or machinery required by publishers. In Ghana, for instance, the Ministry of Information has control over the supply and allocation of almost all media equipment and facilities, from newsprint to telephones and typewriters, rendering all journalists dependent on government approval. In June 1989, charges of profiteering were levelled against Indian officials in charge of the state's newsprint monopoly. In Tanzania, a government requirement that newpapers purchase expensive local newsprint rather than cheaper imports has raised fears that some papers may have to shut down. *See India, Iran, Mexico, Nicaragua.*

Typewriters Governments have placed restrictions on the use of typewriters in order to silence unwanted opinions. In Romania, for example, a 1983 decree gave the authorities power to decide who could or could not possess a typewriter; a register was kept of all owners, and repairs to individual typewriters could only be carried out in appointed workshops; and no-one with a police record was allowed to own a typewriter. On February 20 1987, the Vienna Conference on the implementation of the Helsinki Accords discussed a call to abolish all restrictions on the possession and use of typewriters in the 35 participating states.

In Iraq, importing typewriters (and computer printers) is allowed only after obtaining permission from the General Security Directorate. Foreigners entering Iraq may have their typewriter numbers stamped in their passports. *See Iraq, Romania.*

Photocopiers and Facsimile Machines Since the introduction of the photocopier, duplication and therefore distribution of written materials has become much easier for those with access to such a machine. To combat this process, governments have often required licences to own and operate photocopiers. In Hungary before the revolution of 1989, the Ministry of Industry handled all licences for photocopiers and duplication machinery.

Sometimes photocopiers are crucial to the reporting of human rights atrocities. Such was the case in Cambodia where massive killings were documented by the perpetrators themselves and photocopies of these documents (made under extreme circumstances and a sporadic electricity supply) formed important evidence of the atrocities.

Like photocopiers, facsimile (fax) machines are vital tools for disseminating valuable information. Prior to the United States invasion of Panama in December 1989, fax machines were used to circumvent blanket censorship measures introduced by General Manuel Noriega. In 1989, the Chinese government placed guards at fax machines in Beijing to prevent foreign information about the student uprising reaching the local media. In May 1989, Israeli authorities banned the use of fax machines in the Gaza Strip and confiscated all such machines found in the possession of journalists; they then began to require advance authorization to purchase or operate a fax machine. In Iraq, foreign journalists must send fax transmissions through a government operator. *See China, Iraq, Israel and the Occupied Territories, Panama.*

Restrictions on Access to Information

Control and constraint of the supply of information to journalists and researchers seeking information from public and private sources is exercised through a number of methods, including control of official press releases and authorized briefings; classification or reclassification of information as secret; subjection of government officials to a long-term or even lifetime duty of confidentiality; restriction of the importation and exportation of publications and films; denial or restriction of visas and accreditation for travel between and within countries; denial of access to official or independent sources and independent local assistance; and restriction of information to only major news agencies and bureaux.

News Agencies The five major international news agencies, Associated Press, United Press International, Reuters, Agence France Presse and TASS, account for the bulk of the gathering and dissemination of international news. A sixth agency, Inter Press Service, focuses on news concerning economic and social issues in developing countries. Regional news agencies include Xinhua (New China News Agency), the Pan African News Agency, the Organization of Asian News Agencies, the Union of Arab News Agencies and the Caribbean News Agency.

National news agencies are often closely aligned with the government and may restrict the reporting of domestic affairs to the outside world in compliance with government policy. *See China, Kenya, Mexico, North Korea, Zaire.*

Self-Regulation

Media Self-Regulation In many countries, press or media councils have been established to preserve freedom of the media through self-regulation. These bodies seek to promote and ensure high professional and commercial standards, to respond to complaints and to monitor restrictions on the supply of information of public interest. The success of such bodies depends on the credence given to them by governments, journalists, management and owners of national media bodies, and the general public. In Britain in 1990, government endorsement of the Calcutt Committee's proposals on the press, which appear to foreshadow a shift from self-regulation to statutory control, met with unanimous hostility

from the press. In Portugal, the government's abolition of a statutory press council and its call for journalists and others to engage in self-regulation have been greeted with protests from the media. In single-party states, control of the media is often restricted to members or strong supporters of the ruling party. *See Poland, Portugal, South Africa, Sweden, United Kingdom, Zaire.*

Self-Censorship The term "self-censorship" is used to describe the various reasons why journalists, writers and publishers suppress or withhold information which might otherwise be deemed suitable for publication. Self-censorship operates at various levels and is difficult to identify or monitor. Self-censorship is in operation when an editor or journalist feels obliged not to publish what he or she believes to be true or not to act in accordance with his or her own convictions or sympathies. In many countries, media reporting is based on the understanding that coverage of sensitive issues is to be minimized or dropped and that criticism is to be moderated. Compliance may be secured by physical attacks, threats of dismissal, detention, denial of a licence, closure or (in the case of the foreign press) expulsion or refusal to renew a work permit. The prospect of improved work conditions may contribute to self-censorship; journalists' sympathies may be fostered by salary increases and gifts from the government or other vested interests. *See China, Colombia, El Salvador, Ghana, Honduras, Kenya, Kuwait, Mexico, South Korea.*

Restrictions on Freedom of Assembly and Association

The full exercise of the right to freedom of expression and information requires respect for the closely related rights to freedom of association and assembly. Freedom of association implies the liberty to join with others for the pursuit or furtherance of any of a wide variety of social, artistic, literary, scientific, cultural, political, or religious ends. It also includes the right to form and join trade unions which can be crucial in safeguarding workers' rights to freedom of expression. Freedom of assembly involves the right to assemble peacefully in private or in public. Both rights are protected by Article 20 of the UDHR and by various human rights treaties and may only be restricted for reasons of national security, public order, public health, public morals or the protection of the rights of others.

Banning of Organizations Organizations that challenge the government or the *status quo* are often banned, frequently without reference to whether their opposition is violent or non-violent. Prohibited organizations may be denied access to the media, and sympathetic reporting may be censored, with journalists punished for "condoning terrorism". *See Congo, CSFR, Iran, Iraq, Ireland, Paraguay, Poland, Spain, Tunisia, Turkey, United Kingdom, Zaire.*

Bannings of Meetings and Demonstrations Mass demonstrations are often the only peaceful means by which a movement or organization can capture national and international media attention; that attention, in turn, is often the only means by which groups can bring pressure to bear on a government to respect human rights.

Political meetings, demonstrations and press conferences may be banned or disrupted by government security forces and pressure may be put on the media not to report or to play down sensitive events. An egregious example was the massacre of student demonstrators in Beijing's Tiananmen Square on June 4 1989. Another was the killing of more than 50 students in Kinshasa, Zaire, by troops on May 11 1990. In South Korea, newspapers are instructed to exercise extreme caution when reporting anti-government demonstrations. In Haiti and South Africa, journalists and cameramen have been prevented from covering demonstrations through assault, arrest, and prosecution. *See China, Israel and the Occupied Territories, Romania, Saudi Arabia, South Africa, South Korea.*

Banning of Individuals

Banning orders which deny individuals their freedom of expression and prohibit their right to practice a profession are not uncommon censorship measures. Banned individuals may be prohibited from meeting others and may not be quoted by the media, as was the practice in South Africa until 1990. Prevention of terrorism laws often enable governments to impose restrictions on a person's movements and activities relating to membership in a political organization, such as taking part in any political activity or addressing public meetings. Banning orders are frequently linked

with internal exile. *See South Africa, Soviet Union, Turkey, United Kingdom.*

Banning of Non-Citizens Many countries regularly interfere with the right of their citizens to receive information by denying entry to or deporting non-citizens. Grounds for exclusion or expulsion include the determination that the speaker's views challenge prevailing political ideology or that he or she belongs to a disfavoured organization. In 1989 and 1990, the United States denied entry to Palestine Liberation Organization leader Yasser Arafat, even for the limited purpose of addressing the UN General Assembly, on the ground that he was a leader of a terrorist organization, necessitating the convening of a special session of the General Assembly in Geneva. Other speakers excluded by the United States in recent years include Nobel Laureate Gabriel Garcia Marquez and Hortensia Bussi de Allende, widow of the assassinated Chilean president. The United Kingdom has regularly excluded IRA supporters, including Martin Galvin, publicity director of the IRA's United States support group Noraid.

Illiteracy

Access to books and newspapers is affected not only by government measures but also by national literacy rates and poverty. Illiteracy affects over 900 million adults in the world, over two thirds of them women. A further 100 million children are not enrolled in school. A greater number, perhaps hundreds of millions, are "functional illiterates" (FIL), with severe defects in reading, writing and numeracy. Literacy is often a pre-condition for legal participation in a democratic society and is crucial to the full enjoyment of the right to seek, receive and impart information.

The gap between the literate and the illiterate is widening with the development of information technologies and the spread of electronic data. Even if illiteracy is reduced immediately, the gap will remain because the newly-literate usually only become acquainted with print and not with information technologies or electronic data.

Illiteracy is not just a problem in the developing world. A survey conducted in Canada (Southam Literacy Survey) estimated that 22 per cent of native born Canadians were FIL. UNESCO estimates that approximately 15 per cent of the population of France and 9.5 per cent of the United Kingdom are FIL. **See Literacy Programmes.**

4. Censorship: Targets

Media Workers

Editors and Producers Editorial policy normally reflects a certain political viewpoint, and editorial judgement is often confused with covert censorship. There are, however, many examples of direct proprietorial or state interference in editorial policy. This is particularly evident when the government controls appointments to editorial boards or owns most media outlets. In Viet Nam, where all media outlets are owned by the government, at least six editors of leading newspapers and journals were forced to resign or accept early retirement during 1988 and 1989. *See Chile, China, India, Romania, Viet Nam, Yugoslavia.*

Printers Printers have been the target of forces wishing to stop publication at its material source. In Sri Lanka, printer P D Wimalasena was gunned down at the printing press he managed in Colombo in May 1989. *See Colombia, Panama, Romania, Tunisia, Uganda.*

Journalists By the very nature of their work, journalists are a prime target for censorship and a wide range of measures are employed against them which can be characterized as censorship. **See Attacks and Restrictions on Journalists**.

Investigative Journalists Investigative journalism has emerged as a separate, specialized mode of journalistic inquiry. It involves the investigation and exposure of human rights abuses and of corruption, misconduct and mismanagement in government, bureaucracy, the military, and business; often such exposure generates sufficient outrage to cause a halt or modification of the misconduct. Investigative journalism extends the limits of public debate and political participation. Exposure of the Watergate scandal in 1973 brought investigative journalism to new prominence in the United States, but it has long been a feature of German journalism, exemplified by *Der Spiegel*. The emergence of investigative journalism in other countries such as the Soviet Union and Spain may be viewed as a sign of increasing desire for more openness in government. Journalists engaged in investigative journalism are at particular risk of being subjected to harassment, dismissal, physical abuse and even death. *See Australia, China,* *Colombia, El Salvador, Japan, Mexico, Sweden.*

Writers and Academics

While most writers subjected to imprisonment are arrested for journalistic or political activity, large numbers have been arrested and imprisoned primarily for their novels, poems, plays, teaching activities or scholarly works. In recent years, most of those have been detained in China, Cuba, Guatemala, Iran, the Israeli-Occupied Territories, Myanmar, South Korea, Sudan, Turkey and Viet Nam. Often they are held without charge or trial. Writings which evoke themes critical of the government or considered blasphemous are most likely to place their authors at risk. Several countries have imprisoned leading novelists and poets.

Jack Mapange, a well-known poet, recipient of the Rotterdam Poetry Prize, and head of the Department of Language and Literature at the University of Malawi, has been imprisoned without charge or trial since September 1987 when a book of his poems was banned. Salman Rushdie was forced into hiding on February 14 1988 when Iran's late Ayatollah Khomeini issued a *fatwa*, declaring a death sentence and placing a bounty of $3 million on his head, accusing his novel *The Satanic Verses* of blasphemy. Alaa Hamed, a noted Egyptian novelist, was arrested in March 1990 and accused of "propagating extreme ideas including atheism and contempt of religion" for his novel about a man's imaginary journey to paradise and his meetings with several prophets. Bealu Girma, the former Director-General of Ethiopia's Ministry of Information was dismissed from his job in 1983, reportedly because a book he had written was viewed as containing criticisms of the government. Several months later, Girma disappeared and is believed to have been killed.

Pramoedya Ananta Toer, one of Indonesia's best known novelists was imprisoned for several years and is now under town arrest. His most recent book was banned because it was found to contain "clauses supporting the concept of social classes". Israeli government concerns over "security threats" have led to detention without trial, deportation, exclusion from East Jerusalem or house arrest of over 50 Palestinian poets and writers, including Shafiq Habib, a Palestinian poet who was arrested in June 1990 because his poetry was accused of "inciting violence" against Israel's military occupation. In Iran, following a purge of artists unsympathetic to the current government, Soraya Montaza, a 23-year-old poet, was executed after being found guilty of "advocating sexual freedom". *See India*, **Poems and Novels**, **Book Banning**.

Human Rights Defenders

Human rights defenders around the world are subjected to the abuses they try to prevent and/or document. Defenders, who include judges, defence lawyers, prosecutors, religious workers, members of human rights organizations, teachers, trade unionists, and public officials, in addition to journalists and writers, are threatened, harassed, dismissed from their jobs, imprisoned, tortured and murdered. Human Rights Watch documented 68 murders of human rights defenders in 1989, up from 34 in 1988. Although this obviously shows an increased danger to human rights defenders it may also reflect the spread of human rights activism.

Human rights defenders are most often the subject of violence in countries racked by internal armed conflicts. In Colombia, for instance, where there is an intensive drug war, 24 human rights defenders were murdered in 1989. In Brazil, 14 human rights defenders were killed in 1989, largely due to conflict over land distribution in rural areas. Without accurate reporting of human rights abuses, violations will continue and government officials and "death squad" members could escape responsibility.

Political Opponents

Leaders of opposition political parties or popular movements may form the largest category of people whose rights to free expression are regularly violated. By censoring opposition voices, governments may stifle the aspirations of the majority of their citizens, nullifying not only their own rights to free expression but also to political participation and even self-determination.

Political opponents are people who seek to change the government or modify its policies. They include students, trade unionists, religious leaders, government officials, editors and journalists as well as active members of political parties. Opposition leaders, even those who have not advocated violence, are killed by government troops, executed after summary trials, imprisoned for lengthy periods without charges or on spurious charges,

subjected to unfair, often secret trials, tortured, and held incommunicado. Opposition leaders are also often targets of guerrilla groups and government-tolerated death squads. *See Chile, China, Cuba, Egypt, El Salvador, Ethiopia, Ghana, Guatemala, Iran, Iraq, Israel and the Occupied Territories, Kenya, Mexico, Myanmar, Philippines, Sri Lanka, Sudan, United Kingdom, Viet Nam, Zaire.*

Prisoners

The UN Human Rights Committee and the European Court of Human Rights have decided several cases involving the rights of prisoners to correspond and to receive information, including newspapers and books. They concur that prison authorities may exercise measures of control and censorship over prisoners' correspondence but insist that such measures may not be applied arbitrarily and must be necessary to secure public safety and prevent crime. In 1983, the European Court ruled that various practices in British prisons violated European law, including blanket prohibitions of letters containing complaints about a prisoner's trial, sentence or conditions of confinement; letters to other than friends and relatives; and letters that attempted to stimulate public discussion. In Northern Ireland, correspondence by prisoners in the Irish language is not permitted and there are complaints of severe delays in the receipt of Irish language publications.

Speech

"Freedom of speech" has come to stand for freedom of all types of expression, through any media, including the printed word. However, strict censorship of oral communication is still commonplace. Public speech may be denied to an individual altogether, temporarily or permanently, or doctored to accord with official policy. In many countries certain speech is allowed in small private circles but not in public speeches. In Yugoslavia, the law provides for prosecution of those who commit "verbal crimes", including the spreading of "false news". Under Kenya's sedition law, individuals may be prosecuted for single utterances. In South Africa until 1990, any reference in public speech to members of banned organizations constituted a punishable offence. *See Iraq, Kenya, Morocco, South Africa, United States, Yugoslavia, Zaire.*

Correspondence

Interception of mail is a violation of the right to privacy, as stated in Article 12 of the UDHR, Article 17 of the ICCPR, Article 8 of the European Convention on Human Rights, and Article 11 of the American Convention on Human Rights. In Denmark, the Constitution prohibits any such violation of privacy, unless a judge finds according to strict criteria that special circumstances justify the interference. *See India, Morocco, North Korea.*

Telephone Communications

Opponents of government policy are often subjected to surveillance methods which censor free expression through the creation of an atmosphere of fear and suspicion. In Malaysia, for example, the Special Branch enjoys unlimited powers under the Internal Security Act to investigate and tap the telephones of "subversives". During the Palestinian *Intifada*, Israeli authorities have disrupted, for short periods of time, telephone communications between the Occupied Territories and the rest of the world. In 1989, the European Court of Human Rights held that certain French telephone-tapping practices violated the right to privacy protected under the European Convention. In the United States, evidence of illegal surveillance and telephone-tapping of political groups has come to light under the Freedom of Information Act. *See Argentina, France, Israel and the Occupied Territories, Malaysia, South Korea, Sri Lanka, United States.*

Newspapers and Journals

Freedom of the press is often given a central position in constitutional guarantees related to freedom of expression. For instance, it is a fundamental clause in the First Amendment of the United States Constitution. Despite the ascendency of electronic media around the world, it is generally in the arena of independent newspaper publishing that the most publicized battles for freedom of expression are fought. Magazines and small circulation journals are often targets of censorship, especially in countries with few or no independent newspaper outlets, such as Rwanda. Unofficial or semi-official press organizations in many countries may be the main source of reliable information on national and international issues. *See also separate entries on* **Editors, Journalists, Newsprint, Attacks and Restrictions on Journalists**.

Electronic Media and Technologies

Radio Worldwide, radio is the most important medium of mass communication and the primary source of news and information in countries with low literacy rates and newspaper circulation. *See Rwanda, Brazil.* In some countries, radio operates under the same laws as the press, but is more often regulated by specific rules and guidelines which aim to regulate its programmes. In most countries, all radio stations must acquire a licence and entitlement to use a specific frequency from the state. The licence is usually accompanied by conditions and can be revoked for violation of those conditions. Unlicensed and pirate radio stations have been a major issue in France and Britain and, until recently, in Ireland and Portugal.

In almost all countries, censorship bodies prohibit broadcasting certain subject matter on radio airwaves. In North Korea, most household and work places are equipped not with radio sets but with installed speakers, tuned to the national and local networks. Dials are fixed to prevent reception of external broadcasts.

Radio jamming is used by governments against radio stations within the country which relay opposition views, or against foreign broadcasts thought to carry hostile propaganda. Jamming may take the form of sustained interference of frequencies or sporadic interruptions of programmes with music or other recordings. *See China, Cuba, Mexico, Nicaragua, North Korea, Paraguay, United States; see also* **Transfrontier Broadcasting**.

Television In countries where television broadcasting is widely accessible, it is generally the most popular and influential medium. It is, however, easy to censor. Rapidly changing programmes and images, behind-the-scenes production and editing procedures, and obstacles in obtaining access to original tape material combine to make "watch-dog" activities a particularly difficult task. Scenes may be easily excised or altered and programmes censored or dropped without public knowledge.

In many countries, all TV stations are government-controlled. Independent television may be subject to codes and guidelines issued by the government or independent regulatory bodies. In some countries these guidelines are rigid and must be adhered to, in others they are routinely ignored. Opposition parties are often denied or given minimal TV coverage, particularly during election campaigns.

Transfrontier Broadcasting Article 19 of the UDHR specifically guarantees the right to communicate "through any media and regardless of frontiers". In an age of electronic, computer and satellite technology, communication and information exchange are no longer restricted by national boundaries. The new communications technologies have given rise to two broad areas of freedom of information concerns: government interests in prohibiting the receipt of broadcasts from other countries, and privacy concerns raised by the increased amount of personal information stored in computer files. *See* **New Cable Technologies** and **Satellite Communications**.

The fact that broadcasts from one country can be received in another country gives rise to conflicts between, on the one hand, Article 19's protection of the rights to receive and impart information regardless of frontiers and, on the other hand, limitation clauses in Article 29 of the UDHR and various treaties which permit governments to restrict the communication of information for such reasons as public health, morals, national security and public order. In some cases, governments intentionally broadcast radio and TV programmes into other countries despite the protests of the receiving country. Until 1987, the Soviet Union jammed the BBC Russian and Polish Services and the Voice of America. Beijing authorities jammed the broadcasting of BBC news transmitted from Hong Kong after the Tiananmen Square massacre in June 1989. In 1990, Cuban authorities threatened to broadcast programming into the United States and create problems for smaller United States radio stations, in reaction to the continued operation of Radio and TV Marti, United States-financed stations beaming programmes directly at Cuba, which the Cuban government maintains violates its territorial integrity and political independence.

In other cases, broadcasting into a second country is an unintended consequence of technology the broadcaster has chosen to use. Examples include alcohol, tobacco, drug and firearm advertisements, or programmes showing sexually explicit scenes legal in the broadcasting country but illegal in the receiving country. The receiving country may attempt to block offensive programmes or punish its residents who receive them. The problems involved are significant and largely unresolved.

The European Community Directive on Broadcasting (which incorporates Article 10 of the European Convention on Human Rights) seeks to harmonize the rules governing broadcasting in Europe. The Directive will be made part of the national legislation of all 12 member states by October 2 1991. Although substantially modified in draft to accommodate different national perspectives on standards of taste, decency and advertising airtime, it will nonetheless play an important role in standardizing the practices of EC countries. Under the Directive, national legislation will remain intact but where a conflict arises the Directive will take precedence. For example, the United Kingdom's and Irish government's bans on broadcasts of interviews with members of certain political groups could be thwarted by broadcasts from other countries which "spill over" national boundaries.

The Council of Europe's Convention on Transfrontier Television, agreed to in March 1989, is broadly similar to the Directive but will only bind those countries that ratify the treaty and will come into force only after ratification by seven countries. As of July 1990, it had not yet come into force. *See China, Denmark, France, Hong Kong, Ireland, Mexico, Morocco, Poland, Soviet Union, United Kingdom.*

The European Court of Human Rights has decided only one case concerning transfrontier communication. In *Autronic AG v Switzerland* (1990), Autronic, a Swiss company, applied to the appropriate Swiss authority for permission to broadcast a public Soviet television programme which it received directly from a Soviet telecommunications satellite by means of a private dish aerial. The Swiss authority denied the application on the grounds that the Soviet Union itself had refused permission in order to prevent the disclosure of confidential information. The European Court ruled that the denial violated article 10 of the European Convention which guarantees the free flow of information across frontiers. The Court reasoned that the fact that the programme was publicly broadcast throughout the Soviet Union sufficed to establish that the broadcast was of a public nature. Moreover, the fact that the European Convention on Transfrontier Television authorizes the reception of uncoded broadcasts without requiring the broadcasting country's consent has contributed to the development of a practice that appears to tolerate reception without consent.

Satellite Communications Satellites provide a way of transferring information over long distances to large geographical areas.

They allow the transfer of voice, data, text and image without regard to frontiers. Telephone, fax and telex communications, radio and television transmissions, and data relating to specific purposes such as weather and financial markets can all be relayed by satellite.

Since the introduction of satellites in the 1960s, numerous issues have arisen concerning their ownership and operation, including: the high cost of purchasing and maintaining satellites and the virtual monopoly of a few wealthy countries over their control and use; the limited number of satellites that can be launched into a geostationary orbit (GSO) around the equator and the absence in international law of any recognition of each country's right to have at least one GSO; the fact that it is possible for neighbouring countries to receive information broadcast to a specific country; the potential use of satellites for secret intelligence gathering, including photographs and phone-tapping; and the need for common technical standards to allow easy exchange of information between different satellite communication channels. *See* **New Cable Technologies**.

The rapid development of multinational channels transmitted by satellite makes it possible to receive foreign television broadcasts in individual homes via satellite dish. In the United States alone there are an estimated two million "backyard earth stations". The sale, operation and location of satellite dishes, however, may be subject to government monopoly, authorization or regulation. *See Denmark, France, Soviet Union, Spain, Sweden, United Kingdom.*

New Cable Technologies   Much of the world's information now flows along telecommunications cables. Their significance for the future of communications derives from the spread of digital information. News, data, telephone conversations and television transmissions can all be translated into digital form and transmitted over the same cable network.

Under the name Integrated Services Digital Network (ISDN), old copper analogue telephone networks are being upgraded with fibre optic cables to accommodate high speed data and two-way moving pictures. The ISDN is based on a complex set of international standards promising "full transparency across borders".

While simplifying the communication of text and data, the ISDN raises a host of difficult issues, notably data protection and privacy. With widespread ISDNs, it will become easier to duplicate and disseminate personal information. The ISDN can automatically and undetectably monitor telephone calls, bank transactions and spending habits. Establishing the individual's right to control this information will be a major challenge during the 1990s.

The new network technologies offer new mechanisms by which governments may monitor the actions and communications of their citizens. The sheer volume of data promised by the ISDN, however, seems likely to limit the ability of governments to intercept or censor the great bulk of messages.

Computers   Computers are able to store, analyze, code and decode information to a degree that makes them enormously powerful (and extremely vulnerable) instruments of information collection and dissemination. Computers can be linked together via telephone links and information readily exchanged. Due to high costs, however, development of computer technology and broad access to computers is mainly limited to industrialized countries.

Domestic and international legal principles concerning the use of computers, such as laws on copyright of unpublished works and the right to privacy, are underdeveloped, lagging far behind developments in computer technology. Possession of computer equipment is often restricted and subject to licensing laws. Some countries have passed laws against "computer hacking" in an effort to stop the damage to security and privacy which unauthorized forays into computer data banks can cause. *See France, Iraq.*

Databases   Databases and other computerized information banks allow for huge amounts of data to be processed and made widely accessible. The facility with which data can be accessed and compiled using databases has led to privacy and national security concerns regarding sensitive information and data. Some countries have imposed restrictions on access to and use of databases. In the United States, for example, certain databases cannot be accessed by users based in other countries. A new category of "potentially sensitive" information was created in the United States in 1986, referring to unclassified, non-sensitive data which can be turned into "sensitive" information through compilation and matching. Countries without legislation on "transborder dataflow" (TDF) have been termed "data havens". *See Denmark, United Kingdom, United States; and* **Data Protection**.

Artistic Expression

Article 19 of the ICCPR guarantees freedom of expression "in the form of art" or through any other media. This clause recognizes that art is a traditional target of censorship.

Censorship of art is often based on misapprehensions about artistic substance and intention. It is often art's capacity to say more than one thing at a time that makes it vulnerable to misinterpretation. This is not to deny that some works of art are produced with the firm intention of defying authorities and moral codes; some *avant-garde* art is purposefully designed to shock or disgust. In February 1990 in the United Kingdom, for example, an artist and gallery curator were convicted of "outraging public decency" over an exhibit of earrings made of freeze-dried human foetuses. Art is, however, commonly censored in anticipation of, or as a reaction to, popular disenchantment with a work's style or message. Ironically, art censorship may create conditions in which the art is publicized. A banned film, book, or exhibition may enjoy a wider audience following censorship (provided the suppression is not total) than could have been otherwise expected.

Film and Video Reasons given to justify film censorship vary widely. In Pakistan, for instance, all sexual material in films is censored according to the laws of Islam. In Tunisia, the film *Fatma 75*, by Selma Baccar, was banned because it questioned the government's official policy concerning women. Film censorship may also be motivated by national security considerations. In Egypt, for example, films critical of the government will not pass the censors. In South Africa, the Commissioner of Police may "prohibit any ... film recording or sound recording containing any news ... ", for the purpose of public safety and the maintenance of public order.

Although abolished or weakened in many countries, film censorship boards are still prevalent. In countries that have traditional censorship boards, all films for public exhibition and/or hire must be approved. Films may be banned, approved, or passed subject to cuts being made. In some countries, a censorship certificate must be purchased for each print of a film, but more often only a single certificate is required for all prints. Films are censored twice in Egypt where a department in the Ministry of Culture must approve all films both in their script form and before they are shown to the public. Further censorship occurs before

films can be televised. In some countries, films that are exported are subject to censorship to prevent the country of production being shown in a poor light.

Many traditional censorship boards have become classification boards, which place films into categories for showing to adults only or to both children and adults. Some countries, including the United Kingdom, United States, Ireland, and Australia, have adopted sophisticated systems which employ several guidelines, such as U (unclassified), PG (parental guidance), age restricted to 12, 15 and 18, and R18 (restricted distribution to specially licensed sex shops or cinemas). In Ireland, people over 18 were allowed to view Martin Scorsese's *The Last Temptation of Christ*, but only on the condition that no one would be admitted to the film after it began, to ensure that audiences saw a statement that the film was not based on the Gospels but on a book by a Greek author; this statement was also required to be included on signs outside the cinema.

In the United States, self-censorship by directors is encouraged through studio contracts obligating directors to produce films with no higher than an R rating (no-one under 18 allowed without parent or guardian). In July 1990, a group of respected Hollywood film-makers criticized the rating system of the Motion Picture Association of America, charging that "the taint of an X rating (18 and over only) clearly results in massive and arbitrary corporate censorship" because "an X-rated or unrated film is denied exhibition in thousands of cinemas nationwide".

Recently, the private showing of films has become subject to censorship in the form of video censorship. Britain pioneered this new form of censorship with its Video Recordings Act of 1984, which requires classification of videos before they may be sold or hired. In September 1989, the British Board of Film Classification refused certification to *Visions of Ecstacy*, an 18-minute video depicting the visions of St Teresa of Avila in an erotic manner, because it "was contemptuous of Christ" and contained imagery "the Board has come to associate with soft pornography". The video was the first film or video banned in Britain for blasphemy. The Board's decisions are subject to appeal and the Board issues statements justifying its decisions in detail. The film and video censor in New Zealand also makes a policy of publicizing and explaining censorship and classification decisions. Scandinavian countries are following a different path by linking video censorship to existing film censorship certificates. *See Brazil, Cameroon, Egypt, Iraq, Ireland, Hong Kong, Japan, Tunisia, United Kingdom.*

Theatre In many countries public theatrical performances are subject to censorship. In Indonesia, anyone planning to stage a play, poetry reading or short-story reading must first obtain permits from the local police. Even with a permit, a scheduled performance of a 300-year-old Chinese love story was abruptly cancelled in May 1989 on the grounds that it contained "cultural and artistic values contrary to *Pancasila*", a set of five broad social and political principles elevated by President Suharto to a state ideology. It was the second dramatic production to be cancelled in two months for portraying Chinese values. In Kuwait, a censor is expected to monitor performances and check that actors do not deviate from the written text; actors may be persecuted for offending Islam. Theatre is completely prohibited in Saudi Arabia.

The Israeli Board for Film and Theatre Review supervises all films and plays. In December 1986, a play, *The Last Secular Jew*, was banned because it was "liable to stir up hatred against all religious people". However, after protests the play was permitted with certain cuts. A Palestinian theatre, *Al Hakwati*, in East Jerusalem, has been closed at least 20 times since it opened in January 1986, for allegedly fostering "illegal meetings".

Banning a play may also entail a banning order against the playwright, as in the case of Congolese playwright Guy Menga. Distinctions can be made between staged and televised versions of plays. In South Africa, for example, a play by Athol Fugard could be staged but not televised.

One possible effect of theatre censorship is a cultural "brain drain". Prior to and immediately following the fall of the Berlin Wall in November 1989, many East German actors, theatre directors and producers left their country because of restrictions on artistic expression. In June 1990, artists in the Soviet Union held a strike led by the Minister of Culture to protest lack of state funding for the arts and low salaries. *See Congo, CSFR, Indonesia, Iran, Israel and Occupied Territories, Kenya, Kuwait, Mexico.*

Poems and Novels In many cultures, poets and writers are considered spokespersons for their society. Poetry is censored if it is judged to convey ideas hostile to government policy or to public morals or taste. One of the strengths of poetic language, its ambiguity, is often the source of censors' disaffection for the medium. In Yugoslavia, for example, a collection of poems was withdrawn because they could be "interpreted as having a number of meanings and their content ... (could) bring ideological confusion to the readers". In Pakistan, translations of love poems by the English poets Robert Browning and D H Lawrence are among works deemed offensive to Muslim sensibilities. As part of the policy of *glasnost* in the Soviet Union, once proscribed poets are now being published.

Novels are similarly censored on moral and religious grounds or for their depictions of political-historical movements. In early 1988, the first instalment of Boris Pasternak's novel *Dr Zhivago* was published in a Soviet magazine after being banned for nearly 50 years. Similarly in 1987, Anatoly Rybakov's novel on the effects of Stalinism, *Children of Arbat*, was published. In 1988 the last Irish novel banned in Ireland, *The Cabfather*, by Lee Dunne was unbanned. *See Honduras, Iran, Pakistan, South Africa, Soviet Union, Yugoslavia, and* **Writers and Academics**.

Art Sketches, drawings, paintings and sculptures are censored or their subject matter controlled through the direct interference of authorities or compliance by artists' unions with government policy. In January 1988 in the Soviet Union, reformers attending a congress of the Union of Artists mounted an open challenge to the traditional leadership, stating that despite an explosion of interest in art in recent years, "the union leadership chooses who is to be and who is not to be in artistic life, who is allocated a studio or a workshop, who is allowed to give an exhibition, (and) who should become known through reviews of books". In Pakistan in January 1987, the editor of *Frontier Post* was prosecuted for publishing a photograph of a painting of Adam and Eve by the Renaissance artist Lucas Cranach, considered sacrilegious to Muslim ideology. In the United States in 1989, an exhibition of photographs by Robert Mapplethorpe which contained a strong homo-erotic theme was cancelled by a museum because of concern that the government would cut the museum's grant; in April 1990, a museum and its director were charged with violating state obscenity law for exhibiting the same photographs. In South Korea, art sympathetic to the North Korean state is routinely censored and its creators punished. *See Mexico, United States.*

Music Popular music and musicians have always been targets of censorship. In some countries, music is perceived by the authorities to be such an important medium of communication that special laws on performance and recording have been created. In Zaire, for example, laws proscribing censorship of music are part of the Penal Code. The Zairean Censorship Commission of Music rules on the conformity with *bonnes moeurs* and public order of songs performed, recorded or broadcast live. The Commission determines whether songs are likely to give rise to racial or tribal hatred and whether they contain insults or prejudicial or slanderous imputations. Recording, performing and broadcasting of songs without prior authorization are criminal offences. Commission members are authorized to enter any place, day or night, where musicians play or music is recorded.

In July 1990, Louisiana became the first United States state to pass a law requiring warnings on the covers of record albums which contain sexually explicit lyrics, and forbidding the sale of such records to minors. The law has since been vetoed by the state governor. Similar legislation is pending in 19 other states. In June 1990, a federal judge in Florida declared obscene a recording by the rap group, 2 Live Crew.

Since *glasnost* in the Soviet Union and the revolutions in Eastern Europe, music by hitherto proscribed songwriters has been performed and publicly disseminated. The Music Censorship Department of the Iraq Ministry of Information and Culture maintains a list banning over 200 Iraqi and foreign songs. *See CSFR, Iraq, Israel and the Occupied Territories, Mexico, United States, Zaire.*

Education and Research

Libraries Libraries and librarians perform a vital role in protecting freedom of information and the public's right to know. In many countries, however, governments influence or interfere with the operation of libraries. In Iraq, for example, all libraries are directly supervised by government authorities. In El Salvador in June 1990, a librarian from the military academy said he had been ordered to set aside possibly key evidence in the murder of six Jesuit priests so that it could be burned.

Restrictions on access to library materials on political, moral, or religious grounds can operate on various levels. Pressure can be exerted by government authorities, employers or patrons. Access to libraries may be restricted or library funding made conditional. Librarians may exercise self-censorship through selective acquisition or restrictive dissemination. In the United States it became known in September 1988 that the Federal Bureau of Investigation had engaged in a "Library Awareness Program", pressuring librarians across the country to disclose the names and reading habits of certain library patrons deemed "hostile to the United States". Professionals at both the national and international levels, including the International Federation of Library Associations, have become more active in monitoring and opposing censorship of libraries. *See Iraq, Romania, United States.*

Academic and Scientific Freedom Academics and scientists face limitations on the freedom to practice their profession because research findings are often of a sensitive nature and are restricted by classification rules. Academics and scientists have been dismissed from posts, blocked from publishing, denied funding for research, denied the opportunity to travel abroad to international meetings, and denied contact with foreigners in the name of national security. Rigid ideological control can be exercised over intellectual and scientific life on religious grounds. In some countries, overstepping the dangerous boundary between academic or scientific opinion and political opinion can bring severe penalties, such as subjection to psychiatric abuse, common in the Soviet Union before 1989.

A human rights report on higher education by the World University Service entitled "Academic Freedom 1990" gives an overview of the status of academic freedom in the world. The project, begun with the proclamation of the "Lima Declaration on Academic Freedom and Autonomy of Institutions of Higher Education" in September 1988, documents human rights violations in the education sector and identifies factors and conditions responsible for these violations with a view to searching for durable solutions. *See Germany, Iran, Iraq, Soviet Union.*

Advertising

Article 19 of the ICCPR defines freedom of expression as including the "freedom to seek, receive and impart information and ideas *of all kinds*". This language is clearly wide enough to cover advertising.

Commercial Advertising The European Commission of Human Rights has recognized commercial speech as within the human rights guarantee of freedom of expression (*Wiljenberg*, 1983; *Barthold*, 1985). The United States Supreme Court has held that there is no First Amendment protection for false advertising or advertising which promotes unlawful products, but that otherwise restrictions on commercial speech must be justified by a substantial state interest and be the least restrictive method to advance that interest.

The World Federation of Advertisers campaigns for self-regulation of advertising. The Council of Europe's Convention on Transfrontier Television and the EC Directive on Broadcasting prohibit advertising certain items relating to health products and prescribe how others may be presented. In June 1990, a law banning alcohol and tobacco advertising, including sports sponsorship, was passed by the French National Assembly and will take effect in 1993. In Nicaragua, Law 57, passed in April 1989, forbids the use of women as "commercial" or sexual objects. *See Argentina and* **Transfrontier Television**.

Political Advertising Advertising as a mode of expression need not have a commercial motive alone; advertising for political purposes or to promote knowledge of rights and entitlements is commonplace. Restrictions placed on political advertising are of particular concern because they can potentially limit the free expression of political opinion. In France, heavy protests followed the passing of a Bill by the National Assembly banning political advertising until three months before an election. In South Africa, conveying political messages through advertising was banned after the practice was adopted in response to the Emergency Media Regulations of 1987. *See France*.

Environmental Information

Freedom of information is necessary in order to maintain environmental quality and to use scarce environmental resources efficiently. Sometimes existing scientific data about environmental conditions is made unavailable through government bureaucracy and regulation, often in the name of national security. Lack of access to environmental data and poor government-controlled news distribution has prevented many developing nations from dealing with the effects of rapid deforestation and desertification. No governments are known to censor reports about depletion of the ozone layer and the "greenhouse" effect, but few

have commissioned the necessary studies to determine what roles their own industries have played in the creation of these phenomena. The UN General Assembly passed a resolution in 1983 establishing the independent World Commission on Environment and Development. In 1987 the Brundtland Commission published a report, *Our Common Future*, focusing on "sustainable development", that is, development which meets the needs of the present generation without making it more difficult or impossible for future generations to meet their own needs. The report notes that a prerequisite for such development is "a political system that secures effective citizen participation in decision making". Effective participation requires informed citizens.

Pollution Information Information about pollution is routinely the target of censorship. Until the revolutions of 1989, censorship kept hidden the true extent of the environmental and ecological disaster in Eastern Europe. In Poland, for example, pollution data was considered a "state secret". In Morocco in December 1989, information about a major oil spill off the Atlantic coast was withheld from the Moroccan press and public for 10 days; news of the event eventually surfaced through the French media. *See Morocco*.

Public Health Information The right to health is protected by a number of international instruments. It is recognized in Article 12 of the International Covenant on Economic, Social and Cultural Rights as "the right of everyone to the enjoyment of the highest attainable standard of physical and mental health".

There are numerous examples of the restriction and suppression of health information about which the public has a right to know. These include information on abortion and contraception (in 1987 it became illegal in Ireland to provide referral information on abortion clinics in the United Kingdom); the safety of nuclear power plants and the link between radiation leaks and public health; and the dumping of banned pharmaceuticals and hazardous products in developing countries where information on their danger is not available. The full extent of the health damage caused by the leak of poisonous gas from the Union Carbide factory in Bhopal, India, on December 2 1984 is still unknown, although 3,600 died from the accident and the Indian government has estimated that half a million people were affected.

Many governments seek to hide the number of AIDS cases in their countries and have deliberately suppressed information on the disease. Some African countries, such as Zaire and Kenya, have suppressed such information out of fear that reporting the full extent will damage tourism, foreign investment and national prestige, and will result in governments being blamed for the disease's spread. Until recently, AIDS was dismissed in the Soviet Union as a disease of Western decadence. Suppressing information about how to control and prevent the disease and minimizing its prevalence can accelerate the spread of HIV, the virus that causes AIDS, and hasten the death of those who develop the disease.

Private and religious groups have also taken positions that have resulted in the suppression of life-saving information. In Ireland, for example, religious and legal prohibitions against homosexuality have forced many gay men to marry to conceal their sexual orientation. This has contributed to Ireland having the highest incidence of HIV-positive babies per capita in Western Europe a statistic, however, which is also related to the scale of intravenous drug use. In 1989, Fr Paul Lavelle, an Irish Jesuit priest and co-ordinator of the Catholic Church's National AIDS Task Force, had his book (which dealt with the use of condoms to prevent the spread of the disease) withdrawn on the orders of the Bishop of Dublin. The original edition was pulped and the book now appears without references to use of condoms.

A major challenge to international human rights is the scale of hunger, death through disease and malnutrition, and reduced life expectancy in the developing world. Prevention of famine depends on accurate and timely identification of those threatened with starvation and their location; an informed public who can pressure governments to respond swiftly and effectively to need; and a host government willing to allow the media and aid agencies immediate access. The World Bank stated in its November 1989 report on Sub-Saharan Africa that the success of any long-term development in Africa or other famine-ridden regions depends on a freer flow of information. *See China, Ethiopia, Ireland, Poland, Romania, Soviet Union, Sudan, United Kingdom; and* **Public Health and General Welfare**.

Nuclear Information Discussions about nuclear arms and nuclear safety are often lost in a maze of technicalities, propaganda and secrecy. It has gradually emerged that the early exploitation of nuclear power for weaponry and electricity generation was accompanied by rigorous censorship and systematic disinformation. In 1987, it was disclosed that the British government had suppressed information about the effects of a serious fire at a nuclear reactor at Windscale (today known as Sellafield) for 30 years. One reason was to deny the information to opponents of the government's nuclear policies. In June 1989, a scientific report which showed that plutonium contamination from Britain's nuclear tests had spread far beyond an official test range in South Australia was withheld from publication by the Australian government. On April 26 1988, a United States government report was released which revealed that the Department of Energy had deliberately withheld information about plutonium contamination of the people of Rongelap in the Bikini Islands which had resulted from hydrogen bomb testing in 1954.

When the Chernobyl nuclear power plant accident occurred on April 26 1986, *glasnost* was in its infancy and, throughout the 10 day battle to contain the disaster, Soviet citizens were kept in the dark by their government. The world was first notified by Swedish scientists who detected the radioactive cloud on April 27. Only in 1990, four years after the accident, has the enormity of the disaster begun to emerge. It is now known that at least 31 people died in the accident and its immediate aftermath, 600,000 people were significantly exposed to radiation, 130,000 people had to be relocated and some 5,000 square kilometres (1,930 square miles) were rendered uninhabitable.

In Israel in 1987, Mordechai Vanunu was convicted of treason and espionage (in a trial from which the press and public were excluded) after revealing that Israel has an independent stockpile of nuclear weapons. His appeal to the Israeli Supreme Court was rejected in 1990. Since his arrest, he has been held in a section of the Ashkelon jail reserved for prisoners of the highest category of security risk. No other prisoners are allowed to come near him and, except for exercise periods, he remains in his cell. As members of his family stated at a press conference in early 1987: "The policy of utter secrecy adopted by the Israeli government in all aspects of the Vanunu affair is a direct outgrowth of the policy of secrecy and deception of the whole nuclear issue."

By April 1987, the International Atomic Energy Agency had received more than 250 "hushed-up" reports of nuclear power plant accidents around the world. The World Association of Nuclear Operatives, a 31-nation group concerned with improving the image of nuclear power, agreed on May 15 1989 to prohibit all secrecy in the operation of civilian nuclear power plants.

In both the United States and the Soviet Union, material on the use of nuclear power in space is classified on national security grounds and, therefore, little is known about its potential hazards to the environment and public health. Using, in large part, the United States Freedom of Information Act, Greenpeace reported 200 nuclear accidents involving the world's navies, which were not publicly revealed at the time. In three serious cases which concerned the United States (the loss of an H-bomb from the carrier *Ticonderoga*, off the Japanese coast in 1965, a fire aboard the *Belknap* in 1975, and a reactor coolant leak aboard the submarine *Guardfish* in 1978) the report alleges that United States Navy records had been distorted to hide critical information.

Historical Information

Official archives are generally subject to a rule whereby they are not made available to the public before a certain date. The determination of when it is permissible to release material varies, for example 25 years in the United States, 30 years in the United Kingdom, 50 in Greece. Information deemed sensitive is subject to longer or indefinite restriction, chiefly for reasons of national security or public order.

Restrictions on access to historical information have been criticized for allowing official cover-ups of embarrassing or damaging information, and for lending credibility to inaccurate or partisan versions of history in the absence of accurate source material. The Turkish government continues to deny access to records which many historians believe would provide documentary evidence of the Ottoman Empire's culpability for the killing of more than a million Armenians in 1915. *Glasnost* in the Soviet Union and Eastern Europe has led to the revision of much historical literature and the unbanning of accounts of history that conflicted with offical versions. *See Canada, China, France, Iran, Japan, Norway, Turkey, United Kingdom, Soviet Union.*

5. Defending Freedom of Expression and Information

Non-Governmental Organizations

International, non-governmental organizations have played a significant role in directly or indirectly working to combat censorship. Among such organizations are those with membership or affiliated bodies in several countries, such as Amnesty International, ARTICLE 19, the Committee to Protect Journalists, Human Rights Watch, the International Commission of Jurists, International PEN and Reporters Sans Frontieres.

Other relevant international organizations include Index on Censorship, the International Federation of Journalists, the International Journalism Institute, the International Organization of Journalists, the International Press Institute, the International Committee of the Red Cross (Hot Line), the World Press Freedom Committee, the International Federation of Actors, the Association for the Promotion of the International Circulation of the Press, the Commonwealth Press Union, the International Federation of Library Associations, and the World University Service.

On the regional and national level an increasing number of organizations monitor and document the performance of their governments regarding the rights to freedom of expression and information, and try to mobilize public opinion against abuses of those rights.

Inter-Governmental Organizations

The responsibility for monitoring and promoting compliance with international standards protecting freedom of expression is vested in inter-governmental bodies such as the UN Human Rights Committee, the UN Commission on Human Rights, the Council of Europe, and the Inter-American Court and Commission on Human Rights. Among the UN agencies, UNESCO has particular responsibility for the protection and promotion of rights in the fields of education, science and culture. Other agencies, such as the International Labour Organization, are concerned with promoting the right to freedom of association.

New World Information and Communication Order The concept of a "new world information and communication order" (NWICO) first arose at a symposium on mass media in the non-aligned countries in March 1976. A resolution adopted by the symposium stated: "Since information in the world shows disequilibrium in favouring some and ignoring others, it is the duty of ... countries to change this situation and obtain the decolonization of information, and initiate a new international order in information".

In 1980, the UNESCO General Conference began to debate the implementation of NWICO policies based on the conclusions of the MacBride Commission's report, "Many Voices, One World". Since 1980, there has been deep international division over the validity and interpretation of many aspects of UNESCO's policies for NWICO. By November 1989, however, some degree of consensus had emerged. UNESCO's new "strategy for communications policy and activities in the 1990s" encourages "the free flow of information at international as well as national levels"; seeks to "promote the wider and better balanced dissemination of information, without any obstacle to freedom of expression"; responds to earlier criticisms of one-sided support for government-controlled media by an insistence that support of communication structures should concern both "public, private and other media"; includes a commitment that the industrialized countries would increase their support for the building of communication infrastructures in developing countries; and emphasizes media education in order to "promote a better understanding of the means available to (media) users to know and to defend their rights".

In the late 1980s, many of the issues surroundeding NWICO began to be discussed at meetings of the General Assembly on Tariffs and Trade (GATT) as communications services became a major topic in international trade policy. Some of the current proposals under consideration concern the promotion of expanded free trade in services activities.

However, many of the principles advanced in the GATT proposals run directly counter to those of the NWICO. If its policies are adopted and implemented, GATT is likely to provide the dominant international policy framework which governs the structure and the flow of international information services in the future. *See* **Media Concentration**.

International Measures to Protect Journalists

There is increasing recognition that journalism is a dangerous profession and that journalists place themselves in life-threatening situations when covering wars, terrorism and civil strife. Attempts to provide journalists with greater protection have been made by intergovernmental and non-governmental organizations. Protocol I (1977) to the 1949 Geneva Conventions, ratified by more than 90 governments, provides measures of protection for journalists in areas of armed conflict. In 1985 the International Committee of the Red Cross, which monitors and seeks to promote compliance with the Geneva Conventions, established a "hot-line" to assist journalists on dangerous missions. The International Press Institute has produced a manual to help journalists on dangerous assignments to "avoid death, injury, jail, expulsion and other perils". In April 1990, the International Federation of Journalists (IFJ) produced a 32-page safety manual, in four languages, to assist journalists working in areas of high risk. It provides contact numbers of journalists' unions and human rights agencies around the world. The IFJ has also initiated a programme which provides financial support for threatened journalists and their families; developed a safety training programme for unions in Latin America, Africa and the Middle East; and provided telecommunications equipment to improve contact with unions in those regions. *See Colombia, El Salvador, Iraq, Panama, Peru.*

National Law, Policy and Practice

Freedom of expression and information requires legal protection on the national level based on the full implementation of international standards. Where a country has a written constitution, freedom of expression, freedom of all media, and the right to know should be protected within it and in other national legislation. All measures taken to promote freedom of expression at the national level should adhere to the international principle that "freedom is the rule and its limitation the exception".

Access to Information Freedom of expression includes the right not only to impart but also to seek and receive ideas and information. This "right to know" is fundamental to ensuring open and accountable government. In the Philippines, for example, the right to seek information is enshrined in the Constitution.

Where public access to information is a working principle, countries fall into two broad categories: those which have specific freedom of information laws governing rights of access (Australia, Canada, France, Sweden and the United States, for example), and those which adhere mainly to the principle of discretionary secrecy in the release of information (the United Kingdom, for example). *See Canada, Denmark, France, United Kingdom.*

Freedom of Information Acts The aim of Freedom of Information Acts is to increase the flow of information from governments to their citizens. One difficulty involved in the effective implementation of such acts has been the need to reconcile them with existing secrecy laws. Intelligence agencies, for example, are often granted the right to refuse to produce documents or sections of documents, on national security grounds. Many journalists in Canada, not having access to information on government policies of public interest in their own country, have discovered details of such policies by referring to documents available under the United States Freedom of Information Act. A decade-long campaign to have a Freedom of Information Act enacted in Britain has produced only limited victories. *See Australia, Canada, United States.*

Whistleblower Laws "Whistleblower" laws exist in the United States to protect private employees from reprisals for disclosing illegal activities of their employers. By contrast, the United Kingdom provides no such legal protection. In 1989, Tanzanian journalists received government awards for exposing corruption.

Media Ownership and Access to Media Some countries have laws and government programmes which ensure minority representation and participation in the media. In the United States, for example, preference is given to minority-owned ventures bidding for licences and frequencies for radio and television stations. Companies which are awarded a franchise are often required to provide "community access channels" to air the opinions of local and minority group members of their service region.

Data Protection and Access Increasingly, governments recognize that freedom of information includes the right of access by individuals and organizations to files that contain confidential information about them, held by public or private authorities, to ensure that the data is accurate, up-to-date, relevant for the purpose for which it is kept and withheld from all persons not expressly entitled to it. In some countries, the right of access to personal records excludes records held by public offices such as police, social security, and immigration departments. *See France.*

Concerns about data protection motivated passage of Scandinavian and German legislation in the early 1970s. Concern has increased with the ever-growing power of computers to manipulate data without individuals knowing what data is stored or how it is used. The European Convention on Data Protection (1981) provides an international legal framework for countries to adopt. The Convention, sponsored by the Council of Europe, came into force in October 1985 and is open for ratification internationally. In July 1990, work on a draft Directive on Data Protection, which will address the need to reconcile the free flow of data with the right to privacy, was progressing within the European Community.

Although dealing mainly with information stored on computers, in some countries data protection laws extend to records kept manually. *See France, United Kingdom.*

Right of Reply Article 14(1) of the American Convention on Human Rights allows anyone injured by inaccurate or offensive statements the right of reply in the same communications outlet where the statements were made. The application of this right requires the outlet to publish the reply by the injured party free of charge. An international convention on the Right of Correction has been in force since 1962, but has been ratified by only 11 countries.

The right of reply is enshrined in the law of many countries with legal systems based on French, Spanish and German law. Countries with legal systems based on English law do not usually provide a right of reply, but rely rather on non-legal protection of the principle through self-regulating measures. In 1988 in the United Kingdom, a Bill on "Unfair Reporting and the Right of Reply" failed in the House of Commons. The Bill's supporters argued that suing newspapers for damages was too expensive a remedy for the majority of the population. In 1990 in the United Kingdom, the Calcutt Committee on Privacy and Related

Matters rejected the idea of a statutory right of reply.

In some countries, the right of reply has been extended to government officials and departments. This has led to some abuse of the right by governments which require the media to publish extensive government reports and even propaganda in response to alleged misrepresentations. *See Australia, France, India, Paraguay, Portugal, Singapore, United Kingdom.*

Literacy Programmes

1990 was declared International Literacy Year by UNESCO, which has called on governments and non-governmental organizations to make special efforts to increase action and co-operation to reduce world illiteracy during the 1990s.

Important efforts have been made by some governments to reduce illiteracy, for example, in Somalia, Cuba and Nicaragua. The Sandinista government reportedly reduced the rate of illiteracy in Nicaragua from 53 per cent to 12 per cent during its first three years in office and took steps to integrate the newly-literate into the political arena.

Development Issues

A 1989 World Bank report asserted that freedom of expression and access to information are not only fundamental requirements of democracy but, further, that democracy itself is necessary for economic development. This theme has been further explored in the context of famine (see ARTICLE 19's *Starving in Silence*); deliberate suppression of information on imminent starvation by the governments of the countries concerned as well as by international humanitarian organizations has too often led to slow and inadequate relief responses. Strict censorship in certain countries also prevents potential victims of famine from informing a wider world of their plight and from organizing themselves in order to mobilize relief from the government. By contrast, in those countries which maintain the tradition of freedom of speech (see India), even threatened food shortages immediately become the subject of debate and preventive action.

In other countries, economic or religious imperatives preclude the collection and dissemination of accurate and timely information on the threat to life from disease, lack of pre-natal care and multiple closely-spaced pregnancies. The spread of AIDS in some under-developed countries and the denial of family planning information emphasizes the life-saving role of the right of access to information.

While information necessary for survival is often not available in countries precisely because of the lack of development and therefore the lack of investment in gathering statistics, information which is available is often not accessible to the population. Furthermore, the efficient transfer of information is often limited, due to lack of resources, and there are often severe restrictions on the publication of information. Finally, the international media often fail to publicize early indications of catastrophes due to a perceived lack of news interest; timely publicity can be crucial in mobilizing an adequate response.

Pluralism

Article 25 of the ICCPR proclaims that citizens have the right "to take part in the conduct of public affairs, directly or through freely chosen representatives; (and) to vote and to be elected at genuine periodic elections which shall be by universal and equal suffrage and shall be held by secret ballot, guaranteeing the free expression of the will of the electors". While the ICCPR does not expressly require multi-party democracy, it does require "genuine periodic elections" which in practice have occurred only in democracies where there are competing political parties.

In June 1990 in Copenhagen, the 35 CSCE countries "recognized that pluralistic democracy and the rule of law are essential for ensuring respect for all human rights and fundamental freedoms", including the right to freedom of expression.

In 1989 and 1990, the world witnessed historic transitions from single-party rule to multi-party systems not only throughout Eastern Europe but also in several African countries. Leaders in Zaire, Zambia and Somalia announced their intentions in 1990 to proceed towards multi-party systems and genuine elections, and in Latin America several countries embarked on the path from military dictatorship to democracy.

Selected Bibliography

General: Serials

Amnesty International Newsletter, Amnesty International, London.

Consideration of Reports Submitted by States Parties under Article 40 of the International Covenant on Civil and Political Rights, Human Rights Committee of the United Nations, Geneva and New York.

CPJ Update, Committee to Protect Journalists, New York.

Direct Line, International Federation of Journalists, Brussels.

Guide to the "Travaux Préparatoires" of the International Covenant on Civil and Political Rights, Bossuyt, M., Martinus Nijhoff Publishers, 1987.

Human Rights Monitor, periodical of International Service for Human Rights, Geneva.

Human Rights Watch, Watch Committees and Fund for Free Expression, New York.

Index on Censorship, Writers and Scholars International, London.

Interights Bulletin, Interights, London.

IPI Report, International Press Institute, London.

La Lettre de Reporters Sans Frontières, Reporters Sans Frontières, Montpellier.

Mass Communication Media in the World: Excerpts From the Press, International Journalism Institute, Prague.

Media Law and Practice, Frank Cass and Co, London.

Mediapouvoirs, Reporters Sans Frontières, Paris, 1990.

Minority Rights Group Reports, Minority Rights Group, London.

PEN Freedom-to-Write Bulletin, PEN American Center, New York.

Persecution and Protection of Journalists: News Clippings, International Journalism Institute, Prague.

SIM NEWSLETTER, Periodical of Studie-en Informatiecentrum Mensenrechten (SIM), Netherlands Institute of Human Rights, Utrecht.

SOS Torture, Newsletter of SOS Torture, Geneva.

Summary of World Broadcasts, British Broadcasting Corporation Monitoring, Reading, UK.

General: Books and Reference

Amnesty International Report, Amnesty International, London, 1990.

Attacks on the Press 1989, Committee to Protect Journalists, New York, 1990.

Basic Documents on Human Rights, Brownlie, I., Clarendon Press, Oxford, 1985.

A Compilation of International Instruments, United Nations, New York, 1988.

Country Reports on Human Rights Practices for 1989, US Department of State, Washington DC, February 1990.

Demographic Yearbook 1986, United Nations, New York, 1988.

Europa Year Book 1990: A World Survey, Europa Publications Ltd., London, 1990.

Global Journalism: A Survey of the World's Mass Media, Merrill, J.C. (Ed), Longman, London, 1983.

Human Rights and the Media, Eide, A., and Skogly, S., (Eds.), Norwegian Institute of Human Rights, Oslo, 1988.

The International Law of Human Rights, Sieghart, P., Clarendon Press, London, 1983.

International Workgroup for Indigenous Affairs Yearbook 1989, IWGIA, Copenhagen.

Journalists on Dangerous Assignments: Guide for Staying Alive, Falls Montgomery, L. (Ed), International Press Institute, London, 1986.

La Protection des Journalists en Missions Perilleuses dans les Zones de Conflit Armé, Malherbe, S., Éditions Bruylant, International Committee of the Red Cross, Brussels, 1989.

The Right to Freedom of Opinion and Expression: Preliminary Report, Turk, D. and Joinet, L., United Nations, UN Doc No. E/CN.4/Sub.2/1990/11.

Statistical Yearbook 1985-1986, United Nations, New York, 1988.

Status of International Instruments: Human Rights, United Nations, New York, 1987.

World Communication Report, UNESCO, Paris, 1989.

World Press Encyclopaedia, Kurian, G.T. (Ed.), London, 1982.

World Radio TV Handbook, Billboard Ltd, London, 1990.

Africa, South of the Sahara

Africa Confidential, Miramoor Publications Ltd., London.

Africa Watch Reports, Africa Watch, London.

Cameroon Monitor, Bulletin of Committee for Human Rights in Cameroon, London.

Censorship in South Africa, van Rooyen, J.C.W., Juta and Co, Johannesburg 1987.

Factsheet, Bulletin of the Association of Democratic Journalists, South Africa.

Government Restrictions on the Press in South Africa: The State of Emergency and International Law, Roadstrum Moffett, M., International Human Rights Law Group, Washington DC, 1987.

Journalists and International Humanitarian Law: Seminar Final Report, Union of African Journalists and International Committee of the Red Cross, Geneva, December 1985.

The Nairobi Law Monthly, Kaibi Ltd., Kenya.

Update, Bulletin of Anti-Censorship Action Group, South Africa.

West Africa, West Africa Publishing Co., London.

Where Silence Rules: The Suppression of Dissent in Malawi, Africa Watch, London 1990.

The Americas

Abandoning the Victims: The UN Advisory Services Programme in Guatemala, Lawyers Committee for Human Rights, 1990.

Andean Newsletter, Lima.

Annual Report of the Inter-American Commission on Human Rights, IACHR, Organization of American States, Washington, 1989.

Advisory Opinions, Inter-American Court of Human Rights, OAS, Washington DC, 1989.

Book Banning in America: Who Bans Books? - And Why, Noble, W., Eriksson Publishers, 1990

The Central-Americanization of Colombia? Human Rights and the Peace Process, Americas Watch, New York, January 1986.

Challenging Impunity: The Ley de Caducidad and the Referendum Campaign in Uruguay, Americas Watch, New York, March 1989.

Chile: Human Rights and the Plebiscite, Americas Watch, New York, July 1988.

Chile: No News Allowed, Committee to Protect Journalists, New York, May 1985.

Chile: The Plebiscite and Beyond, International Human Rights Law Group, Washington DC, February 1989.

Civil Liberties in Conflict, Gostin, L., (Ed.), Routledge, 1988.

Colombia: Inside the Labyrinth, Jenny Pearce, Latin America Bureau, London, April 1990.

Honduras: A Journalism of Silence, Committee to Protect Journalists, New York, January 1984.

Human Rights in Panama, Americas Watch, New York, April 1988.

IAPA News, Inter American Press Association, Miami.

Informe Especial-Periodismo en el rincon de los muertos-Estudio de las matanzas de periodistas en Peru y El Salvador, International Federation of Journalists, Brussels, July 1988.

Justicia Militar y Libertad de Opinion, Azrobispado de Santiago Vicaria de la Solidaridad, Santiago, August 1988.

Keeping America Uninformed: Government Secrecy in the 1980s, Demac, Donna A., Pilgrim Press, New York, 1984.

Latin American Newsletters, London.

Latinamerica Press, Latinamerica Press, Lima.

Liberty Denied: The Current Rise of Censorship in America, Demac, Donna A., Rutgers University Press 1990.

Media and Politics in Latin America - The Struggle for Democracy, Fox, E., (Ed.), Sage Publications, London, 1988.

The News Media and the Law, Reporters Committee for Freedom of the Press, Washington DC.

Newsletter on Intellectual Freedom, American Library Association Intellectual Freedom Committee, Chicago.

Nicaragua: The Human Rights Record 1986-1989, Amnesty International, London, October 1989.

The Right to Know, Data Center, Oakland (California), 1985.

School Censorship in North Carolina, People for the American Way, January 1990.

Survey of Press Freedom in Latin America, Council on Hemispheric Affairs and Hemispheric Newspaper Guild, New York, 1987.

Asia

Civil Rights Movement of Sri Lanka Bulletin, Sri Lanka.

Dialogue with North Korea: Report of a Seminar on "Tension Reduction in Korea", Carnegie Endowment for International Peace, May 1989.

Far Eastern Economic Review, Dow Jones and Co., Hong Kong.

Hot-Line Asia, Bulletin of Justice and Peace Co-ordinating Committee for Asia, Hong Kong.

Human Rights in Indonesia and East Timor, Asia Watch, New York, March 1989.

Human Rights in Taiwan, Asia Watch, New York, 1987.

Indonesia and the Rule of Law: Twenty Years of "New Order" Government, International Commission of Jurists and the Netherlands Institute of Human Rights, Frances Pinter Publishers, London, June 1988.

The Journalist, Journal of the Hong Kong Journalists' Association, Hong Kong.

Korea Update, North American Coalition for Human Rights in Korea, Washington DC.

Law and Society Trust, Fortnightly Review, Colombo, Sri Lanka.

Media Asia, Quarterly of the Asian Mass Communication Research and Information Centre (AMIC), Singapore.

Newspapers in Asia: Contemporary Trends and Problems, Lent, J.A. (Ed.), Heinemann Asia, 1982.

People's Republic of China: The Human Rights Exception, Cohen, R., in *Human Rights Quarterly*, Vol 9 No. 4, November 1987.

The Press in Chains, Niazi, Z., Royal Book Company, Karachi, 1980.

Press Freedom Advocate, Newsletter of the People's Movement for Press Freedom, Philippines.

TAPOL Bulletin, Indonesia Human Rights Campaign, London.

Violation of Freedom of the Press, Press Council of India, Indian Law Institute, Bombay, 1986.

Zia's Law: Human Rights Under Military Rule in Pakistan, Lawyers' Committee for Human Rights, New York, 1985.

Europe

Assignment Eastern Europe: The Working Conditions of Foreign Journalists in Bulgaria, Czechoslavakia, Poland and Romania, International Helsinki Federation for Human Rights, Vienna, 1987.

Censoring "The Troubles": An Irish Solution to an Irish Problem, International Federation of Journalists, Brussels, 1987.

The Cultural Obligations of Broadcasting, Shaughnessy, H. & Fuente Cobo, C., Council of Europe, European Institute for Media, University of Manchester, 1990.

Freedom of Expression and the Law, Report by Justice, UK, 1990.

Freedom of Information: The Law, the Practice and the Ideal, Birkinshaw, P.J., Weidenfield & Nicolson, London, 1988.

Free Press, Newsletter of the Campaign for Press and Broadcasting Freedom, London

Human and Citizens' Rights in Poland, International Helsinki Federation for Human Rights, April 1989.

Human Rights in the People's Socialist Republic of Albania, Minnesota Lawyers Committee, USA, 1990.

Human Rights in the United Kingdom, Sieghart, P., (Ed.), Human Rights Network, London, 1988.

Independent Peace and Environmental Movements in Eastern Europe, Helsinki Watch, New York, September 1987.

Is There Censorship in the Soviet Union? Methodological Problems of Studying Soviet Censorship, Golovskoy, V., Kennan Institute for Advanced Russian Studies, Washington DC, 1985.

Judgements of the European Court of Human Rights and European Commission of Human Rights, Council of Europe, Strasbourg.

La Liberté de l'Information en France, Ligue des Droits de l'Homme, Paris, 1990.

Media Law: The Rights of Journalists, Broadcasters and Publishers, Robertson, G., and Nicol, A.G.L., Sage Publications, London, 1990.

Mennesker og Rettigheter: Nordic Journal on Human Rights, Quarterly of the Norwegian Institute of Human Rights, Oslo.

Official Secrets: The Use and Abuse of the Act, Hooper, D., Secker & Warburg, London, 1987.

Rapport au Président de la République et au Parlement 1989, Commission nationale de l'informatique et des libertes, La Documentation Francaise, Paris, 1990.

Reinventing Civil Society: Poland's Quiet Revolution 1981-1986, Toch, M., US Helsinki Watch Committee, New York, December 1986.

Romania: Human Rights Violations in the Eighties, Amnesty International, London, July 1987.

Secrets, Newsletter of the Campaign for Freedom of Information, London.

Violations of the Helsinki Accords - Turkey, Helsinki Watch, New York, November 1986.

Yugoslavia: Crisis in Kosovo, Helsinki Watch, New York, 1990.

Middle East and North Africa

Annual Report: 1989 and 1990 (Arabic), Arab Organization for Human Rights, Cairo.

Annual Report 1989: Violations of Human Rights in the Occupied Territories, B'tselem, Israeli Information Center for Human Rights in the Occupied Territories, Jerusalem.

Human Rights in Iraq, Middle East Watch, New York, February 1990.

Human Rights in the Gulf and Arab Peninsula (Arabic), Annual Report, International Committee for the Defence of Human Rights in Gulf and Arab Peninsula, London, 1989.

Human Rights Update: May 1990, Palestine Human Rights Information Center, Arab Studies Society, Jerusalem, 1990.

Human Rights Vol. 3: Human Rights in the Arab World; Vol. 4: Methods of Teaching Human Rights in The Arab World (Arabic), Dr Mahmoud Sherif Basiouni, Dar al-Ilm Lilmalayin, Beirut, 1989.

Maroc, Repression, Newsletter of le Comité de lutte contre la repression au Maroc, Paris.

Newsletter, Arab Organization for Human Rights, Cairo.

Sudan Democratic Gazette, London.

Sudan Monitor, Research and Communications International, London.

Sudan Update, Bulletin of Committee for Peace and Reconstruction in Sudan, London.

Oceania

Communications, Law and Policy in Australia, Armstrong, Grey & Hitchens, Butterworth, Sydney.

Communications Update, Bulletin of the Communications Law Center, University of New South Wales, Australia.

Developments in Media Law, Media Law, Legal Research Foundation Inc, 1988.

Guilty Secrets: Free Speech in Australia, Pullan, S., Methuen, 1984.

Media Law in Australia, Armstrong, Blakeney and Watterson, Oxford University Press, Melbourne, 1988.

ARTICLE 19 Publications

Bulletin: The ARTICLE 19 Newsletter
Published 5 times per year. Free to Members

Information, Freedom and Censorship: The ARTICLE 19 World Report 1988
(Longman, London 1988, Times Books, New York 1988) £16.95

Journalism Under Occupation: Israel's Regulation of the Palestinian Press
(ARTICLE 19 and the Committee to Protect Journalists, New York 1988) £4.95

In the Shadow of Buendia: Censorship and the Mass Media in Mexico
(ARTICLE 19, London 1989) £4.95

The Year of the Lie: Censorship and Disinformation in the People's Republic of China 1989 (ARTICLE 19, London 1989) £3.95

No Comment: Censorship, Secrecy and the Irish Troubles
(ARTICLE 19, London 1989) £3.95

Starving in Silence: A Report on Famine and Censorship
(ARTICLE 19, London 1990) £3.95

Banned in Ireland: Censorship and the Irish Writer
(Routledge, London 1990, University of Georgia Press, Georgia 1990) £7.99

World Statement: Writers and Readers in Support of Salman Rushdie
(International Committee for the Defence of Salman Rushdie, London 1989) £3.95

The Crime of Blasphemy - Why it Should be Abolished
(International Committee for the Defence of Salman Rushdie, London 1989) £3.95

Violations of Freedom of Expression and Information in the Occupied Territories of the West Bank and Gaza Strip (ARTICLE 19, London 1989) Free

Threats to Freedom of Expression in the United Kingdom
(ARTICLE 19, London 1990) Free

Violations of Freedom of Expression and Information in Turkey
(ARTICLE 19, London 1990) £3.95

Violations of the Right to Freedom of Expression in Guatemala
(ARTICLE 19, London 1990) Free

Censorship in Sri Lanka: Three Women Speak Out (Video), 17 mins. VHS £12.50

The ARTICLE 19 Commentary Series

In-depth reports on the status of freedom of expression and information in individual countries. These reports have been prepared to coincide with consideration of the country's compliance with the International Covenant on Civil and Political Rights by the United Nations Human Rights Committee. Approximately 12 reports are published annually.

Individual Reports: £3.00

Freedom of Expression and Information in:

Australia (1988)	Mexico (1988)
Barbados (1988)	Morocco (1990)
Belgium (1988)	New Zealand (1989)
Bolivia (1989)	Nicaragua (1990)
Cameroon (1989)	Norway (1988)
Canada (1990)	Panama (1990)
Central African Republic (1988)	Philippines (1989)
Chile (1989)	Poland (1987)
Colombia (1988)	Portugal (1989)
Congo (1987)	Romania (1987)
Democratic Yemen (1989)	Rwanda (1987)
Ecuador (1988)	Senegal (1987)
France (1988)	Spain (1990)
German Democratic Republic (1989)	Togo (1989)
Guinea (1988)	Trinidad and Tobago (1987)
Hong Kong (1988)	Tunisia (1990)
India (1990)	Uruguay (1989)
Iraq (1987)	USSR (1989)
Italy (1987)	Viet Nam (1990)
Japan (1988)	Zaïre (1990)
Mauritius (1989)	Zambia (1987)

Please make all payments in UK Sterling or US Dollars.

Further information from
ARTICLE 19
The International Centre on Censorship
90 Borough High Street,
London SE1 1LL, United Kingdom.
Tel: (071) 403 4822 Fax: (071) 403 1943

Index

B

C

Index

G

H

I

J

K

O

Q

R

S

T

W

X

Y

Z

Miscellaneous